BRITISH ENGLISH,
A TO ZED

BRITISH ENGLISH,
A TO ZED

Norman W. Schur

Facts On File Publications
New York, New York ● Oxford, England

BRITISH ENGLISH, A TO ZED

Library of Congress Cataloging-in-Publication Data

Schur, Norman W.
   British English, A to Zed.

   Rev. ed. of: English English. c1980.
   Includes index.
   1. English language—Great Britain—Glossaries, vocabularies, etc. 2. English lan-
guage—Great Britain—Terms and phrases. 3. English language—Glossaries, vocabu-
laries, etc. 4. English language—Terms and phrases. I. Schur, Norman W. English
English.
   II. Title.
   PE1704.S38   1987   423'.1   86-16754

Jacket design: Ed Atkeson

ISBN 0-8160-1635-6
Printed in the United States of America

10 9 8 7 6 5 4 3

For Marjorie—incurable Anglophile

lexicographer. A writer of dictionaries; a harmless drudge . . .
—Johnson's Dictionary

Though a linguist should pride himself to have all the tongues that Babel cleft the world into, yet if he had not studied the solid things in them as well as the words and lexicons, yet he were nothing so much to be esteemed a learned man as any yeoman competently wise in his mother dialect only.
—John Milton

. . . The American language is in a state of flux based on the survival of the unfittest.
—Cyril Connolly in
The Sunday Times (London),
Dec. 11, 1966

When the American people get through with the English language, it will look as if it had been run over by a musical comedy.
—"Mr. Dooley" (Finley Peter Dunne)

I propose, therefore, the institution of a Society for the Prevention of Inadvertent Transatlanticisms (for short S.P.I.T.). No part of its aim would be to assert the existence of anything undesirable in North American English as distinct from English South-East Midlands English. The object is simply to strike a smallish blow for free will. . . .
—Geoffrey Marshall, in
"Appeal to the English,"
Oxford Magazine, 6
Michaelmas (1966) 97

Consider the influence of the USA. There are few families without American connexions today and American polite vocabulary is very different from ours. We fight shy of abbreviations and euphemisms. They rejoice in them. The blind and maimed are called "handicapped," the destitute, "underprivileged." "Toilet" is pure American (but remember that our "lavatory" is equally a euphemism). Remember too that the American vocabulary is pulverized between two stones, refinement and overstatement.
—Evelyn Waugh, "An Open
Letter To The Hon'ble Mrs Peter
Rodd (Nancy Mitford) On a Very
Serious Subject," in *Encounter*

. . . Why, oh why, do we quietly absorb, instead of resisting, these unnecessary . . . transatlantic importations which, far from enriching, nearly always degrade our beautiful language?
—Brigadier R.B. Rathbone,
in a letter to *The Times* (London)
dated Sept. 6, 1971

READERS who think this article is written in English are slightly mistaken. Actually, it's American English they're reading, a respectful but independent daughter of the Mother Tongue. Is the distinction trivial? Certainly not to lexicographers. . . .
—Mort La Brecque
"The Best of Dictionaries,
The Worst of Dictionaries," in
The Sciences, September 1972

American sub-titles
SIR—I wonder how many millions of television viewers find American dialogue baffling?

It is almost like a foreign language. Sub-titles, as in French and Italian films, would be a great help.

Noel Hardwick
in a letter to the *Daily Telegraph* (London) dated
August 25, 1980

The English and the American languages and literature are both good things; but they are better apart than mixed.

—H.W. and F.G. Fowler, in
The King's English
Oxford, 1906

Dick Washington . . . defeated the English at Bunker's Hill . . . After this the Americans made Whittington President and gave up speaking English.

—W.C. Sellar and R.J. Yeatman,
in *1066 and All That*
Methuen, 1930

Giving the English language to the Americans is like giving sex to small children; they know it's important but they don't know what to do with it.

—Morton Cooper
as reported in *The
Times* (London), Nov. 1, 1974

I can't explain to the English that we speak a different language.

—S.J. Perelman
(American expatriate, explaining
why he went back)

. . . The Beelzebub of neologisms . . . is the Americanism . . . Whose language is it? Ours or theirs?

—Lord Disgusted (Michael
Frayn), in the *Observer Weekend
Review* (London), Jan. 27, 1963

If it weren't for the language, you couldn't tell us apart.

—Bob Hope, to the British in
a television program

. . . We are told you also speak English here . . .

—Sir Peter Ramsbotham, British Ambassa-
dor to the United States, on television Mar. 8, 1977

Britons and Americans just have to be different! Their independence is, in most ways, an admirable characteristic: but in a comparative study of language it is rather a nuisance.

—Eric Partridge
Some Aspects of Etymology
A paper delivered to the English
Seminar of the University of Liverpool
Oct. 19, 1953

I am in no way criticising the American language, for, although originally English, admittedly it is today (1958) a separate language. . . .

—Henry Cecil in *Sober as a Judge*
(Michael Joseph, London, 1958)

Perhaps we can compel the deplorably permissive lexicographers to start banning such American solecisms as "hopefully" used absolutely to mean "it is to be hoped"; "different than"; and the ubiquitous flouting of "flaunt" and flaunting of "flout".

—*The Times* (London) June 27, 1981

Look at the process of deterioration which our Queen's English has undergone at the hands of the Americans. Look at those phrases which so annoy us in their speech and books, at their reckless exaggeration and contempt for congruity.

—The Very Reverend Henry Alford, D.D.,
Dean of Canterbury, in *Plea for the Queen's English* (1863)

. . . the English talk funny.

—William Safire, in *On Language*,
New York Times, October 2, 1983

Contents

Acknowledgments

This lexicon first appeared in the form of *British Self-Taught: With Comments in American*, published by Macmillan Publishing Company, Inc., New York, in 1973. Johnston & Bacon Publishers, of London and Edinburgh, a subsidiary of Cassell & Collier-Macmillan Publishers of London, brought out a somewhat revised edition under the same title the following year. Under the new title *English English*, it made its bow under the aegis of Verbatim, Essex, Connecticut in 1980. This incarnation, with the inestimable help of Kate Kelly (who wields the blue pencil at Facts on File, Inc., New York as skillfully as D'Artagnan brandished the sword) appears as *British English, A to Zed*. It has had the advantage of the author's longer experience of life in this scepter'd isle . . . this blessed plot, this earth, this realm, this England . . . this land of such dear souls, this dear, dear land, with the consequent addition of new entries and the correction and amplification of old ones.

For the first edition, help far beyond the reasonable bounds of hospitality came to me from many kind and patient English friends. Besides much painstaking correspondence over the years, there were many long sessions in English homes, gardens and pubs: countless words, gallons of tea, barrels of beer. I was indebted to my great friends John and Sarah (now Sir John and Lady) Freeland, Ronald Smith, Alan Vaughan, Donald Walker and Peter Tanter, and my now dear departed C.E. Thompson, B.T. Flanagan, Kenneth Fearon, Charles Kirby and Philip Harding; not a single philologist in the lot, of immensely varied background, with nothing whatever in common except kindness, intelligence, wit and taste. On the American side, I owed much to Edmée Busch, who helped put the manuscript into intelligible shape, and my secretary, Dorothy Schnur, stubbornly loyal through moments of self-doubt. My friend, the literary agent Robert Lewis, made important suggestions at the outset and urged me on when I faltered. When I first suggested the idea of an Anglo-American glossary to my lifelong friend the late A.C. Spectorsky, then assistant to the publisher of PLAYBOY, as an article for that distinguished ornament of American culture, he countered with, "It's too important for us; there's a book here," and I took him seriously.

For the second edition, there was help from further quarters. My oldest friend, Ralph Berton, a remarkably acute and dogged word buff, was of invaluable aid in supplying new entries and suggestions for improvement. Robert Elwell kept sending a flow of new items accompanied by comments that I gleefully adopted. Dr. Edwin M. Hudson, a remarkably learned man of many parts, plied me with new entries and recondite discussion. Dozens of readers from distant places became, and have remained, pen-pals and have contributed all manner of improvements. Warren Knock, of Johnston & Bacon Publishers, was patient and creative during that episode. After the appearance of the London edition, I received a long and learned letter from Paul S. Falla, a New Zealander with a distinguished background in the United Kingdom diplomatic service, now living in England, and a linguistic wizard of encyclopedic knowledge. His help has been enormous and his family and mine have become fast friends. Ronald Mansbridge, until a few years ago head of the New York office of the Cambridge University Press, has never faltered in his interest and help. I have been fortunate in receiving creative editorial guidance from the noted lexicographer Laurence Urdang. I cannot include the name of everyone who has participated, but I may not leave unmentioned a remarkably learned and witty letter from the late novelist Desmond Bagley of Guernsey overflowing with valuable information and suggestions. His untimely death deprived the world of a wonderful teller of tales and me of a beloved friend. From an avocational lexicographer to this team of pros and semipros, humble thanks.

I must end with a note of gratitude to my wife, Marjorie. Back in the late sixties, right after my return alone from our annual summer in England, my then still sketchy manuscript vanished. I was sure I had brought it back. Letters went back and forth between us. Searches on both sides proved fruitless. Dejected, I was on the point of abandoning the project, but Marjorie never gives up. One day her cable arrived: MANUSCRIPT FOUND, ON ITS WAY. Accidentally left behind, it had been stored in a most unlikely place by an overdiligent *daily* (cleaning woman). For my wife's persistence in the search and for her patient listening thereafter, I give my most loving thanks.

Preface

It was about twenty years ago, during one of many sojourns in the British Isles, that I began more and more to notice how many words and phrases uttered and written by the British were unfamiliar to my American eyes and ears. Occasionally they were unintelligible. Often the context made them clear. Much of the time it was only a question of what appeared to be preferred usage. I had never before heard of being *lumbered (saddled)* with an unwelcome job, but the context left little doubt. On the other hand, I really didn't know what a *lumber room* or a *hoarding* was. (A *lumber room* is a *storage room*, a *hoarding* is a *billboard*). I heard that a young student friend had *gone up*, and, vaguely wondering up where, asked a British friend whether *going up* by any chance meant *being promoted*. His reply was that the boy was much too young to be in the army. (*Promotion* means *advancement* generally, often with a military connotation, and normally has nothing to do with school grades.)

I began to note these peculiarities down. The list grew and grew and eventually reached the proportions of a glossary, and now a dictionary, with occasional reflections on British institutions, customs and idiosyncrasies in cases where it seemed no simple American equivalent could be found or would suffice. The list is still growing, even though, as edition has followed edition, I have had to delete certain entries born in one country and naturalized in the other.

The book is essentially a glossary of Briticisms for the guidance of Americans caught in the entrapment of a common language. I have seen fit to include certain terms and expressions which, though they may be fading from current British use, or may even have disappeared completely from most people's everyday conversation, an American might run up against in the literature of a few years ago, or quite possibly in the conversation of an elderly person, especially in the more remote (and less "with it") parts of the British countryside. In some instances, I have expanded the discussion in an effort to demonstrate not only peculiarities of the language of Britain, but also aspects of her culture as reflected by her language. In a few cases, I must admit, I have been unable to resist the temptation to stray a bit afield and include certain entries that may not be very useful, solely because they amused me, and may amuse you.

Language is so much a living, expanding and contracting thing that there can be no point at which any compilation of this sort ends. Even Dr. Johnson, in the words of John Moore (*You English Words*, J.P. Lippincott Company, Philadelphia, 1962), ". . . knew full well that his dictionary began to be outdated even while the proofs were on their way back to the printer. It is the despair and delight of lexicographers that in language they are dealing with a living thing. . . ."

What began as a pastime took on tangible form and, somewhat to my own surprise, has emerged as a serious compilation. I would be grateful if (in addition to omissions and possible erroneous inclusions and definitions) new items which appear from time to time were called to my attention. Not the least of my rewards has been the volume and tenor of the response I have received from scholars and aficionados in many parts of the world who have written letters ranging from a few words of appreciation to essays full of valuable information and comments. Many of the entries must evoke some controversy and even censure. "A dictionary-maker," said H. W. Fowler in his preface to the *Concise Oxford Dictionary* (reprinted in the sixth edition of that admirable work, 1976), "unless he is a monster of omniscience, must deal with a great many matters of which he has no first-hand knowledge. That he has been guilty of errors and omissions in some of these he will learn soon after publication, sometimes with gratitude to his enlightener, sometimes otherwise." Dr. Johnson, in the preface to his *Dictionary*, expressed the gloomy view that ". . . It is the fate of those who toil at the lower employments of life . . . to be exposed to censure, without hope of praise; to be disgraced by miscarriage, or punished for neglect. . . . Among these unhappy mortals is the writer of dictionaries. . . ." Again and again when I inquired about the precise meaning of an unfamiliar term, I received as many different answers as the number of kind British friends consulted, so that my final choice of American equivalent sometimes represented a compromise, a solution usually satisfactory to no one. I trust, however, that my book will afford a measure of enlightenment and occasionally some pleasure, and if it should serve to prevent even the tiniest bit of Anglo-American misunderstanding, I should feel that my labors were well rewarded.

Norman W. Schur
Hawkhurst, Kent, England
Weston, Connecticut, U.S.A.

Explanatory Notes

For a full discussion of the criteria used in assembling the Briticisms and their American equivalents the reader is referred to the Introduction. The following are brief notes on how to use the dictionary.

Entries

Briticisms, listed alphabetically, are set in boldface on the left-hand side of each entry. American equivalents are set in boldface on the right, opposite the British headword. When there is no American equivalent, SEE COMMENT refers the reader to the comment under the headword.

Labels

Parts of speech are set in italics, immediately following the British headword. Usage labels: when a Briticism is nonstandard this is indicated in italics, either at the beginning of the comment, or, when there is no comment, immediately following the function label. The labels used are: *Slang*, *Inf.* (Informal), *Old-fash.* (Old-fashioned), and *Rare*. American equivalents are similarly labeled. Though it has been the policy to attempt to provide American equivalents of the same usage level, that has not always been possible, and in such cases a comment always follows the headword. When the American equivalent is only an approximation of its British counterpart, it is preceded by *approx*.

Pronunciation

When the pronunciation of a Briticism is idiosyncratic, i.e., not ascribable to general differences between British and American pronunciation, a phonetic transcription in small capital letters is given at the beginning of the comment, following the usage label. The system of notation used is too simple to merit a table of its own.

Sense Distinctions

Arabic numerals separate the senses of a headword, both in the American equivalent and in the comment. Divisions are based on usage rather than strict semantic distinctions.

Comment

Examples of typical usage are set in italics, as are British and American terms that are used hypostatically. Glosses of Briticisms are set in single quotes. Briticisms used in the comments which appear in the alphabetical listing are set in **boldface** when it is felt that referring to them would add to the understanding of the comment.

Cross-References

See, See also, and *See under* refer the reader to other entries and to the Appendices. Cross-reference is based on various criteria: related meanings (similarity and contrast), related subject matter (e.g., pub terms, telephone terminology—in such cases the reader may be referred to the Appendices), morphological similarity (in several cases the American equivalent is itself an entry, e.g., *vest* is the equivalent of the British *waistcoat* and is also a Briticism of which the American equivalent is *undershirt*). Readers are also referred to the Appendices that deal with general differences between British and American English, when they have bearing on the entry. Words appearing in **boldface** type in the text of a comment have their own entries in proper alphabetic sequence.

Appendices

The Appendices are of two kinds: the first section contains short notes on general differences between British and American English. These are far from comprehensive, but the reader is referred to works that deal more fully with the topics discussed.

The second section contains tables and glossaries of terms whose meaning and use are best shown when the terms are grouped together (e.g., currency, measures) and lists of specialized slang terms of which only a few are included in the A-Z section.

Index of American Equivalents

This addition to the new edition of the book should be of special help to users searching for British equivalents of particular American words and phrases. The American equivalents given in the main, A-Z section of the book are listed alphabetically in the Index, together with the equivalent Briticism, which the reader will find treated in full in the main section.

Abbreviations

adj.	adjective	*n.*	noun
adv.	adverb	*pl.*	plural
approx.	approximate	*prep.*	preposition
conj.	conjunction	*v.i.*	verb, intransitive
inf.	informal	*v.t.*	verb, transitive
interj.	interjection		

Introduction

The nature of the relationship between British and American English has been the subject of debate (often heated) for years. *Webster's Seventh New Collegiate Dictionary* defines British English as "English characteristic of England and clearly distinguishable from that used in the United States. . . ." Evelyn Waugh's amusing dedication page in *The Loved One* reads in part: "My thanks are due to Mrs. Reginald Allen who corrected my American; to Mr. Cyril Connolly who corrected my English." The anonymous author of the article entitled "Broadcasting of the Year" in a *Whitaker's Almanack* of the middle twenties talks of the introduction of international broadcasting and characterizes the American emanations as particularly successful "because of the similarity of the languages."

However, in *Memoirs of the Second World War*, Churchill tells how an Anglo-American misunderstanding of a single word at a high-level military meeting resulted in "long and even acrimonious argument." The word was the verb *table*, which means 'shelve' (i.e., 'defer consideration of') to Americans, and the precise opposite: 'bring up for immediate discussion' to the British.* During that war, Admiral Lord Louis Mountbatten made the statement that he believed himself qualified to act as "Anglo-American interpreter" between the Americans and British in Southeast Asia.

Charles Smithson, the English hero of John Fowles's *The French Lieutenant's Woman*, bored and unhappy on the Continent, runs into two Philadelphians and leaps to the "pleasure of conversing with someone in a not too alien tongue." In the same vein, John Eisenhower, in *Strictly Personal* (Doubleday & Co. Inc., New York, 1974), after mentioning a conference among his father, Christian Herter, Harold Macmillan, and Selwyn Lloyd, seems pleased to point out that ". . . meetings with the British were always eased by the fact that the two nationalities speak relatively similar tongues." This is described by Edwin Newman, reviewing the book for *The Washington Post*, as a "rare attempt at humor," but I think that it is a fairly serious characterization of the relationship between the two branches of English. Robert Knittel, then editorial director of Collins Publishing, says that halfway across the ocean the two languages nuzzle up to each other and fraternize enough to become "mid-Atlinguish."

Some reactions to the differences have been far less conciliatory. In *Sir Michael & Sir George*, J.B. Priestly presents one character's thoughts on this subject as follows: "Sir George, not for the first time, thought how difficult it was to achieve real communication with some Americans, just because they used the same words but gave them different meanings." In *Less Than Kin*, William Clark recalls the Shavian quip that Britain and America are two countries divided by a common tongue. Dylan Thomas, in *A Visit to America*, describes himself as "up against the barrier of a common language." Consciously or not, they were all echoing Oscar Wilde's epigram: "The English have really everything in common with the Americans, except of course language."

What, then, is the nature of the relationship between "British" and "American"? Would it offend my compatriots if their idiom were characterized as a dialect of the mother tongue? Mencken thought the shoe was on the other foot. A letter appeared in *The Times* (London) on April 12, 1972, from Mr. Dixon Harry of Nottinghamshire objecting in vigorous terms to the Americanization of "good English words." In a riposte eight days later, Mr. Bernard F. Shinkman of London quoted Fowler quoting Mencken on the subject of what was standard and what was dialect. It was Mencken's theme that Britain, displaced by the United States as the most populous English-speaking country, was no longer entitled to pose as arbiter of English usage. "When two-thirds of the people who use a certain language decide to call it a *freight train* instead of a *goods train*, the first is correct usage and the second a dialect."

According to Marcus Cunliffe, in *The Literature of the United States*, a chauvinistic delegate to the Continental Congress moved that the new nation drop the use of the English language entirely; William Morris, in *Newsbreak* (Stackpole, New York, 1975),

---

*The "opposing" parties were on the same side of the controversy.

1

reports that the more violently anti-British leaders moved to reject English as the national language in favor of Hebrew, until it was pointed out that very few Americans could speak it; and another delegate proposed an amendment providing that the United States retain English and make the British learn Greek!

American claims to the English language are far from being left unanswered. In April 1974, Jacques Chastenet of the Académie française, suggesting Latin as the most suitable official tongue for the European Economic Community (Common Market), expressed the concern that "English, or more exactly American, might otherwise take over." He characterized "American" as "not a very precise idiom." Frederick Wood's attempt at consolation in his preface to *Current English Usage* (Macmillan & Co. Ltd., London, 1962) might seem even more offensive: "Certain words and constructions have been described as Americanisms. This does not necessarily mean that they are bad English." In "An Open Letter to the Honorable Mrs. Peter Rodd (Nancy Mitford) On A Very Serious Subject," Evelyn Waugh, discussing the American influence, writes: ". . . American polite vocabulary is different from ours. . . . [It] is pulverized between two stones, refinement and overstatement." Cyril Connolly went pretty far in *The Sunday Times* (London) of December 11, 1966: ". . . the American language is in a state of flux based on the survival of the unfittest."

Some have expressed more neutral sentiments in assessing the relationship. "British and American English undoubtedly are different," writes John W. Clark, associate professor of English, University of Minnesota, in *British and American English Since 1900* (Greenwood Press, New York, 1968), coauthored by Eric Partridge. "American English, especially today, might be called, I think, a smart-aleck language. Perhaps it would be more accurate as well as more up to date to call it a wise-guy language. . . . Another way of saying it is to say that British English has more *frein* and American English more *élan*. Yet another is to say that British English is stuffy and American English bumptious." Mario Pei refers to the "two major branches of the English language," and a British literary critic speaks of being "bilingual in the two branches of English." Perhaps Peter Strevens (*British and American English*, Collier-Macmillan, London, 1972) has put it even more clearly in asking whether British and American English should be regarded as different forms of one language or as two different languages, and in answering his own question by calling them "varieties of English." American English," he writes, "[is] an equal partner with British English."

Whatever the relationship may be, and however strongly opinions are voiced, it seems clear that in the jet age, what with the movies (the *cinema*), TV (the *telly*), and radio (the *wireless* still, to many Britons), linguistic parochialism is bound to diminish. In *Words in Sheep's Clothing* (Hawthorn Books, Inc., New York, 1969), Mario Pei, after referring to the different meanings given to the same word in the two countries, writes: ". . . In these days of rapid communication and easy interchange, such differences are less important than you would think." The latest edition of the *Pocket Oxford Dictionary* includes a fair number of American terms not found in earlier editions: *teen-age, paperback, T-shirt, supermarket, sacred cow, sick joke*, and many others. And in their recorded dialogue, published under the title *A Common Language, British and American English* in 1964 by the British Broadcasting Corporation and the Voice of America, Professors Randolph Quirk of University College, London, and Albert H. Marckwardt, of Princeton University, agreed, according to the Foreword, that ". . . the two varieties of English have never been so different as people have imagined, and the dominant tendency, for several decades now, has been clearly that of convergence and even greater similarity." And in a similarly optimistic mood, Ronald Mansbridge, manager emeritus of the American branch of the Cambridge University Press, in his foreword to *Longitude 30 West* (a confidential report to the Syndics of the Cambridge University Press by Lord Acton), refers to the two countries as "strongly linked together—let us reject the old joke 'divided'—by the English language."

Sam Vaughan, an American publisher, says, "New York looks more like London every day," in an article entitled "A Tale of Two Cities" which appeared in *The Sunday Times* (London) of April 11, 1976, and to prove that the two cities were beginning to sound alike as well, he offered the following evidence:

> Our dialogue has been influenced. Some words, like "bloody" and "smashing," have long been in use here. Yet they remain English—quaint, different, characteristic over- or under-statement. Others, however, such as "super," have been adopted wholly and have lost their English accent.
>
> If someone answers the phone, saying "Hopkins here," he is no longer mimicking

a Scotland Yard movie. We say "early on" straightfaced. A few years ago either would have been affectation or burlesque.

Novelist and *New Yorker* writer Nancy Hale says that "I've" (as in "I've not been there") is, for us, a new construction. (Almost everybody said "I haven't been there.")

This growing cross-Atlantic contact is not universally welcomed; Michael Frayn, in a tongue-in-cheek polemic entitled "Word Sanctuary" (*Observer Weekend Review*, London, January 27, 1963) signed "Lord Disgusted," strove to prevent the "convergence and even greater similarity" predicted by Quirk and Marckwardt:

> But the Beelzebub of neologisms, Sir, is the Americanism. Let me ask a plain question. Whose language is it? Ours or theirs? It makes me furious when I see our own language larded with words like "editorialise" and "hospitalise." Cannot people say "give as an opinion in an editorial" and "cause to go to hospital"? Are they too lazy to say the extra syllables? Are they too sunk in moral torpor to work out the proper syntax?
>
> And "commuter"! Every time I hear the word "commuter" I can see a red haze of rage in front of my eyes. It is an entirely unnecessary outrage, since there is a perfectly good English expression: "A man who lives in one place and works in another, and who travels back and forth between the two each day." There is simply no need for a new word. A man who lives in the one place and works in another, and who travels back and forth between the two each day, is simply a man who lives in one place and works in another, and who travels back and forth between the two each day—and that is all there is to say about it.

That sentiment is echoed, this time quite seriously, in a letter to *The Times* on September 8, 1971, from no less a personage than Brigadier R. B. Rathbone of Gloucestershire, expressing keen resentment at the "gross misuse" of the word *dessert*. (In the A–Z section of this book, there is a full treatment of the complex relationships among *dessert*, *sweet*, *pudding*, and *afters*.) "Why, oh why," cries the Brigadier, "do we quietly absorb, instead of resisting, these unnecessary (and in this case misleading) transatlantic importations, which, far from enriching, nearly always degrade our beautiful language?" We have already mentioned Mr. Dixon Harry of Nottinghamshire. Outraged, in his letter to *The Times* on April 12, 1972 (headed "Foreigners, be careful of English"), he insisted that "the British will always be British and will not accept Americanized versions of perfectly good English words." He too found the Americanization process "very degrading both to our language and people," referring to the invasion as "such slights." "Our language is for the use of English-speaking people," he proclaims, "it is not for the convenience of foreigners!"

Welcome or not, the process of convergence is slow, and the differences linger. Herbert R. Mayes, in his London Letter in the *Saturday Review* of November 14, 1970, wrote: ". . . There are enough archaisms here to keep an American off balance. . . . The British are stubborn. . . ." And Suzanne Haire (Lady Haire of Whiteabbey, formerly with the BBC, then living in New York), writing in *The New York Times* of January 11, 1972, of her "Study of 'American-English' at its source," mentioned the "bizarre misunderstandings [which] can result from expressions which have different meanings on the two sides of the Atlantic." The example she selected was the informal noun *tube*, meaning *subway* in Britain and *television* in the United States.

American clients of my law office whose book was published in a British edition found their royalty account debited with a "translation fee." A common clause in authors' contracts for the British publication of American books requires the author's consent to "Anglicization" of the text, and it works the other way round as well. When another client's book came out in a British edition, the publisher made seven word changes in the tiny volume: *perhaps* for *maybe*, *stone* for *rock*, *wash* for *do* (dishes), *parcel* for *package*, etc. (It caused a row; she hadn't been consulted. I was called in as attorney to enjoin further printings!) The British edition of Damon Runyon's work included a glossary. (Not a very accurate one: *old tomato* was translated 'loose woman'!) Back in 1926, the producer, Jed Harris, got S. N. Behrman, then his press agent, to prepare a glossary, in Behrman's words, "to explain the esoteric Broadway argot [of Philip Dunning's play *Broadway*] to British audiences." In 1939 Oxford brought out H. W. Horwill's *Anglo-American Interpreter*. The preface begins: "An American, if taken suddenly ill while on a visit to London, might die in the street through being unable to make himself understood." (No one would know what he meant when he asked for the nearest drugstore!) The Behrman glossary and Horwill's dramatic description of the dying American may seem like ancient history, and so might G. V. Carey's expression of concern on the jacket of his *American Into English* (William Heinemann Ltd., London, 1953): ". . . It is well to start by understanding each other's language. . . ." In his London Letter referred to above, Herbert Mayes felt that things were beginning to change: "It is rare that an American novel is Anglicized. The British edition of *Time* is published exactly as it would be in the States; no substituting of *underground* for *subway*, *tin* for *can*, or *express post* for *special delivery*." That letter appeared in November 1970. Yet in the February 14, 1972, edition of *Time* itself, Keith R. Johnson registers the complaint, in his review of the final volume (in translation) of De Gaulle's *Memoirs*, that the American publishers ". . . neglected to alter Anglicisms that will baffle many U.S. readers—for example 'council flats' for public housing."

When we get away from standard English and are faced with the ephemeralness of slang and informal terms, the division widens. In a letter to *The Times* published July 12, 1974, the literary critic and translator Nicholas Bethell, answering objections to his review of an English translation of *The Gulag Archipelago*, wrote: ". . . What I was objecting to was the use of words like 'bums' and 'broads' in a translation. They are too American. 'Yobbos' and 'birds' would be equally inappropriate. They are too British. It is a problem that translators are often faced with, how to render slang without adding confusing overtones. One has to try to find a middle way." To a Briton, a *bum* is a *behind*, and a *broad* a *river-widening*. To an American, *yobbo* (an extension of *yob*, backslang—reverse spelling—for *boy*, meaning *lout* or *bum*) would be unintelligible, as would *bird*, in its slang sense, as a 'character,' in the sense of an *eccentric*, as in *He's a queer bird!*

Whether standard, informal, or slang, and despite the "convergence" theory, the differences are still many and confusing. Bearing a London dateline, Russell Baker's column in *The New York Times* of September 15, 1970, began: "One of the hardest languages for an American to learn is English," and the language he was referring to was British English. About a year later, Henry Stanhope's review of *Welcome to Britain* (Whitehall Press, London, 1971) in the September 3, 1971 [London] *Times* referred to a glossary in the book as going ". . . some way towards bridging the linguistic gulf, broader than the Atlantic Ocean, which still separates our cultures." And on an arrival a few years ago at Heathrow Airport, London, I picked up a copy of *Welcome*, a newspaper available without charge to passengers, and read Sylvia Goldberg's article headed "Perils of the Spoken Word" which began: "One thing American visitors to Britain are seldom warned about is the 'language problem,' " and continued with the observation that the ". . . most mundane negotiation, the simplest attempt at communication with the natives can lead to unutterable confusion."

Whatever the future may hold in store, I have found that many facets of British English are still in need of clarification and interpretation. For despite occasional deletions because the American equivalent has all but taken over, my list of Briticisms has expanded substantially.

Hence this book, which is a comprehensive glossary of Briticisms for Americans, rather than a dictionary of British English in general. *Briticism* is defined by *The Random House Dictionary* as "a word, idiom or phrase characteristic of or restricted to British English, especially as compared to American English." Briticisms fall into three main categories:

1. Those that are used in both countries to mean different things. Thus, *davenport* means 'small writing desk' in Britain and 'large sofa' in America. Some words and phrases in this category have diametrically opposite meanings in the two countries. *Bomb* in Britain is slang for 'dazzling success'; in America it means 'dismal flop.' The verb *table* has already been mentioned as an example of the same phenomenon. Most of these terms have several meanings, some of which are shared and some particular to Britain.

2. Those that are not used at all in America, or extremely rarely, like *call box* and *kiosk* for 'telephone booth'; *hoarding* for 'billboard'; *dustman* for 'garbage man.'

3. Those that are not used (or if used at all, used differently) in America for the simple reason that their referent does not exist there. Examples abound: *beefeater; commoner; during hours; Oxbridge*. Often these refer to social and cultural institutions and have taken on connotative meanings which may have approximate American counterparts: *Chelsea; Bloomsbury; redbrick*. Many in this category reflect the higher degree of class consciousness in "socialist" Britain than the level that exists in "capitalist" America.

The definition quoted above includes the phrase "characteristic of or restricted to Britain," indicating that some terms qualify as Briticisms not because they are exclusively British but because they have a peculiarly British flavor. I lump such terms under the general heading "preferences." For example, if a British girl and an American girl were out shopping together, the British girl, pointing to a shop window, might say (and her mother and certainly her grandmother would have said), "I'd like to go into that shop and look at that frock," while her friend would more likely say, "I'd like to go into that store and look at that dress." The British girl might have said *dress* but would not have said *store*. The American girl might have said *shop* but would never have said *frock*. And the person who waited on them would be a *saleswoman* or *salesman* to the American girl, but a *shop assistant* to her British friend. It is all rather delicate and subtle, and these preferences keep shifting. Here is a sample list of mutually intelligible terms which qualify as preferences:

BRITAIN	AMERICA
blunt (e.g., of a pencil)	*dull*
crash (automobile, train)	*collision*
engaged (busy)	*tied up*
fancy	1. *like* 2. *suppose*
motor-car	*automobile*
position (the way things stand)	*situation*
queer (peculiar)	*funny*
sea	1. *ocean* 2. *beach*
snag (describing a troublesome situation)	*trouble, problem, catch, hitch*
tablet	*pill*
tidy	*clean, orderly, neat*
trade	*business*
wager	*bet*
wretched (e.g., of weather, person, luck)	*awful, terrible*

In addition to matters of preference, there is a category that may best be described by the term *overlaps*, to describe the situation where the British also use the American equivalent, but the Americans do not (or usually do not) use the British equivalent. The British, for example, say both *crackers* and *nutty* (meaning 'crazy'), but Americans do not use *crackers* in that sense. Many American terms are by now used more frequently in Britain than the parallel Briticism which has become old-fashioned. I have preferred to include such entries, but in such cases, have mentioned the increasing use of or total takeover by the American equivalent. See, for example, *aisle; flicks.*

Conversely, Briticisms which may be familiar to many Americans have been included where in my opinion they have not gained sufficient currency in America to be considered naturalized. In years to come, as jets become bigger and faster and the world continues to shrink, many such items will undoubtedly acquire dual citizenship. In this area, too, inclusion was the rule. See, for example, *chap; jolly.*

Most Briticisms have precise American equivalents, in which case they are given in boldface. Occasionally, however, this has not been possible. This applies to terms with figurative meanings; here we are on the slippery ground of connotations, implicit references, social context, and cultural implications. Many of these are slang and informal expressions that are too closely tied to British social and cultural institutions to have American equivalents, and in such cases it has been my policy not to attempt to invent one, but instead, to refer the reader to a comment providing a definition and illustrations of the uses and connotations of the British term. See, for example, *another place; curate's egg; the Ashes.* This policy is also followed in the case of encyclopedic entries, like *the Commons, beefeater; Dame.* (The phrase SEE COMMENT in place of an American equivalent refers the reader to the text immediately below the entry.)

On the other hand, there are a good many Briticisms that have close or approximate equivalents in American English. These are cases where the referents may be different; but the connotative meanings, based on the social or cultural backgrounds of the referents, or the referents themselves, may be similar enough to render the parallel terms approximate equivalents. Thus, though *the City* and *Wall Street* have different referents, it is reasonable to assume that in most contexts in which a Briton would refer to *the City*, an American would say *Wall Street*. The guidelines for deciding when we are justified in regarding the American term as an exact equivalent, when only an approximation, and when there is no equivalent, are by no means cut and dried. And apart from the question of referents, there is the wholly unrelated matter of what may be termed "stylistic imbalance": the problem which exists when the Briticism is slang or informal, and there is no American equivalent on the same level. Here, too, the American term taken from the standard vocabulary must be regarded as an approximation of a sort, even though the meaning of the equivalent may be exact.

While we are on the subject of slang, it is well to point out that that is the most unstable area of language, in which expressions become outmoded in the space of a year and then resurface, sometimes with new or additional meanings. In some cases, the use of slang and informal expressions is indicative of particular social and cultural backgrounds, and in view of the vast differences between the social structures, historical backgrounds, and cultural institutions of the two countries, it must be obvious that this area will produce a good many roadblocks in the search for equivalents. For instance, there is the troublesome category of public school cant, based on a privileged way of life so deeply rooted in British history and so foreign to American traditions. Then there is a vast category of *blimpisms* which are used by ordinary mortals (as opposed to retired army and navy officers) in silent quotes, such as *by Jove, old bean, good show*, and the like. Many of these have been included, as has much Wodehousean jargon, jocular use of which is part and parcel of contemporary British humor. And there are dozens of terms taken into the general language from cricket (just as baseball terms are adopted into general American English) and are used by people who have rarely, if ever, attended a cricket match. When entries are outdated, or specific to particular contexts, this has been indicated.

Many terms have "shared senses," meanings common to both countries. The noun *note*, for instance, can mean 'musical note' (do re, mi), 'written evidence of debt' (promissory note), 'memorandum' (he made a note of it), 'message' (he passed her a note), and so on. In Britain it has an additional sense that it does not possess in America: a 'piece of paper money' (a one-pound note, a banknote). The American equivalent in that sense is *bill* (a one-dollar bill, a five-dollar bill). Correspondingly, the word *bill* has a multiplicity of senses; the *beak* of a bird, the *draft* of a proposed law, etc. In including the pairing *note/bill*, I do not overlook the fact that the British term *note* has other senses shared with America or that the American noun *bill* has other senses shared with Britain. It would unduly lengthen the discussion of such an item to list or refer to all the shared meanings. It is therefore to be assumed that in the case of terms with more than one sense, those not dealt with are common to both countries.

It has been difficult to apply precise criteria of inclusion and exclusion. Many slang and informal terms have been included but others omitted because they seemed too ephemeral or too narrowly regional. A *roke* is a *ground fog*, but only in Norfolk. In certain parts of Surrey they eat *clod and stickin*, an unattractive-sounding stew, but if you asked for it outside of that area you would be met with a totally uncomprehending stare. It is well to avoid Lancashiremen and Yorkshiremen who are *razat*: they're *sore* at you. In parts of Yorkshire a donkey is a *fussock* or a *fussenock*, in Lancashire a *bronkus* or a *pronkus*. Such narrowly restricted dialectal terms, though amusing enough, have been reluctantly passed by. John Knowler, in *Trust an Englishman* (Harcourt Brace Jovanovich, Inc., New York, 1972), tells us that a survey of British dialects has turned up more than 80 terms for lefthanded: *bawky-handed, clicky-handed, coochy-gammy, cow-pawed, cunny-handed, gibble-fisted, kay-neived, kittaghy, scroochy, skiffy, quippy, watty* . . . (to name a few of the more picturesque items). Prof. Ellis of the University of Leeds, in an interview published in *The Sunday Telegraph* (London) of September 21, 1980, mentions *cuddy-wifted, Marlborough-handed, north-handed, squivver-handed*, among others. In the December 1976, issue of *In Britain*, an article by Anthony Grey entitled "Mother Tongues" listed 72 terms for 'runt-of-the-litter pig': *crink, nustle-tripe*, etc., and commented on more than 1285 terms of abuse for *fool*, all the way from *gappermouth* to *joufin-head, stoit, ballitraunt, toot, lollypot*, and other unpronounceable gems; 1050 epithets for *slattern*, and much more of the same. In this connection, interested readers are referred to *A Word Geography of England* (Seminar Press, London, 1975) by Professor Harold Orton of Leeds University, England. His colleagues are bringing out an 18-volume *Linguistic Atlas of England*. Orton's work contains 207 maps drawn by Nathalia Wright, a University of

Tennessee Professor of American literature, showing the "quaint and curious words" to be heard throughout the British Isles. Little wonder that so many fascinating terms from the dialects had to be left out of this book! In the Appendix section, however, we have included certain lists of localized slang.

Inclusion has been the rule in the case of Briticisms which may not be in general current use, but which might puzzle the American reader of a British book written some years ago. For example, *wireless*, for *radio*, is old-fashioned and will undoubtedly be out of current usage within a short time, but an American reading in a British detective story published fifteen or twenty years ago that so-and-so had heard certain news on his *wireless* might be led to believe that so-and-so had an elaborate Marconi system of his own, when all that had happened was that he had turned on the radio. Or take the case of *responsions*, originally the name of the first of three examinations for a B.A. degree at Oxford and later the name of the Oxford entrance exam. Responsions were abolished in 1960, but a novel published before that date, or one published last week describing events before 1960, might well speak of *responsions*, and the fact that the practice had been abolished years before would hardly be a reason for excluding that interesting word from this book. I would rather risk the misdemeanor of inclusion than the felony of omission.

Pronunciation has been indicated by reference to common words presumably familiar to the general reader, rather than through the use of phonetic symbols which remain an unbroken code to all but specialists. There is an index of American terms for the benefit of those seeking British equivalents. There are appendices dealing with general aspects of British English, and special glossaries of related terms better presented in that fashion than as separate headwords.

A separate section, "Explanatory Notes," is devoted to instructions for the most efficient use of the book (page xv).

A

A.A.   **Automobile Association**
    Opposite number to America's *A.A.A.* (*American Automobile Association*). Just about everybody in Britain who drives a car is a member of the *A.A.* or of the *R.A.C.*, which is short for *Royal Automobile Club*.

A.A.A.   SEE COMMENT
1. See **A.A.**
2. Amateur Athletic Association.
3. A film suitability rating, in Britain meaning 'not for persons under 14.'

abandonment, *n.*   **abandon**
    In the sense of 'uninhibited conduct.' *Abandon* is used in Britain as well.

ABC   **alphabetical railroad guide**

about, *adv.*   **around**
    Used as an adverb indicating place, meaning 'near' or 'in the vicinity' as in, *Is your father about?* In the sense of 'approximately' Americans use both terms interchangeably, but the British much prefer *about*. See also **Appendix I.A.1.**

above the salt   SEE COMMENT
    In days of yore, when the family saltcellar among the powerful and wealthy was a massive silver vessel, it was placed in the middle of the dining table and marked the boundary between the classes when people dined together. Those seated *above the salt* were members of the higher classes, the family and their peers; those *below the salt* were seated among the servants and dependents. Today, of course, these terms are used only metaphorically. At a banquet or formal dinner, to sit *above the salt* is to sit in a position of distinction.

absolutely sweet   **delightful**
    Usually applied to people, but it can refer to almost anything.

academicals, *n. pl.*   **cap and gown**

Academy, *n.*   SEE COMMENT
    Royal Academy of Arts. The Academy is usually so understood; *academician* refers especially to that institution. The initials *R.A.* after a name mean that the artist is a member of the institution.

accept, *v.i.*   **agree**
    For instance, *I cannot accept that you have met the conditions of the contract.* A common use in Britain. See discussion under **agree.**

access, *n.*   **visitation**
    Term used in matrimonial law, referring to the rights of the parent without custody to visit the children of the marriage. See a different usage in **except for access**; and note an unrelated use in *Access*, the name of a credit card issued by Lloyds Bank Limited, competing with *Barclaycard*, issued by Barclays Bank Limited.
    Staying access means 'temporary custody,' as when the party with visitation rights is authorized to have the minor child stay with him or her for limited periods, e.g., during every other weekend or on certain holidays.

accident tout   **ambulance chaser**

acclimatize, *v.t.*   **acclimate**
The American form is rarely heard.

accommodation, *n.*   **accommodations**
In the sense of 'food and lodgings,' the British use the singular. They seem not to use the word at all as the Americans do to include travel facilities, such as train and ship staterooms, plane seats, etc.

accommodation address   **temporary mailing address**

according to Cocker   **correct(ly); exact(ly)**
Inf. Cocker was a 17th-century writer on arithmetic. This expression is synonymous with *according to Hoyle,* a term used in both countries. Hoyle was an 18th-century authority on card games.

account, *n.*   **1. bill**
                                                                      2. charge account
1. Notification of an amount owing.
2. The term *charge account* is not used in Britain.

accountant. See **chartered accountant; commission agent; turf accountant.**

accumulator, *n.*   **battery**
Battery, too, is heard in Britain, usually applied to *dry cells,* while *accumulator* is generally reserved for *storage battery.*

ack emma   **A.M.**
And *pip emma* is *P.M.* Both generally outmoded.

act for   **represent**
Lawyers in Britain *act for,* rather than *represent,* their clients.

action replay   **instant replay**
TV term.

actually, *adv.*   **as a matter of fact; to tell the truth**
A pause-word, like *well...,* *you see...,* etc; perhaps intended to lend importance to what follows, but in reality meaningless. Some Britons are addicted to it, using it repeatedly in flowing discourse. Sometimes *actually* is used attenuatively, e.g., in mock-modesty: *Are you the champion? Well yes, I am, actually.* It can also be used in veiled reproof: *Actually, we don't do things that way.* Here the idea is *since you force me to say it.*

adapter, *n.*   **multiple plug**
A double or triple (perhaps even more) plug transforming a single wall outlet into a multiple one so that two or several lamps, appliances, etc., can be plugged into the one outlet. Generally considered unsafe.

A.D.C.   **time and charges**
These letters stand for *Advice of Duration and Charges,* and are what one says to the long-distance operator in order to learn the cost of the call. They share with America the meaning 'aide-de-camp.'

admass, *n.*   **mass-media public**
(Accent on the first syllable.) The gullible section of the public (mass) which is most easily influenced by mass-media advertising (ads); especially the TV proletariat, as it were.

Admiralty, *n.*   SEE COMMENT
The Department of the Navy in the Government, now merged in the Ministry of Defence.

adopt, *v.t.*   **nominate**
At the caucuses and conventions Americans *nominate* candidates who *run* for election. The British nominate potential candidates and finally *adopt* the ones who are going to **stand** for election.

adversarial, *adj.*   **adversary**
A legal term. An *adversarial* (*adversary*, in America) proceeding is a lawsuit involving actual opposing interests, as opposed to a request for a declaratory judgment.

advert, *n.*   *Inf.* **ad**
Inf. (Accent on the first syllable.) Abbreviation of *advertisement*.

advice of receipt; advice of delivery. *See* **recorded delivery.**

advocate, *n.*   SEE COMMENT
An *advocate* is a Scottish **barrister**. It is also the title of a lawyer in some of the Channel Islands, reflecting the influence of the French, who call a lawyer an *avocat*.

aeger, *n.*   **sick note**
(Pronounced EE'-JER or EYE'-GHER.) *Aeger* is Latin for 'sick'; the adjective is here used as a noun, in university circles. When the student is too sick to take an examination, he is given an *aegrotat* (Latin for 'he is sick'; pronounced EE'-GRO-TAT or EE-GRO'-TAT, the latter being the correct stress in Latin), an official certification of illness testifying that he is unable to attend lectures or take an exam. The same word designates a degree granted a student who has completed all other requirements but was too ill to take the final exams.

aerial, *n.*   **antenna**
The British don't use *antenna* except as applied to insects, or figuratively in the plural.

aerodrome, *n.*   **airfield**

aeroplane, *n.*   **airplane**

aesthete, *n.*   *Slang.* **grind**
Inf. A special university term, somewhat pejorative, for a studious student; the very antithesis of a **hearty**. The diphthong *ae* is pronounced EE. See **Appendix I.B.1.**

affiliation order   SEE COMMENT
In a paternity suit, an order of the court requiring the putative father to support or contribute to the support of the child.

afters, *n. pl.*   **dessert**
Inf. Thus: *What's for afters?*

after the break   SEE COMMENT
This is the dreadful pronouncement made by British **newsreaders** on stations that allow commercials, and is the equivalent of "after these messages" or words to that effect, *message* being one of the most hateful of euphemisms, foreshadowing a recital of all the advantages of the wonder-working products you simply can't live without.

aga, *n.*   **kitchen stove**
(Pronounced AH'-GA.) The full name is *Aga cooker* (see **cooker**), a proprietary name of a kitchen stove. *Aga* seems well on the way to achieving the same generic status that **hoover** and **li-lo** enjoy in Britain.

against the collar   **tough going**
 Inf. One meaning of *collar* is the 'roll around a horse's neck.' This meaning gives rise to the colloquial phrases *against the collar* and *collar-work*, both of which indicate *uphill effort.*

agency, *n*   SEE COMMENT
 A special usage, in signs seen at service stations all over Britain. It means that trucks can fill up at a station displaying that sign and have the fuel billed directly to the company owning or operating the truck. The driver simply signs a form, and no money changes hands.

agent, *n*. See **commission agent; estate agent; turf accountant.**

aggro, *n*.   **1. aggravation**
                                                         2. aggressiveness
 1. *Slang.* In the sense of 'exasperation,' 'annoyance.'
 2. *Slang.* A tendency to violence, a readiness to boil over and commit violent acts on the slightest, if any, provocation, e.g., the emotional imbalance that causes the rioting of a **football** (soccer) crowd or the destructive tendencies of a gang of youngsters looking for trouble on the streets. In this sense it is probably derived from *aggression.*

A.G.M. See **Annual General Meeting.**

agree, *v.t.*   **agree to; concede**
 Except when used intransitively (*You say it's a good painting: I agree; You want $100 for that old car? I agree*), this verb, in American usage, is followed by *that* (*I agree that it is so*) or by *to* (*I agree to your terms; I agree to go away*). Those constructions are equally common in Britain, but one British usage not found in America is *agree* followed by a direct object, where Americans would use *concede, admit, accept,* or *approve of,* e.g., *I agree the liability for income tax; I agree the claim for damages; I agree the price; I agree your proposal; I agree your coming tomorrow.* There is a curious relationship between the British uses of *agree* and *accept,* which are more or less the reverse of the American uses, since *agree* is used in Britain where an American would normally say *accept* (*I agree the liability for damages*) and *accept* is used there in the way in which Americans use *agree* (*I accept that he is an honest man*).

agreed verdict   **consent decree**
 Legal term.

agricultural labourer   **farmhand**

agricultural show   **state** or **county fair**
 An *agricultural show* represents roughly the same aspect of British life as an American *state fair* or *county fair.* The Tunbridge Wells Agricultural Show or the Kent (County) Agricultural Show serve about the same cultural and economic purposes as, for example, the Kansas State Fair, the Great Barrington Fair in Massachusetts, or the Danbury Fair in Connecticut.

air bed. See **li-lo.**

airy-fairy, *adj.*   *approx.* **fey**
 Inf. In its original sense *airy-fairy* meant 'light and delicate,' like "airy-fairy Lilian" in Tennyson's poem. It has now acquired a disparaging meaning; 'insubstantial,' 'superficial,' perhaps with connotations of whimsy, artiness, pretentiousness: *This progressive education is a lot of airy-fairy nonsense.* There would appear to be no precise American colloquial counterpart. *Artsy-craftsy* might be close in certain contexts.

aisle, *n.*   **church aisle**
 Americans use *aisle* generically. In Britain, out of context, it refers to churches, although it is now more and more being used for shops and theaters as well. A pas-

sageway in a shop is still sometimes called a *gangway* in Britain, and in trains it is always *corridor*, because the passageway in the great majority of British and European railroad coaches runs along one side rather than down the middle.

ait, *n.*   **islet**
(Pronounced EIGHT; sometimes found in the form *eyot*.) Not a common word, but the darling of crossword puzzle concocters. It usually describes a little island in a river or brook.

albert, *n.*   **watch chain**
Also called an *Albert chain*; if used alone, the *A* drops to lower case. Based on the sartorial habits of Victoria's Prince Consort.

ale-house politician   **cracker barrel politician**

A-levels, *n. pl.*   **approx. college entrance examinations;**
                                                                        approx. **Scholastic Aptitude Tests (S.A.T)**
The *A* stands for *advanced* just as the *O* in *O-levels* stands for *ordinary*. At the age of fifteen or sixteen, students in Britain take their *O-levels*, and at seventeen or eighteen, their *A-levels*. Both are known as *G.C.E.* examinations. *G.C.E.* stands for *General Cerfiticate of Education*, which is required for admission to any university. Oxford and Cambridge have additional examinations of their own, as do several other universities, but the practice is waning in favor of a central clearing-house for university applicants. The American definition must be approximate because of the procedural differences in the two educational systems. A Frenchman who had lived in Britain, after making vain efforts to explain the British school system to a compatriot, finally wound up with: *Ça ne s'explique pas, mais ça marche* ('You can't explain it, but it works.').

alight, *v.i.*   **get off**
Would be quaint in America, and is in Britain as well, except in notices at railroad stations and bus stops.

all found. *See* **fully found.**

all in   **1.** *Inf.* **everything thrown in**
                                                                        2. *Inf.* **anything goes; no holds barred**
1. *Inf. All included*, as in, *The holiday cost us £100 all in* (i.e., travel, **accommodation**, and all other expenses included). Nothing to do with the American and British meaning 'all tuckered out.' An *all-in* policy is an *all-risk* (insurance) policy. A British insurance company advertisement of the early 1900s spoke of such a policy, enumerating the dozen or so risks covered by the omnibus contract. Included as items 7, 8, and 9 were Riots, Strikes, and Civil Insurrections. These three were bracketed by a connecting brace, on the other side of which, in fine print, occurred the phrase: *Except in Ireland*.
2. *Inf.* As in the phrase, peculiar to American ears, *all-in wrestling* in which the gladiators are permitted to do just about anything except resort to knives.

all my eye and Betty Martin!   *Inf.* **baloney!**
Inf. Various derivations proposed. The most likely would seem to be *Mihi beata mater* (which appears to be Latin for something like 'Grant to me, blessed Mother'). According to one legend, the imperfectly understood phrase was reported back to Britain by a sailor who had been abroad and to him it sounded like *all my eye and Betty Martin*. The British often shorten the expression to *all my eye!* Cf. American *my eye!* Other American synonyms are *hogwash* and *eyewash*.

allotment, *n.*   **small rented garden area**
Sometimes allotted free of charge to those living in **council houses** or **alms-houses** for the raising of vegetables for personal consumption and flowers for personal delight.

all over the shop, *Inf.*   *Inf.* **in a mess; in wild disorder**

allowance, *n.*   **exemption**
Income tax terminology, referring to the amounts allowed per taxpayer, dependent, etc.

all-round, *adj.*   **all-around**

all-rounder, *n.*   SEE COMMENT
A sports term, especially in cricket, denoting a versatile player; in cricket, one good at bowling, fielding, and batting. An American approximation, especially in football, would be *triple threat*, a player skilled in passing, kicking, and tackling.

all Sir Garnet   *Inf.* **according to Hoyle**
Inf. An old-fashioned phrase, still used by senior citizens. Sir Garnet (later Viscount) Wolseley (1833–1913) was a famous military man who wrote the *Soldier's Pocket Book*. Anything described as *all Sir Garnet* is *O.K., done by the book*. See also comment under **batman**. A somewhat different derivation of this curious expression is found in James Morris's *Heaven's Command* (Faber & Faber, London, 1973), where he describes Sir Garnet's successful campaign against the Ashanti in Africa. ''. . . Sir Garnet went home once more in glory,'' writes Morris. ''He was nicknamed 'Britain's Only General', and when people wanted to describe something supremely well done, neatly wrapped like the Ashanti War, they called it 'All Sir Garnet'.''

all the fun of the fair   **great fun**
Inf. More damn fun! Often used ironically to describe a tight situation.

almoner, *n.*   **social worker**
(Pronounced AWL'-MONER, AL'-MONER or AH'-MONER.) One still comes across this term occasionally, but it is to all intents and purposes obsolete in current usage. An *almoner* was formerly an official dispensing alms. One function was to determine how much each hospital patient could afford to pay. After the National Health system began to operate, the almoner's main activity was that of a medicosocial worker attached to a hospital. Today the term has given way to the much more descriptive and less patronizing term *social worker*.

almshouse, *n.*   **old people's home**
In America *almshouse* would not ordinarily be used in everyday speech. It might be seen in historical or literary contexts. Originally a charitable home for the poor, the *almshouse* in Britain is today a subsidized home for old folk who live in quite pleasant little apartments at nominal rent, which often includes a garden **allotment**. See also **workhouse**.

alpha (beta, gamma, *etc*).   **A (B,C, etc.)**
Symbols used by teachers in marking grades at universities generally. The Greek letters are preferred. See also **query 2**.

Alsatian, *n.*   **police dog; German shepherd**

ambulance, *n.*   **1.** SEE COMMENT
                                                                        2. tow truck
1. Although there are of course ambulances in Britain similar to those seen in America, the same term is applied to small buses that are used, under the National Health system, to transport ambulatory patients, free of charge, to and from doctors' offices or hospitals for visits. These are sit-up affairs, for those who have no car or who, for financial or physical reasons, can't manage with regular public transportation.
2. *Inf.* Garagemen's terminology, jocular in origin, but now apparently used as technical jargon in some quarters.

amenities, *n. pl.*   **conveniences**
Referring to household facilities. (*Amenities* in the American sense is *civilities* in Britain.) The American term *conveniences* is also used and is found in the abbreviated phrase, *mod. cons.*, which stands for *modern conveniences*. (*Mod. cons.* appears in advertisements and is used conversationally in discussing a house or an apartment in the same literal but half-humorous way in which the British conversationally use the abbreviation *two veg.* (pronounced VEJ), meaning two vegetables accompanying the entrée in a meal.) Another British equivalent is **offices**.

Amenities can be applied more widely, to indicate whatever features of a place make life more pleasant (from *amoenus*, Latin for 'pleasant'; and *amoena* means 'pleasant places'), including view, proximity of theaters or shopping, etc. The abuse of this word by the local authorities in Southampton, who labeled their public dump a "civic *amenity* site," caused Philip Howard to write this angry piece in *The Times* (London) of April 7, 1977, headed "The rubbish talked about amenity":

> In Southhampton, and no doubt other districts whose local authorities prefer dishonest gobbledygook to plain words, the official name for a corporation rubbish dump is a "civic *amenity* site".
>
> *Amenity* comes directly from a Latin root, and means pleasantness, as in situation, climate, manners, or disposition. Concretely it means a pleasing feature, object, or characteristic. It can mean civility.
>
> This harmless, hazy word has been taken up and debauched as a vogue word, frequently in the plural. It is applied, understandably, to the more human and pleasurable aspects of a house, factory, town, and so on, as distinguished from the features of the house, factory, town, or so on, considered by itself. In its modern use it can also be used concretely, usually in the singular, to mean a particular advantageous or convenient feature of this kind. So people speak of social *amenities*, and we understand roughly what they mean.
>
> *Amenity* woodland is said to be uneconomic, though that should not be taken as sufficient reason for not planting it. *Amenity* beds in National Health Service hospitals are for patients who want a little more privacy and luxury than are available in the public wards and are prepared to pay for them. *Amenity* centres probably means places with clubrooms, bars, cinemas, fruit machines, playing fields, and other modern delights, and would be more helpfully described by a less woolly word than *amenity*.
>
> *Amenity* is a word much favoured by estate agents and other branches of the property business. It is the quality that makes a desirable residence desirable; a favoured locality favourable; enchanting views in all directions enchanting; and advertisements for unsellable slum properties that even the rats have deserted glow with promise.
>
> Nevertheless, vague as well as vogue though it is, *amenity* is an incongruous word to apply to a rubbish dump.
>
> *Amenity*, in its new coat of garbage, is a misnomer that reeks of Double Think and Newspeak of 1984, only seven years to go. You will remember that the three slogans of the party in Oceania were: War is Peace; Freedom is Slavery; Ignorance is Strength. The propagandist who thought of those would have been gratified by their latest related slogan: Rubbish dumps are Civic *Amenity* Sites.

American cloth   oilcloth

amongst, *prep.*   among
Not quite so common as *whilst* for *while*.

angel on horseback   oyster wrapped in bacon
Served on toast. This is the English version. There is a Scottish version which substitutes smoked haddock for the oyster. See also **devil on horseback.**

anglepoise lamp   *approx.* **adjustable table lamp**
Originally a trademark, now becoming generic. The term describes a table lamp with a base built of a series of hinged arms with springs and counter-weights that adjust the height, beam direction, and so on.

and pigs might fly!   *Inf.* **Yeah, sure!**
Inf. Expression of disbelief in response to a prediction.

Annual General Meeting   **Annual Meeting of Shareholders**
                                                               (Stockholders)
Usually abbreviated to *A.G.M.* What the British call an *Extraordinary General Meeting* is called a *Special Meeting of Shareholders (Stockholders)* in America.

anorak, *n.*   **light waterproof jacket**
An Eskimo word, stressed on the first syllable.

A.N. Other   *approx.* **John Doe**
A rather weak joke (?) in cricket usage. In the list of players, it denotes one still unchosen or one desiring to withhold his name, which is (to reveal the secret) Mr. A. N. Onymous. *A. N. Other* is not the only weak joke in this category, according to a letter to *The Times* (London, of course) dated June 28, 1932, and reprinted in its issue of September 28, 1983. Sadly, this author is without the information requested in the letter. The letter reads, in part: "Sir,...I am now rather a doddering old man, but still able to take a bat in hand on occasion. Could any of your readers give the date I first appeared before the public, my highest score, and if I have ever batted before No. 10, or ever been used as a **bowler**...I have a score sheet in front of me, when a close connexion of mine in 1859 batted No. 11 for Harrow School against the Town. On the list he figures as T. H. E. Swell. I am, Sir, *A. N. Other.*" No. 10 and No. 11 in the batting order, in cricket, are lowly positions, assigned to poor **batsmen**. Good bowlers, like good pitchers in baseball, are usually inept at the bat.

another pair of shoes (boots)   **a horse of a different color**

another place   SEE COMMENT
This is the way the House of Commons refers to the House of Lords, but it doesn't work the other way around. *The other place* (note the definite article) is the way Oxford and Cambridge refer to each other. In this case it's mutual. These circumlocutions are reminiscent of the old days when CBS and NBC referred to each other as *another network*. Incidentally, *another place* was a Victorian euphemism for *hell*.

ansafone, *n.*   **answering machine**

answer, *v.i.*   **work**
Inf. In phrases indicating inappropriateness: *It won't answer; It didn't answer.* For example, a person reads an advertisement of the help-wanted or houses-for-rent variety, goes to investigate, finds the situation unsatisfactory, and in answer to a friend's question says, *It didn't answer.* An American might have said, *It didn't do the trick.*

anti-clockwise, *adj., adv.*   **counterclockwise**

Any more for the Skylark?   SEE COMMENT
When mother was a girl, people went to resorts like Southend and Blackpool and took rides on the little excursion boats, one of which was bound to be called the SKYLARK. As the SKYLARK was ready to depart, with a few empty seats, the attendant would cry out, *Any more for the Skylark?* This became a cliché in Britain which eventually became applicable to any situation where a last summons for action was indicated: the car is about to leave and there are stragglers; people are about to set out for a hike; Mother, in the kitchen, is about to turn on the dishwasher and there may still be things on the dining-room table that should go in. Or it's time to announce the last round of drinks at the pub. A sweetly reminiscent little joke, this phrase is, sadly, going out of fashion, like the little excursion boats.

apartment, *n.*   **single room**

appeal, *n.*   1. SEE COMMENT
                                                                         2. **fund-raising campaign**
1. for a special meaning in cricket, see **Howzat!**
2. One is frequently asked to contribute to the *appeal* of, e.g., Canterbury Cathedral for construction repair, or of Ely Cathedral to fight the woodworm. *Appeals* are not restricted to cathedrals: they issue from hospitals, schools, charitable institutions and other worthy causes.

appointed to a cure of souls, *Inf.*   **made vicar**

approach, *v.t.*   **service**
What a ram does to a ewe under appropriate conditions.

approved school
See also **borstal**.

reform school

A.R. See **recorded delivery.**

archie, *n.*   *Slang.* **ack-ack**
Slang. World War I for *anti-aircraft gun. Ack-ack* became World War II slang in both
countries for both the guns and the fire.

argue the toss   *Slang.* **argufy**
Slang. To *dispute needlessly.*

argy-bargy, *n., v.i.*   **squabble**
Slang. Derived from *argue.*

armchair socialist, *Inf.*   *Inf.* **parlor pink**

Army and Navy Stores   SEE COMMENT
Army and Navy store in America is a generic term for a type of shop selling low-priced
work and sports clothes, sports and camping equipment, and the like. In London, it is
simply the name of a particular department store selling general merchandise.

arse, *n.*   *Slang.* **ass**
Slang. The anatomical, not the zoological designation. Neither term is in polite use.
Even *ass,* meaning 'fool,' was commonly pronounced ARSE until recently, as in, *You
silly arse,* according to John Knowler (*Trust an Englishman,* Harcourt Brace Jovanovich,
New York, 1972). He tells the story of a schoolboy who, asked by teacher how Samson
slew the Philistines, bent over to a better informed chum. Chum whispered, "Jawbone
of an ass," and "Jobbed them in the arse, sir," came the bright reply. See also **bum.**
Knowler says that under American influence, some Britons are now saying *ass* for *arse.*
This unfortunate development excited the ire and alarm of a contributor to the *Sunday
Times* (London) of March 16, 1975:

> When did the grand old English word "arse" start to be pronounced "ass", Amer-
> ican style, and now, even in *The Times,* so spelled? I remember the pleasure when, as
> a student of English literature, reading that Elizabethan farrago of tedium, Grammer
> Gurton's Needle, I discovered the presumed origin of that traditionally bowdlerised,
> maternal reproach "Faith, an' thou wouldst lose thy arse an' it were loose."
>   I'd like to keep it in the language, though mostly I agree that words are living things
> and cannot be forced to revert to their etymological origins if the spirit of the age is
> against it. So I no longer try to point out that "prestigious" ought to mean adept at
> sleight-of-hand because nobody will believe me. But when "uninterested" and "dis-
> interested" become identical, we lose a valuable term and gain nothing. So, "arse" it
> should remain. Everybody, after all, or sometimes first of all, is born with one. To
> own an "ass", you have to be both rich and probably eccentric.

arse over tip, *Slang.*   *Inf.* **head over heels**

arsy-tarsy, *Slang.*   *Slang.* **ass-backwards**

arsy-varsy, *adv., Slang.*   **vice versa; backwards**

arterial road   **main road**
Synonymous with **major road** and **trunk road**. A common traffic sign used to be:
HALT—MAJOR ROAD. This appeared (sometimes still does) on what Americans call *stop
signs,* at junctions where secondary roads ran into main roads. STOP now generally
replaces HALT on traffic signs not only in Britain, but in many other countries (cf. CTOII
in the U.S.S.R.). See also **Halt.**

articled clerk. See **articles.**

articles, *n. pl.*   **agreement**
Usually expanded to *articles of agreement.* A common use, in this sense, is in the term *articles of apprenticeship.* As a verb, to *article* is to *bind by articles of apprenticeship,* from which we get the term *articled clerk,* meaning 'apprentice.' That is the common term in the legal profession in Britain (see **clerk 1**) whereas the humble novitiate in an American law firm acquires the more flattering title of 'associate.' All that means is 'employed lawyer' as opposed to *partner.* (But the systems in the two countries are quite different, and all analogues are approximate.) When one's apprenticeship is ended, one *comes out of articles.* Accountants, too, have *articled clerks,* who, like those in law offices, are on their way to gaining full professional status. *Clerk,* incidentally, is pronounced CLARK.

articulated lorry   **trailer truck**
The verb *articulate* has been used so widely as an intransitive verb meaning to 'speak clearly' that most people have forgotten that it is also a transitive verb meaning to 'connect by joints.' In truck drivers' vernacular, often shortened to *artic* (accented on the second syllable); also quite graphically called *bender* (which happens to be slang for the old sixpence as well).

as bright as a new penny, *Inf.*   *Inf.* **as bright as a button**

as cold as charity   **biting cold**
Inf. Often applied to human attitudes, the allusion being to the coldness of the administrative procedures of most charitable organizations. When applied to weather conditions, cf. **monkey-freezing.**

as dead as mutton   *Inf.* **as dead as a doornail**
Inf. As everyone knows who remembers the opening lines of *A Christmas Carol,* the British commonly use the *doornail* simile that Dickens applied to Marley.

Asdic, *n.*   **sonar**
Stands for *Allied Submarine Detection Investigation Committee,* just as *sonar* stands for *Sound Navigation Ranging.* Both are marine depth-measuring devices and are used in finding and locating submarines and submarine objects.

as dim as a Toc H lamp   *Inf.* **thick-headed**
Inf. Toc H (initials of Talbot House, *T* being called *toc* in military signaling) is an organization for social service and fellowship with branches throughout the British Commonwealth, so called because it originated at Talbot House, a rest center for soldiers at Poperinghe, Belgium. Talbot House, founded by the Rev. T.B. Clayton (usually referred to as "Tubby Clayton"), was named for Gilbert Talbot, who was killed in action in 1915. In front of each Toc H location hangs a lamp (like an Aladdin's lamp) which is always dimly lit. Sometimes a sign with a lamp replaces the lamp itself. The *dim* in this phrase is short for *dim-witted* and is thus a mild pun. The expression, like the institution itself, is on the way out.

as easy as kiss your hand, *Inf.*   *Inf.* **as easy as pie**

as from   **as of**
As from such-and-such a date, e.g., *The fares will be increased by 10 pence as from December 9.*

(the) Ashes, *n. pl.*   SEE COMMENT
Inf. This is a symbolic term meaning 'victory' in test cricket with Australia (see **Test Match**). Thus we have the expressions *win the Ashes, retain (or hold) the Ashes, bring back* (or *win back* or *regain) the Ashes,* etc., depending upon circumstances. When England and Australia play in a test series for *the Ashes* no physical trophy changes hands. Yet after the term came into use, under the circumstances described below, the abstraction did materialize into a pile of physical ashes which are contained in an urn which is in turn contained in a velvet bag, now resting permanently at Lord's Cricket Ground in

London, the Vatican of English cricket. The story is told in a brochure put out by the Marylebone Cricket Club (always referred to as the *M.C.C.*) which, with its headquarters at Lord's, was the official body in charge of English cricket until 1969, when that function was undertaken by the Cricket Council. (The author once asked a stranger in a country pub what the initials *M.C.C.* stood for and was informed in the same tone of disdain as those in which the stranger at the counter in a Brooklyn bar and grill, in the old days, might have answered a Briton asking the name of the sport practiced by the Dodgers.) Herewith some excerpts from the brochure:

> When the...Australian team...met England...on August 28, 1882, England was still unbeaten on her own soil. Here follows a tragic account of the disaster of that date...In an atmosphere of tension and excitement which mounted as the wickets fell, Australia achieved her first victory in a test match in England by 7 runs. It was a glorious finish and Australia's triumph was well deserved....
>
> The *Sporting Times* reflected the sentiments of English cricketing circles by printing a mock obituary notice, which ran as follows:
>
>
>
> In affectionate remembrance
> of
> ENGLISH CRICKET
> which died at the Oval on
> 29th August 1882,
> Deeply lamented by a large circle
> of sorrowing friends and
> acquaintances.
> R.I.P.
> N.B.—The body will be cremated and
> the ashes taken to Australia...
>
>

So was coined the expression *the Ashes*, which is used whenever a series of test matches is played between England and Australia.

Almost immediately after the match, an English team under the captaincy of the Hon. Ivo Bligh (afterwards Lord Darnley) left for Australia on tour....It had been commonly said that Ivo Bligh had gone on a pilgramage to *recover the Ashes*, and so, after the second defeat of...[the Australian] team, some Melbourne ladies burned and collected the ashes of a bail [one of the parts of a wicket] which they placed in a small pottery urn and presented to him....An additional gift...was a red velvet bag to contain the Ashes....

as near as dammit   *Inf.* **just about**
   Slang. Almost exactly; give or take a bit; very close! We'll get there at seven, as near as dammit. Or, Can we make it in two hours? As near as dammit. The origin of the phrase is *as near as 'damn it' is to swearing.* Cf. **as near as makes no odds.**

as near as makes no odds   *Inf.* **just about**
   Inf. Sometimes *as near as makes no matter.* Either is the equivalent of *give or take a bit.* For example: *I'll get there at nine, as near as makes no odds,* i.e., so near that it makes no difference. Cf. **as near as dammit.**

as nice as ninepence   *Inf.* **as nice as pie**
   Inf. Unexpectedly pleasant and helpful.

as safe as a bank, *Inf.*   **perfectly safe**

as safe as houses, *Inf.*   **perfectly safe**

assessment for. See **suffer an assessment for.**

assessor, *n*   **adjuster**
   One who investigates an insurance claim.

assistant, *n.*   **clerk; salesman; saleslady**
   Assistant, in this British use, is short for *shop assistant,* which usually means a 'sales-person' or 'salesclerk,' but can also mean in a more general sense a 'shop attendant' who may not be there to sell you anything but to help out generally. In Britain one hears of a *bootmaker's assistant,* who would be called a *shoe clerk* in America, a *florist's assistant,* who would be described in America as a *salesman* or *saleslady at a florist's,* etc. *Assistant* and *shop assistant* have always seemed to be euphemisms to raise the spirits without raising the wages of the persons involved. See also **clerk.**

assisting the police   **held for questioning**
   Sometimes *assisting in the inquiry.* These euphemisms are coupled with the practice of withholding names in newspaper reports until the persons involved are formally charged.

assizes, *n. pl.*   **court sessions**
   The periodic sessions of the judges of the superior courts in each county of England and Wales.

association football (soccer). See **football.**

as soon as look at you, *Inf.*   *Inf.* **before you can say 'Jack Robinson'**

as soon as say knife, *Inf.*   *Inf.* **before you can say 'Jack Robinson'**
   Also *before you can (could) say knife.*

assurance, *n.*   **insurance**
   Assurance lingers on, quaintly enough, in the name of the gigantic Equitable Life Assurance Society of the United States (also, note *Society,* rather than *Company*). *Assurance* is the usual term in Britain. The person or firm covered is *the assured,* and the insurance company is the *assurance society.*

as under   **as follows**
   For instance, at the top of a bill for services, one might see, *For professional services as under.*

as well   **too**
   Mostly a matter of preference. *She speaks French as well* would be usual in Britain; *She speaks French, too,* would be more likely in America. *Too* at the beginning of a sentence, meaning 'besides,' occasionally met with in American writing, is a non-British usage.

At, *n.*   SEE COMMENT
   Inf. Partial acronym for (member of) *Women's Auxiliary Territorial Service (A.T.S.)* in World War II, nowadays known as *Women's Royal Army Corps*—*WRAC* for short. See also **WAAC; WREN.** See **fanny.** Comment 3.

at close of play   *Inf.* **when all is said and done**
   Inf. More concretely, it can refer to the end of a certain period or to the conclusion of a situation: *Let me have the memorandum by close of play on Wednesday.* One of the many expressions taken over from cricket. See also **at the end of the day**.

at half-cock   *Inf.* **half-cocked**
   Inf. As in the expression *go off at half-cock.*

athletics, *n. pl.*   **sports**
   Athlete, though used in the broad sense, generally connotes participation in track and field. In a British school one goes *in* for *athletics,* rather than *out* for *sports.*

at risk   **in danger**
   E.g., *If we let this slip by, the whole project is at risk.*

at the end of the day   **when all is said and done**
   Expressing the ultimate effect or result of foregoing activity or discussion: *Large housing units may be more efficient, but at the end of the day people want their separate homes. Hard feelings were expressed by both sides, but at the end of the day, they parted friends.* See also **at close of play.**

at the crunch   *Inf.* **in the clutch**
   Inf. When the chips are down; a favorite of Winston Churchill.

at the side of   *Inf.* **alongside; beside**
   Inf. Used in odious comparisons: *She's ugly at the side of her cousin Betty.*

attract, *v.t.*   **involve; entail**
   A British bank, answering a customer's letter about its rendering a certain service, wrote: *The work on your enquiry will attract a small charge.* Also used in tax terminology: *This stock will attract capital gains tax rather than income tax. Those wishing to pass on capital to their families without attracting any liability to tax....*(Note *to* tax rather than *for* tax; see **Appendix I.A.1.** on preposition usage in Britain.) In this last example, *incur* may be a preferable equivalent and the author of the tax advice might have been better advised to use the word *incurring,* because it is the thing or operation which *attracts* the tax, not the person.

aubergine, *n.*   **eggplant**

au fait   *Inf.* **conversant**
   Fairly common in Britain; rarely used in America, and then only by the literati.

Aunt Edna   *Inf.* **little old lady from Dubuque**
   Inf. Aunt Edna is Terence Rattigan's invention. Like Harold Ross's *little old lady from Dubuque,* she is the prototypically provincial nice old lady with whom one must be very careful when suggesting reading matter or theatrical entertainment. See also **Wigan.**

Auntie, *n.*   SEE COMMENT
   Slang. The affectionate nickname for the BBC, synonymous with **the Beeb.** *Auntie* used to be short for *Auntie Times,* meaning, of course, *The Times* (of London).

Auntie Times. See **Auntie.**

Aunt Sally   1. *Slang.* **patsy**
                                                          2. *Inf.* **trial balloon**
   1. *Inf.* An *Aunt Sally* is a *butt.* The term is derived from the carnival game in which one throws balls at a figure known as *Aunt Sally.*
   2. *Inf.* Since it is something set up to be knocked down, it has acquired the meaning of 'trial balloon,' a proposition submitted for criticism.

au pair   **1. giving services for board and lodging**
                                                          2. SEE COMMENT
   1. (Pronounced OH-PAIR.) This term from French applies generically to service bartering arrangements between two parties, with little or no money changing hands. A doctor and a lawyer might thus make an *au pair* arrangement. British families also exchange children with foreign families in order to broaden the children's experience, this being another type of *au pair* arrangement.

2. The term is heard generally in the expression *au pair girl* (often called just an *au pair*) and refers to the common British custom of a family giving a home to a girl from abroad who helps with the children and the housekeeping. For an unrelated use of *pair*, see **pair**.

Autocue, *n.*   **Teleprompter**
Proprietary names.

awkward, *adj.*   **troublesome; annoying**
Often used in Britain to mean 'difficult,' in the sense of 'hard to deal with,' referring to people who aren't easy to get along with.

B

baby-watcher, *n.*   **baby-sitter**
And *baby-watching* is *baby-sitting.* Cf. **child-minder.**

back bacon   *approx.* **Canadian bacon**

back bench, *n.*   SEE COMMENT
Occupied by Members of the House of Commons or other body not entitled to a seat
on the front benches, which are occupied by ministers (cabinet members) and other
members of the government and oppostion leaders. See also **front bench; cross bench.**

back-dated, *adj.*   **retroactive**
Referring to pay raises (cf. **retrospective**); nothing to do with the unsavory practice
of backdating, i.e., predating, gifts of vice-presidential papers and other documents.

back-end, *n.*   **late autumn**
Mainly North of England.

backhander, *n.*   **graft**
Headline *Evening Standard* (London) June 14, 1973:
"'Corruption' trial hears of payments to officials: Ex-Mayor Tells Of Backhanders To
Councillors."
(**Councillors** *are councilmen.*)

backlog, *n.*   **overstock**
To a British businessman, *backlog* can mean 'overstocked inventory,' an unhappy
condition, as well as a heartening accumulation of orders waiting to be filled.

back-room boy. See **boffin.**

back slang   SEE COMMENT
Slang created by spelling words backwards, an exclusively British pastime. Example:
ecilop is back slang for 'police' and the origin of the slang noun *slop* meaning 'police.'

back to our muttons   *Inf.* **back to business**
Slang. After a digression in a serious discussion, during which they had wandered
further and further afield into tortuous bypaths: *Well now, back to our muttons,* i.e., 'Let's
get back to the subject.' From the French "Revenons à nos moutons," in the old farce
of Maître Pathelin, in which the witnesses keep straying from the matter in dispute,
which involves some sheep.

backwardation, *n.*   **delayed delivery penalty**
A London Stock Exchange term. It consists of a percentage of the selling price payable
by the seller of shares for the privilege of delaying their delivery. See also **contango.**

backwoodsman, *n.*   SEE COMMENT
Inf. The literal use of this word in Britain is the same as the American. Figuratively,
a *peer* who rarely, if ever, attends the House of Lords.

bad hat, *Inf.*   *Inf.* **bad egg**

bad patch   *Inf.* **rough time**
Inf. When things are not going well with someone, the British say that he is in or
going through a *bad patch*; in America he would be described as having a *rough time* (of
it). For other idiomatic uses of *patch*, see **patch** and **not a patch on.**

bad show!   1. *Inf.* **tough luck!**
                                                                                 2. *Slang.* **lousy!**
1. *Inf.* A show of sympathy.
2. *Inf.* A rebuke for a poor performance.
A ghastly show is a *terrible mess.* See also **good show!**

bag, *n., v.i.*   1. **POW camp**
                                                                                 2. **drop off course**

1. *n., Slang.* Prisoner-of-war camp.
2. *v.i.*, Nautical term.

bag a brace. See **duck.**

baggage service   **lost and found**
Also, *Lost Property Office.*

bagging-hook, *n.*   **small scythe**
A rustic term synonymous with **swop.**

bagman, *n.*   **traveling salesman**
This old-fashioned term does not have the abusive meaning of *graft collector*, as in
America. Synonymous with **commercial traveller.**

bags, *n. pl.*   **slacks**
Inf. Oxford *bags* were a 1920s style characterized by the exaggerated width of the
trouser legs.

bags I!   *Slang.* **Dibs on...! I dibsy! I claim!**
Schoolboy slang. Sometimes *I bag!* or *I Bags!* or *baggy!* or *bagsy! Bags, first innings!* is
another variant. *First innings* in this context means a 'first crack at something.' See **first
innings.** Examples: *Baggy, no washing up!* (see **wash up**) which would be shouted by a
youngster trying to get out of doing the dishes, or *I bag the biggest one!* proclaimed by
one of a group of children offered a number of apples or candies of unequal size. **Fains
I!** is the opposite of *Bags I!*

bags of...   *Inf.* **piles of...**
Inf. Usually in the phrase *bags of money.*

bail.   See **wicket; up stumps.**

bailiff, *n.*   1. **sheriff's assistant**
                                                                               2. **estate or farm
                                                                                     manager**
1. A British *bailiff* is one employed by a sheriff to serve legal papers and make arrests.
An American *bailiff* is a minor court functionary in the nature of a messenger, usher,
etc.

bait, *n.*   1. *Slang.* **fit (of anger)**
                                                                               2. *Slang.* **grub (food)**

Slang. Also spelled *bate* for **1.**

bajan, bajanella. See **fresher.**

baked custard. See **custard.**

baked potato. See **jacket potato.**

bakehouse, *n.*   **bakery**
Where bread is baked, not sold.

baker-legged, *adj., Slang.*   *Slang.* **knock-kneed**

balaam, *n.*   *Slang.* **fillers**
Newspaper slang. Miscellaneous items to fill newspaper space; set in type and kept in readiness, in a *Balaam-box.*(The prophet Balaam could not meet the requirements of Balak, king of Moab, when commanded to curse the Israelites, and the curse became a blessing instead (Num. 22–24). Balaam thus became the prototype of the disappointing prophet or ineffective ally.) It was not easy to see the connection until an article by Philip Howard appeared in a December 1980 issue of *The Times* (London) in which he referred to a 'Balaam-basket,' which is another name for a *Balaam-box.* The article starts as follows:

> Let us have a look in the Balaam-basket for something to enliven or vex the day. Balaam is an agreeable obsolete term of the inky trade. Thomas Wright defined it in his magisterial *Dictionary of Obsolete and Provincial English* of 1857: Balaam: this is the cant term in a newspaper office for asinine paragraphs about monstrous productions of nature and the like, kept standing in type to be used whenever the news of the day leave (sic) an awkward space that must be filled somehow.
> A Balaam-basket or box is the receptacle for such useful little "fillers", as we now call them in the trade. The eponym of the term is Balaam's long-suffering and voluble ass. In a perfect world the filler paragraphs would be set in 9 point, so that one could bring out the pun by referring to Balaam's Ass in Nine Point.

Balaclava, *n.*   **woolen helmet**
Short for *Balaclava helmet,* which is made of wool and pulled over the head, leaving the face exposed. Balaclava was the site of an important battle of the Crimean War. That war made two other contributions to fashion; the sleeve named for Lord Raglan, who occupied the town of Balaclava, and the sweater which was the invention of the seventh Earl of Cardigan, commander of the famous Light Brigade. In America, known to the skiing set.

(The) ball's in your court   *Inf.* **It's up to you**
Inf. The ball's in your court means 'It is your move now.' A variant is *The ball's at your foot.* Used increasingly in America.

ballocks, *n. pl.*   *Vulgar.* **balls**
Vulgar. Probably the origin of the American phrase *all ballocksed* (also *bollixed*) *up*, a variation on *all balled up*, and undoubtedly the origin of *ballocky*, American slang for *naked. Bollocks* now the common spelling.

balls, *n. pl.*   1. *Slang.* **crap (nonsense)**
                                                                    2. *Inf.* **mess**
1. *Slang.* This word is used by itself, as a rather inelegant expletive, in America. In Britain it appears in expressions like *That's a lot of balls,* i.e., *stuff and nonsense,* or *balderdash,* or, in rude terms, *crap.*
2. *Slang.* To make a *balls* of something is to make a *mess* of it, to *louse it up.* A variant of *balls* in this sense is *balls-up.* The familiar expressions to *ball up* (a situation) and *all balled up* are of course echoes of this usage. Synonymous with *balls* and *balls-up* in this sense are **cock** and **cock-up**.
Said by a British army general (May 1974), referring to a certain area of organization and planning:

> ...but in case we become complacent, we should remember that it is said that from the ashes of yesterday's cock-up arises the balls-up of tomorrow!

Said by Siegfried Sassoon in April 1922 in answer to T.E. Lawrence's question whether he'd been writing much lately, "in defiant tones (fixing my disgruntled gaze on an upper window of the Junior United Services Club): 'I sit up all night writing **bloody balls.**'" When asked by Lawrence, "Do you burn the *balls?*" S.S. replied "Yes; I burn it." Note the singular *it,* meaning the 'crap' the poet had discarded. (From the *Siegfried Sassoon Diaries 1920–1922* (Faber & Faber, London, 1981).

bally, *adj., adv.*   *Slang.* **damned**
   Slang. (Rhymes with SALLY.) Expressing disgust, like **bloody**. But it can, by a kind of
reverse English, express the exact opposite, i.e., satisfaction, as in: *We bet on three races
and won the bally lot.* One of several euphemistic variants of **bloody**, like **blinking,
blooming, ruddy,** etc. All these euphemisms sound very mild and old-fashioned nowadays. *Bally* itself is practically obsolete.

band, *n.*   **bracket**
   Tax term; synonymous with **slice** and **tranche.**

B & B   SEE COMMENT
   Inf. Short for *Bed and Breakfast.* Sight seen on British roadsides pointing the way, most
often, to pleasant and inexpensive lodgings and a satisfying meal next morning, including amiable chatter. Nothing to do with *Benedictine and Brandy.*

bandit-proof, *adj.*   **bulletproof**
   Bulletproof is also used in Britain.

bandy-legged, *adj.*   *Inf.* **bowlegged**
   Inf. Referring to persons, and occasionally used also in America. When describing
furniture, the British use *bowlegged.*

bang, *adv.*   **absolutely**
   Slang. Evelyn Waugh ends his novel *Put Out More Flags* (Chapman & Hall, London,
1942) with the sentence: "And, poor booby, he was *bang* right." See also **bang-on.**

banger, *n.*   **1. Sausage**
                                                             2. *Slang.* **jalopy**
                                                             3. firecracker
   1. *Slang.* Derived from the tendency of sausages to burst open with a *bang* in the frying
pan. See also **slinger.**
   2. *Slang.* Derived from the backfire emitted by old heaps.
   3. *Schoolboy slang.*

bang off, *Slang.*   *Slang.* **pronto**

bang on   *Slang.* **on the nose**
   Slang. Exactly as planned or predicted. Literally, *bang on target,* of World Wars I and
II vintage. Synonymous with **dead on.** See also **bang; dead on; spot-on.**

banjo, *v.t.*   *Inf.* **beat up**
   Slang. An underworld term heard in London.

(the) Bank, *n.*   SEE COMMENT
   Always capitalized, it means the 'Bank of England,' Britain's central bank, which
presides over the financial system as a whole. *Bank* is the name of a subway (**underground**: see **subway**) station that serves the area around the Bank of England. See **(the)
City.**

banker's order   **money transfer order**
   Written instructions filed with one's bank for the making of periodic payments to a
third party, such as mortgage payments, alimony payments, and other obligations you
had better not default on. This is common practice in Britain, rare in America. The
American equivalent given above is not a term in common banking usage but was
painfully arrived at only after discussions with bank officers. There would seem to be
no American term universally current in banking practice. *Mandate* is a British synonym,
which also seems to cover the case where the order to the bank is for a fixed amount,
subject, however, to such change as may be directed by the payee, on notification to
the depositor, e.g., in the case of an annual subscription which may be increased by
the organization, such as the **A.A.** (*Automobile Association*), or the C.G.A (Country
Gentlemen's Association—a cooperative).

bank holiday, *n.* **legal holiday**
Also used as an adjective, as in *bank-holiday* Monday. *Bank holidays* were introduced in 1871 by John Lubbock, for many years a Liberal Member of Parliament. He wrote a number of books: *The Pleasures of Life, Peace and Happiness, The Beauties of Nature,* and *Ants, Bees, and Wasps.* The connection between these subject matters and an extra day off is obvious. For years the grateful public called *bank holidays* "St. Lubbock's Days."

bank note. See **note.**

bant, *v.i.* **diet**
To *bant* is to *diet.* Dr. W. Banting, who died in 1878, originated a treatment for overweight based on abstinence from sugar, starch, etc. His name became a common noun: *banting* became and remained the name of this dieting procedure. The word ending in *-ing* looked like a gerund, so by back-formation the verb to *bant* came into being. Rare today. See also **slim.**

bap, *n.* **hamburger roll** or **bun**
Somewhat larger than the customary American variety. Originated in Scotland and the North Country; now common in London. The roll is slightly sweet and very tasty, and large enough to be cut in strips top to bottom (rather than horizontally) for toasting.

bar, *n.* See **lounge bar; private bar; pub.**

bar, *v.t.* *approx.* **loathe**
Slang. When you *bar* something, you 'can't stand' it. No equivalent in American slang.

bar, *prep.* **but; except**
Heard more in the country than in the city. After digging holes in the lawn to repair land drains: *We'll fill them all bar the bottom one.* Thus also: *All over bar the shouting.*
A special usage is found in horse racing, where, after the favorites' odds are posted, they put up an entry headed BAR, followed by odds, e.g., BAR 20/1. Here, *bar* is short for *bar the favorites* and means that each of the remaining horses in the rest of the field is at 20 to 1. Sometimes one sees *20/1 bar one* or, *20/1 bar two* (or *three,* etc.) which means the field are all at 20 to 1, and you then have to inquire about the *one* or *two* (or *three,* etc.) who are not in the field, i.e., the favorites, and get their odds from those in charge.

bar billiards. See **billiards-saloon.**

bargain, *n.* **stock market transaction**
A narrow usage. The ominous phrase *unable to comply with their bargains,* usually found in newspaper and radio reports of bankruptcies (especially in the matter of stock exchange firms), comes out in America as *unable to meet their obligations.* However it's said, it's extremely bad news.

bargee, *n.* **barge operator**
Pronounced BAR-GEE'. This is mainly a canal boat term. There is a great deal of canal slang which would have no equivalent in America because the British inland waterways system has no real American equivalent. *Lucky bargee,* like its American equivalents *lucky stiff* and *lucky dog,* implies a certain degree of friendly envy but has no canal connotations. See also **lengthman; navvy.**

barge-pole, *n.* *Inf.* **ten-foot pole**
Inf. That with which a Briton would refuse to touch certain other Britons. Can also be used of an unsavory proposition. Another object left unused by the British in the same connection is a *pair of tongs.*
As to *pole* in this usage, a friend has invented the collapsible ten-foot pole. It telescopes down to six inches in length, so that, fitted with a clip, it can be carried like a fountain pen. On sighting the approach of a particularly unlovable person, the lucky owner pulls out this indispensable gadget, extends it (by whipping it through the air, or, in the more expensive model, by pressing a button that releases a series of springs)

to its exact ten-foot length, and, as the unlovable one approaches, points the pole at him while adamantly refraining from touching him with it. Thus far, the inventor has failed to secure financial backing. Anyone interested in investing write to The Collapsible Barge Pole Company. This is not a prospectus.

barman   **bartender**
The British also say *bartender*. The female counterpart is a *barmaid*—traditionally bright, breezy, and buxom.

barmy, *adj.*   *Slang.* **balmy**
Slang. Sometimes extended to *barmy on the crumpet*. See also **crumpet**.

barmy on the crumpet. See **biscuit; crumpet.**

barney, barny, *n., Slang.*   **squabble**

baronet, *n.*   **(hereditary) knight**
Member of the lowest hereditary order. *Sir* precedes the name; *Baronet* (usually abbreviated to *Bart.*, sometimes *Bt.*) follows it: *Sir John Smith, Bart.* See also **Dame; Lady; K.; Lord.**

baron of beef. See under **sirloin.**

barrack, *v.t., v.i.*   1. *Slang.* **boo**
                                                                                                      2. root for
1. *Slang.* To demonstrate noisily in a public place, like a stadium or a theater, against a team, a player, or a performer; to *jeer;* to *hoot*. Said to come as a back formation from the cockney term *barrakin,* meaning 'gibberish'; or, possibly, derived from *borak,* Australian and New Zealand slang for 'nonsense' or 'banter,' but this derivation is considered questionable. *Barrack* is commonly used in both of those countries.
2. *Slang.* In the proper context, *barrack* can mean just the opposite, i.e., to 'root for' a team or player.

barrage, *n.*   **dam**
The two countries share the other more common meanings, military and figurative, of this word, but even in those cases the British accent the first syllable, as they do in *garage,* and soften the *g* to ZH. In the special British meaning of a 'dam in a watercourse,' the accent stays the same but the *g* sound is hardened to J, as in *jump*.

barrel, *n.*   SEE COMMENT
Weight unit. See **Appendix II.C.1.a.**

barrier, *n.*   **gate**
Railroad term meaning the 'gate' through which one passes to and from the platform. A guard standing at the *barrier* collects your ticket (or glances at it again if it is a *season ticket* or round-trip ticket) as you leave. If you don't have it as you leave, you pay the fare to the guard (who takes you at your word when you tell him where you boarded the train) and get a receipt, or else you throw yourself on his mercy and explain its mysterious disappearance, usually without success. There is usually no *conductor* (an American term, in railroad idiom; *conductor,* in British transportation, is confined to buses) to take your ticket on commuter and short distance trains. On long distance trains, that function is performed by a *travelling ticket inspector*. Occasionally, a ticket inspector will range through first class compartments to root out passengers traveling on second class tickets, and collect the difference in fares (with a stern expression).

barrister, *n.*   **trial lawyer**
A *barrister* is also known as *counsel*. Apart from serving as *trial lawyers, barristers* are resorted to by **solicitors** *(general practitioners)* for written expert opinions in special fields of the law. The *solicitor* is the person the client retains. The *solicitor* retains the *barrister* or *counsel*. The *solicitor* can try cases in certain inferior courts. The *barrister-solicitor* dichotomy is a legal institution in Britain. It exists in practice in America, where, tech-

nically, any attorney may try cases, but most practitioners resort to trial counsel in litigated matters. See also **brief; called to the bar; chambers; counsel; solicitor.**
There is a passage in Henry Cecil's *Settled Out of Court* (Michael Joseph, London, 1959) in which a **solicitor** explains the dichotomy to a client:

> . . .The legal profession in this country is divided into two branches. The superior, that is the Bar; the lowly and inferior, that is the solicitor's profession. But, humble and lowly as we are, we do have the great honour of being allowed to supply the superior branch with the necessities of life, briefs.

This sardonic treatment of the subject was occasioned by the fact that judges are selected only from the bar, and some of them, who, when they were barristers, depended upon solicitors for their living, tend to forget the hand that fed them and adopt a very superior attitude toward their former benefactors.

barrow, *n.*   **pushcart**
This word means 'pushcart' when referring to a street vendor. In gardening, it is the equivalent of *wheelbarrow*, which is also used in Britain. See also **trolley. Pushcart** is sometimes used in Britain to mean 'baby carriage'; but usually means 'handcart.'

Bart. See **Baronet.**

base rate   **prime rate**
Banking term.

bash, *n., v.t.*   *Inf.* **bang (hit)**
Inf. May be a **portmanteau** blend of *bang* and *smash*, common in Britain and becoming standard. All too common in the extremely unpleasant terms *Paki-bashing* and *wog-bashing*. See **Paki** and **wog.** See also the amusing usage of the word in **have a bash at.**

basin, *n.*   **sink**
Basin is used when referring to the fixture in any room other than the kitchen. **Sink** must be used in Britain when referring to a kitchen fixture. Sometimes *wash-basin.*

basket, *n.*   *Slang.* **bastard**
Slang. A euphemism, especially in the vocative, and in the phrase *little basket*, describing a particularly naughty child.

bat. See **carry one's bat; off one's own bat; play a straight bat; batsman.**

bate. See **bait.**

bat first   **go first**
Inf. Start the ball rolling; a term borrowed from cricket. Synonymous with **take first knock.**

bath, *n., v.t., v.i.*   1. **bathtub**
                                                                                                   2. **bathe**
1. In Britain, as in America, one can *take a bath,* although in Britain one usually *has,* rather than *takes, a bath.* One sits or soaks in the *bath* in Britain rather than in the *bathtub,* as in America. Showers are much less common than they are in America.
2. As a verb, *bath* is used like *bathe* in America: one can *bath* the baby (give it a bath) or, simply *bath* (take a bath). See also **bathe.**

bath bun   SEE COMMENT
A type of *sweet bun* which is filled with small seedless raisins called **sultanas** and candied citrus rinds, and has a glazed top studded with coarse grains of white sugar. The term has been heard occasionally in unkind slang usage to mean 'old bag,' i.e., 'crone.'

bath-chair, *n.* wheelchair
Sometimes the *b* is capitalized, showing derivation from the city of Bath where their use originated as pleasure vehicles. Also called **invalid's chair** and **wheeled chair.**

bath chap pig's cheek
A butcher's term. *Chap* is a variant of *chop*. The pig's cheek is usually smoked.

bathe, *n.* swim
In Britain one *swims* in the sea, but one also takes a *bathe* in the sea. See also **bath; front; sea.**

bathing costume bathing suit
Sometimes *bathing dress* or *swimming costume*. *Bathing dress* used to be confined to women's outfits. All these terms are rather old-fashioned. In Britain today *bathing suit* or *swimsuit* are the terms generally used and apply indiscriminately to that worn by either sex.

bathing drawers swimming trunks
Still heard, if rarely, among the elderly.

Bath Oliver SEE COMMENT
A type of cookie or sweet cracker (the British say **biscuit**) invented by Dr. W. Oliver (d. 1764) of the city of Bath. It is about, an eigth of an inch thick, dry and sweetish—not quite as sweet as an American graham cracker. See also **digestive; biscuit.** A vital question relating to the *Bath Oliver* was answered in the following letter published in *The Times* (London) of September 19, 1986:

> **Heads or tails**
> *From Mr Cyril Ray*
> Sir, The answer to Mr. Simon Gray's question (September 13) on which side of his Bath Oliver he should spread the butter when, at the end of the meal, he comes to the cheese is—neither.
> No one who cares about the taste and the texture of cheese allows his appreciation of them to be confused by the taste and the texture of butter. This, indeed, is why the Bath Oliver—best of all biscuits for cheese (save the Aemrican [sic] Bremner Wafer) since the lamented demise of the Romary — is made austerely dry.
> Yours faithfully,
> CYRIL RAY,
> Brooks's
> St. James's Street, SW1.

batman, *n.* military officer's servant
Not to be confused with either the comic book hero or the **batsman** in cricket. The origin of the term was admirably explained in a letter from the late writer Desmond Bagley that initiated a friendship between him and the author:

> In French the appearance of a circumflex accent indicates a dropped *s*, as in the pairs *hôtel-hostel, tête-testa* from *testa*, a 'pot', Roman army slang for a 'head.' The *bat* in *batman* comes from the Norman-French *bast*—a 'saddle.' Hence *bastard*, a 'child of the saddle,' the **byblow** of a travelling man. *Bâtman* retained the circumflex accent as late as 1870 in Sir Garnet Wolseley's excellent *Soldier's Pocket Book*. Wolseley also refers to bât animals, bât camels, bât elephants—the pack animals which accompanied the army. And so a bâtman was the man detailed to look after the saddle and equipment of the officer's charger and the name was later generalized to mean any officer's servant. Incidentally, the proverbial phrase, **All Sir Garnet**, often heard in England, refers to the above *Soldier's Pocket Book*, and means that the job has been 'done by the book.'

baton, *n.*   *Inf.* **billy; nightstick**
(Accent on the first syllable.) Also called a **truncheon.** Carried by policemen.

batsman, *n.*   **batter**
Cricket vs. baseball. The British say *fielder* or *fieldsman,* but never *batter.* Generally, *batsman* is shortened to *bat: Clive is a fine bat!* See also **bat first; carry one's bat; off one's own bat; play a straight bat.**

Battersea box   SEE COMMENT
Cylindrical or bottle-shaped little enameled copper case with decorated hinged top, typically for perfume, bonbons, etc. The authentic antique boxes were produced at Battersea, a part of London, for only a few years (1753–56) and are rare and expensive. Good copies are being made today with traditional or new designs. Siegfried Sassoon, in his *Diaries 1923–1925* (Faber & Faber, London, 1985) tells us, under August 23, 1925: "Very pleasant chat with E.G. [Edmund Gosse, critic, biographer and man of letters, knighted in 1925]. His Golden Wedding was on August 13. Today I gave him a little Battersea enamel box which I bought at Penzance. On it a motto, 'Until the end I am your friend'."

BBC English   SEE COMMENT
The reference is to the speech of the announcers which is considered by some to be the standard pronunciation of English. This situation has changed since the BBC started employing announcers from different parts of the country, especially the Midlands and Scotland, who don't necessarily speak *RP,* which stands for **Received Pronunciation.** The label *BBC English* can, in certain contexts, be pejorative. To say of someone that he has a BBC accent may imply that he has worked very hard to lose his own, indicating social climbing rather than "culture." In a page one article under the facetious headline "BBC's word game a pronounced success," *The Times* (London) of August 19, 1977, quoted the head of the BBC pronunciation unit to the effect that English was particularly rich in alternative pronunciations of equal authority. When the BBC tried to establish pronunciations, there was such disagreement that the experiment was withdrawn and the chairman of the BBC Speech Advisory Panel remarked, "If the announcer can produce the impression that he is a gentleman, he may pronounce as he pleases." A piece by Vivian Ducat in the *Atlantic Monthly* of September 1986 entitled "Words from the Wise," characterized in the heading as "A tale from the archives of the BBC, in which a star chamber of eminences set out to refine, improve, purify and otherwise put aright the Mother Tongue, with consequences that fall far short of those intended and yet somehow amount to more than meets the ear," dwells on the subject:

> It was a valiant effort, even if the results have been disappointing. The English spoken in Great Britain today is by no means homogeneous. Turn on the BBC and you are likely to hear accents very different from those that were prescribed by the advisory committee. A range of "non-standard" accents—Scottish, Northern Irish, and various regional English accents—have joined what is now a somewhat modified version of Received Pronunciation. In England the accents on radio and TV increasingly reflect those of the British population as a group. And yet the advisory committee's recommendations of a half century ago have not been entirely cast aside. Its work, in perhaps unexpected ways, lives on.

See also **Received Pronunciation.**

beach, *n.*   **gravel**
When a Briton wants to close up a ditch with *fill* or *gravel* he uses *beach.* (When he wants to swim at the beach, he goes to the **sea** or *seaside.*)

beadle. See **bumble.**

beak, *n.*   **1. schoolmaster**
                                                                2. magistrate

Slang. No precise American slang for either meaning.

bean, *n.*

1. *Inf.* **cent**
2. *Slang.* **pep**
3. *Slang.* **hell**
4. *Slang.* **guy; fellow**

1. *Slang. I haven't a bean* means 'I'm broke.'
2. *Slang. Full of beans* means 'full of pep.'
3. *Slang.* To *give someone beans* is to *give someone hell.*
4. *Slang.* In the expression *old bean,* rather outmoded and more likely to be encountered in P.G. Wodehouse than in current speech.

bean-feast, *n.*   **company picnic**
Slang. Also called a **beano.** Apparently, pork and beans (in Britain **beans and bacon**) were considered an indispensable element of the annual company celebration. The term has been extended to mean any merry occasion.

beano. See **bean-feast.**

beans and bacon   **pork and beans**

bearing-rein, *n.*   **sidecheck**

bearskin, *n.*   SEE COMMENT
High fur hat worn by the Brigade of **Guards;** much higher than a **busby.**

beastly, *adj., adv.*

1. unpleasant
2. terribly (very)

beasts, *n. pl.*   **cattle**
As used by Katherine Mansfield in her short story *Marriage à la Mode.* A usage that would be understood only in the context of farm atmosphere.

beat up   *Inf.* **pick up**
Inf. In the sense of 'picking somebody up,' by prearrangement, to go somewhere together. Planning to go out to dinner and the theater, one might say, *I'll be around at about 7:00 P.M. to beat you up.* This usage recalls the image of the *beaters* who flush grouse, pheasant, partridge, and other game birds, and more faintly, that of the African beaters who rouse the beasts of the jungle from their lethargy for the benefit of hunters. To *beat up the town,* however, is to *paint it red.*

beck, *n.*   **brook**

bed and breakfast   *approx. Slang.* **wash sale**
Slang. In addition to its standard meaning of 'sleeping accommodations with breakfast thrown in,' this term has a slang meaning in tax law, describing the sale of securities to establish a tax loss followed by an immediate repurchase of the same securities. This wash sale scheme was ruled out in American capital gain taxation years ago, but not until April 1975 in Britain.

bed bath   **sponge bath**
Synonymous with **blanket bath.**

bed-board, *n.*   **headboard**

bedding, *n., adj.*   **annuals**
A single annual plant is called a *bedder.* Americans are occasionally surprised to see *bedding* advertised for sale in plant nurseries. Also used as an adjective, as in *bedding plants.*

bed-sitter, *n.*   **one room apartment**
Inf. *Bed-sitting room,* meaning a 'combination bedroom-living room'; usually called
bedsit when referring to a room in a hotel. It does not have its own bathroom. If one is
included, the unit becomes a *studio. Bedsit-land* is the Earl's Court area of London, where
large mansions have been cut up into tiny units. Bedsits bespeak hard times, a transient's existence, poverty, student and artist life. People speak of their *bedsit period* and
of *bedsit mentality. Bedsit* is also a verb, meaning to 'occupy a bedsit.'

(the) Beeb, *n.*   SEE COMMENT
Slang. Affectionate nickname for the BBC, snynonymous with **Auntie.**

beefeater, *n.*   SEE COMMENT
A *warder* (guard) of the Tower of London. They are dressed in ornately decorated red
uniforms and distinctively shaped top hats, dating from the fifteenth century. For illustration (if you can't get to the Tower), see a performance of Gilbert and Sullivan's
Yeomen of the Guard or the label on a bottle of a popular gin. The Tower of London,
originally a royal fortress and palace, became a prison and the *warders* thus became
jailers. (A related American prison term is *warden,* the head man at a prison.) Nowadays,
the Tower, a huge collection of buildings housing many objects of historical interest,
including the crown jewels, is crawling with tourists, and the *beefeaters* are its official
guides, knowledgeable and literate, who take groups around, dispensing history and
wit in large doses. The name is supposed to have developed from the concept of *well-
fed* (i.e., *beef-fed*) royal servants, but a *beefeater* named John Wilmington, the Raven
Master at the Tower (charged with the duty of feeding and looking after the ravens
which traditionally dwell there) claims that the name was derived from the Norman
French word *buffetier,* meaning to 'wear a leather jerkin.' This seems doubtful, to put
it mildly. In his *Etymological Dictionary* (Oxford, 1879, still in print; good fun and very
good value) W.W. Skeat discusses other possible variations but sticks to *beef* as the
basis.

beer and skittles   *Inf.* **a bed of roses**
Inf. Skittles being, literaly, a ninepins game, *beer and skittles* would seem to be an apt
phrase for *fun and games, high amusement.* Almost always used in the negative: *Life is not
all beer and skittles,* or, *This job is not all beer and skittles.*

beetle-crusher, *n.*   *Slang.* **clodhopper**

beetle off   *Inf.* **take off**
Slang. Sometimes without the *off: It was warm, so we beetled (off) to the sea.*

beetroot, *n.*   **beet(s)**
The table vegetable known in America as *beet* is always called *beetroot* in Britain.
Beetroot does not add an *s* in the plural. *Beet,* in Britain, describes a related plant, the
root of which is white, not red, used for either the feeding of cattle or the making of
sugar, and usually called *sugar beet.*

before you can say knife. See **as soon as say knife.**

beggar, *n.*   *Slang.* **guy; son of a gun**
Slang. The British use *beggar* literally, as we do. They also use it figuratively, in a
pejorative sense, to describe an unsavory character, as in, *a miserable beggar;* or favorably,
to convey admiration, as in, *a plucky little beggar.* Probably a euphemism for *bugger.*

beginners!, *interj.*   **places, please!**
Stage manager's cry.

behindhand, *adj.*   **behind**
As in, *a maid behindhand with her housework.*

Belisha beacon   **street crossing light**
(Pronounced BE-LEE'-SHA). Ubiquitous post topped by a flashing yellow globe to designate pedestrian crossing. They come in pairs, one on each side of the street, usually
reinforced by stripes running across the road (see **zebra**). Named after their innovator,
Leslie Hore-Belisha (1893–1957), Minister of Transport in 1934.

bell, *n.*   *Inf.* **ring**
Slang. To *give someone a bell* is to *give him a ring*, i.e., call him up. Newish criminal
and police slang.

below the salt. See **above the salt.**

belt, *n.*   **girdle**
Belt started out as a shortening of what in America would be known as a *garter belt*
and in Britain as a *suspender belt* (see **braces; suspenders**). But then *belt* became generic
for anything used by ladies to contain a certain part of the anatomy and the equivalent
of the American term *girdle*, which is now also widely heard in Britain.

belted earl (*or* **knight)**   SEE COMMENT
All earls and knights are *belted*, i.e., theoretically they wear sword belts. These are
affectionately jocular terms, like *noble lord* (all lords are noble) and *gracious duke* (all
dukes are *Your Grace*.)

belt up   *Slang.* **shut up**
Slang. The British also say **pack it up** or **put a sock in it; be said.**

be mum   **pour (the tea)**
Inf. Or the coffee. *I'll be mum* or, *Who's going to be mum?* evokes the image of cozy
family groups, with a kindly, beaming mom officiating, but it is used jocularly in entirely
male groups and even (according to Noel Mostert's *Supership* (Alfred A. Knopf, N.Y.,
1974)) in such strongholds of masculinity as the wardroom of an oil tanker. Also, *be
mother*.

bend, *n.*   **curve**
Referring to roads and used on road signs. A *double bend* is an *S curve*. For a different
use, see **round the bend.**

bender, *n.*   1. SEE COMMENT
                                                                           2. **trailer truck**
1. *Slang.* The old *sixpence*. See **Appendix II.A.**
2. *Slang.* Synonymous with *artic*, short slang for **articulated lorry.**

bent, *adj., Slang.*   1. **crooked; dishonest**
                                                                        2. **homosexual**

be quiet! *interj.*   *Inf.* **keep still!**
In this context, the British do not use *still* in the sense of 'keeping one's mouth shut.'
Keep still would be understood to mean 'Don't move.' See also **be said.**

berk, *n.*   *approx. Slang.* **dope**
Slang. A fool who is also unpleasant. This word is heard in mixed company, but
mightn't be if its origin were known. It is a shortening of *Berkeley*, which is short for
Berkeley Hunt, which is rhyming slang (see **Appendix II.G.3.**) for the "very short and
unattractive word" referred to by A.P. Herbert in his celebrated poem "Lines on a Book
Borrowed from the Ship's Doctor," disscussed under **fanny.**

berm, *n.*   **shoulder**
Of a road. Originally, a terrace between a moat and the bottom of a parapet. See also
verge.

Berwick cockles   SEE COMMENT
Very deceptive this. Not cockles at all, but shell-shaped mints made at Berwick-on-Tweed since 1801.

be said   *Inf.* **keep still**
Inf. Tais-toi! A peculiar use of the past participle of *say*, as though *said* were interchangeable with *told: I've spoken; you've been told* (to keep quiet); *you've been said; now be* (or, *stay) said!* A "homely old idiom," to quote C.P. Snow in *The Malcontents* (Macmillan Co. Ltd., London, 1972). He likes *be said:* he used it in *In Their Wisdom* (Scribners, New York, 1974), too. See also **be quiet.**

be sick   **throw up**
See **sick.**

besot, *v.t.*   1. **stupefy; muddle**
                                                                      2. **infatuate**
In America, the principal meaning of *besot* (which also has the two meanings listed above) is to 'get (someone) drunk,' to 'intoxicate,' so that *besotted* would usually be taken to mean 'drunk' or 'drunken.' The context of intoxicating liquor is absent in the British usage. Imagine the author's surprise and alarm on his first reading of a paragraph in *The Times* (London) of July 3, 1981 relating to the risk of fire at the forthcoming marriage of Prince Charles in St. Paul's. The director general of the British Safety Council, concerned about the lack of fire precautions

> . . . visited the cathedral . . . was appalled by what he found and accused the (fire) authorities of being so besotted with security that fire and safety were overlooked.

Obviously, *besotted* was used in its primary British meaning of 'muddled,' or perhaps, in this context, as a synonym of 'preoccupied' (to the extent of becoming muddled). It took a bit of dictionary investigation to dispel the impression of a group of 'authorities' so concerned with 'security' that they rushed to the nearest pub, took to drink, and forgot all about 'fire and safety!'

bespoke, adj.   **made to order; custom made**
Used in the phrases *bespoke clothes, bespoke tailor,* etc.

(the) best of British luck!   *Inf.* **lotsa luck!**
Inf. Said with heavy irony and implying very bad times ahead indeed.

best offer   **at the market**
When you want to tell your stockbroker to sell *at the market* in England, you tell him to sell **best offer.** This instruction permits him to unload at the bid price.

bethel, *n.*   **chapel**
A **dissenters'** *chapel:* also their meeting-house; sometimes *seamen's church,* whether afloat or on *terra firma.* Also called, at times, a *bethesda* or a *beulah.*

betterment levy   **improvement assessment**
Increase in your property taxes (**rates**) when you improve your property.

between whiles   **in between**
In the interval between other actions.

beyond the next turning. *See* **block.**

b.f.   *Slang.* **goddamned fool**
Slang. Stands for *bloody fool* (See **bloody.**) The titles of John Marquand's novel *BF's Daughter* and of the American film based on it were changed to *Polly-Fulton* in Britain. The *b.f.* is not to be confused with the proofreaders' mark for *boldface,* which is simplified to *bold* in Britain.

bib-overall, *n.*   SEE COMMENT
Overalls with a solid front top, known as a 'bib.'

bickie, *n.*   cracker
Slang. Rather simpering, reminiscent of the nursery, and beloved of older ladies, for
biscuit.

big bug. See **insect.**

big dipper   roller coaster
Synonymous with **switchback,** and nothing to do with Ursa Major.

Big Four   SEE COMMENT
This is the short name for the four big banks in Britain, which handle the overwhelm-
ing bulk of personal and corporate accounts: National Westminster, Barclays, Lloyds,
and Midland. There used to be five, until the National Provincial merged into the
Westminster.

big pot. See **pot.**

bike. *See* **motor-bike.**

bill, *n.*   check
In Britain one asks the waiter for his *bill,* rather than his *check.* (The Briton might pay
his *bill* by **cheque,** however.)

bill broker   discounter; factor
One engaged in the business of discounting notes and other negotiable instruments.

billiard-saloon, *n.*   *approx.* **billiard parlor; poolroom**
The game of *pool* in Britain has a set of rules quite different from *pool* (or *straight pool*)
as the term is understood in America, where there are many variations of the game,
each with its own set of rules. *Bar billiards* is a British game, played with balls and cues,
on a table much smaller than a standard American table, and a bar-billiards table is a
frequent and thoroughly enjoyable adornment of British pubs. *Billiards-saloon* has never
had any of the derogatory connotations of the American term *poolroom.*

billingsgate, *n.*   coarse invective
Inf. Foul language characteristic of the type known as *fishwife.* The term, like the word
fishwife in the derogatory sense, stems from Billingsgate Market, the London fish market
famous for its foul language.

billion, *adj., n.* See **Appendix II.D.**

bill of quantity   cost estimate
Especially in the building contracting business.

Billy Butlin's. See **Butlin's.**

billycock. See **bowler.**

bin, *n.*   hop sack
Made of canvas and used in hop-picking. But *bin* has many other uses: see **bread
bin; orderly bin; waste bin; litter bin; dustbin; skivvy-bin; bin ends.**

bind, *n., v.t., v.i*   1. *n., v.t.,* **bore**
                                                          2. *v.i.,* **gripe**
1. *n., v.t., Slang.* A *bind* is a *bore,* whether referring to a person or a job; what teenagers

call a *drag*. As a *v.t.*, to *bind* someone is to *bore him stiff*. In Britain, the victim can be said to be bored *stiff, solid,* or *rigid*.
2. *v.i., Slang*. As a *v.i.*, to *bind* is to 'be a complaining nuisance,' grumbling and griping continuously.

bin ends   SEE COMMENT
Wine merchants keep their supplies in separate **bins** according to label. When the contents of a number of bins run low, suppliers often offer bargains in *bin ends*, i.e., the few remaining cases of certain labels in order to empty those bins and refill them with the same or other labels.

bint, *n.*   *Slang.* **moll**
Slang. From the Arabic word for *girl*, adopted by British soldiers in the Middle East in World War I. It can have the less sinister meaning of 'floozy.' See **bird** for current slang term.

bird, *n.*   *Slang.* **dame**
Slang. Now much more commonly used than **bint**. Synonyms **bint; bit of fluff; judy.** For a wholly unrelated use, see **give (someone) the bird.** Nothing to do with the grace of a bird in flight; rather, a development from *burd*, an obsolete word for *maiden*.

birl, *v.t., v.i.*   **spin**
Birling is a lumberjack's game which tests the players' ability to stay afloat in a river on logs rotated by their feet. In American, to *birl* is to make the log rotate, but in Britain it has the more general meaning of causing something to rotate, i.e., to spin it, or just to move it quickly. The British use *birl* as an informal noun to mean 'try' or 'gamble,' like *whirl* in the expression *give it a whirl*.

biro,*n.*   **ball-point pen**
Inf. (Pronounced BUY'-RO.) A generic use of the trademark of the original ball-point pen, named after its Hungarian inventor.

Birthday Honours   SEE COMMENT
A miscellany of titles and distinctions, hereditary and otherwise, conferred on the sovereign's birthday, including *knight* (the female equivalent is *dame*), *baron, O.B.E. (Officer of the Order of the British Empire), M.B.E. (Member of the Order of the British Empire), C.H. (Companion of Honour), P.C. (Privy Councillor)*. In the case of Elizabeth II, Birthday Honours are conferred on her *official birthday*, June 13. Her real birthday is April 21, but to provide (presumably) more clement weather for outdoor royal festivities, particularly **trooping the colour(s)** at the Horse Guards in London, it was shifted to June 13. (It often rains on June 13.) Titles are also conferred on New Year's Day and at other times at the request of a retiring Prime Minister. With few exceptions (those that are in the Sovereign's personal discretion), honours, though conferred formally by the Sovereign, are in reality bestowed by the Prime Minister of the day, who in turn takes advice from various sources, principally the civil service. The selections are therefore apt to have some political coloring, though this is normally kept within bounds. It is said, however, that because Lloyd George showered honours more or less indiscriminately upon his buddies in Cardiff, that city came to be known as the 'City of Dreadful Knights.'

biscuit, *n.*   **cracker; cookie**
Biscuit, in Britain, covers both *cookie* and *cracker*, depending upon the circumstances. One is offered *sweet biscuits* (cookies) with tea, and unsweetened ones (crackers) with cheese. In America, the British usage lingers on in the trademark *Uneeda Biscuit* (as opposed, e.g., to *Ritz Cracker*). To get cookies in Britain, specify *sweet biscuits, tea biscuits*, or even *petits fours*. If you ask for *crackers*, you may get firecrackers, or explosive bonbons or snappers, the kind used at children's parties. Yet one finds, in Britain, *Jacob's Cream Crackers* and *Crawford's Cream Crackers*; and in George Orwell's *The Road to Wigan Pier* (Victor Gollancz, London, 1937), the Bookers, keepers of an unspeakable boarding-house which always served "pale, flabby Lancashire cheese and biscuits" for supper, "never called these biscuits biscuits. They always referred to them as 'cream crackers.' "

The difference in usage was, however, officially recognized in the radio jingle (to the tune of *Gallagher & Shean*) of the venerable English biscuit firm of *Huntley & Palmer*, which ends with the couplet:
We're not cookies, Mr. Huntley.
No, we're biscuits, Mr. P.

(a) bit missing   *Inf.* **not all there**
Slang. In the sense of 'feeble-minded'; lacking certain of one's marbles.

bit of a knock, *Slang.*   *Slang* **tough break**

bit of fluff   *Slang.* **chick**
Bit of is prefixed to various slang terms for *woman*, which is probably the origin of the elliptical use of *bit* to mean *gal.* See also **bit of goods; bit of stuff.** A *bit of fluff* is not really pejorative; it implies perhaps a wee bit of overdressing or might refer to the relative youth of the female companion of an older man, but no real harm is meant by it.

bit of goods   *Slang.* **number**
Slang. An attractive *bit of goods* in Britain would be *quite a number* or *dish* in America. See **bit of fluff.**

bit of spare   **sex session**
Slang. Used in expressions like *having a bit of spare on the back seat.*

bit of stuff   *Slang.* **chick**
See **bit of fluff.**

bitter, *n*   SEE COMMENT
Bitter is used as a noun to mean 'bitter beer' (as opposed to mild beer) and rivals tea as Britain's national drink. See also **pint.**

(a) bit thick, *adj.*   *Slang.* **going too far**
Slang. The expression *a bit thick* appears in America sometimes as *a bit much*, but the more common expression in America is *going too far.*

black, *v.t.*   **1. shine**
                                                                               2. boycott

1. Referring to shoes. See also **boot.**
                                                                               SEE COMMENT
2. *Slang.* Describes the interference, presumably on union instructions, by employees of one company with the industrial activities of another company in order to exert pressure in labor disputes. To *black* a firm is to refuse to handle its goods or deliver to it. The term is derived from *blacklist.*

blackbeetle, *n.*   **cockroach**
Entomologically speaking, a cockroach is not a beetle at all.

black coat   *Inf.* **white collar**
Inf. Term referring to type of position or worker. The American term has taken over, for the most part. With no reflection on this worthy segment of society, the term *black-coated worker* is British slang for *prune*, in view of that fruit's usual effect on the digestive tract. Please forgive the British slang for this transgression, and note the *-ed* in *black-coated*. The American opposite numbers may feel collared, but there is no *-ed* in *white collar worker.* See also **cloth-cap.**

blackleg, *n., Slang.*   *Slang.* **scab (strikebreaker)**

Black or white?   **Black or regular?**
Black needs no explanation; *white* in Britain means 'mixed with hot milk.' Americans
who don't want it *black* add cream or milk (cold in either case) to their coffee. The British
hostess or waitress usually holds the pot of coffee in one hand and the pitcher (**jug,** in
Britain) of hot milk in the other, and inquires, *Black or white?* The British system would
appear to be universal outside North America. An American hostess might ask, *With
or without?* instead of, *Black or regular?*
The following little item appeared in *The Times* (London) of January 18, 1984, under
the heading "Blacked coffee," an inside joke using **black** in the British sense of 'boycott':

> The colour of coffee has been redefined by the Greater London Council. The staff
> have been told that black coffee should be referred to as "coffee without milk" on the
> grounds, according to a ruling from the council's equal opportunities unit, that "black
> is a political term." It is still permitted to call the other sort white. Those staff who
> think this is all slightly daft have reacted according to the letter rather than the spirit.
> Everything that the rest of the world knows as black, such as raincoats, umbrellas and
> telephones, are now, of course, "without milk,"

The Greater London Council was the local governing body administering the affairs
of Greater London. The Prime Minister was seeking to abolish it, and a battle was
raging [1985]. And the following month, under the heading *"Storm in a coffee cup"*
(another British journalistic 'joke') in another London daily, this tidbit showed up:

> The GLC Equal Opportunities Unit has banned "Black coffee" from the canteens.
> Now it must be "coffee without milk", so as not to give offence to coloured minorities.

The Prime Minister won. The G.L.C. is out of business. For better understanding
of this item, see **G.L.C.** and **coloured.**

Black Paper. See **Paper.**

Blackpool, *n.*   SEE COMMENT
A very approximate equivalent is Coney Island, N.Y. There are never any exact
equivalents. How could there be? It is a seaside resort archetypically reminiscent of
Coney Island, and used symbolically in the same way. Also famous for *T.U.C.* (Trades
Union Congress) annual conferences often held there.

black spot   **1. accident spot**
                                                                2. trouble scot
Sometimes spelled *blackspot*. This is, unfortunately, a common road sign now and
also used metaphorically to mean a 'danger area' or 'trouble spot.' Thus, in a discussion
of the unemployment situation, the reporter referred to a certain industry as a *black
spot.*

blanco, *n.*   **whitener**
Inf. A dressing for buckskin or canvas shoes or sneakers. Also for military webbing
equipment, like belts. In the army, it can come in various shades of buff or khaki. In
the other services, it is white. It comes in the form of a solid dusty block, which is
moistened and then rubbed on whatever needs smartening. One ex-army friend recalls
an injunction relating to general inspection: "If it moves, salute it; if it doesn't, *blanco*
it!" White *blanco* is still used by the **Guards** regiment before ceremonial occasions for
cleaning belts and rifle slings. See also **clean.**

blanket bath   **sponge bath**
The kind given to one bedridden. Synonymous with **bed bath.**

blast!, *interj.*   *Slang.* **damn it!; rats!**
Slang. See **bother.**

bleeding, *adj.*   *Slang.* **damned; goddamned**
Slang. One of the many euphemisms for **bloody.** *See* **blooming; blinking; bally; ruddy; flipping; flaming.**

blether (blather), *v.i.*   **talk nonsense**
Mainly Scottish. With an *-s* added, it becomes a plural noun meaning 'nonsense.' The vowel changes to *i* in *blithering idiot.* See also **witter; haver; waffle.**

blighter, *n.*   *Slang.* **character; pain; pest**
Slang. This word originally described a person of such low character as to *blight* his surroundings; now not quite so pejorative, it has its approximate equivalent in a number of American slang terms of which the above are only a few. Can be used, like **beggar,** in a favorable sense, as in *lucky blighter.*

blighty, *n.*   *approx.* **God's country**
Slang. British soldiers used this word to mean 'back home,' especially after military service abroad, in the same way that the Americans are glad to get back to *God's country* after being abroad. It is derived from *bilayati,* a Hindustani word meaning 'foreign' and was brought back to their own *blighty* by British soldiers returning from service in India. It is also used to describe a wound serious enough to warrant a soldier's return home: a *blighty* one.

blimey!, *interj.*   *Slang.* **holy mackerel!**
Slang This rather vulgar interjection is a contraction of *Cor blimey!* or *Gor blimey!* which are distortions of *God blind me!* See also **lumme!**

blimp, *n.*   *Inf.* **stuffed shirt**
Inf. A pompous, elderly reactionary, from the David Low cartoon character, Colonel Blimp, a retired officer.

blind, *n., v.i., adj.*   1. *n.,* **window shade**
                                                                            2. *n., Slang.* **bender**
                                                                            3.*v.i.,* **curse**
                                                                            4. *adj., Slang.* **damned**
1. In America, *blind* is usually restricted to a venetian blind or some type of shutter, usually made of wood.
2. *n., Slang.* Denoting that which one occasionally goes on (rarely, it is to be hoped), winding up with a hangover.
3. Old army slang.
4. *adj., Slang.* As in *I don't know a blind thing about it!*

blind road   **dead-end street**
Synonymous with **cul-de-sac.**

blinking, *adj., adv.*   *Slang.* **damned**
Slang. Euphemism for **bloody.**

block, n.   **large building**
A *block of flats* is an *apartment house;* an *office block* is an *office building;* a *tower block* is a *high rise.* In America, *block* is used to describe an area, usually rectangular, bounded by four streets. *In the next block,* to a Briton, would mean *in the next apartment house* or *office building.* In giving directions, the British equivalent would be *beyond the next turning.* It appears, however, that the influence of American visitors is having an increasing effect in bringing *block,* in the American sense, into British usage. See also **apartment; flat.**

block of ice   **ice cube**
Obsolescent, if not actually obsolete. The American term appears to have won out.

bloke, *n.*   *Slang.* **guy**
Slang. See also **chap; guy.** *My bloke* means *my boy friend; my man.*

bloody, *adj., adv.*   **1.** *adj., Slang.* **lousy; contemptible**
                                            2. *adv., Slang.* **damned; goddamned**
Slang. This word is now commonly used as an adverb modifying a pejorative adjective, as in, *It's bloody awful.* Used as an adjective, its nearest equivalent in America
would be *lousy,* as in the phrase, *a bloody shame. Bloody,* regarded as a lurid oath, was
formerly proscribed in mixed company, but that sort of inhibition is waning nowadays.
(It never bothered Eliza Doolittle.) Despite popular belief, there is no sound reason to
suppose that it is derived from *by Our Lady.*
  Bloody has a peculiar use in tmesis, as in *any bloody thing, abso-bloody-lutely, John bloody
Smith,* and Noel Coward's unforgettable "A.1 bloody sauce" in Henry's great speech
in Scene 2 of *Fumed Oak. See* **bleeding; blooming; blinking; bally; ruddy; flipping;
flaming.** As to British swearing habits generally, *damn* is less objectionable in Britain
than in America, in polite circles, and *darn* is practically obsolete in Britain. Americans
are freer with religious names like *Christ* and *Jesus* and deformations like *Jeez,* but *Crikey*
(from *Christ*), originally an oath, is now common as an exclamation of surprise, and
sometimes of admiration. *Balls!* is not used as an expletive there, but see **balls** for its
acceptable British uses.

bloody-minded, *adj.*   *Inf.* **pigheaded; stubborn**
  Inf. Willfully difficult; stubbornly obstructive. An awkward but useful adjective to describe persons you simply can't cope with.

bloomer, *n.*   *Slang.* **booboo**
  Slang. Synonymous with **boob,** and sounds like the American slang term *blooper,*
which, however, is generally reserved for an embarrassing *public* booboo, particularly
on the air.

blooming, *adj., adv.*   *Inf.* **damned**
  Inf. Euphemism for **bloody,** like **blinking, bally, ruddy,** etc.

Bloomsbury, *n., adj.*   **1.** SEE COMMENT
                                                    2. *approx.* **highbrow**
1. Bloomsbury is the name of a section of West Central London where writers and
artists, students and aesthetes generally lived and gathered in the early part of this
century. There was a *Bloomsbury set* which included people like Virginia and Leonard
Woolf and Lytton Strachey, and others in or on the fringes of the arts, and there was
a *Bloomsbury accent.*
2. The name became generally descriptive of that sort of person and atmosphere, and
developed into an adjective roughly equivalent to *intellectual* or *highbrow.*

blot one's copybook   *Inf.* **spoil the record**
  Inf. To mar an otherwise perfect record by an act of indiscretion.

blower, *n*   **telephone**
  Slang. One Briton known to the author still calls it *Bell's folly.* Sometimes referred to
in American slang as the *horn.* A special meaning is *central odds bureau,* the agency for
transmitting the total volume of off-track betting back to the track where the race is
taking place, in order to determine the starting odds. *Blow* is sometimes used as a noun
meaning a 'call' or 'ring' on the telephone as in *If you have any trouble, just give me a
blow.*

blowlamp, *n.*   **blowtorch**
  Sometimes *blowflame.* Synonymous with **brazing lamp.**

(be) blown, *v.*   **(be) found out**
  Inf. Can be said of a person, as well as a spy's cover or any spurious identity.

blow (someone) up   **blow up at (someone)**
To *blow* someone *up* is to *blow up at* someone, or to *let him have it*, and a *blowing-up* is what you let him have!

blow the gaff. See **gaff.**

blue, *n.*   **letter;**
letter man
A man who wins his *letter* and becomes a *letter man* in America wins his *blue* and becomes a *blue* at Oxford or Cambridge. At London University he wins his *purple* and becomes a *purple,* and it appears that other universities award other colors; but neither *purple* nor any other color compares even faintly with the distinction of a *blue.* Oxford *blue* is dark blue; Cambridge *blue* is light blue. A *double-blue* is a *two-letter man;* a *triple-blue* is a *three-letter man.* The sport in which the British athlete represents his university (makes the team, in America) determines whether he earns a *full blue* or a *half blue.* Cricket, crew, rugger, and soccer are *full blue* sports. Tennis, lacrosse, and hockey are half blue sports. A *blue* can be a *full blue* or a *half blue,* but (sacrificing accuracy to diplomacy) *blue* generically includes *half blue.* Similarly, in most universities, the American athlete can *letter (v.i.),* that is, *earn his letter,* in a *major sport,* like football, basketball, track, or crew, or a *minor sport,* like tennis or fencing, the distinction between *major* and *minor* being generally equivalent to *full blue* and *half blue.* This award for excellence in athletics bestows upon the British athlete the right to wear certain articles of apparel which are blue in color; cap, blazer, necktie, and socks. The cap awarded in cricket is worn only during the playing of cricket. Socks are awarded in soccer and crew. The blazer can be worn wherever it is appropriate to wear a blazer generally (for instance, out for a walk on a fine Sunday morning). The necktie can be worn wherever it is appropriate to wear a necktie (for instance, when applying for a job, or a bank loan).

blue, *v.t.*   *Slang.* **blow (squander)**
Slang. Past tense is *blued. Blue* is apparently a variant of *blow,* which is used as well in Britain for *squander.*

blue book   **legislative report**
In Britain, a parliamentary publication. See also **Hansard.**

blue-eyed boy, *Inf.*   *Inf.* **fair-haired boy**

Blue Paper. See **Paper.**

BM   SEE COMMENT
The *British Museum,* very frequently abbreviated thus (without periods), and alarming to Americans when a friend says, "I've had a marvelous morning at the *BM.*" The great BM library is now offically called the *British Library.*

board, *n.*   **sign**
For instance, a TO LET *board.* See also **notice board; hoarding.**

boarder, *n.*   **resident student**
As opposed to a *day student* who lives at home. It applies to secondary school, not university. *Boarder* in the American sense is *lodger* in Britain. Cf. **P.G.**

boater, *n.*   **straw hat**

(the) Boat Race   SEE COMMENT
The annual rowing race between Oxford and Cambridge; a sporting event of interest to the British public generally, including many who have not had the benefit of any university attendance. There are lots of boat races, but *The* Boat Race is so understood, just as, for example, *The* Game means the Harvard-Yale game to Harvard and Yale football fans.

bob, *n.*   SEE COMMENT
Slang. One shilling. See **Appendix II.A.**

bob-a-job?   **any odd job?**
British Boy Scouts come to the door and ask *Bob-a-job?* You are supposed to find (or invent) a household chore which the good young man or men will perform for a *bob* (slang for *shilling*). The proceeds are turned over to the organization for the doing of good works.

bobby, *n.*   *Slang.* **cop**
Slang. Named for Sir Robert (Bobby) Peel, Home Secretary, who founded the Metropolitan Police Force in 1829. A former slang term in Britain for *cop*, also named after Sir Robert, was *peeler*, which is, however, still heard in Ireland. *Copper* is another less common slang term for *cop*, which is also used in America but seems to have gone out of fashion. *Robert* (from the same Sir Robert) was another British term for *cop*. See **constable; P.C.; bogey; busies; peeler; pointsman; slop.**

bobby-dazzler, *n*   **something special**
Inf. Anything or anybody outstanding; often applied to a particularly spiffy dresser.

Bob's your uncle!   *Inf.* **there you are!! that's it! voilà!**
Inf. An expression used at the end of instructions such as road directions, recipes, and the like. For example: *Go about 100 yards, take the first turning on your right, then straight on through a little gate; go 40 yards to a gate on your left marked Main Entrance, but that's not really the main entrance (they just call it that, I haven't a clue why), but 20 yards farther on there's a small gate on your right that really is the main entrance; go through that, you"ll see a dismal brown building on your left and—Bob's your uncle!* Or:...*add a few cloves, stir for five minutes, turn down the flame, let simmer for an hour or so, and—Bob's your uncle!* One explanation of this curious phrase is its alleged use in Robert Peel's campaign for a seat in Parliament. he was a ''law and order'' man nicknamed *Bob* (see **bobby**) and *uncle* was used as a term implying benefaction and protection: *Vote for Bob—Bob's your Uncle!* Maybe. *Uncle* is British (as well as American) slang for *pawnbroker*, and a pawnbroker is, presumably, a friend in need. Another educated guess at its derivation relates to the appointment in 1887 of Arthur Balfour as Chief Secretary for Ireland by the then Prime Minister Robert Cecil, Lord Salisbury, who happened to be Balfour's uncle. This obvious act of nepotism was decried by many. The saying then went (if this derivation can be believed): 'You ask for the job—he remembers your name— and *Bob's your uncle!'* Ngaio Marsh, in *Black as He's Painted* (Collins, London, 1974), makes a most elaborate and amusing use of the phrase. The Ambassador (of Ng'ombwana) has been killed. ''And after the shot was fired you stopped the President [of Ng'ombwana] from standing up but the Ambassador *did* stand up, and *Bob*, in a manner of speaking, *was your uncle,''* suggests Inspector Fox to Chief Superintendent Roderick Alleyn, and Alleyn replies, ''In a manner of speaking, he was.'' Six years later, in *Photo Finish* (Collins, London, 1980), Miss Marsh concocted another elaboration of this phrase, when the AC (Assistant Commissioner) of Scotland Yard ends a long sentence with: ''...and *Bob*, so to speak, *is your uncle.''*

bod, *n.*   *Slang.* **character**
Slang. An abbreviation of *body* and somewhat pejorative. Example: *I saw somebody who seemed to be a night watchman or some other type of lowly bod about the premises.*

bodge up   *Slang.* **cook up**
Slang. In the sense of 'think up' or 'contrive.'

bodkin, *n.*   **tape needle**
In Britain the commonest meaning is that of a thick, unpointed needle having a large eye for drawing tape or ribbon through a hem or a loop. (It is familiar to Americans as *dagger*, but it was used that way by Britons too (see *Hamlet*, Act III, scene 1.) Another meaning in both countries is to designate a large and elaborate hatpin, but most of those went out of fashion in Edwardian times. A British use almost unknown in America is seen in the phrases *ride bodkin, or sit bodkin*, which describe the condition of being squeezed between two other persons.

bodyline, *adj.*   SEE COMMENT
Usually in the expression *bodyline bowling.* In **cricket,** *bowling* is the overhand delivery of the ball (see **bowler 2.**). to the **batsman** (*batter*), who must *defend his* **wicket** (keep the ball from knocking the horizontal pegs (called *bails*) off the vertical supports (called *stumps*)). In *bodyline* bowling, the bowler aims at the batsman, rather than the wicket, not so much to hurt him as to frighten him, thus causing him to duck away and so fail to defend his wicket, especially from a ball with **spin** (*English*) on it sufficient to make it swing in or out as it hits the ground in front of the batsman and hit the wicket. There is widespread disapproval of this unsportsmanlike procedure, so uncharacteristic of the true spirit of cricket, and some steps are being taken to curb it.

boffin, *n.*   research scientist
Colloq. Synonymous with **back-room boy,** referring to a person who during World War II worked as a scientist for the war effort, as, for instance, in the development of radar. A gentleman named Jack Rayner of Muswell Hill, a research scientist in the employ of the General Post Office, is of the opinion that he may be the original *boffin* to whom this bit of R.A.F. World War II slang for 'civilian scientist' was applied. The word became generic for 'research scientist' about the middle of 1943. Early that year Mr. Rayner worked with a scientist who liked to give his colleagues nicknames out of Dickens, and the future Mrs. Rayner was his assistant. The name-giver called her *Mrs. Boffin,* after the character in *Our Mutual Friend.* By simple association Mr. Rayner became *Mr. Boffin,* and was thus addressed by his colleagues on a technical visit to Fighter and Bomber Command Headquarters soon thereafter.

bog, *n.*   *Slang.* **john (toilet)**
Slang. Not only slang but vulgar. Used in the plural to refer to a communal latrine, as at school or in the service. See **loo.**

bogey (bogy), *n.*   *Slang.* **cop**
(Hard G.) *Slang.* This old-fashioned word literally means *bugbear,* which should explain its slang use among the criminal element.

bogie, *n.*   **truck (non-driving locomotive wheels)**
(Hard G.) Railroad term. *Truck* is a British railroad term meaning 'gondola car' (open freight car). See **bogey.**

boiled sweets   hard candy
Sweets, as a general term, is the British equivalent of the American general term *candy.* *Boiled sweets* always means the kind of candy that is usually sucked rather than chewed. See, however, **sweet.**

boiler. See **chicken.**

boiler suit   coverall

boiling, *n.*   *Slang.* **shooting-match**
Slang. The *whole boiling,* referring to a group of people, means the 'whole *mob* of them' but *boiling* can refer to the *whole lot* of anything.

boko, *n.*   *Slang.* **beak (nose)**
Rare. As in the expression *biff on the boko.* See also **bonce.**

bollard, *n.*   traffic post
A *bollard* in both countries is a post on a ship or dock around which hawsers are tied. An exclusively British meaning is 'traffic post,' i.e., a post on a traffic island, to regulate traffic by barring passage in certain directions.

bollick, *v.t.*   *Slang.* **bawl out**
Slang. It is a curious coincidence that this word resembles *bollocks* (see **ballocks**) and *bollixed* (as in, *all bollixed up*). Those words and phrases have to do with the noun *ball*, usually found in the plural, whereas this word happens to be associated with the verb *bawl*, in its meaning of 'shout' rather than 'weep.'

bollocks. See **ballocks.**

bolshy, also **bolshie,** *n., adj.*   *approx.* **unconventional**
Inf. Literally, *Bolshevik*, but applied by the older folk to any unconventional act or person. To *go bolshie* is to go one's own unconventional way, to engage in anti-Establishment behavior; to disregard the accepted form; to do one's own thing. The author heard the aged father of a fiftyish son accuse the latter of *going bolshie* for failure to wear a necktie at a family lawn party on a day when the thermometer stood above ninety! The general sense of the term is 'mutinous' (socially speaking); 'acting in defiance of good form.' Some use it to mean 'obstreperous,' and apply the term to any troublemaker. The *Concise Oxford Dictionary* tones it down to merely 'uncooperative.'

bolt-hole, *n.*   **hideaway**
Inf. A *pied à terre*. Used by exurbanites in, *I have a little bolt-hole in Chelsea* and by Londoners in, *I have a little bolt-hole in Dorset. The Bolt-Hole* is a jocular name given to the Channel Islands, a tax haven. All derived from the rabbit's *bolt-hole*.

bomb, *n.*   1. *Slang.* **smash hit**
                                                                           2. **fortune**
1. *Slang.* A *dazzling success*—the exact opposite of its meaning in America: a *dismal flop!* To *go down a bomb* is to *make a smash hit.* See **knock.**
2. *Slang.* To *make a bomb* is to *make a fortune. It costs a bomb* means 'it costs a fortune' or 'an arm and a leg.'

bonce, *n.*   1. *Slang.* **dodo**
                                                                           2. *Slang.* **noodle**
1. *Slang.* A large playing marble.
2. *Slang.* A rare usage, usually in the expression *biff on the bonce.* See also **boko.**

bone, *v.t.*   *Slang.* **swipe**
Slang. To *make off with* something; evoking the image of a dog skulking off with a bone.

bone. See **when it comes to the bone.**

bonkers, *adj.*   *Slang.* **nuts; goofy**
Slang. Also, **certified; doolally; crackers; dotty.**

bonnet, *n.*   **hood**
Automobile term. See **Appendix II.E.**

bonus issue (bonus share)   **stock dividend**

boob, *n., v.t., v.i., Slang*   1. **goof**
                                                                                     2. **jail**
1. Though Americans don't use *boob* as a verb, they commonly use *booboo* to indicate the result.
2. To *get boobed* is to *be jailed.*

book, *v.t.*   1. **reserve**
                                                                                    2. **charge**
1. In Britain one *books* or *reserves* a table, theater seats, hotel rooms, rental cars, etc. A *booking* in Britain is a *reservation*; a *booking office* and a *booking clerk* (railroad terms) appear

in America as *ticket office* and *ticket agent. Fully booked* means 'all seats reserved.'
2. When something is *booked to an account* in Britain, the equivalent in America would
be *charged*. See also **put down, 2.**

book of words   instructions
Inf. America seems to lack a slang or informal expression for the instructions that
come in the package and that often need their own instructions.

book seller   bookstore
In Britain, book advertisements generally advise you that the indispensable volume
can be obtained at your *book seller* (sometimes *book shop*) rather than at your *bookstore*.

bookstall, *n.*   newsstand
Synonymous with **newsagent; kiosk.**

boot, *n.*   1. trunk (of an automobile)
                                                                        2. shoe
                                                                3. SEE COMMENT
1. See **Appendix II.E.**
2. *Boot* for an American denotes a piece of footwear which comes well above the ankle,
anywhere from a few inches to just below the knee. The British use both *boot* and *shoe*;
boot is used generically to include all leather footwear; but *shoe*, as in America, normally
excludes that which comes above the ankle. If a farmhand or a countryman generally
wanted to talk about his *rubber boots*, he would refer to his *Wellingtons*, standard country
footwear even in dry weather. A British *boot* reaching barely above the ankle would be
called a *shoe* in America. A *shoe* reaching over the ankle used to be called a *highlow* in
Britain, but that term is now archaic. An American who would never refer to his *shoes*
as his *boots* or to the process of *shining* them as *blacking* them nonetheless usually refers
to the person who *shines* his *shoes* as a *bootblack*, although he sometimes calls him a
shoeshine boy. Conversely, the British refer to the person who *blacks* their *boots* as a
shoeblack. The British say both *bootlace* and *shoelace*, while in America *shoelace* is used
regardless of the height of the *shoe* and *shoestring* is relegated to the description of a
kind of string necktie worn out West. In both countries companies go broke because
they were started on a *shoestring*, not a *bootlace*, but they sometimes succeed as a result
of a *bootstrap* operation. A *shoe clerk* in America is a *bootmaker's assistant* in Britain even
if the *boots* are not *made* in that shop.
3. *Boot* is used in a variety of British expressions unfamiliar to American ears: See
**another pair of shoes (boots); (the) boot is on the other leg (foot); like old boots; put
the boot in.**

(the) boot is on the other leg (foot)   the shoe is on the other foot

boots, *n.*   hotel bootblack
Inf. He collects (or is it *used to collect?*) the shoes you put just outside your hotel-room
door at night, to be returned, polished, during the night. Like most old-time luxuries,
this one is pretty much a thing of the past. In military slang, *boots* means a 'rookie
officer' in the regiment.

boot sale   SEE COMMENT
As seen from a previous entry, an automobile trunk is a **boot** in Britain. A *boot sale*
partakes of the nature of an American garage or tag sale, in that one offers for sale all
those things one has no further use for, but the procedure is different. It is called a *boot
sale* because you fill the **boot** of your car with the articles you want to dispose of, drive
to an appointed place where others are engaging in the same operation, open the boot,
strew some of the things around your car, leave some stuff in the boot, and hope to
pick up some change while ridding yourself of the stuff you can't stand having around
any longer but had not had the courage to throw away.

(the) Border, *n.* SEE COMMENT
The one between Scotland and England, which is what is meant when Britons or Scots use the expression *south of the Border*. Nothing to do with the Rio Grande. *North of the Border* is heard as well.

bore, *n.* **gauge**
In describing the internal diameter of a gun barrel: 12 *bore*, 16 *bore*, etc.

borough, *n.* SEE COMMENT
(Pronounced BURRA (*u* as in *butter*).) Basic unit of local government. See also **rotten borough**.

borstal, *n.* **reformatory**
Inf. Borstal is the name of a town in Kent where Britain's original juvenile prison is located. It used to be called Borstal Prison but is now referred to as Borstal Institution, reflecting the modern trend toward rehabilitation, rather than retribution, in the case of young offenders. The Borstal System introduced the indeterminate sentence in juvenile cases requiring observation and treatment. Informally, *borstal* (lower case) has come to mean that kind of essentially remedial and educational institution, wherever located. Also called *remand home*.

bos, also **boss,** *n., v.t., v.i.* **bad guess;** *Slang.* **bum shot**
Slang. Boss-eyed is slang for 'cockeyed.'

bosthoon, bostoon, *n.* **boor**
An Irish word for an awkward, tactless, senseless fellow.

bother, *n., interj.* 1. *Slang.* **trouble; row (dispute)**
2. **damn! rats!**
1. *Inf.* A spot of *bother* in Britain is a *bit of trouble* in America, although serious trouble as well can, with British understatement, be lightly referred to as a *spot of bother*. In context a *bother* can mean a 'row' (fight or dispute).
2. *Slang.* Seen in exclamations emphatically rejecting a kind friend's tentative suggestion, as in *Bother the boat train!* after learning that the planes are full. Somewhat milder than *blast!*

bothy, *n.* **hut; small cottage**
Used by farm hands. A term heard mostly in Scotland.

bottle *Slang.* **guts**
Slang. Said of one in dire straits: "Will he have enough *bottle* to face the music?"

bottle screw **turnbuckle**
A nautical term, synonymous with **rigging screw**.

bottom, *n.* 1. **foot (far end)**
2. **pluck**
1. In such phrases as *bottom of the garden; bottom of the street*, etc., in the same way that a British street has a *top* rather than a *head*.
2. *Slang.* May be obsolete in general use, but still occasionally affected by the landed gentry, perhaps half-jocularly and certainly self-consciously, in the expression *a lot of bottom*, indicating a good deal of stiffness of the upper lip.

bottom drawer **hope chest**

bottom gear **low gear**
Logically enough, *top gear* means *high gear*.

boundary, *n.*   1. SEE COMMENT
                                                                    2. limits
1. A cricket term meaning a hit that sends the ball rolling all the way to the white line around the field that marks the boundary and counts as four runs. The ball doesn't have to land outside the line. If it does that, it scores six runs (see **six**). See also **Appendix II.K.** The term, like so many technical cricket terms, has acquired a figurative meaning in general usage; a *fine performance*, a *stellar achievement*. One fine sentence from *M.C.C.—The Autobiography of a Cricketer,* by Colin Cowdrey (Hodder and Stoughton, London, 1976), illustrates the figurative uses of two cricket terms. A little background is in order: Len Hutton was the first professional (as opposed to "gentleman") cricketer to captain the England side in international cricket (see **Test Match**). At his initial press conference while on tour in Australia, this fact, "...since Australians tended to look at the English class system with eyes narrowed by distrust, got him **off the mark** with a *boundary* before he opened his mouth." (Your first run as a **batsman** gets you **off the mark.**)
2. See **city boundary; town boundary.**

bounder, *n.*   **boor**
    A man guilty of unacceptable social behavior; an ill-bred man. The term does not necessarily imply low moral character, but it can.

bovver boots   SEE COMMENT
    These are offensive weapons consisting of horrible, heavy, metal-tipped boots for kicking that are worn by **skinheads.** The usual police remedy is to take away the laces, which makes the boots too loose on the feet for effective kicking. *Bovver* is apparently a corruption of **bother,** meaning 'trouble' in the sense of 'looking for trouble'—that kind of trouble. The *v* sound for *th* is the usual cockney pronunciation that sounds like a speech impediment. *Bovver,* in turn, is sometimes recorrupted to *bovvy.*

Bow Bells   SEE COMMENT
    (Pronounced BO BELLS.) Literally, the *bells of Bow Church,* also called St. Mary-le-Bow Church, in the **City** of London. The church got its name from the bows (arches) of its steeple or from the arches of stone upon which the church was built—those still to be seen in the Norman crypt—and has nothing to do with Bow Street, famed in British detective stories as the address of the principal London Police Court. The most frequent use of *Bow Bells* is in the expression *within the sound of Bow Bells,* which means 'in the City of London' (see **City**). One is said to be a true cockney if born within the sound of Bow Bells, but Burltrop and Wolveridge, in *The Muvver Tongue* (The Journeyman Press, London and West Nyack, N.Y., 1980) deny this, saying, "'Born within the sound of Bow Bells' is a myth long overdue to be exploded... It [cockney] means East End working class," and they go on to establish far wider geographical limits. (For an explanation of *muvver* as the pronunciation of *mother,* see discussion under **bovver boots.**)
    See also **cockney; East End.** The ecclesiastical court of the Archbishop of Canterbury is held in the crypt of Bow Church, and its head is therefore called the *Dean of the Arches.*

bowler, *n.*   1. derby (hat)
                                                                2. SEE COMMENT
1. Also called in Britian a *billycock.* Designed in 1850 by a Mr. Bowler for (the story goes) Mr. William Coke, who somehow became Mr. Billy Cock. The following letter appears in the *Evening Standard* (London) of May 15, 1973 under the heading "The first bowler," sent in by a Bowler:

> I was most interested to read Geoffrey Aquilina Ross's article (May 2) on the famous company of Locks, the hatters, but one point would be queried. While the first bowler hat was sold by Locks, it is most likely that the hat was made by either my great-great-grandfather or great-great-grand-uncle.... Hence the name bowler.—John Bowler, Denewood, Upper Chobham Road, Camberley, Surrey.

This letter is followed in the paper by the following note:

> Geoffrey Aquilina Ross writes: "It would seem by the record that in fact Thomas

and William Bowler, from Stockport, were the suppliers of the felt used in the first Coke."

2. *Bowler* has an entirely distinct meaning in cricket. The *bowler* (from the verb *bowl*) has approximately the same relationship to cricket as the *pitcher* to baseball. He *bowls*, over-arm, rather than *pitches*, side-arm.

bowler-hatted, *adj.*   **demobilized**
Slang. To be *bowler-hatted* is the same as to *get one's bowler,* a **bowler,** of course, being the equivalent of a *derby* and thus a hallmark of civilian attire. *Bowler-hatted* applies to officers only, and is usually restricted to cases resulting from cuts in the defense budget and similar situations. See also **demob.**

bowls, *n. pl.*   **outdoor bowling game**
A *bowl* (in the singular) in sports is a wooden ball not exactly spherical, or eccentrically weighted if spherical, so that it can be made to curve when rolling. Related to *boccie, boules, pelanca* (or *pétanque*), etc., but the bowling-greens of Britain are as meticulously maintained as the putting greens at the best golf clubs.

box, *n.*   **1. intersection area**
                                                                 2. *Slang.* **idiot box**
1. *Box,* or *junction box,* is a British traffic term denoting the grid marked out at a street intersection (**crossroads**). One sees traffic signs reading DO NOT ENTER BOX UNTIL YOUR EXIT IS CLEAR—don't start crossing at an intersection and get stuck in the middle, thus blocking traffic coming at right angles.
2. Short for *goggle-box,* comparable to American *boob tube.*

Boxing Day   SEE COMMENT
First weekday after Christmas, December 26, a legal holiday in Britain, unless Christmas falls on a Saturday, in which event, December 27. As to the exception, tempers rage, some hotly asserting that *Boxing Day* is always December 26, regardless of the day of the week. Many angry letters have been written to *The Times* (London) about this. In any event, this is the day on which Christmas gifts of money are traditionally given to the family's regular delivery men, such as the milkman, **postman** (mailman), **dustman** (garbage man), and, if you live in the country, baker's boy, grocer's boy, newspaper boy, and (if you still have one) gardener, and other miscellaneous roundsmen (see **roundsman**). Christmas gifts of this type are called *Christmas-boxes,* although they are given in money and nowadays have nothing whatever to do with boxes. This type of gift seems to have acquired its misleading name from the practice, in the old days, of the recipients' arrival at the door holding out boxes. The Christmas gifts to friends and relations given on or before Christmas Day, though usually *in* boxes, are called, simply, *Christmas presents.*

box-room, *n.*   **storage room**
The room in your house for odds and ends, whether they are packed in boxes or not. See also **lumber room.**

box-spanner. See **spanner.**

box-up, *n.*   *Inf.* **mix-up**
Slang. Like landing in the wrong seats at the theater and being made to move. Euphemism for *balls-up;* see **balls.**

boy. See **head boy; old boy; pot-boy; wide boy.**

(in a) brace of shakes. See **two shakes of a duck's tail.**

braces, *n.*   **suspenders**
The American equivalent, *suspenders,* is used in Britain as the equivalent of American *garters.*

bracken, *n.*   **large fern**
Also, an area covered with ferns and undergrowth.

bracket, *n.*   SEE COMMENT
American *brackets* are square enclosing marks, thus: [ ]. In Britain, the term is generic
for enclosing marks, and includes parentheses, thus: ( ). To differentiate while dictating
in Britain, one must specify the type desired, square or round.

bradbury, *n. Inf.*   **one-pound bill**
Sir John Bradbury, who became Secretary of the Treasury in 1914, signed the paper
money issued by the Treasury, and his name, often shortened to *brad,* became the
colloquial term for the bills themselves, particularly the one-pound note (see **note, 1.**).
In 1919 Sir Warren Fisher succeeded Bradbury as the signer of the Treasury notes and
the term *bradbury* gave way to *fisher,* until October 1, 1933, after which date all paper
money was issued by the Bank of England and Treasury notes ceased to be legal tender.

Bradshaw, *n.*   *approx.* **national passenger train timetable**
Short for *Bradshaw's Railway Guide,* originally published by George Bradshaw in 1839.
Ceased publication *circa* 1965.

brakesman, *n.*   **brakeman**

brake-van, *n.*   **caboose**
Railroad term, more commonly called *guard's van.* The American equivalent (*caboose*)
was used in Britain to mean 'galley on the deck of a ship,' now obsolete as a ship design
feature. *Brake-van* relates to freight trains (**goods** trains), as opposed to *guard's van,* which
applies to passenger trains.

bramble, *n., v.i.*   **blackberry**
To go *brambling* is to go *blackberry picking.*

branch, *n.*   **local**
Specialized use in trade union circles: *Branch 101* would be *Local 101* in American
union terminology.

brandy-butter, n.   **hard sauce**
Butter, **castor sugar,** and brandy creamed together. Served with plum pudding and
mince pie. See also **rum-butter,** which it resembles. Also called *Senior Wrangler Sauce.*
See **wrangler.**

brandy snap   SEE COMMENT
A type of cookie made according to a special recipe containing a good deal of **golden
syrup.** Flat and thin or rolled with a cream filler. Delicious and fattening.

brash, *n.*   **hedge clippings**
Or *dry twigs,* or both. A rustic term.

brass, *n.*   *Slang.* **dough (money)**
Slang. The more common British slang term is **lolly;** others are **dibs; corn.**

brassed off   *Slang.* **teed off**
Slang. Synonymous with **cheesed off.**

brass plate, *n.*   **shingle**
To *put up your brass plate* in Britain is to *hang out your shingle* in America.

brawn, *n.*   **head cheese**

brazing lamp   blowtorch
Synonymous with **blowlamp.**

bread bin   bread box

bread roll   bun
That which encloses a hamburger (**wimpy**) in Britain. See also **bap.**

break, *n.*   recess
School term. *Break* is used in both countries to mean a 'temporary suspension of
activities' generally. *Recess* usually refers to Parliament in Britain, and the term is not
used to refer to the daily pause at school.

break a journey at...   stop off at...

breakdown gang   wrecking crew

breakdown van or **lorry**   tow truck

break one's duck. See **duck, 1.**

breaktime. See **playtime.**

breast-pin, *n.*   stick-pin

breve, *n.*   double whole note
See **Appendix II.F.**

brew up   1. make tea
                                                          2. burst into flame
1. *Inf.* Also a noun, *brew-up*, for which there is no equivalent American expression,
since the institution of tea and tea-making in general is not, as it is emphatically in
Britain, a vital function of daily life. A *brew-up* is any making of tea, whether in a
priceless China pot or a billycan, at any time of day or night. See also **be mum.**
2. This meaning was originally applied to an army tank that had been hit by a *Panzer-
faust*, but has also been used to describe an auto accident from which a conflagration
ensued.

brickie, also **bricky,** *n., Slang.*   bricklayer

brick up   *Slang.* **fix (spay)**
Slang. From a letter written by a friend who had been given a male kitten which
proceeded to have kittens of 'his' own: "I didn't want to have it **put down,** so it cost
me six pounds to have her *bricked up.*" An example of graphic and picturesque British
invention. See **doctor.**

brick wall   *Inf.* **stone wall**
Inf. That up against which it is frustrating to be.

bridewell, *n.*   jail
An archaic term, from *St. Bride's Well*, in London, an early prison.

bridge coat   *approx.* **velvet jacket**
An old-fashioned garment no longer in common use. A long-sleeved velvet jacket,
usually black, donned by women for bridge in the evening. Perhaps the feminine equivalent of another vanishing garment—the *smoking jacket* (also of velvet, most often ma-
roon).

bridge school   bridge foursome
Inf. Who usually play together.

brief, *n.*   **instructions to trial lawyer**
In America a *brief* is a written outline submitted to the court in the course of litigation. In Britain it is the **solicitor's** instructions to the **barrister.** A *briefless barrister* is an *unemployed* one. See also **solicitor; barrister.** A *dock brief* is one which bypasses the solicitor, consisting as it does of instructions given at the trial by the accused in a criminal case directly to the barrister who is going to defend him, without benefit of solicitor. For the origin of this term, see **dock,** 2. *Dock Briefs* is the title of a column by Matthew Coady which appears occasionally in *The Guardian* (London), devoted to brief reviews of whodunits. (*Brief* notices of murder mysteries involving murderers, or at least suspects, who end up in the *dock.* Double pun—get it?). In Henry Cecil's *Settled Out of Court* (Michael Joseph, London, 1950), a **solicitor** discusses the relationship between his profession and that of the **barrister:**

> I am only a humble solicitor, as you know. But in my humble capacity I have had the inestimable privilege of supplying barristers with **briefs.** You may or may not know that briefs are as necessary for a barrister as water for a fish. Neither can survive without a sufficient and continuous supply of, in the one case, briefs, in the other, water.

(The solicitor's sardonic attitude is explained in another passage quoted under **barrister.**) One's *brief,* in criminal and police slang, is one's lawyer.

brigadier, *n.*   SEE COMMENT
Military rank between colonel and major general.

bright, *adj.*   **1. well**
                                                                  2. pleasant
1. *Inf.* When asked how he feels, a Briton might say, *I'm not too bright,* where an American would use the expressions *not too well,* or *not up to snuff.*
2. *Inf.* When a Briton says, *It's not very bright, is it?* looking up at the sky, he means that the weather isn't very *pleasant.* See also **bright periods.**

Brighton, *n.*   SEE COMMENT
A seaside resort in the Southeast, the archetypical equivalent of Atlantic City in the latter's heyday. Imposing Edwardian hotels and fascinating lanes (known as *The Lanes*) lined with antique shops full of every description of furniture and a bric-a-brac, much of it quite good.

bright periods   **fair with occasional showers**
Synonymous with **sunny intervals.** A more accurate translation might be *rain with brief intermissions.* There is no real equivalent for British weather-report terminology because there is no real equivalent for British weather, which is so often of several sorts within minutes (see *Macbeth,* Act I, Scene 3). Although British conversation about the weather is voluminous and almost always gloomy, British weather reports literally and figuratively look on the bright side of things. See also **bright.**

brill. See **Appendix II.H.**

brill, *adj.*   *Inf.* **terrific**
Slang. Brills! is used as an interjection meaning 'Great!' Said to be derived from the American soapy scouring pad sold under the trademark *Brillo,* which is alleged to make everything clean and shiny and beautiful, but can be simply a truncation of *brilliant.*

brimstone, *n.*   **sulfur**
Brimstone and treacle has its repellent equivalent in *sulfur and molasses.*

bring off a touch, *Slang.*   *Slang.* **make a touch**

Bristol fashion   **in good order**
Inf. Usually, *all shipshape and Bristol fashion.* Nautical slang, taken into informal general usage, and still heard occasionally.

Bristols, *n. pl.*   *Slang.* **tits**
Slang. Bristol City came out of London rhyming slang (see **Appendix II.G.3.**) as the equivalent of *titty.* There is only one Bristol City, but titties come in pairs, so the rhymsters pluralized City, then dropped it in the way they normally eliminated the rhyming word, and then proceeded to pluralize Bristol. See, as another example of this peculiar practice, **daisies** for *boots:* originally *daisy roots.* Another word for this part of the anatomy is **charlies,** also spelled *charleys,* of uncertain etymology.

broad, *n.*   **river-widening**
Specifically, a lakelike body of water, especially in East Anglia, formed by the widening of a river and then narrowing down again into a river. The most famous group is known as the *Norfolk Broads.*

broad arrow   SEE COMMENT
Symbol marking government property, formerly including convicts' uniforms.

broad bean   *approx.* **lima bean**
Similar, but larger, darker and with a coarser skin. The British variety is the seed of a vetch known as *Vicia faba;* the American, that of the plant known as *Phaseolus limensis.*

broadcloth, *n.*   **black woolen cloth**
In America, *broadcloth* is the equivalent of what the British and Americans term *poplin.* British *broadcloth* is the kind of suiting material used for one's Sunday best.

broadsheet, *n.*   **1. handbill**
                                                                             2. large-sized newspaper
1. Also called *throwaway* in America, and, picturesquely, *broadside. Handbill* used to be the common term, but latterly the British more often use *leaflet.*
2. Like *The Times* (London), as opposed to a tabloid.

Brock's benefit   **fireworks display**
Inf. Named for a noted manufacturer of fireworks. By extension, any loud row, air raid, Guy Fawke's Night (see **guy**), etc.

broken ranges   **broken sizes**
Odd sizes, offered in a sale.

broking firm   **brokerage firm**

brolly, *n.*   *Inf.* **bumbershoot**
Inf. The English term is used quite seriously; the American word is humorous. See **gamp.**

brothel-creepers, *n. pl., Slang.*   **crêpe-soled suede shoes**

brown, *n.*   **1.** SEE COMMENT
                                                                             2. covey of game birds
1. *Slang.* Penny. An old British equivalent of *copper,* early American slang for *penny.*
2. *Inf. The brown* means a 'flying covey of game birds,' and *firing into the brown* means, literally, 'aiming at the covey instead of choosing a particular bird,' and by extension, 'firing into a crowd' (any crowd, not just a group of birds).

brown bread   **whole wheat bread**
Hovis, a proprietary brand, is ubiquitous in Britain. Its name is often used generically for any brown bread. It is often served cut thin and already buttered, with smoked salmon, tiny British shrimps in a sauce, potted shrimps, and other mouthwatering delicacies. The *o* in *Hovis* is long.

brown stock   **beef stock**
Cf. **white stock**, a generic term for either chicken or fish stock.

Brum, *n.*   SEE COMMENT
Slang. Short for *Brummagem*, an old slang name for *Birmingham*, and said to approx-imate the local pronunciation of that name, but the *g* is pronounced soft. *Brummagem* came to be used as an adjective meaning 'shoddy,' a sense derived from the counter-feiting of coins there in the 17th century. As a noun, it can also mean the 'Birmingham dialect,' which other Britons (let alone Americans) find extremely hard to follow. A *Brummie boy* or *Brummie* is a native of that fair city. A limerick invented by the late Royal Ballet conductor and composer, Constant Lambert, begins:

> There was a young lady of Birmingham
> who paraded the streets with a dirmingham...

    In this context, the British public were supposed to recognize the nonsense word *dirmingham* as a back-formation of *drum*!

brush up   *Inf.* **brush up on**
Inf. The British *brush* something *up*, while the Americans *brush up on* it.

B.S.T.   SEE COMMENT
British Standard Time, now obsolete. It was a system of all-year-round daylight saving time (called summer time in Britain), tried for a year or two in order to line up with European Standard Time, but abandoned in 1971.

Bt. See **Baronet.**

bubble and squeak   SEE COMMENT
Leftover greens and potatoes, mixed together and fried; name derived from the sounds they make in the pan.

bubbly, *n.*   **champagne**
Inf. Synonymous with **champers**; both terms old-fashioned or humorous.

buck, *n.*   **eel trap**
A basket used to trap eels.

bucket, *v.i.*   **row hard**
A rowing term. In America the same word means to 'ride (a horse) hard,' or generally to 'drive ahead fast' in any conveyance, and in this connection it is usually used in the expression *bucket along*.

bucket down   **rain cats and dogs**
Inf. Synonymous with **rain stair-rods.**

Buck House   SEE COMMENT
Inf. **Buckingham Palace;** an antique expression, but still seen.

buckshee, *adj., adv.*   *Inf.* **for free (gratis)**
Slang. A corruption of *baksheesh*, used in the Near East to mean 'alms' or 'tip.' Also used in expressions like a *buckshee day*, describing a day unexpectedly free as a result of the cancellation of scheduled events or appointments.

buck up   **improve**
Inf. Example: *The railways had better buck up their ideas of service!*

budget, *n.*   SEE COMMENT
The annual statement of projected national income and expenditures, made by the Chancellor of the Exchequer (counterpart of the Secretary of the Treasury) in the House

of Commons. *A mini-budget* is an interim partial statement of the same sort. But in the popular mind, *budget* means 'tax bill,' because the new tax proposals included in the *budget* are the part that most immediately affects the common man.

budgie, *n.*   **small parakeet**
Inf. The common household term for *budgerigar,* a miniature Australian parrot with a long tapered tail, bred in greens, blues, and yellows.

buffer, *n.*   **1. bumper**
                                                                                                   2. *Slang.* **fogy**
1. Railroad term; but an American automobile *bumper* is a *fender* in Britain. See **Appendix II.E.**
2. *Slang.* Like *fogy,* usually preceded by *old.*

buffet, *n.*   **snack bar**
Both countries use *buffet* to mean 'sideboard' or 'cupboard,' and the terms *buffet supper* and *buffet dinner* to describe meals where the guests serve themselves from a buffet. In all these senses Americans approximate the French pronunciation: BOO-FAY'. When it denotes a piece of furniture, the British sometimes pronounce it BUFF'-IT. It is the common British name for a *lunch counter* or *snack bar* at railroad stations, and in that case the British use a quasi-Frenchified pronunciation, educated people saying BOO-FAY, the others BUFFY. In some cases, as at Charing Cross Station in London, the *buffet* is more than just a counter and is what Americans would call a *cafeteria.* When you are still lucky enough to find a dining car with the word BUFFET painted in large letters on its side, it's always the *buffy-car.* And to add to the confusion (a popular sport in Anglo-American linguistics), here is a letter published in *The Times* (London) of September 17, 1986 that brings the once sacrosanct French language into the picture:

Language mix-up
From Mr C. F. Smith
   Sir, Heard recently over the loudspeaker in the lounge of a cross-Channel ferry, the announcement: "Ladies and gentlemen, the *buffet* is now open", followed immediately by the translation: "*Mesdames et messieurs, le* snack-bar *est ouvert maintenant*".
Yours faithfully,
C.F. SMITH,
55 Warwick Crest,
Arthur Road, Edgbaston,
Birmingham, West Midlands.
September 10.

bug, *n.*   **bedbug**
Bug is generic in America for 'insect,' which is the generic British term. Don't use *bug* unless you mean 'bedbug,' except in the context of the microorganisms which cause those dreadful flu and related epidemics that go around every year; thus: *He couldn't come; he's got the bug,* or, *I must have caught a bug: I feel awful!*

bugger, *v.t.*   *Slang.* **foul up**
Slang. But as an expletive *bugger* has many different American equivalents: *I'll be buggered!* means: 'I'll be damned!' *Bugger you!* means 'Go to the devil!' *Bugger off!* means anything from 'Get the hell out of here!' to 'Fuck off!' depending on the circumstances. To *bugger off* is to *get the hell out* of somewhere, to *leave* in more or less of a hurry. There is a legend about a press cable from Delhi or thereabouts reading: EVERYBODY OFFBUGGERED HILLWARDS. And a story is told in Epsom (the site of England's annual Derby—pronounced DARBY) about two bookies who caught sight of a bettor (**punter**) who bore an amazing resemblance to a former Archbishop of Canterbury. They made a bet as to whether or not it was the famous man. One of the two approached him and asked. "*Bugger off,* you stupid **nit**," was the reply, so they never knew for certain and had to cancel the bet. *Beggar* is a common euphemism for *bugger* used as a noun, as in *Lucky bugger!* .

bugger all   *Slang.* **not a goddamned thing**
Slang. A coarse intensification of **damn all**. Joke: A judge asks the convicted murderer
whether he has anything to say before sentence is passed. The unfortunate prisoner
mumbles *"Bugger all."* Judge turns to prosecutor and asks, "What did he say?" Prosecutor: *"Bugger all,* my Lord." Judge: "That's funny, I was sure he had said something."
A British friend of the author, on gazing down at the Sahara from our plane, was heard
to murmer, "Miles and miles of *bugger-all!"*

Buggin's (Buggins') turn   SEE COMMENT
Promotion based on seniority (sometimes rotation) rather than merit. *Buggins,* like
Joe Bloggs, is an arbitrary name used in Britain the way Americans use *Joe Doakes* to
describe anybody who is nobody. *Buggin's* (properly *Buggins'* or *Buggins's) turn* brings
to mind some of the less suitable chairmen of our Congressional and Senate committees.

builder's merchant   **building supply firm**

building society   **savings and loan association**

building surveyor. See **surveyor.**

buller, *n.*   **proctor's assistant**
Slang. Buller is short for *bulldog,* which is slang for **proctor**'s assistant. A proctor at
Oxford or Cambridge is attended by two *bulldogs,* or *bullers,* who do the dirty work.

bully beef. See **salt beef.**

bullock. See **jolly.**

bum, *n.*   *Slang.* **behind (rear end); derrière**
Slang. For obvious reasons, the title of the American film *Hallelujah I'm a Bum* was
modified to *Hallelujah I'm a Tramp* for exhibition in Britain. See **arse.** The British use of
bum is rather neatly illustrated in the following letter to *The Times* (London) of March
7, 1981:

> **Conundra**
> *From Mr J. M. Ross*
> Sir, A mathematics don at Cambridge once sent a note to a colleague in another
> college suggesting that "next Sunday morning we meet to consider some conundra
> about pendula". He received a reply: "I can think of many better ways of spending
> Sunday morning than sitting on our ba doing sa".
> Yours faithfully,
> J. M. ROSS,
> 64 Wildwood Road, NW11.

1.   The letter incidentally demonstrates the British use of **don** and **college** as well,
and the British ommission of the period after Mr (see **Appendix I.D.6.**).

bumble, *n.*   **bureaucrat**
Inf. Literally, a *bumble* is a mace-bearing ceremonial official at British universities or
churches (also known as a *beadle*), who gets all decked out but really serves little purpose. Figuratively, he has given his name to any minor official puffed up with his own
importance. The British use the word pejoratively, as Americans often use *bureaucrat,*
to describe pompous officials (often lowly clerks) in love with red tape who delight in
obstructing the expedition of what should be simple procedures. Another British name
for such a one is *jack-in-office.*

bumf (bumph), *n.*   **1. toilet paper**
                                                                                                         2. worthless paper
                                                                                                         3. rubbish
Slang. An abbreviation of *bum-fodder* (see **bum**), this slang term for *toilet paper* has, apparently in ignorance of its inelegant origin, been extended as a pejorative for *dull paper work, dreary documents, worthless paper* of the kind generally associated with red tape and bureaucratic memoranda, and more recently, to mean 'rubbish,' in a phrase like *Look here, this may be a lot of bumf, but my theory is...*

bum-freezer, *n.*   **short jacket**
Slang. Especially an Eton jacket or a mess jacket. See **bum.**

bummaree, *n.*   SEE COMMENT
(Accent on the last syllable.) Dealer at Billingsgate. See **billingsgate.**

bumping-race. See **May Week.**

bump of direction   **sense of direction**
Inf. In older times, *bump of location or locality.*

bump-start, *v.t.*   SEE COMMENT
Inf. To start a car by getting it to roll and suddenly throwing it into gear.

bump-supper. See **May week.**

bun, *n., Inf.*   **squirrel**

bunce, *n.*   *Inf.* **windfall**
Inf. Originally, just any *profit* (derived from *bonus*?) but latterly an unexpected one, a *windfall*. It has now gained some currency as a verb, especially in the gerund, *buncing*, to describe the practice, in retail stores, of sticking new higher-price tags over the original lower-price labels on articles for sale.

bunches, *n. pl.*   **clearance items**
In periodic sales at clothing shops.

bun-fight, *n.*   *approx.* **tea party**
Inf. Sometimes *bun-feast.* There is no equivalent American colloquialism. Can also apply to a cocktail party or similar get-together.

bung. See under **pimp.**

bungalow, *n.*   **one-story house**
An American *bungalow* is the equivalent of a British *cottage.*

bungfull, also **bung full,** *adj.*   *Inf.* **chock-full**
Inf. Synonymous with *chockablock.* See also **packed out with.**

bung-ho!, *interj.*   **1.** *Inf.* **so long!**
                                                                                                         2. *Inf.* **cheers!**
1. *Inf.* Synonymous with **Cheerio!**
2. *Inf.* Synonymous with lots of nice words, like *Santé, Salute, Skol, Prosit,* etc.

bunk, *n., v.i.*   *Slang.* **take it on the lam; light out**
Slang. Alone, as a verb; or as a noun in *do a bunk.*

bunker, *v.i.*   **refuel**

bunkered, *adj.*   *Inf.* **messed up**
  Slang. In Britain one gets *bunkered* in troublesome situations in which Americans
would describe themselves as *messed up* in the sense of 'entangled'. This word is derived
from the originally Scottish golf term for *sand trap*.

bureau, *n.*   **secretary**
  A writing desk with drawers. An American *bureau* is the equivalent of a British *chest
of drawers*.

burke, also **burk,** v.t.   **suppress**
  Slang. An honest man will not *burke* a fact merely to support a thesis. Sometimes
spelled *burk*, though derived from the name of a Scottish murderer, W. Burke (hanged
in 1829), who went around smothering people to sell their bodies for dissection. The
original slang meaning was to 'kill without leaving marks of violence.'

burn one's boats, *Inf.*   *Inf.* **burn one's bridges**

bursar, *n.*   **scholarship student**
  A *bursar*, as all readers of C.P. Snow would know, is a *college treasurer*, in Britain, as
well as in America. It has an additional meaning in Britain, 'scholarship student,' which
is synonymous with another British word unfamiliar to Americans, *exhibitioner*. The
grant awarded to the *bursar* is called a *bursary*; the one awarded to the *exhibitioner* is
called an *exhibition*. A distinction between the two types of grant is that the *exhibition* is
awarded for a term of years.

busby, *n.*   **high fur hat**
  Worn by Royal Horse Artillery and Hussars. See also **bearskin; Guards.**

busies, *n. pl.*   *Slang.* **cops**
  Slang. See **bobby.**

busker, *n.*   **street entertainer**

butcher, *n.*   *Inf.* **hatchet man**
  Inf. Incidental intelligence: The American term was derived from the use of real
hatchets by the armed forces of Chinese tongs. The On Leong and Hip Lee Sing tongs
were still going at it in New York's Chinatown in the early days of this century. Large
blow-ups of rows of their hatchet men were displayed in their respective territories as
part of their psychological warfare.

butchery, *n.*   **meat department**
  Sign in a supermarket: *Mr Willcutts, Manager; Mr Compton, Butchery Manager. Butchery*
would not generally be applied to a butcher shop (*butcher's* shop, in Britain), but rather
to a *meat department*. American dictionary definitions include the meaning 'butcher business,' but the use of the term *butchery* is normally restricted to signify carnage. See also
family butcher.

Butlin's, *n.*   SEE COMMENT
  Inf. William Butlin conceived and established a type of family holiday camp with
everything **laid on**: separate **chalet**-bungalows around a central community building
where those who wished to mingle participated in fun and games (movies, dancing,
cards, etc.) under the somewhat authoritarian direction of the director of social activities,
that frightening functionary, while nurses took care of the children, leaving the parents
free for their revelry. The camps have proliferated, and, at moderate prices, are a boon
to middle class families of modest means. The term *Butlin's*, sometimes *Billy Butlin's*,
is used pejoratively by snobs, in the way in which their American counterparts, in the
east, at any rate, refer to *the Catskills*. Nonetheless, the founder became *Sir* William. He
died in 1980, his name a household word. Quoting from William D. Smith, in *The New
York Times* of November 10, 1974:

North America has nothing quite like a Butlin's vacation. It combines elements of Grossinger's, an Army camp, a cruise ship and a family reunion. Specifically, though, it is geared to the British temperament and weather, and its appeal is not ethnic but class. Butlin's provides working-class Britons with their own home by the sea, with food, day-long activities (indoors if wet), a jolly mood and nighttime entertainment—all thrown in for one fixed price. For about 22 pounds...a mid-summer week the camper gets a private chalet (a slightly primitive motel-like cottage), three meals a day, maid and babysitter service, and more entertainment than the normal person can digest.

A more recent, and less charitable view was expressed by Paul Theroux in *The Kingdom by the Sea* (Hamish Hamilton, London, 1983):

> ...I saw the bright flags of Butlin's, Minehead [a seaside resort in Somerset] ...Holiday camps were surrounded by prison fences, with coils of barbed wire at the top. There were dog patrols and *Beware* signs stencilled with skulls...I registered as a day visitor...Most of the Butlin's guests wore sandals and short sleeves, and some wore funny hats...It had the prison look of the Butlin's at Bognor [another seaside resort, in West Sussex]...It was not expensive, £178 a week for a family of four...There were about half a dozen bars... The Exmoor Bar had a hundred and fifty-seven tables and probably held a thousand drinkers. It was the scale of the place that was impressive; the scale, and the shabbiness...Everywhere there was a pervasive sizzle and smell of food frying in hot fat...Butlin's...combined the security and equality of prison with the vulgarity of an amusement park...It was a sleazy paradise in which people were treated more or less like animals in a zoo.

Well, *de gustibus...*

buttered eggs   **scrambled eggs**
The American term has gained precedence.

butter-muslin, *n.*   **cheesecloth**
Also called *muslin.* The references to different dairy products indicate that the material in question originated in both countries in dairy farm use. However, in each country the name is used without any conscious reference to happy days at the farm. What the Americans call *muslin* would be called *calico* in Britain; but *calico* in America means what the British would call a *cheap cotton print.*

buttery, *n.*   **larder**
Where wines and food are kept. A special British use: room in a **college,** especially at Oxford and Cambridge, for sale of food and drink to students.

buttons *n. pl., Inf.*   **bellhop**
Sell also **page.**

butty, *n.*   *Inf.* **buddy**
Inf. Pal, friend, chum, especially fellow-soldier. The British consider the usual American term *buddy* a variant of *butty,* and a corruption of *brother.* The Americans consider *buddy* a development from baby talk for *brother.*

buzz off, *v.i.*   *Slang.* **scram**
Slang. Synonymous with **cheese off; cut away; get stuffed; go to bed; push off.**

by all means   *Inf.* **perfectly okay**
Inf. Means 'there is no objection whatever.' The British would not ordinarily use it in the American hortatory sense, as in *By all means visit the Prado.* Philip Howard has this to say about this expression (*Words Fail Me,* Hamish Hamilton, London, 1980, Chapter 26):

'By all means...' is a phrase in which there is an interesting distinction between American and British usage. Americans use it straightforwardly to emphasize their point. 'By all means do it' is an invitation to do it at all costs and whatever the consequences. Britons use it as a reversible lie. If an Englishman says 'By all means...', he is speaking with a forked tongue. He means: 'If you really must.' The phrase signifies grudging acceptance of the unavoidable.

By Appointment   SEE COMMENT
One often sees notices on merchandise labels, shop signs or commercial stationery reading: *By Appointment to...* naming some royal personage—the monarch, the Queen Mother, a duke. This means that the purveyor has received the distinction, by warrant, with attendant public relations value, of supplying that personage with the commodity or service in question.

by-blow, *n.*   **bastard**
A particularly uncharming word—with a hint of *'ditch-deliver'd'*?

(obtaining money) by deception   **(obtaining money) under false pretenses**
The American usage is also heard in Britain, with *by* rather than *under*.

by-election, also **bye-election,** *n.*   **special election**
Of a **Member**, to fill a vacancy in the House of Commons.

by-law, also **bye-law** *n.*   **ordinance**
Used in municipal government. *By-laws* in America usually mean 'corporate by-laws,' i.e., the procedural rules and regulations governing a corporation. The *by-* in the British term is a Scandinavian import meaning 'town' or 'village' and appears in names like Ashby, Gatenby.

byre, *n., Scottish.*   **cowshed**

by the way, *pred. adj.*   **incidental**
By the way is used in both countries adverbially as the equivalent of *incidentally*. Its use as a predicate adjectival phrase is fairly common in Britain, in America very rare.

C

cabbage-looking, *adj.*   *inf.* **green-looking**
Slang. I'm not so green as I'm cabbage-looking, i.e., 'I'm not so green as I may seem.'

caboose,*n.*   **galley (on the deck of a ship)**
See also **brake-van; guard's van.**

cab-rank, *n.*   **taxi stand**

cack-handed, *adj.*   **clumsy**
Slang. Literally, *left-handed.*

cad, *n., schoolboy slang.*   *Slang.* **grind**

Caesar, *n.*   **Caesarean**
Inf. In both countries *operation* or *section* is understood; but the British sometimes use
the name of the author of the *Gallic Wars* while the Americans always use the adjective
derived from his name. Noun or adjective, it has always seemed a strained device to
have the witches' prophecy, on which Macbeth counted so heavily, come true in the
case of Macduff, because this type of operation is by no means untimely in the usual
case.

café   **coffee shop**
Since the word *café* implies a more prestigious establishment many Britons deliberately mispronounce it as KAIF or KAFF when referring, e.g., to a **transport café.**

cage, *n.*   **box**
On forms to be filled out, there sometimes appear a series of boxes that are to be
checked with an *x* or a check mark, and one is instructed to 'check appropriate box,'
or words to that effect. In England, one would be instructed to '**tick** appropriate *cage.*'

cakehole, *n.*   *Slang.* **trap**
Slang. Mouth. Synonymous with **gob.**

calendar, *n.*   **catalogue**
In the sense of a 'list of courses' offered by a university, together with appropriate
regulations and descriptions of the courses, terms, and examination dates.

calendar, station. See **station calendar.**

calico, *n.*   **white cotton cloth; muslin**
Calico as used in America would be called a *cheap cotton print* in Britain. See also **butter
muslin.**

call, *n., v.t., v.i.*   **1.** *vi.,* **visit**
                                                                          2. *n., vt., v.i.,* **bid**
                                                                          3. *v.i.,* **be in heat**
1. Mr. Jones *called,* in America, means that Mr. Jones 'telephoned.' In Britain, it means
that Mr. Jones 'dropped in,' 'came by.' Britons say *rang up* in the case of a telephone
call. An illustration of this difference is found in Delving's whodunit *Die Like a Man*
(Belmont Productions, Inc., New York, 1971). Miss Truce (an Englishwoman) says to
the hero (an American), "Ah, you got my message, Mr. Cannon." "No," answers
Cannon, "as a matter of fact, I didn't. When did you *call?*" She replies, "I didn't *call.* I

telephoned the hotel." Cannon says, "Sorry. That's one of those ways which you can tell there's a difference between English and American." (But see **caller**; and note the term *gentleman caller* meaning 'visitor' as Tennessee Williams used it in *The Glass Menagerie*.) 2. Bridge term: *Let's see, you called two hearts, didn't you? A call* is a 'bid.' 3. Of cats.

call after   name for
The British *call* their babies *after* favored relatives and national heroes.

call at   stop at
Both countries speak of vessels as *calling at* ports. The British occasionally apply the same term to trains. Thus one sees signs in the Charing Cross Railway Station at the gate (**barrier**) describing a particular train as *Not calling at London Bridge*.

call-box, *n.*   telephone booth
Also called *kiosk* or *telephone box*.

called to the bar   admitted to practice
This phrase applies only to **barristers** and refers to persons who have received a license to practice as barristers. See also **Inns of Court; barrister.**

caller,*n.*   calling party
A person making a telephone call is referred to as *caller* and is addressed by the operator as *caller*. In America the *caller* would be referred to as the *calling party* and would be addressed by the operator as *sir* or *madam*. See also **pay for the call; personal call.**

call-out charge   house call charge
What the repair man charges when he visits your home because something's gone wrong.

call to order   rebuke
When a person violates the rules of parliamentary procedure or otherwise offends decorum at any meeting, the presiding officer *calls him to order*. In America it is the meeting that is *called to order*.

call-up,*n.*   draft
Military service term. A *call-up* is a *draft* card.

Calor gas   propane gas
Proprietary name, but used generically for liquefied butane gas in pressurized containers for use in homes, on boats, etc.

camber, *n.*   bank
This word is a general term in both countries describing any upward convexity, but is not common in American traffic terminology. A British road sign proclaiming REVERSE CAMBER means 'road banked wrong way.'

cami-knickers, *n. pl*   SEE COMMENT
All-in-one ladies' undergarment with bodice and wide legs. *Cami* is a shortening of *camisole*. American informants advise that this form of undergarment is obsolete. British informants say the opposite.

camp bed   cot
The British also use the word *cot*, but to them it means what the Americans call a *crib*. Also, *safari bed*, once proprietary.

candidature, *n.*   candidacy

candlestick telephone   upright telephone
The old-fashioned kind.

candyfloss, *n.*   **1. cotton candy**
                                                             2. SEE COMMENT
2. Used metaphorically for 'flimsy ideas.'

cane, *n., v.t.*   **whip; switch**
When an American uses a *cane,* as a gentleman's accessory, he is referring to what
the British prefer to call a *walking-stick.*

cannon, *n.*   **carom**
Term in billiards.

Cantabrigian, *n., adj.*   SEE COMMENT
Of Cambridge, from *Cantabrigia,* the Latin name for Cambridge. In a narrower sense,
a Cantabrigian is a student or graduate of Cambridge University. Informally abbreviated
to *Cantab.,* which is the usual form, and applies in America to Cambridge, Mass., and
particularly Harvard.

canteen of cutlery, *n.*   **silver set**
Contained in a case, usually a fitted one.

canterbury, *n.*   **magazine rack**
Properly speaking, this word means a 'low stand with light partitions, built to hold
music portfolios.' This original meaning is borne out by the fact that the genuine old
ones are usually decorated with woodwork carved in the form of a lyre. People use
them, lyre or no lyre, most often to hold magazines, newspapers, and the like.

Cantuarian, *n. adj.*   SEE COMMENT
This is the name of the official magazine of The King's School, Canterbury, a **public
school** reputed to be the oldest functioning school in the world. The name is derived
from *Cantuaria,* the medieval Latin name for Canterbury, which in Roman times bore
the name of *Durovernum.* Neither a King's School **old boy,** nor a member of the **staff**
(*faculty*), nor a resident of Canterbury would be called a *Cantuarian,* in the way in which
Cantabrigian, Oxonian, etc. are used with reference to Cambridge, Oxford, and other
university cities. However, this rule does apply to Archbishops of Canterbury, who
sign by given name followed by *Cantuar:.* (It appears that the colon, rather than a period,
was medieval Latin usage in this connection.) *Cantuar:* is an abbreviation of *Cantuarien-
sis,* the Latin adjective formed from *Cantuaria.* The King's School is closely connected
with Canterbury Cathedral, situated as it is within the cathedral precincts, and this
cathedral is, of course, the very core of the Anglican Church, the Archbishop of Canterbury being the Primate of All England. It is easy to see why The King's School calls
its magazine *The Cantuarian.* Not only archbishops, but bishops as well sign that way:
given name plus (usually) a Latin place-name, abbreviated; e.g. (as of 1975), *Gerald
Londin:* (London); *Maurice Norvic* (Norwich—and Maurice seems to omit the colon, or
perhaps *Whitaker's Almanack 1975* left it out inadvertently); *David Roffen:* (Rochester). As
to archbishops, we have *Donald Cantuar:* and *Stuart Ebor: (Ebor:* being an abbreviation
of *Eboraciensis,* the adjective from *Eboracum,* the Latin name for what is now York).
There is one other application of *Cantuarian:* the Cantuarian Lodge of Freemasons in
the town. One more note about Cosmo Cantuar:, who was the Archbishop of Canterbury at the time of Edward VIII's crisis and abdication. Here we have to quote from
Noel Annan's review of *Edward VIII,* by Frances Donaldson (Lippincott, New York,
1975) in the January 22, 1976 issue of *The New York Review of Books:*

> But one observation should be pondered upon by all, whether of left, center, or
> right, who have triumphed on some issue after which their opponents have slunk
> discomfited from the field. In the hour of their triumph, as the *Times* **leaders** [editorials]
> thundered against the corruption of society and in particular of an unidentified group
> called the King's friends, one member of the British Establishment overstepped the
> mark. In a Sunday broadcast, the Archbishop of Canterbury, Cosmo Lang, referred
> to Edward's "craving for private happiness" and his choice of a wife from "within a
> social circle whose standard and way of life are alien to all the best instincts and

traditions of his people," and ended by unctuously commending him to the infinite mercy and protecting care of God.

The heavens fell on the Archbishop. The British, who behave better in a calamity than in prosperity, and who put love lower in their worldly scale of values than honor, i.e., the esteem won by obeying society's code, nevertheless had not forgotten Edward's qualities of sympathy for the poor and unfortunate. The mood of the nation was, as Frances Donaldson recalls, funereal rather than critical, and the irritation with Edward was tranferred overnight to Cosmo Cantuar. In her superb study, she rightly quotes the original of the squib by Gerald Bullett on this incident, but I prefer a variant which ran:

> *My Lord Archbishop, what a scold you are.*
> *When a man is down, how very bold you are.*
> *Of Christian charity how very scant you are.*
> *Oh, Old Lang Swine, how full of Cantuar!*

The Bullett version, published (1959) in his *Collected Poems*, went:
> *My Lord Archbishop, what a scold you are,*
> *And when your man is down how bold you are.*
> *Of Christian charity how oddly scant you are.*
> *How Lang, O Lord, how full of Cantuar!*

cap, *n.* **1. letter (in athletics)**
2. diaphragm
1. Sports term, usually in the expression *win one's cap*. It generally indicates that one has played for one's county or one's country. To *be capped* is to *have won one's cap; uncapped*, generally, refers to players who have yet to win their *caps*; but an uncapped county player is one who has not yet been selected to play for England in a **Test Match**. See also **blue,** n., and **international.**
2. For contraceptive use.

(to) cap it all **(to) make matters worse**
In other words, to complete the tale of woe.

Capital Transfer Tax SEE COMMENT
Its opposite number in America is the *Unitax.* In both countries, the one tax comprises the gift and estate or inheritance taxes. *Estate taxes* are *death duties* in Britain.

capsicum, *n.* **green pepper**
The little sign in the country supermarket read CAPSICUMS, and hung over a display of green peppers. (In a quality **greengrocer's** , my informant suggests, it might have read *capsica.*) The young lady in attendance seemed to feel that *capsicum* and *green pepper* were interchangeable and that there was nothing fancy about *capsicums.* The word is the botanical name for a genus of plant of which the fruit is the pepper, and for the fruit itself.

caravan, *n.* **house trailer**
As an automobile term. It is also used in the more original romantic sense. A *caravan park* is a *trailer court.*

car breaker **car wrecker**

cardan shaft **drive shaft**
Automobile term. See **Appendix II.E.**

cardigan. See under **Balaclava.**

cards. See **give (someone) his cards.**

care a pin *Slang.* **give a hoot**
Slang. Almost always used, like its American equivalent, in the negative.

caretaker, *n.* **janitor**
Caretaker, in America, implies the owner's absence. *Gardener* would be the term used by a Briton owning country property.

(in) Carey Street *Slang.* **flat broke**
Inf. The High Court of Justice in Bankruptcy (commonly known as the Bankruptcy Court) used to be located on Carey Street in London. (It is now located around the corner at Victory House, Kingsway.) That is the origin of the peculiar phrase *to be in Carey Street*, which is usually used to describe the condition of being flat broke rather than in technical bankruptcy. Might it be said that one gets to Carey Street via **Queer Street**? (Incidentally, note the preposition *in*. Americans would say *on* such and such a street rather than *in* it. See **Appendix I.A.1.**) Whether *in* or *on*, *Carey Street* is a bad place to be.

cargo boat **freighter**

Carnaby Street SEE COMMENT
A street in the Soho section of London, studded with apparel shops catering to the young. In the 60s the name was used allusively to refer to youthful used clothing; sometime shortened to *Carnaby*, as in *Carnaby styling or attire*. Its heyday as the center of youthful fashion has gone, and it is now becoming identified with the tourist rip-off business.

carny, carney, *v.t., adj.* 1. *v.t., Inf.* **coax; cajole**
2. *adj.,* **sly**

carousel, *n.* **rotating conveyor belt**
Like those seen at airports. Spelled with one *r* in Britain, where it doesn't mean 'merry-go-round' as in America.

car park **parking lot**
See also **caravan.**

carpet, *n.* SEE COMMENT
The British distinguish between *carpet* and *rug* on the basis of size: forty sq. ft. or over is a *carpet*; under that size is a *rug*. The American distinction is based on type of manufacture: a *carpet* is machine made; a *rug* handmade (but the distinction gets a little fuzzy in the case of a good machine-made, imitation Persian rug).

carpet area **floor space**

carriage, *n.* 1. **car; coach**
2. **freight**
1. In Britain a railroad *car* or *coach* is called a *carriage; car* means 'automobile' and *coach* means 'bus'.
2. *Carriage* means 'freight' in the sense of *cost of shipping*. *Carriage forward* means 'freight extra'; *carriage paid* means 'freight prepaid.' See also **forward; freight.**

carriage rug **lap robe**
Has given way to *travelling rug.*

carrier, *n.* **express company carrier bag; shopping bag**
In all but the grandest shops, like Harrods, one pays an extra small amount (3 to 5 pence) for the bag. The alternative free brown paper bag, if available at all, is so flimsy as to be useless.

carrycot, *n.* **portable bassinet**

carry on, *v.i., n.*   1. *v.i.*, **keep going**
                                                                            2. *v.i.*, **flirt**
                                                                            3. *v.i., n.*, **fuss**
                                                                            4. *military*, **as you were**
1. In the giving of road directions, *carry on* means 'keep going straight ahead.' It is the
equivalent of *You first* when one is offering to hold a door or otherwise step aside for
someone. At times it seems to mean little more than 'O.K.' and once in a while it
replaces *so long*.
2. A rather old-fashioned use.
3. Can be used not only as a verbal phrase but also (hyphenated) as a noun meaning
'fuss': *This has been a most trying carry-on* (situation, affair).

carry one's bat   *Inf.* **stick it out**
  Inf. To *carry, carry out,* or *bring out one's bat* is to 'outlast the others,' *to stick it out* and
finally *put it over* or *bring it off*. Stems from cricket as it used to be played: the batsman
who was not put out left at the end of his **innings** carrying his bat out with him instead
of leaving it for the next batsman. In this affluent society, each player has his own bat,
so that a batsman would walk off the **pitch** today carrying his own bat whether or not
he was out; but the symbolism of the phrase lingers on. See also **off one's own bat.**

carry the can   1. *Slang.* **be the fall guy**
                                                                            2. *Inf.* **do the dirty work**
  Slang. In meaning 2, the phrase is often lengthened to *carry the can back.* The *can* in
question is said to be the one containing dynamite used in blasting operations. See also
hold the baby.

cartridge, *n.*   **shell**
  Shotgun ammunition. Used in both countries, as well, to mean the ammunition used
in a rifle or revolver.

carve up   **swindle**
  Slang. Especially, to cut a partner-in-crime out of his "rightful" share of the loot. The
noun *carve-up* has acquired the more general meaning of any 'swindle.' It has been used
in a quite different sense to mean a 'melon' in the sense of 'bonanza,' which may be
the result of the legitimate splitting of a windfall, but somehow the impression lingers
that the windfall may not have been all that legitimate.

case, *n.*   **set**
  For example, a British shop advertises a *case* of dessert spoons where an American
store would speak of a *set*.

cashier, *n.*   **teller**
  Banking term, used interchangeably with *teller* in Britain. In most American banks,
the title *cashier* is reserved for the officer who is the equivalent of the *secretary* in non-
banking corporations.

CASH POINT   SEE COMMENT
  Sign commonly seen in supermarkets and other shops, indicating the place where
you pay. The equivalent American sign would be CASHIER or PAY HERE. *Cashpoint* (one
word) is Lloyds Bank's name for the machines situated on the outside walls of selected
branches which deliver cash when you insert a plastic card and press your code numbers.

casket, *n.*   **small box**
  A *casket* in America means a 'coffin.' It never has this meaning in Britain (*The Merchant
of Venice*, Act II, Scene 7).

cast, *v.t.*   **discard**
  Special military term applied to superannuated cavalry horses. Unhappily they are
usually slaughtered for horsemeat at a **knacker's** yard rather than sent to pasture.

castor-sugar, *n.*   **finely granulated sugar**
   Castor sugar is more finely grained than American *granulated sugar* but not powdery like American powdered or confectioner's sugar, which is called *icing sugar* in Britain. The equivalent in American is called *Verifine,* which is manufactured primarily for iced drinks, cereals, and fruit desserts. Also spelled *caster,* which indicates its origin from the fact that it is fine enough to be *cast* from a *caster* (also spelled *castor*).

casual labourer   **transient or occasional worker**
   This term refers principally to workers like stevedores who show up for work but may or may not get any that day. A rather awkward neologism in this area is *decasualization,* which means putting such workers on a permanent footing, with a guaranteed weekly wage. *Casual labourer* does not apply exclusively to heavy labor: a young nurse who lost a series of steady jobs because of facilities closing down and became a free-lancer speaks of herself as a *casual labourer,* as does a teacher who was retired at 60 and became a roving tutor. See also **casual ward.**

casualty department   **emergency room**
   In a hospital. The person in charge is a *charge-nurse.* The term is often shortened to *casualty,* just as the American equivalent becomes *emergency* ("Dr. Kildare wanted in *emergency!"*). Sometimes *casualty ward;* not to be confused with the next entry!

casual ward   **flop house**
   Synonymous with **doss house;** derived from the extension of **casual labourer** to mean 'pauper' or 'vagrant.'

cat, *n.*   **whipping**
   Inf. Undoubtedly a reference to *cat-o'-nine-tails;* rarer as a practice than a word, but there are still those who advocate "bring back the *cat,"* i.e., 'reintroduce corporal punishment.' Incidentally, in the expression *room enough to swing a cat,* the *cat* is not a screaming feline, but a *cat-o'-nine-tails.*

catalogue company   **mail order house**

cat among the pigeons   *Inf.* **match in a tinderbox**
   Inf. To *put the cat among the pigeons* is to *start a fuss* by introducing a highly inflammatory topic into the conversation.

catapult, *n, v.i.*   **slingshot**
   The British also use this word as the Americans do, as both noun and verb.

cat burglar, *Inf.*   *Inf.* **second-story man**

catch a packet. See **packet.**

catch hold of the
wrong end of the stick   *Inf.* **miss the point**
   Inf. Sometimes *get* instead of *catch.*

catchment area   SEE COMMENT
   In America, *catchment* is the act of catching rainfall, the rainfall caught, or the basin or reservior in which it is caught. In Britain, the word is used in the term *catchment area,* denoting the area from which the rainfall flows into a given reservoir or river, and figuratively (a common use in these days of social planning), the area from which hospital patients, pupils, etc. are drawn into a particular hospital, school, etc.

catch out, *v.t.*   **catch (in a mistake); detect**
   A Briton will *catch you out* if you commit a solecism. He will also *catch out* a solecism. The Americans omit the *out.* See **Appendix I.A.I.**

catch (someone) up, *v.t.*   **catch up with (someone)**
The British *catch you up* or *catch up with you.*

caterer, *n.*   **restaurateur**
The *catering trade* is the *restaurant business.* In America, the term *catering* is confined to the preparation and bringing of food to a home and serving it there, for instance at a wedding, or at some public place for a special occasion. The term *caterer* is broader in Britain, including the more restricted American sense, and would normally be understood as 'restaurateur.'

cat-lap, *n.*   *Slang.* **dishwater**
Slang. Dull people, novels, or movies would never be likened to *cat-lap:* the term is reserved for weak tea and similar outrages.

catmint, *n.*   **catnip**

cat's-eyes, *n. pl.*   **surface road reflectors**
Reflector studs, set at close intervals into road surfaces along the white lines marking the lanes. Enormously helpful on unlighted roads and foggy nights, they are mounted in depressible rubber frames so that they can be driven over without harm. Strongly recommended for adoption on American country roads in climates where destructive snow-plowing doesn't occur. The official word, *studs,* is seen on road signs, e.g., just ahead of a newly resurfaced stretch: NO STUDS OR LINES FOR 2 MILES.

cat's-meat, *n.*   **cat food**

cattery, *n.*   **cat-boarding kennel**
Also *cat-breeding establishment.* The term is heard in America only in cat-breeding circles.

cattleman, *n.*   **cowherd**
A *cattleman* in America is a *rancher* or *cattle owner.* In Britain he works for somebody else.

caucus, *n.*   **political party committee**
A political organization which formulates party policy, election strategy, and the like. In Britain, the word is somewhat derogatory, implying the atmosphere of an unofficial cabal. A *caucus* in America is an *ad hoc* political meeting of party regulars.

caught on the hop, *Slang.*   *Inf.* **caught napping**

caught on the wrong foot   *Inf.* **caught napping**
Slang. A term borrowed from **cricket.** A **batsman** *(batter)* put in this position by the **bowler** *(approx.* pitcher) is in difficulties.

cause-list, *n.*   **trial calendar**
Legal term.

cave!, *interj.*   *Slang.* **cheezit!**
Schoolboy slang. (Pronounced CAVEY.) This is the singular imperative of the Latin verb *caveo.* This imperative form may be familiar from reproductions of the well-preserved Pompeian floor mosaic showing the picture of a dog and bearing the legend *Cave canem* (beware of the dog). To *keep cave* is to *keep watch, act as lookout.* David Daiches has something to say about this in his marvelous book about his youth as a Jewish boy in Scotland, *Was* (Thames and Hudson, London, 1975):

> In school stories he had read boys shouted *cave* to give warning of the approach of a teacher or other intrusive adult, but not in Edinburgh; in Edinburgh you kept *shote,* kept a look-out, and shouted *shote* when you spied someone coming. *Shote! Yon's the parkie!*—a familiar cry in the Meadows when the park-keeper hove in sight to castigate boys for climbing over railings.

ceased to exist   **been disconnected**
   Gloomy intelligence imparted by the telephone operator: *Sorry sir, that line has ceased to exist.* The line, that is, not the subscriber, it is to be hoped. A *ceaseline* is a *disconnected number.*

centenary, *n.*   **centennial**
   Both terms are used in both countries, the above being the preferred usages. Both pronounce *centennial* the same way; but *centenary* is usually accented on the first syllable and has a short *e* in the second syllable in America, whereas in Britain it is usually accented on the second syllable, with a long *e,* though it is permissible there to shorten the *e,* or even to accent the first syllable. During all the radio and television hoopla that went on in Britain in the summer of 1976 about the American bicentennial, their announcers increasingly shifted over to the short *e* in the second syllable of *centenary,* but they all stuck to accenting on that syllable, as in *centennial.*

centillion. See Appendix II.D.

central (centre) reserve (reservation). *See* **centre strip.**

centreplate. *See* **sliding keel.**

centre strip   **median divider**
   Called *central reserve* in the official Highway Code, an appellation which seems as pompous as *median divider.* See also **dual carriageway.**

century, *n.*   **100 runs**
   In a cricket match, the **batsman** who makes 100 runs scores a *century.* See **batsman.**

certified, *adj.*   **insane**
   Inf. A past participle used as an adjective, both literally and hyperbolically, like its American equivalent. An echo is heard in the American phrase *certifiable lunatic.* See synonyms under **bonkers.**

C.H. See **Birthday Honours.**

chair, *n.*   **track socket**
   Metal device to hold railroad track in place on a tie.

chairman (of a company), *n.*   **president (of a corporation)**
   This usage reflects differences in forms of business organization in the two countries. The Americans do not speak of the *chairman* of a company or corporation. They speak of the *chairman of the board,* meaning the 'chairman of the board of directors.' Such a *chairman* is not, strictly speaking, a corporate officer. He runs meetings of the board of directors but has only one vote on the board, and often the term implies more honor than power. Thus, an American corporate *president* is often said to have been kicked upstairs when he becomes chairman of the board. In a British company, the *chairman* is the equivalent of the *president* of an American corporation. See also **managing director.**

chalet, *n.*   SEE COMMENT
   How to describe this unfortunate type of domestic architecture, beloved of real estate agents? It is used to designate a small suburban house that wishes it were in the country. An abomination, far removed from the Swiss mountain cottage from which the name was stolen for this pious misuse. Worse is a *chalet-bungalow,* basically a one-story house with an extra room in the eave-space.

chalk and cheese   **night and day**
   Worlds apart. As different as chalk from cheese is the usual phrase, the equivalent of *as different as night and day.* This is sometimes shortened to *chalk and cheese: Why, they're simply chalk and cheese.*

chambermaid, *n.*   **hotel maid**
Not a *domestic* as in America. See also **char; daily.**

chambers, *n. pl.*   **lawyer's office**
The **solicitor** will invite you to his *office;* a **barrister** more often to his *chambers*. An American lawyer would never speak of his *chambers*, but that term is applied to a judge's private office (usually adjoining his courtroom). See also **Inns of Court.**

champers, *n.*   **champagne**
Slang. Americans may be more familiar with the other British slang for this patrician beverage: *bubbly*. As in *champagne*, the CH- is pronounced SH-. See **Harry.** . .

champion, *adj.*   **fine**
Slang. Champion is used adjectivally in America in sports terminology, as for instance, *champion boxer, champion golfer*. In Britain it is occasionally used as the equivalent of *fine* or *great*. Thus: *Alf is a champion lad!* In the north country, *champion!* is used as an exclamation of approval or agreement.

chance, *n.*   SEE COMMENT
When a member of the fielding side in cricket misses a possible catch off the **batsman's** bat (which, as in baseball, results in an out), or a **football** player misses a possible goal, he is said to have had a *chance*. This has become a technical term in these sports, but it is by no means so black-and-white as an *error* in baseball, and no obloquy attaches to the unfortunate player who was unable to exploit his *chance*. The word merely draws the line between possibility and impossibility. See **misfield.**

chance-child, *n.*   *Inf.* **love child**
Inf. The British term seems harsh beside the romantic American term. Both countries use the unfeeling term *illegitimate child*. The British sometimes use the term *come-by-chance* to mean the same thing.

chance-come, *adj.*   **fortuitous**
Describing anything that happens by *chance*.

chancellor, *n.*   **honorary university head**
University term. See also **vice-chancellor.**

Chancellor of the Exchequer   **Secretary of the Treasury**

chance-met, *adj.*   **met by chance**

chance one's arm, *Inf.*   *Inf.* **try one's luck**

change. See **get no change out of.**

change down   **down shift**
Inf. An automobile term. The British also use the term *change up*, where the Americans would say *shift*, a term which in America is always understood to refer to shifting up, i.e., shifting into higher gear. See **Appendix II.E.**

change the bowling. See **open the bowling.**

changing-room, *n.*   1. **dressing-room**
                                                                        2. **locker-room**
1. In a clothing store.
2. In a gym or at a stadium, swimming-pool, tennis court, and the like.

chant, *v.t.*   **tout**
Slang. To *sing the praises of,* with a strong implication of fraudulent misrepresentation. Usually seen in the phrase *to chant a horse,* i.e., to push the sale of a defective one, concealing bad points like foul temper or poor vision.

chap, *n.*   *Slang.* **guy; fellow**
The use of the word *chap* seems affected to most Americans. Its commonest equivalent in America is *guy,* which is slang and seems even a little vulgar. Americans also use *fellow,* which is less inelegant than *guy* (as opposed to *person,* for instance), but still seems to come off as somewhat deprecatory. *Guy* is common in Britain now.

chapel, *adj.*   **non-Anglican**
Inf. Usually as a predicate and sometimes mildly pejorative, or at least snobbish, to describe a person adhering to a Protestant sect other than the established church, i.e., the Church of England (also known as the Anglican Church). It is a shortening of *chapel-folk* or *chapelgoer,* both of which are informal labels for members of such sects. The standard British nouns for such a person are **dissenter** and **nonconformist,** which are interchangeable and sometimes capitalized. *Free Church* is another synonym.

chap-fallen, *adj.*   **crest-fallen**
Chap is an archaic variant of *chop,* meaning 'jaw' (as in, e.g., *lick one's chops*). *Chap-fallen* describes a person whose jaws are hanging, i.e., who is in low spirits. Shakespeare made a grim pun of the word (hyphenless) in the graveyard scene in *Hamlet* (Act V, Scene 1). Examining Yorrick's skull, Hamlet, before he knows it is Yorrick's, describes it (lines 95/96) as "chapless, and knocked about the mazzard with a sexton's spade." (*Mazzard,* or *mazard,* is archaic for *head* or *face.*) Then, on learning whose skull it is, he says (lines 10/11), "Not one now, to mock your own grinning? quite *chapfallen?*"

chapman, *n.*   **peddler**
Like the itinerant merchant it describes, the word is rarely met with nowadays. Synonymous with *peddler,* which the British spell *pedlar.* They hawked *chapbooks,* little pamphlets containing street cries, short tales, tracts, and ballads, many of which are now common nursery rhymes (such as the ones about the old woman who lived in a shoe and the baby on the treetop). The *chap-* is related to the *cheap* in **cheapjack,** also meaning 'peddler.' *Cheap* itself comes from Old English *ceap,* meaning 'trade.'

char, *n.*   **1. cleaning woman**
                                                                                          2. tea
1. *Inf.* This word is displeasing to the ladies whom it describes. It is also used in the combinations *charwoman* and *charlady.* The latter is minimally acceptable to these ladies, who generally prefer to be called *daily help, daily woman,* or just *daily.* No precise informal equivalent in America.
2. *Inf.* The British love their tea and some of the most cultured of them will affectionately offer it to you in the mildly humorous phrase *a cuppa char.* Sometimes the *char* is omitted in this connection and *cuppa* is used alone. No slang American counterpart. This use of *char* is said by some to be simply an imitation of the Mandarin pronunciation of the Chinese word for *tea,* transliterated *chá* in the Pinyin system (used by the mainland Chinese) and ch'a in the Wade-Giles system (used customarily in English). Other authorities state that *char* is a corruption of the Urdu word for *tea, chāē,* brought back in that form by British troops returning from India.

charabanc, *n.*   **excursion bus**
A term rarely heard today but occasionally seen in old travel books. When used, it is pronounced SHARABANG. Now referred to as a *coach.*

charge-hand, *n.*   **foreman**
The person *in charge.*

charge-nurse, *n.*   **head nurse**
In *charge* of a ward. See also **casualty department; sister.**

charge-sheet, *n.*   **police blotter**
To *take* a person *in charge* is to *arrest* him.

charge (something) to tax   **impose tax on (something)**

charity. See **as cold as charity.**

Charles's Wain   **Ursa Major; Big Dipper**
Other British names for the Big Dipper: *the Plough; the Great Bear.*

charley, *n., Slang.*   *Slang.* **botch job; mess**

Charley's dead. See **slate.**

charlie, *n.*   *Slang.* **jerk**
Slang. Some charlie has broken my vase! Or, I *felt a proper charlie* (i.e., a *real idiot*)! On occasions, *charlie* can take on the connotation of *patsy; fall guy.*

charlies (charleys), *n., pl.*   *Slang.* **tits**
Slang. Synonymous with **Bristols**, but apparently not rhyming slang (see **Appendix II.G.3.**); etymology unknown.

charmer, *n.*   SEE COMMENT
Inf. This word now applies to either sex, to mean an attractive person, but in old-fashioned circles the connotation is still feminine. Used of men, it can imply a studied approach to the art of charming.

chartered accountant   **certified public accountant**
Almost always referred to in America as *C.P.A.*

chartered surveyor   **licensed architect**

chat show   **talk show**
Television term.

chattermag, *n., v.i.*   1. *n.* **chatterbox**
                                                         2. *v.i.* **babble**
Inf. Probably formed of *chatter* and *magpie.* In his *Poems of Rural Life*, the English poet and philologist William Barnes, who wrote poems in Dorset dialect, a *Philological Grammar*, and other books on the English language in the middle of the nineteenth century, defined *chattermag* as a "chattering magpie, a much-talking woman." But the sexual discrimination was eliminated when the English novelist Iris Murdoch, in *A World Child* (Chatto & Windus, London, 1975), characterized the idle chatter of a group of do-nothing young men as *chattermagging.* There is a strong implication of *gossiping* in *chattermagging.*

chat up   *Slang.* **hand (someone) a line**
Slang. In Britain you *chat up* a person in the attempt to *win him* or *her over.* When the *chatting up* is directed by a male to a female, there is generally an implication of a sexual objective. *Sweet-talk* is another American equivalent. *Chat* (without the *up*), as in *chat the girls*, means 'flirt with.'

chaw-bacon, *n.*   **hayseed**
Slang. Jaw-bacon is a variant.

cheap, *adj.*   **inexpensive; reduced (in price)**
In America a lady would express pride in her successful shopping expedition by saying, *The dress was cheap,* or *I bought it cheap.* However, she would not want to refer to the object of her shopping triumph as a *cheap dress.* If she wanted a new dress when the sales were on, she would never ask the saleslady to show her a *cheap* dress. She would ask for a *reduced* dress. Thus, it can be said that, except as a predicate adjective, *cheap* would be avoided in America as a synonym for *inexpensive* because of a reduction. As an attributive adjective, *cheap* in America connotes *tawdriness* in referring to things and persons and has a special slang connotation of *stinginess* when referring to persons, especially in the expression *cheapskate.* These meanings are secondary in the British usage of *cheap.* Thus *cheap tickets,* as advertised on railroad posters, are *excursion fares,* and a *cheap* frock may be a very nice dress indeed, though inexpensive. An interesting development from *cheap* is the word *Chipping* which appears in place names like Chipping Norton, Chipping (also Chepping) Wycombe, etc. The *Chipping* comes from *cheaping* and appears in the names of towns where fairs were held and presumably *cheap* goods (among others) were offered for sale. As to the origin of *cheap,* see **chapman.** See also **on the cheap.**

cheapjack, *n., adj.*   **hawker**
At fairs, etc. Sometimes it means 'peddler.' *Cheapjack goods* are poor quality stuff, *shoddy,* the sort usually offered by this class of merchant. See **chapman.**

cheddar, hard. *See* **hard cheese.**

cheek, *v.t.*   *Inf.* **to sass; be fresh to**
Slang. To *cheek* someone is to be impudent or rude to him. Not used as a verb in America.

cheerio! *interj.*   *Inf.* **so long!**

cheers! *interj.*   **here's how!**
Down the hatch! Here's mud in your eye! Chin chin! Salute! A votre santé. Skol! Prosit! The British form was originally non-U (see **Appendix I.C.6.**) and was frowned on in some U-circles where *Your health!* or *Good luck!* was preferred. It was gradually taken over, perhaps at first facetiously, and is now established practically everywhere.

cheese it!   *Slang.* **pipe down!**
Slang. Rather than *Look out! Somebody's coming!* which Americans mean when they shout *Cheezit!*

cheesed off   *Slang.* **teed off**
Slang. Synonymous with **brassed off.**

cheese off!   **get lost!**
Slang. Synonymous with **buzz off.**

cheese-paring, *adj., n.*   **penny-pinching**
A *cheese-paring* sort of chap is a *stingy* one, and the noun *cheese-paring* describes this sorry attitude toward life. As a plural noun *cheese-parings* means 'junk,' odds and ends that ought to be thrown away. In this connection, see also **lumber.**

cheesy, *adj.*   *Slang.* **swanky**
Slang. In the sense of 'stylish' or 'chic,' the British and American meanings are directly opposite. This British use is going out; some say that it is already obsolete, but it is still heard occasionally in the countryside, among old folk. Along with the passing of its use in the first sense, the word has now acquired the American meaning in Britain. One must be careful to know one's audience before using this word in Britain.

Chelsea, *adj.*   *Inf. approx.* **Villagey**
Inf. One says of a person, *He's very Chelsea,* to connote Bohemianism, genuine or affected. An approximation would be *Villagey* in America, referring to Greenwich Village in New York, the haunt of artists, models, writers, and persons wanting to be taken

for same. Parts of the Village are now as chic and in the swim as parts of Chelsea in London. Like almost everything else about the London-New York Axis, the similarities are tenuous.

Chelsea bun   **currant bun**
Usually with icing.

chemist, dispensing. See **dispenser.**

chemist's shop   **drugstore; pharmacy**
The *shop* can be omitted. See also **dispenser.**

cheque, *n.*   **check**
A matter of spelling. But isn't it peculiar that a *check* (or *cheque*) is a form of *draft*, that *draft* is sometimes spelled *draught*, and that *draughts* is the British form of *checkers*? Perhaps the explanation is that the medieval Exchequer was an accounting system carried out on a squared board. In Britain, a *checking account* is a *cheque account*, a *current account*, or a *running account*. See also **crossed cheque; bill.**

Chequers, *n.*   SEE COMMENT
Official country residence of the Prime Minister, in Buckinghamshire.

chesterfield, *n.*   **sofa**
In America a *chesterfield* is a dark overcoat, usually with a velvet collar. The British *chesterfield* is a large overstuffed sofa, with a back and upholstered arms. In Canada, the term is applied to any large sofa or couch.

chest of drawers   **bureau; dresser**
In Britain a **bureau** is a writing desk with drawers of the sort Americans refer to as a *secretary*, and a **dresser** is a *kitchen sideboard with shelves.*

chevy, also **chivy,** *v.t.*   *Inf.* **keep after**
Inf. Also *chivvy.* To *put pressure* on someone; to *hurry* him *up*, in the sense of 'chase' him. Probably there is some connection with *Chevy Chase*, an old ballad, and a place on the Scottish border.

chewing gum   **gum**
In Britain **gum** by itself would be taken to mean 'mucilage.'

chi-ack, *v.t.*   *Inf.* **give a yell at**
Slang. (Pronounced CHY'-AK.) To *chi-ack* is to *hail*, whether the object of the hailing is a friend you know who might be plowing in the next field or a girl you don't know but would like to. Many variant spellings; *chy-ack, chi-ike,* etc.

chicken, *n.*   **young chicken**
Chicken in America covers any size or age. An old one in Britain would be called a *fowl* (or a *boiler*), and *chicken yard* in America would be *fowl-run* in Britain.

chicken-flesh, *n.*   *Inf.* **goose pimples**
Inf. Also *goose-flesh* in Britain. *Goose pimples* is considered a vulgar Americanism in Britain.

chicory, *n.*   **endive**
In a British **greengrocer's**, ask for *chicory* if you want *endive*—and vice versa! Waverly Roots has gone into great detail on the *chicory-endive* dichotomy, a matter of deep significance to botanists, housewives, and gourmets. His learned article entitled "Investigations into Chicory and Endive" begins with this impressive paragraph:

What is chicory? Or, more pertinently, which plant of the family Cichorium is chicory and which is endive?... There are two contenders, *Cichorium endivia* and *Cichorium intybus*, and as the first carries the very word endive in its stomach, that ought to end the argument. *Cichorium endivia* is endive and *Cichorium intybus* is chicory in England and Germany, but in France it is just the opposite. Popular usage in the United States usually follows the French example, but scientific usage that of England and Germany.

There follows a long and learned discussion involving further etymological and botanical investigation. To the author's astonishment and to muddy the waters further, if possible, the Kroger grocery chain (in Ann Arbor, Michigan, at least) calls *chicory*, in the American sense, *endive lettuce*. That may be local, of course, and time prohibited research in the other forty-nine states. As a practical matter, just remember that the pair switch labels in Britain. As an even more practical matter, just point, if there is an attendant, or pick it up if there isn't.

chief bridesmaid

maid of honor

chief editor

editor in chief

child-battering   child beating
Battering is used for *beating* also in the expression *wife battering*. But note that the American term would imply sexual abuse in Britain.

child-minder, *n.*   daytime babysitter
The connotation is that both parents are working. The term *babysitter*, in Britain, refers to the evening. Also called a **sitter-in.**

chilled distribution   (delivery by) refrigerated truck

Chiltern Hundreds   SEE COMMENT
This name is derived from the term *hundred*, a now obsolete subdivision of a county, with its own court and other administrative features. These courts were abolished over a century ago. (*Hundreds* existed in a few American states in the old days, too.) Three of these English hundreds in the County of Buckinghamshire, named Stoke, Burnham, and Desborough, came to be known as the *Chiltern Hundreds* because of their situation in the Chiltern Hills. The *Stewardship of the Chiltern Hundreds* is a nominal office under the Chancellor of the Exchequer, an "office of honour and profit under the crown," the holding of which has been considered, since 1701, incompatible with membership in the House of Commons. Since the middle of the 18th century a Member who held the office was required to vacate his seat in the Commons. Hence, to *apply for* or *accept the Chiltern Hundreds* (i.e., the stewardship thereof) means to 'resign one's seat' in the House of Commons. Since a Member is not allowed to resign his seat before the expiration of his term of office, the only way he can vacate the seat is to *apply for the Chiltern Hundreds*. This is probably the only reason why the office still exists.

chimney-piece, *n.*   mantelpiece

chimney-pot, *n.*   SEE COMMENT
A pipe added to the top of a chimney; ubiquitous in Britain (and much of Europe). Its function is to improve the draft and disperse the smoke. A *chimney-pot hat* is a *stovepipe.* This is sometimes shortened to *chimney-pot*, omitting the *hat*, like *stovepipe.* See also **ingle-nook.**

chine, *n.*   SEE COMMENT
Apart from its meanings shared with American English (backbone, part of the backbone of an animal cut for cooking, ridge, crest, intersection of sides and bottom of a ship), a *chine* is a deep ravine, but only in the Isle of Wight and Dorset.

chip, *n.*   1. wood sliver
                                                                                  2. fruit basket
1. The material from which fruit and vegetable baskets are made. See **punnet.**
2. The basket itself.

chip, *v.t., Inf.*   chaff; kid
As in, *They chipped me about my boy-friend.*

chip in   *Inf.* **butt in; break in**
Inf. In the sense of interrupting somebody else's conversation, a meaning not used
in America, where it means to 'contribute,' in the way children make up a fund to buy
teacher a gift. The British use it that way too, and also have another phrase for that: to
pay one's whack. Chop in is a variant.

chipolata, *n.*   small pork sausage
(Pronounced CHIPPO-LAH'-TA.) The meat is mixed with meal. The best are those
ground, blended, and stuffed by your own butcher.

chippie (chippy; chips), *n.*   carpenter
Slang. See also **fish 'n' chips.**

chippings, loose. See **loose chippings.**

chit, *n.*   memo
The British use it as well in its American meaning of an 'I.O.U.,' usually for drink or
food in a club or military mess, or at a bar or pub. See **on the slate.**

chips, *n. pl.*   French fried potatoes
Inf. One sees *French fried potatoes* on some British menus nowadays, especially in the
better places. See also **crisps** and **fish 'n' chips.**

chivy or **chivvy.** See **chevy.**

chock-a-block   *Inf.* **chock full**
Inf. Rarely heard in America. Synonymous with **bungfull.** See also **packed out with.**

chocker   *Inf.* **fed up**
Slang. From **chock-a-block.** For the *-er* ending, see **Harry...**

choked, *adj.*   disgruntled
Slang. Synonymous with **chuffed** 2.

chocolate vermicelli   chocolate sprinkles
See also **hundreds and thousands.**

chok(e)y, *n.*   *Slang.* **poky**
Slang. Synonymous with **quod.** See also **porridge,** 2.

choose how   *Inf.* **like it or not**
Inf. A north of England term.

chop, *n., v.t., v.i.*   *approx.* **change**
A special use of *chop* in the expression *chop and change,* which, used transitively, means
to 'keep changing' (e.g., to keep trading in your car for a new one). To *chop and change,*
used intransitively, means to 'shilly-shally.' *Chops and changes* are *variations.* To *chop
about* or *chop round* means to 'veer,' like a suddenly shifting wind. To *chop in* (a variant
of *chip in*) is to 'break into a conversation, to 'put in your two cents' worth,' as it were.
To *chop logic* is to 'argue for argument's sake.' The phrase *chop and change* is said to have

originated from Henry VIII's matrimonial variations, in certain instances of which he had to *chop* before he could *change*, but this derivation smacks of the apocryphal. See also **get the chop.**

chops of the Channel   SEE COMMENT
Inf. Passage from the Atlantic Ocean into the English Channel.

chough, *n.*   **red-legged crow**
(Pronounced CHUFF.) A fairly common crow in some parts of Britain, notable for its plaintive cry like a kitten's. There are many varieties of birds with unfamiliar names, not found in America, like *ouzel* (also *ousel,* a 'black thrush'), *wagtail,* etc., whose inclusion would unduly burden this book. This one is included because of the West Country expression *as the chough flies,* a variant of *as the crow flies.*

Christian name   **first name**
Americans also say *Christian name* and *given name* but *first name* is much more common. It has always seemed a good idea, to the author at least, to avoid this term in addressing a query to people of other religions (*Mr. Nehru, how do you spell your...ahem...Christian name?*) or other persuasions (*What is your Christian name, Mr. Gorbachev?*). See also **middle name.**

Christmas-box. See Boxing Day.

Christmas club   SEE COMMENT
Different from the American scheme of the same name; a special sort of layaway plan. In Britain one can join a Christmas club usually during the summer at a neighborhood butcher shop or grocery store, accumulating modest periodic deposits there to lessen the impact of the holiday bills for the turkey or roast beef and its trappings.

chucker-out, *n., Slang.*   *Slang.* **bouncer**

chuffed, *adj.*   **1. delighted**
                                                                        2. disgruntled
Slang. This curious bit of army slang has two diametrically opposite meanings, depending on the context. In case of ambiguity, one can say *chuffed pink* (tickled pink) to mean 'pleased,' or *dead chuffed* to mean 'displeased.' In the second sense, *chuffed* is synonymous with **choked.** Philip Howard has much more to say about this 'Janus' or 'reversible' word in an article entitled 'English English' in the language quarterly *Verbatim,* Vol. VII, No. 1 (Summer 1980). He quotes Eric Partridge, the authority on British slang, who declared that "...if one needed to distinguish [the two meanings], one said *chuffed to fuck* or *chuffed to arseholes* or *chuffed pink* or *bo-chuffed* to mean 'gruntled,' and *dead chuffed* to mean 'disgruntled.'" He mentions the variant *chuffed as bollocks* (see **bollocks**) and other intensifiers and winds up with these sentiments: "I doubt whether we are ever going to arrive at an explanation of *chuffed* that is going to satisfy everyone. In any case the Janus word is distinctly old-fashioned in British English."

chummery, *n., Inf.*   SEE COMMENT
Starting out in life as a colloquialism for *friendship,* it came to mean 'shared living quarters.' The word is obsolete in Britain, but still heard in India (and in Britain among old India hands), to describe lodgings shared by Britons employed by the same company.

chump, *n.*   *Slang.* **nut**
Slang. Chump, like *loaf, nod,* and other words, is a slang term for *head,* like *bean* in America. *Use your chump* is commonly heard, inviting the party addressed to stop being a fool. To be *off one's chump* is to be *off one's nut.*

chump chop   SEE COMMENT
Type of lamb chop. *Chump* is thought to be a portmanteau word made up of *chunk* and *lump* and literally means a 'small lump of wood.' In the food department it desig-

nates the thick end of a loin of mutton, hence *chump chop*, meaning a 'mutton' or 'lamb chop' which (as opposed to a rib chop) is mostly meat surrounding a little bit of bone in the middle. See **Appendix II.H.**

Chunnel, *n.*   SEE COMMENT
Inf. English Channel tunnel. Dream and dread of Britons and Frenchmen for years and years, reactivated in the first flush of the Common Market, and now (1986) very much in the news, as agreement has been reached between the affected countries to go ahead with the project, to be financed by the private sector rather than the governments, as in the case of the Suez Canal. The inhabitants of the Dover area are horrified. So are all the Englishmen this author has spoken to.

chunter, *v.i.*   *Inf.* **blab on and on**
Inf. Like **rabbit on.**

C.I.D.   SEE COMMENT
The initials stand for *Criminal Investigation Department.* A *C.I.D. man* is a plain-clothes detective: a *Cop In Disguise.*

cider, *n.*   **hard cider**
Cider, in Britain, is always fermented and alcoholic. Americans distinguish between *cider* (which the British call *apple juice,* as do many Americans) and *hard cider,* which is simply *cider* to the British. In addition, there is a delicious British drink called *vintage cider,* which has the consistency of good sherry and is at least as strong. It is a deceptive drink—goes down much too easily—and bears watching. See also **scrump.**

cinecamera, *n.*   **movie camera**

cinema, *n.*   **movie house**
In America, its connotation is technical rather than popular. See also **film; flick; pictures.**

Cinque Ports   SEE COMMENT
(Pronounced SINK PORTS.) Literally (from Old French via Middle English) 'Five Ports' on the southeast coast of Britain. The author was puzzled to learn that there were seven 'Five Ports,' whose names he memorized with the help of a silly mnemonic. Thereafter, he discovered a village (Tenterden) not on the list of seven which, on a decorative roadside sign at its entrance, proclaimed itself to be one of the *Cinque Ports.* Now the puzzlement reached feverish proportions—until his discovery of the following bit of prose supplied by the Ashford Borough Council, a governmental subdivision whose jurisdiction extended to the Village of Tenterden:

> Hundreds of years ago, before England possessed a Royal Navy, the five ports of Hastings, Romney, Hythe, Dover and Sandwich provided ships and men to protect the south coast from invaders. These ports, later joined by the 'Antient Towns' of Winchelsea and Rye, came to be known as the Cinque Ports.
> To the Crown, their service was vital and in 1278, during the reign of Edward I, the duties and privileges of the Confederation of the Cinque Ports were set out in a special charter. The duties were basically to provide a certain quota of fully-manned ships, and the privileges included tax and trading concessions and honours at Court.
> In order to supply its own quota of ships and men, each Head Port looked to a number of 'Limbs' or supporting towns, and extended its privileges to them. However, with the advent of larger ships, the changing coastline and the creation of a permanent navy, the influence of the Cinque Ports gradually diminished. Yet still today, the Confederation (now consisting of the original seven towns plus Tenterden, Deal, Faversham, Folkestone, Lydd, Margate and Ramsgate) sends its Barons to attend at Coronations. The Lord Warden of the Cinque Ports is currently [1987] Her Majesty, Queen Elizabeth the Queen Mother.

cipher. See **nought.**

circs., *n. pl.*   **circumstances**
Inf. One of those abbreviations the British like, not only written, but also pronounced that way (SERKS). See **Appendix I.D.9.**

circular road   **belt highway**
See **arterial road; ring road; orbital.**

circular saw   **buzz saw**
Heard also in U.S., especially commercially.

circumbendibus, *n.*   1. **roundabout route or method**
                                                      2. **long-winded story**
                                                      3. **circumlocution**
Inf. An old-fashioned jocularity involving mock Latin, a favorite British indoor sport. Cf. **omnium gatherum.**

Circus, *n.*   **Circle**
Used in cities where Americans would normally use *Circle;* thus Piccadilly *Circus,* Oxford *Circus,* etc., as compared with, e.g., *Columbus Circle* in New York.

(the) City, *n.*   *Inf. approx.* **Wall Street; financial district**
Inf. The *City* of London is a precise geographical section of London and is chief among several *Cities* (e.g., the *City* of Westminster) which are incorporated in London. The *City* of London includes the financial district, and *the City,* as an abbreviation of the *City of London,* is used in Britain exactly as *Wall Street* is used in America. Geographically the *City* is larger than the London financial district which it includes, whereas *Wall Street* is only a part of the New York financial district in which it is included. The *City* measures one square mile and has 5,000 residents; and the sovereign of Great Britain and Northern Ireland cannot enter it without the Lord Mayor's permission. The *City* *editor* of a London newspaper is what would be called the *financial editor* in America; (but *city editor,* in America, means the person in charge of local news). See also **Throgmorton Street.** For the general meaning of *city* apart from this specialized use, see **village.**

City editor   **financial editor**
See under **City.**

city boundary   **city limits**

civilities, *n. pl.* See **amenities.**

civil servant   **government employee**
The *civil service* is a term familiar to Americans, but in the author's experience, Americans in the civil service have rather uncivilly expressed resentment at being, quite civilly, referred to as *civil servants* and prefer to be known as *government employees.*

(the) Civil War   SEE COMMENT
War between Charles I and Parliament. Nothing to do with the American *War Between the States,* also known as the *War of Secession.* This one was fought in the 17th century between the Royalists supporting King Charles I and the Roundheads led by Oliver Cromwell, ending with the beheading of Charles (or "Charles the Martyr" as true blue Royalists called him).

Civvy Street, *Inf.*   **civilian life**

claim against tax   **take as a deduction**
Tax terminology. It is getting more and more difficult to *claim against tax* the tabs for all those three-martini lunches. (But see also **martini.**)

clap, *v.t.*   **applaud**
Clap, in the sense of 'applaud,' is used intransitively in America. In Britain, one *claps* a performer; in America, one *applauds* him.

clap eyes on, *Slang.*   *Inf.* **set eyes on**

clapped out   *Slang.* **tuckered out**
Slang. Frazzled; beat. See **fag; knock up; cooked; creased; flaked out; jiggered; spun.**

clapper bridge   SEE COMMENT
A primitive type of bridge found in the West Country, consisting of large stones (five or six feet long by two or three feet wide, and about one foot thick) laid flat on boulders spaced about four feet apart across small streams. Some of these bridges are believed to be prehistoric.

clapper-claw, *v.t.*   **beat up**
Slang. Clapper-claw is often used intransitively in a figurative sense to mean 'claw one's way', e.g. to the top in a toughly competitive industry, or in politics.

class, *n.*   **grade**
University term. In America, one's *college class* is the *year of graduation*. In Britain one's *class at university* is the place in the honours examinations, e.g., a *first,* an *upper* or *good second* or *lower second* (sometimes called a 2.1 or 2.2), or a *third. Class* is understood.

classic races. See under **guinea.**

clawback, *n.*   *Slang.* **toady**
Slang. With the emphasis on flattery.

clean, *v.t.*   **shine**
Referring to shoes. See also **blanco.**

clearing bank   SEE COMMENT
A *clearing bank* is one that clears checks (**cheques**) drawn on other banks. The *clearing banks* as of the moment (1987) are Barclays, Coutts, Lloyds, Midland, National Westminster, Williams & Glyn's. See **Big Four.**

clear majority   **majority**
In British voting terminology, *majority* means what in America is called a *plurality.* To indicate an arithmetical majority, i.e., more than 50 percent, the British use the term *clear* or *absolute majority.*

clearway, *n.*   **no-parking thoroughfare**

cleg. *n.*   **horsefly**
Mainly Scottish.

clem, *v.i.*   **starve**
Slang. As in *clemmed for a snack.* Dialect, favored by hoboes; common in rustic novels. Its use is considered by some to be chic.

clench, *adj.*   **rigid**
Slang. A Lincolnshire term, which includes the senses, according to Michael Gilbert in *Flash Point* (Harper & Row, New York, 1974) of "uncompromising, prickly, with a bit of grudge against life. Sometimes it's the result of being bullied at **school.** You spend the rest of your life trying to **get your own back on it.**"

clerk, *n.*   1. **lawyer's assistant**
                                                                        2. **church officer**
                                                                        3. **town officer**
                                                                  4. **office or store worker**

(Pronounced CLARK.) This word originally meant 'clergyman' in Britain, but that meaning is now archaic.
1. It is commonly used by British **solicitors** (*lawyers*) to describe their assistants, and *law clerk* is a term not unknown in America.
2. The job of a lay person who renders miscellaneous services to a parish church.
3. An official, usually a lawyer, in charge of town records, who acts generally as the business representative of a town.
4. *Bank clerks, shop clerks,* and the like, are *general office workers* who keep books, do filing, and take care of miscellaneous office functions. A *clerkess* (rarely used, except in Scotland) is a *female clerk*, just as a *manageress* (e.g., of a restaurant or a pet shop) is a *female manager*. Americans often denote the sex of such disparate groups as actors, sculptors, Negroes, and Jews with *-ess*, a practice much decried by feminists, but they stop short of *clerkess* and *manageress*. See also **assistant.**

clerk of the works   **supply man;**
                                                         maintenance man
   This title denotes a person who acts as overseer of supplies and building materials for a contractor on a particular construction site, and acts as a kind of progress reporter, on site, among customer, contractor, and architect. This term also covers the position of one in charge of repairs and maintenance, such as outside painting and sidewalk repair, for instance, of a municipal housing unit (**council house** *estate*).

clever Dick, *Slang.*   *Slang.* **wise guy**

clinking, *adj.*   *Slang.* **damned good**
   Slang. Thus, a *clinking* game, a *clinking* race, etc. But it can also be used adverbially modifying *good*: a *clinking good game*, a *clinking good race*. See also **rattling; thundering.**

clippie, *n.*   **bus conductress**
   Inf. In Britain there are bus conductors of both sexes. A male conductor is simply a *conductor;* a female *conductor* is a *clippie*. Both male and female bus conductors used to *clip* your ticket, i.e., *punch* your ticket, but only the lady conductors are called *clippies*. The word came into being during wartime when they replaced the men. Usage going out of fashion now.

cloakroom, *n.*   **washroom**
   Both terms are euphemisms for *toilet,* but beware: Following a *cloakroom* sign in a public place in Britain may lead you to another destination, because it is also used literally in that country. The British term *cloakroom ticket* has nothing to do with permission to leave the room. All it means is 'baggage check' or 'hat check'. See **loo.**

clobber, *n.*   **1.** *Inf.* **get-up**
                                                           2. *Inf.* **gear**
1. *Slang.* This word means 'attire' and is generally used when there is something peculiar about the attire, as for example, *He appeared in the strangest clobber,* or *He had borrowed somebody else's clobber.* See **rig-out.**
2. *Slang.* The word aquired the further meaning of 'gear,' 'junk,' 'one's full equipment' in World War I.

close, *n.*   **dead-end residential area**
   (Pronounced CLOCE.) A *close* is a kind of *cul-de-sac* broadened out at its end. The term is used also to describe the enclosed land around a cathedral. The British love addresses involving *crescent, gardens, terrace, mews, close, pavement, parade, vale, grove,* and the like. They stick more or less to the facts in things like *crescent*, but streets miles removed from the humblest buttercup ruthlessly cling to epithets like *gardens*. Sometimes they really go to town and name streets 'The Garth,' 'The Dale,' 'The Vale,' 'The Knoll,' etc. In the town of East Grinstead (which is separated from West Grinstead by many miles and has very little in common with it), one passes in rapid succession streets named *...Park, ...Rise, ...Hollow, ...Way, ...Croft, ...Court, ...Downs, ...Grove* (each following a name), and climactically a circular *cul-de-sac* called simply *The Coronet*. And there is a street in Bromley, Kent, called *Crown Lane Spur*. In a village in Kent, there is a street called *The Weavers*. The British seem to be willing to go to any length to avoid the lowly

designation *street*, for a public road. But conversely, there is a *village* in Kent named *Hamstreet*, a town in County Durham called *Chester-le-Street*, and—for good measure—a village on the border of Herefordshire and Worcestershire with the proud name of *Broadway! Avenue* is common in America, and once in a while Americans indulge in descriptions like *square, circle*, or *drive*, more rarely *boulevard*, very rarely *mews*, and there is a street in Hartford, Conn., known as *American Row*, while Fairfield, Connecticut, boasts streets called *Tunxis Hill Cut-Off* and *Kings Highway Cut-Off*. But on the whole Americans are more prosaic in their designations—to say nothing of their soulless practice of assigning numbers and letters, rather than names, to their streets and avenues.

close crop, *n.*   **crew cut**
Despite the prevailing trend, some British young men still fancy the *close crop*. See also **short back and sides.**

close season   **closed season**
Referring to hunting, fishing, etc. (never to girlwatching). Here, the British omit the *d*. It's turned the other way around in the legal phrase *closed company* (British) for *close corporation*. See **Appendix I.A.3.**

closet, *n.*   **toilet bowl**
A euphemism. *Water closet* is old-fashioned British for *lavatory*. *Closet* (see **pedestal**) is the polite term seen in house-furnishing catalogues for the bowl itself. Never tell a guest in Britain to hang his clothes in the *closet*. The correct term would be *cupboard*.

close the doors, please!   **all aboard!**
Heard in railroad stations and often followed by "Train is about to depart!" In Britain, the one-time maritime power, the nautical term is still used for nautical situations.

closing-down sale   **liquidation sale**
Although sometimes it seems to mean only a 'closeout' of a particular line.

closing time. See **during hours.**

closure, *n.*   **cloture**
The British form is not common in America, and vice versa.

clot, *n.*   *Slang.* **jerk**
Slang. A strong pejorative. "She is suffering from marital thrombosis," quipped the doctor. "She's got a *clot* for a husband." Mild British humor.

cloth, washing-up. *See* **tea towel; washing-up cloth; dish clout.**

cloth-cap, *adj.*   *approx. Inf.* **blue-collar**
Inf. From the sartorial habits of those described. See also **black coat.**

cloth-eared, *adj., Slang.*   *Slang.* **deaf**
Referring to someone who either purposely or through lack of attention misunderstands what is said to him. See also **thick ear.**

clothes-peg, *n.*   **clothespin**

clothes-prop, *n.*   **clothespole**

clotted cream. See **Devonshire cream.**

club-hammer, *n.*   **mallet**

clubland, *n.*   SEE COMMENT
St. James's, an area of London including the palace of that name. It is bounded on the north by Jermyn Street, on the west by St. James's Street, on the south by Pall Mall (pronounced *Pell Mell*), and on the east by Lower Regent Street, and is called 'clubland'

because it houses many of London's famous clubs. Note the spelling of *St. James's*. The palace was once the royal residence, and although it has not been so used since the time of Queen Victoria, the British court is still designated as 'the Court of St. James's.'

club together, *v.i.*   **join up; pool**
Britons *club together* to buy a going-away gift for a friend or a memento for a retiring colleague.

clue, *n.*   **notion**
I haven't a clue is a very common expression in Britain, meaning 'I haven't the slightest idea.' It is interchangeable with another British expression: *I haven't the foggiest. He hasn't a clue,* however, means 'he is hopelessly ignorant or stupid.' If the pronoun is third person, of either gender or number, the expression is pejorative. See next entry.

clueless, *adj.*   *Inf.* **hopeless**
Inf. Describing someone who doesn't know what it's all about or which end is up. See also **clue.**

clutch, *n.*   SEE COMMENT
Inf. Clutch, in addition to its other uses as noun and verb, means a 'set of eggs,' or a 'brood of chickens.' Reflecting the usual untidiness and noisiness of the latter and the disagreeable social institution known as the *pecking order, clutch* is used in the term a *clutch of friends* to indicate the type of swarm of followers that might surround a movie star or other celebrity.

clutter, *n.*   **junk**
Clutter literally means *litter* or any untidy miscellany in both countries. But whereas an American might say, *Our weekend guests arrived with an awful lot of junk,* a Briton would probably describe them as having brought along a great deal of *clutter.* See also **lumber.**

C.M.G. *See* **K.; V.C.**

coach, *n.*   **inter-city bus**
See also **carriage, 1; motor coach.**

coalfish, *n.*   **black cod**
Also called *coley fillet* and *saithe.*

coarse, *adj.*   **common**
A special meaning applied to fresh water fish: *coarse* would exclude salmon and trout and other sporting fish caught with a fly. *Coarse* fish are run-of-the-mill types.

coatee, *n.*   **short coat**
Worn by women and infants. In American, a *coatee* is a short coat with tails, the word being fashioned after *goatee,* a certain type of beard.

cob, *n.*   **wall material**
A mixture of clay, gravel, and straw.

cobble, *n.*   SEE COMMENT
Lump coal the size of smallish cobblestones, whence the name.

cobble, *v.t.*   **run up; put together roughly**
To *cobble* something, or to *cobble* something *together,* is to run it up. A professor in a hurry will *cobble* a lecture together. This verb is used also to mean 'mend' or 'patch,' especially of shoes, indicating its back formation from **cobbler,** which in Britain means not only 'shoemaker,' but also 'clumsy workman,' a sense which is archaic in American usage.

cobblers, *n. pl., interj.* SEE COMMENT
Cockney rhyming slang (see **Appendix II. G.3.**) omitting, as usual, the rhyming word; short for *cobblers' awls*, rhyming with *balls*, so that its meaning as an interjection is 'balls!' particularly in the sense of 'forget it!' in response to a preposterous proposal. As a noun, it is used to describe anything considered rubbish or nonsense, as in *That's a lot of cobblers!*

cock, *n.* *Slang.* **bull**
Slang. Stuff and nonsense. We've all heard of *cock and bull* stories. The British have chosen the *cock,* the Americans the *bull.* Americans are squeamish about using *cock.* Britons have mocked such delicacy by referring to *roostertails* for preprandial drinks, *pet roosters* for *petcocks, roostered hat, go off half-roostered,* and similar conroostertions. However, *cock* is generally taboo in mixed company, except when it clearly refers to the animal, or in **that cock won't fight.**

cock-a-hoop, *adj., Slang.* *Inf.* **on top of the world**

cock a snook *Slang.* **thumb one's nose**
Slang. (Snook rhymes with COOK.) Sometimes *cock snooks.*

cockchafer, *n.* **June bug**
The beetle that usually arrives in May. The British are amused by the American name because **bug,** to them, normally means 'bedbug.' Member of the Scarabeid family.

Cocker. See **according to Cocker.**

cockerel, *n.* **1. young rooster**
2. young tough
1. Americans, too, occasionally use this word to mean a 'young rooster.'
2. Metaphorical extension.

cockney, *n., adj.* SEE COMMENT
Inf. Also used adjectivally meaning, literally, 'characteristic of a born **East Ender.**' A *cockney* accent is not deemed one of the more socially acceptable ways to pronounce English. But those possessing such an accent are often very proud of it and during the 60s it became a fashionable accent to attempt to imitate. See also **Bow Bells.**

cockshy. See **coconut shy.**

cock-up, *n.* *Inf.* **mess; muddle**
Slang. You've never seen such a cock-up in your life! (The bank robbers got away and the police arrested the bank manager by mistake.) See also discussion under **balls, 2.**

coconut shy SEE COMMENT
Like **Aunt Sally,** except that the contestant throws balls at a heap of coconuts (pronounced COKER-NUTS) for prizes. More or less interchangeable with *cockshy,* which is somewhat more general, in that it includes any game in which balls or sticks are thrown at a variety of targets. A *cockshy* may be the target itself, and the word is also used figuratively to mean a 'butt,' like *Aunt Sally. Cockshy* is also used to mean 'trial balloon': *I put up a cockshy memorandum* (to test opinion).

cod, *n., v.t., v.i.* **1.** *n.,* **joke; parody; take-off**
2. *v.t., v.i.,* **tease; spoof**
3. *Slang. v.i.,* **horse around**
Slang. In the first meaning, *cod* is used attributively in expressions like a *cod version of "Hamlet"* or a *cod cockney accent.*

codswallop, *n.* *Slang.* **baloney**
Slang. (Pronounced and sometimes spelled COD'S WALLOP.) *Hot air.* According to Rosie Boycott, in *Batty, Bloomers and Boycott* (Hutchinson, London, 1982), one Hiram

Codd, in *circa* 1870, "designed a bottle which was closed by means of a glass marble stuck in the neck...held in place by the pressure from a fizzy drink...Wallop in those days was the slang name for beer, so *codswallop* was used to refer to a beer bottle that was closed in this fashion." It is to be assumed that *codswallop* acquired the meaning 'hot air' by reference to the compressed air within Mr. Codd's bottle, but the connection does seem somewhat tenuous.

In William Safire's *On Language* column in the *New York Times* of Sept. 1, 1985, entitled *Codswallop, Poppycock and Horsefeathers*, he discussed this entry as follows:

> The word, meaning 'nonsense,' is British English: as a slang synonym for *rubbish, bosh, humbug, hogwash, tommyrot, tripe* and *drivel*, the newer *codswallop* was observed in the *The Radio Times* [an English weekly radio and TV program] in 1963. The Supplement to the Oxford English Dictionary published in 1972 tosses in an etymological sponge with a despairing 'Origin unknown.' Poppycock! James McDonald, in his 1984 book *Wordly Wise*, writes that in the 19th century, 'an inventor called Hiram Codd patented a new type of bottle with a glass marble in its neck. Mineral waters were sold in such bottles and, *wallop* being a slang term for fizzy ale, the contents became known as Codd's Wallop.' An alternative etymology is suggested by Farmer and Henley's slang dictionary, completed in 1904, which describes *cods* as a term of venery [two meanings, both archaic: 'sexual intercourse' and 'hunting']. In Norman W. Schur's 'English English,' the noun *codswallop*, defined as 'hot air,' follows a slang verb, *cod*, meaning 'to horse around.'

(As you can see, it is defined as *baloney*, with the added comment '*hot air*' for clarification.)

There was in interesting exchange of correspondence about *codswallop* in the *Times Literary Supplement* early in 1982. In a letter headed **Codswallop** (published January 29), Mr. Colin Vines wrote:

> . . .The *COD* [*Concise Oxford Dictionary*] defines it as "nonsense". That is both facile and incorrect. Chambers [*Chambers Twentieth Century Dictionary*] has it more accurately: "nonsense put forward as if serious idea or information". . . .The *COD* gives "20th c., origin unknown". That must be simple ignorance. Mr Codd (a northener, I think Lancastrian) sold lemonade and/or "wallop". He watered down this lemonade or wallop, and his products came to be known derisorily as Mr Codd's wallop. And later codswallop. That is to say, something pretending or appearing to be what it was not, with an element of deception; and, derived therefrom, something put forward as if to be taken seriously but being in fact a load of old codswallop. . .

Appearing in the February 12 issue was a letter from none other than Robert Burchfield, editor of the *Supplement to the Oxford English Dictionary* (with whom this author did a telecast from London in 1983 on NBC's *Today Show*, on Anglo-American language differences), who characterized Mr. Vines's letter as "an ill-humoured attack. . .on the *Concise Oxford Dictionary*" and went on to write:

> . . .No reputable dictionary subscribes to the theory that the first element derives from the name of the drinks-manufacturer Codd (the Codd bottle had ceased to be current in Britain before the first recorded use of *codswallop*). . .Amateur etymologists should credit lexicographers with having a professional interest in weighing the availing evidence and rejecting the unsupportable. . .It is regrettable that the *TLS* should on this occasion become a forum for casual and ill-informed comments of this kind.

Mr. Burchfield writes of "weighing the evidence." This author believes that Mr. Burchfield's authority weighs more than all the Codd supporters put together, and votes for "origin unknown." Quite incidentally, the omission of the period after *Mr* and the placing of the period outside the quotation marks are not typographical errors. See **Appendix I.D.3.** and **6.** See also **gammon; rot; balls; rubbish; all my eye and Betty Martin!** and **cobblers.**

C. of E.   Church of England
The established church. See **chapel; dissenter; nonconformist; Free Church.**

coffee sugar   SEE COMMENT
Sugar in large crystals, usually brown or honey-colored; occasionally varicolored.
Americans tend to approach it cautiously and it makes for table talk. The usual name
for it in shops is *sugar crystals.* See also **demerara.**

coffee-stall, *n.*   street coffee stand
Similar to the genus hot dog wagon, or chestnut stand, as seen on the streets of
America.

coiner, *n., Inf.*   counterfeiter

coley fillet. *See* **coalfish.**

collar stud   collar button

collar-work. See **against the collar.**

collections, *n. pl.*   mid-years
Term-end examinations at Oxford and Durham colleges. See **college.**

college, *n.*   school; house (dormitory)
This word, which in American educational terminology always denotes an institution
of higher learning and is roughly synonymous with *university,* does not necessarily
mean the same thing in Britain. Eton and Lancing Colleges are what are known as
public schools, roughly equivalent to what Americans call *prep schools,* and City of
London College is a secretarial school. On the other hand, the Oxford and Cambridge
colleges (about twenty-five at each) are more or less autonomous institutions each with
its own buildings, including hall of residence (see **hall**)—*house,* in the American 'college
dormitory' sense—dining-halls, chapel, principal's residence (see **master** and **Fellow**),
bedrooms and studies for Fellows (see also **don**), tutors (advisers) and undergraduates
(students), senior and junior common-rooms, and campus (**quad** at Oxford, **court** at
Cambridge). An undergraduate will get his basic teaching and supervision within his
own *college,* though he may attend lectures given by dons at other colleges. The colleges
do not specialize in the subjects taught. Some colleges, like All Souls and St Antony's,
Oxford, are for graduates only. Most are now coeducational. (The omission of the period
after *St* is not an error: see **Appendix I.D.6.**). Some of the Oxford *colleges* have nicknames: Brasenose is called *B.N.C.;* Christchurch, *The House;* St. Edmund Hall, *Teddy
Hall;* St. Peter's College, *Pot House.* The *college,* then, is residence, foster parent, and
spiritual home as well as teacher. For an excellent discussion of Oxford Colleges, their
historical origin and present constitution, see Muriel Beadle, *These Ruins Are Inhabited*
(Doubleday & Co., Inc., New York, 1961, p. 77 *ff.*). The phrase *college graduate* would
not be used in Britain. The person would be called a *university man* or *woman,* or *graduate.*
College is also applied to learned or professional institutions, such as the Royal College
of Physicians.

college grounds   campus
Campus is used increasingly in Britain, especially at the newer (**redbrick**) universities.
It is unlikely that it will catch on at **Oxbridge.** See **quad; court.**

college of further education   *approx.* **extension school**
For persons who have left school and wish to continue their general education or
learn a trade.

colleger, *n.*   SEE COMMENT
One of the 70 (out of 1,100) Eton students who live *in college* (i.e., *on campus;* see
college). The others are **oppidans.**

collier, *n.*   **coal freighter**
It means 'coal miner' in both countries, as well.

Collins, *n.*   *Inf.* **bread-and-butter letter**
Inf. Synonymous with **roofer.** See *Pride and Prejudice,* chap. 23. Now obsolescent;
usually *b and b,* or the American term in full.

coloured, *adj., n.*   *approx.* **non-white**
Colored in America signifies black, whether of African or West Indian origin. In Britain
the term includes Indians, Pakistanis, and persons of mixed parentage. Unfortunately,
it has become a noun in Britain, usually in the plural.

colt, *n.*   **1.** *Slang.* **rookie**
                                                               2. *approx.* **junior varsity player**
1. *Inf.* In professional cricket, a player in his first season.
2. *Inf.* At school it can refer to a boy who is a member of any junior team, not necessarily
cricket.

combe. *See* **coomb.**

combination-room, *n.*   **common-room**
Meeting-room at Cambridge University. There is a junior combination-room for undergraduates. The senior combination-room is for **fellows.**

combinations, *n. pl.*   **union suit**
Referring to underwear. *Union suits* are on the way out in America. *Combinations* are
dying out more slowly in Britain. *Combs* (short *o*; the *b* is silent) is an informal abbreviation.

comb-out, *n.*   **intensive search**
Inf. Sometimes the Americans use the term *comb* or *combing.*

combs. See **combinations.**

come, *v.t.*   **act**
Slang. To *come* the hero or the bereaved spouse is to *act* the part, to *put it on.*

come a cropper   *Inf.* **take a tumble**
Inf. Originally a hunting term; now extended to apply to a failure in any endeavor.

come a heavy over   *Slang.* **high-hat**
Slang. Also *come the heavy over.*

come a mucker. See under **mucker.**

come a purler   *Slang.* **fall on one's face**
Slang. Like the American equivalent, used both literally and figuratively. Thus, it
might apply not only to the physical act of stumbling, but also to a business or theatrical
fiasco, or the messing up of plans for a picnic.

comeback, *n.*   *Slang.* **oomph**
Inf. A person who does not have much *comeback* is one who does not have much *on
the ball,* i.e., is dull and not very good company.

come-by-chance, *n.*   **love child**
Inf. See **chance-child.**

come-day-go-day, *adj.*   **shiftless**
Too easygoing, apathetic; a drifter. It sometimes has the additional connotation of carelessness about money—*easy come, easy go.*

come down   **1. graduate**
                                                   2. SEE COMMENT
1. *Inf.* This is a university term. To *come down* is to *graduate.*
2. *Inf.* Used in the expression *come down for the summer vacation.* A vacation from work, generally, is called a **holiday** in Britain; but in university life, holidays at Christmas, Easter, and the summer hiatus are known as *vacations,* and the same is true of the Law Court calendar. The long university summer vacation is known as the **long vac.** *Come down* means the same thing as *go down* and the choice of phrase depends on the vantage point of the speaker: if you are at the university you talk of *going down;* the student's parents, however, would talk to their friends and relations about John's *coming down.* It depends on the position of the speaker in relation to the university. *Come down* and *go down* are not to be confused with **send down,** also a university term, meaning 'expel.' No colloquial American counterpart.

come expensive   *Inf.* **come to a lot**
Inf. To *cost too much.*

come home trumps. See **come up trumps.**

come it rather strong   *Inf.* **lay it on thick**
Inf. To *overdo it.* Applies, e.g., to excessive demands. It has been used about a Trimalchian feast: *That's coming it rather strong, isn't it?* But, the author prefers an elderly female friend's cliché for that type of parvenu party: *Piling on the agony.*

come on   **menstruate**
Inf. One of many euphemisms.

come on to   **begin**
Thus: *It came on to snow last night.*

come over, *v.i.*   *Inf.* **go (become)**
Inf. As in *I was so astounded I came over numb.*

come the acid   *Slang.* **be a wise guy**
Slang. Usually in the negative imperative: *Don't come the acid with me!* as a reproof given to a smart alec who has given a snide answer to a question. Has other shades of meaning as well, depending on context: 'exaggerate,' 'be too big for one's breeches,' 'try to burden someone else with one's own job,' generally, to 'make oneself objectionable.'

comether. See **put the comether on (someone).**

come top   *Inf.* **come out on top**
Inf. To **win.**

come to the horses, *Slang.*   *Slang.* **get down to brass tacks**

come to the wrong shop. See **shop.**

come up trumps   *Inf.* **turn out well**
Inf. Also *turn up trumps* and *come home trumps.* In context, it means 'not fail *or* disappoint,' to 'be there when you're needed': *He came up trumps when the going was bad.*

comforter, *n.*   **1. baby nipple; pacifier**
                                                   2. woolen scarf
Two distinct meanings, as opposed to the American meaning of *comforter,* which is 'quilt.' See also **duvet; eiderdown.**

comic, *n.*   **humorous comic**
Americans use the term *comic* generically, to designate all narrative strips, whether horror, macabre, tales of adventure, or funny. In Britain, the term tends to mean 'funny comics,' unless otherwise specified, e.g., as in *horror comic.*

coming, *adv.*   **going on**
Used adverbially in expressions of age: *Mary is coming seventeen.* Synonymous with **rising.**

command paper. See **Paper.**

commem, *n.*   SEE COMMENT
Inf. Abbreviation of *commemoration,* an annual celebration at Oxford in commemoration of founders. Seen in the expression *commem ball,* a dance celebrating the event during *Commemoration Week,* the Oxford equivalent of *May Week* at Cambridge.

commercial traveller   **traveling salesman**
In the proper context, *traveller* by itself is understood in this sense. Incidental intelligence: The 16,000 members of the *United Kingdom Commercial Travellers Benefit Society* recently voted to change their name to the *British Benefit Society for Representatives and Agents,* after a moving valedictory by the retiring chairman. He justified the change on the alleged popular belief that a *commmercial traveller* was a dirty old man. See also **bagman.**

commission agent   **bookmaker**
A lofty euphemism. See also **turf accountant.**

commissionaire, *n.*   **doorman**
In Britain, *commissionaires,* usually doormen but sometimes also messengers and other types of clerk, are normally pensioned military men. More specifically, they are members of the *Corps of Commissionaires,* an organization formed many years ago to provide decent employment for ex-regular army men, and run on military lines. *Commissionaire* is rarely used in America and is a rather old-fashioned word meaning 'doorman' or other type of attendant in a hotel or other public place. A more common British term is **porter.**

Commissioner for Oaths   **notary public**

commode, *n.*   **chamber pot holder**
This noun, in America, usually means a 'chest of drawers.' It has the secondary meaning there, rarely used, of a chest or box holding the chamber pot. In Britain, it signifies the container of this homely commodity, usually in the form of a chest or chair.

Common Entrance Examinations   SEE COMMENT
Prep school entrance exams. *Prep school,* in the American sense, is what the British call **public school.** *Common Entrance Examinations,* though national in scope, are not prepared by a government agency, but by a private body organized by the public schools of Britain. The same entrance examinations are given to all candidates for the schools, but each public school has its own requirements as to the grades achieved in these examinations. See also **council school.**

commoner, *n.*   SEE COMMENT
Anyone below the rank of **peer.**

common lodging-house. See **Rowton House.**

(the) Commons, *n.*   SEE COMMENT
Common shortening of the *House of Commons,* the lower legislative chamber. The upper one, the House of Lords, is a respected debating chamber but has little power in normal times except to delay or amend non-financial measures. See **Lord.**

company, *n.* corporation
A business term; sometimes called *limited company* or *limited liability company*, the essence of this form of business organization in either country being the *limitation* of its liability to the value of its net worth, thus insulating from risk other assets of the individual(s) involved. *Ltd.* is the British equivalent of *Inc.* It is sometimes used in America to create an atmosphere of chic. *Company* does not necessarily connote incorporation in either country. It may denote a partnership or even a sole proprietorship. The term *and Company* (usually *& Co.*) can be used by someone doing business all by his lonesome, in unincorporated form. As to the use of *corporation* in Britain, see **corporation**. A *closed company* is British for a *close* (or *closely held) corporation*.

company director. See **director.**

compensation, *n.* damages
In America, *compensation* includes not only *damages* but also more generally, *emolument* or *payment*, whether salary or fee. In Britain *compensation* is not used except to indicate *restitution* or *damages* after suffering physical injury or any other kind of loss.

compère, *n.* master of ceremonies; emcee
(Pronounced COM'-PARE.)

completion, *n.* title closing
Term used in real estate transactions.

compliments slip SEE COMMENT
A transmittal slip, usually printed, that is sent with enclosures by professionals and tradesmen, and sometimes accompanies their bills. The slip contains the phrase *With compliments*, followed by the name and address of the sender. The phrase does not mean that the sender is giving anything away, as it might suggest in America, where *With so-and-so's compliments* indicates a gift.

compositor, *n.* typesetter

comprehensive school. See **eleven plus.**

compulsory purchase condemnation
A legal term, meaning the forcible sale to a public authority of property for public use, pursuant to the right of eminent domain.

concert party SEE COMMENT
This term has two entirely distinct meanings.
1. A group who buy shares of stock in the same company separately, for the purpose of combining them into one aggregate holding, or voting them in concert, pursuant to an undisclosed plan based on 'mutual reliance.' This maneuver was concocted to defeat the law requiring a stockholder to disclose any holding to the Department of Trade when it reached 5% of the issued voting capital of the corporation. The House of Commons has been considering a bill to extend that requirement to such a group, treating them as one party in contemplation of law. The difficulty of controlling this type of undercover collaboration is underscored in the following item from *The Times* (London) of May 8, 1986:

> **Westland
> 'concert
> party'
> mystery
> By Teresa Poole**
> Mr Peter Wills, who headed the Stock Exchange inquiry into dealings in the shares of Westland this year, admitted yesterday that the existence of half a dozen foreigners willing to buy blocks of shares for double what the company was worth "screams concert party at me."

But he said there was little the Stock Exchange could have done even if it had been able to prove the existence of such collaboration.

Mr. Wills told the all-party Commons trade and industry committee: "I would accept that, even if we had discovered it, we couldn't have done anything. No-one could have done anything very much."

The six mystery shareholders, including three Swiss bank nominees, held 21 per cent of Westland's shares and played a crucial part in the victory of the £80 million Sikorsky-Fiat rescue package.

The inquiry report, which has not been published in full, said that it was not beyond the bounds of possibility that there were six such ingenious foreigners but that its credibility was sufficiently strained to be sceptical as to the absence of a concert party of some sort. All but one have now written to Westland saying that there was no concert party.

Mr Wills, a former deputy chairman of the Stock Exchange, said that without a legal document a concert party was very difficult to prove. "I don't think that anyone, except in exceptional circumstances, will ever find a way of prosecuting."

Asked about any mutuality of interest between the beneficial owners, Mr Wills requested to be heard in private.

2. A theatrical production by a company, of varied entertainment including singing, dancing, comedy skits, a sort of mini-revue, which plays a season in a particular locality and then moves on. Its eight shows a week, usually delightfully old-fashioned, appeal especially to the old folk.

conchy, *n., Slang.*   **conscientious objector**

confectioner's, *n.*   **candy store**
Synonymous with **sweet-shop.**

confidence trick   **confidence game**

confined to barracks   *Inf.* **confined to quarters**
Int. An ambulatory but slowly convalescing invalid might say: *I'd love to come, but I'm afraid I'm more or less confined to barracks (quarters,* in America) *for the time being.* Or, he might just say: *No can do; I'm stuck here.*

confinement theatre. See **theatre.**

conjuror, *n.*   **magician**
Both terms are used in both countries, but *conjuror* is the common term in Britain.

conk, *n.*   **1.** *Slang.* **beak (nose)**
                    2. *Slang.* **noodle (head)**
Slang. In meaning **2.,** it is used in the expression *off one's conk, i.e., nuts.* Synonyms under **loaf.**

conker, *n.*   **1. horse chestnut**
                    2. rubber
Slang. No American slang equivalent. Meaning **2.** applies exclusively to the game of darts, which is standard equipment at every proper British pub. When the game score is one-all, it there's time (and there always is) someone says, *Let's play the conker,* meaning the *rubber.* In other games except bridge, the word is *conqueror,* from which *conker* must be derived. See also the next entry.

conkers, *n. pl.*   **horse chestnut game**
Each boy has a string with a horse chestnut (called a **conker**) tied to the end, and, in turn, tries to break the other boy's chestnut. Scoring rules appear to vary regionally.

conqueror, *n.*   *Inf.* **rubber**
Inf. Nothing to do with William I. See **conker.**

conservancy, *n.*   river or port commission
For example, the Thames Conservancy.

conservatoire, *n.*   conservatory (music school)
Conservatory, in Britain, would usually mean 'greenhouse,' but it can also be used to
mean a 'music school.'

consignment note   bill of lading
Railroad term.

consols, *n. pl.*   SEE COMMENT
Abbreviation of *consolidated annuities,* government securities of Great Britain which
were consolidated in 1751 into 3 percent bonds, which in Britain are known as stocks.
They have no maturity. There are now both 2½ percent and 4 percent *consols* which
sell at heavy discounts that vary with fluctuations in prevailing interest rates. Accent
on either syllable.

constable, *n.*   policeman;
                                                                            patrolman
A *constable* is a *policeman* and is the usual form of address to a policeman below the
rank of sergeant. *Constables* addressed by Americans as *officer* find that practice quaint.
A *chief constable* would be known in America as a *chief of police.* See also **bobby** for slang
synonyms, and **P.C.**

constituency, *n.*   district
A *Parliamentary constituency* is roughly equivalent, in British politics, to a *Congressional
district* in America. See also **Member.**

construe, *n., v. t.*   construction
The accent may be on either syllable. Used as a noun, it means an 'exercise in syn-
tactical analysis,' as in the teacher's warning: *Next Tuesday, we'll have a construe of an*
unseen (a passage for sight translation).

consultant, *n.*   1. specialist (medical)
                                                                  2. counsel (legal)
These are special meanings, in the respective professions; but the word has the same
general meaning as in America. For those unfamiliar with the American term *counsel* as
used in definition **2.,** it applies to a lawyer sharing quarters and loosely connected with
a law firm but not a partner.

contango, *n.*   delayed acceptance penalty
A London Stock Exchange term. It consists of a percentage of the selling price payable
by the purchaser of shares for the privilege of postponing acceptance of their delivery.
See **backwardation.**

content, *n., adv.*   aye
House of Lords voting terminology. *Not content* means 'nay'. The *contents* are the *aye-
voters.* (Accent on the second syllable.) Cf. **placet.**

continental quilt. See **duvet.**

contract hire   lease
For instance, of office equipment or farm machinery, for a specified period after which
it must go back to the owner, as opposed to *lease,* in the British usage, implying (in this
connection) that after the initial hiring period, the item may be kept under an agreed
extension of the original term.

convener, also **convenor.** See **works.**

convenience, *n.*   rest room
A masterpiece of understatement for one of life's prime necessities! A *public convenience* is a *comfort station*—a battle of euphemisms. See **cloakroom; loo.**

coo!, *interj.*   *Slang.* **gee! gosh!**
Slang. See also **cor.**

cooee, coo-ee, cooey. See within **cooee (coo-ee) of**

cook, *v.t.*   *Slang.* **juggle**
Slang. To *cook* records or accounts is to *tamper with* them. In Britain people *cook the books*. In America this reprehensible practice is known as *juggling the books.* Synonymous with **fiddle.**

cooked, *adj., Slang.*   **1.** *Slang.* **baked**
                                                                  2. *Slang.* **tuckered out**
1. Especially after sitting in the sun.
2. Or *beat,* like an exhausted runner. See **clapped out; fag; knock up, 2.**

cooker, *n.*   **stove**
Cooker is the normal British word for *stove.* A Briton would hardly ever say *electric stove,* but *gas stove* is heard. The generic term for this kitchen appliance in Britain is, however, *cooker.* See also **Aga.**

cookery book   **cook book**
See **Appendix I.A.3.**

coomb, also **combe,** *n.*   **hillside valley**
(However spelled, rhymes with BOOM.) A *coomb* is a valley on the side of a hill, usually a short one, running up from the sea on a coastline.

cop. See **not much cop.**

coper, *n.*   **horse trader**
Also seen in the form *horse-coper.*

copper, *n.*   **laundry boiler**
Neither the word (in this sense) nor the article is much used nowadays; but they exist and persist. The word has two slang meanings: 'cop' (see **bobby**), and 'penny' (see **brown**).

copper-bottomed, *adj.*   *Inf.* **cast-iron; sound**
Inf. Often *one hundred percent copper-bottomed,* and most frequently applied to financial matters. The usage arises from the image of a ship so treated, so that its bottom is immune from damage by teredos (shipworm) and tends to resist the onset of barnacles. This is reinforced by the belief that copper-bottomed pans are more solid and last longer than those not so equipped. In another context, modifying the noun *excuse,* it is the equivalent of *airtight.*

copperplate printing   **engraving**
As on stationery, calling cards, and so on.

copse, *n., v.t.*   **wood (wooded area)**
This is a shortening of *coppice,* a noun shared with America. As a verb it means to 'cover (an area) with woods.'

cor! *interj.*   *Slang.* **gee! gosh!**
Slang. A corruption of *God.* See **blimey; coo.**

coracle, *n.*   **basket-shaped boat**
Welsh and Irish inland waterways wicker boat. The making of these is an old and almost extinct local craft.

cor anglais   **English horn**
The British call it by the French name. *Cor* by itself refers to the *tenor oboe.*

co-respondent shoes   **two-toned shoes**
Old fash. The flashy, raffish type, usually brown and white. In this age of easy no-fault divorce, dispensing as it does with the need for co-respondents, the expression may puzzle people under middle age.

corf, *n.*   **creel**
After you catch a fish in Britain, you keep it alive in a *corf* submerged in water. Plural *corves.*

corn, *n.*   **grain**
The American term *corn* has its equivalent in the British word *maize*, but more and more the British use the term *sweet corn*, though it is hard to grow in Britain and is not nearly as commonly found there as in America. The British term *corn* is as generic as the American term *grain*, and a British *corn factor* is an American *grain broker*; but *cornflour* in England is *cornstarch* in America. See **Indian corn.**

corn, *n.*   *Slang.* **dough (money)**
Slang. Synonymous with **dibs; brass; lolley.**

corned beef   **canned pressed beef**
What the Americans call *corned beef* is known as *salt beef* in Britain.

(The) Corner, *n.*   SEE COMMENT
Slang. The Corner is slang for the betting establishment, known as Tattersall's (betting rooms), which was originally located near Hyde Park Corner.

corner-boy, *n. Slang.*   *Slang.* **tough**

cornet, *n.*   **cone**
Special meaning in conjunction with ice cream. (There was also once the rank of *cornet*—a junior officer—in the British army.)

corn factor. *See* **corn.**

cornflour. See **corn.**

corporation, *n.*   **municipality**
The American *corporation* has its equivalent in the British *company*. The British *corporation* is generally understood to be a *municipal corporation*. Thus, a *corporation swimming-bath* would be a *municipal* or *public swimming pool* in America, a *corporation car park* would be a *municipal parking lot*, etc. A sign reading *Corporation of Greenock Cleansing Department* means *Greenock Sanitation Department. Corporation stock* means 'municipal bond.' (See **shares.**) Of late, however, the British have begun to use *corporation* in the American sense, especially in tax terminology.

corrector, *n.*   **proofreader**
Short for *corrector of the press.*

corridor, *n.*   **aisle**
Referring to railroad cars. See under **aisle.**

corrie, *n.*   **mountainside hollow**
Scottish.

cos lettuce, *n.*   **romaine**
See also **web lettuce.**

cosh, *n., v.t.*   **blackjack**
Slang. A *cosh* is a *blackjack*. To be *coshed* is to be *hit on the head*, whether with a blackjack or some other unpleasant weapon. *Coshed* would find its American equivalent in *beaned.* To be *under the cosh* is to be beleaguered or plagued. A television program that was

listed in *The Times* (London) as "London *under the cosh*" turned out to be a review of the intensive German V-1 rocket raids of World War II when Hitler sent the **doodle-bugs** over southern England.

cost a bomb. See **pay the earth; come expensive.**

costermonger, *n.*   **fruit and vegetable pushcart vendor**
   Sometimes shortened to *coster.* His pushcart is known in Britain as a **trolley** or **barrow.** See also **pearly; fruiterer; greengrocer's.**

costings, *n. pl.*   **costs**
   A business term used in arriving at the price to be charged for a product.

cost the earth. See **pay the earth; come expensive; bomb, 2.**

costume, *n.*   **lady's suit**
   This is somewhat old-fashioned and non-U (see **Appendix I.C.6.**), but still frequently heard, especially in dry cleaning establishments. With most Britons, *suit* applies to both sexes.

costume, bathing. See **bathing costume; swimming costume.**

cot, *n.*   **crib**
   See also **camp bed.**

cotton, *n.*   **thread**
   In the sense of 'sewing thread.' And cotton is not wound on *spools* in Britain but on *reels.*

cotton wool   **absorbent cotton**
   For metaphorical uses, see **live in cotton wool; wrap in cotton wool.**

coul. See *cowl.*

council, *n.*   *approx.* **town**
   Literally, a local administrative body of a village, town, borough, city, county, etc. But the word is used, particularly in the country, exactly as Americans use *town*, in the sense that it is the *council* to which you apply where there is a problem about schools, sewage, roads, and that sort of thing. There are now more extensive bodies called *district councils.*

council house   **municipal or public housing unit**
   So-called because the government agency regulating housing is known as a *council*, whether *district council, county council,* or other. The rent in *council houses* is extremely low. In America, municipal housing is often referred to as *low-income housing* or *middle-income housing.* A multi-family unit of this sort in America is called, generically, a *public housing project.* The equivalent in Britain would be a *council house estate* or *council housing estate.*

councillor, *n.*   **councilman**
   A member of a *council* (e.g., a district council, county council, local administrative bodies) is a *councillor.* A member of the New York City Council is a *councilman.*

council school   **public school**
   The *council school* in Britain is the government-operated facility which Americans call *public school.* **Public schools** in Britain are what Americans call *prep schools* or *private schools.* See also **Common Entrance Examination.**

counsel. See **barrister.**

counterfoil, *n.*　　　　　　　　　　　　　　　　　　　　　　　　　　**stub**
Referring to checks and checkbooks; also to the part of a bill one detaches and keeps.

counter-jumper, *n.*　　　　　　　　　　　　　　　　　　　　　　　**salesperson**
Slang. No American slang for this.

count out the House　　　　　　　　　　　　　　　　**adjourn Parliament**
When fewer than a quorum of forty **Members** are present in the **Commons.**

country round　　　　　　　　　　　　　　　　　　　　　　　　**day's route**
Referring to a delivery route (see **roundsman**) or round of professional visits.

county, *adj.*, *n.*　　　　　　　　　　　　　　　　　　　　**approx. quality**
Inf. This word has no exact equivalent in America. It has the connotation of good breeding and activity in local affairs like riding to hounds and opening flower shows. Such a person is *county*, i.e., a member of the local gentry, and it is hard to say whether *county* in such cases is an adjective or a noun. Never applied to a city dweller.

courgette, *n.*　　　　　　　　　　　　　　　　　　　　　　　　　**zucchino**
Courge is French for *gourd* or *squash. Courgette* is the diminutive. See also **marrow.**

court, *n.*　　　　　　　　　　　　　　　　　　　　　　　　**approx. campus**
Cambridge University term for an area bounded by college buildings. The Oxford equivalent is **quad** (for *quadrangle*).

court card　　　　　　　　　　　　　　　　　**picture card; face card**
Referring to playing cards.

court of inquiry　　　　　　　　　　　　　　　　　　**fact-finding board**

court shoes　　　　　　　　　　　　　　　　　　　　　　　　　　　**pumps**

cove, *n.*　　　　　　　　　　　　　　　　　　　　　　*Slang.* **guy; fellow**
Slang. See also **chap.**

Coventry, send to. See **send to Coventry.**

cover, *n.*　　　　　　　　　　　　　　　　　　　　　　　　　　**coverage**
An insurance term, indicating the aggregate risks covered by a particular policy.

covered goods-waggon　　　　　　　　　　　　　　　　　　　　　**boxcar**
Railroad term.

cowboy, *n.*　　　　　　　　　　　　　　　　　　　　　　SEE COMMENT
Slang. Term applied to an itinerant self-employed workman (e.g., builder, roofer, electrician) who undercuts a skilled man and does a job of awe-inspiring incompetence. *Don't let him anywhere near your roof—he's just a cowboy!* Philip Howard, in *The Times* (London) of August 25, 1986, writes: "Cowboy is a word that has worsened rapidly. When we talk, as it is idiomatic to do, about cowboy builders, plumbers, electricians, drivers and cowboy policing, we imply rough-and-ready and unofficial performers, who take short cuts and may be part of the black economy, and with whom the supper guest should use a long spoon." (The reference to the long spoon is based upon the old proverb: He that sups with the devil must use a long spoon. The idea is that the long spoon will allow you to keep your distance from the unwelcome guest, and keep a close watch on the untrustworthy fellow. In *The Comedy of Errors*, Dromio of Syracuse tells Antipholus of Syracuse: "Marry he must have a long spoon that must eat with the devil." And in *The Tempest*, the drunken butler Stephano shouts at Trinculo: "This is a devil...I will leave him; I have no long spoon." Chaucer and Graham Greene—and others, surely—have made use of the proverb.) In other words, don't put your trust in a *cowboy* worker. In America, the term *cowboy* is applied to a reckless driver.

cracker, *n.*   **snapper**
The kind served at children's parties. The use of the word in the American sense is creeping in, but the British generally call *crackers* **biscuits.** See under **biscuits.**

crackers, *adj.*   *Slang.* **cracked; nuts**
Slang. Predicate adjective only. See synonyms under **bonkers.**

cracking, *adj.*   *Slang.* **full of pep**
Slang. Also expanded to *in cracking form,* but now considered rather old-fashioned. *Get cracking!* means *Get busy! Get going! Get moving! Get to work!*

crammer's, *n.*   **cram school**

cram on   **step on**
Slang. To *cram on* the brakes is to step hard on them.

cramp, *n.*   **clamp**
A portable tool for pressing things like planks together, or a metal bar to hold masonry together. The British use *clamp* as well.

cranky, *adj.*   **eccentric**
The usual meaning in America is 'irritable,' 'ill-tempered.' The British usage reflects the noun *crank* in the sense of 'eccentric person,' a meaning common to both countries.

crash, *n.*   **1. collision**
                                                                                  2. wreck
The British tend to use *crash* to describe both cause and result. *Crash repairs* means 'body work,' and is the sign on establishments where one gets the car repaired after the accident. *Crash barrier* is the *center guard rail* on express highways, synonymous with **centre strip, central reserve,** etc.

crawl, *v.i.*   *Inf.* **cruise**
Inf. Of taxis. See also **gutter crawl.**

crazy pavement. See **pavement.**

cream, clotted. See **Devonshire cream.**

cream off   **take the best (people) out of**
Inf. Skim, as it were, the top talent off a group. The police complained that it was official policy to *cream off* the best talent on the force and put them into administrative jobs, rather than keep them on the regular force to train and set examples for the recruits.

creamed potatoes   **mashed potatoes**

cream tea   SEE COMMENT
Afternoon tea with *Devonshire cream,* which is rich, sweet, delicious, thicker than American whipped cream, and is meant to be piled on top of the jam on top of the scones, creating in all likelihood a dish with more calories than any other substance known to man. See also **high tea.**

crease, *n.*   *approx.* **foul line**
As a sports term, the crease is the line behind which a player must stand in the game of *bowls,* as well as the line which defines the position of both bowler and batsman in cricket.

creased, *adj.*   *Slang.* **tuckered out**
Slang. See also **clapped out.**

create, *v.i.*   *Slang.* **explode; make a fuss**
Slang. Describing the antics of a testy individual who is provoked in the extreme. It would seem to be short for *create a scene.* See **cut up rough.**

crèche, *n.*   **nursery**
(First *e* usually sounds like AY; sometimes like EH.) Used occasionally in America to describe the traditional nativity scene.

credit slip   **deposit slip**
A banking term.

creek, *n.*   **inlet**
In Britain a *creek* usually means an 'inlet on a seacoast' or a 'small harbor.' Its secondary British meaning is the same as its principal American meaning: a 'small stream,' or 'minor river tributary.'

creepy-crawly, *n.*   **insect**
Slang. Most often, a spider; but used the way Americans use *slug,* to describe a disgusting person, the kind that seems to have *crawled* out from under a rock, and gives you the *creeps.*

crib, *n.*   *Slang.* **pony; trot**
Slang. A translation used by students in violation of school rules. This word is sometimes used in America. *Pony* and *trot* do not appear in this connotation in Britain. (*Crib,* the American word for a child's bed, is *cot* in Britain, except in connection with the Infant Jesus.)

cricket, *n.*   SEE COMMENT
Britain's national sport, with vital social overtones and symbolism. Thus, *not cricket* means 'unfair' or 'ungentlemanly,' and *It isn't cricket* must be familiar to millions outside Britain who haven't the slightest acquaintance with the game, so that the very word *cricket* has built into it the strongest implication of fair play. To help Americans more clearly to understand what cricket is all about the following explanation of a **Test Match,** offered by a small British boy to a group of visiting Americans, is offered herewith:

> It's quite simple; you have two sides, one out in the field, one in. Each man on the side that's in goes out, and when he's out he comes in and the next man goes in until he's out. When they're all out, the side that's been out in the field comes in, and the side that's been in goes out and tries to get out those coming in. If the side that's in declares, you get men still in not out. Then when both sides have been in and out including not outs, twice, that's the end of the match. Now do you see?

Crikey!, *interj., Slang.*   *Slang.* **Good heavens!**

crinkle-crankle, *adj.*   **winding**
Inf. A precious, or at least rare, adjective used to describe serpentine red brick garden walls, full of twists and turns. If this sounds Miltonian, you are probably thinking of *quips and cranks* and possibly even of *wanton wiles.* There are fifty-eight *crinkle-crankle* walls in the County of Suffolk and only twenty-eight in all the rest of Britain. *Crinkle-crankle* is an informal variant of *crinkum-crankum,* a lovely, if obsolete word that described anything (not only walls) full of twists and turns and was sometimes used by itself as a substantive.

crisps, *n. pl.*   **potato chips**
Crisps (short for *potato crisps*) are called *potato chips* in America. The British shorten *potato crisps* to *crisps;* Americans rarely shorten *potato chips* to *chips.* British *chips* are *French fried potatoes* in America. The Americans often shorten *French fried potatoes* to *French fries.* See also **chips; fish 'n' chips.**

crit, *n.* review
Inf. In the sense of *criticism,* of which it is an obvious truncation.

crock, *n.* *Inf.* **wreck**
Inf. Often used in the expression a *bit of a crock,* meaning a 'chronically ailing person,' not necessarily a hypochondriac. To *crock up* is British slang for 'break down' and *crocked* means 'broken down,' i.e., 'disabled,' rather than *drunk,* which is its special American slang meaning. The Old Crocks' Run from London to Brighton is for vintage cars.

crocodile, *n.* line of schoolchildren
Inf. Always led or followed (or both) by a teacher or teachers.

croft, *n.* small landholding
A *crofter* is one who rents a *croft.* Mostly Scottish.

cross-bench, *n.* SEE COMMENT
The *bench,* in the Houses of Parliament, occupied by independent members who vote with neither the government nor the opposition. See also **front bench; back bench.**

crossed cheque SEE COMMENT
Cheque means 'bank check.' A *crossed cheque* is so-called because the check is *crossed* by two vertical or oblique lines in the middle of the check, forming a column, or slanted space, within which the mysterious words *& Co.* are printed at the top, and within which the drawer of the check may write additional instructions, such as the name of the bank through which the check must be paid (i.e., the name of the payee's bank if he knows it—this as a safety measure only, and rarely resorted to). Such a check cannot be cashed; it must either be deposited in the payee's bank or endorsed to a third party and deposited in the endorsee's bank. On British checks the line for the payee's name reads *Pay...or order,* not *Pay to the order of...*See also **cheque.**

crossroads, *n.* intersection
This word is used in America to mean the *intersection* of roads, but is more apt to be used figuratively in the sense of a 'dilemma urgently requiring decisions.' It would not be used in America referring to a street *intersection* in a city, and in the country Americans would use *intersection,* or, in deep rural areas, *four corners.*

cross-talk comedians comedy team

crotchet, *n.* quarter note
Musical term. See **Appendix II.F.**

crown, *n.* SEE COMMENT
Five shillings, but there was no crown coin or bill in general circulation even before the decimalization of the currency. From time to time the British mint has struck off commemorative crowns (e.g., the Churchill crown of 1965 and the 1977 Jubilee crown), which though legal tender are cherished rather than tendered. See **Appendix II.A.**

crown stroller, *Slang* *Slang.* **road hog**

crow to pick *Inf.* **bone to pick**
Inf. A disagreeable subject to bring up. The British *pick bones* as well.

crumb, *n.* inside of loaf
That part of a loaf of bread which is not crust.

crumpet, *n.* **1.** SEE COMMENT
2. *Slang.* **nut (head)**
3. *Slang.* **dish (desirable woman)**
1. There are no *English muffins* in Britain, toasted or otherwise. In Britain the *muffin* is a light, flat, round, spongy cake which is toasted and buttered. In America a *muffin* is

a quick bread made of batter, baked in a cup-shaped pan, which does not have to be toasted. The nearest thing to a British *crumpet* is what Americans call an *English muffin.* It is a small individual flat soft yeast mixture cake which is toasted on a griddle. *Crumpet* is an American noun which technically means the same thing, but anyone seeking crumpets in an American restaurant or bakery must go hungry indefinitely.
2. *Slang.* A *crumpet* means a 'head,' for which American slang affords us *nut, bean, noodle,* etc. It is used in Britain especially in *barmy on the crumpet,* meaning 'crazy in the head.' Synonyms under **loaf.** This use is at least obsolescent, and may indeed be obsolete.
3. A *nice bit of crumpet* is the usual phrase. See **bit of fluff.** This usage is definitely vulgar. In a sentence like *Getting any crumpet?* the word is a euphemism for *fucking.* The equivalent American question normally omits the object of the verb: *Getting much lately?*
An article in *The Listener* of March 27, 1975, discussing *Later English Broadside Ballads* (a selection of 127 ballads from the massive Madden Collection at Cambridge), describes the atmosphere of those times—the 17th century—in lively terms:

> Idyllic days of murderers and thieves on the gallows; dying and drunken sailors; Irishmen and girls in trouble; strange and available females encountered, with venereal diseases picked up....The arresting phrase or detail, the inventive prosodic form— these occur with fair frequency: one might for instance breakfast with the girlfriend:
> Fond pleasure the charm of her bosom elates, As the fresh moulded cream the soft crumpet inflates.

> Good—though the editors...think that *crumpet* cannot be given its modern overtone.

crutch, *n.*   **crotch**

cry off   **call off**
In the sense of 'discontinue'.

cry stinking fish   SEE COMMENT
(*Slang.*) The verb *to cry* has the little used meaning, in both Britain and America, of "announce for sale," and in both countries, to *cry* (something) *up* is to *praise* or *extol* it. To *cry up one's wares,* then, is to *boast about one's products;* in the case of a writer, e.g., to praise his own writings. There was an expression in Britain to *cry roast meat,* used to describe a person's announcing to others a piece of private luck or good fortune, like an unexpected inheritance or a windfall on the stock market. That is now archaic. To *cry stinking fish* is to call attention to one's failures (literally, to *condemn one's own products*), which would appear to be a study in masochism, like sucking on a sore tooth. On the subject of *cry,* generally, Samuel Johnson wrote a little poem:

> If a man who turnips cries
> Cry not when his father dies,
> 'Tis a proof that he would rather
> Have a turnip than his father.

C Three, also **C3**   *approx. Inf.* **4F; unfit**
Inf. A term of population classification, designating the class composed of the mentally or physically deficient. The technical term has developed the connotation of *unfit* or even *worthless.* Perhaps the closest equivalent is the former American Selective Service (draft) classification *4F.*

cubby, *n.*   **glove compartment**
Often expanded to *cubby-hole* (in America a general term for any little nook where one stuffs odds and ends), but not much heard any more except among quite senior citizens. It has given way to *glove-box,* sometimes *glove-locker.* The American term is heard as well. See **Appendix II.E.**

cuckoo-pint, *n., Inf.*   *Inf.* **jack-in-the-pulpit**

cufuffle, *n.* See **kerfuffle.**

cul-de-sac, *n.*   **dead-end street**
    Cul-de-sac and *blind road* are British terms for what in America would be called a *dead-end street*, at the entrance of which there is often (but by no means always) considerately placed a sign saying DEAD-END STREET or NO THROUGH ROAD. See also **close.**

cully, *n.*   *Inf.* **pal**
    Obsolescent.

cupboard, *n.*   **closet**
    See **closet** for British meaning.

cupboard love   *Slang.* **sucking up**
    Inf. Describes the activity of a person trying to curry favor, with the strong implication of insincerity and self gain.

Cup Final   SEE COMMENT
    Generally, the final match in any competition awarding a cup. It is usually understood to refer to **football** (*soccer*). See **up for the Cup.**

cuppa, *n.*   **cup of tea**
    Slang. No American slang equivalent. Often used in expressions like *He's not my cuppa,* meaning 'He's not my kind of person.' See also **char, 2.**

curate, *n.*   **vicar's assistant**
    (But see the next entry!)

curate's assistant   **muffin stand**
    Inf. Having three tiers and very useful at teatime.

curate's egg   SEE COMMENT
    Inf. Something both good and bad. This curious phrase originated from a *Punch* cartoon that appeared in 1895. A humble curate is breakfasting with his bishop, overawed by the very presence of that dignitary, and the caption reads:

> "I'm afraid you've got a bad egg, Mr. Jones."
> "Oh, no, my Lord, I assure you! Parts of it are excellent."

    And so, although the original egg was all bad, and it was only the poor curate's brilliant feat of diplomacy that imparted any virtue at all to it, a *curate's egg* came into the language to mean 'something good in parts' (but defective in others); anything with its good points and its bad.

curlies, *n. pl.*   *Vulgar.* **short hairs**
    Vulgar. To have someone by the *short and curlies* is to have him at a considerable disadvantage.

curling tongs   **curling iron**

curly, *adj.*   **gruesome**
    Slang. A brutal murder might be spoken of as *curly*. A reflection of this use may be found in the following American usage: *It would make your hair curl.*

current account   **checking account**
    Synonymous with **running account.** Cf. **deposit account.**

curse of Scotland   **nine of diamonds**
    Inf. Various apocryphal derivations have been suggested.

custard, n.   **custard sauce**

A word of explanation: In America, *custard* is a sweetened mixture of milk and beaten eggs, baked until set, and served as a dessert (**pudding;** see also **dessert; sweet; afters**), with or without a sauce of one sort or another. In Britain, it can mean that too, but normally refers to the same mixture in running liquid form, thicker or thinner, done in a double boiler (**double saucepan**), served as a sauce over pies, compote, and the like. (It *should* be done in a double boiler, but is too often bought in packaged powder form.) To differentiate, the solid stuff is usually called *baked custard* in Britain, and it is often called *cup custard* in America.

custom, n.   **business**

Commonly used in Britain where Americans would say *business* or *customers*, as in: *An attractive shop-front* (see **shop**) *will bring in custom.* See also **trade**.

cut, *adj. Slang*   *Slang.* **tipsy**

cut along, *Inf.*   *Inf.* **run along**

cut (a long story short), *Inf.*   *Inf.* **make (a long story short)**

cut away!   *Slang.* **beat it!**

Slang. See synonyms under **buzz off**.

cute, *adj.*   **shrewd**

In America, *cute* is generally applied to children, especially babies, or things like little girls' dresses, and means 'pretty, dainty, attractive.' In Britain, one speaks of a *cute* maneuver, or describes a lawyer or businessman as *cute*, in the sense of 'shrewd, clever, ingenious.' The American sense is not used in Britain, but the reverse is not true: one does hear in America of a clever move or tactic described as 'cute,' often 'pretty cute,' usually with a note of admiration or even rueful envy.

cutlet, *n.*   **chop**

Butcher's term.

cut one's lucky, *Slang.*   *Slang.* **take a powder**

cutting, *n.*   **clipping**

Meaning 'newspaper clipping.' One resorts to a *cutting service* in Britain, in America to a *clipping bureau*. Sometimes the sense is clarified by amplifying the term to *press cutting*, and *press cutting agency* is synonymous with *cutting service*.

cut-throat, *n., Inf.*   **straight razor**

cut up, *Slang*   **upset**

Slang. Wrought up, broken up, agitated, disturbed. Sometimes *all cut up*.

cut up for   **leave (as an estate)**

Slang. How much did he cut up for? is indelicate slang for 'How much of an estate did he leave?' This usage refers to a decedent's estate.

cut up rough   **make a fuss (row)**

Slang. See also **create**.

D

dab, *n.*   *Inf.* **whiz**
Inf. Used in the expression to *be a dab at,* sometimes lengthened to *be a dab hand at,* meaning to 'be especially adept at.' Samuel Johnson did not approve of the word. In his *Dictionary,* sense No. 4 is "[In low language] An artist; a man expert at something. This is not used in writing." But, as you will see under **penny reading,** Mr. Sullivan's partner Mr. Gilbert did use it in writing.

dabbly, *adj.*   **wet**
Slang. A *dabbly* summer is one with frequent rain. Most people think that *dabble* is used only in the expression *to dabble in,* i.e., 'engage in superficially,' as to *dabble* in the market or in a hobby. But its primary meaning is to 'moisten intermittently'—hence a *dabbly* summer.

dab in the hand, *Slang.*   **bribe**

dabs, *n. pl., Inf.*   **fingerprints**

daddy-longlegs, *n.*   **crane fly**
In Britain, a *daddy-longlegs* is a *crane fly,* an insect of the family *Tipulidae* of the order *Diptera,* resembling an enormous mosquito and popularly called the *mosquito hawk.*

daggerplate. See **sliding keel.**

daily woman   **cleaning woman**
Inf. Often shortened to just *daily.* Sometimes *daily help.* See also **char, 1.**

dainty, *adj.*   *Inf.***picky; finicky**
Inf. About food; a term applied to young children who are hard to please at mealtime. See also **faddy.**

Dame, *n.*   SEE COMMENT
A woman who is knighted becomes a *Dame.* Judith Anderson is now *Dame Judith,* just as Robert Helpmann became *Sir Robert. Dame* is a title conferred, not inherited, and is never coupled directly with the surname: i.e., *Dame Anderson* would be as wrong as *Sir Helpmann.* A *Dame* should not be confused with a **Lady.** See also **Lord** for other titles.

damn all   *Slang.* **not a damned thing**
Slang. This expression is in fairly wide use and would not be considered improper in normal company, even mixed. In the same circumstances Americans might hesitate to say *not a damned thing.* The British expression would be used, for example, by a person looking for a coin to buy a ticket for the underground and finding his pocket empty. He would look at his companion and say, "I've got damn all."

damp course   **insulating layer**
A *damp course* or *damp-proof course* is a layer of tarred felt, slate, etc., placed above the house foundation to prevent deterioration in the walls of a building caused by rising moisture, a troublesome phenomenon usually called *rising damp* in Britain.

dampers, *n. pl.*   **flat cakes**
Slang. Made of flour and water, usually by Boy Scouts, and not recommended for gourmets. *Damper* is used as well in the various senses in which it is used in America in connection with fireplaces, pianos, etc., and figuratively in the sense of a 'wet blanket.'

damp squib   *Slang.* **bust; dud; lead balloon**
Inf. One of those things, like a Church Bazaar or a Charity Ball that was going to be a howling success, but...

darbies, *n. pl.*   *Slang.* **bracelets**
Slang. Handcuffs. The British term is said to be derived from the expression *Father Darby's bands* or *bonds*, a particularly rigid form of debtor's bond extracted by usurers in the old days.

Darby and Joan   SEE COMMENT
Inf. This sentimental nickname for any loving couple of advanced years is supposed to have originated from an allusion in a ballad that appeared in 1735 in a publication called *Gentleman's Magazine.* The poem, entitled "The Joys of Love Never Forgot," went:

> Old Darby, with Joan by his side,
> You've often regarded with wonder.
> He's dropsical, she's sore-eyed,
> Yet they're never happy asunder.

It was written by one Henry Woodfall, who, in his youth, was apprenticed to a printer in London named Darby, whose wife was named Joan. Darby died in 1730. Henry became very fond of the Darbys, as evidenced by his sentimental ballad. There is a line in *She Stoops to Conquer* (Goldsmith) that goes: "You may be a Darby but I'll be no Joan, I promise you," and the following appeared in the June 18, 1894, issue of *Punch:* "Both their Graces were present, Darby-and-Joaning it all over the place." Membership in Darby and Joan Clubs all over Britain is open to those whom Americans so tactfully call *Senior Citizens* and *Golden Agers* and the British *Old Age Pensioners,* usually shortened to *O.A.P.s*; but see **O.A.P.** for the alarming news that *Senior Citizen* is gaining ground in Britain.

darning mushroom   **darning ball**

dashed, *adv.*   *Slang.* **damned**
Slang. Milder than *damned* in expressions like *dashed good, dashed bad,* and the like. Also heard in, *Well, I'm dashed,* where Americans would say, *Well, I'll be damned! Dashed* has a Bertie Woosterish sound and is on the way out as language gets freer in a more permissive society.

daughter concern   **subsidiary**
A company owned by another company. The family relationship of the subsidiary is recognized in the American expression *parent company,* but the Americans keep the sex of the subsidiary a secret.

davenport, *n.*   **writing table; escritoire**
In America this word means 'sofa.'

daylight robbery   *Inf.* **highway robbery**
Inf. Figure of speech, like *holdup,* meaning an 'exorbitant price *or* fee.'

day return. See **return.**

day sister. See **sister.**

day tripper. See **tripper.**

dead-alive, *adj.*   *Inf.* **dead; more dead than alive**
Inf. Sometimes *dead-and-alive.*

dead cert   *Inf.* **sure thing**
  Slang. Cert is short for *certainty.*

dead keen on. See **keen on; mad on.**

dead man's shoes   SEE COMMENT
  This rather grim phrase describes something that somebody is waiting to inherit or
succeed to, like his boss's job.

dead on   *Slang.* **on the nose**
  Inf. See **bang on** for synonyms.

dead set at. See **make a dead set at.**

dead slow   **extremely slow**
  Often seen on traffic signs: *as slow as possible.* In both countries, shipboard signal from
bridge to engine room.

dead stock   **farm equipment and machinery**
  The term *dead stock* is occasionally used to mean 'unemployed capital' or 'unsaleable
merchandise.' However, it has a special use in connection with the sale of country
property. One sees signs advertising an auction of such and such a farm property,
sometimes with *livestock* (which means the same thing in both countries), and sometimes
including *dead stock.* After suffering considerable depression from the image of deceased
cows, sheep and pigs, the author inquired of professional auctioneers and was advised
that *dead stock* meant 'farm equipment.' In its usual sense the word *dead* implies that
the subject has previously been alive; as used in this expression *dead* means merely
'inanimate.' Undoubtedly, the phrase came about as an echo of the common term
livestock.

dead to the wide. See **to the wide.**

deaf aid   **hearing aid**

deals, *n. pl.*   **lumber**
  For British meaning of *lumber,* see **lumber,** *n.*

dean, *n.*   **cathedral head**
  See under **head, 1.**

death duties   **estate tax**
  See **Capital Transfer Tax.**

debag, *v.t.*   *Inf.* **cut down to size**
  Slang. Literally, *debag* means to 'pull somebody's pants off,' **bags** being slang for
'pants,' or as the British say, *trousers.* Figuratively, it means to 'deflate' a person.

debenture, *n.*   **secured bond**
  In America, a *debenture* is a corporation bond unsecured by any mortgage, and only
as good as the credit of the issuer.

debus, *v.t., v.i.*   **get out of an automobile**
  (Accent on second syllable: DEE-BUS, EM-BUS.) *Embus* is to *get in.* Cf. *detrain* and *entrain.*
Military terms.

decasualization. See **casual labourer.**

decillion. See **Appendix II.D.**

decoke, *v.t.*   **decarbonize**
  To *do a ring job* on a car.

decorate, *v.t.*   **paint**
In context, *decorating* a room or a house means 'painting' it, and *house painters* are
sometimes referred to as *decorators*. In this sense, the word has nothing to do with
decoration in its general sense, nor with interior decorating. If the occupant prefers
wallpaper, *decorate* could include *papering*.

deed-poll, *n.*   **unilateral deed**
A legal term describing a document signed by a single party. *Poll* is an old verb
meaning to 'cut evenly,' as for instance, the edge of a sheet. A *deed-poll* is written on a
polled sheet, one that is cut evenly and not indented. The common use of a *deed-poll*
nowadays is as a document by virtue of which one changes one's name. It has to be
advertised in the *London Gazette*. Thus, a lady who wants to live as the wife of a man
who happens to be married to another lady who won't give him a divorce can execute
a *deed-poll*, by virtue of which she changes her last name to his: a very convenient
arrangement especially when it somes to registering the birth of a child born to such a
union, since both parents would now bear the same surname and the registration would
cause no fluttering of eyelids.

degree day   **commencement**
This is a university term and has nothing to do with weather measurements, as in
America.

degree of frost   **degree below 32°F**
In America, *20°F* is *20° above zero*, or simply *20 above*, or even more simply, *20*. In
Britain, *20°F* is announced as *12° of frost*. Formula: X° of frost in Britain = (32 − X)° above
0 in America. To the consternation of most Britons, in the current drive to Europeanize
and therefore decimalize units of measurement, weather reports on TV and radio and
in the newspapers usually state temperatures in Celsius alone, or along with Fahrenheit,
and the *degree of frost* idiom will one day disappear.

dekko, *n., Slang.*   *Slang.* **gander (glance)**

demanding money with menaces   **extortion**
A criminal offense.

demarcation dispute   **jurisdictional dispute**
Between unions, or between different departments in a company.

demerara, *n.*   SEE COMMENT
(Rhymes with SAHARA.) Raw cane sugar, light brown, frequently served with coffee.
Imported from Demerara, in what was British Guiana, now Guyana. See also **coffee
sugar.**

demisemiquaver, *n.*   **thirty-second note**
Musical term. See **Appendix II.F.**

demister, *n.*   **defroster**
Automotive term. See **Appendix II.E.**

demo, *n.*   **demonstration**
Inf. A street *demonstration*, or a *demonstration* of something the demonstrator wants
you to buy. In the U.S., a sample recording by a musician.

demob, *v.t.*   **discharge**
Inf. (Accent on the second syllable.) A military term. See **bowler-hatted.**

demonstrator, *n.*   **laboratory assistant**
At an academic institution.

dene, *n.*   1. **sandy stretch by the sea**
                                                                            2. **dune**
                                                                        3. **wooded vale**

denominational school	parochial school

denture, *n.*   **removable bridge**
A denture, in America, is usually understood to denote a set of upper or lower false teeth. It is used that way in Britain, too, but the term is also used for any removable bridge, whether one or more teeth are involved. *Bridge* means 'fixed bridge' only. *Removable bridge* would be a contradiction in terms. Dentures, in the American sense, are occasionally referred to in Britain, especially by older people, as *dentacles* or *dentals*.

departmental store   **department store**
An example of the British tendency to lengthen (or is it the American tendency to shorten?) the first of the two words in a compound noun. See **Appendix I.A.3.**

deposit account   **savings account**
Cf. **current account, running account.**

deposit-taking institution. See **fringe bank.**

derby duck   *Inf.* **dead duck**
(Pronounced DARBY.) *Inf.* An old-fashioned colloquialism.

de-restricted road   **road without speed limit**
For many years there were no speed limits on British country roads. Now the government has imposed an overall speed limit of 70 m.p.h. However, as one approaches a city, town, or village there are signs reading "30" or "40" restricting the driver to those limits while passing through those areas. Once beyond the geographical limits, you find a de-restriction sign, which means that you are back on the overall speed limit of 70 m.p.h.

dessert, *n.*   **fruit course at end of meal**
In Britain *dessert* is a fresh fruit course (sometimes also nuts and/or trifling sweetmeats) served at the end of a meal either after, or in place of, what the British call a *sweet*. British *dessert* can be any fresh fruit. *Dessert* in America is a generic term for the last course of the meal whether it consists of fruit, pudding, ice cream, or whatever. In spite of the aforementioned restricted use of *dessert* in Britain, the British use *dessert plates*, *dessert knives*, *dessert forks*, and *dessert spoons* to designate the implements involved in the eating of a *sweet*. Very confusing. To make matters just a little bit worse, *dessert spoon* has, in addition, the special technical meaning of a certain unit of measure in recipes, whatever they involve, whether dessert, sweet, or stew! See extended discussion at **sweet.**

destructor, *n.*   **incinerator**

detached house. See **semi-detached; terrace.**

detain, *v.t.*   **1. arrest**
                                                                                          2. keep
1. Not often used in this sense in America. *Three men were detained in connection with the shooting of a policeman. A man was detained after a* **raid** *on a bank.* See also **assisting the police.**
2. Used commonly about people *kept* in the hospital after an accident, as opposed to those whose injuries were superficial. In American you would be *kept in the hospital;* in Britain you would be *detained in hospital* (no article). See also **appendix I.A.2.**

detained during the Queen's (King's) pleasure   **sentenced to an indeterminate term**
Sometimes, *during His/Her Majesty's pleasure.* Predictably, there is the story of the woman so sentenced during the reign of a male monarch: "I thought I was too old for that sort of thing."

developer, *n.*   **real-estate developer**
Used by itself, in Britain, the term describes a person engaged in the purchase of
land and the erection of buildings on it. It sometimes appears in the phrase *property
developer.* As in America, *developer* also means "photographic developing solution.'

development area   SEE COMMENT
Area suffering from temporary or intermittent severe unemployment.

devil, *n., v.i.*   **1. law apprentice**
                                                            2. literary hack
Americans may be familiar with the old-fashioned term *printer's devil* meaning 'printer's errand boy' or 'junior apprentice.' In Britain *devil* has two additional meanings.
1. Assistant to junior legal counsel in the **chambers** of a **leader.**
2. *Hack,* or *ghostwriter.* To *devil* is to act in either of these lowly capacities, often under-
paid in the literary field, and not only unpaid, but a privilege usually paid for, in the
legal field.

devil on horseback   **prune wrapped in bacon**
One of many different types of **savoury,** served on a small piece of toast. Sometimes
a piece of liver replaces the prune. See also **angel on horseback.**

devilry, *n*   **deviltry**
The British say *deviltry* as well.

devolution, *n.*   **home rule**
(The *e* is long in British English, short in American.) Governmental decentralization.
A term that has lately come into vogue in political discussion. A devolutionist is one
who urges decentralization of government. Devolutionists "believe that the creation of
assemblies for Scotland, Wales and the regions of England would lead to improved
government with decisions taken closer to the people." (Geoffrey Smith's page one
report in *The Times* (London) of June 26, 1976.) *Devolution* "would strengthen democratic
participation and help to unload the burden on the centre, thereby producing better
government for everybody." The term had been, and still is, used to describe the
delegation of duties or authority, as in the case of Parliament deputing matters to
committees.

Devonshire cream   **clotted cream**
Clotted cream is made by scalding milk and skimming off what rises to the top. For
one of its delicious applications, see **cream tea.** Incidentally, *clotted* is derived from the
clot or *clout* (cloth) with which the cream is covered during the process, and does not
refer to the consistency of the cream. Real Devonshire cream is a very superior kind of
clotted cream, rarely found even in Devonshire, though imitations abound.

Dewar's flask   **thermos bottle**
Sir James Dewar was a british physicist who invented the 'Dewar vessel,' a double-
walled glass container with the air between the walls exhausted to prevent conduction
of heat in either direction. Various names were given to the contraption, depending on
the shape of the container: *Dewar tube, Dewar bulb,* etc. Rarely heard nowadays.

dhobied, *adj.*   **washed**
Inf. From *dhobi,* meaning an 'Indian laundry man.' Usage restricted to retired old
India hands.

diamond jubilee   SEE COMMENT
The usual meaning in Britain is 'sixtieth anniversary,' though (leave it to the British
to keep things simple!) it occasionally means 'seventy-fifth' as in America. Safest to
investigate.

dibs, *n., Slang.*   *Slang.* **dough (money)**
Lolly is more usual. See **corn; brass.**

dicey, *adj.*   **touch and go**
Slang. A term based on the figurative aspect of the throw of the dice. Applied to the weather in the perennial British problem of whether or not to plan a picnic and similar games of chance. A somewhat less common British slang equivalent is **dodgy.**

dickey, *n.*   **rumble seat**
Slang. This was the familiar name in the old days for the servant's seat in the rear of a carriage. Sometimes spelled *dickie.*

dicky, *adj., Slang.*   *Inf.* **shaky**

diddle, *v.t.*   *Slang.* **do**
Slang. In the sense of 'fleece' or 'gouge,' i.e., to 'do somebody out of something.' See also **do,** *n., 2.*

digestive biscuits   SEE COMMENT
Somewhat close to Graham crackers, and very tasty. Now marketed in America under the trademark *Wheatolo Biscuits.* Sometimes shortened to *digestives.* See also **Bath Oliver.**

digs, *n. pl.*   **place (rooms; lodging)**
Inf. Short for *diggings.* A Briton speaks of his *digs* in the way an American speaks of his *place,* or, these days, his *pad.* Mostly actors' and students' terminology. See **drum.**

dim, *adj.*   *Slang.* **thick; thickheaded**
Slang. Short for *dim-witted.* See also *as dim as a Toc H lamp.*

ding-dong, *n., Slang.*   **1. heated argument**
                                                                                    2. noisy party

dingle, *n.*   **dell**
Sometimes combined as *dingle-dell.* Usually a deep hollow, shaded with trees.

dinky, *adj.*   **cute; cunning**
Inf. This word is the equivalent of the American term *cute* or *cunning* in the sense of 'sweet' or 'adorable,' not in the sense of 'sly.' The word *dinky* in America has the pejorative meaning of 'ramshackle' and is more or less synonymous with the American slang term *cheesy* which, however, in Britain can mean 'swanky.' See how careful one must be? *Dinky Toys* reflect the British meaning.

dinner-jacket, *n.*   **tuxedo**
Americans say *dinner jacket* too, but *tuxedo* is never used in British English.

diplomatist, *n.*   **diplomat**
The shorter form is almost universal nowadays. See **Appendix I.A.3.**

directly, *conj.*   **as soon as**
Immediately after: Directly he left the room, she began to talk freely.

director, *n.*   *approx.* **executive**
To the british layman *director* means about the same thing (in the context of business epithets) as *executive* would mean to an American layman. Directorships in British companies and American corporations (see **chairman; company; managing director)** amount roughly to the same thing, although their duties and prerogatives (as a matter of law) and their day to day functions (as a matter of practice) differ in some respects in the two systems. In both countries important personages are frequently elected to membership on boards of directors as window-dressing and don't participate actively in the affairs of the company. But the general connotation of *director* in Britain is that of an 'operating executive' whose American opposite would be the company's *vice-president-*

in-charge-of-something-or-other. Thus, it is common practice for smaller British companies to list their directors, by name, on their stationery. This is unheard of in America. The term *company director* is often used, particularly in journalese, as a description of a profession. Thus, the swindler, murderer, or victim is (or was) a *company director* without further details. In America, he would have been described in words identifying him with a particular business or profession: '...in the textile business...,' '...manager of a furniture store located at...,' 'head of the international division of...' etc. *Company director* is a vague, all-inclusive term that covers anyone from the struggling proprietor of a one-man cigar store to the moving spirit of a multibillion multinational conglomerate. Perhaps its use indicates a lingering reluctance to denigrate a person by referring to his **trade,** and a healthy respect for anonymity.

directory enquiries. See **enquiries.**

dirty week-end   **amorous weekend**
Inf. Spent with one's lover, with the implications of all those circumspect arrangements. Used light-heartedly in the proper context, it can mean a weekend devoted to making love to one's very own spouse, after shipping the kids off somewhere.

discommon, *v.t.*   SEE COMMENT
A special Oxford and Cambridge term: to bar a *tradesman* (storekeeper, retailer; see **trade, 1.**) who has violated the university rules from doing business with the undergraduates (shopkeeper, retailer).

dish, *n.*   **serving dish; platter**
Although both countries use *dishes* generically, *dish* in Britain usually has the narrower meaning of 'serving dish' and *platter* is considered archaic.

dish, *v.t.*   *Inf.* **stump**
Inf. This verb is used, especially in politics, to mean 'outmaneuver.' *Dished* would have its equivalent in the American word *stumped,* derived from the verb *to stump,* a technical term in cricket describing one of the ways a **batsman** is put out.

dish-clout   **dish rag; dish mop**

dish-washer. See **wash up.**

dishy, *adj.*   *Slang.* **sexy**
Slang. Like its American counterpart, usually applied to people, but also to inanimate objects like sports cars.

dismal Jimmy, *Slang.*   *Slang,* **gloomy Gus; calamity howler**

dismiss, *v.t.*   **put (someone) out; get (someone) out**
Cricket term. One doesn't *get* or *put* the **batsman** *(batter) out.* He (and when he is last in the batting order, his side) is said to be *dismissed* when he is run out, caught, etc. There is something lofty, almost imperial, about this term, which is used by sports writers, but hardly ever in speech. Reminiscent of *retire* in baseball. When the dismissal is the result of an umpire's decision, the player is said to be *given out.* See **give (someone) out.**

dismissal with disgrace   **dishonorable discharge**
A term applied to noncommissioned soldiers and sailors alike. A naval officer would be *dismissed with ignominy,* an army officer *cashiered.*

dispatch, *n.*   **mailing and handling**
As in *Price £1 + 40p. for dispatch.* Cf. **posting (postage) and packing.**

dispensary. See **dispenser.**

dispenser, *n.*
In America a *dispenser* usually means a container that feeds out some substance in convenient units, or a *vending machine*. The British use the word *dispenser* that way, too, but primarily it means in Britain what Americans would call a *pharmacist*, a person in the profession of making up medical prescriptions. *Dispensing Chemist* is a sign commonly seen on the store front of a British drugstore (**chemist's shop**). The related word *dispensary* means the 'drug department' of a drugstore, hospital or doctor's office (**surgery**). Group practice is common in Britain, especially in the countryside. The surgery sometimes includes a *dispensary* manned by a resident *dispenser*.

dissenter, *n.*   SEE COMMENT
A member of a Protestant sect that has split off from the established church, i.e., the Church of England. See also **chapel.**

distemper, *n., v.t.*   **paint with a size base**
In both countries, this word has a totally unrelated meaning: a common and fatal disease of cats and dogs. In America as well as in Britain it can be used to mean 'painting with a size base' (rather than an oil base); but this is a most uncommon American use, while it is its most common meaning in Britain.

divan, *n.*   **sofa; couch**
Divan is not nearly so frequent in America as in Britain, where it is preferred to *sofa*: *couch* is rarely used in this connection by the British.

diversion, *n.*   **detour**
A traffic term. All too frequently one sees a road sign reading DIVERSION leading one away from the main road and only sometimes back onto it. Much more of a nuisance than a diversion in the usual sense.

divi; divvy, *n.*   **dividend**
Slang. Short for *dividend*, especially that distributed periodically by cooperative societies. As used in Britain, *dividend*, which in America applies only to shares of stock, can refer as well to bond interest.

division, *n.*   **1.** SEE COMMENT
                                                          1. SEE COMMENT
                                                          3. voting line-up
1. Area represented by a Member of Parliament: corresponds to *Congressional District* (see **constituency; Member**).
2. A term used in sentencing convicted criminals. Preceded by *first, second,* or *third,* it means 'lenient,' 'medium,' or 'severe' treatment in prison, as prescribed by the sentencing judge.
3. The *division* of the Members of Parliament into two sides for vote-counting. Hence, *division bell,* the *warning bell* in the home or office of a Member of Parliament which rings to let him know that his vote is required in the House of Commons.

division bell. See **division, 3.**

divvy. See **divi.**

D-Notice   *approx.* **press publication restriction**
Notice given by the *D-Notices Committee* (made up of representatives of government and press) to newspapers, requesting them to omit mention of material that might endanger national defense. The *D* stands for *defence*. A wartime institution, now obsolete. Let us hope that it may never have to be revived.

do, *n.*   **1. deal**
                                                                    2. fast one (swindle)
                                                                              3. ruckus
1. *Quite a do* (for instance, that wedding you attended last week) would more likely be *quite a deal,* or *a big deal,* in America.
2. The nasty transaction by which one is *done.*
3. Americans would be more likely to say *ruckus.*

do, *v.t.*   **handle**
   In America a shop does or doesn't *have, sell, keep, stock,* or (sometimes) *make* a particular item. The British often substitute *do* in those cases. A stationer may *do* daily newspapers but not the Sunday edition. An upholsterer may *do* hangings but not slipcovers (which he would call **loose covers**). A certain restaurant will be recommended because, though their soups are indifferent, they *do* a good mixed grill.

do bird   *Slang.* **serve time**
   Slang. In prison. *Bird* here is short for *birdlime* (the sticky stuff nasty people spread on twigs to catch birds) which is cockney rhyming slang for *time.* Synonymous with **do porridge.** See **Appendix II.G.3.**

do (someone) brown   *Slang.* **take (someone) in**
   Slang. To *fool* someone, to *pull the wool over his eyes.*

dock, *n.*   **1. basin**
                                                                          2. SEE COMMENT
1. The British use *dock* to denote the water between what Americans call *docks* and the British call *wharves.* But note the expression *dry dock* which means the same thing in both countries. Generally, *dock* is the term used in a place name, such as *Tilbury Docks.*
2. A *prisoners' detention area* in the courtroom. *In the dock* means 'on trial.'

dock brief. See **brief; dock.**

docker, *n.*   **longshoreman**

docket, *n.*   **judgment roll**
   In British legal parlance a *docket* is a register in which judgments are entered, but the term can be narrowed to mean an 'entry' in such a register.

dockyard, *n.*   **navy yard**

doctor, *v.t.*   **castrate** or **spay**
   Applied to animals of both sexes. Both countries also use the verb *neuter.* See **brick up.**

doddle, *n. Slang*   **cinch**
   Anything easily accomplished. In a narrower sense, *doddle* can mean 'money easily obtained.'

dodge, *n.*   *Slang.* **racket**
   Slang. That's my dodge, meaning 'That's my racket,' can be used, somewhat impudently, to mean nothing more than 'That's the business I'm in.' More generally, a *dodge* is any *shrewd device* or *sly expedient.* Dickens liked the word: remember Mr. Weller's *artful dodge* in *Pickwick Papers* and the *artful dodger* in *Oliver Twist.*

dodge the column   *Slang.* **goof off**
   Slang. To *shirk one's duty.* The British expression, taken from the military, has a somewhat more elegant sound. It is an extension from the original concept of draft-dodging.

dodgy, *adj.*   *Slang.* **touch and go**
   Slang. Risky; doubtful; uncertain. See **dicey.**

do (someone) down   *Slang.* **do (someone) dirt**
   Synonymous with **do (someone) in the eye.**

do for   SEE COMMENT
Inf. No precise American colloquial equivalent. When a British housewife tells you
that Mrs. Harris *does for* her, she means that Mrs. Harris is *acting as her housekeeper,* or
is what the British call her *daily help* (see **char; daily woman**). Can be applied also to
outside helpers, like gardeners, handymen, and others performing similar functions.

dog-end, *n.*   cigarette butt
Slang. Vagrants' cant. See also **end; stump.**

doggo. See **lie doggo.**

dog's body, *n.*   *Slang,* **gofer**
Slang. This quaint term was originally British nautical slang. *Dog's body,* in that idiom,
means a 'dish of dried peas boiled in a cloth.' For reasons apparently lost in history, it
also means 'junior naval officer.' As a matter of obvious practical extension, it came to
mean 'drudge,' hence an *errand boy* (in the slang sense) or in an even slangier sense a
prat boy, or *gofer.* Also spelled *dog's-body* and *dogsbody.*

dog's breakfast   unholy mess
Inf. Unlike a *dog's dinner* (see **like a dog's dinner**).

dog's dinner. See **like a dog's dinner.**

do (someone) in the eye   *Slang.* **do (someone) dirt**
Slang. To play (someone) a dirty trick. Synonymous with **do (someone) down.**

(the) dole, *n.*   unemployment benefits
Inf. Common term, somewhat pejorative, for *unemployment compensation.* The equivalent of welfare and/or unemployment compensation under the British system, with
its own rules, regulations, arithmetic, and heartbreaks. *Love on the Dole* was a very
successful play in the thirties.

dollar, *n.*   SEE COMMENT
Slang. Former expression for 5 shillings, now 25 pence. *Half-a-dollar* was used for the
half-crown, equal to 12 ½ new pence. See **Appendix II.A.**

dollop, *v.t.*   1. serve in large quantities
                                                               2. cover with a large quantity
Inf. From the noun *dollop,* meaning a *blob* of something. In meaning 1, it is usually
found in the expression *dollop out.* In meaning 2, it is usually seen in the passive voice,
as in *dolloped in mud.*

domestic science   home economics
The arts of cooking and sewing are dignified by the educational terminology of both
countries.

domiciliary, *n.*   house call
Adjective used as a noun; short for *domiciliary visit.* Used especially by doctors to
designate what has become a practically obsolete practice.

don, *n.*   *approx.* **college teacher**
A *don* (contraction of *dominus,* Latin for 'lord') is a *teacher,* whether a **Head** (*dean*), a
fellow (*assistant*), or tutor (*adviser*) at a **college,** primarily at Oxford and Cambridge, but
also at other old universities like Edinburgh and Durham. The derivation from *dominus*
is clearly seen in *dominie,* which is Scottish for 'schoolmaster.' *Donnish* is 'school teach-
erish,' 'didactic.' Dr. Fitzgerald, in his bid for the premiership of Ireland, was characterized by a BBC television commentator as an 'intellectual with a touch of donnishness.'

(be) done   *Slang.* **(be) had**
Slang. In the sense of taken advantage of, or even *cheated.* See **do, 2.**

done to the wide. See **to the wide.**

donkey's years   *Inf.* **a dog's age**
Inf. Both expressions mean the same thing, although donkeys live longer than dogs.
See also **moons.**

donkey-work, *n.*   **drudgery**
Slang. Like clearing the weeds under the hedges.

donnybrook, *n.*   *Inf.* **free-for-all**
See under **Kilkenny cats.**

doodle-bug, *n.*   **flying bomb**
Slang. Hitler's V-1 rocket, the 'flying bomb' sent over southern England in World War
II. See **cosh.**

doolally, *adj.*   *Slang.* **nuts**
Slang. Deolali was a sanitorium in Bombay to which British soldiers were sent when
their time of service expired, and where time hung heavily on their hands while waiting
for a troopship to take them home. Boredom sometimes got them into trouble and jail,
and not too rarely into the hospital for treatment of venereal disease. The boredom in
the camp produced all sorts of peculiar behavior, for which the expression *the Doolally
tap* was coined, *tap* being Hindustani for 'fever.' All this happened a long time ago; the
army stopped sending men to Deolali soon after the turn of the century. See synonyms
under **bonkers.**

doom, *n.*   **painting of the Last Judgment**
A *doom* may also be a sculptural group depicting the Final Day.

doorstep salesman   **door to door salesman**
Synonymous with **knocker.**

do one's nut, *Slang.*   *Slang.* **1. work like mad**
                                                              2. blow one's top

do porridge   *Slang.* **serve time**
Slang. In jail. Synonymous with **do bird.** See also **porridge.**

DORA, *n.*   SEE COMMENT
Acronym for *Defence of the Realm Act,* passed in August 1914, giving the government
very wide powers during wartime. Between the wars, chiefly associated with pub opening hours. See **during hours.**

dormitory, *n.*   **commuting town**
Used by itself, but more commonly in the phrase *dormitory town.* Of late, the term
bedroom community, meaning the same thing, has come into usage in America. The
equivalent of the American sense of *dormitory* is *hall of residence.*

dorothy bag   **tote bag**

doss, have a. See **have a doss.**

dosser. See **doss house.**

doss-house, *n.*   *Slang.* **flophouse**
But a *doss* is not a *flop. Doss* is British slang for a 'bed' in what Americans call a
flophouse. Doss house is common to both languages, but it is hardly ever used in America.

In British slang, the word *doss* is also a verb meaning to 'sleep in a flop house' but, less specifically, to *doss down* is to 'go to bed,' usually in rough, makeshift circumstances. A *dosser* is a *down-and-outer*, which the British call a *down-and-out*. See also **casual ward; have a doss.**

dot and carry one   *Inf.* **gimpy**
   Inf. A lame person who walks with a limp or drags a leg, based on the supposed rhythm of one walking with a wooden leg.

dot, off his. See **off his dot.**

dotty, *adj.*   *Slang.* **loony**
   Slang. See synonyms under **bonkers.**

double, *adj., n.*   1. SEE COMMENT
                                                                           2. SEE COMMENT
                                                                           3. double portion
                                                                           4. heavy; thick
1. *Double* and *treble* are used in giving telephone numbers in Britain. Thus, Belgravia 2211 was Belgravia *double two double one;* Grosvenor 3111 was Grosvenor *three one double one* or *three treble one.* As in America, the telephone companies have terminated named exchanges. Farewell to Belgravia, London Wall, etc., as well as to Butterfield and Murray Hill! At least the British have not yet begun to change Piccadilly and Regent Street to First Avenue, etc.
2. In oral spelling, one always says *double* the letter (*double-b* for b-b, etc.) rather than repeat it.
3. A wholly different use of *double* is heard in the pub. If you ask for a whiskey you get what Americans would consider a smallish quantity and the proof is less as well. One British friend who ordered a whiskey at the Savoy was politely asked by the waiter whether he wanted a single or *double.* "Good God, man!" was the reply, "Drinking a single is like talking to yourself!" When you want a decent drink of whiskey you ask for a *double.* Even the thirstiest Briton, however, would never ask for a treble. A common synonym of *double* in this sense is *large.* A *large* or *double* drink is twice a single portion, which is by law, in England, one-sixth of a gill, and a gill is one-fourth of a pint, which means that a single is one-twenty-fourth of a pint! But all is not lost: the pint in question is an imperial pint, which is 1.20095 American pints. (See **Appendix II.C.2.**) After a few drinks, you ought to be able to measure out one American pint, divide by twenty-four, then multiply by 1.20095, then double that, and **Bob's your uncle**—you've arrived at an English *double.* But north of the Border (see **(the) Border**) the normal measure is one-fifth of a gill. But wait: not everywhere in Scotland; there are some fortunate localities where you are still fed one-fourth of a gill.
4. And then there's *double (heavy)* and *single (light)* cream.

double-barrelled, *adj.*   **hyphenated**
   Inf. Referring to surnames, like Sackville-West.

double-bedded, *adj.*   **with a double bed**
   When you reserve **(book)** a hotel room for two in Britain the clerk usually asks you whether you want a *double-bedded room* or a *twin-bedded room. Single-bedded room* is used to describe what would be called a *single room* in America.

double bend. See **bend.**

double blue. See **blue,** *n.*

double cream   **heavy cream**
   Very heavy cream, much thicker and richer than American heavy cream, which is called just plain *cream* in Britain.

double Dutch   *Inf.* **"Greek"**
   Inf. Unintelligible gobbledygook, as in *It's all double Dutch to me!*

double figures   **double digits (ten or more)**
Inf. But not over ninety-nine, where one gets into *treble figures. Double figures* is used commonly to indicate the attainment of a new plateau, as in *He's gone into double figures,* about a **batsman** *(batter)* in cricket who has broken nine, i.e., made his tenth run, or, *We've gone into double figures,* by someone who has just increased the staff from eight to eleven. The British don't usually use *figures* as American credit sources do in expressions like *He keeps an account in the low four figures* or, *the high five figures,* but one does occasionally run across it in, for instance, the financial pages of British newspapers. The phrase *double figures* has become current in America as a result of its use by television announcers uttering dire predictions relating to unemployment and inflation.

double-gaited, *adj.*   *Slang.* **AC-DC**
Slang. Bisexually inclined. Ambidextrous is sometimes heard in America.

double-glazed, *adj.*   **fitted with storm windows**
The storm windows generally move sideways rather than vertically. Incidentally, they don't use screens in Britain to keep out the flies, mosquitoes, etc. Whether it's the climate, or government control of pests, or whatever, no screens, as far as the author has been able to observe.

double saucepan   **double boiler**

doughnut, *n.*   **jelly doughnut**
With jam or cream inside, instead of a hole and sugar on the outside, like an American jelly doughnut. The regulation American doughnut is called *ring doughnut* in Britain. But Philip Howard, in *Words Fail Me* (Hamish Hamilton, London, 1980) has this to say:

> ...We might mourn the Americanization of the English doughnut. In British English or Bringlish, *doughnut* or *doughnut-shaped* is now universally used to describe a torus, which is shaped like a quoit, or, well, a *doughnut.* But that is the American doughnut, used for dunking in coffee and other distasteful practices. The true, the jamful English doughnut is a sphere. But you would not guess it, reading British journalists referring to the torus-*doughnut,* which is universal in maths and physics.

Note the *-s* in **maths.** Also, for the benefit of the unenlightened (including the author), the *Random House Dictionary* defines *torus*—as a geometrical term—as follows: "a. Also called **anchor ring,** a doughnut-shaped surface generated by the revolution of a ...circle about an exterior line in its plane. b. the solid enclosed by such a surface." The definition is accompanied by an illustration that resembles a geometrically—if not culinarily—perfect doughnut.

do (someone) up   **do (someone) in**
To *exhaust, wear out: The long walk did us up.*

do (someone) well, *v.t.*   *Inf.* **treat (someone) right**
Inf. In the British phrase *they do you well* (referring, for example, to one's experience at a little hotel), the *do* is equivalent to *treat* in America, but an American would be more likely to say *they treat you right,* or, *they do all right by you,* or *they take good care of you.* To *do yourself well* means to 'live comfortably.'

dowlas, *n.*   **heavy linen or muslin**

down, *adv.*   SEE COMMENT
Inf. From London; conversely, **up** means *to London.* A person living outside of London might ask his friend, "How often do you go up?" and the meaning would be quite clear: "How often do you go to London?" *Come up* would be used if they were talking in London. *Go down* and *come down* would be used, depending on the vantage point of the speaker, to mean 'go' or 'come to the country,' i.e., to somewhere outside of London. (See also the university use of **come down.**) But people living in Scotland or in the north of England may talk of *going down* (i.e., south) to London—to the confusion

of southerners, the despair of geographers, and the discomfiture of certain northerners, as expressed, for example, in a letter from David C. Speedie published in the November-December 1981 issue of *Harvard Magazine:*

> ...I recall that as students in Scotland we invariably sought adventure and seasonal employment by going "up to London" for the summer—a process that involved a southward journey of four hundred miles.
>
> In this instance (and the phrase was uniformly used throughout Britain), South, in the form of the political, commercial, and social hub of power, was most definitely "up"—a fact that deeply offended our Scots Nationalist sensibilities!

See also **down train.**

down, *n.*   **dislike**
Inf. To *have a down on* someone means to 'be prejudiced' against him. Shades of Dr. Fell.

down at heel   *Inf.* **down at the heels**
Inf. Note singular of *heel.* See **Appendix I.A.2.**

down-market, *adj.*   **lower class**
Inf. But sometimes it means only 'lower priced.'

downs, *n. pl.*   **uplands**
An American asked a Briton what the *downs* were and the Briton answered: "The *downs* are the ups." They are, and the South Downs are the open rolling hills of southern England, which are usually dotted with cattle and sheep. *Downs* can be *ups* because the word is etymologically related to *dune* and has nothing to do with the direction *down.* With an upper case *D, the Downs* is the name for a part of the ocean opposite the North Downs off the eastern part of the County of Kent.

down train   SEE COMMENT
Train from London. A train in Britain goes *up* to London even if it has to travel south (or east or west) to get there; and it goes *down* from London no matter what direction it has to take to leave that fine city. Most people would think that *up* implied northwards and *down* southwards, but Americans confused by British train terminology should remember how confused Britons are when they hear Yankees say *Down East,* which really means 'up north in Maine.' The *up* end of something seems somehow or other to be more important that the *down* end. Since there can be no more important end to a British railway trip than arrival in London, London must be the *up* end, and one therefore takes the *up train* to London no matter where one starts the journey. *Up* and *down* are not mere oral colloquialisms, but appear in printed timetables and are standard terms on station bulletin boards. However, it so happens that civic spirit has sought to apply the same rule to other large cities. Starting out from London, one would take the *down train* to Manchester, and even a Mancunian in London would not think of the train from London as the *up train;* but a patriotic denizen of Manchester might talk of any train *leaving* Manchester as a *down train.* When far enough away from London, be careful. In the time of Thomas Hardy it was still safe to use these terms in relation to London exclusively. Thus, in *Jude the Obscure,* in discussing a meeting between Jude and Sue on a mythical road in a mythical town in the mythical County of Wessex, arrangements were made for him to meet her "at the Alfredston Road...on his way back from Christminster, if she should come by the up-train which crossed his down-train at that station."

downy, *adj.*   *Inf.* **sharp**
Slang. A *downy card* is a *smart cookie.*

doyen, *n.*   **dean**
(Pronounced DOY'-EN, or as in French.) Indicating the senior member of the group, like the *doyen* of the diplomatic corps, the *doyen* of the London Bar. *Doyen* is rarely used in America; *dean* is sometimes used in Britain. See **dean** for an exclusively British use of *dean.*

dozy; dozey, *adj.*   *Slang.* **dopey**
Slang. Indicating slow-wittedness.

drabbit, *n.*   SEE COMMENT
This material, a type of drab light brown woven or twilled coarse linen, was used in
the old-fashioned British field-laborer's smock, a garment seen in old paintings and
engravings, which has gone out of style and was known as a *smock-frock.*

drag from the burning   *Inf.* **save by a hair**
Inf. As the United States Cavalry does it again, in movies about the old West.

drain, *n.*   *Slang.* **nip**
Slang. An undersized drink of something.

drain, laugh like a. See **laugh like a drain.**

drains, *n. pl.*   **plumbing; sewerage system**
The *drains* of the house are its *drain pipes,* or *plumbing and sewerage system.* When a
real estate advertisement in Britain uses the term *main drainage,* it means that the house
is connected to a public sewer system.

draper's shop   **dry goods store; haberdashery**
The *shop* can be omitted, and the *draper's* can also mean a 'haberdashery,' in the
American sense of 'men's shop.' But a British **haberdashery** would be called a *notions
store* in America. See also **Manchester; fancy goods; haberdashery; soft furnishings.**

draughts, *n. pl.*   **checkers**

drawing office   **drafting room**

drawing-pin, *n.*   **thumbtack**
Synonymous with **push-pin.**

drawing-room, *n.*   **living room**
Living-room and **sitting-room** are also used in Britain. **Lounge** is provincial and considered **non-U** (see **Appendix I.C.6.**) except in a hotel, on board ship, or in the expression *lounge bar.*

draw it mild!   **don't exaggerate!**
Term derived from *drawing* of beer.

draw stumps. See **up stumps.**

draw tab   **French tab**
A theater curtain in a single piece which is opened by being drawn aside across the
entire stage, as opposed to the usual double curtain which opens in the middle and
disappears in the wings.

draw the long bow   *approx.* **exaggerate**
Inf. There is no exact American equivalent. Usually found in the expression *I'm not
drawing the long bow,* where Americans might say, *I'm not kidding.*

dreadful warning, *Inf.*   **movie trailer ("coming attractions")**

dree, *v.t., adj.*   **1. suffer**
                                                                              2. dreary
1. In the sense of 'endure.' Usually in *dree one's weird,* Scottish for *put up with one's fate.*
2. With the emphasis on being *tiresome, tedious.* A North Country and Scottish term,

spelled in all sorts of ways: *dreegh, dreigh, driegh, driech*. It seems to combine both the verbal and adjectival meanings and connotes patience and long-suffering. Applied to animals, it means only 'tame.'

dress circle   **first balcony**
Of a theater; in America, confined to concert halls. *Balcony* is not used in this context in Britain, where the *dress circle* would be described as the 'first gallery' of a theater. The term *gallery*, in theater parlance, is restricted to the topmost balcony housing the cheapest seats, called the **gods** in Britain, *le paradis* in France, *el paraiso* in Spanish—all terms denoting proximity to the heavenly regions. **Dress circle** is still to be found in some older (and larger) U.S. theaters and concert halls.

dressed to the nines   *Slang.* **all dolled up; dressed to kill**
Inf. Sometimes *dressed up to the nines*. Synonymous with **(got up) like a dog's dinner.** *To the nines* is a British expression meaning 'to perfection.'

dresser, *n.*   SEE COMMENT
Kitchen sideboard with shelves. Americans use *dresser* principally to mean a 'bureau' or 'dressing table.'

dressing gown   **bathrobe; wrapper**
In America *dressing gown* refers to something a little fancier than *bathrobe*. *Bathrobe* is not used in Britain; there, both men and women wear *dressing gowns*.

dress show   **fashion show**

drill. See **what's the drill?**

drive, *n.*   **driveway**
This word runs contra the tendency of British equivalents to be longer than their American counterparts. See **Appendix I.A.3.**

drive a coach and horses through   *Inf.* **knock holes in; flout**
Inf. Generally applied to Acts of Parliament.

driver, *n.*   **motorman**
British **trams** (tramways) and American trolleys (trolley cars) are both practically obsolete, but when they were in common use the man who operated them was known as a *driver* in Britain and a *motorman* in America. The same distinction exists today with respect to the **underground** or **tube** (*subway*). On a bus, however, he is the *driver* in both countries. On a British train, he is the **engine-driver;** on an American train, the *engineer*.

driving seat   **driver's seat**

drive (someone) up the wall   *Slang.* **drive (someone) crazy**
Slang. He (she) *drives me up the wall* is commonly used in Britain to describe neighbors, bosses, teachers, and other annoying specimens.

driving licence   **driver's license**

drop, n., v.t.
Slang. In the sense of the bonus given to waiters, barbers, etc.

drop a brick   *Slang.* **make a booboo**
Slang. In the special sense of committing a gross indiscretion.

drop a clanger make a gaffe
Slang. See also, **put up a black; howler.**

drop down dead drop dead
The direction would have to be *down*, wouldn't it? Heard in the country.

drop-head, *adj., n.* convertible
Referring to automobiles. See also **Appendix II.E.**

drop off the hooks, *Slang.* *Slang.* kick the bucket

drop-scene, *n.* backdrop
Sometimes *drop-curtain.* Theatrical lingo. The British term covers not only a whole painted scene, but occasional scenery.

dropsy, *n.* bribe
Slang. Often with the implication of hush-money.

dross, *n.* scrap coal
A mining term. A Scottish housewife will buy *dross* to use with household coal as an economy measure.

drug, *v.i.* take drugs
The intransitive use is becoming common in America, informally, in the teen set.

drum, *n.* *Slang.* **pad**
Slang. Living quarter. Hippie equivalent of **digs.**

drunk in charge drunken driving
The official charge for the offense.

dry martini. See **martini.**

D.S.O. See **V.C.**

dual carriageway divided highway
See also **centre strip.**

dubbin, *n.* leather dressing
A greasy preparation for softening leather and making it waterproof, according to most people and some dictionaries; but James Morris, in *Farewell the Trumpets* (Faber & Faber, London, 1978) quotes from Flora Annie Steel's *Complete Indian Housekeeper* (1892) to the effect that the only correct recipe for boot-dubbin is "fish-oil, mutton suet and resin." Sometimes spelled *dubbing.*

duck, *n.* 1. *approx. Inf.* **goose egg**
2. *approx.* **honey**
1. As a cricket term, to *get a duck* is to *be bowled (put out,* approximately) without scoring a single run. If this happens on the first ball bowled (first pitch, approximately), you get a *golden duck.* This type of *duck* is short for *duck's egg.* (*Love* as a term in tennis scoring used in both countries, meaning 'nothing' in America (**nought** in cricket and **nil** in other sports, in Britain), is a corruption of *l'oeuf,* French for 'the egg' but what kind of egg— goose or duck—is an open question.) To be *out for a duck* is the same thing as *getting a duck.* If the match consists of two innings and you fail to score in either **innings,** i.e., *get a duck* or are *out for a duck* in both innings, you *get* (or *make) a pair of spectacles,* usually shortened to *get* (or *make) a pair,* or you *bag* (or *take) a brace,* a term borrowed from grouse-shooting. The moment you make a run in cricket, you *break your duck.* These terms are, of course, technical cricket talk, but they are used figuratively in all kinds of ways, just as Americans borrow expressions like *make a hit* or *couldn't get to first base* from baseball. Thus, to *break your duck* is to *break the ice,* i.e., to 'make a start.' See **off the mark.**

2. *Inf. Duck* is used as a form of address traditionally by barmaids and frequently by purveyors of other types of merchandise, especially the older ladies of that group. It is used by females to persons of both sexes, but by males only to females. It is a term of extremely casual endearment, and in this use is synonymous with *love, lovey, dear, deary,* and *darling* as forms of address. *Duck* (or *ducks),* in this use, sometimes becomes *ducky* or even *ducky diamond,* but the latter, fortunately, is comparatively rare. See also **love.**

dud cheque   *Slang.* **bum check; rubber check**
Slang. Note spelling of *cheque.*

dues, *n. pl.*   **fee(s)**
Dues, generally associated in America with the cost of membership in an organization, has the general meaning in Britain of *fee* or *charge* as in *postal dues (postage), university dues (tuition),* etc. Agents' commissions are also called *dues* in Britain.

duff, *v.t.*   **fake**
Slang. To *duff* merchandise is to make old stuff look new in order to fool the customer.

duffer, *n.*   **peddler of faked merchandise**
A *duffer* in Britain is a con man specialist who, selling shoddy goods, claims them to be of great value because they were stolen or smuggled. It is sometimes used in Britain generically, to mean any *peddler* (spelled *pedlar* in Britain). In both countries it also commonly means a 'person inept at games.'

duff gen. See **gen.**

dug-out, *n.*   *Slang.* **old duffer**
Slang. More specifically, a superannuated officer reluctantly taken back into military service.

dull, *adj.*   **overcast**
A term used all too frequently in describing the weather.

dumb-waiter, *n.*   **lazy Susan**
An American *dumbwaiter* is a British **service lift.**

dummy, *n.*   **baby pacifier**

dumpling, *n.*   **yokel**
Slang. Used in the phrases *Norfolk dumpling* and *Devon dumpling,* Norfolk and Devon being counties in Britain. The seemingly libelous implication is that of a rather slow and cumbersome person or hayseed. The coupling of *dumpling* with the name of other British counties may exist but if so, has escaped the author's notice. In any event, one must not confuse a **Norfolk dumpling** with a **Norfolk capon.**

dunnage, *n.*   *Inf.* **duds; personal luggage**
Inf. More generally, *personal belongings;* one's *stuff. Dunnage,* in standard English, means the 'loose material packed around cargo.'

during hours   SEE COMMENT
Inf. Pubs used to be open more or less at all hours, but during World War I they were forced to close during certain hours. This provision was included in **DORA.** DORA also included a provision, still unrepealed, like many New England blue laws, making it illegal to treat another to a drink in a pub. The establishment of pub closing hours was deemed necessary to prevent workers from stopping at a pub for a quick one in the morning on the way to the munitions factory and somehow never getting there. Nowadays, country pubs are generally open from 10:00 A.M. to 2:00 P.M. and from 6:00 P.M. to 10:30 P.M., except Saturday nights when they close at 11:00 P.M. London pub hours are 11:00 A.M. to 3:00 P.M. and 5:30 P.M. to 11:00 P.M. weekdays; 12 noon to 2:00 P.M. and 7:00 P.M. to 10:30 P.M. Sundays. All this refers to England; Scotland and Wales

have their own schedules, which are on the whole more restrictive. The *hours* in *during hours* refer to those happy ones when the pubs are open. *Opening time* and *closing time*, without express reference to pub schedules, but in proper context (e.g., *I had a few minutes to spare, but it wasn't yet opening time so I popped into a book-shop to browse,* or *It was just past closing time and I still had twenty minutes to wait for the next train*) would be generally understood, respectively, as the times when the pubs open and shut their doors. *Time!* in the **publican's** or **landlord's** *(saloon keeper's)* announcement (which always has to be repeated several times and eventually becomes an entreaty: *Time gentlemen, please!*) means that the legal closing hour is at hand—or, more often, past.

dust, *n.*   **household refuse**
In addition to its more usual meaning in both languages.

dustbin, *n.*   **garbage can**

dustcart, *n.*   **garbage truck**

dustman, *n.*   **garbage man**
Upgraded to *refuse collector,* then *sanitation officer.*

dust road. See **metalled road.**

dust-up, *n.*   **brawl**
Slang. Kick-up and *punch-up* are synonyms.

dutch, *n.*   **wife**
Slang. Especially in *my old dutch,* a term of endearment, like *my old girl, my dear old better half.* Perhaps an abbreviation of *duchess,* with the *t* thrown in by reference to *Dutch.*

duvet, *n.*   **eiderdown quilt**
(Usually pronounced DEW'-VAY, but DOO-VAY' and DOO'-VET are also heard.) A French word, heard often now because of the Common Market. It differs from an **eiderdown** in that it has a removable washable cover, hangs over the sides of the bed, and is used as a complete bed covering without top sheet or blankets. It is also called *continental quilt* in Britain.

D.V., W.P.   *approx.* **God willing**
These initials stand for *Deo volente, weather permitting.* This is an old-fashioned British joke and reflects the Briton's firm belief that British weather is so uncertain that, when plans are being discussed, appeal should be made not only to the Almighty but to the elements as well. William IV is quoted as saying at a church service in Brighton, "No use praying for rain when the wind's in the south-east." *Deo volente* is Latin for *God willing,* and is an example of the grammatical construction known as the ablative absolute, involving the present participle. How many Britons saying "D.V." know that?

dye stamp   **engrave**
Stationery, for example. A term used in printing.

dynamo, *n.*   **generator**
See **Appendix II.E.**
In the U.S., *dynamo,* formerly much used, especially to describe a D.C. generator, is now rarely heard; an A.C. generator is now usually an *alternator,* especially as an automotive part; a *generator* can be A.C. or D.C.

E

---

each way. *See* **have a quid each way.**

eagre, eager, *n.*   **tidal bore flood**

early closing   SEE COMMENT
1:00 P.M. weekday closing. Just about every British village or town has an *early closing day*. This custom is observed in a few parts of America, but even in those towns there are often nonconforming individual holdouts, a practice rare in Britain. In the smaller British villages and towns, all the shops close for lunch, usually from 1:00 P.M. to 2:00 P.M. or 2:15 P.M. every day, but on *early closing day* they shut at 1:00. for good, and many are the frustrations experienced by the unwary visitor or absentminded native. The **A.A.** Book, the familiar useful handbook issued to every member of the British *Automobile Association (A.A.)*, which is about as ubiquitous as the Bible and is to be found in the **cubby** of practically every car in the British Isles, gives the *EC (early closing day)* of each place in its exhaustive list. Watch out for Wednesday particularly; Thursday is a fairly close second. Look out for places like Sturminster Newton, with two early closing days a week. An *early closing day* is also known as a **half-day.**

early days   **too soon;** *Slang.* **jumping the gun**
Inf. This phrase connotes *prematureness.* Thus: *It's early days to reach that conclusion.*

early on   **early in the picture**
This expression is being adopted in America.

earth, *n., v.t.*   **1. ground**
                                                      2. cover with soil
                                                      3. run to earth
1. Term used in electricity. The Americans *ground* a wire; the British *earth* it. The same distinction occurs in the noun use of this electrical term.
2. To *earth* the roots of a plant is to *cover* them *with soil.*
3. *To earth* a fox is *to run* it *to earth.*
Note that *dirt* is not used in Britain as a synonym for *earth* or *soil.*

earth floor   **dirt floor**

earthly, *adj.*   **chance; hope**
Inf. Often used elliptically, always in the negative, to mean '(not a) chance;' '(not a) hope.' A slang American equivalent in some contexts is *no way.* For example, *Do you think he'll succeed?* might be answered, *Not an earthly!* in Britain, and *No way!* in America.

East, *n.*   **Orient**
The British do not speak of the *East* as the *Orient* except poetically. Often lengthened to *Far East.*

East End   SEE COMMENT
The Eastern part of London, which, like its Manhattan parallel, the Lower East Side, was the area in which immigrants settled during the first half of the century. It is still a predominantly working-class area.

east end of a westbound cow   **south end of a northbound horse**
A euphemism. Another is *back (end) of a bus.*

easy about it. See **I'm easy about it.**

easy as kiss your hand. See **as easy as kiss your hand.**

easy meat   1. *Slang.* **a cinch**
                                                                              2. *Slang.* **sucker**
1. *Slang.* Something easily obtained, attained, or mastered, as in, *It was easy meat getting it right,* or *getting the tickets.*
2. *Slang.* Originally the phrase was applied mainly to people, connoting passivity or gullibility, as in, *The immigrants were easy meat for the politicians. Pushover* and *easy* pickin's are other American equivalents. It is still used occasionally of a susceptible woman—a tasteless and regrettable usage.

eat one's dinners   **study for the bar**
To *study for the bar* is a less general term in Britain than in America. It refers only to preparation to become a **barrister.** An aspiring barrister *eats his dinners* (three dinners in the Hall of his **Inn of Court** each of four Terms per year) in order to **keep his terms** in compliance with British bar admission requirements. This phrase is a pleasant survival from the days when the Inns of Court more or less constituted residential universities where, naturally, the students took their meals.

eddy forth   **sally forth**
The British use the American term as well.

edge-to-edge, *adj.*   **wall-to-wall**
See **fitted carpeting.**

effects not cleared   **uncollected funds**
Banking term; see **refer to drawer.**

eiderdown, *n.*   **quilt; comforter**
Used generically for all quilts, not necessarily those filled with the soft feathers of the female eider. See also **duvet.**

Eights Week. *See* **May Week.**

Elastoplast, *n.*   **Band-Aid**
The proprietary name for *plaster.*

electric fire   **electric heater**
See under **fire.**

elementary school   **grade school**
Or *primary school* in America, where the term *elementary school* is going out of fashion.

elephant's, *adj.*   *Slang.* **tight**
Slang. Drunk. Short for *elephant's trunk.* Cockney rhyming slang; see **Appendix II.G.3.**

elevator, *n.*   **lift**
An *elevator* in Britain is not a device for vertical conveyance of people or things. Its generic meaning is 'anything that lifts,' but its common meaning is 'shoe lift.' (This use is seen in America, too, in the term *elevator shoes.*) Conversely, British **lift** is an American *elevator.*

eleven, *n.*   **cricket team; soccer team**
Inf. In American sports terminology, an *eleven* would mean a 'football team' (using *football* in the American sense; see **football**). An *eleven* in Britain refers to cricket or soccer and means a 'side.' Roman numerals are often used: first XI (the first choice

team), second XI (the reserve team). Similarly, a rugby team is a XV, but note that a rowing crew is an *eight*, not a VIII, though in listing their order, crews might be designated *1st VIII, 2nd VIII*, etc.

eleven plus SEE COMMENT
An examination, in the nature of an aptitude and attainment test. Meant to be taken at the end of primary school, it determined what type of secondary education was most suitable for the child, with the most academically gifted going to *grammar schools*, those exhibiting a practical bent to technical or vocational schools, and the remainder, a majority, to *secondary modern schools*. In practice, the examination was looked upon by parents as a pass/fail exam for the prestigious grammar schools. Formerly widespread but now largely eliminated except for scattered pockets of resistance in Britain, this system has been largely replaced by nonselective *comprehensive schools* which claim to provide for all aptitudes and levels of ability. Public education (called *state education* in Britain) is free. Parents may opt out of the state system by sending their children to fee-paying private schools. Those catering to children aged 8–12 are called **prep schools;** those for 13–18 year olds are called **public schools.** The entrance examination for public schools is called the **Common Entrance Examination.**

elevenses, *n. pl.* *approx.* **morning coffee break**
Inf. Also called *elevens* and *elevensies*. The light refreshments consumed in this widespread British morning exercise consist usually of a cup of coffee and a **biscuit** or two. The coffee is usually very tasty and is made with hot milk instead of cream as in America (See **black or white?**). *Morning coffee* is another term used by the British to describe this social practice, which takes place at home, in hotels, and in tearooms. It is almost impossible to get a cup of tea for *elevenses* at most tearooms.

embus. See debus.

Employment Secretary *approx.* **Secretary of Labor**

encash, *v.t.* **cash**
One **encashes** (accent on the second syllable) a **cheque** (*check*). The noun is *encashment*, about which William Safire writes in his language column carried in the *International Herald Tribune* of June 1, 1981:

"Citibank has coined a new and unnecessary word," Mrs. Winsome Adams of St. Albans, N.Y., wrote last year. "In several branches, the bank has signs which state that no two-party checks will be accepted for 'deposit or encashment.' 'Encashment?' What is wrong with the old-fashioned word cashing?"

The wheels of the vaults grind slowly, but a vice-president of Citibank, Nathaniel Sutton, investigated the matter and reports: "We plead guilty on 'encashment.' We did use it, but we didn't coin it. The British did. And two recent editions of Webster's are keeping the word alive and well." The word is listed in Webster's III as a Briticism. "I believe the British are more fond of 'encashment' than we are, but you still hear it all the time in banking circles."

Does Citibank endorse this pretentious import? "While the dictionary confers legitimacy, it does not confer appropriateness," said Sutton, caving in without admitting a bank error in our favor. "I agree with Mrs. Adams that 'encashment' has a jargonish ring, and that 'cashing' is simpler and more appealing." He then deposited his policy directive: "In fact, 'encashment' is one of the taboo words we urge employees not to use in the communications seminars our department conducts. But as you know, portentous words die hard."

end, *n.* **butt**
London theaters and other public places are usually provided with wall receptacles, partly filled with sand, bearing the legend "Cigarette *Ends*." See also **stump; dog end.**

endive, *n.* **chicory**
In a British vegetable store (**greengrocer's**), if you want *chicory* ask for *endive*, and vice versa. See discussion under **chicory.**

endorse, *v.t.*   **record on license**
Under a point system similar to that used in America, a British operator's license is
said to be *endorsed* with a record of the offense.

engage, *v.t.*   **hire; employ**
A Briton *engages* a chauffeur and *hires* a car; an American *hires* a chauffeur and *rents*
a car. In America, one *rents* a house to or from another. In Britain, you *rent* a house
from the owner and *let* your own *to* a tenant. However, the sign TO LET is seen in both
countries.

engaged, *adj.*   **busy**
It is just as frustrating to be told by a British telephone operator that the line is *engaged*
or to hear the *engaged tone* as it is to hear the word *busy* or the *busy signal* in America.
He's engaged, used by a British **telephonist,** is just as irritating in Britain as the dreary
American equivalents *He's busy talking* or *He's on the wire.* This maddening word *engaged*
is also the British equivalent of the exasperating American term *in conference* or *in a
meeting.*

engine driver   **engineer**
Railroad term.

enquiries, *n. pl.*   **information**
(Stressed on the second syllable.) This is the term you use in Britain when you want
Information to look up a telephone number for you. It also appears on signs in offices,
railway stations, etc., where the American sign would read INFORMATION. *Trunk enquiries* means 'long-distance information.' Sometimes the term *enquiries* in telephone
context is expanded to *directory enquiries.* When you dial *information* in America now the
operator answers, *Directory assistance,* which somehow sounds British rather than American. As the British tend to adopt freer and easier American phraseology and customs,
in certain instances the Americans begin to appear almost stuffy. See **Trunk Enquiries.**

enquiry, *n.*   **investigation**
(Stressed on the second syllable.) This word is often used where *investigation* would
be used in America, e.g., in discussing an attempt to ferret out wrongdoing in a government department. A similar sense is found in the British term *enquiry agent,* which
would be *private investigator* or *private detective* in America. It is also used as the equivalent of the American term *hearing,* e.g., *planning enquiry,* which is the British equivalent
of *zoning hearing.* An *enquiry office* is an *information bureau.*

ENSA, *n.*   *approx.* **USO**
A pronounced acronym. Stands for *Entertainments National Service Association.* Like
the American *USO* (stands for *United Service Organizations*) it supplied entertainment to
the armed forces. ENSA gave its final show on August 18, 1946, the last of two and a
half million performances.

ensure, *v.t.*   **make sure**
Instructions from a travel agency: "Please *ensure* your baggage is correctly labelled."
(See **Appendix I.E.** for the third *l* in *labelled.*) This usage of *ensure* would be found in
commercial, government or other 'official' communications, rarely, if ever, in ordinary
writing or speech.

entrance fee   **initiation fee**
This is the term used by the British to describe the initial fee paid on joining a club.

entry, *n.*   **entrance**
Sign over a door in a public building. See **no entry.** The American term is used as
well.

erk, *n.*   *Slang.* **rookie**
Slang. Absolute bottom of the totem pole in the Royal Navy and Air Force.

Ernie, *n.*   SEE COMMENT
Used in selecting **premium bond** winning numbers; an acronym for *electronic random
number indicator equipment.*

escape lane (road)   SEE COMMENT
A means of egress off a main highway for a vehicle in difficulties, usually, at least in the U.S., a fairly sharp upgrade.

Esq., *n.*   **Mr.**
Short, of course, for *Esquire*. In addressing letters, *Esq.* follows the name, and is simply the equivalent of *Mr.* preceding the name. The *Concise Oxford Dictionary* defines *Esquire* as the "title appended to name of one regarded as gentleman by birth, position, or education, esp. in address of letter (abbr. *Esq.*)." But who is to make these fine distinctions? How address one's courteous and gentlemanly plumber, or polite and well-spoken cesspool cleaner? Play safe: use *Esq.* Samuel Pepys expressed delight at receiving an envelope with *Esq.* on it. During World War II, an American correspondent of the British Information Service in New York was equally delighted and thought he had been awarded a British decoration. *Esq.* is not used where the name is preceded by a title (e.g., Prof. C.E. Jones, Sir Charles Smith). See **Appendix I.D.7.**

(the) Establishment   SEE COMMENT
The Establishment describes those British institutions (and their representatives) that symbolize tradition and conformity, and, whether or not actually in control of the country, wield considerable social, financial, and political influence: the upper classes, the Church of England, *The Times*, **Whitehall,** and the Marylebone Cricket Club (see under **Ashes**). *The Establishment* is used roughly the same way in America, but its components are quite different, omitting the church and any (but there isn't any) equivalent of the Marylebone Cricket Club (see **(the) Ashes**). According to Leonard and Mark Silk (*The American Establishment*, Basic, 1980), the Establishment, American style, is a "bringing together of intellectuals, under the benevolent governance of (big) business, rather than that of the state." The **intellectual** in that description sounds more flattering than accurate.

estate, *n.*   **real estate development**
Usually found in the terms *housing estate*, meaning a 'residential development,' or *industrial estate*, signifying an area designated for industry, work shops and offices. British housing officials and experts use *estate* or *housing estate* as the exact equivalent of the American term *housing project*, to denote any development of one or more buildings comprising a number of households. By itself, *estate* is occasionally used as a flattering description of any old house and lot, particularly in real estate advertisements.

estate agent   **real estate broker**
Synonymous with **land agent.**

estate car   **station wagon; suburban**
It also used to be called *estate wagon*, but that term is rarely heard nowadays. Another synonym, now practically obsolete, was *shooting-brake* (also *shooting-break).*

evens, *n. pl.*   *Inf.* **even money**
*Inf. Evens on...*means 'I will lay you *even money* on...'

ever so   **very**
He's ever so handsome. She was ever so kind. **Non-U.** See **Appendix I.C.6.**

everything in the garden's lovely   *Inf.* **everything's hunky-dory**
Inf. An old-fashioned catch phrase.

everything that opens and shuts   *Inf.* **everything but the kitchen sink**
Inf. The price of my new car includes everything that opens and shuts. The expression could apply as well to a hand at cards full of trumps and honors.

except for access   *approx.* **no through trucks**
Preceded by numerals indicating width or weight (e.g., 6′ 6″, or 3 TONS) on a sign
at the ingress of a back road, forbidding entrance (**entry**) to a vehicle over the specified
width or weight, unless it is in fact headed for a destination on that road. See **access**,
for a different usage of that word by itself. The *through* in the American road sign is
often spelled *thru*, alack. See **pinch-point.**

exchange contracts   **close contract**
There are two principal steps in a purchase and sale of real estate: *closing of contract*
and *closing of title.* In Britain, these are respectively *exchange of contracts* and **completion.**

Exchequer, *n.*   **Treasury Department**
The *Chancellor of the Exchequer* is the British equivalent of the *Secretary of the Treasury.*
The term is used facetiously to refer to the family budget.

exclamation mark   **exclamation point**

exclusive line   **private line**
Telephone term. Sometimes the telephone department (of the **G.P.O.**) in its literature
uses the quaint phrase *exclusive working* to describe this luxury. The less fortunate have
shared lines or *party lines.*

ex-directory, *adj.*   **unlisted**
Referring to telephone numbers.

exeat, *n.*   **temporary school leave**
(Pronounced EX′EE-AT.) Term used in schools and colleges. The connotation is that
of a short holiday. Like the more familiar word *exit,* it is a form of the Latin verb *exire,*
'to go forth'; in this case the third person singular present subjunctive used in Latin as
a third person imperative—literally, *let him go out.*

(the) Executive, *n.*   **(the) Executive Committee**
Used the way Americans use *the Management* at the end of notices posted in public
places, like railroad stations and post offices.

exercise book   **notebook**
Sometimes referred to as a **jotter.**

exhibition; exhibitioner. *See under* **bursar.**

export carriage   **overseas shipping**
Seen as an extra charge item on bills for goods sent overseas, like tea bought at
Fortnum & Mason's and shipped to America.

express, *adj., adv.*   **special delivery**
Post office term. The American designation has now been adopted by the **G.P.O.** See
recorded delivery. The U.S. Post Office now has 'Express Mail,' a premium overnight
service available at a price.

ex-service man   **veteran**

external painting   **outdoor painting**
Builders' and contractors' term.

extractor fan   **exhaust fan**

extra-mural studies   **extension courses**

Extraordinary General Meeting. See under **Annual General Meeting.**

F

fab, *adj.*   *Slang.* **cool**
Slang. A teenage truncation of *fabulous* and synonymous with **gear** and **kinky,** all of
which are out of fashion now, though they can be used as jocular exaggerations. *Kinky*
has another grown-up meaning.

face-glove, *n.*   SEE COMMENT
A very convenient type of *washrag* or *facecloth,* consisting of a square terrycloth mitt.
The British call an ordinary washrag or facecloth a **flannel.**

facer, *n.*   *Inf.* **poser**
Inf. Facer is rarely heard in either country in its literal meaning of 'blow in the face.'
In Britain it has the special meaning of 'poser,' i.e., a difficulty that you suddenly come
up against.

facia. See under **fascia.**

faculty, *n.*   **college department**
In America (unless qualified as in the case of graduate faculties of specific subjects
such as law, medicine, social science, etc.), the *faculty* of a college is its entire teaching
body. In Britain, this is called **staff,** and *faculty* is confined to groups of academically
related subjects, i.e., departments, as in *Faculty of Medicine, Law,* etc.

faddy, *adj.*   *Inf.* **picky**
Inf. Often used to describe persons who are fussy about their food and difficult to
please. See also **dainty.**

fadge, *v.i.*   **suit**
Slang. Especially in the expression *It won't fadge,* meaning 'It won't suit' (or 'do' or
'fit'). "How will this *fadge*?" asks the sleuth, trying out a new theory of the crime. "No
good, it won't *fadge,*" is the unhappy reply.

fag, *n., v.t., v.i.*   1. *v.i.,* **toil**
                                                                                  2. *v.i.,* **exhaust**
                                                                                  3. *n., Slang.* **drag**
                                                                      4. *n., Slang.* **butt (cigarette)**
                                                                                  5. SEE COMMENT
1. *v.i., Slang* To *toil painfully.*
2. *v.t., Slang.* To *tire* or *wear (someone)* out.
3. *n., Slang.* In the sense of 'drudgery'; a painfully boring job.
4. *Slang. Cigarette* in both countries, though archaic in America. More common than
another British slang term: **gasper.**
5. *Slang.* In **public school** slang, when seniors *fag,* it means that they are using the
services of juniors; when juniors *fag,* it means that they are rendering services to seniors
and the junior so serving is known as a *fag.* The last-named usage goes back quite far.
(*Mr. Fag* in Sheridan's *The Rivals.*) America's use of *fag,* in the sense of 'male homosexual' is not used in Britain, though *faggot* is heard increasingly.

faggot, *n.*   1. **crone**
                                                                                  2. **spiced meatball**
1. *Inf.* Chiefly a country term, summoning the image of a battered old slut.
2. Mostly Wiltshire and Somerset. Made of chopped pig innards (see **offal**) and fairly
heavily spiced. The common American slang use of *faggot* to mean 'male homosexual'
has caught on in Britain, particulary in entertainment circles and among the jet set. A

sign on a Marlborough **High Street** market stall reading BAKED FAGGOTS (this writer then being unfamiliar with the second sense of *faggot* listed above) evoked in his mind the frightening image of cannibalistic homosexuals, but this is not the only instance of confusion arising from the British use of *faggot* in that sense. In David Lodge's novel *Small World* (Secker & Warburg, London, 1984), a Japanese translator is working on a translation into Japanese of an English novel and keeps bombarding the novelist with queries. One sample: "P 107, 3 down. '**Bugger** me, but I feel like some *faggots* tonight.' Does Ernie mean that he feels a sudden desire for homosexual intercourse? If so, why does he mention this to his wife?" See also **fag. 5.**

fains I! SEE COMMENT
Slang. Also *fain I! vains I!* and other regional variants like *fainites! vainites!* and even *cribs! scribs! crosses! keys!* and goodness knows what else, usually accompanied by conspicuously crossed fingers. All these are truce words meaning that the crier wants his little pals to wait a minute while he attends to a personal need like pulling up his socks or looking for a dropped coin—calling for a halt, for example, in a fast children's game. Any of these cries has the force of law. Only an unscrupulous bully would take advantage of a call for truce: it would be like shooting at an enemy advancing with a white flag. See a special use of *fains* under **quis? Bags I!** is the opposite of *fains I!*

fair, *adv.* *Inf.* **sure**
Inf. That sermon fair set us thinking! Substandard; mostly rustic.

fair do's! *Slang.* **divvy up!**
Slang. Used by children anxious to secure their fair share.

fair-light, *n.* **transom**

fair old..., *adj.* *Inf.* **quite a...**
Inf. A *fair old job* means 'quite a job' (*a major chore); a fair old mix-up* means 'quite a mix-up' (a snafu of major proportions).

fair's on *Inf.* **what's fair is fair**
Inf. To the kind friend who paid for the previous round of drinks, a Briton might say: "*Fair's on...*, this one's on me".

fairy cake **cupcake**

fall about laughing *Slang.* **die laughing**
Slang. Sometimes shortened to *fall about,* with *laughing* understood, especially in the **cockney** idiom.

fallen off the back of a lorry *Slang.***hot**
Slang. A **lorry** is a *truck.* The idea is that the thief (or black marketeer), seeking to dispose of his ill-gotten wares, approaches the pedestrian and out of the side of his mouth assures him that *it* (the fur coat or wristwatch or whatever it may be) *fell off the back of a lorry.*

fall over backwards *Inf.* **lean over backwards**
Uncharacteristically, in this case the British overstate.

family butcher **butcher shop**
Often *first-class family butcher.* An American friend walked into a shop bearing that sign and timorously assured the man in the white coat behind the counter that she came from a first-class family. See also **butchery.**

fancy. See **fancy one's chances.**

fancy goods **notions**
See also **draper's shop; haberdashery.**

fancy one's chances   *Inf.* **have high hopes**
Inf. The hopeful swain *fancies his chances* with the girl; the team with a comfortable margin *fancy their chances* for the cup. One may fancy one's own or another's chances, but when the expression applies to a third party, it is usually found in the negative. After attending a disappointing first night: *I don't fancy its chances,* or, about a friend about to enter a tennis tournament: *I don't fancy his chances.* An echo of this usage is found in the use of *fancy* as a noun meaning 'favorite' in horse-racing parlance, as demonstrated by the following item from *The Times* (London) of May 29, 1981:

Derby fancy out
Beldale Flutter, the second favourite for next weeks's Derby, is out of the race after bolting on the gallops and injuring himself yesterday. . .

As to the *Flutter* in the horse's name, see **flutter.** The *most fancied* contestant in a horse race is the *favorite;* in a political contest, the *front-runner.*

fanny, *n.*   **1.** *Slang.* **backside**
                                        2. cunt
                                   3. SEE COMMENT
1. *Slang.* Originally, this word meant the female pudenda (see below), but the American sense—'backside,' 'behind,' 'derrière'—appears to have become its primary meaning now in Britain, as a result of importation from America, where it has never had the second meaning. Yet it might be just as well to avoid its use in Britain, because there are those, among the elderly at least, and perhaps the not-so-elderly in less chic circles who, unacquainted with Coward and Rattigan (who were among those who innovated its use in the American sense), might be shocked, and certainly puzzled, if it were applied to a male–an anatomical paradox, like applying **sod,** in its original meaning, to a female. The fact that sense 3. originated as long ago as 1918 indicates that sense 2. had become practically obsolete that far back. Writing in the BBC weekly program magazine, *The Listener,* issue of August 8, 1985, in his *Endpiece* column, Fritz Spiegl has this to say: "...in a recent broadcast of *Mansfield Park* it might have been better to alter 'I'm going to make 'my' little *Fanny* feel as she's never felt before.' What a pity it was when that pretty girls' name met its ruin...and although the latest OED supplement gives the American 'backside,' it has so far refused to admit the equally vulgar but more forward British meaning. According to BBC folklore, Frank Bough [an announcer] once wound up a cookery demonstration by Fanny Craddock [Britain's Julia Childs] with 'Well, that's all we have time for, and I hope *your* doughnuts will look like Fanny's.' "
2. *Slang.* This is the original British meaning, and the word is still understood or may be understood that way in some circles. Its shortened form, *fan,* must have been so understood by the audience who attended the Globe Theatre and guffawed when, in *Romeo and Juliet* (Act II, Scene 4), Nurse entered with Peter and met Romeo and Mercutio. "Peter!" cries Nurse, "My fan, Peter," and Mercutio comes out with: "Good Peter, to hide her face; for her fan's the fairer of the two." The American equivalent, derived from an old Middle English word, was also in the vocabulary of the English at that time as demonstrated by the plays on words in *Hamlet* (Act III, Scene 2, "country matters") and *Twelfth Night* (Act II, Scene 5, "her very C's, her U's, and her T's"). It is identifiably referred to, though not mentioned, in a bit of doggerel entitled "Lines on a Book Borrowed from the Ship's Doctor" by Sir Alan Herbert (A.P. Herbert), which, after describing the female equipment in mock-rhapsodic terms, ends with the following quatrain:

What a pity then it is that, when we common fellows chatter
Of the mysteries to which I have referred,
We should use for such a delicate and complicated matter
Such a very short and unattractive word!

The same short and unattractive word is said to be the British schoolboy's mnemonic acronym for Nelson's memorable victories (Copenhagen, Ushant, Nile, Trafalgar). If so, he gets them in the wrong order.
3. (Member of) *First Aid Nursing Yeomanry,* sometimes in the phrase *old Fanny.* An acronym based on F.A.N.Y. (inaccurately doubling the *n*) which developed in World War I, and used in polite society, despite the risks mentioned above. Its use (with one

N), and some background information, can be found in the following report from the *New Standard*, issue of April 16, 1981, under the headline ROYAL TASK:

> Hopes are high among the FANYs that Lady Diana Spencer will soon take up the post of Commandant-in-Chief...Today FANY has little to do with nursing. Founded in 1907 they are the oldest voluntary women's organisation in the country. In wartime, rather like the Brigade of Guards, they are regarded as very special. During the Last War the FANYs became a driving element in the A.T.S....and SOE...Of the seven GCs awarded to women's services during the War, three were won by Fannies. In peace-time the FANYs operate a radio telephone team on call to the City Police and Tower Hamlets in case of Thames flooding. They are taught First Aid, and there is a linguists' section, whose members can speak 12 languages between them...

A.T.S. (also know as *the Ats*) stands for *Auxiliary Territorial Service; S.O.E.* for *Special Operators' Executive* (roughly the equivalent of the American O.S.S. (Office of Strategic Service) in World War II; *G.C.* for *George Cross*, a very high military decoration. The A.T.S. was superseded by the WRAC (Women's Royal Army Corps).

Fanny Adams. See **sweet Fanny Adams.**

Far East. See **East.**

fare stage   **bus fare zone limit**
   In both countries *stage* appears in the phrase *stage of a journey*, and as part of *stagecoach*, especially in American movies about the Wild West. In Britain, *fare stages* are the *zone limits* for purposes of computing bus fares.

farthing *n.*   SEE COMMENT
   One fourth of an old penny, a coin long since demonetized; but the term is still used figuratively to mean a 'bit' in expressions like, *It doesn't matter a farthing.* See **Appendix II.A.** and, for idiomatic use, **halfpenny.**

fart in a colander, *Slang*   **restless soul**
   Describes one who jumps around from one chore to the next, unable to make up his mind what to start first. This indelicate expression is supposed to evoke the image of an anal wind emission unable to decide which hole in the colander to pass through. Synonymous with **tit in a trance.**

fascia   **1. dashboard**
                                                                         2. store sign
   Also spelled *facia.* In meaning 1. it is sometimes lengthened to *fascia-board* or *fascia panel.* See also **Appendix II.E.**

fast, *adj.*   **express**
   Applied to trains and to roads (express or limited highways). A local train is called a **stopping train,** or **slow train.**

Father Christmas   **Santa Claus**
   The British also use *Santa Claus.*

fat rascal   **soft bun**
   Inf. Stuffed with lots of black currants.

faults and service difficulties   **telephone repair department**
   This is what you ask for on your neighbor's telephone when yours isn't working. A *faulty* telephone is one that is out of order.

feed, *n.*   **1. feeding**
                                                                       2. straight man
   1. Usually in the context of formula feeding. To *go onto feeds* is to *go onto formula,* e.g.,

My little one is on six feeds a day. Technically, a *feed* can be any variety—breast, formula, or mush.
2. The member of the comedy duet who *feeds* the stuff to the gag man.

feeder, *n.*   **child's bib**

feel, *v.i.*   **feel like**
   E.g., *I feel a perfect fool!*

feeling not quite the thing, *Inf.*   *Inf.* **not feeling up to par**

felicitate, *v.t.*   **congratulate**
   Used when the subject of good wishes (i.e., the object of the verb) is the lady. One *congratulates* the fiancé or groom but *felicitates* the fiancée or bride.

fellow, *n.*   **member of college governing body**
   In Oxford and some other universities, also called **don**. The chairman of the governing body is called the *Master* in most **Oxbridge** colleges, but in addition to the eight Masters, there are seven Wardens, five Principals, three Provosts and two Rectors. At Cambridge, *Master* is the title with only four exceptions: one each of Provost, President, Mistress and Principal—all of this being a shining example of British nonconformity. C.P. Snow has a great deal to say about *fellows* and Masters in his novel *The Masters*, one from his great series, *Strangers and Brothers*. It should be remembered that **college** is not synonymous with *university* in Britain, but is rather a constituent unit of a university. At Oxford and Cambridge *fellow* can best be defined as 'senior teaching or administrative member' of a college. There are all sorts and varieties of *fellow: Research Fellows, Junior Research Fellows, Honorary Fellows, Emeritus Fellows, Quondam* (or *ex-*) *Fellows*.

fender, *n.*   **bumper**
   Old automobile term; but American *fender* is British **wing. Bumper** is now universal. (See also **Appendix II.E.**)

(the) Fens, *n. pl.*   SEE COMMENT
   Name given to the marshy district of the eastern part of the country, west and south of *the Wash*, a shallow bay in that section of England.

fetch, *v.t.*   **bring**
   As in, to *fetch* a price in an auction. The British use *make* in the same way.

fête, *n.*   **fair**
   (Pronounced FATE.) An important part of British life. Not only churches and organizations like the **W.I.** (*Women's Institute*) or the Young Conservatives Club (roughly equivalent to the Young Republicans Club), but apparently every village in Britain, down to the smallest, organizes a fête. The village fête is annual and is a small scale country fair, sometimes preceded by a parade with floats. Attendance at village fêtes has been spotty in many cases, and in some villages, talk of discontinuing the practice is almost as regular as the fête itself.

fib, *n., v.t., v.i., Boxing slang.*   **rain (of) blows**

fiddle, *n., v.t., v.i.*   **swindle**
   To *fiddle* is to *cheat* and to *fiddle the books* is to *engage in shady dealings.* A *fiddle* is usually a minor cheat. To *be on the fiddle* is to engage in minor swindling. A newly coined bit of rhyming slang (see **Appendix II.G.3.**) is *Nelson Riddle*, as in *He's got a few Nelson Riddles going*—i.e., he's got some *fiddles* going. When the offense is of major proportions, the British use *swindle*. See also **diddle; do; carve up; ramp; sell a pup; swizz; take down; cook.**

fiddling, *adj.*   **petty; futile; picayune**
  Slang. Eric Partridge, in *A Dictionary of Slang and Unconventional English*, his ground-breaking work on British slang usage, defines *fiddling* as "a livelihood from odd street jobs; esp. the selling of matches in the streets," and after defining the verb *to fiddle* as "to cheat," goes on to say, "Hence, to make a living from small jobs done on the street." Partridge related *fiddler*, which he defined as "a sharper or cheat," to its obsolete meaning of 'sixpence,' and to *fiddler's money*, defined as "small change, esp. sixpences." Note: as to *sixpence* itself, a coin long since demonetized, see **Appendix II.A.**; incidentally, the *picayune* included in the above definition of *fiddling* was once the name of a nickel in the American South. Paul S. Falla (for his extraordinary qualifications see the Acknowledgments in this book, and, more importantly, the "Acknowledgements" [note the inclusion in British English of the *e* after the *g*; like *abridgment, judgment, lodgment*, it's spelt with or without that *e* in Britain] in Sir Ernest Gowers's revision of *Fowler's Modern English Usage*) says, in referring to the predecessor of this book, *English English*, "I dare say you have already revised the 'fiddling' entry. The first half rings no bell wth me and I would delete it." That 'first half' read: "A *fiddling business* is a *nickle-and-dime* [note misspelling of *nickle* in that edition] operation', a *catch-as-catch-can* way of making a living, like street vending or occasional odd jobs..." This "first half" came to Mr. Falla's attention when he saw a copy of it used by Thomas H. Middleton as the subject of an acrostic puzzle in Simon & Schuster's *Acrostics 91*—other passages of this book and its predecessor "British Self-Taught" had been used by the indefatigable Mr. Middleton in the New York *Sunday Times* at long intervals. Well, that first half is hereby deleted and *fiddling* is hereby defined as above, and can mean 'contemptible' as well. *Fiddling* sometimes emerges as *fiddly*, meaning 'awkward to do or use; exacting, finicky,' with the implication that it denotes the exasperation that often occurs when one is working on delicate things like small, intricate machinery or, for example, fine watches, though, according to Paul Falla, "a master-jeweller [note the double *l*: see **Appendix I.E.**] would not use it of his own work, unless in mock-modesty [note the hyphen: see **Appendix I.D.1.**]." This excellent advice from friend Falla was, only a few days later, followed by the following note: "Dept. [note absence of apostrophe, which is going out of style in British abbreviations] of coincidence: 'fiddler' for 'sixpence' has turned up in the [London] Times crossword [of January 21,1986]. It doesn't affect my advice, however: crossword language is often old-fashioned [in this word, both countries use the hyphen]. Does this sort of coincidence happen to you?" (The answer is Yes!) And he enclosed *Times* crossword puzzle No [note absence of period, which is called **full stop** in Britain; the symbol # for 'number' is not used in Britain] 16, 949, in which the clue for 18 Down reads: "He cheats players for sixpence" and the answer is—you guessed it—*fiddler*! After all this, see also **fiddle**.

fiddly. See **fiddling**.

field, *v.t.*   **put up**
  Speaking of political candidates. Americans and Britons alike *field* teams or armies, i.e., put them in the field, but only the British *field* candidates.

fieldsman, *n.*   **fielder**
  Cricket vs. baseball (See also **batsman**.) *Fielder* is commonly used in Britain, but *fieldsman* is unknown in America.

fifty-fifty sale   SEE COMMENT
  You collect all those things you want to get rid of, take them to a scheduled charity sale, and split the proceeds *fifty-fifty* with the charity. Everybody's happy.

file, *n.*   **loose-leaf binder**
  A British schoolboy or university student will keep his notes in a *file*.

filibuster, *n., v.i.*   **buccaneer**
  Filibuster originally meant the same thing in both countries: as a verb, to 'engage in unauthorized warfare against a foreign power,' as a noun, a 'buccaneer' or 'pirate' engaged in that activity. In Britain, it does not have the specialized American sense of an endless speech, especially in the Senate and the House of Representatives, designed to obstruct the proceedings and prevent unwanted legislation.

fillet, *n.*   **tenderloin**
(Rhymes with MILLET, not MILLAY.) On an American restaurant menu the equivalent
would be *tenderloin steak,* or perhaps *filet mignon.*

fill in   **fill out**
The British fill *in* or fill *up* a form; the Americans fill *in* or fill *out* a form. See **Appendix
I.A.1.** *Fill out* is creeping into Britain.

film, *n.*   **movie**
A *film* is a *movie* (i.e., a motion picture). A **cinema** is the theater that shows them. In
old-fashioned slang, one went to the **flicks** to see a *flick.*

filter sign   **green arrow**
Traffic signal, the kind that permits a turn while the straight-ahead light is red, and
lets you *filter* into the merging stream of traffic.

(the) filth   *Slang.* **(the) fuzz; (the) cops**
Slang. The police. *Look out! Here comes the filth!* Underworld argot.

filthy, *adj.*   *Inf.* **lousy**
Inf. As in *Filthy weather we're having; She's had a filthy time of it; He's got a filthy temper.*

financial, *adj.*   *Inf.* **well-heeled**
Inf. Mainly Australian and New Zealand, but used jocularly in Britain on occasion.
Let me buy the drinks; I'm financial tonight or, *I'm feeling financial.*

financial year   **fiscal year**
An accounting term.

find, *v.t.*   **like**
At times. When the manager of the inn, in Britain, asks you as you are leaving, "How
did you *find* us?" he may not be asking you how you *located* the place. Quality, not
location, may be the issue. The answer would then not be "With a road map," or
"Through friends." He is asking you how you *liked* his inn. The question "How do you
find the new **greengrocer's?**" may not be seeking directions. The reply might be "Very
good, but **pricey,**" or "Not nearly so good as when old Mr. Higglesworth ran it!" The
context should make things clear.

fine down   *Inf.* **thin down; clear up**
Inf. To *fine* (something) *down, away* or *off* is to make it thinner. Transitively, referring
to the brewing of beer, it means to 'clear up.' Intransitively, referring to any liquid, it
means to 'become clear,' as in the case of a wine whose sediment has settled.

finger-food, *n.*   SEE COMMENT
The kind of food you get at cocktail parties, which can be eaten with the fingers, i.e.,
without benefit of implements. Cf. **fork supper** and **knife-and-fork tea.**

fingerling, *n.*   **young salmon**
In America it means anything small and specifically any fish no longer than your
finger.

fingers, *n. pl.*   **bread strips**
Inf. Strips of bread, to be dipped into soft-boiled egg. See **soldiers.**

fire, *n.*   **heater**
As in *electric fire; gas fire;* but also used eliptically meaning either. See also **fired.**

fire brigade   **fire department**

-fired   SEE COMMENT
The British speak of *oil-fired, gas-fired,* etc., *central heating.* This is shortened to *oil heat,
gas heat,* etc., in America. See also **fire.**

fire-flair *n.* stingray

fire-guard, *n.* fire-screen

fire-irons, *n. pl.* fireplace implements

fire office fire insurance company office

fire-pan, *n.* brazier

fire-raising, *n.* arson
A *fire-raiser* is an arsonist.

firewood, *n.* **kindling**
Firewood, in America, is a generic term for any wood for burning, usually in a fireplace for heat, but also outdoors for cooking. The American term includes *kindling*. In Britain where most fireplaces contain grates for the burning of coal, *firewood* denotes merely wood to start the fire with, and is either gathered outdoors or is bought at the **iron-monger's** (*hardware store*) in small wire-bound bundles of thin, short sticks-called **pimps**.

first, *n.* *Inf.* **summa**
Inf. First is a university term which is short for *first-class honours* and is roughly equivalent to *summa* in America, which is short for *summa cum laude.* There are *seconds* and *thirds* as well. See **class**. One says, *He got* (or *took*) *a first in physics.*

first class *approx.* **major league**
Sports terminology. This pairing is as approximate as the respective national games; *first-class* cricket, *major league* baseball. There is also *second-class* cricket, very roughly analogous to *minor league* baseball, involving the second **elevens** of first class counties and the first **elevens** of second class counties, each category with its own championship; also village cricket, club cricket, and God knows what other kinds of cricket. For further elucidation on this arcane subject please consult *Wisden*, the annually published Bible of cricket. For another use of *first-class*, as in *first-class honours*, see **first**.

first floor **second floor**
Americans use *first floor* and *ground floor* interchangeably to describe an apartment on the ground level, and *main floor* or *street floor* to describe the ground level of a shop or office building. The British use *ground floor* to describe all of those things, but when they say *first floor*, they mean the next floor up, i.e., the floor above the ground floor, or what Americans call the *second floor*. This difference continues all the way to the top, of course. Though Americans call the floor above the ground floor the *second floor*, inhabitants of that floor are also heard to say that they live *one flight up*. In this difference between the American and British usage, the British are one with the Europeans against their former colony. For example:

	Ground level	One flight up
American	first floor	second floor
British	ground floor	first floor
French	rez-de-chaussée	premier étage
Spanish	piso bajo	primer piso
Italian	pianterreno	primo piano
German	Parterre;	erster Stock
	Erdgeschoss	

The German usage is highlighted in the title of Johann Nepomuk Nestroy's comedy, *Zu ebener Erde und im ersten Stock (Downstairs and Up;* literally, in the American usage, *On the First Floor and on the Second Floor).* One must be careful also to distinguish between *floor* and *storey* (note the *e* in the British spelling) in Britain: a *two-storey* house has a ground floor and a first floor, and so on. Thus, in a fifty-story skyscraper in America, the top floor is the fiftieth. It would be the forty-ninth in Britain (if you could find one that high). When **pair** is used in the sense of *floor* (*first pair, second pair,* etc.), remember that *first pair* relates to those dwelling on what would be the *second floor* in America, and so on all the way up.

first knock. See **take first knock.**

fish, *n.*   **fish and seafood**
In Britain *fish* usually includes *seafood.*

fisher. See **bradbury.**

fish fingers   **fish sticks**

fishmonger's   **fish store**

fish 'n' chips   SEE COMMENT
This national delicacy consists of fish fried in batter and served with French fried potatoes (see **chips**). This fish used to be cod, most of the time, in the cheaper places, and plaice, a European flatfish, in the better places, and here and there other varieties of fish. As a result of the "cod war" the price of cod has rocketed, and haddock and hake are the normal fare in the usual fish 'n' chips place. Worse, still, potato prices have risen so high that many chips 'n' fish shops have been forced to close down. In fact, a Labour **M.P.** made a motion to subsidize potato prices in order to prevent the disappearance of the working Briton's national symbol. In the more casual type of establishment, this dish used to be served wrapped in a piece of newspaper (a practice long since made illegal), and specialist gourmets insist that the newspaper ink lent an incomparable flavor that cannot be duplicated and that fish 'n' chips on a plate is a dish fit only for tourists. The normal procedure is to drown this dish in vinegar, Brown Sauce, or Daddy's Sauce, which are, like ketchup in America, ubiquitous. Another component of the experience of this dish, in a proper establishment, is the ineradicable smell of the establishment itself. A slang term for a fish 'n' chips shop is *chippie*—which happens also to be slang for 'carpenter,' but there shouldn't ever be any confusion. Fish 'n' chips shops are edging into the U.S. fast-food market. See **chippie.**

fish-slice,   **spatula**
Inf. Literally, a cook's implement for turning fish while it is cooking, and for removing it from the pan; but used informally to mean 'spatula' generally. In that sense, synonymous with **palette-knife.**

fish, wet. See **wet fish.**

fit?, *adj.*   *Inf.* **all set?**
Inf. Usually asked in the form, *Are you fit?*

fitments, *n. pl.*   **fixtures**
Of a shop or factory.

fits. *See* **give (someone) fits.**

fitted, *adj.*   **wall-to-wall**
Used of carpeting. Another phrase, though less common is *edge-to-edge.* *Wall-to-wall* is beginning to be used frequently, especially in its extended senses.

fitter, *n.*   **plumber; mechanic**
Americans use the phrase *steam fitter* to refer to a mechanic who installs or repairs steam pipe systems but do not use *fitter,* as the British do loosely, to mean a 'repairman' or 'plumber.' In Britain you send for the *fitter* whether your home radiator or your boat engine, as just two examples, is out of order.

fittings, *n. pl.*   **fixtures**
Shop fittings in Britain are called *store fixtures* in America.

fit-up, *adj.*   *Slang.* **pick-up**
Slang. Theatrical slang, to describe a temporary touring company, assembled from hither and yon. The term can be applied to other types of organization.

five honours. See **four honours.**

fiver, *n.*   *approx.* **five**
A *fiver* is a *five-pound note* (see **note**), at present (February 1987) worth about $7.75. A *fiver* (more commonly a *five*) in America is, of course, a *five-dollar bill*.

fives, *n.*   **handball**
The games are roughly similar.

five-star. See **four-star.**

fixing, *n.*   SEE COMMENT
The *fixing* is the twice-a-day ritual, held at N.M. Rothschild, whereby representatives of the five London gold-bullion firms fix that day's price for gold.

fixings, *n. pl.*   **hardware**
What Americans call the *hardware* on a window, swinging gate, or other such contraption, is called the *fixings* in Britain.

fixture, *n.*   **scheduled sporting event**
In the British sports world what the Americans call an *event* is called a *fixture*.

Flag Day   **Tag Day**
The day on which people solicit you for contributions to a cause and give you something to put on your lapel to prove you've come through. In Britain you get little flags; in America you get other little things on the end of a pin.

flaked out   *Slang.* **fagged**
Slang. Worn to a frazzle.

flaming, *adj., adv.*   *Slang.* **damned**
Slang. Synonymous with **flipping, ruddy, bloody**, etc., but heard more among the working class.

flan, *n.*   SEE COMMENT
Sponge cake or pastry with fruit filling, usually with a layer of whipped cream as well. In Italy and Spain *flan* is *crème caramel*, in France, any custard. Seen in America only in Hispanic restaurants.

flannel, *n.*   **face cloth**
Also known in America as *washcloth* or *washrag*. But when the British talk of a **washcloth**, they mean what is known in America as a *dishcloth*. See also **face-glove**.

flannel, *n., v.t., v.i., Slang.*   1. *n., Slang.* **soft soap; flattery**
                                                   2. *v.t., Slang.* **soft-soap; flatter**
                                                   3. *v.i., Slang.* **talk one's way out**

flapjack, *n.*   1. SEE COMMENT
                                                              2. **lady's flat compact**
1. Type of cookie. *Flapjack* does not mean 'pancake' in Britain.

flash, *adj., Slang.*   **flashy**

flat, *n.*   1. **apartment**
                                                                    2. **fool**
1. A *block of flats* is an *apartment house*. See **block; apartment.**
2. *Slang.* A *foolish person*, especially a *dupe*. An old-fashioned usage.

flat, *adj.*   **dead**
Describing batteries that have come to the end of their useful lives.

flat out   **at full speed**
   Inf. Flat out to a Briton suggests a race, particularly a horse race, with the winner (by
a nose) going *all out,* using every ounce of power. In Britain, it does not have the sense
of 'plainly' or 'directly,' as in (American) *I told him flat-out what I thought of him.*

flat spin. See **in a flat spin.**

fleck, *n.*   **lint**
   Inf. The odds and ends that cling annoyingly to dark woolen clothing; also called
flick. Fluff is the usual term in Britain. See also **lint.**

fleet, *n., adj.*   **1. creek**
                                                                                   2. shallow
   Heard in the countryside.

Fleet Street   **the press**
   Inf. See **Throgmorton Street, Wardour Street,** and other street names used symbolically, or should one say metonymically, or better, synecdochically, to indicate various
businesses and professions. However, as to *Fleet Street,* see the following letter carried
in *The Times* (London) of September 29, 1986:

   Streets ahead
   From Mr Martin Knapp
      Sir, Now that the editorial offices
   and presses of so many newspapers
   have a new location, how long will
   "Fleet Street" remain as a synonym
   for the Press?

   What, if anything, will take its
   place?
   Yours sincerely,
   MARTIN KNAPP
   1 Brooking Barn.
   Ashprington.
   Totnes. Devon.

The headline **Streets ahead** is a pun contributed by *The Times.* See **street, 1.** A few days
later, on October 3, two letters appeared in *The Times,* under the same paronomastic
headline:

   From Mr C.W. Pratley
      Sir, Let "Fleet Street" continue...
   "Whitehall" still serves
   without confusion, though
   most Government offices are else-
   where.
   Yours etc.
   CLIVE PRATLEY.
   The Old Chapel.
   Aldfield.
   Nr Ripon, North Yorkshire.
   September 29.

   From Mr N. Leverton
   Sir, Flight Street?
   Yours sincerely.
   N. LEVERTON
   66 Teignmouth Road. NW2.
   September 30.

As to Mr Pratley's letter, see **Whitehall** and **nr;** as to the omission of the period after
Mr and *nr* see **Appendix I.D.6.**

Finally (*The Times*, October 9) we read:

> **Streets ahead**
> *From Mr P.E.L. Fellowes*
> Sir, "Fleet Street" may become an
> anachronism, but "Grub Street" will
> live forever.
> Yours faithfully.
> PEREGRINE FELLOWES.
> The Court.
> Chipping Campden, Gloucestershire.

Grub Street is the former name of a London Street, changed to *Milton Street* in 1830. Samuel Johnson described it as "Much inhabited by writers of small histories, dictionaries, and temporary poems; whence any mean production is called *grubstreet*." The term is now used metaphorically for starving writers, literary hacks and their output.

flex, *n.*   **electric cord; extension**
Abbreviation of *flexible,* used as a noun.

flexible (table) lamp   **gooseneck lamp**

flextime, *n.*   SEE COMMENT
A system whereunder the employee worked a fixed number of hours but at times partly as the worker chose.

flick. See fleck; fluff.

flick-knife, *n.*   **switch-blade**

flicks, *n. pl.*   **movies**
Slang. Old-fashioned. See **film.**

flies, *n. pl.*   **fly**
The *fly* of a man's trousers is commonly *flies* in Britain. To American ears, a strange use of the plural.

flimsy, *n.*   **thin copy paper**
Inf. Particularly the type favored by Her Majesty's ministries. The word can also mean a carbon copy of something typed on such paper.

flipping, *adj., adv.*   **darn**
Slang. More or less equivalent to **bloody** but more polite. Pejorative and intensive. See synonyms under **bloody.**

flit, *v.i.*   **move**
Inf. To change residence. (See also **moonlight flit.**) *Flit* by itself is mainly Scottish.

float, *n.*   **petty cash fund**

flog, *v.t.*   1. *Slang.* **push**
                                                                     2. **sell illegally**
                                                                3. *Slang.* **lick (vanquish)**
                                                                     4. *Slang.* **swipe**
1. *Slang.* In Britain *flog* describes the hard sell, whether the insistent effort to *dispose of goods* or to *press an idea.*
2. *Slang.* Applies to stolen or smuggled goods *flogged* on the black market, for example. See also **fallen off the back of a lorry.**

3. *Slang.* To *flog* one's competitors, whether in sports or competitive examinations, is to *trounce* them, to *beat them all hollow*.
4. *Slang.* To borrow without the owner's permission, with only the vaguest intention of returning.

flog it   **plod**
Military slang. To *flog it* is to *walk* or *plod*. See also **foot-slog**.

floor, *v.t.*   SEE COMMENT
Inf. When a British schoolboy stands up to recite and isn't prepared, the teacher (**master**) *floors* him, i.e., tells him to sit down. *Floor* shares the general American colloquial meaning 'overcome' or 'shatter' someone with a devastating riposte.

Floral Dance. See **furry dance.**

florin, n.   SEE COMMENT
Two shillings. See **Appendix II.A.**

fluff, *n.*   **lint**
A *bit of fluff* is British slang for *chick* in the sense of *gal.* A *bit of fluff* is not really pejorative; it implies perhaps a wee bit of overdressing or might refer to the relative youth of the female companion of an older man, but no real harm is meant by it. See **fleck; bit of; lint.**

fluff, *v.t., v.i.*   1. *Slang.* **juggle**
                                                                                2. **lie; bluff**
1. *Slang.* As in, *fluff the books* (accounts).
2. *Slang.* As in, *Don't take him seriously; he's fluffing.*

flutter, *n., v.i.*   **gamble**
A *flutter* is a *bet.*

fly, *adj.*   **sharp**
Slang. With rather unpleasant connotations of craftiness: a bit on the dishonest side. The current American term *street-wise* is a close equivalent.

fly a kite, *Inf.*   *Inf.* **send up a trial balloon**

fly on the wall   **invisible onlooker**
Inf. When someone says he'd give anything to be a *fly on the wall*, he means that he'd love to witness a meeting, confrontation, etc. unobserved. There are occasions, it seems, when almost anyone would like to be a voyeur (in the non-sexual sense, of course). *Mouse in the corner* is one American equivalent.

fly-over, *n.*   **overpass**

fly-post, *v.i.*   SEE COMMENT
To put up notices (rapidly and surreptitiously) on unauthorized walls. Sign on Tottenham Court Road (London): FLY-POSTERS PROHIBITED. Cf. STICK NO BILLS (**stick** 4).

fobbed off (with)   *Slang.* **stuck (with)**
Slang. Both countries use *fob off* in the sense of palming off inferior merchandise, but only the British use the past passive participle this way to indicate the resulting situation of the victim.

fob pocket   **watch pocket**
Tailor's term.

fogged, *adj., Slang.*   **befuddled**

foggiest, *adj.*   *Inf.* **faintest**
Inf. Usually met with in the negative expression *I haven't the foggiest,* meaning 'I haven't the slightest (idea)'. In this expression, *foggiest* is used as a substantive, like *slightest* or *faintest* when the modified noun (*idea* or *notion*) is omitted.

Follow?, *v.i.*   **See?**
Usually in the question *Do you follow?* meaning 'Do you see?' or 'Are you with me?'

folly, *n.*   **whimsical structure**
A peculiar, nonfunctional structure built for no apparent reason other than the whim of an estate owner with too much leisure and money and lots of whimsy (some people simply *have* to have a project going); usually found on 18th-century English estates. The subject, with illustrations, is covered in a section of *Odd Aspects of England,* by Garry Hogg (Arco Publishing Co., Inc., New York, 1969), and an entire book is devoted to it in *Monumental Follies, An Exposition on the Eccentric Edifices of Britain* (British Book Centre, Inc., New York, 1973).

fool, *n.*   SEE COMMENT
A dessert. Blanch, mash, and strain berries or other fruit, mix with custard or cream and serve cold. *Gooseberry fool* is the most common of these desserts, and has nothing whatever to do with **gooseberry** in its slang sense of *fifth wheel* or *chaperon.*

football, *n.*   **soccer**
As the name of a game, *football,* in Britain, is short for *association football,* the game that Americans call *soccer.* This is the game, which, in Britain and increasingly in America, attracts audiences that fill those incredibly large stadiums. The nearest equivalent in Britain to American football is the game called *Rugby football,* or simply *Rugby,* but most commonly called *rugger.* This game is played in uniforms like the ones used in *soccer,* without helmets, padding, nose guards, etc., and how a game of rugger is completed without multiple injuries and even deaths is a great mystery. Rugby is the name of a very old **public school.** A kind friend who, like his forefathers, is a Rugby **old boy,** has offered the following comment:

> Do you know why a rugger ball, British or American [sic], is oval? Because the original ball was based on a pig's bladder. Have a look at the next pig you see and you will find its bladder oval. The original manufacturer of rugger balls, Gilbert, confirms this and it was so in my father's day at the home of the Rugby game, 1880-83. There is a plaque on the school wall to William Webb Ellis, commemorating his exploit of October 23, 1823, who with a fine disregard for the rules of football as played in his time first took the ball in his arms and ran with it, thus originating the distinctive feature of the Rugby game.
> The plaque was up when I was there (1916–20) and is no doubt still there. Father and I went to the Centenary of the October 23, 1823, match when England and Ireland played Scotland and Wales. Quite a match in the lovely original setting, but I do not propose to go to the 400th anniversary of the foundation of Rugby in 1567 by a London grocer...

footer, *n.*   **soccer**
Schoolboy slang. See **football.**

footpath. See **footway.**

footplate, *n.*   **engineer's and fireman's platform**
Railroading. The engineer (**engine-driver,** in Britain) and fireman are known collectively as *footplatemen.* Loosely used to designate the whole locomotive cab.

foot-slog, *v.i.*   **trudge**
Slang. A *foot-slogger* is a hiker; the word sometimes means 'infantryman'. See also **flog it.**

footway, *n.*   **sidewalk**
An old-fashioned term, still seen on street signs threatening pedestrians with fines if they permit their dogs to "foul the *footway.*" Also *footpath.* In the countryside, where there aren't any sidewalks, both words refer to any path for walkers. **Pavement** is the common British term.

(the) forces, *n. pl.*   **(the) service**
In the sense of the *armed forces.* A Briton would speak of 'leaving the forces.' An American would more likely say something like 'When I got out of the army (navy, marines, air force),' specifying the branch.

forecourt, *n.*   **front yard**
Applied to a service station, *forecourt* means the 'area where gas **(petrol)** is pumped.' Thus one sees help-wanted ads for a *forecourt attendant,* i.e., somebody to man the gas pumps.

Foreign Office   *approx.* **State Department**
Now called the Foreign and Commonwealth Office (FCO).

forged, *adj.*   **counterfeit**
The British speak of a forged **note,** the Americans of a *counterfeit* bill.

for it   *Inf.* **in for it**
Inf. In deep trouble. *Oh, he's for it now!* See also **for the high jump.**

fork supper   **casserole meal**
Inf. This term is applied to a meal that can be eaten without a knife. *Fork lunch* is also used. Roughly speaking, the American equivalent of *fork* in this context might be thought to be *buffet,* as in a well-planned *buffet lunch* or *buffet dinner,* at which a knife is not needed. A *fork meal* in Britain is definitely one in which a knife is superfluous. For the converse of this situation, see **knife-and-fork tea.**

form, *n.*   **1. grade**
                                                                                             2. class
1. A school usage. Used in America, but rarely.
2. As in, *He was punished for laughing in form.*

form-master. See **master.**

for nuts. See **toffee.**

for the high jump   *Slang.* **in for it**
Slang. A grim echo of a hanging (the *high jump*) and nothing to do with a track meet. The phrase is now used to refer to any threatened punishment.

for the matter of that   **for that matter**
The American form is used in Britain as well.

fortnight, *n.*   **two weeks**
This is a common word in Britain, somewhat archaic or formal in America. *Today fortnight, Monday fortnight,* etc., mean 'two weeks from today, two weeks from Monday,' etc. *Week* is used in the same way in Britain: *today week, Friday week,* etc. *This day fortnight* (or *week*) is still heard, too. *I'd rather keep him a week than a fortnight* is a quaint, if mildly callous, way of saying, *He's a big eater.* See also **Appendix I.D.5.**

for toffee. See **toffee.**

forward, *v.t.*   **ship**
Ship and *shipment* are not used in Britain of transportation by land or air, but are confined to sea consignments. In land and air freight, *forward,* and sometimes *consign,* are the terms used. See also **freight; goods.**

fossick, *v.i.*   *Slang.* **mess around**
   Slang. With no very clear goal. To *fossick after* something is to *rummage about* for it.
The word derives from an Australian term for those who picked over abandoned gold
workings. In some British dialects *fussock* means 'bustle about,' and that may be reflected
here as well. See also **frig about.**

found, all (*or* **fully.**) See **fully found.**

foundation, *n.*   **founding**
   The Briths use *foundation* in the sense of the establishing of an institution, where
Americans would use *founding*. Usually, but not necessarily, the British term carries the
connotation of financial endowment in addition to merely getting something started.

foundation member   **charter member**

foundation-stone, *n.*   **cornerstone**

fourball, *n.*   **foursome**
   Golf term. When the British say *foursome*, they mean a 'Scotch foursome,' a two ball
match, in which the partners on each side take alternate strokes at their one ball.

four honours   **100 honors**
   A term used in bridge, meaning any four of the top five cards in the trump suit. *Five
honours*, as you might expect, means 150 honors.

fourpenny one   *Slang.* **sock on the jaw**
   Slang. Sometimes a **tuppenny one.**

four star   **premium**
   Designation of gasoline (**petrol**) octane rating. *Two star* is *regular*. *Four star* and *two
star* are the only grades obtainable at gas pumps these days (1986). A higher rating, *five
star*, and an intermediate *three star* were formerly available.

four up. See **make the four up.**

Four Wents   **Four Corners**
   This is not a general term meaning 'intersection' but a very common place name in
the British countryside. The *Four Wents*, or the *Four Went Ways*, is always a place name
designating a specific intersection. The *Four Corners* is a classic bucolic general term
rather than a specific place name in the American countryside. The *Went* in the British
expression is derived from the word *wend*, in the sense of 'turn' or 'direct.'

fowl, *n.* See under **chicken.**

fowl-run, *n.* See under **chicken.**

F.P. See **old boy.**

fraffly   SEE COMMENT
   From Alistair Morrison's *Fraffly Well Spoken*. See **Appendix I.B.1.**

fraternity *n.*   **religious organization**
   Never has the sense of 'male college society' (*frat*), an institution unknown in Britain.

frazzled, *adj.*   *Inf.* **roasted**
   Slang. Applied to a person who has tarried too long in the sun, on a beach, for
instance. It can also be applied to an overdone hamburger or anything overcooked.

Fred Karno's Army   *approx. Inf.* **Coxey's Army**
   Inf. Fred Karno was a **music-hall** (*vaudeville*) comedian during World War I and did
an act involving a joke army. Jacob Sechler Coxey was a U.S. political reformer who
led a civilian march on Washington in 1894 to petition Congress for unemployment

relief. (He died in 1951 at the age of 97.) Old-fashioned Americans still use the phrase *Coxey's Army* to describe any motley throng. Among old-fashioned Britons, *Fred Karno's Army* is a term usually applied to any sort of chaotic organization. In 1913, Fred Karno came to New York with "A Night in an English Music Hall," accompanied by a small troupe which included newcomers Charlie Chaplin and Stan Laurel.

Free Church. See **Chapel.**

feefone, *n.*   **tollfree number**
You dial the operator, give her the number, and the connection is free of charge.

freehold, *n.*   *approx.* **title**
This term, as opposed to *leasehold*, means 'title to real estate,' whether outright or for life. It implies *ownership* as opposed to *tenancy*. A person enjoying such ownership is a *freeholder*. In 1430, Parliament limited the right to vote in the election of Members of Parliament to *forty-shilling freedholders*, i.e., those owning real property whose rental value was at least forty shillings per annum. Forty shillings was a respectable sum in those days, so that this law effectively disfranchised "almost everyone below the small gentry, and the result of a diminished county electorate was to increase the power of the great nobles over Parliament." (Trevelyan, *Illustrated History of England*, Chapter VIII, Longman, Green & Co. Ltd., London, 1926—dedicated, incidentally, to President Abbott Lawrence Lowell of Harvard University.) The Reform Bill of 1832 abolished this limitation. Today, of course, every British subject has the vote, except **peers**, lunatics, and other special categories.

free house   SEE COMMENT
Most pubs are tied in with a particular brewery, at least in the beer and ale department, serving only that brewery's brand. The brewery owns the premises and leases the pub to the operator, who is known as the **landlord** (though he is, legally speaking, the tenant), or **publican**. The pub has its own historic name (White Swan, Queen's Head, Eight Bells, etc.) and a standing or hanging decorative pub sign, sometimes beautifully painted and occasionally ancient, but the effect is somehow a little marred by the appearance of another sign, attached to the building, of the name of the brewery, which has the effect of depersonalizing the management. A *free house* is a pub not affiliated with a brewery. They are few and far between, and serve whatever brands of ale and beer they choose. All other pubs are **tied houses**. See **tied; pub.**

free issue of new shares   ·   **stock dividend**

free line   **line**
You ask your switchboard operator (**telephonist**) for a *free line* when you want to dial the number yourself. In both countries, you may request a *line*.

free of   **entitled to the use of**
To make someone *free of* something is to give him the right to use it. A person *free of* a company or a city is one entitled to share in the privileges of membership in the company or citizenship in the community. To make someone *free of* your house, car, library, etc. is to allow him the free use of it, to make free of it. *His wife is free of more money than he will ever earn* indicates that she has at her disposal a lavish income compared to his earning capacity.

free-range eggs   **eggs from uncooped hens**
As opposed to battery eggs. This usage is increasingly common in the U.S.

freight, *n.*   **cargo**
In Britain, *freight*, by itself, is applied to transportation by water or air, though railroads use the terms *freight rates*, *freight sheds*, etc. In America the term is applied to transportation by land or by air, and *cargo* is the marine term. See also **forward; goods.**

French, gin and. See **martini.**

French beans   string beans

French toast   fried bread
A particularly delicious morsel, simple enough to concoct, but never met with in America, where the term refers to bread soaked in a mixture of eggs and milk, fried, and eaten with syrup or molasses or sprinkled with cinnamon and sugar. *Fried bread* is also heard in Britain. All you do is fry it in butter. Try it!

fresh butter   sweet butter

fresher, *n.*   *approx.* **freshman**
Slang. A British university term and a little more restricted than *freshman*. *Freshman* applies to the entire first year; *fresher* normally covers only the first term. *Freshman* (despite its second syllable) and *fresher* apply to both sexes. Some universities have their own special terms. At the University of Aberdeen in Scotland, for example, a first year male student is a *bajan* and his opposite female number is a *bajanella*, from *béjaune*, French for 'greenhorn.'

fret, *n.*   *Slang.* **tizzy**
Inf. People, when agitated, *fret* in both countries. The word is used as a noun in Britain in the expression *in a fret* in situations where Americans would be apt to use *in a tizzy*.

fridge, *n.*   refrigerator
Inf. Also spelled *frig* and *frige*, but always pronounced *fridge*. The universal term in Britain for *refrigerator* or *icebox*. Even the young children in America who have never seen an old-fashioned affair of the sort that actually used ice use *icebox*.

friendly, *n.*   *approx. Inf.* **exhibition game**
Inf. Adjective used as a substantive; *match* understood. It means a game (usually **football** or **cricket**, but it can be applied to any sport)—even one between two **first-class** teams—the result of which is not reflected in any official record and has no effect on championships. Like exhibition baseball games, except that they are not confined to preseason contests and can happen at any time when the boys decide to get together.

friendly action   action for a declaratory judgment
A legal term, meaning a lawsuit brought to get a point decided, rather than for money damages or other relief.

friendly society   mutual insurance group
A common and extremely useful type of organization, even in an advanced welfare society. Its members are pledged to provide assistance to one another in old age, in illness, and in similar situations.

Friendship Town. See **twin with...**

frig about   *Slang.* **mess around**
Slang. The British use *frig* also in the sense common in America. The above permissible usage is unknown in America. See also **fossick.**

frightfully, *adv.*   *Inf.* awfully; very, very
Inf. A **Mayfair** word, but it hangs on tenaciously, and not only among the genteel.

frillies, *n. pl.*   *Inf.* **undies**
Inf. Going out of fashion—the word, that is.

frilling *n.*   ruching

fringe, *n.*   bangs
Coiffeur term.

fringe bank   SEE COMMENT
A *fringe bank* is a small deposit-taking institution, a bank or other organization licensed to accept deposits (for example, a leasing company) but lacking a bank charter. Some of them were so badly hurt in the 1974 real estate collapse that the **Bank** forced mergers or liquidations and set up financing for some of them, in a **lifeboat** operation.

Fringe Theatre. See under **West End.**

frock, *n.*   **dress**
The everyday word in Britain for a *woman's dress* among older people. Common among people of all ages for little girls' dresses. Note that misbehaving clergymen get themselves *unfrocked*, while misbehaving ladies get themselves *undressed*.

frock-coat, *n.*   **Prince Albert**

from the off   **from the word go**
Somewhat old-fashioned, but still used, though jocularly at times.

front, *n.*   **seaside promenade**
Referring to seaside places, and also called *sea front*. A *front* or *sea front* is like an American *boardwalk*, except that the walking surface is not made of wood. People in Britain do not talk about going to the *beach* or *shore*; they go to the *sea-side*. When you get to a British sea-side town, to find the ocean follow the signs reading FRONT.

front bench   SEE COMMENT
Describes the benches in the House of Commons and the House of Lords occupied by **ministers** (*cabinet members*) and other members of the government and members of the opposition **shadow** cabinet. Those who occupy them are *front-benchers*. See also **back bench.**

frontier, *n.*   **border**
The word means *border between nations* in both countries, but in Britain it does not have the special meaning of that part of the country which forms the outer limit of its populated area. In view of Britain's history, it is understandable that the connotation, having had no application for so long a period, would now be lost. But both countries use the term symbolically, as when John F. Kennedy spoke of the New Frontier.

frost, *n.*   *Slang.* **bust**
Slang. If an American went to a party that he would later describe as a *bust* (or a *dud*), his English counterpart would have characterized it as a *frost*.

frosted food   **frozen food**
Sign in Harrods, the great department store (**departmental store**) in Knightsbridge, London: FROSTED FOODS. A refrigerator salesman (**shop assistant** in a **fridge shop**) would point with pride to a large *frosted foods compartment*, which Americans would call a *freezer*.

frowsty, *adj.*   **musty**
Inf. Frowst is a British colloquialism meaning the 'fusty stale heat in a room.' As an intransitive verb, to *frowst* means to 'stay in and enjoy frowst,' i.e., to like it stuffy, or to put it another way, to be the opposite of a fresh air fiend. From this colloquial word we get *frowsty*, which describes the way the unfortunate room smells. *Frowsty* is related to the adjective *frowzy*, also spelled *frouzy* in America, which means 'close,' in the sense of 'musty,' 'fusty,' and 'smelly,' and by association 'dingy.' But nowadays in either country it is most commonly used in the sense of 'unkempt' and evokes the image of a slatternly woman with her hair in disarray. See also **fug.**

frowzy. See **frowsty.**

fruiterer, *n.*   **fruit seller**
The *fruiterer's* is a *fruit store*. Not to be confused with *fruiter*, which covers *fruit-bearing tree, fruit-ship,* and *fruit-grower*. See also **costermonger; greengrocer's.**

fruit machine   *Slang.* **slot machine**
Slang. A one-armed bandit. What you get out of a **slot machine** in Britain is neither exhilaration nor despair: simply merchandise—because that is what they call *vending machines* there.

fruity, *adj. Slang.*   *Slang.* **spicy; sexy**

fry-up, *n.*   *approx.* **fry**
Slang. A *fry* in America is any fried dish, or more generally a social function involving the eating of a fried dish (e.g., *fish-fry*; cf. *clambake*). A *fry-up* is what Dylan Thomas's widow called the result of his late night excursions into the kitchen, where he would throw together and fry a concoction of kippers, eggs, potatoes, and anything else lying around.

F.T.I.   SEE COMMENT
These initials stand for *Financial Times Index* of thirty leading industrial common stocks; analagous to the Dow Jones Index in America.

fubsy, *adj.*   **fat and squat**

fug, *n.*   **1. stuffiness (room)**
                                                      2. fluff (dust ball)
Inf. In addition to these two quite distinct meanings as a noun, *fug* sometimes appears as a verb. To *fug* is to like to have it stuffy, in a room, a car, or any other enclosure, and in this sense is synonymous with **frowst**. See **frowsty**.

(in) full fig, *Slang.*   *Slang.* **all decked out; (in) full regalia**

full marks   **full approval**
Inf. I give him full marks for that! or *Full marks to him!* expresses the appreciation of a performance beyond criticism.

full out   **full time**
In both countries *full out* can also indicate maximum speed, *full throttle*.

(a) full plate. See **have enough on one's plate.**

full stop   **period**
The British never use *period* for the dot at the end of a sentence, though they generally understand this Americans usage. Americans avoid *stop* except in dictating telegram and cable messages. *Full stop* is peculiarly British except that Americans do sometimes use it when reading printed proof aloud. In view of the inclusion of this entry, this old English schoolboy riddle shouldn't be too difficult: "If the B m t put: If it b."

full bookable. See **book.**

fully found   **all expenses paid**
Salary £15, fully found means that you get £15 per week, and all expenses, like transportation, board and lodging, and so on. *All found* is also used.

funeral furnisher   **undertaker**
Americans have their euphemisms too, e.g., *mortician*.

funky, *adj.*   *Slang.* **chicken**
Slang. This word comes from *funk (n., v.t., v.i., Slang* in Britain and *Informal* in America), which, however, is used much more commonly in Britain than in America. The noun has one meaning in Britain which it does not have in America: 'coward.' *You're a funk* would be *you're chicken* in America. The adjective *funky* is not commonly used in America in this sense, nor is the slang term *funk-hole* (literally, *trench dugout* of World

War I fame) which figuratively describes a job that gets you out of military service, or in other words a *draft dodger's dodge*. A *blue funk* is an American expression meaning 'in the dumps,' i.e., a *depression*.

funniosity, *n.*
A jocular term for anything that makes one laugh.

fun of the fair. See **all the fun of the fair.**

furnishings, soft. See **soft furnishings.**

furry dance
An ancient ritualistic folk dance similar to the **morris dance**, seen these days only at Helston in Cornwall on certain days of the year; also called the **Floral Dance**, and pronounced as though it rhymed with HURRY (U as in BUT).

fuss, *v.t., Inf.*   faze

fuzz. See **in a fuzz.**

G

gadzookery. See **Wardour Street.**

gaff, *n.*   *Slang,* **honky-tonk**
   Slang. Sometimes *penny gaff.* An entirely different British use is seen in the slang expression *blow the gaff,* which means 'spill the beans.' An American slang use is found in *stand the gaff,* where *gaff* means 'strain' or 'rough treatment.' None of these *gaffs* has anything to do with *gaffe,* from the French, meaning *faux pas.*

gaffer, *n.*   1. *Slang.* **old duffer**
                                                                                        2. boss
   1. *Inf.* With the implication of the countryside, and humorously affectionate rather than in any sense pejorative.
   2. *Inf.* When used by a gang of unskilled laborers, *the gaffer* means the 'mean in charge,' the 'boss' of the gang, the 'foreman,' and, if anything, is mildly pejorative, without the slightest trace of humor or affection. But the expression *good gaffer* has been used to describe a *good boss.* And *gaffer* is sometimes used as schoolboy slang for 'headmaster,' a special kind of boss. In the U.S., he is the senior electrician on a film unit.

gain on swings, lose on roundabouts   *Inf.* **you win some, you lose some**
   Inf. Or, *gain on roundabouts, lose on swings.* The *roundabouts* in question are *merry-go-rounds* (see **roundabout, 2.**) and the expression is taken from the playground scene. It expresses resignation to the approximate effect that *you can't win 'em all;* there are pros and cons to most of life's decisions. Perhaps *six of one and a half a dozen of the other.*

gall, *n.*   **rancor**
   In Britain *gall* (apart from its medical implications) is also slang for *impudence* or *effrontery,* as it is in America.

gallon, *n.* See **Appendix II.C.2.a.**

gallop, *n.*   **bridle trail**
   TRESPASSING ON THESE GALLOPS FORBIDDEN; sign seen on a southern *down.* See **downs.**

gallows, *n. pl.*   **boom crutch**
   Inf. A nautical colloquialism, plural in form but usually treated as singular.

galoshes, *n. pl.*   **rubbers**
   In America *galoshes* are *overshoes,* waterproof boots that are worn over shoes and reach to about the ankle. They would be called *snowboots* in Britain, though *galoshes* is sometimes used by Britons in the American sense. See also **Wellingtons; boot; gumboots; snowboots.**

game, *n.*   **kind of thing**
   Inf. Game is much used in Britain in a variety of phrases and a variety of ways. A man says to his much-divorced friend who is contemplating another plunge, *I should think you'd have enough of that game! A mug's game* (see **mug**) is *something for the birds,* an activity that only a fool would engage in. *I wonder what her game is* means *I wonder what she's up to* i.e., *what's her angle? Play the game* means 'do the right thing.' *On the game* means 'living as a prostitute.' *She's on the game* means 'She's a whore.' See also **Stuff that for a game of soldiers!**

game, *v.i.*   **gamble**
Americans speak jocularly of the *gaming table*, but rarely if ever use the verb *game*.
The verb is not commonly used but it still heard in Britain.

gammon, *n.*   **ham**
Not only good to eat, but much celebrated in British letters. We all know about *The
Love-Sick Frog*, who "...would a-wooing go...whether his mother would let him or no."

> With a rowley, powley, gammon and spinach,
> Heigh ho! says Anthony Rowley.

The poem goes on and on, involving a rat, a mouse, a cat and her kittens, and the
lily-white duck who did Froggy in, and

> So there was an end of one, two, three,
> Heigh ho! says Rowley,
> The rat, the mouse and the little frog-ee.
> With a rowley, powley, gammon and spinach,
> Heigh ho! says Anthony Rowley.

Our good friend *gammon* appears in the refrain of every one of the fourteen verses. And
then, years later, we come to *David Copperfield*, and we hear Miss Mowcher exclaim with a
sigh, "What a world of gammon and spinnage it is, though, ain't it it!" So we'd better know
what *gammon* is, shouldn't we? But...see next entry for slang uses.

gammon, *n., v.t., v.i.*   **humbug**
Slang. Nonsense intended to deceive. The verb, used intransitively, means to 'engage
in talking humbug'; transitively, to *gammon* someone is to *pull his leg, put him on*. Slang
of a bygone day. But see **humbug**, which has nothing to do with any of this.

gammy, *adj.*   **lame; game**
Slang. Usually in the expression *gammy leg*, meaning 'game leg.' An arm can be *gammy*
as well, but this is not a common usage.

gamp, *n.*   *Inf.* **bumbershoot**
Inf. A big one, named after Sarah Gamp, in *Martin Chuzzlewit*, a bibulous lady who
carried a large cotton umbrella. The common slang term in Britain is **brolly**.

gang. See **breakdown gang; navvy.**

ganger, *n.*   **gang foreman**
In charge of a gang of workers. Often applies to foremen in charge of men working
on the railroad.

gangway, *n.*   **aisle**
In theaters, ships, stores and in the House of Commons. See also **aisle** for especially
British sense of the word.

garden *n.*   *approx.* **yard**
Garden is used, in its literal sense, the same way in both countries. But the British
use *garden* to refer to one's property outside his house, the way Americans use *yard*.
Those fairies at the bottom of Beatrice Lillie's garden are, in American prose, simply
fairies at the end of her property. Also, the British often use *garden* as a synonym for
lawn; How nice your garden looks! is said of your *lawn* even when there isn't a single
flower showing.

garibaldi, *n.*   **currant cookie**
Inf. The popular name of this hard rectangular cookie (**biscuit**) is *squashed fly* (jocular,
if just the least bit unappetizing). The old **public school** name for them was *fly cemeteries*.
Legend hath it that Garibaldi (1807–1882) was intensely popular in England, and was

feted everywhere, including the venerable McVitie bakery. McVitie had devised a new product, the current cookie in question, which was to be launched on the very day of Garibaldi's visit. They therefore named it in his honor. The *garibaldi*, otherwise, used to be the name for a sort of loose blouse worn in the mid 1800s by women and children in imitation of the garb worn by Garibaldi's soldiers.

Garibaldi lived for a while in exile in Uruguay. In the capital, Montevideo, he raised an Italian Legion to help his hosts in their war with Argentina. The market suddenly became flooded with red woolen shirts. The grateful government of Uruguay bought them up at a very low price and presented them to the Italian patriot and freedom fighter. Thus the Garibaldi 'redshirts' were born.

garneting, *n.*   *approx.* pebbling
A type of architectural decoration common in the Hamsphire-Surrey region of England. It consists of inserting pebbles (usually a very dark garnet-colored iron oxide) about an inch apart in the mortar around stones in the wall of a building, giving the mortar a checkboard appearance. In Mayan and Aztec ruins in Mexico, this device has become an archeological convention for the marking of restored parts.

gash, *n., adj.*   1. *n.* **waste; garbage**
                                                               2. *adj.* **superfluous; extra**
                                                               3. *adj.* **free**
Slang. Originally nautical slang; a shortening of *gashion.*

gashion. See **gash.**

gasper, *n.*   *Slang.* **butt (cigarette)**
Slang. Now generally outmoded. The current slang term is **fag.**

gate, *v.t.*   **confine to quarters**
Inf. That is, to punish by confinement. To be *gated* is to be *confined to college* (see **college**) during certain hours, or in some cases entirely, for a certain period, varying with the severity of the offense committed. The principal aspect of the punishment is the interruption of one's evening social life. The term is derived from the symbolic shutting of the precinct gate against the offender. The term applied originally to Oxford and Cambridge only, but was extended to other universities and now to **public schools**, where the punishment consists of the student's being deprived, for a limited period, of the privilege of leaving the school grounds and going into town. The practice is waning in universities and the term now applies mainly to public schools.

gaudy, *n.*   SEE COMMENT
Oxford college alumni dinner and celebration. From *gaudium*, Latin for 'joy' (and *gaudeo*, 'rejoice,' whence *Gaudeamus igitur, juvenes dum sumus*). The incomparable Dorothy Sayers wrote a novel entitled *Gaudy Night* involving just such a celebration. Literally, *gaudy* means any feast, but it is usually understood in the narrower sense. The dinners themselves are normally anything but gaudy.

Gawdelpus, *n.*   *Slang.* **pain in the ass**
Slang. An exasperating person; intentional mispronunciation of *God-help-us.* Synonymous with **Gawdf'bid,** which was originally Cockney rhyming slang (see **Appendix III.G.3.**) for *kid*, i.e., *child,* the kind known as a *little terror.*

Gawdf'bid. See **Gawdelpus.**

gazette, *v.t.*   SEE COMMENT
There are three official journals for the publication of official notices in the United Kingdom: the *Belfast Gazette, Edinburgh Gazette,* and *London Gazette.* They come out twice a week with official public notices of such things as government appointments, bankruptcies, etc. To *gazette* something is to have it published in one of these publications.

gazump, *v.t.*   *Inf.* **jack up**
   Slang. A nasty word. The accent is on the second syllable. To *jack up* the price of a
piece of real estate after the asking price has actually been met, just before the contract
is signed. This current usage to describe such unworthy methods appeared first in the
spelling *gazoomph,* and was derived from the more general meaning of the term *gazumph*
(*gezumph*) which covers the various kinds of swindling that go on at dishonest auctions.
As recently as April 10, 1973, the Court of Appeal refused to countenance this practice.
Lord Justice Buckley said that the seller's "attempt to evade obligations in which he
had entered to sell Dingleberry Cottage...were deplorable," and ordered him to fulfill
his oral understanding with the buyer, despite Section 40 of the Law of Property Act,
1925, requiring a written note or memo of the contract, signed by the seller, in the case
of real property.

G.C.E.   SEE COMMENT
   Stands for *General Certificate of Education.* See under **A-levels.**

G.C. See **V.C.**

gear, *adj.*   *Slang.* **cool**
   Slang. A teenage term, synonymous with **fab** and with **kinky** as used by youngsters.
Not much heard any more.

gearbox, *n.*   **transmission**
   Automotive term. See also **Appendix II.E.**

gearing, *n.*   **leverage**

gear-lever, *n.*   **gearshift**
   See also **Appendix II.E.**

gee, *n.*   *Inf.* **horsie**
   Inf. Gee! and *gee-up!* are used in both countries to urge a horse on. In Britain *gee-ho!,*
and *gee-wo!* are heard, too, and *gee-gee* was originated by children as a juvenile colloquialism equivalent to *horsie. The gee-gees* is used jocularly in the way the Americans
say *the ponies,* i.e., *the horses,* as in the expression *play the ponies.*

gefuffle. See **kerfuffle.**

gen, *n.*   *Slang.* **inside dope**
   Slang. (Pronounced JEN.) *Gen* is short for *general information,* and like so many slang
expressions, started in the armed forces. *Duff gen* means 'bum dope,' 'misleading information.' See **gen up; duff; griff.**

general election   **countrywide election**
   The election of members of the House of Commons (Members of Parliament, usually
shortened to *M.P.s*) throughout the country. This must take place at least every five
years but can be brought on sooner by the resignation of the Prime Minister and his
(or her) Government, normally as the result of a defeat in the House of Commons,
whereupon there would be a dissolution of the incumbent Government. Technically,
the monarch may at any time dissolve Parliament, but for 150 years this right has been
exercised only upon the official advice of the Prime Minister, and it doesn't look as
though that were going to change. See also **go to the country.**

general meeting. See **Annual General Meeting.**

general post   *approx.* **circulation**
   A mass changing of places, as at a party where the guests are just sitting around.
The hostess suggests (or orders, as some hostesses will) a *General Post!* meaning that
the guests should start moving around, circulating. Appears to be derived from the
children's game of Post Office, which involved complex rules determining who kissed
whom. Under *general post* everybody kissed everybody.

General Post Office. See **G.P.O.**

general servant   **maid of all work**
Sometimes informally shortened to *general.*

gentle, *n.*   **maggot**
As used for fishing bait.

gentry, *n. pl.*   SEE COMMENT
The class just below the nobility. See **landed,** 3.

gen up   **1.** *Inf.* **fill in**
                                                                    2. *Slang.* **bone up**
1. *Slang.* To *fill (someone) in,* in the sense of 'putting (him) in the know.'
2. *Slang.* To *acquire the necessary information* about someone or something before taking
a step. See also **gen.**

geography of the house   **location of the john**
    Inf. A considerate host in an expansive mood may ask a guest, under appropriate
circumstances, *"Do you know the geography of the house?"* A guest unfamiliar with the
layout might elicit the same information through the use of the same euphemism. Cf.
have a wash, under **wash** and **wash up.** Said to be **non-U.** For a discussion of *non-U* see
Appendix I.C.6.

Geordie, *n., adj.*   SEE COMMENT
    Native of Tyneside. Also the dialect they speak in that part of northeastern England.
In Scotland especially, the term can be applied to any coal miner.

George, *n.*   **automatic airplane pilot**
    Slang. Believed by some to have been derived from the old saying *Let George do it.*

get. See **git.**

get across (someone)   *Inf.* get (someone) riled
                                                                                    up
    Inf. The British as well as the Americans also speak of *getting a person's goat.*

get a duck. See **duck, 1.**

get a rocket. See **rocket.**

get knotted!, *Slang.*   *Slang.* **stop bugging me!**

get much change out of   *Inf.* **get anywhere with**
    Inf. These expressions (in their respective countries) are almost always in the negative.
When a Briton says, "He didn't get much change out of me," he is saying, in the
American idiom, "He didn't get anywhere (or very far) with me." Like **wash** in *That
won't wash* or **wear** in *The boss won't wear that for a minute, get much change out of* is rarely
encountered in the affirmative.

get off   SEE COMMENT
    Slang. (No American equivalent without a long circumlocution). To make initial head-
way in the eternal struggle with a member of the opposite sex, stopping short, however,
of what grandmother used to call, with a shudder, "going the limit." Cf. **have it off,**
4, which includes the attainment of the limit.

get one's bowler. See **bowler-hatted.**

get one's cards. See **give (someone) his cards.**

get one's colours   SEE COMMENT
  Be made a member of a team, in sports. To *give (someone) his colours* is to include him or her in a team, usually as a permanent or regular member rather than as a temporary substitute.

get one's eye in   SEE COMMENT
  Inf. The **batsman** in **cricket** must initially 'feel out' his adversary, the **bowler**, before changing his stance from defensive to aggressive, and begin to make runs. This initial period is known as *getting his eye in* and is more fully explained under **play oneself in.**

get one's head down. See **put one's head down.**

get one's head in one's hand   *Slang.* **catch hell**
  Slang. In other words, to get your head chopped off and handed to you.

get one's skates on   *Inf.* **get going**
  Slang. To start moving, to hurry. It has a special meaning in the armed forces: to 'desert.'

get one's own back on   *Inf.* **get back on**
  Inf. That is, to *get even with*, to *avenge oneself.* Also, *get something back on.*

get on (someone's) wick   *Slang.* **bug (someone)**
  Slang. Or, to *get on someone's nerves.* (Not recommended in mixed company.)

get on with   **get along with**
  A different sense from that in which one *gets on with* one's work. It applies to human relations. Also not to be confused with **Get on with it!**

get on with it! *Inf.*   *Inf.* **get going!**

get-out, *n.*   *Inf.* **out**
  Inf. In the sense of an *avenue of escape*, one's *way out* of a jam.

get out of it!   *Slang.* **come on!**
  Slang. Meaning *'quit your kidding!'* Synonymous with **give over!**

get stuck in   *Inf.* **get going**
  Slang. To *get stuck in again* means to 'resume an interrupted task.' Thus, plotting our next year's vacation together, a friend writes: *I can get stuck in again when the new year's schedules are to hand. Get stuck in!* or *get stuck into it!* means 'get going!' or 'quit stalling!' when spectators are exhorting their team who appear to have slowed up.

get stuffed. See **stuff.**

get the better of   **get the best of**
  You *get the better of (triumph over)* somebody in Britain but the Americans use the superlative. Lest you think that Americans always resort to superlatives, the reverse is true in the following sense: an American says, *I'd better leave now*, while his British friend will sometimes say, *I'd best leave now*, especially if he's the lit'ry type and given to recherché-isms.

get the bird. See **give (someone) his cards.**

get the chop, *Slang.*   1. *Slang.* **be bumped off (get killed)**
                                              2. *Slang.* **get the gate (be fired)**

get the push. See **push.**

get the stick   *Slang.* **catch hell**
Slang. When a person has been severely criticized, the British say he *got the stick, got a lot of stick* or *got a bit of stick.* Derived, presumably, from the custom (happily dying) of caning schoolchildren for misbehavior. One hears *take the stick* as well.

get the wind up   *Inf.* **be jumpy**
Inf. In a situation where an American is nervous about something, the Briton *gets the wind up* about it. To *have the wind up* is to be 'scared' rather than merely 'nervous.' To *put the wind up* somebody is to 'scare him.' Strangely enough, to *raise the wind* is to *raise the money. Windy*, by itself, means 'nervous' or 'jumpy.'

getting on for   **well nigh**
Inf. Thus: *Getting on for thirty years before, Elsie had married into the peerage.* Or, *It's getting on for one o'clock.*

get upsides with   *Inf.* **get even with**
Inf. To *turn the tables* on someone, or to *avenge oneself.*

get up (someone's) nose, *Slang.*   *Slang.* **get in (someone's) hair**

get weaving, *Inf.*   *Inf.* **get going**

get your knickers in a twist. See **knickers.**

geyser, *n.*   **water heater**
Geyser is a geological term in both countries denoting a hot spring which shoots up a column of steaming water at fixed intervals. The most famous of these is Old Faithful in Yellowstone National Park. But to a Briton the primary meaning of *geyser* is 'water heater,' and the word evokes the image of a smallish white cylindrical tank with a swiveling faucet underneath, located on the wall next to the kitchen sink or in the bathroom. To an American coming across a British *geyser* for the first time, the apparatus looks precarious. However, it is a dependable gadget, and many of them have been working well for so long a time that they, too, deserve the adjectives *old* and *faithful.* In this specialized meaning, the word is pronounced as though spelled GEEZER. See also **immersion tank.** In a column in the August 16, 1973, issue of *The Times* (London) headed "How an old geyser fell on hard times," Bernard Levin tells the story of his mother's *geyser* "of ancient design and dilapidated condition" and her long-unavailing efforts to obtain its conversion from electricity to gas. In the article he tells a joke: "Mornin' lady: 'ave you got an old geyser 'ere what won't work?" "Yes, 'e's just gone down to the Labour Exchange to draw the **dole.**" Mr. Levin vigorously disclaimed the authorship of this chestnut in a kind letter to the author. Incidentally, his efforts on his mother's behalf were swiftly rewarded with success after August 16, 1973. In his *Diaries 1923-1925* (Faber & Faber, London, 1985) Siegfried Sassoon describes someone at a tea party as "silly old *geyser.*" An American would have written "geezer."

ghastly show. See **bad show!**

giddy fit, *Inf.*   **dizzy spell**

giddy-go-round, *n.*   **merry-go-round**
More commonly **roundabout.** See also **carousel.**

gig-lamps, *n., pl.*   *Inf.* **specs**
Slang. Meaning 'eyeglasses.' *Pebble gig-lamps* are thick ones, *pebble* in this sense being old English for 'natural rock crystal.'

gill, *n.*   **1. ravine; torrent**
                                                                              2. See Appendix II.C.2.b.
1. The *g* is hard. Usually a *deep ravine* and wooded. When it means *torrent*, it refers to a *narrow mountain torrent.*

gilts   **government bonds**
See also **shares**.

gin and French; gin and It. See **martini**.

gin and Jaguar belt   **expensive suburb**
Inf. Of London; synonymous with **stockbroker belt**.

ginger, *n.*   **homosexual**
Slang. Rhyming slang (see **Appendix II.G.3**). Short for *ginger beer*, which rhymes with
queer.

ginger biscuit, also **ginger-nut,** *n.*   **gingersnap**

ginger group   *Inf.* **young Turks**
Inf. Any activist group that thinks its own political party or organization is moving
too slowly and wants to push it forward or to move ahead on its own.

ginger-up, *n., Inf.*   *Inf.* **pep talk**
Inf. Without the hyphen, to **ginger up** means 'give a pep talk to.'

gin-stop, *n., Inf.*   *Inf.* **gin mill**

gippo, *n., Slang.*   **army stew**

gippy tummy   **diarrhea**
Slang. Also spelled *gippie, gyppy, gyppie. Gippy* was common British slang for an Egyp-
tian soldier or cigarette. *Gippy tummy* describes what happens to travelers visiting trop-
ical countries.

girdle, *n.*   **griddle**
A variant heard in the north.

Girl Guide   **Girl Scout**
Boy Scouts are Boy Scouts in both countries, but *Girl Scouts* become *Girl Guides* in
Britain.

Giro, *n.*   SEE COMMENT
A system of credit transfer between banks, widely used by the **G.P.O.** (*Post Office*).
From *giro*, Italian for (*inter alia*) *circulation*.

git, *n.*   *Slang,* **jerk**
Slang. Occasionally *get*, and often coupled with a deprecatory adjective, as in *you silly
git...!* Synonyms: **poon; swob; twit; jobbernowl; juggins; muggins**.

give (someone *or* **something) a miss**   1. *Inf.* **pass (something) up**
                                                        2. *Inf.* **do without (someone)**
Inf. One *gives a miss* to a play that has had bad notices or a restaurant where one's
friends have had a poor experience. One might do the same thing in the case of the
fifth wedding of a dear pal: here Americans might say, *I'll sit this one out!* But to *give
someone (or something) a miss* doesn't necessarily imply distaste. One can have seen the
Tower of London once too often and decide this time to *give it a miss*, despite past
happy experiences there. Or, if you've borrowed too often from your friend Tim and
have lost again at poker, while you are wondering where to get it this time, you might
reflect, *This time I'll give Tim a miss*.

give (someone) a shout   *Inf.* **sing out**
Inf. A Briton will promise to *give you a shout* when he is ready, where an American
would promise to *sing out* or *let you know*.

give (someone) best   *Inf.* **bow to (someone)**
Inf. To *give* somebody *best* is to *admit his superiority*, and in that sense to *bow to him.*

give (someone) fits, *Slang.*
                                                      Slang. **cream (someone)**

give (someone) gyp (gip; gyp), *Slang.*
                                                      Slang. **hurts (someone) like hell**

give (someone) his cards   *Slang.* **give (someone) his pink slip** or
                                                 the gate or **his walking papers**
Slang. To *fire (someone)*. Synonyms: **give (someone) the bird;** *give (someone) the chop,*
which can have the far more sinister meaning of 'bump off' (see **get the chop**). Conversely, to *get one's cards, the bird,* or *the chop* is to *be fired* (unless *chop* is being used in
the more drastic sense). One can also be said, somewhat wryly, to *collect one's cards.* To
ask for one's cards is to *give up one's job,* to *resign.*

give (someone) his colours. See **get one's colours.**

give (someone) in charge   **turn (someone) in**
To *turn a person over to the police.* See also **charge-sheet.**

give in part exchange   **trade in; turn in**
In Britain you *give* your old car, television set, or vacuum cleaner *in part exchange*
when you buy a new one, in the same way in which you *trade it in* in America.

give (someone) out   **call (someone) out**
A cricket term. The American term is not used.
The *someone* in the cricket term is the player who is (in the American term) called out
by the umpire after an appeal (see **howzat!**) by the other side. *Give* is thus used in
cricket where *call* would be used in baseball. In an article entitled "Conversations with
Wilfred Rhodes" (a legendary cricketer) by Humphrey Brook in the August 7, 1980 issue
of the English magazine *Country Life,* we read about another all-time great, W.G. Grace
(a name in cricket history known to every English schoolboy—Babe Ruth might be his
American opposite number), whom the umpire called out on a technicality. (Rhodes
was bowling to Grace—see **bowler 2.**) "He [Grace] didn't like the decision," said Rhodes,
"and stood his ground. 'I've given you out and you were out,' said the umpire. That
settled it." This expression appears also in a letter to *The Times* (London) dated July 12,
1934, reprinted in its issue of September 28, 1983. Before reading it, please look up **six**
and **wicket** (def. 1). The score book entry term *c.* stands for *caught; b.,* for *bowled* (see
bowler def. 2). The letter, headed 'Caught Fish,' tells of "a strange incident in far Sohar
[a seaport town in Oman], where we were wont to peg down a mat on the seashore
and play cricket as an antidote for nostalgia. The last wicket stand on a memorable
afternoon was troublesome indeed, for the temperature was 110 deg., maybe more...
At last a ball was hit for six into the sea; but it fell not into the sea, for it was swallowed
by a shark. I...*gave* the man '*out.*' 'c. Fish, b. Birkat Ullah' was duly entered in the score
book by a soldier clerk. I am, sir, your obedient servant, R. TOWNSHEND STEPHENS."
See also **dismiss.**

give over!   **come on!**
Slang. Synonymous with **get out of it!** Can also mean 'stop it!'

give (someone) some stick   *Slang.* **give (someone) hell**
Slang. A severe dressing down.

give (someone) the bird   *Slang.* **give (someone) the gate**
Slang. See synonyms under **give someone his cards.**

Give Way   **Yield**
Road sign in Britain, meaning 'Yield right of way.' In many parts of America there
are road signs to the same effect, reading YIELD in large letters, sometimes followed by
RIGHT OF WAY in smaller letters.

glass, *n.*   **crystal**
Referring to watches and clocks. The term *crystal* is used in Britain, too, but only in
the trade.

glass fibre   **fiberglass**

glasshouse, *n.*   **1. greenhouse**
                                                                        2. stockade
                                                                        3. lock-up
1. The standard meaning.
2. *Military slang. Army prison.* The naval equivalent in both countries is *brig.*
3. The term has been extended to mean any sort of detention center, such as those
proposed for the confinement and treatment of young offenders. Headline in *The Times*
(London) of August 10, 1977: "Tories plan 'glasshouses' for young delinquents."

glasspaper, *n.*   **sandpaper**

Glaswegian, *n., adj.*   SEE COMMENT
Of Glasgow. An illogical echoing of *Galwegian, Norwegian,* etc.

G.L.C.   SEE COMMENT
Stands for *Greater London Council,* the administrative body that governed Greater
London before it was abolished in 1985. See also **council.**

glove-box, glove-locker, *n.* See **cubby.**

G.M.T.   **Greenwich Mean Time**

go, *n.*   **turn; try**
If you are caught dozing on your feet during a slow game of croquet on a British
lawn when your turn comes around, your adversary will most likely politely notify you,
It's your go. If a child is demonstrating his new bicycle to his little British friend, the
friend will, after a certain interval, ask anxiously, *May I have a go?* In America, he would
ask if he might *try* it. *Go* is used in Britain also in the sense of 'taking a shot' at
something, like a stuck window or something in your eye. When used in America,
always accompanied by *at it: Have another go at it. Have a go!* is sometimes used by
policemen as an exhortation to the pubilc to try and stop thieves, etc.

go, *v.t.*   **bid**
Inf. Bridge term. *We went two, partner* means 'we bid two.' Same as **call.**

go a mucker. See **mucker.**

goat, n.   **fool**
Slang. To act the *goat* or to play the *goat,* or the *giddy goat,* is to play the *fool.*

gob, *n.*   *Slang.* **trap**
Slang. Mouth; thus; *Shut your gob!*

gob, *v.i.*   **spit**
Slang. Extremely vulgar; only from the mouths (the word as well as the expectoration)
of louts.

gobstopper, *n.*   SEE COMMENT
A large hard long-lasting sucking candy, so big that it **stops** (*fills*) one's **gob.**

God-bothering, *n., adj.*
Slang. There's an old Yiddish story about the terribly pious man who complained bitterly to the Archangel Michael that his neighbor, an utter rascal, had been admitted into heaven while he, who had prayed twelve times a day, was refused. Michael's explanation: "You nagged him." A *God-botherer* is a *parson* and a *God-pesterer* a *bishop* (R.A.F. slang). A better reply from the Archangel might have been: *You pestered him.* What he actually said was: *You noojied him,* because Michael was (what else?) Jewish.

go down. See **come down.**

godown, *n.*   **warehouse**
Used in Asia, especially India.

gods, *n.*   *Inf.*(peanut) heaven; peanut gallery
Inf. The *gallery* of a theater, the part nearest heaven. (Cf. *le paradis* in France).

go for six   **get smashed**
Slang. Describes the accidental destruction of breakable ornaments around the house, like porcelain objets d'art, as the result of careless dusting or rampaging kiddies or large tail-wagging doggies. See **six;** cf. **gone for a burton.**

goggle-box, *n.*   *Slang.* **boob tube; idiot box**
Slang. In both countries affectionately perjorative terms have been invented for the TV. Now usually shortened to *the box.*

going spare   *Slang.* **on the loose**
Slang. Referring to girls who are available, easy to get. But see **go spare.**

golden duck. See **duck, 1.**

golden handshake   **dismissal with bonus**
Inf. Applies to executives let go with a generous severance allowance. The Americans give this colorful phrase an entirely different meaning. Jack Anderson, in the *New York Post* of December 18, 1972 had this to say:

> Those multi-million dollar cost overruns are often approved in advance with a "golden handshake" in the back room of the Pentagon. Explains [*sic*] our sources: A defense contractor will sign a contract, with a secret understanding that the Pentagon will bail him out if his costs exceed the stipulated figure, and then shake hands on the deal. This is known within military-industrial circles as the "golden handshake."

golden-knop *n.*   **ladybug**
The more common British name for this insect is *ladybird.*

golden syrup   *approx.* **corn syrup**
Lyle's Golden Syrup is a trademark; but *golden syrup* is used generically and is something like American *corn syrup.*

goloshes. See **galoshes.**

go missing, *Inf.*   **disappear**

go nap on. See **nap.**

gone, *v.i.*   *approx.* **become; turned**
Used in expressions of time, like *It had gone four o'clock by the time Frank arrived.* Americans would say *It was after four when Frank arrived.* More generally, in expressions other than those of time, the American equivalent would be *turned,* for example, in an expression of this sort: *The Dead Sea Scrolls had gone all black.* See also **just going.**

gone for a burton *Slang.* **finished; killed**
Slang. Originally Royal Air Force slang perhaps referring to Burton ale, describing the men who failed to return from the mission. Now applied to less serious situations, like a broken glass. See **go for six.**

gongs, *n. pl.* *Slang.* **hardware**
Slang. Humorous service terms for *medals*; jocular, affectionate military slang, with the accent on understatement and self-deprecation. The *gongs*, usually in miniature form, are worn with military evening dress on festive occasions at places like the Naval and Military Club. *Ribbons* are *fruit salad* in American slang.

gony, *n.* *Slang.* **dope**
Slang. In the sense of 'dunce.' Also in the forms *goney* (rhymes with BONNY) and *gawney* (rhymes with BRAWNY).

good innings **long life; good spell**
Inf. One who has had a *good innings* (**innings** is singular in Britain and simply means 'inning') has had a *good long life*, or a *good spell* of something, like a term of office.

good in parts **good and bad**
For origin see **curate's egg.**

good job *Inf.* **good thing**
Inf. As in *Good job it didn't rain during the picnic.*

good party? *Inf.* **how'd it go?**
Slang. Asked of someone returning from a mission.

goods, *n. pl.* **freight**
A railroad term. A *goods-waggon* is a *freight car.* See also **covered goods-waggon; freight; forward.**

good show! *Inf.* *Inf.* **nice work!**

good value *Inf.* **good stuff**
Inf. Thus: *That lad is very good value.*

go off, *Inf.* **get tired of**

go off the boil **quiet down**
Inf. Said, for instance, of an official inquiry that starts off like a house afire but turns out to be only a nine-day wonder.

goolies, *n. pl.* *Slang.* **balls**
Slang. Also spelled *ghoulies*, and very low usage.

gooseberry, *n.* *approx. Inf.* **fifth wheel**
Inf. The superfluous third party who sticks like glue to the (un)happy couple who are aching to be alone. To *play gooseberry* is to *act as chaperon.* All this has nothing to do with *gooseberry*, the fruit, or *gooseberry fool*, the dessert discussed under **fool.**

goosegog, *n.* **gooseberry**
Inf. A common jocular corruption of *gooseberry* the fruit (not of **gooseberry** in its colloquial sense); in some families, the only name for it used by children until they grow up to learn the real name. *Goosegog* is sometimes used metaphorically in a phrase like *goosegog eyes* (watery eyes, that remind one of gooseberries).

go racing **go to the races**

gormless, *adj. Inf.* *Slang.* **dumb (stupid)**

gorse, *n.*   **furze**
 A common yellow-flowering shrub which grows wild on open waste lands over much
of Europe.

go spare, *Slang.*   1. *Slang.* **get sore (angry)**
                                                            2. go beserk
                                                            3. be baffled
                                                    4. *Slang.* **go AWOL**
 But see **going spare**; and see **send (someone) spare.**

Go to bath! *Slang.*   *Slang.* **Go to hell!**

Go to bed! *Slang.*   *Slang.* **Shut up!**
 See synonyms under **buzz off.**

go to ground   *Inf.* **lie low**
 Inf. Hide out; from fox hunting, when the poor pursued beast takes to its earth or lair.

go to the bad, *Inf.*   *Inf.* **go to the dogs**

go to the country   **have a general election**
 This is a political idiom. General elections (for **Members** of Parliament) are held every
five years. The Government, however, can resort to a general election short of that time
in order to test public opinion, usually in case of a crisis, and must do so if it loses its
majority in the **Commons.** To hold such an election is to *go to the country*, a procedure
sometimes informally known as a *snap election*, an expression which implies undue
opportunism on the part of the Government.

goulash, *n.*   *Slang.* **goulies**
 Slang. Bridge term: dealing the next hand without shuffling, so as to produce extraordinary hands.

go up   **1. enter university**
                                                    2. be promoted
1. *Inf.* College term.
2. *Inf.* Secondary school term.

government, *n.*   **administration**
 The British talk about the *Thatcher government*, the Americans about the *Carter administration*. Each phrase refers to the people ruling the country at the moment.

governor, *n.*   **1. warden**
                                                    2. *Slang.* boss; mister; dad
1. Head man at a prison.
2. *Slang.* A British worker might speak of his *boss* as his *governor*. He would address
him that way but would always pronounce it GUV'NOR, and that is the way it would
appear in the dialogue of a novel. A cab driver might well address his passenger in
Britain as *guv'nor* and that would be equivalent to the American familiarity *doc*, or *mister*.
As a form of address, however, *guv'nor* seems to be going out of fashion in favor of *sir*,
although one still hears *guv* in London. Old-fashioned Britons still use *guv'nor* in the
sense of *dad*, and the **publican** or **landlord** of a **pub** is sometimes referred to or addressed as 'guv'nor,' often pronounced *guv'na*.

gownsman. See **town and gown.**

G.P.O.   SEE COMMENT
 Stands for *General Post Office*, which handles not only the mail but also the telephone
service, telegrams, old age pension payments, as well as maintaining savings accounts,
and a credit transfer system known as **Giro.** Nothing to do with **general post.**

grace and favour   SEE COMMENT
  Describing a residence occupied rent-free by permission of the royal family, like a cottage within the area of Kensington Palace grounds, or the residence of the person in charge of the **race-course** at Ascot, which was established by the sovereign in 1711. Sometimes hyphenated, and note the *u* in *favour* (see **Appendix I.E.**).

gradient, *n.*   **grade (hill)**
  Gradient can mean 'grade' or 'slope' in America, too, but it is not as commonly used. *Gradient* would be the more common term in Britain as, for instance, in an automobile instruction book advising which gear to use when starting up a hill.

graduate, *n.*   **college graduate**
  In America a *graduate* can refer to a person who has completed the course at any school, whether elementary school, high school, or college. Used alone, *graduate* in Britain means one who has graduated from university, or what Americans would call a *college graduate*. See also **university man.**

graft, *v.i. Slang.*   **knock oneself out**

grammar school. See under **eleven plus.**

gramophone, *n.*   **phonograph**

granary bread   SEE COMMENT
  A delicious dark bread. They remove most of the roughage, refine some of it, and put the refined part and some of the unrefined part back into the dough. Different from **whole meal**, where they take nothing out of the grain but refine the whole of it.

granny waggon, *Slang.*   *Slang.* **jalopy**

grasp the nettle, *Inf.*   *Inf.* **take the bull by the horns**

grass, *v.i.*   *Slang.* **squeal (inform)**
  Slang. This word is derived from Cockney rhyming slang (see **Appendix II.G.3.**) *grasshopper,* meaning 'copper,' i.e., *policeman. Grass* sometimes appears as a noun, meaning both 'informer' or 'stool pigeon' and the 'act of informing' itself. It has shown up in the new form *supergrass,* describing an I.R.A. member who turns *queen's evidence* (see **king's (queen's) evidence**) and names his former comrades to the police in exchange for immunity. The Northern Ireland security forces have caught and imprisoned an impressive number of terrorists as the result of evidence supplied by *supergrasses.*

gratuity, *n.*   SEE COMMENT
  Government bonus to war veterans; a special British usage, in addition to meanings shared with America.

grease-proof paper   *approx.* **waxed paper**
  Not quite the same but generally serving the same functions. The British variety comes not in rolls but in sheets, is more nearly opaque, heavier, and stiffer, and it crackles.

greasy, *adj.*   **slippery**
  Slippery generally, not only because of the presence of grease. A wet road or a lawn tennis court after a sudden shower would be described as *greasy.* The same distinction exists in the figurative sense; be just as careful of dealing with a *greasy* Briton as with a *slippery* American. Americans also use *oily* in the same uncomplimentary sense.

Great Bear   **Big Dipper**
  Other British names for the *Big Dipper: Charles's Wain,* the *Plough.*

Greats, *n. pl.*   SEE COMMENT
  Inf. Oxford classics finals. *Greats* refer to the course of study as well as to the exams, and the course includes philosophy in addition to classical literature and history. See also **moderations; responsions; smalls.**

Great War   **World War I**
Not heard much any more. Britons now often call it the *'14-'18 war*. Younger people,
to whom it is now more or less ancient history, chiefly say 'World War I' or 'First World
War.'

green belt   *approx.* **no-building zone**
The *green belt* is the area around a British municipality which is kept green, i.e., where
building and development are not allowed, lest the overpopulated little isle develop
into one megalopolis.

green card   SEE COMMENT
Insurance card covering motorists against accidents in foreign countries.

green fingers, *Inf.*   *Inf.* **green thumb**

greengrocer's, *n.*   **vegetable store**
See also **fruiterer; costermonger.**

Green Paper. See under **Paper.**

green pound   SEE COMMENT
A unit of value applicable to British transactions in connection with the Common
Agricultural Policy of the European Economic Community, commonly known as the
Common Market. This pound has a higher value, vis-à-vis the currencies of the other
Common Market members, than the free-floating pound sterling, since it has not been
devalued in line with sterling. The use of the *green pound* makes food imports from
Common Market countries cheaper for the British consumer, and conversely, British
food exports to those countries harder to sell.

greens, spring. See **spring greens.**

Gretna Green   SEE COMMENT
The name of a small village in Dumfriesshire, Scotland, near the border with England,
where runaway young couples from England could be married according to Scottish
law by a simple declaration before witnesses, made to a **landlord,** toll-keeper, blacksmith, etc. When the blacksmith officiated, the couple were said to be 'married over
the anvil.' In 1856, a law was enacted which impeded impulsive couples by requiring
residence in Scotland of one of the parties for a minimum of 21 days before the ceremony. In 1940, marriage by declaration was abolished by Scottish law, but the place
still attracts young couples because minors may marry there without parental consent.
The Standard (London) of August 10, 1981, contained the following report:

> **Popping**
> **in**
> THERE'S no disputing the pulling power of marriage. One of the Gretna Green
> establishments that dispensed matrimony to fugitive English couples until the un-
> romantic Marriage (Scotland) Act of 1939 put an end to it is now up for sale. It
> includes the traditional blacksmith's shop, an hotel and a motel and the owners
> want £625,000 for it.
>   Records show that an innkeeper there married 1134 couples in 30 years. None
> is married there now but 100,000 tourists a year, inexplicably, still seek out the
> place.

greycing, *n.*   **greyhound racing**
Inf. A **portmanteau word:** *grey(hound + ra)cing.*

grid, *n.*   **map reference system**
The *National Grid*, a system of vertical and horizontal lines superimposed on the map
of the country, divides it into lettered squares with numbered subdivisions, providing
a reference system for all regional maps.

griff, *n.* *Slang*. **dope; info**
  Slang. Synonymous with **gen**: originally navy slang, and thought to be derived from *griffin* (meaning 'tip on the horses,' or, more generally, 'hint'), which became World War II slang for 'warning,' in the phrase *give the griffin*. Possible connection with *griff*, past tense of the German verb *greifen* (to 'grasp,') from which they get *begreifen* (to 'comprehend').

griffin. See **griff.**

grig, *n.* **small eel**
  The other meaning, 'grasshopper' or 'cricket,' and figuratively a 'lively person,' are American as well as British. *Merry* (or *happy*) *as a grig* is a common phrase equivalent to *gay and lively, bright and merry, happy as a lark.*

grill, *v.t.* **broil**
  A lady who asks her butcher in Britain for a *broiler* might get a chicken but might instead be referred to the **ironmonger** (*hardware store*). If she wants to be sure to get a chicken for broiling, she should ask for a *grilling-chicken*. See also **chicken.**

grills, *n. pl.* **steaks and chops**
  GRILLS (from *grill* meaning to 'broil') is a common British restaurant sign and is the equivalent of *steaks and chops*. This usage is found in both countries in the term *mixed grill*.

grind, *n.* 1. *Slang*. **drag**
2. *Slang*. **lay**
1. *Slang*. In the sense of a boring *task*, not *person*; usually in the expression *a bit of a grind*. *Grind*, in America, implies *tough going* (which is usually boring as well).
2. *Slang*. A crude word usually used pejcratively in the phrase *not much of a grind*, i.e., an unsatisfactory sexual partner.

grinder, *n.* **crammer**
  To *grind*, in the sense of 'study hard,' is common to both countries; also to *cram*, in the sense of 'preparing intensively for a particular examination.' But where Americans would describe as a *crammer* one who waits until the last moment to *bone up* (**mug** or *mug up* in Britain), the British call him a *grinder*, the American equivalent of which is not *grind*, because that describes (among other things) a student who continually works hard, exam, or no exam. See **crammer** for British use of the word.

grip, *n.* **narrow ditch**

grip, hair. See **hair grip.**

grip, Kirby. See **Kirby grip.**

griskin, *n.* **lean bacon**
  More particularly, the *lean part of the loin.*

grit, *n.* **fine gravel**
  A *gritting truck* or **lorry** is a *sanding truck*. GRIT FOR ICE, a roadside sign, calling attention to a supply of the stuff (usually contained in a barrel), offers sand to motorists in need of traction. *Gritting truck* or *lorry* is sometimes shortened to *gritter*.

grizzle, *v.i., Slang*. **whimper**

grockle, *n.* SEE COMMENT
  Slang. West Country pejorative for **tripper**, reflecting the local xenophobia.

grotty, *adj.* *approx. Slang*. **cruddy**
  Slang. A grotty little schoolboy pinched her **knickers**. *This is a grotty little restaurant—look at the stains on the table-cloths.* From *grotesque*. See also **ropy; tatty; tinpot; twopenny-halfpenny.**

ground, *n.*   **field**
A sports area: a cricket *ground*, a **football** *ground* (or **pitch**), etc. *Nevill Ground* in Tunbridge Wells would be called *Nevill Field* in America.

ground, spare. See **spare ground.**

ground floor. See **first floor.**

ground-nut, *n.*   **peanut**
Synonymous with **monkey-nut.**

group of companies   **conglomerate**
The term (*So-and-So*) *Group of Companies* (seen on signs, letterheads, etc.) indicates a *conglomerate*. American conglomerates usually retain the name of the corporation which bought up all the others. Sometimes the British term is shortened to (*So-and-so*) *Group*.

Grundyism. See under **wowser.**

guard, *n.*   **1. conductor; brakeman**
                                                                            2. stopper
1. A railroad term. *Conductor* is used in Britain to mean the official in charge of passengers on a bus.
2. Term used in contract bridge.

guard dog   **watchdog**

Guards, *n. pl.*   SEE COMMENT
Also known as *household troops* (comprising the regiments of Foot Guards, Horse Guards and Life Guards), part of whose duty is to attend the sovereign ceremonially. A member of any of these regiments is known as a *guardsman*. See **Life Guard.**

guardsman. See **Guards.**

guard's van   **caboose**
See under **brake-van.**

gubbins, *n. pl.*   **1. innards**
                                                                  2. *Slang.* thingamajigs
1. *Slang.* The *insides* of something: the *gubbins* of a car—all the bits and pieces mechanics have to get at.
2. *Slang.* Also used as a vague reference to any old junk, equivalent to *thingamagigs* or *whatchamacallits*.

guffy. See *jolly.*

guggle, *v.i.*   **gurgle**
The British use *gurgle*, too. *Guggle* appears to be pejorative, as applied to a person in a state of impotent rage or hysterics.

guide dog   **Seeing Eye dog**

guildhall, *n.*   **town hall; city hall**
The *Guildhall* in the **City** of London is what Americans would call the *City Hall* if London were an American city. In other municipalities, whether town or city, the British use the expression *town hall* rather than *city hall* to refer to the municipal office building.

guillotine, *n., v.t.*   **1. cloture**
                                                                   2. limit by cloture
1. *Inf.* Limitation of debate in Parliament by fixing the times at which specific parts of a bill must be voted on.
2. *Inf.* The act of thus limiting debate.

guinea, *n.*   SEE COMMENT
  One pound, one shilling. The *guinea* was originally a gold coin created for use in the African trade. It was theoretically pegged at twenty shillings (the same as the pound) but after a certain degree of fluctuation was fixed at twenty-one shillings. This happened relatively recently as British history goes (1717), and the *guinea* was last coined even more recently (1813). Thereafter, no longer the denomination of either a coin or a bill (**bank note** or **note** in Britain), it became simply a measure of money used in pricing certain goods and services. It appeared on price tags in shop windows and advertisements and on bills (**accounts,** in Britain) sent out by professional people like doctors, lawyers, and such. Stating a price in *guineas* instead of pounds was a convenient way to keep the numerals down and the prices up. Thus, twenty-one guineas was twenty-two pounds, one shilling (£22.1.0). The *guinea* became obsolete on February 1, 1971, when the British money system was decimalized, eliminating shillings altogether. Incidentally, before decimalization, lots of things in Britain were priced the way they are in America, one penny less than a round amount, to make them seem cheaper. For example, shoes priced at £9.19.11 (one penny less than £10.0.0), in the same way that they might be priced $29.95 in America. This has now become £9.99. See **Appendix II.A.** *The Guineas* is the familiar name of two of the five classic British horse races, all for three-year-olds, consisting of the *One Thousand Guineas* and the *Two Thousand Guineas*, both run at Newmarket in Suffolk each April. The other three are the Derby (pronounced DARBY), run at Epsom Downs in Surrey on the first Wednesday of June, the Oaks, also at Epsom the following Friday, and the St. Leger at Doncaster in Yorkshire each September.

(a) guinea to a gooseberry   *Inf.* **ten to one**
  Inf. Long odds.

gum, *n.*   **mucilage**
  If you want something to chew, ask for *chewing gum.*

gumboots, *n. pl.*   **rubber boots**
  See also **snowboots; wellingtons; boots; galoshes.**

gump, *n.*   *Slang.* **horse sense**
  Slang. Short for *gumption.*

gum tree. See **up a gum tree.**

gun, *n.*   **hunter**
  A *member of a shooting party* in Britain where they **shoot,** rather than *hunt,* game birds. See **shoot.**

gut, *n.*   **river bend**
  At Oxford and Cambridge, referring especially to bends in the boat-race course.

gutter-crawl, *v.i.*   **cruise for a pickup**
  Slang. **Crawl** is used by the British the way Americans use *cruise* to indicate the slow driving of a car. *Gutter-crawl* describes the nasty conduct of a motorist on the prowl for women foolish enough to accept his invitation to hop in. **Kerbside-crawl** is synonymous. (*Kerb* is spelled *curb* in America.)

guy, *n., v.t., v.i.*   1. *n., Slang.* **fright; sight**
                                                 2. *n., Slang,* **slip (vanishing act)**
                                                 3. *v.t.* **ridicule**
  1. *n., Slang.* As a noun it means a 'grotesquely dressed person' in such a weird getup that onlookers would call him a *fright,* a *sight,* a *scarecrow,* or something of that sort. Literally, a *guy* is a *scarecrow* of a special sort: a limp, shapeless bundle of rags often propped up against walls, wearing frightful masks and caps, surrounded by street-urchins begging *a penny* or *alms for the guy.* The word is derived from Guy Fawkes and his famous gunpowder plot to blow up King James I, the Prince of Wales, and all the

Members of Parliament on November 5, 1605. Like so many other historical events which occurred centuries ago, the gunpowder plot is very much alive in British memories as though it were part of last week's news. In 1826 handbills were passed out imprinted with the following doggerel:

> Please to remember the fifth of November
> Gunpowder treason and plot;
> We know no reason, why gunpowder treason
> Should ever be forgot!

There was a time when every inhabitant of the City of London (see **City**) received a notice on Lord Mayor's Day Eve reading as follows:

> Sir,
> By Virtue of a Precept from my Lord Mayor, in order to prevent any Tumults and Riots that may happen on the Fifth of November and the next ensuing Lord Mayor's Day, you are required to charge all your Servants and Lodgers, that they neither make nor cause to be made, any SQUIBS, SERPENTS, FIRE BALLOONS or other FIREWORKS, nor fire, fling nor throw them out of your House, shop or Warehouse, or in the Streets of this City, on the Penalties contained in an Act of Parliament made in the Tenth year of the late King William. Note. The Act was made perpetual, and is not expired, as some ignorantly suppose.

This occurs no longer and a word of caution must be added: the American usage of *guy* meaning 'fellow' is now common throughout Britain. For instance, in a recent advertisement for men's sportswear and under a picture of a very elegant, casually dressed young man, the copy included the sentence: "What more could a *guy* want?" This was, of course, the American use of *guy* and since it referred to a very elegantly attired person, *guy* in that sentence meant, of course, the exact opposite of a *grotesquely dressed person!* Yet as recently as the late 20s, G.K. Chesterton dined out on an anecdote about an American interviewer who characterized him as *a regular guy*, which at that time could have meant nothing other than a *really grotesque individual* to the general British public.
2. *n., v.t., vi., Slang.* In the British slang expression *give the guy* to someone, *guy* means 'slip' and to *do a guy* is to 'perform a vanishing act.' As an intransitive verb (*Slang*), to *guy* means to 'take it on the lam,' i.e., to 'decamp.'
3. *v.t., Slang.* As a transitive verb, to *guy* is to *exhibit in effigy* and by extension, to *make a monkey of,* i.e., to *ridicule.*

gymkhana, *n.*   **horse show**
   This peculiar word is occasionally used in America to mean a 'sports car meet.' Technically, it refers to any public sports field or sports meet. The word is derived from the Hindi *gendkhana,* meaning a 'racket court,' but somewhere along the line it was influenced by *gymnasium*—an understandable mongrelization. Its common meaning in Britain, however, and one little used in America, is 'horse show.' You can see signs all over Britain reading *Gymkhana,* followed by the name of a town or village, a date, and road directions; and if you follow the instructions on such a sign you will wind up attending, or even participating in, a local *horse show.*

gym shoes   **sneakers**
   See also **plimsolls.**

gym slip (gym tunic)   **gym suit**

gym vest   **T-shirt**
   Old-fashioned. *T-shirt* is far more common now. See also **singlet.**

gyp, *n.*   **college servant**
   This is a special term restricted to the universities of Cambridge and Durham. The same functionary is called a *skip* at Trinity College, Dublin, and a *scout* at Oxford.

gyp, gives me. See **gives me gyp.**

H

haar, *n.*   **sea mist**
   Cold sea fog on the east coast of England and Scotland.

haberdashery, *n.*   **notions store**
   In America a *haberdashery* is a men's outfitter. In Britain it is one of those shops,
getting harder and harder to find, that sell pins, needles, thread, tapes, and a little of
this and a little of that. Nowadays the term is used mainly to describe the merchandise
sold in such establishments, and, increasingly, in the haberdashery departments of
department stores. See also **draper's shop; fancy goods.**
   According to Lady Diana Cooper, as quoted by Bernard Levin in *The Times, haberdashery* "came from the cry of immigrant German pedlars [*sic*—the usual British spelling]
who, adorned Autolycus-like with trays of pins and ribbons, would shout their wares
to the passers-by in the form 'Ich habe das hier (I have it here).' " Levin adds: "Se non
è vero, è bellissima e immortale." ("If it isn't true, at least it's beautiful and immortal.")
Autolycus was a Greek astronomer and mathematician who flourished *circa* 310 B.C.
and wrote on subjects like the motion of points on a revolving sphere and the apparent
rising and setting of fixed stars. Apparently his drawings were adorned with designs
resembling trays of pins and ribbons, unless Mr. Levin has another explanation.

habit-shirt, *n.*   **corset cover**
   Corset covers must be very rare nowadays, because so few ladies wear corsets anymore.
A good many years ago, Mrs. Abbott Lawrence Lowell, the wife of the president of
Harvard College at the time, told the wife of a faculty member, in hushed tones, that
the British word for *corset cover* was *habit-shirt.*

had for a mug. See **mug, 1.**

haggis, *n.*   SEE COMMENT
   A popular English dish until the 18th century, now considered specially Scottish;
made of the heart, liver, and lungs of a sheep, minced and mixed with oatmeal, suet,
and seasoning, and then boiled in the sheep's stomach. In one dictionary after another
the definitions are strewn with *etc.'s: hearts, liver, etc., stomach of a sheep, etc.,* etc. This
sort of thing tends to make one suspicious. There are fierce partisans on both sides of
this particular *de gustibus* specialty.
   The Scottish poet Robert Burns was an enthusiast. In *We, the British* (Doubleday &
Co., Garden City, N.Y., 1983), Ivor Richard has this to say about Burns and *haggis:*

   The worship of Burns by Scots (including those who have never read him) is little
   short of adulation. I cannot imagine the English celebrating a Shakespeare Day the
   way the Scots celebrate Burns Night. Perhaps they should. I am never quite sure,
   however, whether the ceremonial eating of haggis on that occasion is a tribute to the
   fact that it is an excellent way of eating otherwise inedible offal or to the fact that
   Burns succeeded in writing a poem in its honour.
       Fair fa' your honest sonsie face,
       Great chieftain o' the puddin'-race!

hairdresser's, *n.*   **1. barber shop**
                                                                                               2. beauty parlor
   The British term is used for both types of establishment, but nowadays the British
male usually talks of going to the *barber;* the female, to the *hairdresser.*

hair grip   **hairpin; bobby pin**
   Also *hair-slide* and *Kirby grip.*

hair-slide, *n. pl.*   **bobby pin**
Also known in Britain as *Kirby grip* and *hair grip.*

half, *adv.*   **half past**
Inf. In expressions of time, e.g., *half twelve,* meaning 'half past twelve.' *Half eleven* means 'half past eleven.' The British use of *half,* in this connection, is nonstandard and confusing, and certainly not to be imitated. Note that *half after* is American, as is *quarter of,* which in Britain is always *quarter to.*

(a) half, *n.*   SEE COMMENT
A half pint on beer. Form of address to a **publican.** See also **(the) other half.**

(not) half. See **not half.**

half-and-half, *n.*   **ale and stout mixed**
But some **publicans** say it can mean 'mild and bitter' mixed, so that when a customer who is not a regular asks for one, it is wise to request a fuller description. There is a legend about a **publican,** in bed with his wife upstairs over the **pub,** long after closing time (see **during hours**), who, annoyed at drunken customers standing under his window shouting for more half-and-half, emptied his chamber pot on their heads, announcing, "There you are, mates—half mine and half hers."

half a tick, *Slang.*   **half a minute (right away)**

half-cock. See **at half-cock.**

half-crown. See under **crown.**

half-day, *n.*   SEE COMMENT
Day of the week on which shops close for the day at 1:00 P.M. See **early closing.**

half hunter. See under **hunter.**

halfpenny, *n.*   SEE COMMENT
The old one was discontinued on August 1, 1969, as a step in the decimalization of the British currency system. (See **Appendix II.A.**) It was then pronounced HAY'-PNY. The word is still used in its old pronunciation to describe things of contemptible worth, as are *twopenny, threepenny,* and *farthing.* A *halfpenny* or *halfpenny's worth* is what a halfpenny will buy; hence, a very small amount. The plural of *halfpenny* as it used to be pronounced was HAY'-PNS. One who was *three ha'pence short of a shilling* was *not all there.* A later *halfpenny* has also been discontinued. See **ha'p'orth.**

half-term, *n.*   SEE COMMENT
Brief **school** vacation. See under **term.**

half, the other. See **(the) other half.**

half-yearly, *adj., adv.*   **semiannual; semiannually**

hall, *n.*   **large public room**
In the context of country **gentry,** *hall* refers to the ample residence of a **landed** proprietor in Britain. In British universities a *hall* is a building for student living or teaching, and in British **colleges** a common *dining-room.* When it is equivalent to *passage* as used in America, it means only an 'entrance passage.' In its general sense, *hall* finds its equivalent in the British word **passage.** *Hall* is used in both countries in the names of concert halls, as in Carnegie Hall (New York) and Albert Hall (London).

hall of residence   dormitory
See under **dormitory.**

Halt, *v.i.*   **Stop**
The equivalent of an American *Stop* sign used to be and sometimes still is a British
road sign reading HALT, but STOP is now coming into general use. See **arterial road.**
Once in a while *Halt* appears coupled with a place name to indicate a railroad stop in
the middle of nowhere, but near the designated place.

hammer, *v.t.*   **declare insolvent**
Inf. And suspend from trading. An informal expression in financial circles, to describe
the suspension of a brokerage firm unable to meet its commitments. The verb is derived
from the London Stock Exchange practice of declaring a person or firm bankrupt with
three taps of a gavel or hammer on the rostrum.

hampton, *n.*   *Slang.* **prick**
Slang. The male member. Shortening of *Hampton Wick;* cockney rhyming slang. See
Appendix II.G.3. *Wick* is an archaic word meaning 'town' or 'district,' still found in
place names like *Hampton Wick, Warwick,* etc., and in the word *bailiwick,* the sphere of
operations of a bailie (a Scottish magistrate) or a bailiff (a sheriff's officer).

hand, *n.*   **handwriting**
As in *His hand is impossible to decipher; She writes a fine italic hand.*

hanger, *n.*   **hillside woods**
This special British meaning is used to describe a wooded area on the side of a steep
hill or mountain.

hanging matter   SEE COMMENT
Inf. Literally, a capital crime (and hanging was the penalty). Used after a negative,
usually in the expression *It's not a hanging matter,* meaning 'It's not all that serious.'

hang up one's hat   *Inf.* **settle down**
Inf. The context is matrimonial.

Hansard, *n.*   SEE COMMENT
The name of the official Parliamentary report (analogous to the *Congressional Record*)
initiated in 1774 by Luke Hansard (d. 1828) and published until 1889 by Messrs. Hansard; now by *Her Majesty's Stationery Office (HMSO).* To *Hansardize* (now archaic) was
to confront a Member of Parliament with previous statements inconsistent with his
most recent utterance.

ha'p'orth, *n.*   **trifle**
Inf. (Pronounced HAY'-P'TH.) Contraction of *halfpenny worth,* as much as one could
buy for a halfpenny in the old days (before August 1, 1969, when the old halfpenny
was demonetized). Cf. the old adage: *Don't spoil the ship for a ha'p'orth of tar,* i.e., 'Don't
be penny-wise and pound-foolish.' Also used occasionally as a term of endearment in
an expression like 'You daft *ha'p'orth!*' See also **halfpenny; Appendix II.A.**

happy as a sand-boy   *Inf.* **happy as a clam**
Inf. The words *at high tide* are often added, and always implied, in the American
version.

hard, *n.*   **1. firm beach**
                                                               2. sloping stone jetty
                                                                      3. hard labor
1. The sort one can drive on, as opposed to a soft or mushy one.
2. Across the sand of a beach, down to the water's edge.
3. *Slang.* In prison.

hardbake, *n.*   **almond taffy**

hard-baked, *adj.*   **hard-boiled**
The British use both terms interchangeably. Also, *hard-cooked.*

Hard cheese!   *Inf.* **Tough luck!**
Slang. Occasionally, *Hard cheddar!; hard lines!*

hard-cooked, *adj.*   **hard boiled**
Of eggs, not of people.

hard done by   *Inf.* **done dirt**
Inf. Ill-used.

Hard lines! See **Hard cheese!**

hare off, *Inf.*   *Slang.* **vamoose**

hare, put up the. See **put up the hare.**

hare, start a. See **start a hare.**

Harley Street   SEE COMMENT
Used synecdochically to describe the British medical profession at its most specialized
and expensive best. On this street the fashionable doctors flourish, while ordinary
mortals go along with the **National Health.**

Harrovian, *n., adj.*   SEE COMMENT
Of Harrow; a *Harrovian* is either an *inhabitant of Harrow* (the town where the famous
school is located) or a *member of Harrow,* the **public school** which takes its name from
the town, whether student or graduate (**old boy**). Its playing-fields, together with those
of Eton (a similarly outstanding school), are alleged to supply the future leaders of
Britain.

harrow, under the. See **under the harrow.**

Harry. . .   SEE COMMENT
This is a word used in conjunction with another word in slang expressions once
favored by the "with-it" element in chic society. Why *Harry?* The only answer obtainable
was, Why not? Could it be a corruption of *very?* The second word in the combination
is usually a corrupt form of a standard word. Thus: *Harry spaggers* is *spaghetti; Harry
champers* (see **champers**) is *champagne; Harry Roughers* is a *rough sea* and *Harry Flatters* a
calm (flat) sea. Harry Blissington is *quite marvelous, absolutely glorious.* As to the *-ers* in
champers, starkers, stark ravers and goodness knows how many others: this quaint bit
of philological zanyism seems to have started at Rugby, a **public school,** over a century
ago, then passed to Oxford along with one or more **old boys,** and thence into chic
young society along with one or more Oxford graduates. The standard word is cur-
rupted, usually truncated, and then inflicted with an *-ers. Pregnant* to *preg-* to *preggers*
and so on. On the whole, these concoctions seem to have a simpering sound and appear
to be well past their zenith.

Hatton Garden   **the diamond industry**
Inf. The name of the London street where most of the diamond merchants are located
is applied colloquially to designate the industry generally. A common British practice,
like *Fleet Street* for the press, *Wardour Street* for the film business, and others.

hat trick   **triple achievement**
Slang. This is cricket slang which originated as the description of the feat of taking
three wickets (i.e., getting three men of the opposing team out) with three successive
bowls (i.e., three successive balls bowled—Americans would say *pitched,* but the tech-
niques are quite different). It still means that, but the term has been extended not only
to any triple achievement in sports, but to the bringing off of any series of three suc-
cesses, like three company acquisitions or a lawyer's winning three cases in a row. The

derivation of *hat trick* has been explained as follows: In the old days, there was a distinction between gentlemen players and professionals. The gentlemen were the more proficient *batsmen;* the professionals handled the bowling. (See **bowler, 2.**) When (rarely enough!) a bowler took three wickets with three balls, the gentlemen passed the *hat* to reward him for the achievement. Another explanation—that the triumphant bowler was presented with a *hat,* a high hat, like those worn by cricketers in the old prints—appears to be apocryphal. Americans use *hat trick* only in (ice) hockey.

haulage contractor   **trucking company**

haulier, *n.*
(Pronounced HALL'-YER.)

haulm, also **halm,** *n.*
(Rhymes with HAWM.) A collective noun, meaning the 'stalks' or 'stems' of growing things generally, and especially thatching material. It can be used in a singular sense, too, meaning 'one stem' or 'stalk.'

have a bash at   *Slang.* **take a shot at**
Slang. To *have a bash at* something is to *give it a try.* Synonymous with **have a go at.** See **go.**

have a doss, *Slang.*   *Slang.* **get some shut-eye**

have a down on, *Inf.*   *Inf.* **be down on**

have a go at. See **have bash at.**

have an early night, *Inf.*   **go to bed early**

have a quid each way   *Inf.* **bet across the board**
Inf. At an American track, you can bet to win, place, or show, or any combination of the two, or all three. Betting on all three in America is called *betting across the board.* In American horse racing, to *place* means to 'come in second,' to *show* to 'come in third.' In British betting, *place* describes any of the first three to come in (or in a race with very few horses entered, either of the first two). At a track in Britain (incidentally, *track* is **course**), if you *have a quid each way* and your horse comes in, you win two bets: the odds on the winner, plus a proportion of those odds. In America if you *bet across the board* and have picked the winner, you win three bets, at descending odds, for win, place, and show, respectively. **Quid** is British slang for *pound,* but the *quid* in this phrase is used figuratively, the way Americans use *buck* in an expression like: *Some days it's hard to make a buck.*

have a read   **be reading**
Inf. To *have a read* connotes settling in a comfortable armchair, and the common expression is *have a good read,* i.e., be wholly absorbed in that activity. *The book is a good read* connotes that the book is substantial, entertaining and not too demanding—an emetic phrase now creeping into American reviewers' jargon.

have a rod in pickle for   *Inf.* **be laying for**
Inf. This is rather ominous stuff. *Pickle* usually evokes the image of cucumber preserved in brine, and there are many varieties in both size and flavor. But that is an extension of *pickle's* primary meaning in both countries, which is the flavored *brine* or *vinegar* in which the preserving is done. The *rod* in this phrase is the type of sparing of which spoils the child, and presumably one soaked in *pickle* would hurt more than an unpickled one. Since brine is a strong solution of salt, a rod thus treated would both inflict and rub salt into a wound in one quick, easy operation. There are those who say that this explanation of *pickle* is apocryphal, the brine being used merely to keep the rod supple, because inflicting an actual wound, even in a British **public school,** would be regarded as going too far. In any event, to *have a rod in pickle for* someone is to be *nursing a grudge and aching to punish him, and waiting to pounce on him at the first opportunity;* or to put it as Gilbert and Sullivan did, to *have him on your list.*

have a slate loose, *Slang.*   *Slang.* **have a screw loose**

have a time of it. See **rare time.**

have a word with   **speak to**
About a particular matter, with the object of accomplishing something. *I'll have a word with him* implies that the speaker is about to try to get something done about something, with a degree of assurance (whether justified or not) about the outcome.

have enough on one's plate   **have plenty to do**
Inf. Often in the expanded form *enough on one's plate as it is*. A *full plate* means the same thing. A form sometimes used is *a lot on one's plate*, which connotes the state of being busy rather than overworked.

have everything in the shop window. See **shop.**

have (someone's) guts for garters   *Inf.* **let (someone) have it**
Slang. To *given someone the works: If the boss hears about this, he'll have my guts for garters.*

(to) have had one's chips   *Inf.* **(to) have had it**
Slang. To *be beaten; licked,* e.g., If you miss the last train out of Charing Cross Station, you've *had your chips* till tomorrow morning.

have (something) in one's eye   *Inf.* **have (something) lined up**
Slang. Referring, for instance, to a better job than the one you have now.

have it off   1. *Slang.* **pull (bring) it off**
                                                                     2. **win a bet**
                                                               3. *Slang.* **make it**
                                                                  4. **have an affair**
1. *Slang.* Referring to any achievement.
2. *Slang.* At the track, usually.
3. *Slang.* With a girl. Sometimes *have it away*. Both expressions indicate sexual performance.
4. *Slang.* Intransitive use, referring to either sex.

have jam on it   *Inf.* **have it easy**
Inf. To *be in clover, be feeling no pain,* etc. To *want jam on it* is to *want egg in your beer*.

have no mind to   *Inf.* **not care a rap about**
Inf. For example, *He is so old that he has no mind to women.*

have no time for   *Inf.* **have no use for; not think much of**
Inf. Americans commonly use the expression: *I don't think much of him,* or *I have no use for him,* where the British might say *I have no time for him*. Predictably, to *have a lot of time for* someone is to *have a high opinion of* him.

have (someone) on, *Inf.*   *Inf.* **kid (someone)**

have (something) on, *Inf.*   *Inf.* **have (something) going**

have one over the eight   *Inf.* **get somewhat tight**
Inf. When somebody has *had one over the eight,* he is not terribly drunk but is certainly under the influence. The inference may be that one ought to be able to put away eight pints of beer without effect—no mean feat for the inexperienced beer drinker!

have (someone) on toast, *Slang.*   **have (someone) at one's mercy**

have (something) put in hand   *Inf.* **get (something) under way**
Inf. If a Briton needed a secretary, he would mention it to friends, put an advertise-ment into the newspaper, apply to agencies, and would thus *have* the operation *put in hand;* while an American would *get* it *under way.*

haver, *v.i.*   **talk nonsense**
(Pronounced HAY'-VER.) Like **blether,** with which it is synonymous, it is mainly Scot-tish, and with an -*s* added becomes a plural noun meaning *nonsense.* The admirable Sir Ernest Gowers discusses it in *The Complete Plain Words* (Penguin Books, Ltd., Har-mondsworth, Middlesex, England, 1969; a combination of *Plain Words,* 1948, and *The ABC of Plain Words,* 1951), which is required reading. In Chapter 4 he speaks of words that drop out of English and change their meanings and new words that are admitted, which he calls "gatecrashers." About *haver* he has this to say:

> Some words gatecrash irresistibly, because their sound is so appropriate to the mean-ing they are trying to acquire....*Haver* does not mean *vacillate* (it means *blather*), but almost everyone south of the [Scottish] Border thinks it does; there is no withstanding its suggestion of simultaneous hovering and wavering. The dictionaries do not yet recognize this, but doubtless they will soon bow to the inevitable...[There follows this footnote of Sir Ernest's:] When this book was first published a Scottish friend wrote to me: "As a Scot I wept bitter tears over your defeatist attitude in the matter of *haver.* I think it is utterly damnable that a perfectly honest word with a clearly defined meaning should be taken by 'havering bodies' and given a meaning, quite arbitrarily, which violates all its past history...I deplore your weak-kneed acquiescence."

have square eyes   **be a television addict**
Slang. See also **goggle box; telly.**

have the penny and the bun, *Inf.*   *Inf.* **eat your cake and have it**

have the pull of. See **pull.**

have the wind up. See **get the wind up.**

have (someone) up   **bring charges against (someone)**
To bring someone before a court of justice or a government agency.

Have you been served?   **Is someone helping you?**
Question asked (or which should be asked) by a salesperson (shop *assistant,* or simply **assistant**). Sometimes, *Are you being served?*

hawkie, *n.*   **white-faced cow**
North Country, and sometimes applied to any cow, whose face is any color. Also spelled *hawkey.*

hayter, *n.*   **rotary mower**
This proprietary name is almost universal, at least in Kent and Sussex, as generic for *rotary lawnmower,* the way **hoover** has come to mean any vacuum cleaner and **li-lo** any air mattress.

head, *n.*   **1. principal; dean**
                                                                 2. top of the bottle

1. *Head* is a shortening of *headmaster* or *headmistress,* both of which terms are used in America where, however, *principal* is the common term in secondary schools and *dean* in colleges. **Dean,** in Britain, usually denotes a church official, although it is sometimes used there in the American sense of a *college* faculty head or department head. *Principal* is seldom seen in Britain in this connection, where its definitions include, only incidentally, *headmaster* (of a **college**). The February 24, 1967, issue of the *Kent and Sussex Courier,* a rural weekly, contained an alarming headline, which did not rattle local residents in the least: INFANTS TO GET NEW HEAD. No miracle of surgery was involved. The article had to do simply with a change of staff at the Rusthall Infants' School, whose current *principal* was leaving to take up the **headship** at Bishop Down's Primary School, i.e., become *principal* there. And *Punch* reprinted a sentence from the *Times Educational Supplement* which proclaimed: "A fifteen-year-old Croydon boy has been suspended by his head since last September because of his long hair."
2. In Britain, the cream still rises to the top of the bottle (remember the old pre-homogenization days?) and is called the *head.* As in America, the same word also describes the *froth on beer.*

head boy; head girl   *approx.* **top boy; top girl**

In British schools generally, below the university level, the headmaster (*principal*), with the recommendations of the **staff** (*faculty*), designates one student as the *head boy* or *head girl,* as the case may be. This fortunate student is not necessarily the one with the best academic record or the best sports record or the best anything specific, but the one who has made the best all-round contribution to school life. The title is an honorable one and involves the burden of exemplary conduct with no special privileges except that of leading the cheers on the occasion of the visit of a notable personage. Incidentally, leading the cheers has nothing to do with *cheerleading* in the American sense. All it means in Britain is uttering solo the "hip, hip" part to which the ensemble "hooray" is added. There really should be a third *hip.* On that subject, a letter to *The Times* (London) of May 7, 1977, in connection with the cheers for the Queen which followed her speech to Parliament officially opening her Silver Jubilee, is relevant:

> **Three cheers**
> *From Mr H. Faulkner*
>   Sir, Three cheers for the Lord Chancellor for reminding us all that there are three "Hips" to each "Hooray".
> Yours faithfully,
> H. FAULKNER,
> National Liberal Club,
> Whitehall Place, SW1.

headed paper   **letterhead**

headlamp, *n.*   **headlight**
See also **Appendix II.E.**

headmaster. See **head.**

headship, *n.*   **office of school principal** or **college dean**

health visitor   *approx.* **health inspector**

An official of the Health Department of the County Council (see **council, councillor**) who visits homes after childbirths, children's clinics, schools, and elderly people to check up and advise on matters of health. The author is advised by his **chemist** (*druggist*) that in addition to these officials, there are volunteers who make the rounds checking up on new mothers and babies and on elderly persons living alone, with no compensation except the satisfaction of good works.

heaped, *adj.*   **heaping**
Teaspoonsful, tablespoon, etc.

hearty, *n.*   *Slang.* **jock**
Inf. A university term for an athlete or sportsman; the opposite of an **aesthete.**

heath, *n.*   **wild open land**
Usually covered with shrubs. *The Heath* in London refers to *Hampstead Heath,* a beautiful, very large park in northwest London.

Heath Robinson   **Rube Goldberg**
Applicable to a mechanical contrivance of amusingly superfluous complexity.

heavy gang   **third degree squad**
Slang. Tough police interrogators. The *heavy gang* or *heavy mob* are the rough boys in the force.

heavy over, come a. See **come a heavy over.**

he bought the farm   **he was shot down**
Slang. A very sad bit of R.A.F. argot, for which there would appear to be no American slang equivalent. The expression alludes to the many pilots who were "going to settle down and buy a farm" when it was all over. In some cases it was all over too soon. *He's bought it* has apparently superseded the longer phrase, and it can now refer to a premature death as a result of any disaster, like that of a racing driver in flames.

hedge, *n.*   **stone wall**
Inf. A special West Country usage. In some cases the wall is level and wide enough to walk on cross-country. Stone walls take the place of hedges (green, living ones, ubiquitous in most of Britain) in the West Country, but they are called *hedges* anyway.

hedge-barrister, *n.*   SEE COMMENT
A **barrister** who attends court daily, prepared to take on any case that might come his way.

heel bar   **while-U-wait shoe repair shop**

Heinz hound   **mongrel**
Slang. Alluding, of course, to the 57 varieties.

helter-skelter, *n.*   **carnival slide**
Inf. One sits on a mat and travels down a dizzying spiral slide (if one likes that sort of thing).

hemidemisemiquaver, *n.*   **sixty-fourth note**
Musical term. See **Appendix II.F.**

hemlock, *n.*   *approx.* **poison**
To an American *hemlock* usually evokes the image of a species of evergreen seen all over the country. To a Briton it means a fatal potion made from a poisonous herb, *Conium maculatum* (*maculatum* means 'spotted' and the stems of the plant have spots); and to a scholar it calls to mind Socrates, whom the Athenian court sentenced to die by drinking a cup of it in 399 B.C.

Her Majesty's
Stationery Office   **Government Printing Office**
Often shortened to *HMSO.*

hessian, *n.*   **burlap**

hi!, *interj.*   *approx. Inf.* **hey! look here!**
Inf. Designed to call attention; often a remonstrance. Not a greeting, as in America, though it is beginning to catch on.

hiccup, *n.*   **hitch**
Slang. A snarl, any sudden obstruction that interferes with the best laid schemes of mice, etc.

hide, *n.*   **hiding place**
Of a specialized type—for the observation of wild life. It is sometimes used also to mean 'hunting blind.'

hidey-hole, *n. Inf.*   **hideaway**

hiding to nothing. See **(be) on a hiding to nothing**

highly-strung   **high-strung**
See **Appendix I.A.3.**

High Street   **Main Street**
The British commonly name the principal thoroughfare of their villages and towns *The High Street,* and in referring to it, they still retain the definite article (see **Appendix I.A.2**). British *High Streets* are about as common as American *Main Streets.*

high tea   **light supper**
High tea includes something cooked: eggs or sausages or Welsh rarebit or any combination of these. It is the equivalent of a *light supper.* It is appropriate to quote from Nancy Mitford's novel, *The Blessing.* Sigi (short for Sigismond), the small son of an Englishwoman and a Frenchman, is brought up in Britain. When his parents separate he divides his time between them and is now in Paris with his elegant Gallic father. The following colloquy occurs while the two are dining in Paris:

> "In England," said Sigi, "little boys don't have dinner."
> "No dinner?"
> "Supper. And sometimes only high tea."
> "What is this, high tea?"
> "Yes, well, it's tea, you know, with cocoa and scones, and eggs if you've got hens and bacon if you've killed a pig, and marmalade and Bovril and kippers, and you have it late for tea, about six."
> "How terrible this must be!"
> "Oh no—high tea is absolutely smashing. Until you come to supper-time, and then I must say you do rather long for supper."

Hilary. See under **term.**

hip, *n.*   *Inf.* **the blues**
Inf. Also used as a transitive verb meaning to 'give the blues' to someone, i.e., to 'depress' him. As a noun, it is sometimes spelled *hyp,* revealing its derivation (*hypochondria*). Rarely used now; by some considered archaic. See also **(the) hump.**

hire. See under **engage.**

hire-and-drive, *n.*   **rent-a-car**

hire-purchase, *n.*   **installment plan**
Also known colloquially as the **never-never.** That which is repossessed is known as *hire-purchase snatchback.*

hit (someone) all over the shop, *Inf.*   *Inf.* **run rings around (someone)**

hit for six. See under **six.**

Hitler's War   **World War II**
Inf. See also **Great War.**

hit off, *Inf.*   **mimic**

hive off   **split off**
Inf. Used of a group that splits off from the main organization, like a swarm of bees
deserting the hive. Also used transitively, and, with a hyphen, as a noun designating
the procedure.

HMSO. See **Her Majesty's Stationery Office.**

hoarding, *n.*   **billboard**
The primary meaning of this word (apart from its use as present participle of *hoard*)
is 'construction site fence,' the roughly built temporary type, on which people are so
fond of posting notices despite the customary advice to the contrary, and through the
holes or chinks of which people are so fond of peering. *No Hoarding* is not an injunction
in times of shortages of commodities; it means *Post No Bills,* which sometimes appears
as *Stick No Bills.*

hob, *n.*   **runner (sled)**
See also **on the hob.**

hockey, *n.*   **field hockey**
To a Briton *hockey* means 'field hockey'; to an American, 'ice hockey.' If a Briton wants
to talk about the type played on ice, he calls it *ice hockey.* If the American means the
game played on the ground, he says *field hockey.*

hogget, *n.*   **yearling sheep**
Hogget would seem more naturally to mean a 'young hog' than a 'young sheep.' Its
meaning stems from the fact that in certain British country dialects the name *hogget* is
applied to a *young sheep* before the first shearing of its coat.

hoick, *v.t.*   **jerk**
Slang. Particularly, to *raise* or *hoist* with a jerk. Possibly a combination of *hoist,* and
hike. The noun *hoick* comes from rowing slang: a *jerk* at the end of a poorly executed
stroke.

hoist, *n.*   **freight elevator**
See also **lift; elevator.**

holdall, *n.*   **carryall**

hold a watching brief. See under **watching brief.**

Hold on!   **Just a minute!**
In Britain, a pure interjection, without the sense of 'wait!' or 'be patient!' or 'hold
your horses!', though it has these meanings as well.

hold the baby   *Slang.* **hold the bag**
Slang. Usually in the phrase *be left holding the baby.*

hold the ring   **stay out of it**
Inf. To *hold the ring,* or *keep the ring,* is to *stay out of a situation* or to *remain on the
sideline.* The expression is also used in the context of keeping third parties from inter-
fering in a fight. The ropes forming the prize ring in the old days were not attached to
posts but were held by the spectators, thus forming the ring. The derivation then
becomes obvious.

hold-up, *n.*   **traffic jam; delay**
Inf. Any delay, whether as a result of heavy traffic, fog, road construction, etc.

hole-and-corner, *adj.*   **underhand**
Inf. A *hole-and-corner man* is a *shady character* or *operator,* and *hole-and-corner work* is *shadiness* generally.

hole-in-the-corner, *adj., Inf.*   **played down**
Imparting a slight connotation of shabbiness. *The wedding had a hole-in-the-corner air.*

holiday, *n.*   **vacation**
An employee in Britain looks forward to his *holiday,* and while on vacation is a *holiday-maker.* But the university student in Britain speaks of his *vacations* and the summer recess is the *long vacation,* often shortened to *long vac* or simply *long.* See also **come down.**

hols, *n. pl.*   **vacation time**
Inf. Short for *holidays;* mainly **public school** jargon.

home and dry   *Inf.* **safe and sound**
Inf. Or *over the hump,* or *home free,* i.e., *doing all right.* Sometimes *home and dried,* and even extended occasionally to *home and dried on the pig's back.*

Home Counties   SEE COMMENT
Counties nearest London, especially Surrey, Kent and Essex. Used to include Middlesex, but that is now part of London, and no longer a county except for its cricket side and a postal address.

home-farm, *n.*   **residence farm**
The farm lived on by a farmer who owns several farms which he rents.

home from home   **home away from home**

homely, *adj.*   *Inf.* **homey**
Homely is used in Britain to mean 'simple,' 'unpretentious,' 'nothing fancy.' A *homely* woman in Britain is a friendly, unassuming, domestic type. It is quite possible to be attractive and homely in Britain. *Homely,* applied to the atmosphere of a place, comes close to the German *gemütlich. Homely,* in America, is uncomplimentary and means *not good looking* or even *ugly.* One wonders about the social implications of the evolution in America of the adjective *homely* from the proud noun *home.* See **plain,** for American sense of *homely.* C.P Snow seems particulary aware of the different meanings in the two countries. In *Last Things* (Macmillan Co. Ltd., London, 1970) he describes a young lady in these words; ". . .she wasn't, either in the English or the American sense, *homely."* Again, in *The Malcontents* (Macmillan Co. Ltd., London, 1972) he describes a character as *homely* "in the English sense." Yet again, in *In Their Wisdom* (Scribner, New York, 1974), a person's face is depicted as "...in the American sense *homely."*

homeminder, *n.*   **house-sitter**
Cf. **child-minder; house-minder.**

Home Office   SEE COMMENT
Performs some of the functions of both the U.S. Department of the Interior and the State Department.

home run   **homestretch**
Racing term.

honk, *v.i.*   **throw up (vomit)**
Slang. Britons are startled to see the sign NO HONKING as a warning to motorists on New York City streets.

Honourable, *adj.*   SEE COMMENT
Usually abbreviated to *Hon., Honble,* or *Honble.* For the use of this term in the system of British titles, see **Lord.**

Honours. See **Birthday Honours.**

Honours, Birthday. See **Birthday Honours.**

honours even *Slang.* **even Stephen**
Inf. Synonymous with **level pegging.**

honours, four. See **four honours.**

hon. sec. SEE COMMENT
Abbreviation for *honorary secretary*, a noble term bestowed upon long-suffering, unpaid, general factotums of nonprofit organizations. There are *hon. treas.* as well, who handle the money.

hood, *n.* **convertible top**
Automobile term. See also **Appendix II.E.**

hoo-ha, *n.* **uproar; row**
A *to-do.* See also: **shemozzle; scrum; dust-up; kick-up; punch-up; shindig; slanging match; Kilkenny cats; barney.**

hook it *Slang.* **take a powder**
Slang. The Americans *take a powder, get out of town, take it on the lam,* and do lots of other picturesque things to get away from the police, their wives, and other unfriendly people. Synonymous with **leg it.**

hook off **uncouple**
Railroad term.

hooligan, *n.* **hoodlum**

hoop, *n.* **wicket**
In croquet. See **wicket** for British uses of that term, both literal and figurative.

hooter, *n.* **1.** *Slang.* **schnozzle**
2. automobile horn
3. factory whistle

hoover, *n., v.t., v.i.* **1.** *n.,* **vacuum cleaner**
2. v.t., v.i., **vacuum (clean)**
Originally *Hoover* was a trademark, but the word has now become generic, like aspirin, thermos, etc. It is also used as a verb: one hurries home to *hoover* the carpet because guests are coming. The trademark was derived from the name of the pioneer in the field, William Henry Hoover (1849-1932). Most Britons would be startled to learn that Mr. Hoover was an American—in fact, he was the first mayor of North Canton, Ohio. He was impressed with a crude prototype put together by a fellow townsman and organized the Electric Suction Sweeper Company. The excellence of the product apparently overcame the dullness of its slogan: "It Sweeps as It Beats as It Cleans."

hop; hopper. See under **oast.**

hop-garden, *n.* **hop field**
See also **oast.**

horses. See **come to the horses.**

hospital job **made work**
Inf. When there's a smallish job to be done on your house in no great hurry, and you ask a friendly local contractor to squeeze it into his regular schedule from time to time as opportunity arises, you are giving him a *hospital job.* This was the original usage and

is still the respectable version. But the term has come to acquire a dishonorable connotation and now much more commonly signifies an unscrupulous worker's conversion of a simple straightforward assignment into a "career," a sort of malingering operation: He came to fix a shutter in May and is somehow still around in August replacing perfectly good shingles, putting up superfluous lattices, and rectifying the traditionally satisfactory plumbing system.

hospital nurse   **registered nurse**
Still addressed and referred to in Britain as **sister**, whether or not the hospital or the nurse in question is connected with a religious order. The order of rank in Britain is *nurse, sister, matron;* and *sister* is applied properly only to a nurse of sister rank, but it is often loosely used to describe or address any nurse. This is true among the laity, but see discussion of technical terms under **sister.**

hostelry, *n.*   **inn**
The shorter form *hostel* in both countries indicates a specialized type of *inn* for young people.

hotel page   **bellhop**
Often shortened to *page*. An informal term is *buttons*.

hot ice   **dry ice**
Dry ice is the more usual term in Britain.

house, *n.*   **1. building**
                                                                                                2. show
1. As part of the title of an office building, with a capital *H*. For instance, the British speak of *Esso House*, the Americans of the *Empire State Building.*
2. If there are two shows a night, the British talk of going to the first *house* or the second *house*, whereas Americans go to see the first *show* or the last *show*. See also **House Full.**

hot on   **1.** *Inf.* **tough on**
                                                                                          2. good at
1. *Inf.* Thus: *The boss was hot on latecomers.*
2. :*Inf. He's hot on gardening*, i.e., *expert at it.* Synonymous with **dab.**

House Full   *approx.* **Sold Out**
Sign seen outside Covent Garden and certain theaters, imparting the gloomy intelligence that there isn't even any standing-room. The *Standing Room Only* sign goes up first, succeeded, when appropriate, by *House Full.* See **house, 2.**

household troops. See **Guards.**

housemaid, *n.*   **chambermaid**
A **chambermaid** in Britain is a *hotel maid.*

houseman, *n.*   **intern**
A hospital term.

house-minder, *n.*   **house-sitter**
Cf. **child-minder.**

housewife, *n.*   **sewing gear kit**
Pronounced HUZZIF in this meaning.

housing estate   **residential development**

Hovis. See **brown bread.**

how, *n.*   **small hill**
Obsolete as a common noun, but still found in some place names in the north of England, e.g., *Brant How; Silver How.*

How are you keeping?   How have you been?

howler, *n.*, *Inf.*   *Inf.* **boner**

Howzat!, *interj.*   SEE COMMENT
Corruption of *How's that?* The cry, called an *appeal,* to the umpire in a cricket game
by one or more of the team (**side**) in the field demanding a ruling that the batter
(**batsman**) is out on one technicality or another. Usually just a shout or scream, sort of
rasping soprano.

hoy, *v.t.*   drive
Inf. Hoy! is an interjection used in herding or driving cattle. To *hoy* a herd is to *drive*
it by gestures and shouts of *hoy!* or whatever else comes to mind.

huggery, *n.*   SEE COMMENT
Inf. Activities of *barristers* wooing *solicitors.* Rhymes with SKULDUGGERY (which can
be spelled *skullduggery* or *sculduggery* or *scullduggery* and is a variant of *sculduddery*—or
vice versa).

hullo! *Interj.*   hey! (what's going on?)
(Accent on the first syllable.) It is not only a simple greeting; it can also be an expression of surprise—*what's happening here?*—possibly with a lifting of eyebrows and interchangeable with *I say!* and **hi!**

hum and ha, *Inf.*   *Inf.* **hem and haw**

humane society   lifesaving service
A *humane society* man would be called a *lifeguard* in America. A **Life Guard,** or more
properly, *Life Guardsman* in Britain is a member of an elite cavalry regiment attached to
the royal household. A *humane society* in America is a benevolent organization for the
care and shelter of pets.

humble pie   crow
People eat *crow* in America, and, rarely, *humble pie;* in Britain it is never *crow,* always
humble pie. Both terms signify *humiliation,* especially that of *eating one's words,* i.e., having
to retract a previous categorical assertion. The *humble* in *humble pie* got there by mistake.
It is corruption of *umbles,* a word now obsolete in both countries, and a variant of
numbles, an archaic English word for the entrails of a deer. *Umble pie,* long ago, was a
pie of the inferior parts of a deer served to the huntsmen and other servants. The
inferior parts included the heart, the liver, and the lights. *Lights* is a little known plural
noun meaning the *lungs* of animals, now usually used as food for domestic pets. The
confusion between the obsolete word *umbles* and the *humble* status of the servants who
were served the pie in the old days is quite understandable, especially in view of the
problem certain Englishmen have with the letter *h.* Incidentally, the current English
word for *umbles* is the rather nasty sounding word **offal.** The pie itself probably tasted
pretty good.

humbug, *n.*   mint candy
Hard, with white and brown stripes, and very tasty.

(the) hump, *n.*   *Slang.* **(the) dumps**
Slang. You can wake up with *the hump,* or get it or have it. People and things that
give you *the hump* would be said to *get you down.* The *hump* would seem to imply a
certain amount of irritation combined with depression, like *the sulks. I've got the hump*
means 'I'm fed up.' If you're *humpy,* you're *down in the mouth, in the dumps.* See also
hip.

hump, *v.t*   *Inf.* **lug; schlepp**
Inf. The image is that of one wearily carrying a heavy burden. *Schlepp* is heard increasingly in Britain.

humpty, *n.*   **cassock**

hundred, *n.*   SEE COMMENT
Subdivision of a county in the old days. See **Chiltern Hundreds.**

hundreds and thousands   *approx.* **multicolored sprinkles**
Tiny candies spread on top of cookies. See also **chocolate vermicelli.**

hundredweight, *n.*   SEE COMMENT
112 pounds in Britain; 100 pounds in America.

hunt, *v.i.*   **skip; miss**
Inf. If your motor is *hunting* in Britain you had better get your spark plugs (**sparking plugs**) looked at.

hunt, in the. See **in the hunt.**

hunt, out of the. See **in the hunt.**

hunter, *n.*   **watch with hinged covers**
If it has hinged covers front and back, it is a *hunter;* if only a front cover, a *half hunter.* These names derive from the function of the cover(s): to protect the watch on the hunting field.

hurroosh, *v.i.*   **zoom**
Inf. Hurroo is old-fashioned slang for a cry of triumph or happy excitement. It gave rise to the informal equivalent *hurroosh.* Kipling used it in *Plain Tales:* "There was a wild *hurroosh* at the Club." *Hurroosh* became a verb as well, and in his *Dairies 1923-1925* (Faber & Faber, London, 1985), Siegfried Sassoon made a **portmanteau** use of it, combining *hurry* and *rush,* as it were, with a sense of triumph and happy excitement, when he wrote: *"*Left Castle Acre at 5.30 and *hurrooshed* to Downham Market (eighteen miles) in thirty-four minutes." He loved his little car, a new acquisition, and in those days 18 miles in 34 minutes was quite an achievement, especially on English country lanes. Incidentally, note the period rather than colon in *5.30* (see **Appendix I.D.4.**). For another Sassoon coinage, see **reynardism.**

huss. See **Appendix II.H.**

hyp. See **hip.**

hyper-market, *n.*   **mall**

hy-spy, *n.*   *Inf.* **hide-and-seek**
Inf. A corruption of *I spy.*

I

ice, *n.*   **ice cream**
   In most British restaurants, *ices* means *ice cream*, and *ices, various* is the name for *assorted flavors* thereof. The British use *sorbet* for *sherbet*, but *sherbet* in Britain means 'powdered candy,' a sweet sugar-like substance which children suck up through licorice sticks. *Water ice*, meaning 'sherbet' in the American sense, is sometimes seen on British menus instead of *sorbet*.

icing sugar   **powdered sugar**
   See also **castor sugar.**

identification parade   **police lineup**

identity disc   *Slang.* **dog tag**
   The Americans prefer the slang expression, for which there is no British slang equivalent. The British are not required to carry I.D.s and indeed do not have them at all. They are quite shocked when they come across this Big-Brotherish system in other countries.

I have to say that...   **I beg to say that...**
   Have here does not express necessity, any more than the *am* in *I am to say*, in officialese, expresses futurity, or the *beg* in the corresponding American phrase implies a request for permission. The entire phrase, in each country, should be omitted. See the reference to Gowers under **I shall be glad if you will....**

ilk. See **of that ilk.**

ill, *adj.*   SEE COMMENT
   The British use *ill* in the usual American senses, but also in ways in which it would not appear in America. Thus, one often hears a television announcer describe the victim of an accident or a shooting as 'seriously ill,' where an American would have been likely to use a phrase like 'in a critical condition.' Where a car hit a bump and a passenger's head hit the roof, he was said to have 'been made ill for a fortnight.' Here, an American would probably have said that the victim had 'been laid up for a couple of weeks.' Note that **sick** is generally not used as a synonym for *ill*, but much more narrowly, to mean *nauseous*, and to *be sick* is to *throw up*.

I'll be bound   *Inf.* **I bet**
   Inf. This expression comes only at the end of a sentence so that it never takes a dependent clause.

I'm easy (about it)   **It's all the same to me**
   Inf., I'm easy (about it), in answer to a question posing a dilemma or an alternative: e.g., *Would you rather I came at 10:00 or 11:00?* means *I don't care*, or *It's all the same to me. I'm easy about it* has a British equivalent in *I don't mind.* Usually shortened to *I'm easy.* See also **mind, 2.**

immersion tank   **hot water heater**
   An *immersion tank* is not for a baptism. It heats the water for the whole house, as opposed to a **geyser,** which provides a supply of hot water in a particular room, usually the kitchen. Often referred to as the *immersion heater* or just the *immersion*.

immigrant, *n.*   **non-white**
Inf. Used by some as a pejorative synonym for **coloured,** which in Britain includes Asians and persons of mixed ancestry as well as blacks. Properly speaking, in either country, any person entering another country to settle there permanently is an immigrant.

imperial, *adj.*   *Inf.* **terrific**
Inf. As in, an *imperial balls-up* (see **balls**) which is *one lousy mess.*

importune, *v.t.*   **solicit**
In America, *importune,* in addition to its primary meaning of 'beset, ply, dun,' can mean 'to make improper advances toward' someone. In England, *importune* is used in the special sense of 'solicit for immoral purposes,' and is commonly used to describe the activities of prostitutes.

impot, *n.*   **punishment task**
Schoolboy slang. An informal shortening of *imposition,* sometimes written *impo,* referring to an unpleasant task assigned as a punishment at school, like having to write, *I shall not pass notes during Scripture* 500 times.

impression, *n.*   **printing**
Thus: First published January 1968
      Second *impression* February 1968...
In a book printed in America the *second impression* would be called the *second printing.*

imprest, *n.*   SEE COMMENT
Funds advanced to a government employee for use in official business. Formerly, it meant an advance payment to a soldier or sailor on enlistment. Cf. *imprestare,* Italian for *lend,* and *prêter,* the French equivalent. (In French spelling, the circumflex indicates the dropping of an *s* that in Old French used to follow the vowel so accented.)

in a cleft stick   *Slang.* **in a pickle**
Inf. The two branches of a *cleft stick* are like the *horns of a dilemma.*

in a flap, *Inf.*   *Inf.* **het up**

in a flat spin   *Slang.* **rattled**
Slang. Usually in the expression *going into a flat spin,* and obviously taken into the language from R.A.F. slang.

in a fuzz, *Slang.*   *Slang.* **in a tizzy**

in aid of   **for (used for)**
What's that in aid of? 'What's that for?'—asked by someone pointing to an object whose purpose is unclear. Can also be asked about intangibles like a shout or a trip.

in a merry pin   **in high spirits**
Inf. Really archaic, or at least dialectal, but heard among literary folk who like this sort of thing. The phrase occurs in the *Ballad of John Gilpin.*

in a way; in a great way. See **way.**

in (someone's) bad books   *Inf.* **in dutch with (someone)**
Inf. Variant: *in (someone's) black books.* Synonymous with **in the cart.**

in baulk, balk   *Inf.* **in a spot**
Inf. Meaning 'in difficulties.'

in care   **in a foster home**
Said of children, and applies equally to an orphanage.

incident room   *(approx.)* **situation room**
  A term beloved of English detective stories; temporary headquarters set up during
the investigation of the crime; a sort of control room where the hero-detective and his
assistants meet and discuss things. There is a permanent Situation Room in the White
House.

indent, *n., v.t.*   **requisition**

indexed. *See* **index-linked.**

index-linked, *adj.*   **adjusted to inflation**
  Describes savings programs, investments, etc. where the income and/or capital are
geared to the British cost-of-living index (the *UK General Index of Retail Prices—RPI* for
short). One of the most popular programs is the SAYE arrangement (SAYE stands for
Save as You Earn). Index-linked is sometimes shortened to *indexed,* and the process has
been dubbed *indexation,* which can be applied to wages and salaries as well.

Indian. *See* **red Indian.**

Indian meal   **corn meal**
  Corn in the American sense is usually called *maize* in Britain at the agricultural or
trade level (see **corn**), but another British name for it, at the gardener's or householder's
level, is *Indian corn* (sometimes *corn on the cob*). Hence *Indian meal* for *cornmeal.*

industrial action   **union protest activity**
  Anything from a slow-down to a full-fledged strike. Philip Howard (*Words Fail Me,*
Hamish Hamilton, London, 1980) has this to say about the phrase:

> *Industrial action:* a strike or disruptive action by employees in any occupation, not
> necessarily industrial. Civil servants, teachers, firemen, postmen, journalists, and oth-
> ers who are not horny-handed sons of toil take industrial action frequently, when it
> would be more accurately described as non-industrial inaction. But the metaphor from
> the factory implies that all trade unionists are brothers under the jargon.

industrial estate. *See under* **estate.**

ingle-nook, *n.*   **chimney-corner**
  A word greatly favored by estate agents, it summons up an irresistibly cozy, even
stirring, image of the quintessential Briton by his hearth. Rooms in old houses sometimes have fireplaces as much as eight or ten feet wide, with a grate or stove in the
center from which the smoke runs into a narrow flue. Comfortable chairs can be placed
on either side, within the fireplace.

ingrowing, *adj.*   **ingrown**
  Referring to toenails. The Americans seem resigned to a *fait accompli.*

in hand   1. **at one's disposal**
                                                               2. **under control**
1. As in, *Aberdeen still has two games in hand,* and though trailing at the moment, might
yet win the Scottish first division **football** (**soccer**) championship. In this sense, *in hand*
would be *to go* in America: *…two games to go.*
2. *Being attended to:* **Not to worry;** *the matter is in hand.*

inland, *adj.*   1. **domestic**
                                                                      2. **internal**
The British speak of *inland* postage rates and *inland* revenue. The opposite number of
an American *internal revenue agent* is the British *inland revenue inspector.* But see **internal.**

in low water   1. *Inf.* **hard up**
                                                                  2. *Slang.* **in hot water**
1. *Inf.* Financial stress is the usual connotation.

2. *Inf. Difficult straits* or a *depressed state* generally (e.g., the weak position of a political party out of favor) is the broader implication, and in this sense its American equivalent would be *in hot water*. **Low in the water** is a variant, meaning 'up against it.'

innings, *n. sing.*   **inning**
Note the *-s,* which does not make *innings* plural. An American *inning* is a British *innings.* The standard British plural is the same as the singlular; informally, it is *inningses.*

Inns of Court   SEE COMMENT
These are the four legal societies which alone may admit persons to the bar (in the restricted British sense of allowing them to practice as **barristers** as distinguished from **solicitors**). These societies are the Inner Temple, Middle Temple, Lincoln's Inn, and Gray's Inn. The term *Inns of Court* denotes not only those societies but also their buildings in London. In addition to the examination procedures for admission to the bar, the Consolidated Regulations of *Inns of Court* (as revised on July 22, 1963) provide for the *Keeping of Terms* (synonymous with the *Eating of Dinners,* in this context) as follows:

KEEPING TERMS
12. The word "Terms" in these Regulations...shall mean the Terms fixed by the Inns of Court for the purpose of Calls to the Bar...[Four Terms are designated, each of twenty-three days' duration.]
13. A student may keep terms by dining in the Hall of his Inn of Court any three days in each Term.
. . . . . .
15. No day's attendance in Hall shall be available for the purpose of Keeping Term, unless the Student shall have been present at the grace before dinner, during the whole of dinner, and until the concluding grace shall have been said, unless the acting Treasurer, on any day during dinner shall think fit to permit the Student to leave earlier...

The full import of these Regulations would hardly be complete without the following comment of a friend and barrister, a member of Gray's Inn, who kindly took the trouble to clarify some obscurities:

The clue to these strange customs is that they are a survival of the medieval college system, still in full operation at Oxford and Cambridge, the college being residence, parent, and spiritual home rather than teacher, which is the function of the faculty or "school." The English attach great importance to belonging to some institution with traditional standards of conduct. It make them feel good and even act good (or pretend to, which is near enough for practical purposes). Dining in Hall, which is the way Terms are kept, is the outward manifestation of the inward and spiritual truth of belonging to a sort of vestigial university and a far from vestigial profession. Dinners are eaten (and drunk) with some ceremony, particularly in my Inn, Gray's, and are in fact quite pleasant occasions where one gets to know those who are or will become one's "learned friends" or, if one reaches the eminence of the Bench, one's "brothers."
The teaching and examining functions of the Inns as a body are now exercised by the Council of Legal Education, though individual Inns do hold "moots" or mock trials which are quite valuable and usually amusing.
Perhaps I should add, in case it is not clear from the documents, that the governing body of an Inn is the Benchers (judges and other distinguished lawyers), who correspond roughly to the "dons" of an Oxford college.

in one's gift   **at one's disposal**
With particular reference to a **living.**

in pod   *Slang.* **knocked up**
Slang. Both countries use inelegant terms for "pregnant." See also **preggers** and **pudding club.** See **knock up** for its various British meanings, all of which are much less serious matters.

inquiry. See **enquiry.**

insect, *n.*   **bug**
Americans use *insect* and *bug* more or less interchangeably. In Britain *bug* means
'bedbug.' *Bug* has slang meanings in both countries. In British slang a *big bug* is what
Americans call a *big gun*, a *VIP*.

inside (of a bus)   **bottom**
And the *outside* of a bus is its *top*. These terms refer to double-deckers and are reminiscent of the days when the top was uncovered, and therefore the *outside*. Nowadays
it's all inside, literally speaking, but *outside* is still often heard from conductors.

inspectorate, *n.*   SEE COMMENT
Governmental body for inspection of schools and education generally. Performs some
of the functions of a Board of Education.

in store. See under **store.**

instruct, *v.t*   **retain**
Term used in the legal profession. In Britain a client instructs a **solicitor,** that is,
engages him. In America a client *retains* a lawyer.

intake, *n.*   **entrants**
Inf. Those recently *taken in*. Covers entrants into a university, the ministry, the armed
forces, etc. The slang American equivalent in military and sports usage would be *rookies*.

interfere with   **criminally assault**
To *rape* or *sodomize* (e.g., a child). The British circumlocution is even more euphemistic
than the American.

interior-sprung, *adj.*   **inner-spring**
Type of mattress.

internal, *adj.*   **domestic**
Term applied to air travel. But see **inland.**

international, *n.*   SEE COMMENT
Also *internationalist*. An athlete who has represented his country abroad, especially
at soccer, rugby, or cricket, although for cricket the proper term is *test player* (see **Test
Match**). In soccer and rugby Britain is not one nation but four—England, Scotland,
Wales, and Northern Ireland.

interval, *n.*   **intermission**
The pause between acts at the theater or between the halves of a concert. *Tea in the
interval?* (at the matinee) or *Coffee in the interval?* (at an evening performance) used to
be the courteous and comforting question addressed to members of the audience by
British usherettes in most theaters, and if the question was answered in the affirmative,
you were served at your seat. Stronger beverages may be procured at the bar with
which every British theater appears to be equipped.

in the basket   *Slang.* **no soap; no dice**
Slang. When a proposed project is *in the basket,* its's *no soap (rejected, discarded, nothing
doing)*.

in the cart, *Slang.*   *Slang.* **in the soup**

in the club. See **pudding club.**

in the dock. See **dock, 2.**

in the driving seat, *Inf.*   *Inf.* **in the driver's seat**

in the event   **as it turned out**
Thus: *In the event, the vote was much closer than expected.* The phrase does not connote futurity, as in an expression like *In the event of rain...*, but refers to something which actually came to pass despite predictions or expectations to the contrary. *Event* is thus used in the sense of its Latin forbear to mean 'result' or 'outcome.'

in the hunt   *Inf.* **in the running**
Inf. And *out of the hunt* is *not in the running.*

in the picture   **au courant**

in the same case   **in the same situation**
Used when comparing one person's situation with another's.

in trade. See **trade.**

in train   **coming along**
Sometimes *on train. In train* is not often heard in America, and when it is it sounds rather stuffy and means 'in good order' or 'in proper form.' In Britain the phrase is heard quite frequently and is the normal response of merchants or contractors to whom one is complaining about delay: *It is in train,* meaning that he has done all he can, and that you must be patient.

introduced by...   *approx.* **presented by...**
Not exactly. Often, at the end of a TV show, the announcer states that the show was *introduced* by So-and-so. This does not mean that So-and-so made an introductory statement at the outset, but rather that it was So-and-so's show; he was the m.c. This has always sounded somewhat misleading.

in two shakes of a duck's tail, *Inf.*   *Inf.* **in two shakes of a lamb's tail**
Inf. Lamb's tail, as well, in Britain. *Shake,* by itself, can mean 'moment' in either country (*of a duck's* or *lamb's tail* being understood). *In a brace of shakes* is synonymous with *in two shakes of a lamb's* or *duck's tail.*

inty, *n.*   **(school) recess**
Schoolboy slang. The *interval* of freedom.

invalid carriage   **electric tricycle**
They are issued by the Ministry of Health, in some cases to working people who could not otherwise get around.

invalid's chair   **wheelchair**
Also called **bath-chair** and **wheeled chair.**

inverted commas   **quotation marks**

invigilator *n.*   **proctor at school examinations**
To *invigilate* is to *keep vigil,* i.e., watch over students during examinations.

ironmonger's, *n.*   **hardware store**

I say!   1. **Say!**
                                                                        2. **My!**
In the French children's humorous comic series *Astérix,* about Roman Gaul, the ancient Britons go about saying, "Je dis!" See also **hullo!; hi!**

-ish, *adv.*   somewhat; sort of; rather; about

Inf. Tacked on to an adjective or adverb, it adds an attenuating nuance, with the same force as placing *somewhat, fairly,* or *sort of* before the word, or *about* or *around* in expressions of quantity or time. Americans are familiar with *-ish* after adjectives of color: *reddish, greenish,* or of general age: *youngish, oldish,* although these are heard infrequently. But the British are prone to add *-ish* to almost anything: *tallish, fattish, poorish;* to numerals in expressions of quantity: *How many people were at the party? Oh, fiftyish;* in general or specific expressions of time: *earlyish, latish; I'll get there elevenish* ('around eleven o'clock'); and with adverbs: *The play began slowish* ('got off to a rather slow start'), but **smartish** is used instead of *quickish.* There are several British uses that do not occur in American speech: 1. After a name, meaning *characteristic of,* as in *That's a Maryish gesture* ('one characteristic or reminiscent of Mary'); *That's a Teddyish reaction* ('the way Teddy would react'). 2. By itself, as an answer or reaction, meaning 'well, sort of,' or if you say so,' or 'somewhat,' to someone else's statement or question: *She's pretty. Well, -ish. I found the food in that restaurant quite good. How about you? -Ish,* or, *Only -ish.* Or: *Will you get here by noon? -Ish. Did the market go up today? -Ish.* 3. The British have invented a sillyish kind of word: *It's mor(e)ish,* to describe yummy food, to which Americans would react with the equally insipid expression: *It tastes like more.* Both countries commonly use *-ish* extensions of common nouns as adjectives, like *childish, feverish, foolish, sheepish,* and extend those to make adverbs, like *childishly,* etc.

I shall be glad if you will...   Please...

Officialese, properly objected to together with lots more gobbledygook, by Sir Ernest Gowers in his wonderful book *The Complete Plain Words* (Penguin Books, Ltd., Harmondsworth, Middlesex, England, 1969).

issue, *v.t*   furnish

Used as follows: *There is no charge for issuing you with our credit card.* The British might also have said: *...for issuing our credit card to you.* The Americans might say *furnishing you with* or *supplying you with* but would not use *issue* in the British construction.

It. See **martini.**

item, *n.*   plank

An *item* in a political *program* in Britain is what Americans would call a *plank* in a political *platform.*

It isn't true!   That's or It's incredible!

Inf. Example: *He's so stupid it isn't true!*

izzard, *n.*   (letter) z

Archaic, but occasionally used jocularly.

J

jack, *n.*   *Inf.* **odd-job man**
   Inf. Not much used (the word, that is—and the man in question is hard to come by these days).

jacket, matinee. See **matinee jacket.**

jacket potato   **baked potato**

jack-in-office. See **bumble.**

jakes, *n.*   *Slang.* **can (privy)**
   Slang. A very old bit of British slang, going back to at least Elizabethan times, but still heard on occasion. In 1596, Sir John Harington (1561–1612) incurred the displeasure of the court on the publication of his Rabelaisian work *Metamorphosis of Ajax* (a pun on *a jakes*). He was eventually restored to grace. In the old days, contractors who cleaned out privies were known as *jakes-farmers.*

jam, *n.*   **treat**
   Slang. A real *jam* is British slang for a *real treat.* A *jam sandwich* in Britain can mean what it does in America, but it is also a term used to mean the kind of layer cake which has jam between the layers. See also **jam sandwich.**

jam, money for. See **money for jam.**

jam on it. See **have jam on it.**

jam sandwich   **police car**
   Slang. So named because the vehicles are white with a red stripe along the middle, looking like jam between two slices of white bread. Cf. **panda car; Z-car.**

jam tomorrow, *Inf.*   *Inf.* **pie in the sky.**
   Shades of Lewis Carroll! (*Through the Looking-Glass:* "The rule is, jam to-morrow and jam yesterday—but never jam to-day.")

Janeite, *n.*   **Jane Austen fan**
   Sometimes spelled *Janite.*

jankers, *n., pl.*   **stockade**
   Slang. In the special sense of *military jail. Jankers* has other meanings in military slang: 'defaulters'; their 'penalty' or 'punishment'; the 'cells' themselves. To get ten days' *jankers* is to be confined to the *stockade* for that period.

jasey, *n.*   **wig**
   Slang. This word is old British slang, and the wig it describes is usually made of worsted, which in Britain does not mean primarily the tightly woven material made from woolen yarn, as it does in America, but rather the yarn itself. *Worsted* is derived from a town in Norfolk now spelled *Worstead. Jasey* is probably a corruption of *jersey* and is considered a jocular word.

jaunty, *n.*   **master-at-arms**
   Naut. Slang. Head policeman on a naval vessel. The official title in both the Royal Navy and the United States Navy is *master-at-arms,* often abbreviated to *M.A.A.*

jaw, *n.*   **talking to**
  Slang. A *pi-jaw* (*pi-* is short for *pious*) is one of those lectures or sermons delivered by a schoolteacher or a scout leader on a "man-to-man" basis to prepare the nervous youngster for life's lurking pitfalls.

jaw-bacon. See chaw-bacon.

jaw-jaw, *n., v.i.*   **1. endless discussion**
                                                                        2. drone on and on
  Slang. See also **jaw.**

jelly, *n.*   **gelatin-type dessert**
  Jelly is used in Britain as in America, but in a British restaurant if you wanted Jell-O or its equivalent for dessert, you would ask for *jelly.*

jelly-bag cap   **stocking cap**
  Inf. Jelly-bags are used for straining jelly and are made of the kind of stretchable material associated with what Americans call *stocking caps.*

jemmy, *n.*   **jimmy**
  British burglars use *jemmies;* their American colleagues use *jimmies. Jimmy* is also used as the British slang name for a dish made from sheep's head.

Jeremiah, *n.*   *Inf.* **gloomy Gus**
  Inf. Everybody knows (or should know) who Jeremiah was. Does anybody know who Gus was?

jerry, *n.*   *Inf.* **potty**
  Slang. A *chamber pot.* With a capital *J* it is British slang for a *German,* but *jerry-faced* does not denote the possession of a Teutonic countenance. See **po-faced.**

jersey, *n.*   **pullover; sweater**
  See also **jumper; woollies.**

jib, *v.i.*   **buck**
  Inf. Normally applied to balking horses and in Britain, informally, to cars as well or even to stubborn persons.

jiggered, *adj.*   **1.** *Slang.* **pooped**
                                                                      2. *Slang.* **up the creek**
                                                                      3. *Slang.* **damned!**
  1. *Slang.* After a long day's work, you're *jiggered.*
  2. *Slang.* In a tough situation, like running out of gas in the middle of the night, you'd feel *jiggered.*
  3. *Slang.* The exclamation *I'm jiggered* means 'I'll be damned' as in *Well, I'm jiggered—fancy meeting you here!*

jiggery-pokery, *n., Inf.*   *Inf.* **hanky-panky**

jim-jams, *n. pl. Slang.*   *Slang.* **willies**

jimmy. See jemmy.

Jimmy, dismal. See dismal Jimmy.

jink, *v.t., v.i.*   **dodge**
  To *dodge about* jerkily, to avoid being hit. Said of game birds and slangily extended to warplanes.

job, *v.t.*   **1. rent (horse and carriage)**
2. prod
3. hit

1. The British used to *job* horses and carriages in the old days, the verb being applied to both supplier and user (the way Americans use *rent*). *Jobbing,* in this sense, described an arrangement for a specified period of time, and the supplier was called a *jobmaster.*
2. Standard British English, from which we get
3. *Slang.* To *smite* or *hit.* See **arse,** for this slang use of *job.*

jobber, *n.*   SEE COMMENT
   On the London Stock Exchange, there are a dozen firms that act as wholesalers, and have no counterpart on any other stock exchange, though they are analogous to oddlot firms on the New York Stock Exchange, in that they are principals, acting for their own account, rather than brokers acting only as agents for buyer or seller. The rules of the London Stock Exchange enforce the 'single capacity' trading system, forbidding member firms to combine the roles of *jobber* and broker.

jobbernowl, *n., Inf.*   *Slang.* **dope; jerk**
   See synonyms under **git.**

job of work   **job**
   Inf. In the sense of *work to be done.*

Joe Bloggs   **Joe Doakes**
   Mr. What's-his-name; anybody who isn't anybody; Tom, Dick, or Harry.

joey, *n.*   SEE COMMENT
   Slang. Threepenny bit; after Dr. Joseph Hume (1777–1855), just as **bobbies** got their name from Sir Robert Peel, **bowlers** from a Mr. Bowler, and so on. Hume was a radical politician who served many years in Parliament and was known as "Adversity Hume" for his dire predictions of national disaster. *Joey* (with a lower case *j*) originally meant a 'fourpenny piece,' but only until that coin was replaced by the *threepenny* (pronounced THREPPENNY), often called *threppenny bit* or *threepence* (pronounced THRUPPENCE).

John Dorey
   See **Appendix II.H.**

johnny, *n.*   *Inf.* **guy**
   Slang. Usually pejorative. For the British meaning of *guy,* see **guy.**

John Thomas   *Slang.* **cock**
   Slang. Low slang for the male member. Sometimes abbreviated to *J.T.*

join, *v.t.*   **board**
   To *join* a train, ship, plane, etc. is to *board* it.

joiner, *n.*   **carpenter**
   Technically speaking, *joiners* in both countries, as distinct from *carpenters,* engage especially in interior light carpentry (doors, shelves, etc.) and cabinet making. The British appear often to use the terms interchangeably, but *joiner* is rarely heard in ordinary American conversation.

joint, *n.*   **roast**
   In Britain that tasty leg of lamb or roast of beef or loin of pork is known as a *joint.* Popular for Sunday lunch, hence the *Sunday joint.*

jollop, *n.*   *Slang.* **guck**
   Slang. Any witches' brew you take for whatever ails you, like patent medicines and home remedies.

jolly, *n.*   *Slang.* **leatherneck**
   Slang. A Royal Marine. Synonymous with **guffy** and **bullock** in this context. A kind
correspondent suggested this entry in the plural: *jollies.* When asked whether it couldn't
appear in the singular, he replied:

> There is no *logical* reason why the word cannot be used in the singular; but then, if
> the language were always logical, the comparative of *good* would be *gooder* and the
> plural of *mouse* would be *mouses.* What I am getting at is that I never heard it used in
> the singular. A single Marine was never referred to as *a* jolly, but rather as '...one of
> the (those) jollies, guffies,' etc. The point of this, as I see it, is that a sailor's work is
> *individual.* Even when working in a group, each sailor does *his* job, which he under-
> stands as a job—a fact about which, he is naturally, proud. The marines, however—
> at least in the eyes of a sailor—do everything by the numbers because they do not
> understand anything and can only do what they are told. Hence, they are seen as a
> mass. Hence, the terms used are plural terms, and an accidental individual is just
> '...one of *them.*' About the only time that a singular form might ever be used would
> be for *bullock* (not *jolly* or *guff(e)y*) and that would be in a face-to-face slanging match,
> as in 'you **ruddy** great bullock, you, why don't you **get stuffed...**', etc.

   One use of *jolly* in the singular does occur in Kipling's rollicking poem *Soldier and
Sailor Too (The Royal Regiment of Marines),* which starts:

> As I was spittin' into the Ditch aboard o' the *Crocodile,*
> I seed a man on a man-o'-war got up in the Reg'lars' style.
> 'E was scrapin' the paint from off of'er plates, an' I sez to 'im, '''Oo are you?''
> Sez 'e, "I'm a Jolly—'Er Majesty's Jolly—soldier an' sailor too!"
> Now 'is work begins by Gawd knows when, and 'is work is never through;
> 'E isn't one o' the reg'lar Line, nor 'e isn't one of the crew.
> 'E's a kind of a giddy harumfrodite—soldier an' sailor too!

   (The *Ditch* mentioned in the first line is the Suez Canal.) Incidentally, cf. U.S. Navy
slang for *marines: grunts; jarheads.*

jolly, *adv., Inf.*   *approx.* **mighty (very)**

joskin, *n.*   **bumpkin**
   Slang. Sailors use this term to describe any lubberly hand. The exact meaning of *joskin*
is a man from the Norfolk area who works as a farmhand during the summer and on
trawlers in wintertime, and is therefore, presumably, a green hand on board. But there
are also those who maintain that *bump* means 'jostle,' so that *jos(tle)kin* means 'bumpkin.'
Rarely ecnountered.

josser, *n., Slang.*   *Slang.* **geezer**

jotter, *n., Inf.*   **1. steno pad**
                                                                                                2. notebook
2. Also **exercise book.**

J.T. *See* **John Thomas.**

judder, *v.i.*   **shake**
   Violently and noisily. A bit of onomatopoeia, also influenced by *shudder.* It can apply
to anything from a jalopy to an opera singer, and is also used as a noun to denote the
phenomenon.

judy, *n.*   *Slang.* **broad**
   Slang. A more or less uncomplimentary word for *woman,* often implying that she's
no beauty.

jug, *n.*   **pitcher**
   In Britain it is the milk *jug* or water *jug* which is placed on the table.

juggernaut, *n.*   **large truck**
Inf. Very large; short for *juggernaut lorry.* (See **lorry**.) Usually refers to an enormous trailer truck (see **articulated lorry**). There is a great controversy about their use on country lanes and city streets where they make a deafening noise, shake the fabric of old buildings, etc. The word is related to *Jagannath,* an idol of the Hindu god Krishna which was drawn in processions on vast carts under whose wheels fanatics threw themselves in their esctasy, to be crushed to death.

juggins, *n.*   *Slang.* **dope; fool**
Slang. Synonymous with **muggins**. See also **git**.

jumble, *n.*   SEE COMMENT
Goods sold at a *jumble sale* or unwanted things in the house allocated to the local *jumble sale.* Can also be used loosely to mean 'junk.'

jumble sale, *n.*   **rummage sale**

jumper, *n.*   **pullover**
This term is used to describe a woman's *pullover sweater.* See also **jersey; woollies.**

jump jockey, *Inf.*   **steeplechase rider**

jump to it, *Inf.*   *Inf.* **hop to it**

junction box. See **box.**

junk   **worn-out rope**
Old, worthless stuff, rubbish, which is called *junk* in America, is generally referred to as *rubbish* or **lumber** in Britain, where *junk,* though now extended to mean 'rubbish' generally, is still more especially a nautical term meaning 'worn-out hawsers' or 'cables' which are either discarded or picked apart for use as calking material or in making swabs.

just, *adv.*   *adv.* **right**
Where an American would say, "I can't find it now, but it was *right* over there," i.e., no farther than that, a Briton would say "...*just* over there." Were the Briton to say, "...*right* over there," he would mean '...way over there,' i.e., no nearer than that. If he said, "Drink it *right* up," he would mean 'drink it all,' whereas an American would mean "drink it at once, *right* now.' Cases of ambiguity like this deserve close attention.

just a tick!   *Inf.* **right with you!**
Inf. See also **hold on!**

just going   **just about**
Used in expressions of time of day: *it's just going twelve* means *it's just about twelve,* or, *practically twelve.* The expressions *just on* and *going on for* are used by the British in the same way: *it's just on nine o'clock,* or *it's going on for nine,* i.e., *it's not quite* or *it's just about nine.* See also **gone.**

just here   **right here**

just on. See **just going.**

K

K., _n._   SEE COMMENT
Inf. To _get one's K._ is to _be knighted_ (see **Birthday Honours**). This applies, however, not to common or garden knights (_Knights Bachelor_), but to members of the Orders of Chivalry. Thus, in the Civil Service, or elsewhere, Mr. John Smith, C.M.G. (Companion of the Order of St. Michael and St. George), acquires the magical 'Sir' by being promoted to K.C.M.G. (Knight Commander of the Order of St. Michael and St. George). There are the inevitable wags who insist that C.M.G. stands for _Call me God_, and that when you go up in the world, the K. in K.C.M.G simply stands for _Kindly_. The letters G.C.M.G. after a name indicate that the proud person entitled to them is a Knight or Dame Grand Cross of the Order of St. Michael and St. George. In this case the impious insist that the letters signify 'God calls me God.' _Get one's K._ is an expression that reflects the more or less automatic progress up the ladder of the more accomplished, once they succeed in getting their feet on the first rung.

K.B.B.   **bad soldier or sailor**
Stands for _King's Bad Bargain;_ sometimes _K.H.B._, for _King's Hard Bargain_. Applied to one in the service who has turned out undesirable. The term, still used, goes all the way back to George II. The _K_ didn't change to _Q_ under Victoria, and is still _K_ under Elizabeth II.

K.C. See under **take silk.**

K.C.M.G. See **K.**

kedgeree, _n._   SEE COMMENT
(Accent on the first or third syllable.) Composed of fish, usually smoked haddock, cooked with rice and eggs, and other variable ingredients. The word is derived from the Hindi word _khichri_. The recipe and word were imported from India in the days of the Empire. It is normally a breakfast dish, and not very common in any but upper class households.

keel, _n._   **1. barge**
                                                                2. 21 tons 4 cwt.
                                                                3. ruddle (reddle)
1. Type of boat used, usually to carry coal, on the Rivers Tyne, Humber, etc. Still seen, but going out of use.
2. Weight of coal that can be carried on a _keel_, and still used as a wholesale coal measure. Since a British _ton_ is 2240 lbs. and a British cwt. (**hundred-weight**) is 112 lbs., a _keel_ is, in American terms, 47,488 lbs., or a sliver under 23¾ tons, all of which is about to become totally immaterial under the fast-encroaching metric system. See also **Appendix II.C.1.**
3. A red ochre stain, used to identify sheep, lumber, etc.

keelie, _n._   _Inf._ **tough**
Slang. A Scottish term, derived from the Keelie Gang, a band of hoodlums that terrorized the streets of Edinburgh in the early 19th century. It is applied particularly to street ruffians from Glasgow and environs. Some people say the name comes from the word _keel_, and referred originally to the tough characters who worked in Brown's Shipyard, in Glasgow; but this piece of folk etymology is contested by others who believe that the word is connected with the Scottish word _gillie_, meaning a 'hunter's or fisherman's guide,' a term which is in turn derived from the Gaelic word _gille_, meaning 'lad.' In certain contexts the meaning is softened to 'boor' or 'vulgarian,' rather than 'ruffian.'

keenest prices   **biggest bargains**
Inf. Often seen in advertisements: *For keenest prices shop at So-and-So-'s.*

keen on   **enthusiastic about**
Inf. *Dead keen on* and *mad keen on* indicate mounting degrees of enthusiasm.

keep, *v.t.*   **raise**
A Briton who *keeps* pigs is not simply having them as pets; he is in business and in America would be said to be *raising* them.

keep a straight bat   *Inf.* **play fair**
Inf. One of many expressions borrowed from **cricket,** which is itself synonymous with *fair play* in the mind and idiom of a Briton.

keep cave. See **cave.**

keeper, *n.*   **custodian; guard**
When Americans use the word *keeper* they think in terms of a prison, an insane asylum, or a zoo. *Keeper* is the usual British term for a *museum guard* or *zoo employee.* To a Briton, **guard** would normally invoke the image of a railroad conductor or a sentry.

keeping. See **How are you keeping?**

keep obbo on   *Inf.* **keep an eye on**
Slang. An *obbo* was an observation balloon in World War I. *Keeping obbo* is policemen's slang for *surveillance.*

keep one's terms. See **eat one's dinners; Inns of Court.**

keep the ring. *See* **hold the ring.**

keep your eyes skinned. *Inf.*   *Inf.* **keep your eyes peeled**

Keep your pecker up!   *Inf.* **Chin up!**
Inf. In this expression, *pecker* means 'spirits' or 'courage.' This connotation of *pecker* is probably derived from its original meaning of a 'bird that pecks' (cf. *woodpecker*), and by extension that with which it pecks, i.e., its beak, which became slang for 'nose.' It is obviously impossible to *keep your pecker* (in this sense) *up* without simultaneously *keeping your chin up.* However, the vulgar American sense of *pecker* is not unknown in Britain. This usage occurs in an article in the *Sunday Times Weekly Review* (London) of August 30, 1980, on Gertrude Vanderbilt Whitney entitled *The Secret Life of an American 'Royal'*:

> A close friend of the prince (the then Prince of Wales, later Edward VIII) who had often gone swimming naked with him, added (to a report from a female friend that the prince was "a most unsatisfactory sexual partner") the information that "to put it bluntly, he had the smallest pecker I have ever seen".

The article does not disclose whether the 'close friend' was American or British. Despite the familiarity of many Englishmen (and women) with the common American meaning, the exhortation *Keep your pecker up!* is freely used in polite and mixed society.

Kendal green   **green woolen cloth**
Coarse in texture. Takes its name from Kendal, a town in Cumbria (formerly West-morland).

Kentish-fire, *n.*   SEE COMMENT
Prolonged rythmic applause to express disapproval. The expression is attributed to anti-Catholic demonstrations in Kent in the early 1800s.

Kentish man   SEE COMMENT
   Native of the County of Kent, England, born west of the River Medway. If born east
of it, he is a *man of Kent.*

kerbside-crawl. See **gutter-crawl.**

kerfuffle, *n.*   fuss; commotion; dither
   Slang. Found also in the spellings *cufuffle* and *gefuffle,* and probably in others as well,
as so often occurs with slang and colloquial terms. It is sometimes used loosely as
synonymous with **shemozzle.**

kettle-boy, *n.*   tea maker
   In a special context. The author's friend and occasional gardener, Jack Potter, was
kettle-boy in 1908–09 at the age of fourteen, to the building crew engaged in adding a
ballroom on to a great country residence. His sole function was to keep the tea kettle
going all day long...all twelve hours of it.

kettle-holder, *n.*   pot-holder

keyless watch   stem-winder

kibble, *n., v.t.*   1. *n.,* **mine bucket**
                                                           2. *v.t.,* **grind**
   Kibbled wheat is *cracked wheat.*

kick the beam   lose out

kick-up. See **dust-up.**

Kilkenny cats   **squabblers**
   Inf. Based on an old Irish legend about two cats who fought each other so long and
so murderously that finally there was nothing left but their tails. The figurative meaning
of the phrase retains reference to the audible squabbling of the cats, rather than to their
gruesome end. Kilkenny is a county in southeast Eire, and also the name of its capital;
it was the scene of long and ancient internecine struggles which began in the 13th
century and went on between the Anglo-Irish and the original Irish. If there were a
real free-for-all going on, it might be referred to as a **donnybrook,** from *Donnybrook Fair,*
an annual event which used to take place in the town of Donnybrook, also in Ireland,
and was famous for the drinking of much whiskey and riotous fighting.

king's (queen's) evidence   state's evidence
   In Britain, the accused cooperates with the prosecution by *turning king's* or *queen's
evidence,* the phrase being determined by the sex of the sovereign at the time, unlike
K.B.B.

kinky, *adj.*   1. **sexually unconventional**
                                                       2. **twisted; odd**
                                                     3. **sophisticatedly off-beat**
                                                              4. *Inf.* **cool**
1. *Slang.* Or appealing to such tastes.
2. *Slang.* Peculiar; *kooky.*
3. *Slang.* As of clothes, for instance.
4. *Teenage slang.* Synonymous with **gear** and **fab.**

kiosk, *n.*   1. **newsstand**
                                                            2. **telephone booth**

kip, *n., v.i.*　　　　　　　　　　　　　　　　**1. rooming-house**
2. room in a rooming-house
3. bed
4. sleep
　Slang. The *house*, the *room* in the house, the *bed* in the room, the *sleep* in the bed;
sometimes seen in the expressions *go to kip, have a kip, take a kip,* or *kip down,* meaning
to *'turn in.'*

kipper, *n.*　　　　　　　　　　　　　　　　　　　　　　*Inf.* **kid; tot**
　Slang. Synonymous with a like-sounding British slang word—**nipper.**

kipper tie　　　　　　　　　　　　　　　　　　　　　**wide necktie**
　Inf. In the wide style, which suggests the outline of a knipper.

Kirby grip *n.*　　　　　　　　　　　　　　　　　　　**bobby pin**
　Also known in Britain as *hair-slide* and *hair grip.*

kissing gate　　　　　　　　　　　　　　　　　*Approx.* **cattle gate**
　Kissing gates found in rural Britain are gates hung with the side away from the hinge
swinging within a V-shaped or U-shaped enclosure in such a way that people can get
through but cattle can't. You push the gate away from the nearside of the V or U, step
into the latter, slide over to the other side,' and push the gate back. This quaint device
acquired its romantic name (one is told) because it was often the place where a swain
said goodnight to his lady love, and a certain amount of lingering and incidental activity
was in order.

kiss of life　　　　　　　　　　　　**1. mouth to mouth resuscitation**
2. boost
1. The life-saving procedure.
2. *Inf.* Probably modeled on the phrase *kiss of death,* it has acquired the meaning of
something that revitalizes or provides new hope for an ailing project, situation, etc.

kiss your hand. See **as easy as kiss your hand.**

kit, *n., v.t.*　　　　　　　　　　　　　　　　　　　　　　　**outfit**
　As a noun, *outfit* in the sense of special dress, like *skiing kit, camping kit,* etc. As a
verb, *outfit* in the sense of *equip.* Sometimes lengthened to *kit up.*

kitchen garden　　　　　　　　　　**family fruit and vegetable garden**

Kitemark, *n.*　　　　　　　　　　　　　　　　　　　　SEE COMMENT
　The certification mark given by the *British Standards Institution (BSI)* to products that
comply with its standards.

knacker, *n.*　　　　　　　　　　　　　　　　　　　　　SEE COMMENT
　One who purchases animal carcasses and slaughters superannuated livestock for
rendering into various products. The plant is called a *knackery* or *knacker's yard.*

knackered, adj.　　　　　　　　　　　　　　*Slang.* **beat (tuckered out)**
　Slang A grim image, derived from the previous entry.

knave, *n.*　　　　　　　　　　　　　　　　　　　　　　　　**jack**
　In playing cards. *Jack* is considered substandard in Britain.

knickers, *n. pl.*　　　　　　　　　　　　　　　　　　　　*Inf.* **panties**
　Inf. In America *knickers* would be understood as short for *knickerbockers,* which is the
British term for *plus fours,* an article of wearing apparel still seen there. See also **cami-
knickers.** To *get your knickers in a twist* is to *get all het up* about something or to *make a
muddle* of things. See also **nicker,** which is slang for *pound* (the unit of currency, not

weight); and this brings up a dull joke (?) that would be incomprehensible to Americans unfamiliar with either Briticism: Question: Why is it a waste of time to ask a one-legged woman for change of a one-pound **note**? Answer: Because you ought to know she'd only have half a knicker.

knife-and-fork tea   *Approx.* **light supper**
  Inf. A **high tea** at which meat or fish is served and a knife is required. The converse of a **fork supper**. See also **high tea; cream tea.**

Knight. See **K.**

knob, *n., Slang.*   *Slang.* **scab (strikebreaker)**

knob, *n.*   **lump**
  Of butter, sugar, etc.

knobble. See **nobble.**

knobs. See **with knobs on.**

knock, *n.*   *Slang.* **hit (success)**
  Slang. Synonymous with the British sense of **bomb.** But see **bit of a knock.**

knock, *v.i.*   *Slang.* **wow (impress)**
  Slang. To *knock* someone in American slang is to *disparage* him, but in British slang it means to *impress* him greatly, i.e., to *knock him dead,* and is probably short for *knock for six* (see **six**).

knock acock   *Inf.* **bowl over**
  Inf. To *astonish,* to present with the unexpected.

knocker. See **up to the knocker.**

knocker, *n.*   **door to door salesman**
  Slang. To *work on the knocker* is to *work from door to door.* Synonymous with **doorstep salesman.**

knocker-up, *n.*   **1. arouser**
                                                         2. SEE COMMENT
  1. *Inf.* A special type of arouser, one whose function is to summon sleeping railroad workers or miners to their jobs. *Knocking-up slates,* fixed to the outside wall beside the front doors of miners' cottages, still survive in colliery villages like Leasingthorne in County Durham. The waking time would be chalked on the slates.
  2. *Inf.* The term is used also in political circles, to describe a party worker charged with the function of getting out the vote. The following passage, from Ivor Richard's *We, the British* (Doubleday & Co., Garden City, New York, 1983) explains:

> The last four hours of election day are confused and hectic. The names of those who have not voted are given to teams of volunteer workers who then physically call on them. When I first came to the United States I was describing the process at a small midwestern university and could not understand the hilarity my description evoked. I later discovered why. The activity on the evening of polling day in Britian is called a knocking-up campaign and the volunteers are known as knockers-up.

knock for six. See **six.**

knocking-house, *n., Slang.*   **whorehouse**

knock on *Inf.* **turn up**
Inf. To *knock on* for work is to *turn up for work*; generally applied to **casual labourers;** an echo of the more common *knock off* (work), used in both countries.

knock-on effect side effect
The concomitant result, incidental consequence.

knock oneself up knock oneself out
To *overdo it.*

knock-out, *n.* 1. volleying
2. elimination contest
1. A tennis term, synonymous with **knock-up.**
2. A competition involving the elimination of losers, on the way to the finals.

knock up 1. wake up by knocking
2. exhaust; wear out
3. *Inf.* throw together
4. earn
1. *Inf.* The use of this term by Britons in America is fraught with danger. A respectable American will go to great pains to avoid *knocking up* a lady friend, as he understands the term, because in his country it is an indelicate expression for getting a lady into a delicate condition. In Britain, *knocking* people *up* is a far less serious matter. All it means there is to wake people up by knocking on their door. Some years ago, the author was startled when a male friend told him that he had been knocked up quite early that morning.
2. *Inf.* Another common British usage to be avoided in America: *I'm quite knocked up*, or *He does knock me up.* This refers merely to exhaustion, physical or emotional.
3. *Inf.* An unrelated British meaning is 'throw together,' as in, *Don't stand on ceremony, come along, we can always knock something up*, referring to the preparation of an impromptu meal. This usage was originally American, and was used by Louisa May Alcott in *Little Women*, but is now exclusively British.
4. *Inf.* As in, *He knocks up twenty thousand* **quid** *a year*, **I'll be bound.**

knock-up, *n.* volleying
Tennis term, synonymous with **knock-out, 1.**

know the form, *Inf.* *Inf.* **have the inside dope**

K.O. kickoff
Inf. A British football abbreviation. Thus, on a poster advertising a football game, "K.O. 3:00 P.M." It also means 'knockout,' a boxing term, as in America.

L

label, *n.*   **sticker; tag**

labourer. See **agricultural labourer; casual labourer.**

labour exchange   *approx.* **state employment office**
In this meaning, the words are often capitalized: *Labour Exchange.* In lower case, the term can denote any union building which houses its headquarters, meeting rooms, etc.

lacquer, *n.*   **hair spray**

lad   SEE COMMENT
Americans are familiar with this word in the sense of 'boy' or 'youth,' but do not use it commonly as the British do. Examples: 'He's a good lad.' (about a dependable, or a generous, or an honest *man*). 'Good lad!' (said to a mature man who has come through with a good deed or a nice gesture). 'Get your lads out.' (spoken in a TV drama by a police captain to a subordinate as instructions to get his men out on the street to hunt for the villain). Americans might use *boy* in some of these cases. *The lads* is the almost universal term in which British labor leaders refer to their members, rather than 'the men' or 'the members.' Used that way, the term suggests loyalty, solidarity and affection.

ladder, *n.*   **run**
This term applies to ladies' stockings and pantyhose (**tights**). *Ladder-proof* hose, etc., are advertised in Britain just as *run-proof* articles are advertised here, but the ladies remain skeptical on both sides of the Atlantic.

Lady, *n.* (in titles)   SEE COMMENT
The daughter of a duke, marquess or earl (in which case *Lady* is used with the forename, e.g., *Lady Jane Smith*); *or* the wife of a *peer* (except a duke), a *baronet* or *knight* (in which case *Lady*, without the forename, is followed by the name of the peerage or surname as the case may be, e.g., *Lady Bloomsbury, Lady Smith*). (Coincidentally, Lady Bloomsbury may also be a peeress in her own right.) If Lady Jane Smith marries Mr. Bloggs, she becomes *Lady Jane Bloggs.* See also **Lord; Dame; K.; baronet; peer.**

ladybird, *n.*   **ladybug**
Also called a *golden-knop.*

Lady Day   SEE COMMENT
March 25, so called because that is the day of the Feast of the Annunciation. See **quarter-day.** There is a tale that a letter addressed simply "March 25th, London" was promptly delivered to the wife of a well-known High Court judge (knighted) whose last name was *Day.*

ladyfy (ladify), *v.t.*   SEE COMMENT
To *ladyfy* or *ladify* a woman is to make a lady of her (as Prof. Higgins tried to do in *Pygmalion*), though it can mean merely to lend dignity to a woman by calling her a lady. *Ladified* describes a woman exhibiting the airs of a refined lady.

Lady of Threadneedle Street. See **Old Lady of Threadneedle Street.**

lag, *n., v.t.* 1. *Slang.* **jailbird**
2. *Slang.* **send up; pinch**
Slang. A *lag* is a *jailbird* and the word is usually found in the expression *old lag.* To be *lagged* is to be *sent up,* although *lagged* sometimes means merely 'pinched,' 'arrested,' whether or not the unfortunate is eventually *sent up.* A *lagging* is a *stretch.* There exists an organization called the *Old Lags Brigade,* which consists of hardened criminals placed on last-chance probation before they are imprisoned. It was founded in the fifties by a London judge named Reginald Ethelbert Seaton.

lambert, *n.* **giant**
Inf. Daniel Lambert (1770–1809) grew to a weight of 739 pounds and had a 102 inch waistline. His name has become a synonym for Gargantuan vastness. George Meredith called London the "Daniel Lambert of cities," and Herbert Spenser described someone as "a Daniel Lambert of learning." Apparently, people forgot about the *Daniel* and the upper case *L,* and *lambert* at one time became a common noun. Daniel's vest is still in the Leicester museum, but his name has gone out of figurative use.

lambs' tails **catkins**
Inf. Lambs' tails in Britain, in addition to making good soup, also refer to *catkins* hanging from certain trees such as the hazel and willow, and *catkins* in both countries are *downy flowerings* or *inflorescences.* The word *catkin* is a rather cloying diminutive of *cat* (formed like *manikin, pannikin,* etc.) and was invented because of the resemblance of those inflorescences to cats' tails. In any event, none of this is to be confused with *Lamb's Tales,* which are synopses of Shakespeare's plays by Charles and Mary Lamb, for children.

lame duck 1. *Slang.* **hard-luck guy**
2. **stock exchange defaulter**
1. *Slang.* A *person in difficulties, unable to cope.* The narrow American usage, describing an incumbent political official or body still in office after losing an election but only because the winner has not yet been seated, is a highly restricted application of this British meaning. This narrow American usage, however, appears to have been adopted by British political pundits, at least on the air. The term can also be applied to a firm in financial difficulties, or a troubled industry.
2. *Slang.* This term also describes a person unable to meet his obligations on the London Stock Exchange. Also a *lossmaking company.*

land agent **real estate broker**
Synonymous with **estate agent**.

landed, *adj.* 1. *Inf.* **O.K.; in good shape**
2. *Inf.* **out of luck; lost**
3. SEE COMMENT
Depending on the context, this participial adjective can have two exactly opposite meanings, even if used in identical sentences.
1. *Inf.* If one were waiting for the last available table in a restaurant which was being held until 8 o'clock for someone else, one could say, *If he doesn't show up by eight, we're landed,* meaning *we're okay.*
2. *Inf.* If one's friend who had the tickets to a show or match were alarmingly late, the same sentence could be expressed, and *...we're landed* would mean 'we're out of luck'; 'we've had it.'
3. *Landed gentry* describes those of the **gentry** possessed of land.

landlord, *n.* **innkeeper; pub keeper**
In addition to its wider general meaning in both countries, *landlord* has the special British meaning and flavor of 'inn-keeper.' Many **pubs** were once real *inns* and a few still have rooms for rent, but some that no longer let rooms still have names that include the word *hotel.* The keeper of such a pub (who used to be a *landlord* in the literal sense when rooms were available) is nonetheless still called *landlord* and is so summoned and addressed by clients not familiars of the establishment who don't feel privileged to

address him by name. **Publican** is synonymous with *landlord* in this sense (though never used in the vocative) and comes from *public house*, a term still in use but far less common than its shortened form *pub*. See **free house** for a discussion of the landlord's business arrangements. See also **pub; during hours**.

land of the leal   heaven
    Leal is a Scots form of *loyal*.

landslip, *n.*   landslide

land (someone) with   saddle (someone) with
    Often used in the passive form, *landed with*. Synonymous with **lumbered with**, though the latter invokes an added dimension of inconvenience.

larder, *n.*   pantry

large, *adj.*   double
    As used in ordering a drink at the pub or restaurant. A *large* whiskey (*whisky* in Britain for Scotch; Irish *whiskey* has the *e*), gin, vodka, etc. is a *double* portion. See under **double, 3.**

lark, *n.*   job; type of activity
    Inf. "It's too hot for this *lark*," says a sweating laborer doffing his jacket, using *lark* as a sardonic synonym for *job* or *task*—the same type of British humor as found in "Are you happy in your work?" addressed to one who is palpably miserable as he plugs away at an unwanted task. In Siegfried Sassoon's *Diaries 1920–1922* (Faber & Faber, London, 1981), we see the possibilities of *lark* somewhat broadened. Sassoon is lunching with Arnold Bennett, H.G. Wells and the critic Frank Swinnerton: "...Swinnerton got on to 'Hughie Walpole.'...'He will have no literary reputation at all in five years.' ...A. B. [Arnold Bennett]: 'But Hughie's a great *lark*!'" What he meant was that Walpole was a *lot of fun*, a *character*, always amusing.

lasher, *n.*   pool
    Particularly, one formed by water spilling over a *weir*.

lashings, *n. pl., Slang.*   *Slang.* scads

lash out, *v.i.*   *Inf.* **throw money around**
    Slang. To *lash out* on something is to spend money on it recklessly and without stint.

lash-up, *n. Slang*   1. fiasco
                                                                                      2. improvisation

last post   taps
    Virtually the same as *taps*—not the tune, but the function. There are two *posts*, called, reasonably enough, *first post* and *last post*. The first one comes about ten minutes before the other, as a sort of ready signal.

laugh like a drain, *Slang.*   *Slang.* **horselaugh**

lavatory roll   roll of toilet paper
    Delicacy, like the American use of *tissue*.

Lawk(s)!   *Inf.* **Lordy!**
    Rather vulgar. Used jocularly by the upper classes. *Lawks-a-mercy* is the fuller expression.

Law Society   *approx.* **Bar Association**
    There is a national *Law Society* and also many local ones in Britain just as there is a nationwide *Bar Association* and many local ones in America. In certain matters such as the setting of ethical standards of conduct, the furtherance of legal education, and so

on, the functions of the British and American bodies coincide. Membership in *law societies* is confined to **solicitors** only. **Barristers** have their own group which is known as the **General Council of the Bar**. No such division exists in America. In neither country is membership compulsory.

lay, *v.t.*   1. **set**
                                                                                                          2. **impose**
1. The table.
2. A tax, as in a tax laid on wealth by certain governments.

layabout, *n.*   **loafer; hobo**

lay-by, *n.*   **rest area**
Roadside parking space. When you see a road sign reading LAY-BY as you drive along in Britain, you know that up ahead on your left, there will be a turn-out which broadens into a parking area. People use it for short-term parking, e.g., to take a nap, to look at the view, or as a picnic area. The British are very fond of stopping by the side of the road and having a picnic lunch or **high tea** complete with folding chairs, folding table with tablecloth, tea kettle, and very elaborate outdoor eating equipment, to say nothing of all that good food. If there is no *lay-by* handy, any **verge** (*shoulder*) will do.

lay (someone) by the heels   **track (someone) down**

lay on   **provide; arrange for**
Very commonly seen in the participial form *laid on* meaning 'provided for in advance.' Thus, office quarters can be rented in Britain with or without a secretary *laid on*.

lay (oneself) out to   **put (oneself) out to**

laystall, *n.*   **rubbish heap**

lea. See **ley.**

leader, *n.*   1. **editorial**
                                                                                                      2. **chief counsel**
                                                                                                      3. **concert master**
This word has three distinct British meanings that are not found in America:
1. It means 'newspaper editorial,' especially the principal one. There is a related (and rather unattractive) word *leaderette*, which has nothing to do with female leaders but means a 'short editorial paragraph' following the main one. The expression *fourth leader* is a British inside joke, originated by *The Times* (London). It denotes a humorous discursive essay, and came about in the following way: *The Times*, since more or less time immemorial, published three daily *leaders* (editorials) on serious matters. (See **Establishment** and **The Times**.) In the period 1922–1966 they often entitled the third one 'fourth leader' (leave it to the British to find ways to puzzle benighted, struggling Americans!) to indicate to the cognoscenti that what was really the third editorial was tongue-in-cheek and not to be taken seriously. This practice has recently been revived on occasion. A sample from a recent (mid-June, 1986) edition follows:

FOURTH LEADER
There is word from NASA; well there usually is. The two previously undiscovered asteroids which were recently found to be going round the earth at much the same distance from it as the moon are said to be rich in nickel. So far, so good; but the discovery has given NASA an idea. The idea is to send mining expeditions to them, to obtain supplies of this rare but essential metal for the orbiting space stations which, we are assured, will be filling the heavens by the end of the century, if only they have enough nickel. Plain folk may say that the problem of the nickel-shortage for space stations can be easily solved by abandoning the plans for space stations. But that is why they are just plain folk instead of NASA officials...Mining needs miners; everybody knows that. Miners have unions; every body knows **that**...A stiff drink may be needed to face what follows: how would the NASA officials feel if they arrived on the

nickel-rich moonlet and found a replica of Mr Scargill [a notorious leader of the miners' union who caused great disruption in the long-lasting miners' strike in 1985 and whose very name strikes terror in conservative circles] but with fourteen legs and one huge eye in the middle of his forehead, shouting (from half a dozen mouths) about defending miners' communities?...The plain folk might be right, after all. We would not advocate the abandonment of the entire space programme; we recognize that there must be progress, even if we are sometimes not sure why. But before the mining expedition sets off, it might do well to sit down and think the project through rather more fully. Brother, can you spare a nickel?

Other offerings were concerned with topics as diverse as homing cats (able to find their way home from distant points); the purchase tax on false beards and moustaches (analogous to the American sales tax, but now replaced by **V.A.T.**); the pelicans in St. James's Park (originally a community of two, renewed and enlarged by kindly donations from Texas and Louisiana); the plight of the male parent sent to fetch his little daughter from her friend Ursula's birthday party, finding himself the only male amidst a horde of young mothers; the mysterious delivery, on mule-back, of a consignment of cricket bats to Lhasa in Tibet. Among regular contributors were Peter Fleming (brother of Ian) and Douglas Woodruff (a Catholic journalist and biographer with a vast fund of curious historical knowledge). An anthology of *Fourth Leaders* was published by *The Times* Publishing Company in 1952. It is not an easy book to find. Young English readers, and without doubt any American or other foreign reader who happens to see the editorial page of *The Times*, may well wonder why the *third leader*, on certain days, is labeled 'Fourth.' Now you know. A *Fourth Leader* appeared in the August 2, 1986 issue of *The Times* that starts: "G.K. Chesterton used to say that if he ever felt like taking any exercise, he would lie down until he got over it." It seems that a new English branch of a Japanese company encouraged its employees to start the day with five minutes of "physical jerks." "The mistake," says the editorial, "is to say that the workers should do it. A firm with more experience of the people of this country would have issued a strict order that they shouldn't. There is in the British...something we like to think of as the bulldog spirit, but which others might call **bloody-minded**ness. This happy breed, let Nippon know, does not like doing what's good for it..." In the same issue of *The Times* there appears the following engaging letter:

Lightening of spirit
From the Reverend S. G. Luff
  Sir, It is a pleasure to recognise the old "Fourth Leader", albeit third, in the traditional vein of *Times* humour ("Reigning cats—and dogs", July 28).
  I cannot recall when this feature was suppressed, but in the forties, when I was a novice in a Benedictine monastery, it was the practice to read the Fourth Leader, subject to approval, in the refectory, while the brethren were taking their first substantial meal.
  Any student of monasticism knows the significance attached by the early Fathers to the "noonday demon" or *accidie*. Hard to define, it has been described as "don't careishness" and "torpor", though the latter is more appropriate to the time after lunch. The *Times* reading would follow a passage from Scripture and the combination of divinity, levity and a full platter seemed to be just the thing for getting the brethren through this small daily crisis.
  Vocations to the monastic life have notoriously declined. One hazards a guess that the absence of this special brand of light relief may be a contributing factor. Would a guaranteed revival of the Fourth Leader lead to a strengthening of our monastic communities at the present time?
Yours faithfully,
STANLEY G. LUFF,
Our Lady's Church,
College View,
Llandovery, Dyfed.

2. Another meaning is 'leading counsel' on a team of lawyers trying a case.
3. Finally, it means the 'concert master' of an orchestra, i.e., the first violinist who sits to the conductor's left and is his right-hand man, acting as his liaison with the rest of the players. This meaning sometimes confuses Americans, because *leader* is popularly

used in America to mean 'conductor' when it refers to a small orchestra (as compared with a symphony orchestra), and also because *leader*, in America, is properly used to describe the baton-wielder in a band, large or small.

lead for the Crown act as chief prosecuting attorney
See also **leader, 2.**

leadswinging. See **swing the lead.**

league table performance record
Originally applied to tables ranking the records of teams or clubs constituting an athletic league, it has been extended to refer to tabulated comparisons of performances in any field of endeavor.

leasehold. See **freehold.**

leat, *n.* open watercourse

leather, *n.* chamois
For wiping off automobiles, etc.

leave, *v.t.* graduate from
In the expression *leave school,* which in America connotes dropping out, but in Britain means simply that the student is graduating. *Geoffrey has left Staples High School* would sound ominous in America. *Geoffrey has left King's School Canterbury* means only that he has completed his course of studies there. See also **leaver; school-leaver.**

leave alone let alone
In the sense of 'leave undisturbed.' *Leave me alone!* for *Let me alone!* is nonstandard in America; not so in Britain.

leaver, *n.* *approx.* graduating student
One about to complete the curriculum at a **prep school** or **public school** at the end of that term. During that final term the student is known as a *leaver*. On the completion of the term the *leaver* becomes an **old boy** or **old girl**. See **school-leaver; leave.**

leave the metals. See **metals.**

leave (someone) to it desert
Inf. As in *He went off to America, leaving his family to it.* See **shoot the moon.**

leave well alone leave well enough alone

leaving gift retirement present

lecturer, *n.* instructor
In a British university. See also **reader.**

left-arm, *adj.* left-handed
To describe a left-handed **bowler** (*approx.* cricket counterpart of a pitcher); but a left-handed **batsman** (*batter*) is called *left-hand.*

left luggage office baggage room

lefty, *n.* *Slang.* leftist
Slang. The American usage meaning 'left-handed person' is not common in Britain.

legal aid SEE COMMENT
In Britain, *legal aid* is supplied from Government funds made available to litigants who otherwise could not afford to pay for legal services. In America, there are Legal Aid Societies supported by private contributions.

legal figment   **legal fiction**
A proposition accepted as fact for the sake of argument or convenience, though without foundation in fact. *Legal fiction* is used in Britain also. Gilbert used it in *The Grand Duke.*

leg it   *Slang.* **beat it**
Slang. Synonymous with **hook it.**

legitimate drama   **classical drama**
This phrase means very different things in the two countries. In Britain it refers to dramatic works of established merit as opposed to melodrama or farce, no matter how well known, e.g., *Hamlet* vs. *East Lynne,* or *The Rivals* vs. *Charley's Aunt.* In America the *legitimate theater* means the 'stage' as opposed to any other form of dramatic representation, and *legitimate drama* includes any play produced on the stage or, in today's idiom, *live.*

Lego *n.*   SEE COMMENT
Building game consisting of plastic building blocks that fit into one another. Military dispatch: *Repairing the pontoon bridges was as easy as slotting in pieces of Lego.*

legpull, *n., Slang.*   **hoax**

lengthman, lengthsman, *n.*   **road maintenance man**
A *lengthman* is a laborer charged with the duty of keeping a certain *length* of road in good condition. The word developed in the old days before the creation of a country-wide system of hard-surfaced roads requiring the services of teams of road workers equipped with all kinds of heavy machinery. It evokes the image of the solitary worker equipped with only a spade, a high degree of independence, and a noble sense of responsibility. As used today it can sometimes be taken as synonymous only with *streetcleaner.* There is a highly specialized category of *lengthman,* however, which relates to the maintenance of British inland waterways or canals. These wonderful canals are quite a story in themselves, one which has been beautifully written by L.T.C. Rolt, and in his second book on the subject, *The Inland Waterways of England* (George Allen and Unwin, Ltd., London, 4th ed., 1966, pp. 110–111), he writes of the canal *lengthman* in the following prose, which is offered for the reader's delight:

If a canal overflows or bursts its banks the consequences may be serious as it may run upon embankments high above thickly populated areas...
In October 1939, 3 inches of rain fell in one night at the Daventry area, and despite every effort to discharge the surplus flood water, a breach occurred in the Weedon embankment of the Grand Union Canal. The local lengthman, who had been on duty all through the night, was aware of this danger-point, discovered the breach almost as soon as it carried away in the early hours of the morning, and dropped the stop planks. Only minor local flooding occurred and damage to property was negligible, but had it not been for this prompt action, fifteen miles of waterway could have poured out through an ever widening gap.
Of all the many never-before jobs upon which the security and comfort of our lives and property depend, that of the canal lengthman is probably the least known or appreciated. When we sweep to the north in a night Scotch express or awake from sleep to hear a locomotive whistle and the clash of buffers we do occasionally remember the signalman's vigil in his lonely cabin or the endless work of shunters and train crews on the steel webs of the marshalling yards. We sometimes hear the roar of night lorry traffic on a trunk road, or flick a switch in the small hours and think of those who tend the turbo-alternators and switchgear in some distant power station. But when a great storm lashes rain against the panes and booms in the chimney it merely induces, by contrast, a sharpened sense of comfort and security. Yet a quarter of a mile away there may be a canal whose water level is higher than our roof top, and we do not realize that we are only being saved from a catastrophic flood by the vigilance of one man. He may have forfeited a night's sleep to plod, storm lantern in hand, through the blinding rain along the towing path watching his levels, regulating his paddles, looking for danger signs. He is often a solitary taciturn old man, accustomed to keeping his own company, for his little red-brick cottage dating from the

day the canal was built is often remote even from the village by-road, accessible by land only along the towing path or by a footway over the fields. Sometimes if you are walking the towpath in the daytime you will meet him, a slow-moving, heavy-booted figure bow-hauling his small punt-shaped boat with a load of hedge trimmings or some clay puddle to stop a small leak in the bank. You may perhaps see his weather-beaten face in the village pub of a night, the beer froth whitening the fringe of his heavy moustache. He may not talk to you about his job, for he is seldom a conversationalist, preferring a contemplative **pint,** but even in these surroundings you can generally recognize him by the queer little hump between his shoulder-blades. It is caused by the end of the lock windlass which he habitually carries tucked over the shoulder under his coat. He is a countryman just as the canal has become a part of the countryside, and yet in a sense he stands apart from the village being a member of that unique amphibious community of the canals. Probably he gets his winter coal by water, and if he ever moves house he will do so by boat. His job of regulating the water over a wide area calls for considerable local knowledge, a knowledge which he inherited from his father before him, a knowledge of sluices, weirs, culverts and streams of which his mind is often the only chart. The canal is his life and his first thought. When his time comes, and he must make way for a generation whose first thought is the contents of the weekly pay packet, it is probably that much of this inherited knowledge will go with him. So much the greater will be our loss.

let. See **engage.**

let alone   *Inf.* **count on**
Inf. As in *You can let him alone for producing the goods.*

let-out, *n.*   *Inf.* **loophole**
Inf. Often used attributively, as in the phrase *let-out clause* meaning 'escape clause.'

letter-box   **mailbox**
See also **pillar-box; post-box.**

letter post   **first-class mail**
The terms *first-class mail* and *second-class mail* are now current in Britain to indicate priorities for delivery.

let the shooting. See **shooting.**

let the side down. See **side.**

levant, *v.i.*   **abscond**
Usually after welshing on a gambling loss.

level, *adj.*   1. **even**
                                                                                              2. **close**
1. When players are *level* in a game, it means that they are *even.*
2. However, a *level* race is not a *tie* but only a *close* race.

level crossing   **grade crossing**

level par   **par**
Golf term used (tautologically, it would seem) by sports announcers to mean 'par,' in describing the performances of tournament contestants.

level pegging, *n., adj.*   **even Stephen**
Inf. A term borrowed from cribbage, in which the score is kept by advancing *pegs* along a series of holes in a board. It applies to equal scores in games or mutual obligations between friends or businessmen which wash each other out. Synonymous with **honours even.** To *level-peg* is to *be even.*

levels (A-levels; O-levels). See **A-levels.**

ley, *n.*   **temporary pasture**
(Pronounced LAY or LEE.) *Ley-farming* is the system of putting a given area into grazing pasture for a few years, then *catching the fertility,* as they say in East Anglia, and using that area for a particular crop. A *ley* is a *rotating pasture;* variant of *lea.* In Cambridge *The Leys* is the name of a well-known private school.

Liberal Jew   **Reform Jew**
In America, the three branches of Judaism are Orthodox, Conservative, and Reform; in Britain, Orthodox, Reform and Liberal.

Lib-Lab, *adj.*   SEE COMMENT
Inf. Anything involving both Liberal and Labour party supporters. Originally it applied to members of the Liberal party in the beginning of the century who supported the new Labour party. *Lib-Labbery* was coined to describe an alliance between the two parties and is now usually used to connote shady political dealings.

(on) licence   **(on) parole**

licenced, *adj.*   **having a liquor license**
Sign seen on most British hotels and restaurants. See also **off licence.**

liche- (lych-) gate, *n.*   SEE COMMENT
A roofed churchyard gate, under which the coffin is placed while awaiting the arrival of the officiating minister. Also called *resurrection gate.* *Lich,* derived from Old English *lik,* is an obsolete English word for 'body,' and survives also in the place name *Lichfield* and in the term *lich door.*

lick, *n.*   *Inf.* **dab**
Inf. Term used in house painting, meaning a *light wash.* Cf. *lick* in a *lick and a promise.* For British use of *dab, n.,* see **dab.**

lido, *n.*   **public open-air swimming pool**
The *Lido* is Venice's famous bathing resort. A *lido,* in Britain, is a public swimming pool (**swimming-bath**). One sees the term **corporation** *swimming-bath,* meaning 'public swimming-bath.' *Corporation* in that phrase is the equivalent of the American term *municipal.* A *deck lido* is a *ship's swimming-pool.*

lie doggo   *Inf.* **lie low**
Slang. Literally, to *lie doggo* is to *lie motionless,* the way a dog does; to *play dead.* Figuratively it means to 'lie low,' to 'bide one's time.'

lie down under   *Inf.* **buckle under**
Inf. To *give way* to the other party, to *kowtow.*

lie in   **sleep late**
Inf. In the morning. One can *lie in* or *have a lie-in.* Synonymous with **sleep in.**

lie up   **Inf. take to one's bed**
Inf. With the connotation of not feeling well.

life-belt, *n.*   **life-preserver**
For British sense of *life preserver,* see **life preserver.**

lifeboat, *n.*   SEE COMMENT
Rescue operation for **fringe banks,** managed by the **Bank.**

Life Guard   SEE COMMENT
Member of one of the two regiments of Household Cavalry. (The other regiment is called the *Blues and Royals*.) The household involved is the royal household. Properly speaking, a member of this elite cavalry regiment is called a *Life Guardsman*. *Lifeguards* in the American sense (people who save other people from drowning) are still sometimes called **humane society men** but the American term is becoming common in Britain. The context, it is to be hoped, will preserve the British from confusion.

life-preserver, *n.*   **blackjack**
In America a *life preserver* is an instrument of mercy called a **life-belt** in Britain.

life vest   **life jacket**
The British say *jacket*, too, but British Airways' pamphlets and signs remind you that there is a *life vest* under each seat.

lift, *n.*   **elevator**
To go higher in a building (without walking) the British use *lifts*, the Americans *elevators*. To stand up higher, the British put **elevators** into their shoes, the Americans *lifts*.

light come light go   **easy come easy go**
Hyphenated, it is used by C.P. Snow as an adjective meaning 'casual' in the expression 'a light-come-light-go affair.'

lighting-up time   SEE COMMENT
Time of day when lights must be lit by vehicles on the railroad.

like a dog's dinner   *Inf.* **all dolled up**
Inf. To be *got up like a dog's dinner* is to be *dressed to kill*. Somewhat pejorative; not quite synonymous with **dressed to the nines**. See also **dog's breakfast**.

like old boots, *Inf.*   *Inf.* **like a house afire**

like one o'clock   **1. promptly; quick and lively**
                                                                       2. *Inf.* **to a T**
(Main stress on *one*.)
1. *Inf.* Sometimes it has the sense of 'vigorously.'
2. *Inf. Does that suit you, sir? Like one o'clock!* Synonymous with **to a dot**.

li-lo, *n.*   **air mattress**
(Pronounced LIE-LOW.) *Li-lo* is in fact a trademark for a make of air mattress. There are other brands, but *li-lo* is becoming generic, like **hoover** for *vacuum cleaner*. The nonbrand British equivalent for *air mattress* is *air bed*.

limb, *n.*   *Inf.* **little devil**
Inf. Limb is a shortening of the phrase *limb of the devil* or *limb of Satan* and is used to mean 'mischief-making youngster,' the way *little devil* is used in America. See also **kipper; basket**.

limb of the law   **arm of the law**

limited company   **corporation**
Also called *limited liability company*, more usually just *company*. See **company; corporation**.

line, *n.*   **track**
In Britain it is the *line* one mustn't cross, according to the signs, whereas Americans use the word *line* to mean a whole railroad company, rather than the track itself. Passengers in America are warned not to cross the *track*.

line of country   *Inf.* **line**
Inf. Very often in the negative, to indicate that something is beyond one's capabilities:
I'm afraid that's not my line of country. Alternatively, *That's not up my street.* An American
equivalent would be *not in my line.* Used in the affirmative, in a sentence like, *I'd take
it to Jones; that's just his line of country,* the American version would be *That's just up his
alley.*

line (of stock), *n.*   **block (of stock)**

liners, *n.*   **underpants**
Inf. Worn under **knickers.**

lines, marriage. See **marriage lines.**

lining, *n.*   **striping**
Term used in painting, e.g., the painting of automobiles.

link, *v.t.*   **link arms with**
To hook one's arm through another's. There would seem to be no single American
word with which to avoid the circumlocution. One might *link* a besotted friend to guide
him to his couch, or a sober one just to stroll familiarly with him.

linked signals   SEE COMMENT
Traffic lights graduated so that you always have a green light if you drive within the
proper speed limit.

link house   **row of joined houses**
Synonymous with **terrace.** Not in common use.

linkman   **1. anchorman; moderator**
                                                                       2. go-between
1. In radio and television.
2. Originally described a position in soccer (**football**); now extended to mean any 'go-
between.'

lino, *n.*   **linoleum**
Inf. (Pronounced LIE'-NO.) The British almost always use the informal shortening.
Linoed means 'covered with *linoleum.'* A *linoed* floor is a *linoleum* floor.

lint, *n.*   **surgical dressing**
Ian Ball, the New York correspondent of *The Daily Telegraph* (London), comments on
this Briticism in his witty and informative article entitled *Amerenglish* in the October
1974 issue of *Encounter,* a London publication:

> I once witnessed the horror on the face of an American when an English doctor
> treating him for an open wound said he was about to put some *lint* on it. To the
> patient *lint* meant only one thing—non-sterile flecks of fabric that must be brushed
> off a dark suit. Its English-English meaning—surgical dressing—has never entered
> American-English. If this wounded American had been told he was being taken to the
> *operating theatre,* staffed by *theatre sisters,* his alarm probably would have deepened. In
> American-English, *operating room* is the only term used and our adaptation here of the
> word *theatre* makes them shake their heads over the skittishness of the Mother Tongue.

For the British equivalent of American *lint* see **fleck.** (See also **sister** and **theatre.**)

lip-balm, *n.*   **chapstick (proprietary name)**

listening room   **control room**
Where the engineer of a radio station sits.

list office   **calendar clerk**
Legal term.

literal, *n.*   **misprint**
Typographical error, usually called *typo*. The word is used by Americans as an adjective in *literal error*, meaning 'misprint,' but not as a noun.

litter bin   **trash basket**

little basket. See under **basket.**

little-go, *n.*   SEE COMMENT
Inf. Former term for the first examination for the B.A. degree at Cambridge or Oxford; now archaic.

little Mary, *Inf.*   *Inf.* **tummy**

live in cotton wool   **live a sheltered life**
Inf. **Cotton wool** is *absorbent cotton*, used here as a metaphor for careful packing to provide insulation from the traumata of life in this harsh world. See also **wrap in cotton wool.**

live like a fighting cock   **be a gourmet**
Inf. To insist on the best of fare.

liverish, *adj.*   **bad tempered**

Liverpudlian, *n., adj.*   SEE COMMENT
Of Liverpool. They speak **Scouse.**

liver sausage   **liverwurst**

livery, *n.*   **costume**
Livery has a number of historical and distinctly British meanings having to do with ancient **City** of London companies or guilds called *Livery Companies* which used to have distinctive costumes or *liveries*. *Livery* is still used generically in both countries to describe certain types of uniform, such as those worn by chauffeurs. In Britain it is now also applied to characteristic *color schemes* like those of the various divisions of the British railway system.

living, *n.*   **benefice**
Ecclesiastical term for the position of rector, vicar, etc.

loaf, *n.*   *Slang.* **bean (head)**
Slang. Short for *loaf of bread*, cockney rhyming slang for 'head' but now adopted as general slang as in such expressions as *Use your loaf!* See **Appendix II.G.3.** From *The Times* (London) of July 27, 1985, under the headline **Using his loaf:** 'Lyons (AP)—A bank customer who produced a pistol from inside the long *baguette* loaf he carried under his arm forced the **cashier** [teller] to hand over 25,000 francs (about £2,000). The robber is still at large.''

loan share; loan stock   **bond**

lobbyist, *n.*   **political journalist**
One frequenting the hall of the House of Commons to pick up political news. Sometimes called *lobby correspondent*. By now the term has acquired the common American meaning as well, though perhaps with less suggestion of impropriety.

local, *n.*   **1. neighborhood bar**
                                                   2. native
1. *Inf.* Britons often talk of nipping down to the *local (local pub)*.
2. *Inf.* Usually heard in the plural, the *locals* is a rather affectionate term meaning the *natives*, the people in a particular community who look as though they haven't just moved out from the city, have been around a while, really belong there, and are going to be around for some time to come.
Compare **tripper; grockle.**

loch; lough, *n.*   **1. lake**
                                                   2. inlet
1. In Scotland. Americans usually pronounce it LOK, the way Maxine Sullivan did when she swung *Loch Lomond*. The Scots pronounce *loch* like the Germans. *Lough* is the Irish form of *loch*, pronounced the Scottish way.
2. *Loch* can also mean 'narrow inlet,' known then correctly as *sea loch*. See also **lough.**

locum, *n,*   **doctor covering for another**
   Inf. The term is also applied to a clergyman's temporary replacement. *Locum* is an informal shortening of *locum tenens*. A literal translation of *locum tenens* would be 'one holding a place,' and by inference, a 'person taking somebody else's place,' i.e., a 'replacement.' *Lieutenant* was taken over intact from the French, in which language *lieu* means 'place' and *tenant* is the present participle of *tenir*, to 'hold.' It is easy to see how that word acquired not only its military connotation, but even more particularly its general meaning of 'deputy,' 'substitute,' and at times 'replacement.' Be all that as it may, while your British doctor is off on a Scottish salmon fishing holiday or just playing village cricket that afternoon, his *locum* will take good care of you.

lodger. *See* **boarder.**

loft, *n.*   **attic**

lofty catch   *approx.* **pop fly**
   A cricket term.

loiter with intent   SEE COMMENT
   Short for *loiter with intent to commit a crime;* more specific than *vagrancy*.

lollipop man (woman; lady)   *approx.* **children's traffic guide**
   Employed to assist children across the street. The *lollipop* label is derived from the form of the stick carried, which is surmounted by a disk reading: STOP. CHILDREN CROSSING.

lolly, *n.*   **dough (money)**
   A piece of the lolly has its American slang equivalent in *some of the gravy*. See also **brass; brown; corn; dibs.** A *lolly* in Britain (reminiscent of *lollipop*) is also ice cream or water ice on a stick.

Lombard Street   *approx.* **Wall Street; money market**
   Inf. London's money market, named after its principal street for banking and finance; analogous to *Wall Street* used that way. But *the* **City** is the more usual expression for the financial community generally. *It's all Lombard Street to a China orange* means *the odds are a hundred to one* (or *a thousand to one*). Variations are: *all Lombard Street to a Brummagen sixpence* (see **Brum**): *...to ninepence,...to an egg-shell*.

long chalk. *See* **not by a long chalk.**

long firm, *Inf.*   *Inf.* **set of deadbeats**

long-head, *n,*   *Slang.* **smart cookie**
Inf. The adjective is *long-headed.*

long odds on   **heavy favorite**
This is a sports term, used as a phrasal noun.

long pull   **extra measure**
Inf. In a **pub,** the *long pull* is a measure of beer or other liquid refreshment over and above the quantity asked for; in other words, a drink with a built-in dividend. Sometimes the *long* is omitted, so that a *pull* means the same thing as a *long pull. Long pull* is not used in the American sense to mean 'the future'; 'the years to come.'

long sea outfall   **remote sewage disposal pipe**
This awkward phrase describes a sewage pipe that sticks way out into the ocean in order to dispose of the effluent of a seaside town without polluting the beaches.

long-sighted, *adj.*   **farsighted**
In Britain *far-sighted* is hardly ever used literally to describe corporeal optical capacity. It is almost always used in the figurative sense of *looking ahead,* a figurative use shared with America. The British term for *nearsighted* is *short-sighted,* which is always used figuratively in America to describe a person who doesn't plan ahead, and this figurative use, too, is shared with Britain. In other words, the British use *long-sighted* and *short-sighted* literally where the Americans would say *farsighted* and *nearsighted.* The British use *far-sighted* figuratively, as the Americans do; and the Americans use *shortsighted* figuratively, as the British do.

long-stay, *adj.*   **long term**
Applied, e.g., to hospital patients.

long stop   **1.** SEE COMMENT
                                                          2. backstop; reinforcement
1. The fielder back of the wicket-keeper (rough opposite number of *catcher* in baseball) who is there to stop the balls that get away from the wicket-keeper.
2. *Inf.* Extended to describe any person or thing that serves to prevent or check an undesirable result in case the person primarily in charge is wanting.

long vac. See under **come down; holiday.**

loo, *n, Inf.*   *Inf.* **john**
Bathroom, lavatory, washroom, rest room, convenience, boys' room, little boys' room, girls' room, little girls' room, gents', gents' room, ladies', ladies' room, privy, water-closet, w.c., powder-room—the euphemisms have proliferated like mushrooms after a shower. The **non-U** British (see **Appendix I.C.6.**) use the word *toilet,* a term usually avoided by U-Britons as too euphemistic and by most Americans as indelicate. In public notices in Britain, *toilet* is the usual term, perhaps because *toilet* or a recognizably similar term (*toilette, toiletta, toiletten*) is thus used in many foreign countries whose nationals often come to Britain. The present position in Britain is that the educated and literary say *lavatory* or *W.C.* (or **bog** if they are self-consciously identifying themselves with the proletariat); the middle class (and almost everyone) says *loo;* the lower middle class and the genteel say *toilet.* The common American euphemism is *bathroom,* and its use is pushed to ridiculous lengths. Children are heard to say *The doggie went to the bathroom on the rug,* or, *I'm sorry, I went to the bathroom in may pants,* or, *Kitty's going to the bathroom on the flower bed. Bathroom* is not so used in Britain, where in so many homes, especially the older ones, the bathroom proper, i.e., the room containing the bathtub (and usually a wash-basin) and the smaller room containing only the—shall we say—*toilet,* are quite separate, so that one would *go to the bathroom* only for a bath or to wash one's hands. (Incidentally, to confuse the issue, see **wash,** *n.* and **spend a penny.**) When Evelyn Waugh, in "An Open Letter to the Hon'ble Mrs Peter Rodd (Nancy Mitford) on a Very Serious Subject," said that *toilet* was pure American, he must have meant that that was the literary Americanism for it. He may have been right about that, but surely Ameri-

cans, within the memory of the author, have gone to extremes to avoid it in social speech. As to the derivation of *loo*, the editor has been assured that it is a corruption of *l'eau* (French for 'the water') as used, in the good old days, in the expression "Gardez l'eau!" shouted down at pedestrians by people throwing slops out of the window. Some support for this view may be gained from the following passage in David Daiches's *Was* (Thames and Hudson, London, 1975):

> But some Scots was French: gardyloo, watch out for the water, they had cried from the windows of the high flats of Edinburgh when they emptied their unsavoury slops over unwary passers-by in the street below; Dr. Johnson was not the only visitor to find the practice offensive. *Tsei u-l'mad*, go out and learn, the rabbis used to say, and many an unsuspecting visitor to Edinburgh in earlier times had gone out and learned about gardyloo to his cost.

Another source considers *loo* a truncated pun derived from *Waterloo* (cf. the *water* in *water closet*). Another theory is the following: In hotels, the French used to put the number *00* or *100* on the door of the toilet, as a variant of the letters *w.c.* which stand for *water closet*. *Numéro cent* and *w.c.* (pronounced DOOBLEVAY SAY) were used interchangeably in French by the anxious guest looking for the facility. British soldiers returning from France during and after World War I, according to this hypothesis, misinterpreted the number *100* and came back with *loo*. However, Alan S.C. Ross (mentioned in **Appendix I.C.6.** as the author of *U and Non-U*), in an article entitled simply "Loo," published in *Blackwood's Magazine* (Edinburgh), October 1974, says of this derivation, "This seems an altogether improbable suggestion." Prof. Ross lists seven theories (including the "*Room 100*" story) and rejects them all in favor of a "sporadic French joke," to wit: *le waterloo*—but then goes on to express his doubts about that one as well.

Other suggested derivations: The French noun *lieu* (place). There are signs in some French public *loos* reading: *On est prié de laisser ce* lieu *aussi propre qu'on le trouve*. (Please leave this *place* as clean as you find it.) In the late 18th century the term *lieu d'aisances* (public convenience, comfort station) was in use. The transformation of *lieu* into *loo* might occur quite readily; but there is a problem: the term *loo* seems to date back only to the late 1800s. Another possibility put forward is a nautical source: *leeward*, pronounced *looward*, meaning 'on the sheltered side,' and a *loo* is a shelter of sorts. One of the more interesting theories comes from Lady Constance Cairns. In 1867 the first Duke of Abercorn was Vicerory of Ireland, and he gave a large houseparty at the Viceregal Lodge. The guests included the Lord Lieutenant of County Roscommon and his wife Lady Louisa, a not very amiable soul. The Duke had a number of sons, the two youngest being Lord Frederick and Lord Ernest. They took Lady Louisa's namecard off her bedroom door and tacked it onto the door of the sole bathroom in the entire guest wing. The guests coined the discreet phrase *going to Lady Louisa*. This degenerated into *going to Lady Lou* among the aristocracy, who by that time had lost track of who Lady Lou was. The expression spread to less exalted circles, who democratically dropped the title, and eventually turned the *Lou* into *loo*. This anecdote comes from Frank Muir's *A Book at Bathtime* (Heinemann, London, 1982). The author would be receptive to further theories.

looby, *n, Slang.*   simpleton

look like...   **look as if...**
Look like, plus a gerund, is used as the equivalent of *look as if* followed by a subject and a subjunctive: *Next week looks like being crucial for the Labour Party* (*looks as if it were going to be*). *That company looks like becoming the leader in the field* (*looks as if it were becoming* or *looks as if it were going to become*). *Nancy looks like being the next Mrs. Grant* (*looks as if she were going to be*). *That party looks like getting more support from the workers* (*looks as if it were getting* or *seems to be getting*). This practice sounds nonstandard to American ears, but is perfectly acceptable in British informal speech.

look out   1. pack
                                                                                                        2. select
Look out has a good many British uses shared with America, but there are two not so shared:
1. While watching you pack for a trip, your British friend might say, "*Look out* your

woollies; it's cold where you're going". (*Woollies* are *sweaters* in Britain, *heavy underwear* in America.) *Look out,* in that sense means 'pack,' and your friend is advising you to *take along* a few sweaters. Better follow the advice.
2. One can also *look out* facts in reference works while engaged in a research project. Here, *looking out* means 'looking up,' and then 'selecting' the data you find for use as authority to prove whatever it is you're trying to prove.

look-out, *n,* **outlook**
Inf. Prospect, as in stock market forecasting: *The look-out for that group of companies is bleak.* It also has the connotation of *lot* or *fate* when it refers to something then future, now past: *To die at 18—that had been a poor look-out,* i.e., *a sad fate. Look-out* has the ordinary American informal meaning as well ('responsibility,' 'concern'), as in: *Keeping petrol in the car is your look-out.* Conversely, the standard American meaning of *lookout* (no hyphen), a *point* from which one gets a wide view of the landscape, is often **viewpoint** in Britain, which of course (again without a hyphen) refers to things abstract rather than concrete in America.

look-out window **picture window**

look-round, *n.* **look**
As a noun: a *good look,* an *inspection.* See also **recce; shufty.**

look slippy! *Slang.* **be quick**

look smart! *Slang.* **get a move on**

look-through window **picture window**

look-up, *v.t.* **look up**
I looked-up myself in "Who's Who," said a famous Briton. An American celebrity would have said, *I looked myself up...* So would most Britons.

loopy, *adj., Slang.* *Slang.* **loony**

loose-box, *n.* **horse stall**

loose chippings **loose gravel**
That over which the motorist is enjoined, in both countries, to drive slowly, please.

loose covers **slipcovers**

loose waterproof **slicker**

Lord, *n.* (in titles) SEE COMMENT
A marquess, earl, viscount, or baron (i.e., any peer except a duke) is referred to socially not by these full titles but as *Lord So-and-so* (without forename); his wife is *Lady So-and-so* (see **Lady**). The eldest son of a duke, marquess, or earl takes a spare title of his father's (known as a *courtesy title*) and is therefore *Lord Somebody-or-other.* Other sons of dukes and marquesses have names of the form *Lord John Smith,* and their sisters are *Lady Jane Smith* and so on. The other children of earls, and all the children of viscounts and barons, are merely *Honourable,* which means that in conversation they are plain *Mr* or *Miss;* but in addressing an envelope to them one should write "The Hon. John Smith," and "The Hon. Mrs John Smith" to their wives. (Lest you think the occasional absences of periods are typographical errors, see **Appendix I.D.6.** for the rule in British English.) In addition to members of the peerage, the title *Lord* also belongs to certain dignitaries such as the Lord Chancellor, the Lord Chief Justice, etc., and judges in court are addressed as *My Lord,* pronounced M'LUD or M'LORD. A Lord's signature consists of his title without a forename, e.g., Lord Smith will sign simply "Smith." Bishops are *Lords Spiritual.* For their signatures see **Cantuarian.**
A **commoner** raised to the peerage may take a title different from his surname. Thus Benjamin Disraeli became the Earl of Beaconsfield (Lord Beaconsfield). Nowadays, how-

ever, it is increasingly the practice to keep the surname (to avoid the risk of one's identity being eclipsed). Thus Mr or Sir R. Grey may become Lord Grey. The Labour statesman Mr George Brown elected to become Lord George-Brown, and the ex-diplomat Sir Gladwyn Jebb became Lord Gladwyn (thus, intentionally or not, putting back to square one anybody who was in the habit of addressing him by his first name).

On the other hand, in an article by Frank Johnson in *The Times* (London) of May 8, 1981, there is a reference to the Mater of Peterhouse (a **college** of Cambridge University—also known as St. Peter's College, founded in 1284), followed by the following parenthesis: "(He is still better known by the rather arid-sounding name of Professor Hugh Trevor-Roper, which somehow befitted a figure of such scarifying [sic] scholarship although he has lately assumed the romantically evocative title of Lord Dacre of Glanton. . . .There has been no such transformation since blunt, bleak Mr Ted Short became lilting, seductive Lord Glenamara of Glenridding.)"

The House of Lords has few political powers and the career of a politician could be stopped in midstream by his succeeding to a peerage. To permit such persons to keep their memberships in the **Commons,** a 1963 Act permitted peers to disclaim their peerages for life. A 1958 Act authorized the creation of life peers, male and female. No hereditary ones have been created since 1965. (*Whitaker's Almanack,* 1980.) As to the importance (or lack thereof) of the House of Lords, the reader is referred to the song about it in *Iolanthe.*

Present day attitudes towards titles vary. One sample of a negative reaction is the following letter to *The Times* (London) dated August 26, 1981, which appeared in the September 4, 1981, issue. The writer, Ludovic Kennedy, is the husband of the renowned ballerina Moira Shearer and a well-known and influential television interviewer and commentator.

Title discourtesy
From Mr Ludovic Kennedy
    Sir, Mr Brian Fothergill (August 20) is spitting into the wind. Correct styles of address are now of little concern to anybody. For years the BBC have been putting up misleading captions over the faces of titled contributors, giving the wives of knights the status of daughters of earls (eg "Lady Isobel Barnett") and the younger sons of dukes the status of barons (eg "Lord Douglas-Hamilton") presumably because production staff know no better. And increasingly newspapers—even the top ones, as Mr Fothergill points out—have been following suit.
    Such errors however are only a reflection of the diminished importance that title-holders themselves now attach to their titles. Some years ago Mr John Grigg divested himself of the title of Lord Altrincham because, not having earned it, he regarded it as an irrelevance. The same motive has prompted the children of some peers, particularly life peers, to forgo the use of the prefix "Hon." The Earl of Ancram, MP, prefers to be known as Michael Ancram. Conversely, Lord Matthews signs himself in autograph books "Lord Victor Matthews."
    Does any of it really matter? To master the intricacies of the correct forms of address requires an effort which, in this egalitarian age few people think it worth while to give.
Yours etc,
LUDOVIC KENNEDY,
3 Upper Dean Terrace,
Edinburgh 4.
August 26.

    Inevitably, dissent followed in the form of two letters dated September 4 which appeared in *The Times* (London) of September 8, 1981:

Title discourtesy
From Dr A.R.D. Mathias
    Sir, Every hereditary peerage is a piece of history, about which the distinctions of address are informative and therefore interesting. Mr Ludovic Kennedy's aggressive desire to swim with the tide of coarse indifference to accuracy in these matters (letter, September 4) is saddening; sadder still his wish that others should copy him.
    I have the honour to remain, etc.,
A.R.D. MATHIAS

Peterhouse,
Cambridge.
September 4.
From the Reverend D.G. Richards.
Sir, Mr Ludovic Kennedy (September 4) may not think titles to be of much importance but surely civilization depends upon standards and to a large extent standards are upheld by courtesy.
Yours faithfully.
DEREK RICHARDS,
The Rectory,
Barmouth,
Merioneth.
September 4.

On September 12, *The* (good old) *Times* kept the pot simmering with the following from Lord Glendevon:

Title discourtesy
From Lord Glendevon
Sir, There is nothing new in people getting titles wrong. The subject is highly complicated and it always was.
I sat in the Commons for 20 years as Lord John Hope and was constantly addressed by constituents as Lord Hope. Favourite among my constituency correspondents was perhaps the lady who wrote that it was blasphemy to call myself Lord as the title belonged only to God. She wished me to know that I would certainly go to Hell. I replied that in that case we would be able to continue the argument face to face. I heard no more.
Yours faithfully,
GLENDEVON,
House of Lords,
September 9.

and on the 22nd kept it going with Mrs. Wansbrough's amusing anecdote:

Title discourtesy
From Mrs E. Wansbrough
Sir, It has lately become the fashion, especially among Labour peers, to use their Christian names as well as their surnames when signing (see Lord Caradon's letter, September 10). I remember being with a peeress who, wanting to cash a cheque of her husband's at a shop, was told by the assistant that the Christian name was missing from the signature, to which she answered haughtily: "His Lordship *has* no Christian name".
Yours faithfully,
ELIZABETH WANSBROUGH,
Broughton Poggs,
Lechlade,
Gloucestershire.
September 12.

See also **Dame; Lady; K.; peer.**

Lord Chamberlain   SEE COMMENT
Head of management of the Royal Household; formerly the authority who granted play licenses, a censorship office now happily abolished.

Lord Chancellor   *approx.* **Chief Justice**
Also called *Lord High Chancellor.* He presides in the House of Lords when it is acting as Britain's Supreme Court. Not to be confused with the Lord Chief Justice of England, who presides over the Queen's Bench Division of the High Court, from which appeals are taken to the Court of Appeal, and from there to the House of Lords. Although

America (apart from Louisiana, whose law descends from the Napoleonic Code) inherited its common law (general body of basic law) from the mother country, their court systems developed differently; and short of a long historical treatise on the subject, not of general interest, one will have to be content with approximations. In rough terms, the American Chief Justice and the British Lord Chancellor are each other's opposite numbers, in that they are the top judicial officers of their respective countries, and both take office by appointment, the American for life, the British for a term dependent on the vicissitudes of politics.

lords and ladies   **jack-in-the-pulpits**
Also called *cuckoo pints*.

lorry, *n*,   **truck**
To *lorry-hop* or *lorry-jump* is to *hitchhike*. An **articulated lorry** is a *trailer truck*. See also **bender; juggernaut**.

lost property office   **lost and found**
Also, **baggage service**.

lot, *n*.   **1.** *Slang.* **The works**
                                                                                        2. group
                                                                                 3. *Slang.* **bunch**
1. *Inf. The lot* means 'the whole lot,' 'the whole kit and caboodle,' 'the works.' Thus, *They gave me a beautiful room, marvellous food, wonderful service...the lot! The gift was all wrapped up in fancy paper, gold string, the lot. The lot* also means 'all' of something. At a sale, there are three dresses hard to choose from. You ponder and ponder and finally say (recklessly), "I'll take *the lot*," i.e., 'all' of them.
2. *Inf.* It also has the meaning of 'group.' In an American Chinese restaurant, they are fond of arranging dishes into Group A, Group B, etc. They do it in Britain too, and there you would say, "We'll have two from the first *lot*, three from the second *lot*," etc. From directions written by a friend: "At the first traffic lights you turn right, at the second *lot*, left."
3. *Inf. Lot* means 'group' in another sense, too, the sense in which Americans use the slang term *bunch*. Thus, if a Briton saw a group of unsavory-looking characters on a street corner, he might think, *I don't like the looks of that lot*, where an American would refer to them as *that bunch*. *You lot* means 'the lot of you,' i.e., 'all of you,' in addressing a group of people, and might come out in America as *Hey, you guys*. Director of ballet company to the group leaving the dressing-room just before they are about to go on stage: "Best of luck to you *lot!*" *Lot* is usually a collective noun but it can refer to a single person as well, especially in a *thoroughly bad lot*.

(a) lot on one's plate. See **have enough on one's plate**.

loud-hailer, *n*,   **bullhorn**

lough, *n*,   **1. tidal stream**
                                                                                       2. duck
1. Particularly in the *Fens*.
2. The kind often found in *loughs*. See also **loch**.

lounge, *n*,   **living room**
Considered **non-U** in this sense (see **Appendix I.C.6.**; see also **drawing-room**).

lounge bar   SEE COMMENT
Synonymous with **saloon bar**. *Lounge bar* is sometimes used instead of *saloon bar* to indicate the fancier and more exclusive part of a **pub**. But, like so many other things in Britain, it isn't quite that simple, because some bars boast *saloon bars* as well as *lounge bars*, and even *saloon lounges*.

lounge suit   **business suit**

love, *n,* *approx.* **honey**
Inf. Often spelled *luv* in allusion to its Northern (North of England) origin and pronounced LOOV (-OO- as in LOOK) for the same reason. Widely used as a very informal term of address in the North of England: by men only to women, but by women without distinction as to sex, a primarily lower-class vocative (when applied to strangers). The nearest American equivalent would be *honey,* which used to have a particularly Southern flavor, but by now has spread all over the country.

lovely!, *interj.* **great! fine!**
Lovely! is heard all the time in Britain and is by no means the exclusive property of the cultured. A gnarled old parking lot (**car park**) attendant of distinctly proletarian mien and attire, guiding you into a narrow space will say, "Cut to the left, cut to the right, straighten out, back a little more, stop, that's it. *Lovely!*" The same exclamation would be used by a friend to whom you had just announced the news of your daughter's engagement. *Lovely!* covers a multitude of expletives: *fine! great! wonderful! marvelous! terrific! that's it!* and even *wow!* It can also be used in place of *thanks.*

low in the water. See **in low water.**

(Her Majesty's) Loyal Opposition **party not in power**
Loyal to the monarch; *opposed* to the party in power.

(the) Loyal Toast SEE COMMENT
As the coffee is served at a meal which is part of the proceedings at a regular meeting of an organization like a guild, Rotary Club, and that sort of thing, the chairman stands up and announces, in stentorian tones: *"The Loyal Toast!"* Thereupon all stand, raise their glasses, and say in unison: *The Queen!* They take a swallow and sit down, and thereafter—and only then—is smoking permitted. The word *loyal,* as used in this connection, was best explained by one of its definitions in the first five editions of *The Concise Oxford Dictionary:* "enthusiastically devoted to the sovereign's person and family." This has disappeared from the current (sixth) edition, which has merely "as evidence of allegiance to sovereign."

L plate SEE COMMENT
There should be an American equivalent. A large red *L* (standing for *learner*) on a square white plate attached to the rear of an automobile gives fair warning to all and a very sensible idea it is. An *L-driver* is one who has not yet passed his driving test, and is allowed to drive only with another person in the car and with the L-plate as a warning. The *L plate* is seen attached to the rear of motorcycles as well.

£ s.d. **dough (money)**
(Pronounced ELL-ESS-DEE.) Spelled £ *s.d.* (or *L.S.D.*) it means 'pounds, shillings, pence.' These three letters are the initials of the Latin ancestors of those three words: *librae, solidi,* and *denarii.* The Roman occupation of Britain, of course, occurred a good many years ago, but the symbols remained until February 15, 1971, when Britain put its money on the decimal system (see **Appendix II.A.**), shillings were abolished, and the abbreviation of *pence* changed from *d* to *p.* However, £ *s.d.* remains a British expression synonymous with **lolly,** equivalent to *dough. L.S. Deism,* meaning 'money worship,' is a pretty good British pun. (Nothing to do with the hallucinogen.)

lucern (lucerne), *n.* **alfalfa**

lucky bargee. See **bargee.**

lucky-dip, *n., Inf.* *Inf.* **grab bag**

lud, *n.* **Lord**
Old-fashioned pronunciation of *Lord* in addressing a judge; see **Lord.**

Luddism (Ludditism), *n.*   SEE COMMENT
  Opposition to mechanization, after Nat Ludd, an 18th-century worker from Leicestershire who originated the formation of workers' groups for the purpose of destroying
machinery that caused loss of jobs. Members were called *Luddites.*

Luddite. See **Luddism.**

lug. See **lughole.**

luge, *n.*   **toboggan**
  Inf. A word taken over from a French dialect, Swiss or Savoy.

luggage, *n.*   **baggage**
  Britons *register luggage,* Americans *check baggage.* On a British train, it goes into the
luggage **van;** on an American train, into the *baggage car.*

lughole, *n.*   **ear**
  Slang. Sometimes hyphenated; sometimes simply *lug.* No American slang equivalent.

luke, *n.*   **alley**
  Sometimes *loke,* or *lyke.* The Norfolk equivalent of **twitten.**

Luke's Little Summer   *Inf.* **Indian summer**
  Inf. Other British names: *St. Luke's Summer; St. Martin's Summer.* As to the period in
St., see **Appendix I.D.6.**

lumber, *n., v.t.*   **1. junk**
                                                                                 2. clutter
  Lumber is old furniture, stuff, doodads, and general junk around the house not good
enough to use or be seen by your guests, not bad enough to throw away; you never
really want to see it again but you can't bear to part with it. So you put it into your
lumber-room (*storage room;* see also **boxroom**), the way Americans stuff their attics, and
wish with all your heart but none of your mind that you had never been *lumbered* with
it. The British use *lumber,* especially *lumber up,* also as a verb. To *lumber up* a room is to
clutter it up. Incidentally, the British use **clutter** also as a noun meaning 'miscellaneous
junk' or 'gear.' *Lumber,* in common usage, has none of these connotations in America
where it means only 'wood' for use in carpentry, which is called **timber** in Britain. But
timber in America usually connotes 'standing timber,' i.e., living trees grown for eventual cutting and use as *lumber* in the American sense. Old beams, especially the hand-
hewn variety found in old buildings, barns, and ships, are called *timbers* in both countries. A beautiful example of the British use of *lumber* is found early in chapter 3 of
Jerome K. Jerome's classic *Three Men in a Boat.* The three neophyte sailors have made
a list of theoretically indispensable accouterments for a proposed river trip, but it becomes clear that "the upper reaches of the Thames would not allow of a boat sufficiently
large" to accommodate the list. Then George reflects: "We must not think of the things
we could do with, but only of the things we can't do without." "I call that downright
wisdom," says the author, "not merely as regards the present case, but with reference
to our trip up the river of life generally." Then follows a ruminative passage, quite a
long one, which the author himself wants us to believe he never intended, for at the
end he says to the reader: "I beg your pardon, really. I quite forgot." The passage is
all about *lumber:*

> How many people, on that voyage [the 'trip up the river of life generally'] load up
> the boat till it is ever in danger of swamping with a store of foolish things which they
> think essential to the pleasure and comfort of the trip, but which are really only useless
> lumber.
> How they pile the poor little craft mast-high with fine clothes and big houses; with
> useless servants and a host of swell friends that do not care twopence for them and
> that they do not care three ha'pence for; with expensive entertainments that nobody
> enjoys, with formalities and fashions, with pretence and ostentation, and with—oh,
> heaviest, maddest lumber of all!—the dread of what will my neighbour think, with

luxuries that only cloy, with pleasures that bore, with empty show that, like the criminal's iron crowns of yore, makes to bleed and swoon the aching head that wears it! It is lumber, man—all lumber! Throw it overboard. It makes the boat so heavy to pull, you nearly faint at the oars. It makes it so cumbersome and dangerous to manage, you never know a moment's freedom from anxiety and care, never gain a moment's rest for dreamy laziness—no time to watch the windy shadows skim lightly o'er the shallows, or the glittering sunbeams flitting in and out among the ripples, or the great trees by the margin looking down at their own image, or the woods all green and golden, or the lilies white and yellow, or the sombre-waving rushes, or the sedges, or the orchis, or the blue forget-me-nots.

Throw the lumber over, man! Let your boat of life be light, packed with only what you need—a homely home and simple pleasures, one or two friends, worth the name, someone to love and someone to love you, a cat, a dog, and a pipe or two, enough to eat and enough to wear, and a little more than enough to drink; for thirst is a dangerous thing.

You will find the boat easier to pull then, and it will not be so liable to upset, and it will not matter so much if it does upset; good, plain merchandise will stand water. You will have time to think as well as to work. Time to drink in life's sunshine—time to listen to the Aeolian music that the wind of God draws from the human heartstrings around us—time to—I beg your pardon, really. I quite forgot.

lumbered with   *Inf.* **saddled with**
Slang. See **landed with.**

lumber-room, *n.*   **storage room**
See also **box-room.**

lumme! or **lummy!,** *interj.*   *Slang.* **whew!**
Slang. Corruption of *love me!*

(the) lump, *n.*   *approx.* **independent contracting**
Slang. The practice of workers in various phases of the construction business (e.g., bricklayers, painters, carpenters) who decline to be hired as employees on a wage basis and instead, subcontract on their own as independent contractors, paid by the main contractor without deduction for income tax, health insurance, or anything else. This seems to send the prices sky high. The name of this practice derives from the giving of a *lump* sum to the group, regardless of the time involved or any other factor. The **lumper** is the middleman who handles the arrangements.

lumper, *n.*   **contractor**
Slang. See under **lump.**

luncheon voucher   **lunch coupon**
A fringe benefit granted employees by some employers. They are redeemable at certain restaurants up to a certain value. Often abbreviated to *L.V.* on the signs appearing in the windows of the establishments which honor them.

L.V. See **luncheon voucher.**

M

ma'am, *n.*   SEE COMMENT
This highly specialized form of contraction of *madam* is used as the proper form
of addressing the Queen, and when it is so used it is pronounced M'M by servants
and MAM by all others. You ought to know this, just in case... Also used in addressing other ladies in the royal family, and as the equivalent of *sir* in the women's
military services.

mac, *n.*   **raincoat**
Slang. Short for *macintosh* (sometimes *mackintosh*), a waterproof material patented in
the early 19th century by Charles Macintosh, an amateur chemist. A young man named
James Symes had invented a type of cloth made waterproof by rubberizing. Macintosh
improved Symes's process and was awarded the patent for waterproofing cloth by
cementing two pieces together with rubber dissolved in a chemical solvent, thus making
it suitable for a number of uses including raincoats.

macadam, *n.*   **blacktop**
After J.C. McAdam, who late in the 18th century invented the building of roads with
layers of crushed stone. **Tarmac,** short for *tar macadam,* added tar to the crushed stone
layers. But since tar is almost universally added to the crushed stones these days,
macadam road is used in Britain the way Americans use *blacktop road.* The British also
use the expression *made-up road* to mean the same thing. See also **metalled road.**

machinist, *n.*   **machine operator**
This term, used by itself in Britain, can mean 'sewing machine operator.' The British
also use the term *machine-minder* where Americans would say *machine operator.*

made-up road. See **macadam.**

mad on   *Inf.* **crazy about**
Inf. Americans also say *mad about* and the British also say *crazy about,* but only the
British say *mad on,* and when a Briton wants to be emphatic, he says *mad keen on,* or
sometimes *dead keen on,* or even **struck on.**

maffick, *v.i.*   **exult riotously**
Mafeking is a small town in Cape Province, South Africa. During the Boer War it was
besieged by Cronje and defended by Baden-Powell from October 13, 1899, to May 17,
1900, when the siege was raised by Mahon and Plumer. The relief of Mafeking was
cause for great rejoicing and the populace of London and elsewhere celebrated the
happy event with extravagance and exultation. The *-ing* ending was mistakenly believed
by the general public to indicate a gerund, and *maffick* came to mean, to the many who
had never heard of the place, 'celebrate hilariously' usually with the assistance of alcoholic stimulants. However, you can't "mafek," you must *maffick.* Somehow in the
back-formation from the supposed gerund, the spelling went wrong too. The details of
both the military operation and the antics back home are set forth in a delightful article
by Jan Morris in the *The Times Saturday Review* of May, 1975, the seventy-fifth anniversary of the event. The article begins:

> Seventy-five years ago today, the dictionary tells us, the name of Mafeking went
> into the English language, "treated jocularly as a gerund, or present participle": *Maf-
> ficking, indulging in extravagant demonstrations of exultation on occasions of national rejoicing.*
> In fact, I have never in my life seen the word used in anything but a lexicographic
> context....

Then, a long and learned article appeared in the October 1975 issue (Vol. Two, No.

Four) of *British History Illustrated*, entitled "Mafeking Relieved," by Prof. Lowell J. Satre of the history department of Youngstown University, Ohio. This fascinating article, graced by several contemporary photographs and drawings, begins:

At seventeen minutes past nine on the evening of 18th May 1900 the Reuter's office in London received a telegram from Pretoria. The contents of the message were immediately dispatched to Fleet Street newspaper offices, which informed the public through placards set in their windows. Within minutes London and, indeed, most of the empire as it heard the news, began almost a week of revelry and celebration.
The article includes a drawing with this caption: Mafeking night in Piccadilly Circus 1900. All class barriers were dropped as London took to the streets; hats were thrown in the air and the density of the crowds brought traffic to a standstill.
Later on we read:
Both the young and old danced in the streets. Excitement was unsurpassed. According to one newspaper, there was "Wholesale kissing by consent," and under the heading "Mafekites" (short descriptions of unusual events that supposedly happened during the celebrations), the *Daily Express* reported that: "A young lady in the West-end was so overcome with excitement that she rushed at a negro who was coming towards her, threw her arms around his neck, and kissed him."

mag, *n.*   SEE COMMENT
Slang. The old halfpenny. The new halfpenny is something else again: See **Appendix II.A.**

magistrate, *n.*   *approx.* **justice of the peace**
Some of their duties coincide; others do not.

magsman, *n.*   *Slang.* **con man**
Slang. Obsolescent.

maiden over   SEE COMMENT
A cricket term which, like so many other cricket terms, has crept into the general language. In cricket there are two **bowlers.** Each bowler bowls to the opposing **batsman** six times. This constitutes an *over.* If the batsman fails to make a single run during the *over,* the result is called a *maiden over,* and the bowler is said to have *bowled a maiden over*—an expression that lends itself to an obvious pun. *Maiden* is used differently from its use in such a phrase as *maiden voyage.* In *maiden over, maiden* evokes the Victorian image of *virgo intacta,* the idea being that the score was not touched either. Metaphorically *maiden over* can be used as an elegant and dramatic way of describing any achievement of consistent skill, one in which the protagonist triumphs over the assaults of his opponent.

maid of honour   1. **lady in waiting**
                                                                                                    2. **cheesecake**
1. An unmarried woman who attends a queen or princess.
2. The edible variety; a small round one.

maiden's (maid's) water, *Slang*   **a weak drink**
Maiden's water usually refers to beer; *maid's water* to tea.

mains, *n. pl.*   **electric power source**
The outside (light and power company) source. Thus, directions on an electric appliance: *Disconnect mains before adjusting controls.*

maisonette, *n.*   SEE COMMENT
This term is sometimes applied to any small house or apartment, but generally refers to a part of a house (usually on more than one floor) rented separately from the rest of the dwelling. It is gaining some currency in the United States, to describe something different: a luxury duplex with a separate entrance on the ground floor, embedded in a highrise apartment building.

maize, *n.*   **corn**
See discussion under **corn.**

maizie, *n.*   *Inf.* **flower frog**
Inf. An improvised *flower frog* consisting of a ball of crushed chicken wire. See also **rose.**

major, *adj.*   **(the) elder**
Used after a surname. In a British **public school** the eldest of three or more students then attending who have the same surname has *maximus* (the superlative form of the Latin adjective *magnus,* meaning 'large' or 'great') placed after his name; thus Smith *maximus,* i.e., Smith *the eldest,* to distinguish him from the other Smiths then at the school. The youngest would be Smith *minimus* (*minimus* being the superlative form of *parvus,* Latin for 'small'). The corresponding Latin comparatives, *major* and *minor,* are used when there are only two with the same surname. Sometimes English cardinal numerals, rather than Latin comparatives and superlatives, are used: thus *Smith One, Smith Two, Smith Three,* if there were three Smiths at the school. At some public schools, *major* has been used to mean 'first to enter,' even if an older Smith enters the school later, while the first Smith is still attending; and at other schools *maximus* and *minimus* have been used to refer not to age but to academic standing. These various terminologies are used not only by public schools but also by some British **prep schools.** These varying uses, like so many other carefree British departures from uniformity in practice, can be confusing, but the safe assumption is that these Latin adjectives (or English numerals) following youngsters' surnames indicate seniority in years rather than priority in enrollment or academic rank.

majority, *n.*   **plurality**
A voting term. When the British use the term *majority* in discussing an election they mean what the Americans call a *plurality.* If they want to indicate an arithmetical majority (i.e., more than 50 percent), they use the term *clear majority.*

major road. See **arterial road.**

make, v.t.   **bring**
Bring a price in an auction sale. *Fetch* is used in the same way.

make a balls of   *Inf.* **mess up**
Slang. See also **balls, 2.**

make a dead-set at, *Inf.*   *Inf.* **make a play for**

make a (the) four up   **make a fourth**
For instance, at bridge or tennis doubles.

make all the running   *Slang.* **go the limit**
Slang. Refers to the degree of sexual intimacy permitted by the lady. Not to be confused with *make the running.*

make a meal of. See **make heavy weather of**

make a pair of spectacles. See **duck, 1.**

make game of, *Inf.*   **make fun of**

make hay of   *Inf.* **make a hash of**
Inf. Muddle up, make a mess of. Sometimes the meaning is closer to *make short work of;* someone goes on and on trying to prove a point, you come up with a decisive refutation and *make hay of* his thesis.

make heavy weather of   SEE COMMENT
Inf. Applies to a situation where one finds something harder than anticipated. The implication is that one finds a situation very trying, and is making it unnecessarily

difficult, and that one is making a big fuss over little or nothing; making a big deal out of what should have been easy going; not getting on with a relatively simple task, through bumbling stupidity. Also, **make a meal of. Cf. hospital job.**

make off with   Inf. **run through (money); squander**
   Inf. As in I made off with my salary in one day. In both countries the phrase is also used to mean 'steal.'

make old bones   Inf. **live to a ripe old age**
   Inf. Gloomily enough, seen almost exclusively in the negative: He'll never make old bones.

make one's number with   contact
   Inf. The person you make contact with is often your opposite number (e.g., in another department of the government, or perhaps someone a bit senior). The implication is that of 'getting across' to someone whom it is important to be in touch with; to 'register,' as it were, to 'make your existence known.' There is history behind this expression. When a naval ship spotted another sail on the horizon—if it was a British ship, perhaps to make sure the other was as well—the Captain made his number to the other ship by means of signal flags. As soon as the answering number was received, each Captain consulted his Admiralty schedule to find out which ship was senior, and therefore could take command with the right to give orders to the other. This would have been of particular importance to the British navy since they were the most likely to be cruising around the seven seas and coming across one another.

make out a case for   **make a case for**

make the running   **take the lead**
   Inf. In a competitive situation; but to make some running (not in common usage) would mean to 'make some headway.' For another kind of headway, see **make all the running.**

make up   **fill**
   British **chemists** (druggists) make up prescriptions rather than fill them.

-making   SEE COMMENT
   Hyphenated with such words as shy-, shame-, sick-, to create a series of mildly precious, jocularly expressive adjectives. Cf. the adjective off-putting, under **put (someone) off.** This construction is said to have been the invention of Evelyn Waugh.

malicious wounding   **crimes of violence**
   Term from criminal law.

man, n.   **valet**
   As obsolescent as the institution itself. If a woman today speaks of my man she presumably means 'the man I am living with' or 'the man I sleep with.' Of course, there is also the patronizing my good man.

manager, n.   **producer**
   In speaking of the theater, manager is the equivalent of producer in America. See also **producer.**

managing director   approx. **executive vice president**
   In a British company, the offices of **chairman** and managing director can be combined in one person. This is not common and the division of functions and authority, as between these two offices, will vary from company to company, as it does between chairman of the board and president in American corporations. Roughly speaking, the chairman makes policy, while the managing director runs the show day by day. See also **chairman.**

Manchester, *n.*   **dry goods**
Short for *Manchester goods,* denoting cotton textile wares such as draperies, curtain materials, bedspreads, and the like. Signs reading simply MANCHESTER appear in some department stores. See also **draper's shop.**

Mancunian, *n., adj.*   SEE COMMENT
Of Manchester: the Romans called the place *Mancunium.*

mandate. See **banker's order.**

manhandle, v.t   **handle by hand**
The British use this the way it is used in America to mean 'handle roughly,' 'deal roughly with,' but it has also the more literal meaning in Britain shown above.

manifesto. See **party manifesto.**

mankie, *adj.*   **rotten**
Slang. A strong term for *quite inferior;* also spelled *mankey* and *manky.* It is said to be a corruption of the French word *manqué,* in its sense of 'spoilt,' or 'defective.'

man of Kent. See **Kentish man.**

man of the match   *approx.* **most valuable player**
Unlike the American practice, the title is conferred (together with a cash prize) upon the player chosen by an outside authority, usually a veteran player himself, as the best achiever in a particular match rather than during a playing season. This is the common procedure in cricket matches of special significance. See **match.**

manor, *n.*   *Inf.* **beat**
Inf. In the sense of 'domain, bailiwick.' As a police usage, it is synonymous with **patch** used in this sense.

mantelshelf, *n.*   **mantelpiece**
The terms are used interchangeably in Britain.

marching papers   *Inf.* **walking papers**
Inf. Also *marching orders.*

marge, *n.*   *Inf.* **oleo**
Inf. Each country has its own way of abbreviating *oleomargarine.*

mark, *n.*   **type (sort)**
The phrase *of much this mark* means 'very much like this.' Thus a Briton might be heard to say, *At school we slept in beds of much this mark.* This use of *mark* to mean 'type' has been extended to include 'model,' as used in the expressions Mark I, Mark II, etc., especially in descriptions of new models of cars as brought out year after year. *Mark* has been used in the sense of 'model' in a sentence like *We don't want the Social Democratic Party* [a new political party organized in 1981 by moderate members of the Labour Party] *to be nothing but a Mark II Labour Party.* See also **save the mark!**

mark, *v.t.*   *Inf.* **cover**
Inf. A term used in **football.** In the British game, a player is said to *mark* an opposing player who may be receiving the ball; in the American game that would be called *covering* the receiver.

market, *n.*   **weekly market**
Many British towns have a *weekly market day,* a particular day of the week on which a market, usually open-air, is held for the sale of all kinds of wares, arranged in stalls. As might be expected, these markets, which constitute normal commerce among the natives, seem like fairs to the visitor for they crackle with the festive air of a bazaar.

Such a town is called a *market town*. A number of market towns still have names that include the word *market:* Market Drayton, Market Harborough, Market Weighton, etc. But the names of most towns with weekly markets do not reveal the fact: Stourbridge (market day on Friday), Guisborough (market day on Saturday), etc. Occasionally, as in the town of Stone, the market is held only once every other week. In Stratford-on-Avon, however, there are markets three days a week: Tuesday, Wednesday, and Friday. The **A.A.** Book (the handbook issued to each member of the *Automobile Association* in Britain), which practically every British motorist keeps religously in the **cubby** of his car, gives all sorts of miscellaneous information about the towns it lists, including the *market day (MD)*. The *R.A.C. (Royal Automobile Club)* issues an almost identical handbook.

market garden   **truck farm**
And a *market gardener* is a *truck farmer.*

marking name   **street name**
The broker's name, in which securities are registered for trading convenience. The true owner's name is posted in the broker's books and records.

Marks & Sparks   SEE COMMENT
Inf. A joke name for *Marks & Spencer,* a chain store (**multiple shop**) reminiscent of J.C. Penney. Cf. **Woollies.**

Mark Tapley   **Pollyanna**
One who sees only the bright side. See *Martin Chuzzlewit* by Dickens, which is also the source of **gamp.**

Marlburian, *n., adj.*   SEE COMMENT
Of Marlborough. Marlborough is the site of a famous **public school** in Wiltshire. An *old Marlburian* is a graduate of that school. Marlborough is pronounced MAWL-BRUH.

marquee, *n.*   **large tent**
In America *marquee* generally denotes a rigid canopy projecting over the entrance to a theater or other public hall, and the word evokes the image of large illuminated letters spelling out the names of stage and movie stars, double features, and smash hits. This significance is never attributed to the word in Britain where it means a 'large tent' of the sort used on fair grounds and brings to mind Britain's agricultural fairs (see **agricultural show**), village **fêtes**, the Henley Regatta, and all those garden parties of Katherine Mansfield's childhood. At the annual regatta at Henley-on-Thames, for example, there are little *marquees* for staff, sanitation facilities, and that sort of thing, middle-sized *marquees* for champagne and that sort of thing, and what must be one of the largest *marquees* in history for luncheon. *Marquee* is sometimes used in America, too, in the same sense in connection with outdoor wedding receptions and entertainments.

marriage lines   **marriage certificate**
The American term is now common in Britain.

marrow, *n.*   *approx.* **squash**
A kind of oversized *zucchini,* to put it mildly. (Some marrows grown in country gardens reach positively indecent proportions—one of those things the British have competitions over, like leeks in Yorkshire. The British are very **keen** on vegetable or **kitchen gardens**, and *marrows* are ubiquitous.) The British do not use the term *zucchini* (except possibly gourmets at Italian restaurants in Soho) and do not ordinarily say *pumpkin* (except when telling their children at bedtime the story of Cinderella or possibly each other the sad tale of Whittaker Chambers and Alger Hiss); they might say *courgettes;* and when they say *squash,* unless they are using it as a sports term, they mean a 'soft drink,' usually lemon squash or orange squash (see **squash**).

martini, *n.*   **vermouth**
If you ask for a *martini* in a British pub, you will probably get a glass of *vermouth.* Whether it is dry or sweet will depend upon chance, but in either event it will be warm. If you ask for a *dry martini,* you will get a glass of *dry vermouth.* If you want a *dry martini*

in the American sense, better ask for a *gin and French*, specify extremely little French, and that it be served very cold, by stirring the mixture over ice cubes (formerly, **blocks of ice**), but further specify that the ice be removed (unless you want it on the rocks); and furthermore, if it would grieve you terribly not to find an olive or a piece of lemon rind in it, you had better remain in America. (A *gin and It*—*It* being an abbreviation of *Italian vermouth*—is still occasionally ordered, but not by Americans). As to the dry martini, this would appear to be the present (1986) state of affairs, especially in country establishments and private homes, despite some evidence to the contrary dating from an earlier time. Henry Cecil, in *Sober as a Judge* (Michael Joseph, London, 1958—note date), telling the experiences of an unhappy guest at a small hotel in the South of England who sued the hotel, includes the following excerpt from the judge's opinion in the case: "Not long afterward the plaintiff and his wife came downstairs and went into the bar. There was a girl—munching something and painting her finger-nails— behind it. The plaintiff ordered—to use his own language—'Two dry Martinis.' The plaintiff complains that that is exactly what he got, that is, two glasses containing dry Vermouth and nothing else. The days have, I think, long past when a judge should ask: 'What is a dry Martini?' It would certainly be feigned innocence on my part—an innocence which I do not feel that the short time I have been on the Bench would in any case entitle me to assume. A dry Martini consists of gin mixed with dry Vermouth, and stirred or shaken up [sic!] with ice with a squeezed piece of lemon peel put into it. The Vermouth may be French or Italian, provided it is dry, but whatever the nationality or brand of the Vermouth, the drink is known as a dry Martini. I do not have to enquire why a drink, which, for example, may consist so far as the alcohol is concerned, of an English brand of gin and a French brand of Vermouth, should be called a dry Martini, although the firm of Martini e Rossi has supplied no part of its contents. But, of course, the firm of Martini e Rossi do make a dry Vermouth, and it is true that there are places where, if you ask for a dry Martini, that is all you will get. No doubt it is an admirable drink…But if a person wants gin and Vermouth, shaken up [sic again!] or stirred with ice, he is entitled to be dissatisfied if he is given instead some dry Vermouth rather warm. I think that…an establishment which can properly describe itself as *de luxe* and which charges what I may call *de luxe* prices should know what is meant by a dry Martini." Henry Cecil must have had dry martinis on his mind, for in a book of his published by the same publisher a year earlier (*Much in Evidence*), one character says to another: "You've treated us awfully well and, if I may say so, you mix a jolly good dry Martini." Getting closer to the present, Kingsley Amis, in the *Illustrated London News* of October 1985, describing the Ritz Hotel bar in London, writes: "The Dry Martini was not only expertly prepared but for **once in a way**, proportioned very dry as asked for." (Note: *vermouth*, like most two-syllable French words that Americans stress on the second syllable, is generally accented on the first in Britain, thus: *gar' age, bro' chure*; and the accent moves back similarly in Britain in three-syllable French words, thus: *con somm' é, ré sum' é*, etc. Further note: the British idiom *once in a way* would be shortened to *once* in America.) It is just possible that, given the influx of American visitors to the sceptered isle during the last few decades, in a deluxe, particularly a **West End** hotel, restaurant or bar, an order for a martini, especially if delivered in an American accent, might result in the real thing (except, in many cases, for far too much vermouth), but— *pace* Henry Cecil—better specify. And this cautionary note is confirmed in a 1981 article in *The Times* (London) by Michael Leapman headed *Diary of American English*, discussing the new *Oxford American Dictionary*, in which he writes: "Martini is uncompromisingly given only the American definition: a cocktail made of gin or vodka [sic!] and dry vermouth. Many visitors, believing they have ordered only the vermouth, have choked on their olives at the first taste of this fierce potion." Mr. Leapman may be exaggerating as to the choking, but it makes one wonder about the justice of the judgment given in the lawsuit described above, to the extent that it relied on Henry Cecil's definition of a martini. In a letter to the *Spectator* (issue of August 9, 1896), the eminent author Graham Greene, aroused by a letter from writer John Mortimer that appeared in the July 19 issue, writes: "…Mr Mortimer seems to think I was carrying the shaker to drink from on the battlefields of Vietnam—not very likely. I had a miniature shaker made because during four or five years I was forced to take long distance planes in those days 15 to 24 hours between London and Saigon and I preferred to make my own Dry Martinis (15 gin to 1) rather than drink the English Dry Martini (often about 6 to 4!)…" The letter, as printed in the *Spectator*, was headed "**Cocktail Shaker.**" What is all this talk about martinis (whatever the proportions) and cocktail shakers? Proper martinis (at least

proper American martinis) are stirred, not (heaven forbid!) shaken.
   The American writer Bernard De Voto, in *The Hour,* had this to say about the American concoction: "You can no more keep a martini in the refrigerator than you can keep a kiss there. The proper union of gin and vermouth is a great and sudden glory; it is one of the happiest marriages on earth and one of the shortest-lived." Final warning: take no chances; be specific; when ordering, supply details; don't let anybody *shake* your martini (!); and when it comes to bloody Marys, better order a double vodka with tomato juice and Worcestershire (often shortened, in Britain, to *Worcester*) sauce and plenty of ice, or forever after hold etc.

mash, *n.*   **mashed potatoes**
   Inf. More elegantly, *creamed potatoes* in Britain. A Camberwell pub used to present *sausages and mash* in the **public bar** at three shillings and *sausages and creamed potatoes* in the **saloon bar** at four shillings, sixpence. Same dish.

masses of, *Inf.*   *Inf.* **tons of**

master *or* **mistress,** *n.*   **teacher**
   Below university level. For the meaning of *Master* at the university level, see **fellow.** A *form-master* has about the same functions as a *home-room teacher.*

match, *n.*   **game**
   Two **sides** (teams) play a *match,* rather than a *game,* in Britain.

match, test. See **test match.**

matchcard, *n.*   **scorecard**

mate, *n.*   *Inf.* **buddy**
   Inf. Matey or *maty* is a slang adjective for *chummy.* A *penmate* is a *pen pal.*

mater, *n.*   **mother**
   Slang. Old-fashioned **public school** usage.

maths, *n.*   **math**

matinee jacket   **baby cardigan**

matron. See **sister.**

maximus. See under **major.**

may, *n.*   **hawthorn**

Mayfair, *n.*   SEE COMMENT
   Used attributively, rather in the same way as *Park Avenue* in America, to describe mannerisms and speech, as in, *Her accent's terribly Mayfair.* This use will fade, however, because Mayfair is, in fact, no longer the fashionable part of London it once was. The scene has shifted to Sloane Square and Belgravia. See also **Chelsea; Sloane Rangers.**

May Week   SEE COMMENT
   May Week is a Cambridge University function which lasts several days longer than a week and is celebrated in June. It is a festive period after finals are over, the principal festivities being a series of balls and *bumping-races. Bumping-races* are boat races among eights representing the various colleges (see **college**) in which a boat which catches up with and touches another (called *bumping*) scores a win. A *bump-supper* is held to celebrate four wins. The British are pretty casual in their use of approximations like *May Week* and **Cinque Ports.** *Bumping-races* are held at Oxford as well where the occasion is called **Eights Week.** This type of sport owes it origin to the narrowness of the Rivers Cam (from which Cambridge gets its name) and Isis (the Thames at Oxford).

maze, *v.t.*   **bewilder**
Related to *amaze* but now archaic in America.

M.B.E. *See under* **Birthday Honours.**

M.C. See **V.C.**

M.C.C. See under **(the) Ashes.**

m.d.   **retarded**
Inf. Stands for *mentally deficient;* no slur on the medical profession.

mean, *adj.*   **stingy; petty**
In America *mean* is most commonly understood as 'cruel' and 'ill-tempered.' In Britain
it means 'stingy' or 'petty', 'ignoble.' *Mean* has an additional slang use in America,
especially in jazz circles and among the youth: *He blows a mean horn.* Here, *mean* has
the implication of *punishing:* something that makes a deep impression, that you won't
soon forget—something that almost hurts. Curiously, the British, to express the same
reaction, would say, *He blows no mean horn,* introducing a negative, and here *mean*
probably signifies 'average' or 'mediocre,' its original meaning.

means test   SEE COMMENT
A test establishing the financial means of disabled or unemployed people in order to
determine their eligibility for welfare benefits. *Means-test* is used as a transitive verb
meaning to 'apply a means test' to someone.

meant to   **supposed to**
A Briton asks, for instance, *Are we meant to throw rubbish in that* **bin?** Or he might say,
The Russians are meant to be good chess players, i.e., *reputed* to be.

mear. See **mere.**

meat and drink   *Inf.* **just what the doctor ordered**
Inf. Or *made to order,* i.e., just the opportunity one was waiting for, particularly in a
competitive situation like sports, a court trial, an election, etc.; a source of great pleasure
to the protagonist, when the adversary plays into his hands, and he can pounce.

meat-safe   **food cupboard**
Built of wire mesh and fast becoming obsolete, giving way to the refrigerator. Although it is called a *meat safe,* it can be used to preserve any food.

mediatize, *v.t.*   **annex**
This historical term means to 'annex a smaller country, (usually a principality) to a
larger one.' The former ruler retains his title and may be permitted to keep some governing rights. Hence, the expression *mediatized prince.*

megger, *n.*   SEE COMMENT
Device for the measurement of insulation resistance; from *megohm,* meaning '1,000,000
ohms.'

Melton Mowbray pie   SEE COMMENT
A pork pie from the town of that name in Leicestershire. Round in shape, with a
covering of hard pastry made with hot, rather than the usual cold water. Taken over
by a commercial bakery, they don't come from Melton Mowbray any more.

Member, *n.*   SEE COMMENT
The British opposite number of a *congressman* is a *Member of Parliament,* colloquially
abbreviated to *M.P.* and commonly shortened to *Member.* The area represented by *M.P.*
is known as a **division** or a **constituency.**

memorandum and articles of association   **corporate charter**

mend, *v.t.*   **repair**
You may hear Britons talking about having their shoes, flat tires (**punctures**), and chairs *mended*, but their cars, plumbing, and television sets *repaired*. The distinction would appear to be arbitrary. Nowadays the upper classes tend to have most things *repaired* rather than *mended*, though really old-fashioned types, especially in the country, still tend to have many things *mended*. Thus in the villages, you often hear references to the *shoe mender, the watch mender,* and so on. One word the British rarely use as the equivalent of *mend* or *repair* is *fix*, an Americanism so common as to give rise to the label *Mr. Fixit* for one who is handy at repairing things. *Fix* is commonly used in Britain to mean 'arrange,' as in the TV series *Jim'll Fix It*. An echo of this usage is seen in **fixture,** meaning 'event' in sports, i.e., an 'arrangement.'

mental, *adj.*   **crazy**
Inf. An American will speak of a disturbed person as a *mental case*. The British content themselves with the adjective alone. This usage is generally considered substandard.

mentioned in dispatches   **cited for bravery**
A military term. To be *mentioned in dispatches* is to be honored by being mentioned by name in a military report for bravery or other commendable acts of service.

mercer, *n.*   **textile dealer**
Usually designates an exclusive shop, dealing in expensive high-style fabrics, with the emphasis on silk.

merchant, *n.*   **wholesaler**
The usual implication is that he deals principally in international trade.

merchant bank   *approx.* **investment bank**
Specializing in the acceptance of bills of exchange in international commerce and investment in new issues.

mere; mear, *n.*   **lake**
Or *pond;* almost never used in America. A rather poetic term, one often applied to the Norfolk Broads. Another meaning of *mere* is 'boundary' or 'boundary marker,' but this is country dialect and rare.

mess (someone) about   **obstruct; interfere with (someone)**
Slang. Can also be used in the sense of sexually molesting a child. See **interfere with.**

mess-up, *n., Slang.*   **mess**

metalled road   **paved road**
The British speak of *unmetalled, unpaved, unmade,* and *dust roads,* all synonymous. *Road-metal* is a British term for the crushed stone which constitutes the layers of macadam roads (see **macadam**).

metals, *n. pl.*   **rails**
When a train *leaves the metals* in Britain it has been *derailed.*

meteorological office   **weather bureau**
And the much reviled official whom the Americans call the *weatherman* is the *clerk of the weather* in Britain.

meths. See **methylated spirit.**

methylated spirit   **denatured alcohol**
Usually shortened to *meths,* which is also used to refer to the unhappy derelicts who drink it.

metricate. See **metrification.**

metrification, metrication, *n.*   **adoption of metric system**
Giving rise to the verbs *metrify* and *metricate.* This process, spurred by Britain's entry into the Common Market, has caused something of an unheaval in British society, especially among older people who cling to their *shillings* (see **Appendix II.A.**), *gallons* (see **Appendix II.C.2.a.**), *stone* (see **Appendix II.C.1.f.**), etc., to say nothing of yards, feet, and inches and the Fahrenheit thermometer. *(Fancy asking for a litre of milk!)* See, however, **pint.**

metrify. See **metrification.**

metropolitan district   SEE COMMENT
A phrase used to express the concept of incorporation of surrounding areas into a city unit, creating a governmental subdivision larger than the old city. Americans express the same concept by the use of *Greater* as in *Greater New York, Greater Chicago,* etc., as do the British.

(the) Met(s)   **(the) London Police**
Inf. Short for *the Metropolitan Police,* which is the London police force; nothing to do with either opera or baseball.

Michaelmas   SEE COMMENT
(Pronounced MICKLE-M'S.) September 29. See under **term; quarter day.**

midden, *n.*   **dunghill**
Or *garbage heap. Kitchen midden* is used in both countries to describe a heap of seafood shells or other refuse marking the site of a prehistoric settlement.

middle name   *approx. Inf.* **nickname**
Inf. In America John Henry Smith has a *first* name, a *middle* name, and a *last* name. In Britain he would commonly be said to have two *Christian* or *given* names or *forenames* and a *surname.* John Henry Samuel Smith would be said to have two *middle* names in America, three *Christian* or *given* names in Britain. The term *middle name* itself may also be used either jocularly or bitterly in both countries but usually in somewhat different ways. In America (rarely in Britain) a wife speaking of her husband's favorite dish (or sport) might say about him, *Apple pie* (or *hockey) is his middle name!* In Britain a person complaining of another's hypocritical conduct might say, *His middle name is Heep!* (after the knavish Uriah in *David Copperfield*). The corresponding expression in America would be: *He's a regular Uriah Heep!*

mike, *v.i.*   **Slang. goof off**
Slang. To *idle;* also expressed by *be on the mike.*

milk float   **milk truck**
Probably so called because of its stately gait, required to prevent churning. Not a good vehicle to get behind at the beginning of a long, winding hill.

milliard, *n.*   **billion**
See **Appendix II.D.**

mince, *n.*   **chopped meat**
The common name by which a British housewife orders from her butcher what her American opposite number would call *chopped meat* or *hamburger.* Sometimes the British use the term *minced meat* instead. *Mincemeat* generally means, in both countries, the mixture of chopped apples, raisins, candied orange rind, suet, etc., which goes into mince pie. A *mincer* is a *meatgrinder.*

mincemeat tart   **mince pie**
Mince pie would be understood in Britain to mean a small individual one. See also **pie.**

mincer. See under **mince.**

Mincing Lane SEE COMMENT
Inf. An actual street in London, which has given its name to the *tea business,* just as other London streets have become symbols and nicknames for other lines of endeavor.

mind, *v.t., v.i.*
1. **watch out for**
2. **care**
3. **mind you**

1. When a train stops at a curved platform at a British railroad station, there are attendants who say, or signs that read, *Mind the gap!* Where there is an unexpected step, you will be enjoined to *Mind the step,* i.e., *to watch out for* it. In *Mind you do! mind* means 'make sure.' As for *mind* meaning 'watch out for,' a correspondent writes about a delicious sign in Gloucestershire reading: MIND THE VIPERS, IF BITTEN, PLEASE CALL THE CIRENCESTER FIRE BRIGADE. (He added: "How I have mourned not stealing that sign!")
2. In America, *I don't mind* means 'I don't object.' In Britain it also means 'I don't care,' in the sense of indifference when an alternative is offered. Thus, if asked, *Would you rather stay or go?* or *Do you want chocolate or vanilla?,* a Briton who would be happy either way says, "I don't mind." See also **have no mind to.**
3. **In the imperative,** *mind* often omits the *you* in Britain: *I don't believe a word of it, mind!* The British do not use *mind* in the sense of *obey.* British parents *mind* (*look after*) their children. American children *mind* (or should mind, i.e., *obey*) their parents.

minder, *n.* **bodyguard**
A *minder* is a *personal bodyguard;* in underworld slang, a *lookout.* Nothing to do with **child-minder.**

mineral, *n.* **soft drink**
One sees MINERALS on signs in British restaurants, tea rooms, etc. They are not trying to sell you iron, steel, or copper—all they are offering is *soft drinks.* This use of the term is related to the term *mineral water* which one still hears in America. See also **squash.**

mingy, *adj.* *Slang.* **tight (stingy)**
Inf. A **portmanteau** word: combination of *mean* and *stingy.* It applies not only to persons but also to things, like a *mingy* portion of something. See also **mean.**

mini, *n.* **Mini Minor**
The *Mini Minor,* a small car produced by the British since 1960, was the origin of the popularization of the prefix *mini* to describe anything small. When used alone, as a noun, it refers to any of the various miniature cars produced by British firms.

mini-budget. See **budget.**

minim, *n.* **halfnote**
See **Appendix II.F.**

minimus. See under **major**

minister, *n.* **cabinet member**
A term relating to government officials. The officials whom Americans describe as *cabinet members* are known as *ministers* in Britain. But not all *ministers* (in the political sense) are in the British cabinet, only the most senior ones. See also **Member.** Incidentally, the British would not refer to a *minister* as an 'official,' a term reserved by them to denote a **civil servant,** not an elected representative of the people.

minor. See under **major.**

mis; miz, *adj.* *Slang.* **down**
Slang. Short for *miserable.*

misfield, *n., v.i.t.*   *approx.* **error**
A cricket term, just as *error* is a baseball term; but *misfield* is simply a characterization of a fielding blunder, rather than an official ruling or statistic that goes into the imperishable archives. To *misfield* is to be guilty of the blunder. See **chance.**

missing. See **go missing.**

miss out   **1. skip**
                                                                                2. miss
1. To *omit.* If you don't like artichokes, for instance, you *miss them out* at the dinner table. Often lengthened to *miss out on* with the same meaning: 'intentional passing up,' rather than 'missing something to one's regret.' See also **give (someone or something) a miss.**
2. Automotive term: *The engine is missing out on one cylinder.*

mithered, *adj.*   **hot and bothered**
Inf. Of Lancashire origin. See also **moider.** *Moithered* is heard as well.

mixed, *adj.*   **coed(ucational)**
Applies to secondary schools, many of which are still for girls or boys only. As for the universities, they are coeducational, but some of the colleges within the universities are not, e.g., the Catholic ones at Oxford and most of the women's colleges at Oxford and Cambridge, though many colleges voted in favor of becoming *mixed,* beginning with the academic year 1978/79.

mixed bag   **assortment**
Inf. Of persons or things, implying a considerable variation in type or quality. In the U.S., commonly refers to a situation with both good and bad features. See **curate's egg.**

mixture as before   **same old story**
Inf. When you have a prescription renewed in Britain, the label often bears the expression *"The mixture as before."* The phrase is jocularly applied to situations which amount to the *same old story,* as when delegates to labor negotiations or peace conferences return after an interval and present each other with nothing new.

miz. See **mis.**

mizzle, *n., v.i.*   **drizzle**
Apparently a **portmanteau** concoction of *mist* and *drizzle.*

mobile police   **patrol cars**

mobile production   **traveling show**

mobility unit   SEE COMMENT
Public housing adapted to meet the needs of handicapped persons.

mod. cons. See under **amenities.**

moderations, *n. pl.*   SEE COMMENT
First exams for B.A. degree especially in classics at Oxford. Often abbreviated to *mods.* The examiner is called a *moderator.* See also **greats; responsions; smalls.**

moderator, *n.*   SEE COMMENT
1. Officer presiding over math tripos. See **tripos.**
2. Examiner for moderations. See **moderations.**
3. Presbyterian minister presiding over church group.

mog, moggy, moggie, *n.*   **kitty**
Inf. A *kittycat,* especially one without a pedigree. If one were distinguishing between a Burmese of venerable ancestry and a garden variety pussycat, one might be tempted

to characterize the latter as 'just a moggy,' but it would be preferable to eliminate the 'just' in all other cases. *Mog, moggy*, etc. are highly respectable designations, even if they are corruptions of *mongrel*.

moider, *v.t.*   **bother**
Inf. Moidered is north of England dialect for *hot and bothered*. See also **mithered.**

mole, *n.*   **little hill**
Nothing to do with spies.

Mondayish, *adj.*   SEE COMMENT
Describing the feelings of one facing the prospect of the week's work ahead, after the festivities or relaxation of the weekend. Applies as well to a clergyman weary as a result of his Sabbath labors.

money for jam   *Inf.* **easy pickings**
Inf. Like taking candy from a baby. Description of a task embarrassingly easy. See also **easy meat; piece of cake; as easy as kiss your hand; snip.** Sometimes *money for jam* appears to mean 'something for nothing,' in the sense of a good return for negligible effort. Synonymous, in this sense, with *money for old rope.*

money for old rope. See **money for jam.**

money-spinning, *n., adj.*   1. **money raising**
                                                                                         2. **moneymaking**
1. A *money-spinning* event is one that enriches the treasury of a do-good organization. 2. A *money-spinning* play is simply a hit which is raking it in. A *money spinner* is a *money maker*, anything that makes money, a financial success. See also **word spinning.**

monger, *n.*   **dealer**
This word is almost always used in combination with the word that denotes the particular trade involved. Examples: *cheesemonger, fishmonger, ironmonger* (for hardware merchant), and the usual practice is to put an apostrophe *s* after the combination word: *I'm going to the fishmonger's; I have to get my lamp repaired at the ironmonger's. Monger* fits into other combinations of a derogatory nature: *scandalmonger, warmonger*, and the new pejorative term *peacemonger*, for a *dove*. A *verse-monger* is a *poetaster*.

monkey, *n., Slang.*   **£500**

monkey-freezing, *adj.*   *Inf.* **biting cold.**
Slang. Euphemistic ellipsis of *cold enough to freeze the balls off a brass monkey.* Cf. **cold as charity.**

monkey-nut, *n.*   **peanut**
Synonymous with **ground-nut** and thought by some to be slang or at least mildly jocular.

monomark, *n.*   **registered identification mark**
An arbitrary symbol, consisting of letters, numbers, or both, for purposes of identification.

moonlight flit   **flight by night**
Inf. To *do a moonlight flit* (or **shoot the moon**) in Britain is to *blow town at night* with all your belongings, with no forwarding address, in order to get away without paying the rent or settling with your creditors. It is like *doing a bunk* (see **bunk**), but at night.

moonraker, *n.*   *Slang.* **blockhead**
Inf. The legend is that certain Wiltshire hayseeds tried to rake the moon out of a pond, mistaking the reflection for a piece of cheese.

moons, *n. pl.*   *Inf.* **ages**
Slang. I haven't seen him in moons. See also **donkey's years.**

moonshine, *n.*   *Inf.* **castles in the air**
Inf. Visionary ideas. These can result from *moonshine* in the American sense.

moor, *n.*   **wasteland**
Open and overgrown, often with heather. See also **heath.**

mop up   **sop up**
That which Frenchmen do in public, and most other nationalities do in private, in
order to gather up that irresistible last bit of gravy on the plate.

morally certain   **quite sure**
About 90% certain: almost convinced, much stronger than *reasonably sure.*

(it's) mor(e)ish, *adj.*   *Slang.* **(it) tastes like more**
Inf. See **-ish.**

more power to his elbow, *Inf.*   *Inf.* **more power to him**

morning coffee. See **elevenses.**

morning tea   SEE COMMENT
Very sad that there is no American equivalent. In British country hotels, when asked
the night before, "Will you be wanting morning tea?" The reference is to the tea brought
up by the **chambermaid** when she **knocks you up**—before you go down to breakfast.

morris dance   SEE COMMENT
A ritual folk dance performed all over England, usually during May Day ceremonies,
by persons in costumes representing set characters said to refer back to the legend of
Robin Hood. The term *morris* is a corruption of *Moorish.*

most secret   **top secret**

Mothering Sunday   **Laetare** or **Mid-Lent Sunday**
Fourth Sunday in Lent, called *Laetare Sunday* because on that Sunday the *introit* in
the Latin Mass began *Laetare Jerusalem* ('Rejoice, Jerusalem'). The British name was
derived from the custom of children bringing gifts to mothers on that day—the original
Mother's Day.

mother-in-law, *n.*   SEE COMMENT
Inf. An old joke; a way of asking for an *old and bitter* (*ale* understood). Not current.

mother's ruin   **gin**
Inf. Much deplored and much drunk. Sounds Hogarthian in origin; also ascribed to
rhyming slang (see **Appendix II.G.3**) by some, but *ruin* and *gin* don't really rhyme.

motion, *n.*   **bowel movement**

motor, *v.i.*   **drive**
The British also use *drive,* but no American would ever say, "We *motored* across the
country."

motor-bike, *n.*   **motorcycle**
Inf. Now usually shortened to *bike,* which also means 'bicycle.'

motor coach   **intercity bus**
Usually shortened to *coach.*

motorway, *n.*   **turnpike**

mouch; mooch, *v.i.*   *Inf.* **hang around**
   Slang. Both forms rhyme with HOOCH. To *mouch round* or *mouch about* a place is to *hang around* it or in juvenile American slang to *hack around* in it. *Mouch* also appears as a noun in the expression *go for a mouch* meaning the same thing.

mount, *n., v.t.*   **mat**
   Term used in framing.

mouse-trap, *n.*   *approx. Slang.* **rat cheese**
   Slang. Describes any humble type of hard cheese, like Cheddar, Leicester, Lancashire, and the like (as opposed, for example, to Stilton and the fancier numbers). Usually the word implies a left-over bit, going somewhat stale, but edible; something you'd be willing to offer an old friend who dropped in, but not the vicar.

move house   **move**
   The British occasionally use the shorter American form for *change residence;* but see **Appendix, I.A.3.**

moving stairway   **escalator**
   Interchangeable with *moving staircase,* and the British are familiar with *escalator* as well.

M.P. See **Member.**

Mrs Grundy. See **wowser.**

Mrs Mop   **cleaning woman**
   Inf. Not necessarily disrespectful; on the contrary, often affectionate. *My Mrs Mop is a jewel...,* etc. Mrs Mopp (two *ps*) was a character in the interminable radio program *It's That Man Again* (familiarly known as *ITMA*) during World War II. Her oft-repeated line was, *Can I do you now, sir?* See also **char.** *See* **Appendix I.D.6.** for absence of periods.

much of this mark. See under **mark.**

muck, *n., v.i.*   **mess**
   Slang. The British government makes a *muck* of things, in about the same way the American government makes a *mess* of things, and in the same way in which all the other governments seem to be making whatever-it-is-they-call-it these days. Whereas Americans *mess around*, Britons *muck about*. To *muck in* is to *pitch in*, with the connotation that the task in question is a menial one. To *muck out* (a stable, e.g.) is to *clean it out*, get rid of the *muck* (like Hercules). To be *in a muck sweat* about something is to be *terribly upset* about it, deeply concerned and awfully worried.

mucker, *n.,*   1. *Slang.* **spill**
                                                                            2. spending spree
                                                                                  3. *Inf.* **buddy**
   1. *Slang.* To *come a mucker* is to *take a spill*.
   2. *Slang.* To *go a mucker* is to *go on a spending spree* or *throw your money around*. Fairly obviously derives from *run amok*, with its variant *run amuck*.
   3. Army *slang.*

mudlark, *n.*   *approx.* **scavenger**
   Of a special sort: a person—usually a child—who searches the mudflats between high and low tide for whatever may be found in the way of flotsam or jetsam or lagan.

muff, *n.*   **oaf**
   Inf. Muff is used in both countries as a verb meaning 'miss.' One can *muff* any kind of opportunity, in life generally. In sports, one *muffs* a catch. From this the British developed the noun *muff*, meaning 'awkward, rather silly person.' Apparently, however, in context, it can be used almost as a term of endearment, as in, *What a silly little muff you are!* From *muff* came the slang use of **muffin.**

muffetee, *n.*   knitted wrist cuff

muffin, *n.*   **1. small spongy cake**
                                               2. *Slang.* **dope (fool)**
1. This has nothing whatever in common with what Americans call *English muffins,* which are unknown in Britain. Instead, it is a light, flat, round, spongy cake, served toasted and buttered.
2. *Slang.* See under **muff.**

mug, *n., v.i.*   **1.** *Slang.* **dope; fool**
                                               2. *Slang.* **grind; bookworm**
                                               3. quiz
1. *Slang.* To be *had for a mug* is to be *taken in,* i.e., taken for a *dope.* A *mug's game* is *something for the birds; my idea of nothing at all; a profitless endeavor.*
2. *Slang.* The British also use *mug* and *mug up* verbally, meaning 'bone up,' e.g., for an examination (see also **sap; swot**).
3. *Slang.* The school term, now obsolescent.

muggins, *n.*   *Slang.* **dope; fool**
Slang. Synonymous with **juggins.**

mull, *n., v.t., v.i.*   **mess; mess up**
To *mull* (or *mull over*) in America is to *ponder* or *cogitate,* an activity that often winds up in a *mull* in the British sense.

multiple shops   chain store

multi-storey, *adj.*   **high rise**
Note the *e* in storey. See **Appendix I.E.**

mumchance, *adj., adv.*   **tongue-tied**
Doltishly silent. Said to be archaic or dialectal, but still heard, if rarely, among older folk who speak standard English.

mummy, *n.*   **mama; mommy**
Also **mum** (non-U; see **Appendix I.C.6**). *Mummy* and *mama* start in childhood, but *mummy* lingers on longer in Britain than *mama* does in America, where it usually becomes *mother.* The Queen Mother is facetiously called the *Queen Mum* and sometimes preciously, but always affectionately, *Queenie Mum. Mums,* in the mouth of a "U-person," (See **Appendix I.C.6.**), means 'lower-class mothers.'

mump, *v.t.*   *Slang.* **cadge**
Slang. To *mump* something is to get it by begging, to *cadge* or *wheedle* it out of someone. The same verb, used intransitively, has two separate meanings in standard English: 1. to *mope,* and 2. to *go begging,* from which the slang transitive use is clearly derived. *Mumping* is a British police term, of which the nearest American equivalent is *freeloading,* the practice, sternly disapproved by the majority of the force, of accepting minor gifts from people on the beat, like a cup of tea in the back room of a shop, or petty graft in the form of discounts on goods or services.

mum's help, *Inf.*   **mother's helper**

muniment room   SEE COMMENT
Very British: the storage and/or display room of a castle or church or other ancient monument where historical records and treasures are kept.

music centre   SEE COMMENT
Combination record-player, cassette player, and radio. See also **radiogram.**

music-hall, *n.*   **vaudeville theater**
A *music-hall* **turn** is a *vaudeville act.* **Variety** is a usual British term for *vaudeville.* *Vaudeville* is the name of a famous theater in London and is not commonly used as a common noun.

muslin, *n.*   **cheesecloth**
See also **butter-muslin; calico.**

mustard-keen, *adj.*   **enthusiastic**
Inf. Also, *keen as mustard.* This phrase involves a pun on Keen's Mustard, a popular product. See also discussion of *keen on* under **mad on.**

mutes, *n. pl.*   **professional pallbearers**

muzz, *v.t., Slang.* See **muzzy.**

muzzy, *adj.*   *Slang.* **woozy**
Slang. The implication in *muzzy* is that the unfortunate condition it describes is the result of too much drink. The slang British verb *muzz,* used transitively, means to 'put somebody *hors de combat,*' not in one fell swoop by slipping him a micky, but in nice, easy stages.

My dear...   **Dear...**
In America, the addition of *My* in the salutation of a letter makes it more formal; in Britain, more intimate.

my old dutch. See **dutch.**

N

N/A   **not applicable**
Abbreviation used in filling out forms; for instance, the blank space for *maiden name*, in a form being completed by a male.

NAAFI, *n.*   SEE COMMENT
Slang. (Pronounced NAFFY or NAHFY.) Standing for *Navy, Army, and Air Force Institutes,* an organization that operates canteens and service centers for members of the British armed forces, similar to an American PX.

naff, *v.i., adj.*   SEE COMMENT
Slang. Anything *naff* is shabby or cheap, or **tatty**. *Naff off!* is the equivalent of **Bugger off!** or in America, *Fuck off! Naffing* began in the R.A.F. as a substitute for *fucking* in its adjectival and adverbial uses. There is a theory that it all started as an armed forces gibe against **NAAFI.**

nailed on, *Slang.*   *Slang.***nailed down; all set**

nail varnish   **nail polish**

nannie, *n.*   **child's nurse**
Nanny is the dictionary form but *nannie* appears frequently.

nap, *n.*   *Inf.* **tip (on the races)**
Inf. To *go nap* is to *bet your stack.* A *nap selection* is a racing expert's list of betting recommendations. *Nap* is an abbreviation of *napoleon* (lower case *n*), a card game in which players bid for the right to name the trump, declaring the number of tricks they propose to win. A *nap* or *napoleon* in this game is a bid to take all five tricks, the maximum. *Nap hand* has acquired the figurative meaning of being in the position where one is practically sure of winning big if willing to take the risk. There are those who allege that the association of *nap* with *winning* results from *nap* being an abbreviation of *Napoleon,* who was a winner for a time but appears not to have done so well at the end. A wholly coincidental association of Napoleon and horses is found in the old vaudeville ditty, "Giddyap Napoleon, it looks like rain." See also **pot.**

napper, *n., Slang.*   *Slang.* **noodle (head)**
Synonymous with **bean; loaf; noddle.**

nappy, *n.*   **diaper**
Inf. A diminutive of *napkin,* and the everyday word for *diaper,* which is seldom heard in Britain. *Didie,* the American diminutive baby talk for *diaper,* is unknown in Britain.

nark, *n.*   *Slang.* **stool pigeon**
Slang. Originally *copper's nark.* i.e., *informer.* Jocularly and pejoratively extended to the publishing business, where a *publisher's nark* means a 'publicity man.' *Nark* is not related to the American term *nark* or *narc* meaning 'federal narcotics agent'. The British term came from the Romany word *nak* (pronounced NAHK) meaning 'nose.'

narked, *adj.*   *Slang.* **sore**
Slang. In the sense of 'angry'; to *be narked* is to *get sore.*

narky, *adj.*   *Slang.* **bitchy**
Slang. Probably related to an Australian sense of *nark:* 'spiteful person.'

nasty, *adj.* disagreeable
In America, *nasty* means something a good deal stronger than *disagreeable:* 'foul,' or 'filthy.' *Nasty* (usually in the plural) has been used to mean 'gremlin' or 'bug' in the sense of 'defect' in computer programs. *Nasties* was a facetious name for *Nazis* in the thirties and forties.

nasty piece (bit) of work *Slang.* **louse**
Inf. An unspeakable person.

National Assistance. See **National Insurance.**

National Health Service socialized medicine
The idea and the British terminology are both gaining a foothold in America. See also **health visitor.**

National Insurance Government Insurance System
State-regulated compensation to the sick, aged, and unemployed based on a system of compulsory contributions from workers and employers, including certain supplementary benefits formerly known as *National Assistance.*

nation of shopkeepers. See under **shop.**

natter, *n., v.i.* chatter
Inf. As a verb, it can still mean 'grumble' (when someone goes on endlessly nagging, you shut him up with *Natter, natter, natter!*) but this sense appears to be increasingly less common. *Nattering* on the High Street as one meets neighbors is what makes shopping such a pleasure and wastes so much time. Don't be misled by *natterjack,* which is not a male gossip but rather a *yellow striped toad* indigenous to Britain.

naturist, *n.* nudist
And *naturism* is *nudism.* But the British do use *nudist beach.*

naught. See **nought.**

naughty, *adj.* wicked
In both countries, *naughty* is also a word usually associated with children. Shakespeare used it in the sense of *wicked*:
How far that little candle throws his beams!
So shines a good deed in a *naughty* world.
Merchant of Venice (Act V, Scene 1).
And Dogberry calls Conrade "Thou *naughty* varlet!" in *Much Ado About Nothing* (Act IV, Scene 2). It is still heard in Britain in that sense, but usually as an exercise in jocular understatement which seems somewhat affected, thus (referring to a particularly bloodthirsty murder): *That was a naughty thing to do.* At one time it meant 'wicked' in America too, but that usage is obsolete. Obscene words are rather coyly called *naughty words* in both countries, but in Britain the usual term would be *rude.* See **rude 3.**

navvy, *n.* construction worker
Especially a road, railway, or canal worker. A *gang of navvies* is a *construction crew.* Nowadays mechanical excavating machines are operated by gasoline or diesel fuel. In the old days when they were operated by steam, they were known as *steam-navvies.* The term *navvy* reflects a bit of British history. Britain has a complex and beautiful inland waterway system dating back to the 18th century (but, alas, of uncertain future). The earliest canals, dug with pick and shovel, were called *navigations* and the hordes of diggers *navvies.* See also **lengthman.**

N.B.G. *approx. Inf.* **N.G.**
Inf. The *B.* stands for **bloody** and the three letters really work out to mean 'no goddamned good.' See **bloody** for use of *bloody* in tmesis.

near-side lane   **slow lane**
Since traffic keeps to the left in Britain, and the *near* refers to the edge of the road, the *near-side lane* refers to the leftmost one for regular driving. The one nearest the center is called the *off-side lane*, and is used for passing. The terms *near-side* and *off-side* can also refer to the sides of a vehicle: e.g., the *off-side front wheel*.

near the bone. See **near the knuckle.**

near the knuckle   *Inf.* **off color**
Inf. Somewhat indecent; getting there, anyway. Synonymous with **near the bone.**

neat, *adj.*   **straight**
Referring to undiluted alcoholic beverages. Some Americans say *neat*; no Briton says *straight*.

neck, *n.*   *Inf.* **nerve**
Inf. In the sense of 'cheek' or 'gall' or 'impudence.' Often found in the expression *brass neck.*

neck and crop   **headfirst**
Inf. The way people get thrown out of the barrooms in western movies.

(the) needle, *n.*   *Slang.* **(the) jitters**
Slang. The kind of nervousness one gets when kept in suspense.

needle match   **grudge match**
A game or match which is hotly contested, with a background involving a certain amount of acrimony. A county cricket match between Lancashire and Yorkshire is such a match. (Here, the background involved a certain amount of bloodshed: they are still fighting the War of the Roses.) Such a match is said to *have a lot of needle*. There is a story about a Lancashire-Yorkshire match during which a certain gentleman in the stand jumped up and down and applauded enthusiastically whenever Lancashire scored a **boundary** (four runs). An unhappy Yorkshireman went over to him during a lull and asked, "And what part of Lancashire do ye coom froom?" The enthusiast replied, "As a matter of fact, I'm actually a Londoner," to which the other responded hotly, "Then why don't ye mind yer own bloody business?" Yet another 'Roses' story (and you must remember that Len Hutton—Hoot'n in the Yorkshire accent—the *oo* as in *good*—was Yorkshire's legendary opening **batsman**, i.e., first in batting order): Father and young son go to the match. Dad finds he has forgotten his pipe and asks son to fetch it (they live close by). Son returns with pipe and announces, "Mother's in bed wi' lodger." "Booger (**bugger**) lodger," says dad, "Hooten's out."

Nelson Riddle, See **fiddle.**

nervous nineties, *Inf.*   SEE COMMENT
In cricket, it is a signal accomplishment for a **batsman** to make 100 runs, known as a **century**. As he approaches this desideratum, a batsman sometimes tightens up, and when he makes his 90th run, becomes understandably nervous, or, as the British say, **nervy**. At this point, he is said to be *in the nervous nineties*. The term has been extended to other sports, as in the case of a **football** (soccer) team leading its league towards the end of the season or to any situation where the protagonist is close to triumph, but with pitfalls looming.

nervy   *Slang.* **jumpy**
Slang. Britons express themselves as feeling *nervy* or describe someone as looking *nervy*. In each case, the American equivalent would be *jumpy*. The American slang meaning 'cheeky' is not shared with Britain. A less common British slang sense, not shared with America, is hard to describe by a one-word equivalent but is used to describe something that gets on your *nerves*. In other words, a *nervy* person in Britain can be *jumpy* or *wearing*, depending on the context. Come to think of it, there is no reason why the same person cannot be both at the same time.

network, *v.t.*   **broadcast over a network**

(the) never-never, *n.*   **installment plan**
  Slang. The serious British equivalent for *installment plan* is **hire-purchase.** *The never-never* is popular, wistful, jocular slang.

Newmarket, *n.*   SEE COMMENT
  Newmarket is a horseracing town. It is also the name of a card game. A *Newmarket* or *Newmarket coat* is a *tightfitting overcoat* for either sex.

new penny.
  See **Appendix II.A.**

newsagent, *n.*   **newsdealer**
  See also **kiosk, 1.**

news editor, *n.*   **city editor**
  For British use of *city editor,* see **City editor.**

newspaper post   **second-class mail**
  Second-class mail now refers in Britain to nonpriority letters sent at a cheaper postal rate than first-class mail.

newsreader, *n.*   **newscaster**
  Often shortened to *reader* on radio and TV.

news-room, *n.*   **periodical room**
  The reading room in a library where newspapers and magazines are kept. (*Newsroom* in America is a newspaper term referring to the news section of a newspaper office or a radio or television station.)

New Town. See under **overspill.**

New Year Honours. See **Birthday Honours**

next turning. See **beyond the next turning**

nice bit of work   *Slang.* **quite a dish**
  Slang. Other complimentary slang in the same vein: *nice bit of crumpet* (see **crumpet**); *nice bit of stuff; nice bit of skirt.* Apparently, *a nice bit of* almost anything would do. *Nice bit* is often *nice piece* in these expressions. *Nice bit of homework* is the author's favorite. See also **bit of; nasty piece (bit) of work.**

nice to hear you   **nice to hear your voice**
  A common telephone phrase. Americans say, *How nice to hear your voice,* or *How nice to hear from you.*

nick, *n.*   **1. station house**
                                                          2. *Inf.* **shape**
  1. *Slang. Police station.*
  2. In the sense of 'physical condition.' Usually in the phrase *in the nick,* sometimes *in good nick,* meaning 'in the pink.'

nick, *v.t.*   *Slang.* **pinch**
  Slang. In both senses: to *steal* something, or to *arrest* someone.

nicker, *n.*   **pound**
  Slang. Unit of currency, not weight. Low-class, petty criminals' cant. The common slang term is **quid.** See **Appendix II.G.1** See also *knickers.*

nide, *n.*   **pheasant brood**

night-cellar, *n., Slang.*   *Slang.* **dive**

night on the tiles   *Slang.* **night on the town**
Slang. This phrase is derived from the custom among cats of having fun at night on rooftops, which in Britain are often made of tiles.

night sister. See **sister.**

night watchman   SEE COMMENT
Inf. Cricket term. If a player is out just before close of play that day (e.g., if there is time left for only a dozen balls to be *bowled*—see **bowler, 2.**), a weak **batsman** is put in at that point, out of batting order, to preserve the stronger batsman, who would have been next in the regular order, from the risk of getting out in the failing light of evening, or the strain of an overnight gap in his batting and the consequent risk of his getting out early the next morning. The poor chap thus burdened—who probably will be out early the next day—is called the *night watchman.*

nig-nog, *n.*   *Slang. Derog.* **nigger**
Slang. Derog. This word has lost its former meaning of 'fool' or 'dolt,' and presumably, by association with the deplorable word *nigger*, has become a highly objectionable way of referring to black people.

nil, *n.*   **nothing**
Used in game scores where Americans would use *nothing*, e.g., *six to nil*, except in cricket, where *nought* is the term. See also **nought; duck, 1.**

nil norm   SEE COMMENT
A standard set by the government, limiting price and wage increases. Also, *zero norm.*

nineteen to the dozen   *Slang.* **a blue streak**
Inf. Usually seen in the expression *talk nineteen to the dozen.* See also **talk the hind leg off a donkey.**

nipper, *n.*   *Inf.* **kid (tot)**
Slang. Sometimes *kipper.* See also **limb.**

nippy, *adj., n.*   1. *adj., Slang.* **snappy**
                                                                    2. *n.* **waitress**
1. *adj. Slang.* Look *nippy!* means *Make it snappy!*
2. *n., Slang.* As a noun, *nippy* is slang for *waitress.*
The term was confined originally to the nimble girls at Lyons Corner Houses (a restaurant chain), but then became generic. *Nippy* is just about on its way out.

nip round   *Inf.* **pop over**
Inf. One *nips round* to the pub for a quick **pint.** One can nip *up* as well as *round.* To *nip up* somewhere is to make a hurried trip there and back.

nit, *n.*   *Slang.* **dope; jerk**
Slang. Short for *nitwit.*

nix!, *interj.*   *Slang.* **cheese it!**
Slang. Nix! is an interjection used in Britain to warn one's colleagues that the boss is snooping around. As in America, it is used also to signify a strong *No!*, i.e., *Nothing doing! Cheese it!* (or *Cheezit!*) has become rather old fashioned in America. There would seem to be no modern equivalent, perhaps because people are so much less afraid of the boss these days. *Look busy!* (in a hoarse whisper) is probably the closest equivalent.

nob, *n., Slang.*   *Slang.* **swell**

nobble, *v.t.,*   1. **tamper with**
                                                                    2. *Slang.* **fix**
                                                                    3. **scrounge**

4. *Slang.* **nab**
5. *Slang.* **rat on**

Slang. Sometimes spelled *knobble.* In any of its meanings, a thoroughly unpleasant bit of British slang:
1. One *nobbles* a racehorse to prevent its winning.
2. One *nobbles* a jury to get the desired verdict.
3. *Nobble* also means "scrounge," with the implication of getting something away from somebody through sly, dishonest maneuvering.
4,5. To *nobble* a criminal is to *nab* him, or get him *nabbed* by *ratting on* him.

noddle, *n.*   *Slang.* **noodle (head)**
Slang. Often shortened to *nod.* Synonymous with **bean; loaf; napper.**

no effects   **insufficient funds**
Banking term; for the more up-to-date term, see **refer to drawer.**

No Entry   **Do Not Enter**
Road sign indicating one-way street.

nog, *n.*   SEE COMMENT
Strong ale, once brewed in Norfolk; sometimes spelled *nogg.* In America *nog* is used as short for *eggnog* and refers to any alcoholic drink into which an egg is beaten.

no hoarding. See hoarding.

no joy   *Inf.* **no luck**
Inf. Words announcing *no success,* as you turn to a friend standing by while you vainly try to reach someone by dialing one number after another, or when you call the box office and they're sold out. Applicable to the announcement of any of life's endless frustrations.

nonconformist, *n., adj.*   **non-Anglican**
As a noun, synonymous with **dissenter.** See also **chapel.**

non-content, *n.*   *approx.* **nay-voter**
One who votes against a motion in the House of Lords.

nonnillion. See Appendix II.D.

non-resident, *n.*   *approx.* **transient**
One often sees a sign in front of a British hotel, or attached to its wall, reading MEALS SERVED TO NON-RESIDENTS, or words to that effect. In that use, *non-resident* is used in the sense of a 'person not living at the hotel,' and has nothing to do with national domicile.

(a) nonsense, *n.*   **(a) muddle; fiasco**
Preceded by the indefinite article, especially in the expression *make a nonsense of.* Evelyn Waugh used it in *Put Out More Flags* (Chapman & Hall, London, 1942). In describing a military embarkation that went wrong and turned into a fiasco, a character says, "It was all rather a *nonsense.*" At another point we read: "Everyone said, 'Lyne made a *nonsense* of the embarkation.' "(Strangely, the Penguin paperback omitted the *a* in that sentence—a misprint.) A *nonsense,* in the sense of *fiasco,* is the more elegant equivalent of a **balls** or its variant, a *balls-up,* which is synonymous with **cock-up.** In her novel *A Word Child* (Chatto & Windus, London, 1975), Iris Murdoch's protagonist wants to end the relationship with his mistress: "I wanted now to clean the whole business off myself and be done with it. It had become *an idle nonsense.*" A *nonsense*— a muddle, a fiasco.

non-U   See **Appendix I.C.6.**

no reply   **no answer**
   A telephone term. In America the operator exasperates you by saying *They don't answer*. In Britain the unhappy formula is, *There's no reply*. See also **ceased to exist.**

Norfolk capon   *Inf.* **red herring**
   Inf. A false issue.

Norfolk dumpling   SEE COMMENT
   Inf. Norfolk type, synonymous with *Norfolk turkey*, meaning a native of the county of Norfolk.

Norfolk sparrow   **pheasant**
   Inf. So called because pheasant are so plentiful in the area.

norland, *n.*   **north**
   Norland is a common noun and is simply short for *northland*. *Norland* with a capital *N* is the name of a training college for children's nurses (see **nannie**), which turns out a very superior product who eats with the family.

North Country. See under **West Country**

nose to tail, *Inf.*   *Inf.* **bumper to bumper**

nosey-parker, *n., v.i.*   *Inf.* **rubberneck**
   Inf. When used as a verb, it means to 'be a rubberneck' or 'be a busybody' and take much too great an interest in other people's affairs. This term is said to originate with Dr. Matthew Parker, a 16th century Archbishop of Canterbury who was once chaplain to Anne Boleyn and Henry VIII. He was a religious fanatic and stuck his nose into every aspect of church affairs.

(is) not a patch on   *Inf.* **doesn't hold a candle to**
   Inf. Doesn't come anywhere near; isn't in the same league with.

not a sausage   *Slang.* **not a damned thing**
   Slang. Usually refers to money.

Not at all   **You're welcome**
   The American term used to sound peculiar to British ears. *You're welcome* is now heard increasingly, undoubtedly as a result of its constant use by American visitors. In small matters, the British often say nothing at all (to the surprise of most Americans, some of whom mistakenly consider the silence somewhat rude) in response to *Thank you*. In more important matters, they say *Not at all!* or *That's all right!* A warmer response is *Pleasure! Thank you,* incidentally, is heard all the time from persons serving you, like waiters and waitresses, salespersons, tailors taking your measurements, and the like. It is sometimes so often repeated that it seems more like a nervous tic than a spoken phrase. *Thank you!* from a porter pushing a baggage cart (**trolley,** in Britain) is the equivalent of *Gangway!* See **Pleasure!**

not best pleased   **not too happy**

not by a long chalk, *Inf.*   *Inf.* **not by a long shot**

note, *n.*   **1. bill**
                                                            2. tone
   1. Referring to paper money: a one-pound *note*, a five-pound *note*, and so forth.
   2. In musical terminology, the English use the term *note* in instances where Americans would use *tone*. Examples: 3 *notes* lower; 5-*note* scale. When an Englishman uses *tone* in such expressions, he means what the Americans would call a *whole tone*.

notecase, *n.*   **billfold**
   See also **pocketbook.**

not half   1. **not nearly**
                                                               2. **not at all**
                                                               3. **terrifically**

One must be extremely careful in interpreting the expression *not half:*

1. *Inf.* When a Briton says to a departing guest, "You haven't stayed *half long enough*," he means *not nearly long enough.*

2. *Inf.* When a Briton criticizes his friend's new necktie and describes it as *not half* bad, he means 'not at all bad,' i.e., 'quite satisfactory,' 'pretty good.'

3. *Slang. Not half* has a peculiar slang use as well. Thus, in describing the boss's reaction when he came in and found everybody out to lunch, a British porter might say, "He didn't half blow up," meaning that he did blow up about as completely as possible. In other words, *not half* is used ironically, meaning 'not half—but totally.' As an expletive, by itself, *not half!* might find its American equivalent in *not much!* meaning, of course, the exact opposite: 'very much!' 'and how!' as in, *Would you like a free trip to California? Not much!*

nothing (else) for it   **no alternative**
There's no choice, no other way out or *nothing else to do about it.*

nothing starchy   *Inf.* **no fuss or feathers**
*Slang.*See **starchy.**

nothing to make a song about, *Inf.*   *Inf.* **nothing to write home about**

notice, *v.t.*   **review**
In Britain a book can be spoken of as *reviewed* or *noticed. Noticed* implies that the review was brief.

notice board   **bulletin board**
For instance, the one at railroad stations listing arrivals and departures. See also **hoarding.**

notional income   **imputed income**
Tax term: income attributed to a taxpayer whether or not received (and therefore taxed to him, poor chap). The usual term in the American tax idiom is *constructive income.*

not much cop   *Slang.* **no great catch**
Slang. Not worth much; referring to persons or objects.

not on   1. **impracticable**
                                                          2. *Inf.* **bad form**
1. *Inf.* An employee asks to have his salary doubled. Answer: "It simply isn't on."
2. *Inf.* Denoting impropriety. Synonymous with **off, 1.**

not on your nelly   *Slang.* **no way!**
Slang. **From rhyming slang (see Appendix II.G.3.),** *not on your Nelly Duff* (whoever she was), the rhyme being with *puff,* old slang for 'life.'

not so dusty   *Inf.* **not so bad**
Inf. In answer to the question *How are you?*

Not to worry!, *Inf.*   *Inf.* **Don't let it bother you! No problem!**

nought (naught), *n.*   **zero**
It is used in scoring—*ten to nought.* In that sense Americans would probably use *nothing* instead of *zero.* As a term in arithmetic, a British synonym is **cipher.** Among uneducated Scotsmen—and perhaps elsewhere—one can hear 'ought' instead of *nought.* See also **nil.** *Naught* is archaic and poetic for *nothing. Nowt* is north country for *nothing.* Cf. **owt.**

noughts and crosses   **tick-tack-toe**
Also called OXO, a trademark of a beef soup concentrate.

nous, *n.*   *Slang.* **savvy**
Slang. It looks French, but is the Greek word for 'mind' and rhymes with HOUSE. Upper class, on the whole. Can also mean 'gumption.'

nowt. See **nought.** *Cf.* **owt.**

nr   **near**
A term used on envelopes in addressing letters: thus, Sandhurst, *nr* Hawkhurst, to differentiate that Sandhurst (which has nothing whatever to do with the military academy) from Sandhurst in Surrey. *Nr* in Scotland becomes *by*: thus, Giffnock *by* Glasgow. See also **Appendix I.D.9.**

nude contract   **void contract**
Unenforceable because lacking in consideration, if not signed under seal.

nullity, *n.*   **annulment**
Term is matrimonial law. If you can't stand your spouse but have no grounds for divorce, your American lawyer can look into the chances of obtaining an *annulment.* His opposite number in Britain would determine whether you had grounds for a *nullity suit.*

number. See **make one's number.**

number plate   **license plate**

Number 10 Downing Street   SEE COMMENT
Usually shortened to *No. 10.* The seat of executive power and residence of the prime minister. Like *the White House,* it is not only an address but is also used figuratively when referring to the chief executive's office.

nurse, *v.t.*   **fondle**
A use not met with in America: to hold a baby on one's lap caressingly. The verb is also used to describe the attentions of a politician to his constituency to convince the voters of his devotion to their interests.

nursing home   **private hospital**
Also *convalescent home.*

nutcase, *n.*   *Slang.* **nut; case**
Slang. The Americans refer to a nutty person as a *case* or a *nut.* The British make sure of being understood by a using a combination of the two words.

nut, do one's. See **do one's nut.**

nutter, *n.*   *Slang.* **nut**
Slang. A crazy character: synonymous with **nutcase.**

O

O.A.P.   *approx.* **senior citizen**
Inf. Stands for *old age pensioner,* and refers to those entitled to draw old age
pensions from the government; in addition they are granted reductions in certain
public conveyance fares, prices of admission to some entertainments, sports events,
and the like, a practice not unknown in America. The following question was asked
by an ancient ticket-taker at St. Lawrence Cricket Ground entrance gate, Canterbury, of the more or less middle-aged occupants of an entering automobile: "Meaning no offense, ladies and gentlemen, but are there any *O.A.P.*s in your midst?"
(The tickets were half-price for pensioners.) The British are now replacing *O.A.P.*
with *pensioner,* and occasionally with the unattractive and futile euphemism *Senior
Citizen,* undoubtedly borrowed from America. Be thankful they haven't so far
borrowed *Golden Ager.* See also **Darby and Joan.**

oast, *n.*   **hops kiln**
The *oast* (the *kiln* itself) is housed in an *oast-house,* a red brick tower almost always
cylindrical like a silo. The oast-house is topped by a cone-shaped vented cap, painted
white, which is rotated by the action of the wind pushing against a protruding vane.
The part of southeastern England known as the *Weald,* particularly the hilly Kent and
Sussex countryside, is dotted with hundreds of these structures, usually single but often
in pairs or clusters of several, lending a special character to the landscape. A native of
this part of England returning to his homeland feels he has arrived when he spots his
first *oast*-house. More and more, as the raising of hops has fallen victim to the law of
diminishing returns, oast-houses are being decommissioned, as it were, and converted
to dwellings, often attached to the original farmhouse and making for a most attractive
structure. The County of Kent became known as the Garden of England because of the
fruits, especially apples and strawberries, and the concentration of hops grown there
in enormous hop-gardens, called *hopyards* in Herefordshire and Worcestershire. Early
each September, the countryside used to come alive with the picking of the hop vines,
called *bines,* which were carted to the oast-houses, there to be stripped of their greenish
white blossoms that were then dried over a slow fire in the oasts. In the few decades
since the author acquired a Tudor farmhouse in a Kentish village, the hop-gardens have
become fewer and fewer, alas. Only a few diehards still grow and dry hops in that part
of the country nowadays. Up to about thirty-five years ago, thousands of Londoners,
mostly **cockney**—and the majority of them from London's **East End**—invaded that part
of the country to have a few days' *hopping* (hop-picking) holiday in the open air and to
drink in their wages in the local pubs. Nowadays the London *hoppers'* (hop-pickers')
annual invasion is history. Local housewives and children still occasionally get temporary employment picking the bines, rather than the individual blossoms, to be carted
to the oasts and fed to ingenious machines that strip them of the blossoms. And still
another picturesque country custom has become lore.

oats, *n. pl.*   **oatmeal (uncooked)**
The proper term when you shop at the grocery. Cooked and on the breakfast table,
it is **porridge.**

obbo. See **keep obbo on.**

O.B.E. See under **Birthday Honours.**

oblique, *n.*   **slash**
Sometimes called *oblique stroke* or simply *stroke* in Britain, and many names in America,
including *virgule, diagonal, slant,* and even *solidus,* the latter being the Latin ancestor of
shilling, a reference to the *shilling stroke,* as it was sometimes called in Britain in the old

days before the monetary system was changed, when the *stroke* meant 'shilling(s).' Thus: 15/- meant '15 shillings'. With the abolition of the shilling, the name *shilling stroke* has more or less died out—though these things die slowly, especially in Britain—and it is still used, for example, among printers. *See* **Appendix II.A.**

O.C. Officer Commanding
Subordinate to the C.O., who commands an established group such as an infantry battalion, while an O.C. commands an *ad hoc* unit such as a demolition training center, a rations dump, an intelligence group, etc.

occupier, *n.* occupant
In Britain one who occupies a house is its *occupier*. One occupying a room, railroad compartment, etc., is an *occupant* in both countries. *Occupier* always refers to a dwelling. When the occupier owns the house, he is called *owner-occupier*.

octillion. See **Appendix II.D.**

octingentenary, *n.* 800th anniversary
(Pronounced OCTINGENTEEN'-ARY). America has only just celebrated the bicentenary of her independence from the mother country, which can indulge in words like *octingentenary*.

odd, *adj.* 1. peculiar
2. occasional
1. *Odd* is used much more in Britain than in America to describe a person as *peculiar* in the sense of 'eccentric.' The British, generally speaking, like to regard themselves as *odd* in that sense. Americans conform a great deal more than Britons, despite a lot of nonsense to the contrary.
2. *The odd* is the equivalent of *an occasional*, in sentences like, *He makes the odd trip to town*, or, *I work mainly in my office, but do have the odd meeting with a client elsewhere*, or, *The odd novice will chance swimming in these dangerous waters.*

odd-man, *n.* odd job man

oddments, *n. pl.* odds and ends
Especially applied to broken sets of merchandise for sale. (Used in America not with the British meaning, but two others: 1. *oddities*, like strange people or things, and 2. *eccentricities*).

odd sizes broken sizes
Not all sizes available (referring to merchandise for sale).

off, *n.* start
Inf. For instance, the start of a horse race or a TV program. *It was ten minutes before the off.*

off, *adj.* 1. bad form
2. spoiled
1. *Inf.* Thus: *It was a bit off to be doing her nails at the restaurant table.* Synonymous with **not on, 2.**
2. *Inf.* In the sense of 'rancid' or 'rotten,' referring to food. Thus: *The butter's gone off.*

offal, *n.* viscera
A butcher's term covering liver, kidneys, tongue, etc., or animal insides generally.

off cut remnant
Store sign: RETAIL OFF CUT CENTRE would read REMNANTS in America as applied to textiles, and probably ODD LENGTHS referring to lumber, etc. *Off cut* refers primarily to lumber, but can apply to textiles, carpeting, pipe, etc.

offer for sale secondary issue
Of stock.

offer for subscription   **public issue**
  Of stock. See also **offer for sale.**

offer-up, *v.t.*   **put in place**
  In instructions for a proprietary soft plastic substance for making screw fixings in
masonry: After inserting the material into the masonry opening, one is to "...*offer-up*
the fixture and drive home the screw."

office block. See **block.**

offices, *n. pl.*   **conveniences**
  Synonymous with another British word which has a meaning unknown in America—
amenities in the sense of *conveniences,* as applied to a house. A real-estate agents'
term: *All the usual offices,* i.e., electricity, hot and cold running water, kitchen, lavatory, etc.
See discussion under **amenities.**

official, *n.*   **officer**
  E.g., *bank official.*

off licence   **1. license to sell bottled alcoholic beverages**
                                                          2. package store
1. Sign on shop indicating it can sell liquor all day long for consumption off the premises. See under **during hours.**
2. The shop itself.

off-load, *v.t.*   **1.** *Slang.* **bump**
                                                          2. *Inf.* **saddle**
1. *Inf.* To *displace* an ordinary airplane passenger in favor of a VIP—usually the victim
is a civilian and the VIP is military or government personnel.
2. In the sense of 'passing the buck,' i.e., *saddling* someone with an undesirable burden.

off one's chump; off one's dot;
off one's onion, *Slang.*   *Slang.* **off one's rocker**

off one's own bat   **on one's own**
  Inf. Used in expressions indicating doing things without anybody else's help. A term
derived from cricket. See also **on one's pat, on one's tod,** both of which mean 'on one's
own,' but only in the sense of 'being alone.'

off-putting. See **put (someone) off.**

off-side lane   **passing lane**
  See under **near-side lane.**

off the boil   **past the crisis**
  Inf. When a situation is *off the boil,* it is coming under control, calming down, past
the crisis stage.

off the mark   **off to a start**
  Technically, a cricket term. To be *off the mark* is to have made your first run after
coming to bat. Synonymous with **breaking your duck;** see **duck 1.** Taken over into
general language, like so many other cricket terms, it means 'off to a start,' signifying
at least initial success. See **slow off the mark.**

off-the-peg, *adj., Inf.*   *Inf.* **off the rack; ready-to-wear**

of that ilk   SEE COMMENT
  This curious phrase, as used in Scotland, has an extremely restricted sense. It applies
to persons whose last names are the same as the name of the place they come from;

historically they were chiefs of clans. Thus, in a letter to *The Times* (London) published in the edition of January 7, 1977, Sir Iain Moncreiffe of Easter Moncreiffe, Perthshire, signed himself "Ian Moncreiffe Of That Ilk," meaning 'Ian Moncreiffe of Moncreiffe.' A friend of the author named Hector Cameron was a Cameron of Cameron, and once announced himself over the telephone as "Cameron of that ilk." The uneducated (at that time) author, to his shame, ascribed it to drink. There are MacDonalds *of that ilk* (MacDonalds of MacDonald), Guthries *of that ilk* (Guthries of Guthrie), and so on. From a **Sassenach** misunderstanding of this usage, *ilk* has acquired the meaning 'sort,' or 'kind'; used generally in a pejorative sense: *Al Capone, and people of that ilk*, or even (heaven forfend!) *Freudians* (or *communists*, etc.) *and their ilk.*

...of the best   1. strokes
                                                                   2. pound note(s)
1. *Inf.* To give a schoolboy *five of the best* is to give him *five strokes of the cane.*
2. *Inf.* A wholly different (and much pleasanter) meaning: *A thousand of the best* is £1,000. The context will cure any possible ambiguity.

old, *adj.*   SEE COMMENT
Inf. Used especially in addressing intimates (or persons you would like to be intimate with), coupled with a variety of nouns, thus: *old man, old chap, old bean, old thing, old fruit, old egg, old top,* but *old boy* (not as a form of address) has the special meaning of 'alumnus' (see **old boy**). *Old man* and *old chap* are mildly old-fashioned; the rest have a 1920-ish flavor.

(the) Old Bill   *Slang.* **(the) cops**
Slang. Newish underworld usage. *Watch it! Here comes the Old Bill!*

old boy; old girl   **alumnus; alumna**
Inf. In the frame of reference of secondary education, *old boy* would be *alumnus* or *graduate* in America. When you get to the university level, *old boy* no longer applies. At **Oxbridge**, the British would refer to a graduate as an *Oxford (Cambridge) man (woman)* or *graduate,* or say, simply, "He (she) was at Oxford (Cambridge)." It would remain *alumnus* or *graduate* in America in formal terms, but *old grad* colloquially. The American term *old grad* is a much narrower term than *old boy,* connoting unduly intense college patriotism, especially religious and vociferous attendance at football games. In Scotland, an *old boy* is referred to, with rather more dignity, as a *Former Pupil,* sometimes abbreviated to *F.P.* The *old-boy net* or *network* refers to the bonds established among the boys at **public school,** which are supposed to operate throughout life in social, and, particularly, in business and professional life. Related, of course, to the *old school tie,* in which the *tie* appears to be an accidental pun referring to both the necktie displaying the school colors and the connections establishing the upper-class kinship characteristic of British public school boys. Its importance has diminished in the last twenty years. *Old girls* do not normally form links similar to the *old boy network.* Girls' public schools lack the glamour and legend of the boys' schools, and *old girls* have not been conspicuous in public life to the same extent as *old boys.*

old cock   **old man**
Slang. Used vocatively. See also **old.**

old dutch. See **my old dutch.**

Old Lady of Threadneedle Street   SEE COMMENT
Inf. Bank of England; the expression is derived from its address.

old man of the sea   SEE COMMENT
A person one cannot shake off. From the legend of *Sinbad the Sailor.*

old mossyface, *adj.*   **the ace of spades**

old party   *Inf.* **old-timer**
Inf. In the sense of an *old person,* not quite doddering but not too far from it. The term is jocular, and usually slightly pejorative, but without malice. "How did the ac-

cident happen?" "Well, this *old party* came along in a 1965 Austin, and ..." *Party,* generally, means 'person' in colloquial conversation, derived in this usage from *party* in legal parlance, as in *party of the first part, guilty party,* etc.

old school tie. See **old boy.**

old soldier   *Inf.* **old hand**
   Inf. Implying that he's a crafty fellow. *Don't come the old soldier over me,* means 'Don't try to put one over on me.' A variant is *old stager.*

old stager, *Inf.* See under **old soldier.**

old sweat, *Inf.*   **old soldier**

O-levels. See under **A-levels.**

omnium gatherum   **1. mixture**
                                         2. open house
   Slang. Mock Latin. *Omnium* is the genitive plural of *omnis,* Latin for 'all'; *gatherum* is a phony Latinization of 'gather.' Applied to:
1. Any motley collection of persons or things.
2. A party open to all comers.

on, *prep.*   **over**
   A poker term used in the description of a full house. Thus, aces *on* **knaves,** which in America would be aces *over* jacks. See **Appendix I.A.1.**

(be) on a hiding to nothing   **face annihilation**
   Or, less dramatically, *face insuperable odds, be without a prayer,* i.e., *with no hope of success.* *Hiding,* in this expression, is synonymous with *thrashing,* and *a hiding to nothing* means 'a thrashing to bits.'

on a lobby basis   **off the record**
   Describing the basis on which politicians supply information to newspaper reporters. See **lobbyist.**

on a piece of string   *Inf.* **in a tight spot**
   Inf. A bad place to be on either continent. Usually in the phrase to *have someone on a piece of string,* describing someone being manipulated by someone else.

on a plate   **on a silver platter**

on appro   **on approval**
   Inf. Describing merchandise taken but returnable at the customer's option. *Appro,* unlike *approval,* is accented on the first syllable.

once in a way   **once in a while**
   A favorite usage of the author Anthony Powell. Siegfried Sassoon (*Diaries 1923-1925,* Faber & Faber, London, 1985) had used it differently, to mean, simply, 'once.' "While weeding the lawn, I was thinking about Communism. For *once in a way* I really did seem to be *thinking,* instead of ruminating, meditating, or wool-gathering from one reverie to another." Kingsley Amis used it the same way in 1985; see **martini.**

one-eyed village   *Inf.* **one-horse town**
   Inf. Also known in America as a *whistle stop.*

one hundred percent copper-bottomed   **absolutely sound**
   Inf. Especially applied to financial matters. The usage arises from the belief that a copper-bottomed pan or broiler is much more solid and longer lasting than one made of other metals; or it may have arisen from the image of a ship sheathed with copper. In another context, modifying the noun *excuse,* it is the equivalent of *airtight.*

one in the eye   *Slang.* **a crusher**
  Inf. That's one in the eye for you means 'That'll hold you for a while.'

one-off, *n., adj.*   **one of a kind**
  The *only one made,* or *run off,* referring to manufactured goods. In a BBC commentary
on a boat show, after demonstrating the So-and-So Company's *Speeding Star,* a popular
model at £1,800, they show a terrific job at £45,000 and say, "Now, if you want something special, and can afford the ticket, here's So-and-So's Meteor. This is a *one-off*
model..."

oner, *n., Slang.*   **1. outstanding person or thing**
                                                                2. K.O. blow
                                                                3. *Inf.* **big fib**
  (Pronounced WUNNER, from *one* (as in *one of a kind*); possibly influenced by the careless
pronunciation of *wonder.*)

on form   **in form**
  See also **Appendix I.A.1.**

on heat   **in heat**
  See **Appendix I.A.1.**

o.n.o.   **or nearest offer**
  Usually seen in real estate advertisements and used car ads, written in earnest hope.

on offer   **on sale**
  Indicating a special offer, thus: *Yardley's bath soap is on offer this week.* In America there
would most likely be a sign on the counter or in the window reading SPECIAL or TODAY'S
SPECIAL or SPECIAL THIS WEEK. Not to be confused with **under offer**, meaning 'for sale,'
but only subject to rejection of a pending offer.

on one's pat   **on one's own**
  Slang. From rhyming slang (see **Appendix II.G.3**). *Pat Malone* for *alone.* Synonymous
with **on one's tod.** See also **off one's own bat.**

on one's tod   **on one's own**
  Slang. Rhyming slang (see **Appendix II.G.3**) from *Tod Sloan* (a famous jockey) for
alone. Synonymous with **on one's pat.** See also **off one's own bat.**

on second thoughts   **on second thought**
  How singular of the Americans! But they do have second thoughts.

on strike   **at bat**
  Nothing to do with industrial relations; just a **cricket** term. Two batsmen are always
"up" at the same time, one at either end of the **pitch.** The one to whom the bowler is
bowling at a given moment is said to be *on strike.*

on the cards   **in the cards**
  See under **Appendix I.A.1.**

on the cheap   **cheaply**
  Inf. Something bought *on the cheap* is a *bargain.* The phrase can mean 'on a shoestring'
in certain contexts, thus: *We started the business on the cheap; We were getting along on the
cheap.* See also **cheap.**

on the day   **when the time comes**
  Thus: *On the day, the people will see the light and vote the other way.* A favorite usage of
politicians. Also *on the night:* famous last words of (usually amateur) theatrical performers when things aren't going well at rehearsal: *It'll be all right on the night,* i.e., when
the curtain really goes up.

(be) on the game   **(be) a prostitute**
Slang. Synonymous with **(be) on the knock.**

on the hob, *Slang.*   *Slang.* **on the wagon**

on the hop. See **caught on the hop.**

(be) on the knock   **(be) a prostitute**
Slang. Not to be confused with *be on the knock-off,* which is underworld jargon for *living by thievery.* Synonymous with **(be) on the game.**

on the loose   **on a spree**
Inf. Rather than merely *fancy-free,* which the expression connotes in America.

on the right lines   **on the right track**

on the slate   *Inf.* **on the cuff**
Inf. Synonymous with **on tick.** Usually heard in pubs, in the expression *Put it on the slate,* said to the **landlord** by a **local** out of funds. In the old days, the reluctant landlord actually had a slate on which such transactions on credit were recorded.

on the spot   **alert**
Inf. Right there when he's needed. There is a flavor of this British usage in the old-fashioned expression, familiar to Americans, *Johnny-on-the-spot.*

on the stocks   *Inf.* **in the works**
Inf. Already started, describing any project on which work has already begun. Borrowed from shipbuilding.

on the strength   **on the payroll**
The strength is the working force of an organization. The use of *strength* in this connection is related to the use of *strong* in an expression like *twenty strong,* to describe the size of a group. (See **strong.**) The author first came across this usage while being shown around a friend's large factory. It was a Sunday and the only living being other than the two of us was a lovely black and white tomcat named Charlie, whose function was rat control. Asked whether Charlie was on the payroll, the friend replied; "Oh, Charlie's *on the strength,* all right. Yes, Charles is certainly part of the *strength.*"

on the teapot, *Inf.*   *Inf.* **on the wagon**

on the telephone   **having a telephone**
In America *on the telephone* means 'speaking on the telephone.' In Britain if you want to get in touch with someone and want to know whether or not he has a phone, you ask him, *Are you on the telephone?* In America you would ask, *Do you have a phone?*

on the tiles. See **night on the tiles.**

on the up and up   *Slang.* **going places**
Slang. Quite a different meaning in Britain! Describes a person or company moving ahead satisfactorily.

on thorns, *Inf.*   *Inf.* **on tenterhooks**

on tick   **on the cuff**
Inf. See also **on the slate.**

on train. See **in train.**

On your bike!   *Slang.* **Get lost!**
Slang. Short, according to Bernard Levin in *The Times* (London), for 'It would be better for you if you get on your bike promptly and pedal fast.'

oo-er!, ooer!, *interj.*   **gee!**
   An exclamation of surprise, fear, disgust, etc. A variant of *ooh!*, which in turn is a
variant of *oh!*

oof   *Slang*.**dough**
   In the sense of 'money.' This word is at the least old-fashioned; it may now be
obsolete. It is short for *ooftish*, a Yiddish corruption of *auf dem Tisch,* which is German
for 'on the table.' In other words, *money on the table,* also known as *cash on the barrelhead.*
The current slang term is **lolly.**

open-cast mining   **strip mining**

open goods-waggon   **gondola car**
   See **truck.**

opening time. See **during hours.**

open the bowling, *Inf.*   **set the ball rolling; get things started**
   A term borrowed from **cricket.** One starts the game by bowling (over-arm) the first
ball, which 'opens the bowling,' and thus gets things under way. See **bowler, 2.** To
change the bowling (another cricket term; literally, to put in a new bowler) is to *make a
change* generally, as when a firm has to replace an executive or any employee, a technique, its image, the advertising, etc. A government might have to *change the bowling*
by shifting things around in the cabinet, or pursuing a different course.

Open University   SEE COMMENT
   Correspondence courses involving written materials and reading lists, supplemented
by live tutorial sessions and television and radio lectures, and in some courses a week's
attendance at a regular university. These courses are open to anyone without regard to
scholastic qualifications. There are examinations and an A.B. degree can be earned in
a minimum of three years. This term, in America, refers simply to the removal of
entrance qualifications at regularly constituted colleges.

operating-theatre, *n.*   **operating room**
   See comment under **lint.**

oppidan, *n.*   SEE COMMENT
   An Etonian living off campus. At Eton there are seventy *collegers,* also known there
as **scholars** or *foundation scholars,* and 1,030 (or thereabouts) *oppidans* (from *oppidum,*
Latin for 'town'). The *collegers,* or *scholars,* are the privileged few who live in *college.* The
oppidans attend the same courses but live in school boardinghouses in town.

opposite prompt   **stage right**
   Short for *opposite prompter* and often abbreviated to *o.p.* This archaic circumlocution
was based on the position of the prompter's box in the old days. *Prompt* (short for
prompt side, often abbreviated to *p.s.*) naturally means 'stage left.' Maddeningly enough
these terms sometimes means the exact reverse, particularly in the older theaters, where
the prompter's box was located on the other side of the stage.

(the) opposition, *n.*   **(the) competition**
   The opposition is the *competing firm* in one's profession or business.

ops room   **operations planning room**
   Inf. A military expression. A *tour of ops* is an R.A.F. term meaning the number of
missions to be completed in order to earn a rest period.

optic   SEE COMMENT
   Measuring device fastened to the neck of liquor bottles in pubs. (The legal standard
measure in England is one-sixth gill.) The device is called an *optic* because the liquor
flows out of the upside-down bottle into a transparent vessel and is thus visible to the

naked eye. In this fashion, not a micron over one-sixth gill escapes into the waiting glass, whereas American bartenders tend to be more liberal, on the whole, in dispensing their shots. See **double, 3; Appendix II.C.2.b**

orbital, *n.*   SEE COMMENT
A fancy new name in Britain for what used to called a 'circular road' or 'ring road,' to describe a bypass encircling a town. The adjective is used as a noun.

orderly bin   **street litterbox**

order paper   **calendar**
An *order paper* is the Parliamentary equivalent of an American Congressional *calendar*.

order to view   **appointment to look at**
Term used in house hunting. A written order issued by the real estate agent.

ordinary, *adj.*   **regular**
Regular mail, to a Briton, sounds like *mail at regular intervals* rather than *normal* mail (i.e., not special delivery—which the British call *express*—or registered, etc.). Possibly the pejorative sense of *ordinary* (meaning 'vulgar,' 'coarse,' 'inferior') made the Americans choose *regular*. Thus, *regular coffee,* to an American counterman, means coffee with cream (not black); *ordinary coffee* would imply an inferior drink.

ordinary call   **station-to-station call**
Telephone call. In Britain a *person-to-person* call is known as a *personal* call.

ordinary shares   **common stock**

ordnance datum   **sea level**
Above sea level is commonly seen in Britain; *above ordnance datum* is never seen in America.

organize, *v.t.*   *Inf.* **round up**
Inf. As in, *It's too late to organize a baby sitter,* when you get a last-minute invitation to play some bridge. To *organize* somebody or something is to 'get hold of,' to 'arrange for,' the person or thing that fills the need.

(the) other half   **another drink**
Inf. When your kind friend notices that you've finished your drink—the first one, anyway—he asks solicitously, "How about the other half?" And when you've done with that one, the kind friend is known to repeat the delightful question, in the same words, thus demonstrating not only British hospitality but also creative British mathematics.

other place. See **another place.**

other ranks   **enlisted men**
Non-officers. Frequently referred to as *ORs.*

outdoor relief   SEE COMMENT
Aid given by a poorhouse to an outsider. Also known in Britain as *out*-relief; now obsolete.

out for a duck. See **duck, 1.**

outgoings, *n. pl.*   **expenses**
This British word is used to cover not only *household expenses* but also *business overhead*. Note that *overhead* is *overheads* in Britain, a real plural taking a plural verb.

outhouse, *n.*   SEE COMMENT
Any building incidental to and built near or against the main house; not an outdoor privy, as in America.

out of bounds   **off limits**
Applies principally to military personnel.

out of the hunt. See **in the hunt.**

outwith, *prep.*   **outside**
A Scottish usage, as in, *This pay-rise* (raise in pay) *cannot be allowed as it is outwith the pay code* (wage ceiling).

oven glove   **pot-holder**

over, *n.*   SEE COMMENT
Cricket term; explained under **maiden over.**

overall, *n.*   **1. coverall**
                                                                      2. smock
The British use *overall*, or **boiler suit,** in the sense of a 'one-piece work garment' and also to describe what Americans would call a *smock.*

overbalance, *v.i.*   **lose one's balance**
The British sometimes use the verb transitively as well, meaning to 'make (someone) lose his balance.' The usual American meaning is 'outweigh.'

overdraft, *n.*   **bank loan**
The universal British term for a bank loan, with none of the implications of faulty checkbook maintenance. This type of overdraft is arranged in advance (a banking practice now spreading in America). The inadvertant type, or an intentional one not previously arranged for, results in a swift letter from the bank.

overleaf, *adv.*   **on the reverse side**
Of a page or printed notice. See also **P.T.O.**

overspill, *n.adj.*   **surplus population**
An *overspill* city is a new British sociopolitical phenomenon. It is a made-to-order city designed in accordance with blueprints drawn up under the New Towns Act to take care of surplus urban population. Thus, there exist the New Towns of Crawley, Stevenage and Basildon. Milton Keynes in North Buckinghamshire has absorbed many villages and towns and has provided homes for almost 100,000 souls formerly living in London and other parts. This particular *overspill* city was named after one of the little villages it engulfed that had had a population of 159.

overtake, *v.t., v.i.*   **pass**
A traffic term. DO NOT OVERTAKE is the British road sign equivalent of NO PASSING.

over the eight. See **have one over the eight.**

over the moon   **in raptures**

over the odds   **above market value**
To *ask* or *pay over the odds* for something is to demand or pay a price in excess of the generally accepted price for the commodity in question.

over the road   **across the street**

over the top   **going too far**
Inf. Excessive, as in *Calling him a thief was over the top.* To *go over the top* is to *overact,* especially in the theater, in which context it would mean to 'ham it up.' Nothing, in this connection, to do with the boys in the trenches.

owner-occupier. See under **occupier.**

owt   **anything**
North country. Cf. *nowt* (discussed under **nought**).

Oxbridge, *n. adj.*   SEE COMMENT
Oxford and Cambridge; obviously a **portmanteau** concoction. Used when contrasting Oxford and Cambridge with the provincial universities such as Birmingham, Manchester, and Sheffield, which are referred to as the **redbrick universities,** originally a pejorative term. The image of these universities, however, has been greatly enhanced. No comparable term is yet current to describe a third group of new universities which has recently been established. Of several terms heard, the most pleasant is the *Shakespearean universities,* so-called because their names (Essex, Sussex, Warwick, Kent, Lancaster, York) suggest the dramatis personae of his historical plays. Also heard is the term *plate-glass universities,* reflecting their contemporary architecture. *Oxbridge* might be defined—more or less—as *Ivy League,* and is used as an adjective in such expressions as *Oxbridge type, Oxbridge accent,* etc., with the same connotations as *Ivy League. Oxbridge* is also used on its own to refer to the special *A-level* examinations for students applying for admission to Oxford or Cambridge. See also **redbrick.**

Oxford bags. See **bags**

Oxonian, *n. adj.*   SEE COMMENT
Of Oxford. From the Latinized name of the city, *Oxonia.* In a narrower sense, an *Oxonian* is a student or graduate of Oxford University. Abbreviation: *Oxon.*

oxter, *n.*   **armpit**
Mostly North of England and Scottish, but used occasionally in other parts by obscurantists.

P

p., *n.*   SEE COMMENTS
Abbreviation of *penny* or *pence*, and pronounced simply P. See **Appendix II.A.**

P.A.   **secretary**
Abbreviation of *personal assistant*, a rather lofty title in vogue in the British Foreign
and Civil Services for long-suffering secretaries. The title *secretary* would be confusing
because of hierarchical semantics. Now used in advertisements for positions in ordinary
businesses as well.

pack, *n.*   **deck**
In the expression *pack of cards. Deck* is not used in Britain.

package deal   **turnkey deal**
Package deal is used interchangeably with *turnkey deal* in Britain in the oil industry to
indicate a fixed price, without overcalls, for the drilling of an exploratory well to an
agreed depth. It is not so used in America, where *turnkey* is the invariable term.

packed out with   *Inf.* **packed full of**
Inf. For instance, a popular restaurant in London may be *packed out with* people at
lunch time. See also **bung full; chockablock.**

packet, *n.*   **package**
The delivery man in Britain leaves a *packet* at the door; in America this would be a
package. Applied to cigarettes, the American term is *pack. Pay packet* is the British equivalent of *pay envelope. Packet* has a number of slang uses as well. To *pay a packet* is to *pay
a fortune* (or *an arm and a leg*); synonymous with **pay the earth;** and things that cost a
lot are said to *cost a packet.* If you win a lot of money at a British track or on the London
Stock Exchange, you *make a packet.* The American equivalent of this would be a *pile.* A
proper packet of something is a *great big bunch* of it. If you have been having all kinds of
unpleasant experiences, for instance while making the rounds looking for a job, you
might announce at the end of such a day, *I've had a packet,* meaning a 'bellyful.' One
thing not to do with a *packet* is to catch one, because *catch a packet* means 'stop a bullet.'
See also **twenty.**

pack it in   **desist; retire**
Slang. Synonymous with **pack up** as that term applies to persons. *I used to garden, but
because of my bad back, I packed it in.* Sometimes, *pack it up.* Also means to 'leave,' 'depart,'
or 'quit' (e.g., for the day).

pack it up. See **pack it in.**

pack up   *Slang.* **quit; conk out**
Slang. Applies to both persons and things. Of persons, it means to 'retire,' 'throw in
one's hand.' Also, to 'leave,' 'depart'; see under **pack it in.** Of machines, for example,
to *conk out.*

paddle, *v.i.*   **wade**
To go wading in salt water. The British use *wade* in the sense of walking through
water, mud, snow, or any obstructive material, rather than engaging in a pleasant
aquatic pastime.

paddy, *n.* **tantrum**
Inf. Paddywhack is a variant. *Paddy* is a nickname for *Padraig,* which is old Irish for *Patrick,* and there are so many Patricks in Ireland that Patrick or Pat is usually the protagonist in Irish jokes. Apparently, Irish tempers are shorter than British ones, so somehow *paddy* came to mean 'tantrum.'

paddy factor SEE COMMENT
Slang. Used of the careless habits of I.R.A. terrorists, e.g., in leaving clues, like a note at a pub telling a colleague where the writer is busy working mischief that night. The *paddy factor* is said to be of great help to the British police. Terrorists are very bad people, whatever their nationality, but this phrase has an unpleasant ethnic ring, like the *Schlamperei* ('sloppiness,' 'carelessness') label which Germans pin on Austrians.

page, *n.* **bellhop**
Sometimes *hotel page* or *page-boy.* Occasionally called *Buttons,* especially in the **pantomime** *Cinderella.*

Pagett, M.P. **whirlwind tourist**
Inf. Pagett, M.P. is a Kipling character who thinks he gets to know all about a country by visiting it for a short time. It is used generically to designate that type.

pair, *n.* **floor**
Pair is used on building directories to indicate what *floor* a tenant occupies. A person on the *third pair* means a person 'three flights up.' Old-fashioned building directories usually put the number of the pair first, followed by the name of the occupants.

pair of tongs. See **barge-pole.**

Paki, *n. adj.* **Pakistani**
Slang. (Rhymes with WACKY.) An abbreviated form with unpleasant racist connotations. *Paki-bashing* is an extremely unpleasant word for the extremely unpleasant activities of roaming gangs looking for Pakistanis to beat up.

palaver **affair; business**
Slang. A *palaver,* literally, in both countries, is a *powwow,* a prolonged parley, usually between parties of different levels of culture. In America, the term might suggest long discussions between Indians and white men; in England, between African natives and traders. In both England and America, it has acquired the significance of *idle talk* or *chatter,* but in England alone it is common slang for *affair* or *business* in the sense of 'big deal' or 'fuss'; anything complicated by miles of red tape or tremendous confusion. The word almost always appears in the expression *such a palaver. I'd love to go to the opera but getting tickets is such a palaver! Exchanging Christmas gifts for something you really want is such a palaver!*

palette-knife, *n.* **spatula**
It can also mean what it does in America: a metal blade with a handle, used for mixing and sometimes applying artists' colors. Synonymous with **fish-slice** in kitchen parlance.

palliasse, *n.* **straw mattress**
Also *paillasse,* from the French.

panache, *n.* **flair; swagger**
Panache has the literal meaning of 'plume,' as on a helmet. It is found in Britain in phrases such as *professional panache,* describing, for instance, a doctor or lawyer who acts as though he were very sure of himself; in America, too, for *flamboyance.*

pancake roll **egg roll**
Chinese restaurant fare.

panda car   **police car**
A familiar sight on residential beats is the small police car, usually light blue with white doors and a large POLICE sign on top. They are all blue in London. See also **jam sandwich; Z-car.**

panel, *n.*   SEE COMMENT
List of **National Health Service** doctors for a given district. A *panel doctor* is one on such a list; a *panel practice* is one consisting of National Health patients.

pannage, *n.*   **pig food**

pantechnicon, *n.*   **moving van**
Technically a *pantechnicon* is a furniture storage warehouse, and *pantechnicon van* is the equivalent of *moving van;* but popularly the *van* is dropped so that *pantechnicon* has come to designate the van rather than the storage house. This strange word was the name of a London building known as *The Pantechnicon* (an obsolete word for 'bazaar' or, 'exhibition of arts and crafts') which, over a century ago housed a collection of the wonders of the Victorian age. It failed as a commercial venture and the building was turned into a furniture warehouse while keeping the name, which was inevitably transferred to the vehicles used. See also **removals.**

pantomime, *n.*   SEE COMMENT
Sometimes *panto* for short. This is a peculiarly British form of show, produced during the Christmas season, based on fairy tales or legends, involving singing, dancing, clowning, topical humor, and almost anything but the silence which is associated with the word in its ordinary sense. Adults are admitted if accompanied by children.

pants, *n. pl.*   **underpants**
The British equivalent of American *pants* is *trousers*. In Britain *pants* are *underwear*, usually men's shorts; but *pants* in Britain can also include ladies' *panties*. See also **shorts; frillies; knickers; liners; smalls.**

Paper, *n.*   *approx.* **government publication**
There are White, Blue, and Green *Papers*. White and Blue Papers are official documents laid before Parliament by command of one of the Secretaries of State and are known as *command papers*. When the Foreign Office wanted to tell the British public and the world about the pending negotiations for the independence of India, for example, it compiled its account in a paper to be put before Parliament and given a command number. *Command* is abbreviated to *Cd., Cmd.,* or *Cmnd.,* according to date, so a paper is known, e.g., as *Cmd. 1000*. The short ones are bound in a white cover, the long ones in a blue cover. *White* and *Blue* are simply a matter of binding. *Green Papers,* issued in green bindings, a later development, cover government plans to be placed before the public as a basis for discussion in advance of decision.
Black Paper is a relatively new term, meaning a 'pamphlet' (unofficial, nongovernmental) issued by an *ad hoc* group on any given subject, expressing a view contrary to that of the government or analyzing what they consider to be a scandal. The most familiar one (first of a series) and, as far as the author can determine, the first one published (1969) was on the subject of public education in Britain.

paper knife   **letter opener**

parade, *n.*   **promenade**
A *shopping parade* is a *line of shops* along a street, especially where there is an arcade or colonnade. The British also use *parade* the way the Americans do, complete with brass bands and martial music.

paraffin, *n.*   **kerosene**
The British equivalent of American *paraffin* is **white wax** or *paraffin wax*.

parish, *n.*   *approx.* **town**
The parish was formerly the subdivision of a county constituting the smallest unit of local government, and was regulated by what was known as a *parish council*. Originally,

the term had the familiar religious connotation; but when used alone, it was, in proper context, understood to mean 'civil parish'. The American approximation of *parish* in that sense would have been *town*, in rural areas. *Parish* is now obsolete as a unit of government because of the reorganization acts, pursuant to which the smallest governmental unit is now the *borough*. In informal speech, *parish* can mean 'domain,' 'sphere of operation,' 'job specialty,' the way Americans might use *bailiwick*, for which the British would use *beat*, **pitch** in it slang sense, **turf**, or **manor**. In Louisiana, it means *county*.

park, See **car park; caravan park.**

parking bay   **parking space**
   The space covered by a parking meter, or an outdoor parking space for rent.

parky, *adj.*   **chilly; brisk**
   Slang. Meteorological slang.

parson's nose   *Inf.* **pope's nose**
   Inf. That part that goes over the fence last.

part brass rags   *Inf.* **break things off**
   Slang. Originally a naval expression, based on buddies' sharing their brass-cleaning rags. When the friendship ceased, they *parted brass rags*. The term implies that the parting, if not final, was acrimonious.

part exchange. See **give in part exchange.**

parting, *n.*   **part**
   Both British and Americans *part* their hair, but the result is known as a *parting* in Britain and a *part* in America. Cf. **turning** for *turn, n.* See **Appendix I.A.3.**

party candidate   SEE COMMENT
   When Americans go to the polls they vote for all sorts of offices, from president down to dogcatcher, and they either vote the *straight ticket* or *split their ticket*. A Briton votes only for his *M.P.* (**Member** *of Parliament*), and if his vote is based on party rather than choice of individual, he votes for his *party candidate*.

party manifesto   **political platform**
   Also, **programme.**

pass, *n.*   **passing grade**
   Referring to school examinations: thus, *O-level pass, A-level pass*, etc. See **A-levels.** A *pass degree* is a lower level of academic distinction than an *honours degree*. See also **class; first.**

pass, *v.t.*   **1. leave (a message)**
                                                                                    2. refer
   1. As in, *He isn't in now. Would you care to pass a message?*
   2. As in, *I'll pass you to the person who handles your account.*

passage, *n.*   **corridor**
   See also **landing.**

passbook, *n.*   SEE COMMENT
   In addition to its meaning shared with America ('savings bankbook'), this word has two further meanings in Britain: 1. A book supplied by a bank for the recording of deposits and withdrawals in a checking account (**current account**) as well as in a savings account (**deposit account**). 2. The document formerly issued to non-white persons by the South African government, which they had to carry at all times; a type of identity card. According to *The Times* (London) of July 15, 1981, a *passbook* (in this sense of *identity card*) is now being issued by the Pakistani government to Afghan refugees.

pass current   be generally accepted as true or genuine

passing, *n*   **passage**
Referring to a bill in Parliament.

passman   SEE COMMENT
Not a common word; it describes a person who takes a degree at a university without
hono(u)rs.

pass out   **graduate**
Usage confined to the military, meaning to 'complete military training.' In this sense,
nothing to do with the curse of drink, though *pass out* is used (and happens) in Britain
that way as well.
A rather startling headline appeared in the *Daily Telegraph* (London) of August 20,
1980:

ROYAL MARINES PASS OUT

but the story that followed was prosaic enough:

> The following Royal Marines Young Officers passed out from the Commando Train-
> ing Centre, Lympstone, Devon, when Lieut.-Gen. Sir John Richards took the sa-
> lute. . . [followed by a list of the names of the graduates].

The act itself is not called *passing out*, but rather *passage out*, as indicated by a story in
the same newspaper, issue of July 25, 1981, about the Queen's watching an R.A.F.
(Royal Air Force) 'passage out parade.'

past a joke   *Inf.* **not funny**
Slang. Intolerable. Describes a situation which can no longer be laughed off or tolerated.

past praying for   **in desperate straits**
Inf. Beyond hope; up the creek (without a paddle).

pasty, *n.*   SEE COMMENT
The only one-word American approximation (very approximate) is, in certain parts
of the country, *knish*. The most famous *pasty* of all is the *Cornish pasty*, which originated
in the Duchy of Cornwall but is now ubiquitous in Britain and is usually filled with
seasoned meat mixed with vegetables. *Knishes* are usually filled with mashed potatoes,
which would seem to make for a very unbalanced diet indeed. *Pasties* can be filled with
almost anything—there are *jam pasties* and *fruit pasties* as well as *meat pasties*. Tastes
good even though it rhymes with NASTY (the *a* can also be pronounced as in FATHER).
See also **pie; tart.**

patch, *n.*   *Inf.* **beat**
Inf. A special usage, as where a policeman says of a particularly unpleasant homicide
case, *I'm glad it isn't on my patch.* Synonymous with **manor** used in this sense. For other
idiomatic uses of *patch*, see **bad patch** and **not a patch on.**

Pater, *n.*   **father**
Slang. Old usage; **public school** style.

Paternoster Row   SEE COMMENT
Inf. The *publishing industry.* The British often use a street name figuratively to indicate
a profession centering about that location. Cf. **Throgmorton Street, Fleet Street,** etc.
(Americans do it too: *Wall Street, Broadway,* etc.). Destroyed in World War II. The phrase
is rarely used today.

patience, *n.*   **solitaire**
Name for the endless varieties of card game played by a lone (and usually lonely)
player. *Patience* is the British name and *solitaire* the usual American name, although

patience is occasionally heard among older people in America. The game *solitaire* in Britain describes a game played by a lone player with marbles on a board containing little holes into which the marbles fit.

patrial, *n.* SEE COMMENT
One having the right of abode and exemption from control in the U.K. under the Immigration Act 1971. The important innovation was to confer such rights on Commonwealth citizens who have a parent born in the U.K. Descendants of patrials have the right of free admission to the U.K. For details, if desired, see *Britain 1976: An Official Handbook*, published by **HMSO,** pp. 11/12.

Patrol, *n.* *approx.* **School Zone**
Along the road one sees signs reading PATROL 150 YARDS, PATROL 125 yards, etc., often with a picture of a child. These are the equivalent of SCHOOL ZONE signs in America. The implication is that a **lollipop man** or **woman** may be on duty.

pavement, *n.* **sidewalk**
Sidewalk is not used by the British. *Crazy pavement* (more often *crazy paving*) denotes irregularly shaped, sometimes varicolored flat stones used in the building of garden paths, patios, etc. *Pavement artists* make very elaborate colored chalk drawings in London and other cities on sidewalks and hope for tips from passersby. In London, where it rains so often, this would seem to be a particularly ephemeral medium. The British equivalent of American *pavement* is **roadway.**

pawky, *adj.* **sly**
Inf. Mainly North of England and Scottish. Its usual application is to Scottish humor. The Scots have spread two legends about themselves which are not borne out by the facts: 1. that they are stingy; 2. that they are humorless. Simple jokes are sometimes referred to by the English as "easy jokes for Scotsmen." *Pawky humor* is Scottish humor according to their own *pawky* legend, the kind that encourages the victim to make a fool of himself.

pay bed **paid hospital bed**
As opposed to a free bed under the **National Health Service.**

pay-box, *n.* **box office**

pay code **wage ceiling**

P.A.Y.E. **pay as you go**
These dreary initials stand for *pay as you earn,* which is the British name for the income-tax system which provides for the withholding of income tax by employers.

pay for the call **accept the charge**
This is the term used by the operator in the process of putting through a collect call (**reverse-charge call,** in Britain). The American operator asks the person at the other end of the line, *Will you accept the charge?* The British operator asks, *Will you pay for the call?* (In matters of money, the British are much more direct and tend to avoid euphemisms.) There are many differences between the two countries in telephone idiom (see **caller; ordinary call; personal call; through; trunk enquiries**). Incidentally, Americans often have difficulty at first in understanding one word used by British operators while attempting to place the call: *trahnkneckchew.* This is British operator-ese for *trying to connect you,* the oft-repeated placatory term they use to soothe the nerves of the impatient caller.

paying-in slip **deposit slip**
Banking term.

pay one's shot **chip in**
Inf. Synonymous with *pay one's whack.* See **whack 3.** *Shot* is a variant of the old word *scot,* now obsolete except in *scot-free.*

pay one's whack. See **whack, 3.**

pay on the nail, *Slang.*   *Slang.* **pay spot cash**

pay packet See **packet.**

pay policy   **wage control**
   In Britain, an arrangement between the government and the trade unions, as opposed
to formal legislative control. Also referred to as *wage restraint.* See also **social contract;
wage restraint.**

pay (someone) in washers   *Slang.* **pay (someone) peanuts**
   Slang. A contemptuous idiom used by people connected with engineering, *washers*
being of negligible value.

pay the earth   *Inf.* **pay a fortune**
   Inf. Americans also *pay an arm and a leg,* a particularly gruesome expression happily
not used by the British. The British do not say *pay a fortune,* but they do say *cost a
fortune,* as well as *cost the earth.*

P.C.   **1. Privy Councillor
                                                                       2. Police Constable
                                                                       3. postcard**

1. See under **Birthday Honours.**
2. If your daughter's going out with a *P.C.,* you may hope for 1. but must be prepared
for 2. See **constable.** *P.C.* is the official title, as in *P.C. Smith.*
3. Usually in lower case. For other British abbreviations, see **Appendix I.D.9.**

peak viewing time   **prime time**

pearly, *n.*   **fruit and vegetable pushcart vendor**
   Inf. Called a *pearly* when dressed in *pearlies,* a holiday costume richly adorned with
mother-of-pearl buttons. When so attired, pearlies and their wives are sometimes called
Pearly Kings and *Pearly Queens.* The prosaic name for these flamboyant street vendors
is **costermonger,** and their costumes date back more than a century. They often appear
in their bright and heavy (as much as 70 pounds) outfits at carnivals in the **East End** of
London which raise money for good causes.

pea stick   **bean pole**

pebbledash, *n.*   **pebble-coated stucco**
   A not very good-looking and all too frequent building surfacing in Britain. It gets
dirty rather quickly and appears to be totally unwashable because of the rough texture.
Whole industrial villages of *pebbledash* structure are seen here and there, often in the
Midlands, apparently covering up bad brickwork, and one wonders how in the world
this miserable invention ever came about. Luckily, as far as present construction is
concerned, its day is over.

peckish, *adj.*   *approx. Inf.* **empty**
   Inf. Peckish means 'faintly hungry,' 'wanting a snack,' hankering after a little something to fill the void (but not by any means a real meal). Undoubtedly, *peckish* is derived
from *peck* as in *pecking* at food, a little of this and a little of that, the way a chicken eats.

pedestal, *n.*   **toilet bowl**
   Sometimes *w.c. pedestal,* a terribly polite euphemism for *toilet bowl,* seen, for example,
in lavatory signs on certain British railroad cars requesting passengers not to throw
various objects into the *w.c. pedestal.*

pedlar, *n.*   *Slang.* **blabbermouth**
   Inf. Pedlar is usually spelled *peddler* in America. Its literal meaning is the same in both
countries, evoking the image of a *pack-carrying* or *wagon-driving hawker* of small and

extremely miscellaneous merchandise—an image which is fast vanishing from the land-scape. In Britain it has a figurative meaning: 'gossip' (as indeed most *pedlars* must have been, since they saw everything that was going on). *Pedlars' French* is archaic British slang for 'thieves' jargon,' or more generally, 'underworld lingo.'

pee, *n., v.i.*   **1. urination**
                                      2. urinate
Inf. Surprisingly, to Americans at least, this word is fast becoming acceptable in familiar speech, even in mixed company, while Americans go to almost any length to dream up euphemisms.

peeler. See **bobby.**

peep-behind-the-curtain. See **Tom Tiddler's ground.**

peep-toes, *n. pl., Slang.*   **open-toed shoes**

peer, *n.*   SEE COMMENT
A member of the titled nobility. A peer's wife or a female peer in her own right is a *peeress.* See also **Lord; Lady; Dame; K.**

peg away   *Inf.* **plug along**
Inf. To *stay with* a job, no matter how tired you get. See also **soldier on.**

peg out, *Slang.*   *Slang.* **kick the bucket**
See also **drop off the hooks; pack it in; turn up one's toes.**

pelican crossing   **pedestrian crossing**
Pe(destrian) li(ght) con(trolled) crossing: it ought to be spelled *pelicon,* but close enough. See also **zebra.**

pelmet, *n.*   **valance**

penny, *n.* See **Appendix II.A.**

penny dreadful   *Inf.* **dime novel**
Inf. Sometimes called a *penny blood* or a *shilling shocker.* All these terms have an old fashioned ring, but are still in use, often jocularly.

(the) penny dropped   *Slang.* **I (he, etc.) got the message**
Slang. Something clicked. Used to describe the situation where the protagonist is at first unimaginatively unaware of the significance of what is going on, can't take a hint or two, and then—finally—the veil lifts: *it dawns on him; he gets the point; it clicks.* Metaphor from a vending-machine (which the British call **slot-machine.**) See also **penny in the slot.**

penny-farthing, *n.*   **high-wheeler**
Inf. Primitive bicycle.

penny gaff. See **gaff.**

penny in the slot   *approx. Inf.* **took the bait**
Inf. Said when one succeeds in evoking a predictable reaction from someone, by baiting him. Three persons are sitting around. One is a deadly earnest women's lib partisan. To bait her, one of the others says, "But after all, isn't woman's place really in the home?" and succeeds in getting a terrific rise out of the one addressed. The successful baiter turns to the third member of the group and says, not quite sotto voce, *Penny in the slot!* Can also be said to the angry victim. See also **(the) penny dropped.**

penny plain   **simple**
 Inf. As opposed to **twopence coloured.** The meaning is 'unadorned,' 'without frills.'

penny reading   SEE COMMENT
 An old-time show consisting of a series of short skits and sketches, usually comic. The price of admission was a penny. The practice is kept alive at some of the **public schools.** Despard Murgatroyd, in *Ruddigore* (Gilbert and Sullivan), became, after his reformation, a "**dab** at *penny readings*."

pennyworth, *n.*   SEE COMMENT
 Sometimes *penn'orth,* or *pennorth.* A *pennyworth* is, literally, as much as can be bought for a penny. The expression *not a pennyworth* means 'not the least bit.' *Pennyworth,* in the expression *a good* or *bad pennyworth,* means 'bargain.'

pension cover   **pension benefits**

pensioner, *n.*   **senior citizen**
 See **O.A.P.**

pepper-castor (-caster), *n.*   **pepper shaker**

pepper-pot, *n.*   **pepper shaker**

perambulator, *n.*   **baby carriage**
 But practically always shortened to *pram.*

pergola, *n.*   **trellis**
 Pergola, in America, evokes the image of a rather rustic garden house to escape into out of the rain or for children to play house in or adolescents to daydream in. Technically it means an 'arbor' or 'bower.' But in Britain, especially in the country, it is the name for a *trellis* running in a straight line and usually constructed of slim tree trunks as uprights and branches as crosspieces and Y-shaped supports, all still wearing their bark, and forming a frame for the training of climbing roses.

period return. See **return.**

perish, *v.t.*   **destroy**
 Perish is, of course, common in and to both countries as an intransitive verb. The transitive use is very rare in America and is now heard only in dialect. In Britain one still is *perished* by (or with) cold, thirst, etc. This does not mean one has died of it but merely been distressed or at least made seriously uncomfortable. When heat or cold *perishes* vegetation, it does mean 'destroy.' *Perishing* can be used in Britain as an adverb, as in *perishing cold.* It's *perishing cold,* which means 'terribly cold,' is another British way of saying **bloody** cold. *Perisher* is synonymous with **blighter,** and both are British slang that originally described a person of low character, but now are not so pejorative as formerly, as in *little perishers* (or *blighters*) applied to children in a humorous and still mildly pejorative way. *Perisher* is derived from the transitive use of the verb.

perks, *n. pl.*   **fringe benefits**
 Inf. Shortening of *perquisites.* Gaining currency in America.

permanent way   **roadbed**
 Railroad term. It means the 'roadbed' or the 'rails' themselves. In view of the shutting down of one branch line after another in Britain (as well as in America), the *permanent* seems naive, an echo from a happier time when all good things, like railroads, were going to endure forever. In fact, the epithet *permanent* derives from the earliest days of railroad construction, when the gangs laid temporary trackage, and then later put in the *permanent* tracks, after the right of way had consolidated.

perry, *n.*   **pear cider**
 A fermented pear juice drink which the author has never heard of in America. See also **cider; scrump.**

personal allowance   personal exemption
Income tax term.

personal call   person-to-person call
See also **pay for the call; caller.**

perspex, *n.*   plexiglass

peterman, *n. Slang*   peteman
A *safe-cracker.*

petrol, *n.*   gasoline
A *petrol station* is a *filling station.*

petrol bomb   *Inf.* molotov cocktail

petty, *n.*   *Slang.* john
Slang. A lavatory. Understandably, the title of the American film *Petty Girl* was changed to *Girl of the Year* when it was exported to Britain. Heard mostly in the North of England.

pewter, *n.*   *Slang.* loot
Slang. Nothing stolen: used in this context it means only 'prize' (money or any object), the kind of *loot* you bring home from a church bazaar. This use was derived from the fact that the prize was often a tankard, usually of pewter.

P.G.   boarder
Inf. Stands for *paying guest,* a euphemism for what Americans would call a *boarder* and Britons call a **lodger.** *Paying guest* would seem to be close to a contradiction in terms. Can be used as a verb: to *p.g* (or *PG*) with someone is to *board* with him. This term appears to be confined to a person of the same social class as the proprietor, perhaps a friend or relative, who lives with one in the same fashion as an ordinary house guest, but pays.

picotee, *n.*   SEE COMMENT
A variety of carnation having a border of a color different from the main color of its petals. The border is usually darker. According to some authorities, the term can be applied to tulips and roses as well.

pictures, *n. pl., Inf.*   movies
See also **films; cinema.**

pie, *n.*   meat-pie; deep-dish pie
An ordinary American pie would be called a *tart* in Britain (see **tart**). In Britain, unless otherwise specified, *pie* means 'meat pie' (see **pasty**), rather than anything involving fruit, and a request for a fruit-pie (*apple pie, cherry pie, etc.*) would produce the equivalent of an American *deep-dish pie.* A true story: An American asked the waitress in a small London restaurant for pie with ice cream and got just what he asked for (in British English)—a pork pie with a side order of vanilla ice cream. The waitress understood *ice cream* (on most menus the term would be **ice**), but *pie* was a different matter.

pie and pint man   SEE COMMENT
Slang. A person of extremely modest means. The *pie* in question is a *meat pie* (see **pie**); the *pint* is a *pint of bitter* (see **bitter; pint**). A meat pie and a pint of bitter (*beer*) would make the meal, presumably at a **pub,** of one living on a low budget.

piece of cake   *Slang.* cinch
Slang. An easy thing to do, like rolling off a log. See synonyms under **money for jam.**

pie shell   **pie crust**
Especially the prepared type for sale at the grocer's.

pig-in-the-middle, *n. Inf.*   SEE COMMENT
The *innocent victim* of a situation; one caught in a difficult situation not of his own
making, like a dispute between good friends both of whom appeal to him for support.
From the children's game *piggie-in-the-middle*, in which a child is caught in a circle of
his peers and must struggle to get out.

pig it   1. **live like a pig**
                                                         2. **eat like a pig**
Slang. Becoming current in America. To *pig it* with someone is to share his quarters,
with the connotation of having to squeeze in and live untidily for the time being.

pigs might fly, and. See **and pigs might fly.**

pi-jaw, See **jaw.**

pikelet, *n.*   SEE COMMENT
A crumpet-like type of pancake, originating in Wales. In many families, served mainly
at Christmas.

pile on the agony   *Inf.* **spread the gory details; lay it on thick**
Inf. To intensify the painful narrative, sparing no detail; but it may be used to indicate
any excessive or exaggerated action or display, such as, e.g., a painfully lavish entertainment or feast à la Trimalchio. See also **come it rather strong.**

pillar-box   **mailbox**
In the form of a high, hollow, red pillar. Invented by Anthony Trollope, as indefatigable in the service of the **G.P.O.** as in the writing of novels. See also **letter-box; post-
box.**

pimp, *n.*   **small bundle of kindling**
Inf. Sign in a Kentish hardware store (**iron-monger's**) window: PIMPS—2 PENCE. In
the county of Kent and neighboring sections of Sussex, a *pimp* is a small, cylindrical
roll (also called *bung* because it is shaped like a big stopper) of kindling, usually called
firewood in Britain. In *The Edwardians,* by Vita Sackville-West (Hogarth Press, London,
1930), we find a passage in which the young nobleman, Lord of the manor, "…looked
into the *pimping-shed,* where old Turnour [one of the domestic staff] was chopping
faggots." (Here, *faggot* is used in a sense shared with American usage: a bundle of sticks
or twigs bound together for use as fuel. The favored American spelling is *fagot*. This
shared sense is not listed in entry **faggot**.)

pinch, *v.t.*   *Inf.* **swipe**
Slang. Pinch and *swipe* meaning 'steal,' and *pinch* meaning 'arrest' are used in both
countries; but in the meaning 'steal,' *pinch* is favored in Britain and *swipe* in America,
where *pinch* more commonly means 'arrest.' In America you're *pinched* if you are caught
swiping; in Britain, you're *nabbed* if you are caught *pinching.*

pinch-point, *n.*   SEE COMMENT
Restriction on vehicles beyond a certain width. See **except for access.**

pink, *v.i.*   *Inf.* **ping; knock**
Inf. Describing the sound made by an automobile engine when the ignition is over-
advanced.

pink gin   SEE COMMENT
Gin and bitters, with water added.

pinny, *n.*   **apron**
Inf. Abbreviation of *pinafore.*

pint, *n.*   *approx.* **beer**
If a Briton asks for a *pint* he means a 'pint of **bitter.**' (As a unit of liquid measure, the *pint* in question is an Imperial pint of twenty oz., as opposed to the sixteen oz. American pint. See **Appendix II.C.2.**) If his thirst or budget is of more modest proportions, he will ask for a **half,** or *half a bitter,* which means 'half a pint,' i.e., ten oz. The two sizes of glasses are standard pub equipment, hanging on row after row of ceiling hooks or lined up on shelves and always spotless. Since *bitter* is usually of two grades, *ordinary bitter* and *best bitter,* the regular client, whose taste in the matter is a known quantity, need not specify. Otherwise he will volunteer the grade, or the person behind the counter will ask. Standing by itself, in this context, a *pint* in Britain means about the same thing as a *beer* means in America. One may ask: what will happen to the *pint* when Britain goes entirely metric? Well, householders will eventually buy their milk and motorists their gasoline in litres, and people will shop for kilos of this and grams of that, but a *pint* will stay a *pint,* no matter what its metric equivalent may be, as long as there stand a single pub in Britain and a single Briton ordering his bitter. In fact, at one of the meetings of the E.E.C. in 1976, the British were formally allowed to hang on to *pints* in beer, so long as they went metric in everything else. See also **pub; during hours.**

pinta, *n.*   **pint of milk**
Slang. (The *i* is long as in *ice.*) Originated in the National Dairy Council's advertise-ment *Drinka pinta milka day!* Never to be confused with **pint.** Probably in analogy to **cuppa.**

pip, *n.*   *Slang.* **beep**
Slang. When you make a call from a telephone booth, as your party answers, you hear a series of rapid *pips* and must promptly insert your coin in order to be heard. Certain BBC news programs are preceded by six *pips,* five short and one long, as a time signal. Short *pips,* called *beeps,* are the sounds you are supposed to hear, in America, every 15 seconds, if your call is being recorded. It is an offense to omit them.

pip, *v.t.*   1. *Slang.* **blackball**
                                                    2. *Slang.* **wing (wound)**
                                                    3. *Slang.* **pull rank on**
                                                    4. *Slang.* **nose out**
Slang. For use 4. see **pip-at-the-post.**

pip-at-the-post, *v.t.*   *Inf.* **nose out**
Inf. The post referred to is the winning post in a horse race.

pip emma   **P.M.**
Ack emma is *A.M.* Both now generally outmoded.

pissed, *adj.*   *Inf.* **blind drunk**
Slang. Usually reserved for cases of advanced inebriation. A vulgarism like **pee** which is, however, heard in "polite" society. See also **sloshed; squiffy; to the wide; well away.**

pit *n.*   **rear of orchestra**
What is called (strangely enough) the *orchestra* in America turns up in Britain as the **stalls.** The *pit* used to be the name for the rear of that part of the theater, and a *pittite* was a rarely used word for a person occupying a seat in the *pit.*

pitch, *n.*   SEE COMMENT
A technical term in **cricket:** the narrow rectangular strip between the **wickets** along (or parallel to) which the **batsmen** run; often confusingly to neophytes, itself called the *wicket.* In **football** *(soccer),* however, the whole field is called the *pitch.* Hard to follow, at first. *Pitch* is sometimes used colloquially, like *wicket,* to mean *situation:* to be *on a*

good pitch (or *wicket*) is to be *in a good spot*. It is also slang for *hangout* or *spot*, to describe the established location of a beggar, peddler, prostitute, pimp, tout, or other street person whose living strongly involves the territorial imperative, and in this use is synonymous with **turf.**

pitch upon   **pick on**
Inf. Not in the sense of 'nag' but rather in the sense of 'select:' *The police pitched upon him as the likeliest suspect.*

placeman, *n.*   **office holder**
With the strong implication that the appointment was motivated by self-interest and produced a rubber stamp.

placet, *n.*   **aye**
Affirmative vote in ecclesiastical or university bodies. It is a noun (an *aye* vote), in this use, but is actually the impersonal third person singular of the Latin verb *placere* (to *please, be acceptable*). Cf. **content.**

plain, *adj.*   **homely**
See under **homely.**

plain as a pikestaff, *Inf.*   *Inf.* **plain as the nose on your face**

planning permission   **building permit**
Short for *town and country planning permission*. A *town and country planning committee* is the British opposite number to an American *zoning board*.

plantation, *n.*   **planted grove**
Of trees or shrubs.

plaster, *n.*   **Band-aid**
See **Elastoplast.**

plate-glass university. See **Oxbridge.**

platelayer, *n.*   **tracklayer**

play a straight bat   **play fair**
Inf. Act correctly; do the right thing. A term from **cricket.**

play for safety   **play safe**

play for (someone's) side, *Inf.*   **be on (someone's) side;
                                                                  side with (someone)**

play oneself in   **settle down**
Inf. There are, throughout this book, many references to the English national sport of **cricket**: *inter alia*, **(the) Ashes; at close of play; bag a brace; bat a brace; bat first; batsman; boundary; bowler; cap; carry one's bat; chance; century; duck; fieldsman; first class; friendly; get one's eye in; ground; knock for six; maiden over; night watchman; off one's own bat; off the mark; over; pitch; play a straight bat; rot; run out; run-up; six; sticky wicket; stump; take first knock; Test Match; ton; up stumps; wicket; Appendix II.K.** [The author is an avowed cricket fan, and has the distinction of being one of the exceedingly few foreign—especially American—members of the Marylebone Cricket Club, universally referred to in Britain as the 'M.C.C.' (see **(the) Ashes.)**] Just as baseball, in America, has contributed many of its technical terms to the general language: *inter alia*, **bush-league; get to first base; go to bat; (a) lot on the ball; make a hit; off base; pinch hit; rain check; right off the bat; strike out; throw a curve,** so has cricket in Britain, from among the long list of cricket references given above. One of

these is *play oneself in*. In cricket, the **batsman** has, first of all, to 'defend' his **wicket**, i.e., prevent the **bowler** from 'breaking' it by causing one of the two bails (the horizontal pieces resting atop the stumps—see **wicket**, 1) to fall off the stumps. This the batsman does by simply deflecting the ball away from his wicket; but sooner or later, he must begin to make runs, by striking the ball hard enough to permit him to run between the wickets and thus gain points for his side. (To explain the rules of cricket more fully would require a book almost as long as this one.) Thus, the batsman, initially, feels out the bowler in order to 'get his eye in' (see **get one's eye in**), and thus settle down before he feels that it is now safe to start to attempt runs. This initial period of settling down is known as *playing oneself in*—one of the many cricket terms lent to the general language. Thus, a detective interviewing a nervous witness gives him time to *play himself in* before serious, pointed questioning begins. He talks about the weather (always a prime topic in Britain), the curse of heavy traffic on the roads, the current political crisis, and then—wham!—goes into the active phase: "You knew the deceased for many years, didn't you, Mr. Wiggins?" and "Where were you on the night of...?" and so on and so on. If he's successful, the detective has given the witness an opportunity to *play himself in*.

play-pit, *n.*   sandbox

play the game. See **game.**

playtime, *n.*   recess
   School term, applicable to kindergarten and first grade, children four to six years old. In **prep school** (ages eight to thirteen) the term is *breaktime.*

play (something) to leg   **brush (something) off**
   Inf. A term borrowed from **cricket.** When the **batsman** (batter) **plays** a ball **to leg,** he turns or sweeps it away with his bat, rather than attempt to hit it hard and try to make runs. Thus, to **play** a ball **to leg** is a defensive tactic; and to **play** an embarrassing question **to leg** is to brush it off somehow and evade the issue.

play truant   **play hookey**
   The American term is almost unknown in Britain.

play up!, *interj.*   *Inf.* **come on!**
   Inf. Yelled by sports fans to urge on their team, as in, *Play up, United!*

play (someone) up   1. **play up on (someone)**
                                                                                                        2. **pester**
1. In Britain your trick knee or your hi-fi *plays you up;* in America it *plays up on you.*
2. Pupils who deliberately annoy their teachers are said to *play them up.*

PLC/Plc/plc   SEE COMMENT
   Stands for *public limited company,* one whose shares (under the Companies Act of 1980) can be traded on the Stock Exchange. The three letters follow the name of such a **company,** as opposed to *Ltd.* following the name of a private limited company. In America, *Inc.* is used whether or not the corporation's stock can be traded on an exchange.

Pleasure!   **Don't mention it!**
   A somewhat warmer response than the usual *Not at all, Pleasure* is a contraction of *It's a pleasure* or *My pleasure. Don't mention it* is heard, and sometimes *Think nothing of it. You're welcome,* which until recently was never heard and immediately marked the user American, is now uttered more and more frequently by Britons, doubtless as a result of the influx of American visitors. See also **Not at all.**

plimsolls, *n.*   sneakers
   Another British term is **gym shoes.** *Plimsolls* is the common British word for *sneakers,* so named after Samuel Plimsoll, who also lent his name to the expression *Plimsoll's Mark* (or *Plimsoll Line*), which is the line showing how far a ship is allowed by law to

be submerged when loaded. In addition, he is known as one of the moving forces behind the British merchant Shipping Act of 1876. This connection between Mr. Plimsoll and shipping leads to the conclusion that *plimsolls* got their name from the fact that they were the kind of cheap canvas soft-soled shoes worn on deck. But there are those who say that the name stems from the resemblance between the Plimsoll Line on a ship and the upper edge of the rubber bottom of a sneaker.

plonk, *n.*   **cheap wine**
Slang. Plink-plonk was a variation on *blink-blonk,* a jocular play on *vin blanc* by the British Tommy in World War I. It is possible that the British murdered as many French words as German soldiers. When the *plink* was dropped, the *plonk* that stayed on should still have been reminiscent of *blanc,* but somehow came to apply to any cheap wine, regardless of race, color, or country of origin.

Plough, *n.*   **Big Dipper**
Other British names for the *Big Dipper* are *Charles's Wain* and *Great Bear.* But see **big dipper.**

plough, *v.t.*   *Slang.* **flunk**
Slang. That is, to *flunk* a pupil, not an exam. Undoubtedly short for *plough under.* Sometimes used intransitively, in which case it does mean 'flunk an exam,' but *exam* is understood.

ploughman's lunch   *approx.* **bread and cheese**
Inf. A large piece of French bread, an enormous slab of Cheddar cheese, a vast chunk of butter, and a couple of sour pickled onions. A favorite at **pubs,** and still a terrific bargain.

plough the sand(s), *Inf.*   **work in vain**

ploy, *n.*   **1. job**
                                                                                     2. toy
Inf. The second meaning given above refers specifically to *educational toys,* and looks like a **portmanteau** formation of *play* and *toy,* which was probably helped along by the first meaning: in other words, a *toy* that keeps the kids busy with a *job,* like fitting things together. Since the appearance of Stephen Potter, *ploy* means a 'move,' like a gambit in chess, a feint in boxing, a calculatedly misleading step in the business world, or an act of oneupmanship at a party: anything calculated to get results by outwitting or upsetting the other fellow.

plum, *n., Slang.*   **£100,000**

plum duff   **plum pudding**
(The *duff* is *dough* pronounced like ROUGH.)

plump, *v.i.*   **vote for a single candidate**
When two or several are to be chosen. The vote in such a case is known as a *plumper.* Related, of course, to *plumping* for a particular person or cause.

po, *n.*   *Inf.* **pottie**
Slang. Short for the *pot* in *chamber pot,* and pronounced like the POT in *pot de chambre.* The French pronunciation is supposed to make it amusing and therefore less clinical.

pocketbook, *n.*   **1. pocket notebook**
                                                                                2. billfold
In Britain a lady's handbag is always called a *bag* or a *handbag,* never a *pocketbook.* That term is reserved there for a *pocket notebook* or a *folding wallet,* which the British also call a *notecase.*

podge, *n.*   *Inf.* **fatty**
Inf. Podge gives rise to the adjective *podgy,* which has its American equivalent in *pudgey.* See also **fubsy.**

po-faced, *adj.* *approx.* **impassive**
Slang. A difficult word to pin down. It must be pejorative, based as it is on **po**, which is slang for *pot*, or *pottie (chamber pot)*, and is itself based on the French pronunciation of *pot*, as in *pot de chambre*. A *po-faced* person is one who exhibits a deliberately blank expression to his audience. There is more than a hint of hauteur in this epithet. Quintin Hogg may have fallen prey to an apocryphal derivation when he called Harold Wilson *po-faced*, meaning 'poker-faced.' In a letter published in the *Times Literary Supplement* of December 23, 1977, Brian Pearce writes about the 'delightful piece of "Frenglish" ' in Sir Terence Rattigan's *French Without Tears: une figure de vase de nuit*, purporting to describe the face of a *po-faced* person:

> What the first audience actually heard (and what was printed when the play was published in 1937) was this. Brian, speaking to Alan, describes Commander Rogers as 'pie-faced.' Maingot demands [*sic*, as opposed to *asks*, apparently under the influence of the French atmosphere: author's note]: 'Qu'est-ce que ça veut dire, pie-faced?' Alan replies: 'Nous disions que Monsieur le Commandant avait une figure de vase de nuit, Monsieur.' When I asked Sir Terence why, when what was clearly meant was 'po-faced', it was necessary to have the actors say 'pie-faced' instead, he explained that the Lord Chamberlain would not have allowed 'po-faced'!

The **Lord Chamberlain** (full title: *Lord Chamberlain of the Household*), who is in charge of the management of the Royal Household, used to be the play-licensing authority in England, a censorship now abolished.
The meaning of *po-faced* has lately been somewhat extended to mean 'coldly, stonily expressionless,' and from that, to 'pompous' and even 'arrogant.' *Po-faced* having achieved a degree of popularity, it was only a short step to *jerry-faced* (see **jerry**); it had to happen, and it did. Even *boot-faced* (also for *impassive*) has made its appearance. Whether either of these will catch on is a matter of conjecture.

pogged, *adj.* *Slang.* **stuffed**
Slang. After too much food: *I'm pogged!* A bit of Yorkshire slang.

point, *n.* **1. electrical socket**
2. railroad switch
1. *Point* often appears as *electrical point* or *power point*. Sometimes it is used in combination with another word, as in *razor point*, thus indicating an electrical outlet to be used for a particular purpose.

point duty. See **pointsman, 1.**

pointsman, *n.* **1. traffic policeman**
2. switchman
1. *Point-duty* is the *traffic detail* and a *policeman on point-duty* is a *traffic cop*.
2. The railroad man in charge of switches.

poke, *v.t* *Slang.* **screw**
Slang. Unlovely word for the act of love.

poker school **poker session**

policy, *n.* **landscaped ground**
The landscaped part around a country house. Usually in the plural, the *policies*, and more common in Scotland than in England.

politician, *n.* **1.** *approx.* **government official**
2. political scientist
These were, at least, the old meanings, but confusion has arisen about their continuing validity. Going back a few years, a *politician* was one, whether or not in power at the moment, skilled in the science of government and politics generally. The term had little, if any, pejorative implication as in America, where it brings to mind the scheming

and manipulation characteristic of party politics: unenlightened self-interest, the smoke-filled room. Until recently in Britain, a *statesman* was merely a higher order of *politician* in the British sense, the recognition of whose service, experience, wisdom, and resulting power entitled him to the more eminent label. Indeed, if one can go along with the definition of *politician* in the sixth edition (1976) of the *Concise Oxford Dictionary*, the distinction between the American and British usages still exists. In the last previous edition (the fifth) (1964), a *politician* was 'one skilled in politics, statesman; one interested or engaged in politics; one who makes a trade of politics.' (**Trade** is British for 'busi-ness.') Interestingly enough the 1976 edition uses identical words in its definition, but takes pains to indicate that the ensuing words—'one who makes a trade of politics'—constitute the American definition! What this amounts to is that as late as 1976, accord-ing to the wisdom of the *Concise Oxford, politicians* in Britain were still *statesmen*, whereas in America, *politicians* were, well, *politicians!* But much earlier, Benjamin Disraeli himself used *politician* in the pejorative American sense: "The world is weary of statesmen whom democracy has degraded into politicians." Bernard Levin, a most sensitive prac-titioner of the Queen's English and a properly cynical observer of those in high places, writing in *The Times* (London) of September 15, 1976, decrying the paucity of great leaders in the contemporary world, says: "...there aren't any statesmen; only politi-cians," obviously using the latter term pejoratively, in a manner inconsistent with the allegedly up-to-date *Concise Oxford.* Perhaps Watergate inspired those responsible for the new edition of that estimable dictionary to underline the differences noted between the American and British usages, a distinction which had theretofore been ignored. *Concise Oxford* to the contrary notwithstanding, one must go along with Levin and sadly conclude that there remains very little distinction attached to the respective labels in either country—or for that matter, in any other part of the world. It may be that Am-brose Bierce hit on the true distinction in his definition of *politician:* "As compared to the statesman, he suffers the disadvantage of being alive." In Ireland, they say, "Will the last person leaving the country please switch off the *politicians?"*

polling-day, *n.*   **election day**
The British also use the term *voting-day,* as well as the American term. Signs reading POLLING STATION appear where VOTE HERE signs would be posted in America.

polo neck   **turtleneck**
Applied to sweaters with high collars which are folded down, so that there is a close-fitting double layer around the neck. See also **turtleneck; rollneck.**

polytechnic, *n.*   *approx.* **community college**
A vocational or technical high school or college. Often shortened to *poly.*

Pompey, *n.*   SEE COMMENT
Slang. Affectionate slang for *Portsmouth,* the naval base.

ponce, *n., v.i.*   **pimp**
Slang. A much fancier British synonym is *souteneur,* taken over from the French, in which language its literal meaning is 'upholder,' indicating something or other about certain French attitudes. To *ponce about* is to *swagger,* apparently on the assumption that ponces make a very good living and have the wherewithal to live it up.

pond, *n.*   **pool**
Man made. In America, *pond* usually describes a body of water smaller than a lake, like Thoreau's Walden Pond. In Britain, it means a 'pool made by hollowing or em-banking.' The British also use it as a verb. Transitively, it means to 'dam up' (e.g., a stream); intransitively, of water, to 'form a pool.'

pong, *n.*   *approx.* **stink**
Slang. No slang American equivalent. Used, for example, about Emmenthal cheese—"Tangy without the pong."

pontoon, *n.*   **blackjack**
   A card game. *Pontoon* is a corruption of the French name for the game, *vingt-et-un.*
The British apparently made the common mistake of omitting the *et* in *vingt-et-un, trente-et-un,* etc., and then proceeded to corrupt the corruption phonetically. The game is also known as *twenty-one.*

pony, *n., Inf.*   **£25**

poodle   **puppet**
   Slang. Pejorative used in political circles.

poodle-faker, *n.*   SEE COMMENT
   Slang. A quite specialized word, describing a naval officer who, in civilian clothes, paid social visits ashore to curry favor in certain quarters. Wilfred Granville, in *Sea Slang of the Twentieth Century,* gave this definition: "...a payer of polite social calls; a balancer of tea cups ashore."

poof, *n.*   *Slang.* **pansy**
   Slang. Derogatory term for male homosexual. Sometimes spelled *pouf; pouffe; poove; puff.*

poon, *n.*   *Slang.* **jerk**
   Slang. **Public school** slang, describing a *middle class jerk* (**twit**)—one of those hopelessly middle class types frowned upon by those superior *public school* chaps. The adjective *poonish* is applied to genteel middle-class activities and functions, like sherry parties and flower shows. According to authorities at Winchester, one of the most distinguished public schools, the noun and adjective derive from the nickname of a teacher (**master**) at another distinguished school who "being unaware of what the boys have christened him, should perhaps be left in ignorance." See synonyms under **git.**

poop, *n.*   *Slang.* **dope**
   Slang. Short for *nincompoop.*

poopnoddy, *n., Slang; archaic.*   *Slang.* **fuck**

poor tool   *Inf.* **total loss**
   Inf. To be a *poor tool* at such and such an activity is to be a *total loss* at it, a *bust: He's a poor tool at providing for his family.*

poove. See **poof.**

pop, *n., v.t.*   1. *n., v.t., Inf.* **hock (pawn)**
                                                                                                 2. *v.t.,* **fasten**
   1. *Slang. Popshop* means 'hockshop.'
   2. *Slang.* To fasten with **poppers.** Also, *pop up.*

poplin, *n.*   **broadcloth**
   In Britain, *broadcloth* describes a special kind of woolen material. See **broadcloth.**

popper, *n.*   **snap**
   Used to fasten articles of apparel. See also **press stud; snapper; pop, 2.**

poppet, *n.*   *Inf.* **sweetie**
   Inf. A term of endearment used especially in describing or addressing little ones and pets.

popsie, *n.*   *Slang.* **cutie**
   Slang. Originally the epithet for an *old man's darling,* but now extended to include anybody's *cutie.*

porch, *n.*   **covered approach to doorway**

porlock, *v.i.*   SEE COMMENT
   To *porlock* is to interrupt an artist engaged in aesthetic creation. This word, as a verb, appeared in print for the first time in *Bruno's Dream* (Chatto & Windus, London, 1969),

a novel by the great contemporary English novelist Iris Murdoch. This author suspected that *porlock*, as a verb, was an invention of Miss Murdoch, and dictionary research revealed only the following entry in Volume 3 (0 to Sez) of the *Supplement* (1982) to the *Oxford English Dictionary:*

> Porlock...The name of a town in Somerset [an English county], used allusively (see quot. 1816) in phr. *a person* etc. *from Porlock* a person who interrupts at an inconvenient moment. [**1816** COLERIDGE *Kubla Khan* in *Christabel* 53 At this moment he [*sc.* Coleridge] was unfortunately called out by a person on business from Porlock, and detained by him above an hour.] **1959** *Listener* 1 Jan. 37/3 All the incidental distractions— the telephone-bell, the Christmas carollers at the door, the gentleman or lady 'from Porlock'—to which one is subject.

It seemed, therefore, that to *porlock* was to interrupt at an inconvenient moment. But correspondence with Miss Murdoch brought forth a graciously prompt fuller explanation, if a narrower definition (her letter posted February 7, 1985):

> ...The verb "to porlock" is my coinage. (I know of no other use of it.) It fills a terminological gap and I hope it will pass into general parlance. The Coleridge story, upon which the idea entirely rests, is that Coleridge 'dreamt' *Kubla Khan* and on awakening started to write it down but was interrupted by a person on business from Porlock. To *porlock* is to interrupt an artist engaged in aesthetic creation. By extension, it can mean to interrupt any sustained and serious reflective thinking, that of a scholar or philosopher for instance. I would be against weakening it to mean any sort of unwelcome interruption.

This author can only express the hope that in this (and previous) correspondence with Miss Murdoch, he has not been guilty of *porlocking*—and delaying even for a moment the completion of her next and eagerly awaited novel!

A reference to this rather obscure village of Porlock appears in *The Kingdom by the Sea*, a travel book by the American writer Paul Theroux (Hamish Hamilton, London, 1983):

> I left Lynton on the Cliff Railway, a cable car that descended to Lynmouth [incidentally, a short but terrifying ride experienced by this author and his wife many years ago]. I took a bus to Porlock, ten miles away. The road cut across the north of Exmoor, a rather brown forbidding place, and down the long Porlock Hill...Porlock, the home of the man who interrupted the writing of 'Kubla Khan', was one street of small cottages, with a continuous line of cars trailing though it. Below it, on the west side of the bay, was Porlock Weir...A hundred and seventy years ago a man came to Porlock and found it quiet. But he did not find fault. He wrote: 'There are periods of comparative stagnation, when we say, even in London, that there is nothing stirring; it is therefore not surprising that there should be some seasons of the year when things are rather quiet in West Porlock.'

Porlock seems to be on writers' minds, undoubtedly because of the Coleridge incident. In his *Diaries, 1920–1922* (Faber & Faber, London, 1981), the English poet and novelist Siegfried Sassoon notes under dates April 27, 1921, ff.: "...Thinking of taking Gabriel [Gabriel Atkin, the English artist and Sassoon's great friend] to Porlock next week," and he did so on May 5 following. Ten days later, he sent this poem to the English poet and critic Edmund Blunden:

> KNOW YOU EXMOOR? Have ye heard tell of PORLOCK?
> Whence started out, one morn in 1800 (?),
> A man, on *business* bent, at Nether Stowey.
> Sought there one Samuel Coleridge; knocked and blundered
> Through green-leaf-shuttered parlour into garden;
> Coughed; made his errand palpable; surmised
> Tomorrow's rain or rainlessness. 'Beg pardon

If I've disturbed your nap, sir!' Coleridge smiled;
Seemed half-attentive. Murmured like the stream
Descending Quantock, sloping toward the Channel.
And is he known in Hell—that oaf from Porlock?
Do flames attend him? Is he crucified
Upon Mount Abora? Plagued from feet to forelock
By parasitic friends? Or has he tried
To earn atonement? Did his phantom go,
With necroscopic clichés simplified,
To irritate poor Edgar Allan Poe?

porridge, *n.*   **1. (cooked) oatmeal**
                                                    2. SEE COMMENT
1. To *keep your breath to cool your porridge* is to 'keep your advice for your own use,' i.e.,
to practice what you preach. When shopping, don't ask for *oatmeal;* raw oatmeal is *oats*
in Britain.
2. *Slang.* To *do porridge* is to 'serve time.' Synonymous with **do bird.** A popular television
comedy series about life in prison is entitled "Porridge."

porter, *n.*   **doorman**
    The British often use *hall porter* to distinguish a *doorman* from a *railway porter. Porterage*
is used to describe the services of a doorman. Where an American would say that his
apartment house has a *doorman,* the Briton would say that there is a *porter* at his **block
of flats** or *porterage* is **laid on** *with his flat.* See also **commissionaire.**

portmanteau, *n.*   **blend word**
    The figurative meaning is that of a made-up word combining the sounds and mean-
ings of parts of two other words, like *squarson,* combination of *squire* and *parson; mingy,*
combination of *mean* and *stingy; smog,* combination of *smoke* and *fog,* etc. One would
guess that Lewis Carroll's *slithy toves* had been not only *slimy* but also *lithe.* He invented
this usage of *portmanteau* in *Through the Looking-Glass:* "You see, it's like a *portmanteau*—
there are two meanings packed into one word."

posh, *adj.*   *Inf.* **swanky**
    Slang. From the initials *P.O.S.H.,* which stand for *port out, starboard home,* i.e., the
north side of ships traveling between Britain and India. It was the shady, and therefore
the preferable, side. (There are some authorities who vigorously contest this etymology.
Might be just a contraction of *polished.*)

position, *n.*   **situation**
    Position has two British uses which one almost never hears in America: it means
'situation,' in the sense of 'location,' of a house or other building. The other British
meaning is also 'situation' but in the figurative sense of the 'way things stand.' For
instance: *The position is that the company is insolvent,* or, *Do you understand the position?*

positive discrimination   **affirmative action**
    The promotion and encouragement of increased employment of members of minority
groups and women, a much debated labor practice in both countries.

post, *n., v.t.*   **mail**
    See also **G.P.O.; letter post; newspaper post; recorded delivery.**

postage (posting) and packing   **handling and mailing**
    As used in mail order advertising, where the 'handling' charge often appears to ring
in a wee bit of extra profit. See also **dispatch.**

postal course   **correspondence course**

postal shopping   **mail order buying**

postal van   mail car
Railroad term.

postal vote   absentee ballot

post-box   mailbox
The smallish red iron boxes in rural areas bear the initials of the sovereign in whose reign they were erected. A Briton will announce with pride that the box near his home is a **V.R.** box! Occasionally called *posting box* or *letter box*. See also **pillar-box**.

post-code, *n.*   zip code
In Britain, a combination of numbers and letters. Example: TN18 5DE.

poste restante   general delivery
Permanently borrowed from the French. Literally it means 'mail remaining' ('waiting to be picked up'). The French have a pun for what so often happens when one follows the dangerous course of asking another to mail a letter for him: *poche restante (poche* means 'pocket').

post-free   postpaid

post-graduate, *adj.*   graduate
As in *post-graduate student, degree,* etc.

postman, *n.*   mailman

postman's knock man   unskilled hunter
Inf. The phrase means an 'unskillful hunter' (**shooter,** in Britain) who fires two barrels at almost everything he spies on the wing and rarely hits anything. The analogy is to the **postman's** (mailman's) traditional *rat-tat*. Remember *The Postman Always Rings Twice*, James Cain's thriller, first produced in 1934, later a motion picture? Incidentally, *postman's knock*, burglars' rhyming slang for *lock* (see **Appendix II.G.3.**), appeared in a Chubb advertisement in *The Daily Telegraph* (London) or March 5, 1962.

post-mortem   autopsy
More commonly used in Britain.

Post Office   SEE COMMENT
Usual name for the **G.P.O.** Americans think of their post office as a place to mail letters and parcels and buy stamps and money orders. The *Post Office* in Britain has a much wider scope; see **G.P.O.**

pot, *n.*   1. *Slang.* boodle
                                            2. *Slang.* favorite (horse racing)
                                                           3. SEE COMMENT
1. *Slang.* Used alone or in the expression *pots of money*. To *put the pot* on a horse at a British **race-course** is to *shoot your wad* or *bet your stack* at an American track. The British also use the expression to *go nap* on a horse to describe the same vice (see **nap**).
2. *Slang.* The *pot* is also British slang for the *favorite* in a horse race.
3. *Slang.* A British slang usage sometimes heard (occasionally lengthened to *pot-hunter*) is to describe a person who enters a contest not for the sport of it but only for the prize. Another British slang use is in the expression to *put* someone's *pot on*, which means to 'squeal on' him, or 'spill the beans,' for which the British also use the expression *blow the gaff*. A *big pot*, however, means something entirely different: *VIP*.

pot, *v.t.*   *Inf.* **potty**
Inf. To attend to a very young child's need.

potato, *n.*   hole in one's sock
Slang. **Wellingtons** are said to cause *potatoes.*

pot-boy, *n.* bartender's assistant
Potman means the same thing. Literally, someone who helps out in a pub, but sometimes used figuratively in the sense of *prat boy* as a pejorative term meaning somebody at anybody's beck and call. See also **dog's body.**

pot-house, *n., Slang.* *Inf.* **pub**

potted lecture *Slang.* **canned spiel**
Inf. A pre-set brief spiel, usually in the nature of a demonstration, often with slides. The author's dentist asked his hygienist to deliver, for the author's benefit, her *potted lecture* on a new method of brushing teeth. She did, with slides, models, brushes, and gestures. (The teeth are much improved.)

potty, *adj.* *Slang.* **nutty**
Inf. The implication is eccentricity rather than outright lunacy. Not quite so strong as **dotty** or **bonkers.**

pouf, also **pouffe.** See **poof.**

poulterer, *n.* poultry dealer
Sometimes POULTER (very high class) appears on store signs.

pour with rain pour
It would be hard to know what else the impersonal *it* could pour with; surely not hail or frogs (see *Exodus* 9:10). See also **bucket down; rain stair rods.**

power point. See **point.**

poxing, *adj.* plaguing
Slang. Annoying, irritating. That poxing stuff about French irregular verbs...! Cf. the archaic *a pox on...!*

practical, *n.* lab test
Inf. Like being given a frog to dissect in a biology exam. School cant.

praeposter, preposter. See **prefect.**

pram, *n.* baby carriage
Inf. Short for *perambulator.*

prang, *v.t* 1. crash land (an aircraft)
2. bomb (a target)
3. lay (a girl)
Slang. 1. and 2. are presumably onomatopoeic; but. 3.?
From meanings 1. and 2. the use of the word has been extended to cover nonaeronautical accidents as well, and even minor ones. One can *prang* a car in a collision, or merely one's knee or arm while working around the house. *Bump* would be the equivalent here.

praties, *n. pl.* *Slang.* **spuds**
Inf. Borrowed from the Irish, and according to some authorities, given back.

prawn, *n.* small shrimp
Small in American terms, because *shrimps* in Britain are generally tiny things compared to what Americans mean by the term. A Briton would consider a *prawn* a large, rather than a small, shrimp. What Americans think of as shrimps are generally called *scampi* in Britain, a term usually confined in America to cooked shrimps in restaurants with continental cuisine.

prefect, *n.* *approx.* **monitor**
A school boy or girl who attains a quasi-official position to help keep order. In some **public schools,** called *praepostor* or *prepostor.* See also **head boy** or **girl.**

preference shares	**preferred stock**

preggers, *adj.*   *Slang.* **knocked up**
Slang. Great with child; derivation obvious; discussed under **Harry... Knock up** is far less serious in British usage. See also **in pod** and **pudding club.**

premium bond   **government lottery bond**
   Monthly lottery drawings are held with cash prizes going to the holders of the bonds with lucky serial numbers. They bear no interest. In America the same phrase describes regular interest-bearing corporate bonds callable before maturity, on short notice, for redemption at a premium.

prentice, *adj.*   **amateurish**
   Inf. As in, *It's only a prentice job,* or, *The novel is a prentice piece of work.* A *prentice hand* is an *inexperienced worker.*

prep, *n.*   **1.** *approx.* **homework**
                                                              2. study hall
   Inf. Short for *preparation. Prep* is the name for both the work the student does to prepare for the next day's (or less frequently, that afternoon's) classes and for the session at boarding school at which he does it. *Prep* is usually supervised by a **prefect** or **master** who not only keeps order but is available to help the struggling student. Work to be done at home is called *homework,* even in Britain.

prep school   **pre-preparatory school**
   In this phrase, *prep* is an abbreviation of *preparatory.* A *prep school* is a private school for boys or girls who enter at the age of eight and remain for five years. It is called a *prep school* because it *prepares* the children for **public school** which they enter at thirteen and where, too, they usually stay for five years.

presenter, *n.*   **newscaster**
   Or *commentator* generally. Sometimes heard as a credit at the end of a television program. See also **newsreader.**

press stud   **snap**
   To fasten articles of apparel. Synonymous with **snapper** and **popper.**

press-up, *n.*   **push-up**

pressure, *n.*   **voltage**
   So used by the Royal Navy in World War II.

prezzy, *n.*   **present (gift)**
   Inf. A horrid colloquialism.

pricey (pricy), *adj., Inf.*   **expensive**

principal boy   *approx.* **star**
   A special designation pertaining to **pantomimes,** usually called *pantos.* The *principal boy* is always a girl, or should be. There is a *principal girl,* too; also a star; also a girl. The *principal boy* tradition has been broken occasionally in recent years, usually in the un-traditional glamorous pantos at the London Palladium.

printed paper rates   **third-class mail**

prison van   **police wagon**
   See **van.**

private, *adj.*   **personal**
   On envelopes, meaning that nobody but the addressee is to open.

private bar. see under **pub.**

private school   SEE COMMENT
The author has been informed that Etonians use the expression *private school* exclusively for *prep school* (in the British sense). See **prep school; public school.**

private treaty   contract
In advertisements of real estate for sale, one often sees the phrase *for sale by private treaty*, which means that the common British practice of putting up real estate for sale at auction is not being followed in that case.

privy purse   SEE COMMENT
Funds supplied by the British Government for the private expenses of the sovereign.

prize, also **prise,** *v.t.*   **pry**
Prize is known in America but *pry* is more common; vice versa in Britain.

Prize Day. See **Speech Day.**

P.R.O.   **PR man**
The British call them 'public relations officers' for some strange reason.

proctor, *n.*   *approx.* **college monitor**
A *senior proctor* and a *junior proctor* are selected each year at Oxford and Cambridge as officials charged mainly with disciplinary matters. To *proctorize* is to exercise that function. The word is used in somewhat the same sense in some American colleges, with the emphasis on dormitory and examination discipline, but the American verb is *proctor*, same as the noun. The British have a special use of the word *Queen's* (or *King's*) *Proctor*, designating an officer who may intervene in certain lawsuits, mainly matrimonial, where collusion or other skullduggery is suspected. *Prog* is the slang form, and can be used as a transitive verb, as in *He was progged*, university slang for 'reported by the proctor.'

prodnose, *n., v.i.*   **rubberneck**
Slang. The noun is sometimes applied to detectives.

producer, *n.*   **1. director**
                                                                      2. producer
1. In the British theater, *producer* and *director* are both used to mean 'director' in the American sense, and *theatrical manager* means 'producer' in the American sense.
2. In the film industry *producer* and *director* are used as in America.
This word has undergone a change of meaning in theatrical circles since the old days. Lord Laurence Olivier has this to say about original and current usage in his *Confessions of an Actor* (Simon & Schuster, New York, 1982):

> The title of "producer" enjoyed its original distinction at this time [1932] meaning the person who ordered the actors' moves, prescribed their inflections, set the tempo and generally interpreted the author's intentions. In the old actor-manager days this was part of the stage-manager's job, carried out, of course, in accordance with his chief's desires. This new influence in the theatre was made significant at the turn of the century by Granville Barker in England, Fay in Ireland, Copeau in France, Reinhardt in Germany, Stanislavsky in Russia, Frohman in New York, etc. Gradually, under the influence of the silent film as well as that of Broadway, the meaning of "producer" changed emphatically. It was seized by the no doubt deserving individual whose money, influence or ownership of the play entitled him to it. It took most of the 1950s for the British theatre to be generally converted to this usage.
>   The title of the person with more technical métier became the "director," who in films, by tradition, claimed the position of honor in the credits, namely, the last before the beginning of the photographed story.

prog. See **proctor.**

programme, *n.* **platform**
What Americans call the *platform* of a political party is called its *programme* in Britain. Also, *party manifesto.*

prompt, *n.* **stage left**
See **opposite prompt.**

(the) Proms, *n. pl.* SEE COMMENT
Inf. Short for *Promenade Concerts*, a series started by Sir Henry Wood in 1895, held annually during the summer. Originally at the Queen's Hall, but when that was bombed out, moved to the Royal Albert Hall. The name derives from the removal of seats from part of the orchestra section to allow some of the audience to walk around. But in practice, because these low-priced concerts are so popular, that part of the audience, usually the younger element, stands just below the orchestra itself which plays on a raised stage. Applause is supplemented by much cheering and a good time is had by all.

propeller shaft **drive shaft**
Automobile term. See also **Appendix II.E.**

propelling pencil **mechanical pencil**

proper, *adj., adv.* *Inf.* **regular; real**
Inf. Used by the British as an intensive. If a pal should see you sipping lemonade in a pub, he might ask you why you're not having a *proper* drink, i.e., a *real* drink, an *honest to goodness* drink. A *proper pushing lad* is a *real go-getter*. Less complimentary is an expression such as a *proper fool*, where the adjective emphasizes the degree of folly. *Good and proper* is an adverbial phrase heard mainly among countryfolk, or humorously, in a sentence like, *I told him off good and proper!*

property, *n.* **real estate**
A *property dealer* would be called a *real-estate operator* in America.

provinces. See under **regions.**

proxy bomb **dummy bomb**
For example, a bag of fertilizer left in a suspiciously parked car, to effect a bomb scare.

P.T. *Inf.* **phys. ed.**
Inf. Stands for *physical training*; usually abbreviated like its American counterpart.

P.T.O. **over**
Placed at the bottom of the page and indicating *please turn over*. See also **overleaf.**

pub, *n.* SEE COMMENT
Inf. A very approximate equivalent is *bar*—the institution of the British *pub* is so dismally, nay, tragically lacking in American life. *Pub* is short for *public house*. Everybody in Britain has "his" *pub*. A synonym for *pub* is the **local**, which is, of course, short for the *local pub* (Note that *local* can also mean 'native'; see **local**). Every pub has at least two bars: the *public bar* and the *saloon*, or *private bar*, which is appreciably more elegant; and drinks served in that room cost a little bit more. One is apt to find a carpet on the floor of the *saloon bar*, but the darts board, the bar-billiards table, and the shove-halfpenny board would normally be found in the *public bar*. See also **free house; tied; during hours; bitter; pint; landlord; pot house; shebeen.** Anthony Powell, in *Temporary Kings* (Little, Brown and Company, Boston, 1973—the eleventh and penultimate work in Powell's sequence, *A Dance to the Music of Time*) describes a pub (full name *The Hero of Acre: Hero* for short) characterized by an unusual degree of compartmentalization:

The Hero, one of those old-fashioned pubs in grained pitchpine with engraved looking-glass…was anatomized into half-a-dozen or more separate compartments, subtly differentiating, in the traditional British manner, social subdivisions of its clientele, according to temperament or means: saloon bar: public bar: private bar: ladies' bar: wine bar: off-licence: possibly others too.

This passage indicates a differentiation between *saloon bar* and *private bar*, which has thus far escaped the author's notice in actual experience. *Ladies' bar*, too, would seem to be an obsolete institution, for ladies appear to have been liberated in this area earlier in Britain than in America. As recently as the late 60s, in some parts of America, women were not allowed to sit at the bar. 'That sort of thing was over in Britain long before that.

pub-crawl, *n., v.i.*   **make the rounds (of pubs)**
Inf. To *pub-crawl* is to visit (and presumably give one's custom to) one pub after another, and *pub-crawl* is also the noun describing this activity.

publican, *n.*   *approx.* **saloon keeper**
The *publican*, also known as the *landlord* or *pubkeeper*, is the *proprietor* of a **pub.** See also **landlord.**

public bar; public house. See **pub.**

public convenience   **comfort station**
A battle of euphemisms, both meaning 'public toilet'; a municipal institution which still flourishes in British towns and villages but seems to be disappearing in America.

public prosecutor   **district attorney**

public school   *approx.* **private school**
In some ways a closer approximation might be *prep school*, but one must be careful to remember that in Britain **prep school** means 'pre-prep school' in the American sense. The school system derived its name not, as did the American public school system, from the fact of public, i.e., government support, but rather from the fact that, centuries ago, certain gentlemen thought it preferable to have their children educated in a group away from home, rather than by private tutors at home. Hence the term *public school* in the sense of 'group (rather than individual) education.' The British public schools are specially endowed and though highly individualistic in their traditions have organized a type of association and in common subscribe to certain standards. They are *private schools* in the American sense. In Britain, too, there are also certain fee-charging schools that are called *private schools*, but they are not *public schools* and are therefore not *public* in either the British or the American sense. See also **prep school; council school; Common Entrance Examination.**

pudding, *n.*   **dessert**
Pudding is often shortened to (*Inf.*) *pud*, rhyming with GOOD. But see **dessert**; see also **sweet; afters.**

pudding club   **pregnancy**
Vulgar. In the pudding club (or simply *in the club*) means 'pregnant.' See also **preggers** and **in pod.**

pudsy, *adj.*   **plump**
See also **podgy; fubsy.**

puff, *n.* See **poof.**

pukka, *adj.*   **genuine**
Of Hindu origin, occasionally spelled *pucka* or *pukkah*; sometimes wrongly used to mean 'super' and 'smashing.' A *pukka sahib* is a real *gentleman*.

pull, *n.*   **1. extra measure**
                                                                   2. advantage
1. When you get more beer (or other liquid refreshment) than you ask for in a pub,
you get a *pull*, also known as a *long pull*. See also metaphorical use of **long pull.**
2. To have a *pull* over someone is to have an *advantage* over him.

pull, *v.t., Slang.*   *Slang.* **make (seduce)**

pull down   **tear down**
  House-wrecking term.

pulled down, *Inf.*   *Inf.* **under the weather**

pull one's socks up   *Inf.* **shape up; get going**
  Inf. To *start moving*, to *show more stuff: He'd better pull his socks up if he wants to keep his*
job. Americans might say *pull himself together.* See also **buck up.**

pull-up, *n.*   **diner**
  Diners, in America, can be anything from shabby to magnificent. *Pull-ups* are usually
quite shabby shacklike establishments. See also **café; transport café.**

pull up   *Slang.* **bowl over**
  In the sense of "make a deep impression on.' Thus: *It was a good play, but what really*
pulled me up was Derek's performance.

pull up sticks   *Inf.* **pull up stakes**
  Inf. Fold one's tent and move on. Cf. **up stick.**

pull (take) your finger out. See **take your finger out.**

pumpship, *n. v.i.*   **(take a) pee**
  Inf. (Stressed on the first syllable.) Sometimes two words: *pump ship.* Originally nautical, for *pump out the bilge*, it was extended to the general language as a gentlemen's
colloquialism.

pun, *v.t.*   **tamp**
  Pun appears to be a variant of *pound.* A *punner* is a *tamper*, i.e., a tool with which one
tamps the earth, rubble, etc.

punch-bag, *n.*   **punching bag**
  Note the shorter British form, as in *sunk garden, spring-clean, swing-door*, all of which
run counter to the usual tendency of the British to use the longer form, as in *banking-
account, rowing-boat,* etc. This is discussed in full at **Appendix I.A.3.**

punch-up. See **dust-up.**

puncture, *n.*   **flat**
  Puncture would sound old-fashioned or at least pedantic in America. *Flat* is slowly
being adopted by the British.

punka(h), *n.*   **ceiling electric fan**
  Old-fashioned. An Anglo-Indian term for a large fan, usually of cloth in a rectangular
frame, hanging from the ceiling and operated by a rope pulled by a servant known as
a *punka(h)-walla(h).* By extension applied to ceiling electric fans, the kind you see mostly
in period movies, now obsolescent because of the ever-widening use of air conditioning.
See **walla(h).**

punner. See **pun.**

punnet, *n.*   **small fruit basket**
  A *small basket* for vegetables or fruit, woven of thin pieces of wood which are known
in Britain as **chip.** Strawberries and raspberries are sold in Britain by the *punnet*, which

allegedly comes in one-pound and half-pound sizes, but the boxes often have crumpled paper at the bottom and thus contain as little fruit as the vendor can get away with. Nobody seems to object.

punter, *n.* **bettor**
Technically, to *punt* is to *bet against the house* in a card game; but informally it means to 'bet on a horse race' or 'speculate on the stock market,' and the usual meaning is 'bettor' or 'speculator' as the case may be. See **Appendix II.G.5.** for British betting terms. *Punter* can also mean 'John' or 'trick' in the sense of 'prostitute's client.'

purchase, hire. See **hire purchase; never-never.**

purchase tax *approx.* **excise tax**
Now replaced by the *Value Added Tax*, usually abbreviated to *V.A.T.* or *VAT*. Pronounced either way.

purler. See **come a purler.**

purpose-built, *adj.* **built to order**
Especially built for a given purpose, according to specifications, like a movie theater built as such instead of having been converted from an opera house.

purse, *n.* **money pouch**
Not used in Britain to mean 'lady's handbag.' See also **pocket book.**

push, *n.* *Slang.* **gate**
Slang. To *get the push* is to *get the gate, be fired.* See **sack.**

push along, *Inf.* *Inf.* **get moving**

push-bike *Inf.* **bike**
Inf. As distinguished from *motor-bike* and *moped.* Also *push-bicycle* and *push-cycle.*

pushcart, *n.* **baby carriage**
An occasional use; *pushcart* usually means 'handcart' and the usual term for *baby carriage* is **pram.** *Pushcart* in the American sense is **barrow** in Britain.

push-chair **stroller**

pushed for *Inf.* **pressed for**
Inf. In Britain, one is *pushed*, rather than *pressed*, for time, money, etc. *Pushed*, used alone, generally means 'pressed for time.'

push off! *Slang.* **scram!**
Slang. Synonyms under **buzz off.**

push-pin, *n.* **thumbtack**
Synonymous with **drawing-pin.**

push the boat out 1. *Inf.* **outdo oneself**
2. *Inf.* **treat**
1. *Inf.* to act more generously than the occasion requires; to be lavish, but not ostentatious. Often used in commenting on splendid entertainment one has enjoyed, particularly as a dinner guest. E.g., after a dinner party with all the stops out: *They didn't half push the boat out!* See **half, 3.**
2. *Inf.* Often heard in the expression, (*so-and-so's*) *turn to push the boat out*, meaning that it's his turn to pay (for the next round of drinks, this trip to the movies, and that sort of thing).

put about   1. *Inf.* **put out (be a nuisance)**
                                             2. *Inf.* **plant (a rumor)**
1. *Inf.* As in: *I hate to put you about, but I really need the stuff this very minute.*
2. *Inf.* As in: *It was put about that they had had an affair.*

put a bung in it!   *Slang.* **shut up!**
    Slang. An alternative to **put a sock in it!** *Bung* is easier to visualize than *sock,* somehow.

put a foot wrong   *Inf.* **slip up**
    Inf. Happily enough seen almost exclusively in the negative: *He'll never put a foot wrong,* indicating a meticulous person. Sometimes one sees *put a foot right,* also in the negative: *I can't put a foot right today* means 'I shouda stood in bed.'

put a sock in it!   *Slang.* **stow it!**
    Slang. Or a *bung.* if you prefer. The equivalent of *Belt up!* or *Pack up!* in Britain or *Shut up!* in America.

put (someone's) back up   *Inf.* **get (someone's) back up**
    Inf. The American form is used as well.

put by   **brush aside**
    As in: *The difficulties facing us cannot be put by indefinitely.*

put down   1. **put to sleep**
                                                            2. **charge**
                                                            3. *Inf.* **fold**
    Three wholly unrelated meanings:
1. Euthanasia of pets. Sad. The British expression has now become common among professional dog breeders in America.
2. *Put it down, please,* is the way the customer asks the shop to charge it. Alternatively he might have said, *Please book it to me,* or, *Book it to my account.* See also **on the slate; on tick.**
3. What a wise man does in a poker game when he senses that his chances are slim.

put down the 'phone   **hang up**

put in hand. See **have (something) put in hand.**

put (someone) in the picture   **explain the situation to (someone); bring (someone) up to date**

put it across (someone)   *Inf.* **let (someone) have it**
    Inf. To *punish.* The teacher became angry at the obstreperous pupil and really *put it across him.* To *put (something) across* also has the usual American meaning of 'put it over,' i.e., *accomplish the objective.*

put (someone) off   **disturb**
    Inf. To *put one off* one's balance, or *off* one's stride. *Off-putting* is an adjective describing the person or thing that has that effect. It seems just the least bit precious, perhaps jocularly, like other hyphenated adjectives ending in the participial *-ing,* like *shame-making.* It has the special flavor, sometimes, of *appetite-spoiling,* both literally and figuratively; it always connotes enthusiasm-dampening.

put one's arse to anchor, *Slang.*   **sit down**

put one's back into   *Slang.* **knock oneself out at**
    Slang. Expressing the idea of arduous devotion to a task at hand. See also **do one's nut, 1.**

put one's feet up   **relax**
Inf. A dinner hostess might say to a tired businessman: *Come earlier and put your feet up*. Putting one's feet up connotes easy chairs, possibly a brief nap, freshening up, and in the case of a really kind hostess, even a drink.

put one's head down   *Inf.* **get some shuteye**
Inf. Also *get one's head down*.

put one's hoof in, *Inf.*   *inf.* **get a word in edgewise**

put one's shirt on, *Inf.*   *Inf.* **bet one's bottom dollar on**

put on side   *Slang.* **put on the dog**
Slang. See also **side, 2.**

put paid to   *Inf.* **finish**
Inf. In the sense of 'put an end to.' Thus: *The rain put paid to our picnic.* Derived from the image of stamping 'paid' on a bill, thus putting an end to that transaction.

put (someone's) pot on   *Slang.* **squeal on (someone)**
Slang. To *put* Harry's *pot on* is to *squeal on* Harry.

put the boot in, *Inf.*   **1. kick hard**
                                                            2. take a decisive step

put the comether on (someone)   *Inf.* **have (someone) under one's thumb**
Inf. Sometimes it means simply to 'cajole'; generally, to 'have a strong influence over.' A contraction of *come hither* and suggestion of feminine wiles; therefore usually applied to women. Pronounced CUM-EH'-THER, rhyming with HEATHER.

put the 'phone down   **hang up**
Not as in America, where it means putting it down for a moment, as when interrupted by a knock on the door.

put the pot. See pot.

put the shutters up   *Inf.* **fold**
Slang. To *go broke* and, if necessary, into bankruptcy.

put the wind up. See get the wind up.

put-to, *n.*   *Slang.* **brass tacks; crunch**
Slang. *Harold Wilson makes brave speeches and fine promises, but when you get down to the put-to... Is there an animal-breeding connotation? Probably not; or is it an echo of the old meaning, 'harnessing horses to a carriage,' and by extension 'taking action'?*

putty, *n.*   **muddy bottom**
Nautical slang. The kind of stuff you should be careful not to get your keel stuck in.

put up   **1. *v.t.*, raise**
                                                            2. *v.i.*, run for office.
1. The rent is *put up* in Britain, *raised* in America.
2. Short for *put up the deposit* required of candidates.

put up a black   *Inf.* **fall on one's face**
Inf. To *get a black mark*; close to **blot one's copybook.**

put up the hare, *Inf.*   *Inf.* **get something going**

put up the shutters, *Slang.*   **go into bankruptcy**

put-U-up, *n.*, *Inf.*   **convertible sofa**

pyedog, *n.*   **mongrel**
  Also *pie-dog* and *pi-dog*. Term used in India for an *ownerless mongrel*, running wild.

pylon, *n.*   **high tension tower**

Q

Q.C. See **take silk.**

Q Division   SEE COMMENT
A division of Scotland Yard. See also **(the) Yard.**

quad, *n.*   *approx.* **campus**
Oxford University term, short for *quadrangle*. It denotes a square bounded by college
buildings rather than the whole campus. Some American colleges use the term *quad*.
The Cambridge equivalent is **court.**

quad, *adj.*   **quadruple (stamps)**
Inf. A now obsolete special usage in the seventies on gas station signs meaning
'quadruple trading stamps,' the kind given by retailers to customers and exchangeable
in quantity for various articles. These signs were practically ubiquitous as price wars
began in the early seventies, but started to disappear during the alleged energy crisis
of 1974. When the "crisis" was over, more modest stations revived the practice offering
treble stamps, but the spring of 1975 produced a spawning of signs reading *5-fold* and
6-fold, which logically should have read *quint* and *sext*; but when was language or gas
economics ever logical? (Gas, of course, was and is **petrol** throughout Britain.) By 1976,
despite dire warnings of new gas embargoes, a really vicious price war developed and
the old *quad* seemed pale beside such signs as *8-fold* and *10-fold,* to say nothing of
extravaganzas like *30-fold,* sometimes even coupled with discounts on the gallon price.
All ancient history by 1979 thanks to OPEC. *Sick transit.*

quadrillon. See **Appendix II.D.**

quango, *n.*   SEE COMMENT
Acronym for *Qua*si-*N*on-*G*overnment *O*rganization, coined by Anthony Barker, originally to describe American agencies in contract with the United States government. It
is now applied to a variety of advisory committees and groups working in conjunction
with governmental administrative agencies. They vary in type, procedure, effectiveness
and longevity.

quant, *n., v.t., vi.*   **boat pole**
A *quant* is a pole with a flange near the tip to prevent its sinking into mud, used to
pole or punt the boat along. As a verb, to *quant* is to pole the boat, or to punt.

quantity, bill of. See **bill of quantity.**

quantity surveyor   **materials appraiser**
Particularly in the contracting business.

quarrel with one's bread and butter   *Inf.* **bite the hand that feeds one**
Inf. Generally, like its American equivalent, restricted to negative statements, e.g.,
One shouldn't quarrel with one's bread and butter.

quart, *n.* See **Appendix II.C.2.**

quarter, *n.*   **quarter of a pound**
Inf. One asks for a *quarter* of those chocolates (pointing) at the **sweet-shop.** *Quarter
of a pound* would sound ponderous in Britain. This would apply equally, of course, to
mushrooms at the **greengrocer's,** nails at the **ironmonger's,** etc.

quarter-day, *n.*   *approx.* **due date**
Quarter-days are the four days in the year when quarterly payments traditionally fall due in Britain and are the common dates for tenancy terms. They are: **Lady Day** (March 25); Midsummer Day (June 25); Michaelmas Day (September 29); Christmas Day (December 25).

quartern, *n.*   SEE COMMENT
Four-pound loaf of bread; but they don't make them anymore.

quaver, *n.*   **eighth note**
Musical term. See **Appendix II.F.**

(the) Queen   1. SEE COMMENT
                                                                                      2. SEE COMMENT
1. *Inf.* To stay at a dance through *the Queen* is to stay to the very end. It is usual to play *God Save the Queen* to close the proceedings, and *the Queen* in this context is simply short for the title of the national anthem.
2. *Inf.* The toast to the Queen, known as the **Loyal Toast.**

Queen Mum. *See* **mummy.**

queer, *adj.*   *Inf.* **queasy**
Inf. Unwell or *indisposed,* not really ill. *I went queer* has no homosexual connotations whatsoever. There's an amusing music hall (vaudeville) song made famous by Stanley Holloway called, "My word, you *do* look queer!" See also **sick.**

queer card, *Inf.*   *Slang.* **oddball**

(in) Queer Street   *Inf.* **hard up**
When the British talk of somebody's being *in Queer Street,* they mean that he is in bad trouble, in a bad way, and usually in bad odor as well. The expression originates in the custom of writing *Quaere* ('enquire') against a person's account when it was considered advisable to make enquiries about him before trusting him.

queer the pitch   **stymie; thwart**
To *queer someone's pitch* is to *thwart him,* to *spoil his chances.* A *pitch* is part of a **cricket ground** (*field*); in **football** (*soccer*) *pitch* is used to describe the entire playing field. To *queer someone's pitch,* then, is to *mess up his game,* not literally, but figuratively in the sense of 'spoiling his chances.' There are some however, who claim that this term is not derived from cricket, but from **pitch** in the sense of the territorial prerogative of bookmakers and outdoor entertainers on the streets of London and other cities.

quench, *v.t.*   *Inf.* **squelch**
Slang. to *shut* (somebody) *up.*

query, *n., adv.*   1. *n.* **complaint**
                                                                                      2. *adv.* **approximately**
1. *n.* This connotation of *query* is not met with in America. It appears most frequently in the phrase *query department* of an organization.
2. *adv. Query,* after an adjective, indicates that the adjective is only approximate, and the quality or quantity expressed is somewhat doubtful or questionable. A teacher might characterize a student's performance (the British often use **alpha**, beta, gamma, rather than *A, B, C* in marking) as *beta-alpha query,* or *beta, query alpha,* i.e., *somewhere between A and B but I don't know exactly where,* or *beta, query minus* (*B, but perhaps* a bit closer to B minus). The newer universities prefer the A, B, C system.

question in the House   SEE COMMENT
There'll be a question in the House means, 'This is going to be brought up in Parliament at question time' (the period when **members** may question **ministers**). The nearest American equivalent would be: *This is going to be brought up in Congress,* but more likely before a House or Senate committee.

queue, *n., v.i.*   line; line up
(Pronounced CUE.) The verb sometimes takes the form *queue up*. Foreigners are often surprised at the self-imposed discipline which leads the British to form *queues*. Queue-jumping leads to very positive remonstrations. Americans stand either *in* or *on* a line; but Britons stand only *in* a queue. See **Appendix I.A.1.**

quick as thought, *Inf.*   *Inf.* **quick as a wink**

quid, *n.*   SEE COMMENT
Slang. One pound (£), referring to British money, not weight. No American slang equivalent except *buck* for *dollar*. In general use, unlike many other slang currency terms; see **Appendix II.G.** See also **have a quid each way.**

quid each way. See **have a quid each way.**

quieten, *v.t., v.i.*   quiet down

quintillion. See **Appendix II.D.**

Quis?   Who wants this?
Inf. Public school and upper middle class cant, pronounced *quiz,* addressed by an individual amid a group of his peers. The 'this' can be anything from the remains of something he has been eating (or is still eating, in which case it means 'Who wants some?') to a comic book he's through with or any old bit of anything he comes across while cleaning out his desk and wants to get rid of. The affirmative answer is *Ego* (a suitable Latin answer to a question in Latin); the negative response is *fains*. See **fains I!**

quite, *adj.*   *Inf. approx.* **up to snuff**
Inf. Quite used as an adjective—not an adverb modifying an adjective or an adverb—is found in negative expressions only, such as: *He isn't quite,* meaning, 'He isn't quite acceptable socially.'

quite, *adv.*   absolutely
Used alone, as a response, expressing more or less emphatic agreement; roughly equivalent to *That goes without saying.*

quiz, *v.t.*   *Inf.* **poke fun at**
Quiz originally meant to 'make fun of' and also to 'look curiously at,' but because of the popularity of American television quiz programs, the more common meaning of the word in Britain now is the American one, i.e., to 'interrogate.'

quod, *n.*   *Slang.* **poky**
Slang. Synonymous with **choky.** *Clink,* a slang term in both countries, is derived from an actual prison of that name in Southwark (SE London) where there is still a *Clink Street.* The old prison is long since gone. See also **porridge, 2.**

quoit, *n.*   dolmen
Quoits are stone uprights supporting a capstone. They are prehistoric, and found in the West Country, often covered with earth forming a tomb. Derek Parker, in *The West Country* (Batsford, 1973), speaks of the Lanyon *Quoit,* near Penzance, and Trevethy *Quoit,* at St. Cleer.

R

rabbit, *n.*
Inf. In sports, a beginner or a player of little skill; a *duffer.*

Inf. **dub**

rabbit on
Slang. On and on; and on. Originates from rhyming slang (see **Appendix II.G.3.**) *rabbit and pork* (shortened to *rabbit*) for *talk.*

jabber away

R.A.C. *See* **A.A.**

race-course, *n.*
The British never use *race-track* for horse racing but do use the term for auto racing and use *dog-track* for greyhound racing, which is sometimes colloquially shortened to **greycing.**

racetrack

Rachmanism, *n.*
Inf. The despicable practice of taking over lower-class residential property and deliberately creating intolerable living conditions in order to force the poor tenants to get out, so that the landlord can then turn the property to more profitable commercial uses. The term is derived from a man named Rachman, who in the 1960s pioneered in this type of manipulation.

SEE COMMENT

racialist, *n., adj.*
And *racialism* is *racism.*

racist

rackety, *adj., Slang.*

Slang. **harum scarum**

rackrent, *n.,*
Rackrenting is the wicked practice.

extortionate rent

R.A.D.A.
(Pronounced RA'DA—A as in HAT—as an acronym.)

Royal Academy of Dramatic Art

radiogram, *n.*
By *radiogram* Americans mean 'wireless message.' *Radiogram* is no longer heard much in Britain. See **music centre.**

radio-phonograph

R.A.F.
This doughty band, who fought the Battle of Britain, are almost invariably referred to by their initials. The veterans are entitled to, and often do wear a characteristic moustache, very full and long, with the ample ends curving upwards. This is known as an *R.A.F. moustache.* A ten-year-old once described someone to the author as 'a man with an R.A.F. moustache.' The little chap didn't know what *R.A.F.* stood for, had never heard of the Royal Air Force, and was puzzled by the expression *Battle of Britain.*

Royal Air Force

rafferty, *adj.*
Slang. All mixed up; confused. Apparently derived from *raff,* meaning 'refuse' (the noun), and *raff* seems to have been extracted from *riff-raff,* though some say that it comes from the Irish family name, and others base it on a corruption of *refractory. Rafferty rules* are defined as *no rules at all,* especially in the boxing world, and appear to have been invented in Australia, which, after all, is a pretty wild place. Something that has happened or is done *according to Rafferty* (or *Rafferty's*) *rules* occurs as jungle instincts dictate, without regard to discipline or restraint.

disorganized

rag, *v.t., v.i., n.*   1. *v.i., v.t., Inf.* **fool around; tease**
                                                 2. *n., Inf.* **stunt; gag**
                                                 3. *n.,* **coarse stone**
1. *Inf. Rag* is used intransitively to mean 'fool around' or 'kid around,' in a manner involving a little mild horseplay. Transitively it means to 'tease' or to 'pull someone's leg.'
2. *Inf.* A *rag* is a *stunt* or *gag* and from this use we get *rag-week*, which is a week at the university during which students put on *stunts* in aid of charity, especially dressing up and riding around on weird and grotesque floats.
3. *Rag* is also a variety of hard coarse stone.

rag-and-bone man, *Inf.*   *Inf.* **junkman**

raglan. See under balaclava.

raid, *n.*   **burglary**
In America *raid* brings up the image of a group assault of one sort or another, particularly military or police. One often reads in British newspapers of a *raid* made last night on a house or shop. All it means is a 'burglary' effectuated by one or more persons called *raiders*. A *share raid* is something different: an attempt to gain control of a corporation by buying up shares through tempting offers to shareholders, a takeover attempt.

railway, scenic. See scenic railway; switchback.

rain stair-rods   *Inf.* **rain cats and dogs**
Inf. Synonymous with **bucket down; pour with rain.**

raise the wind. See get the wind up.

rake up   *Inf.* **dig up**
Inf. In the sense of 'procuring with difficulty.' Also used in Britain in the usual American sense of 'bringing up an old sore subject,' like a complaint or a scandal.

rally, *v.t., Inf.*   *Inf.* **pull (someone's) leg; kid**

ramp, *n.*   **1. bump**
                                                        2. *Slang.* **racket**
1. A special use, to denote a bump deliberately built into a private or restricted road to encourage people to drive very slowly; synonymous with **rumble strip.** The term is used as well to denote the point at which the true and the temporary surfaces join where road repairs are going on. The road signs say BEWARE RAMP. The *bump* in question is occasioned by the fact that the temporary surface is at a somewhat higher level.
2. *Slang. Ramp* is also sometimes used as transitive or intransitive verb meaning 'swindle.'

randy, *adj., Slang.*   *Slang.* **horny**

ranker, *n.*   **1. soldier in the ranks**
                                                 2. officer risen from the ranks

rape, *n.*   SEE COMMENT
Dont' be alarmed if you see one *rape* after another when you look at an old map of the County of Sussex, England. That is what the old divisions of the county used to be called.

rare, *adj.*   *approx. Inf.* **great**
Inf. Rare is an informal intensive. A *rare* lot of something is a *helluva* lot of it. *Rare* also implies *excellence.* A *rare* something is a *splendid* something. A *rare* time is a *swell* time; a *rare old* time is even sweller. But watch out, because in the expression, have a *rare time of it, rare time* means quite the opposite: a 'tough time.'

rate, *n.*   **local tax**
Usually in the plural, meaning 'local real estate taxes.' A *ratepayer* is a local *taxpayer*.

Rather!, *interj., Inf.*   *Inf.* **And how!**

rating, *n.*   **able seaman**
Low form of human marine life.

rat rhyme   **doggerel**
Inf. Pronounced RATRIM, and heard mainly in Scotland.

rats!   *Slang.* **baloney!**
Slang. Not *oh hell!* as in America, especially among followers of *Peanuts.*

ratten, *v.t.*   **molest by stealing or damaging tools**

rattling, *adj., adv.*   **1. brisk**
                                                                                                                     2. *Slang.* **damned**
1. *Inf.* A *rattling* pace is a *brisk* one.
2. *Inf.* A *rattling* good wine is an *unusually* good one or more likely a *damned* good one.
In the adverbial use, *rattling* has about the same meaning as **ripping.**

raver, *n.*   *Slang.* **knockout**
Slang. In the sense of *raving beauty.* Synonymous with the old-fashioned Briticisms
stunner, smasher, etc.

ravers. See **stark ravers.**

(have a) rave-up, *n.*   *Slang.* **(have a) ball**
Slang. A helluva good time.

razzle, *n.*   *Slang.* **spree; binge; toot**
Slang. Americans (the lucky ones) go on a *spree*; happy Britons go on *the razzle*. They
also go on *the spree* (note the definite article). See **Appendix I.A.2.**

R.D.   **insufficient funds**
These letters are an abbreviation of **Refer to drawer.**

R.D.C.   SEE COMMENT
These letters are short for *Rural District Council,* the governing body of a *rural district,*
once an area comprising a group of parishes, now become obsolete since the creation
of *district councils.* See **council; parish.**

reach-me-down, *adj.*   *Inf.* **ready-made**
Slang. As a plural noun *reach-me-downs* became slang for *ready-made clothes.* It must
have come from the image of a salesperson *reaching* to get a stock garment *down* off a
shelf. Not heard now: *off-the-peg* is the common term, and *ready-made* is creeping in.
Unrelated to American *hand-me-down.*

read, *v.t.*   **major in**
One *reads* philosophy at Oxford, for example, or law, or chemistry.

read, *n.*   SEE COMMENT
A *read* is a spell of reading, time spent in reading, an opportunity to read. Like the
noun **spend,** *read* in this sense is an example of a verb that becomes a noun.

reader, *n.*   *approx.* **associate professor**
In a British university, the order of academic hierarchy is assistant lecturer, lecturer,
senior lecturer, *reader,* and professor. The term *professor* is more exclusive than in America, where it covers the grades of assistant professor and associate professor, as well as
(full) professor. See also **don; fellow; master.**

reading glass   magnifying glass

read (someone; something) up   **read up on (someone; something)**
E.g., *I read him up before interviewing him*, or, *I read the subject up before lecturing on it.*

(the) ready, *n.*   *Slang.* **dough**
Inf. Ready is colloquially short for *ready cash.* Sometimes, *the readies.* Synonymous with
brass; dibs; lolly.

ready for off, *Inf.*   **ready to go**

reafforest, *v.t., v.i.*   **reforest**
The noun is *reafforestation.* Lawrence Durrell, in *The Greek Islands* (Faber & Faber,
London, 1978) uses a hypen in speaking of the "re-afforestation" of the Island of Crete.
Both countries use *afforest* to describe the planting of land with trees, but they differ as
above in describing the renewal of forest cover. The British may have been influenced
by *reaffirm.*

real jam. See **jam.**

rebate, *n.*   **rabbet**
Term used in framing. But **joiners** (*carpenters*) say *rabbet.*

recce, *n.*   *Inf.* **gander (look-see)**
Inf. An abbreviation of *reconnaissance* which became the offical term among the military
from World War I days, when one *went out on a recce.* It is pronounced RECKY and is in
the general language. *Shall we try that pub? Let's have* (or *do*) *a recce first.* See also **shufty.**

Received Pronunciation   SEE COMMENT
Commonly called *R.P.* This term is described by Barbara M.H. Strang in her book
Modern English Structure (Edward Arnold Ltd., London, 1962) as "...an accent which
can be heard from speakers originating in any part of England, but still local in the
sense that it is confined virtually to English people and those educated at English **public
schools.**" She believes that this accent "...can best be called by the name assigned to it
by Daniel Jones [author of *Outline of English Phonetics* and *English Pronouncing Dictionary*],
Received Pronunciation (RP)." She goes on to quote from David Abercrombie's *Problems
and Principles* (Longmans, Green & Co. Ltd., London, 1955) as follows:

> RP, as a matter of fact, is an accent which is more than unusual: it is, I believe, of
> a kind which cannot be found anywhere else. In all other countries, whether English-
> speaking or not, all educated people have command of the standard form of the
> language, but when they talk it they have an accent which shows the part of the
> country from which they come. One of the accents of the country, perhaps, is pop-
> ularly regarded as the "best" accent, but that is always an accent which belongs to
> one locality or another....In England, RP is looked on as the "best" accent, but it is
> not the accent of the capital or of any other part of the country. Every town, and
> almost every village, contains speakers of RP whose families have lived there for
> generations. It is significant that the question "Where is the best English spoken?" is
> never debated by the English. Those who speak RP are set apart from other educated
> people by the fact that when they talk, one cannot tell where they come from. See
> also **Appendix I.B.; BBC English.**

Prof. Stanley Ellis of the University of Leeds confirms this in an interview published
in *The Sunday Telegraph* (London) of September 21, 1980:

> ...there are really no traces of regional accent in upper-class speech anywhere in En-
> gland, and haven't been for quite a long time.

But he adds a reservation:

> The concept of "standard English," or what is nowadays called RP (Received Pro-
> nunciation) is useful but misleading. I have another category which I call Super-RP,
> the speech of the landed aristocracy. I should find it easier to distinguish the borderline
> between RP and Super-RP than between RP and the rest.

reception, *n.*   **1. office**
       2. front desk
1. A sign on a place of business reading *Reception* would read *Office* in America.
2. *Reception* at a hotel would be known as the *desk* or *front desk* in America; and the *reception clerk* or *receptionist* at a hotel is called *room clerk* in America.

reception room, *n.*   SEE COMMENT
There is no single American word covering this category. It is used almost exclusively by professionals engaged in real estate brokerage and in advertisements for the sale or rent of houses. *Reception room* is a generic term embracing living room, dining room, library, study, den, and so on.

record, *v.i.*   **score**
(Accent on the second syllable.) A term in contract bridge: *We've recorded!* cries the hitherto scoreless player to his partner.

recordal, *n.*   **recording**
The *recording* of a document.

record card   **index card**

recorded delivery   *Approx.* **certified mail**
The post office (**G.P.O.**) gives you a *certificate of posting (mailing)* but holds on to the *certificate of delivery. Registered post* is the approximate equivalent of *special handling,* and allows insurance up to a certain sum. An *A.R. (advice of receipt,* also known as *advice of delivery)* is the approximate equivalent of a *return receipt* in America.

recorder, *n.*   **criminal court judge**

recovery van   **tow car**
Also called *wrecker* in America. Cf. **ambulance** 2.

red as a turkey-cock, *Inf.*   *Inf.* **red as a beet**

red Biddy   **dago red**
Slang. Any cheap red wine. See also **plonk.**

redbrick university   SEE COMMENT
This term designates a British university other than Oxford and Cambridge; but London, Durham, and certain other universities, though they came later, often qualify as well for exclusion from this somewhat pejorative appellation. The name is derived from the use of red brick in the building of the first universities established after the original old ones, which were constructed of gray stone. Now, happily, *redbrick universities* are built of whatever pleases the architect, including at times even gray stone. Used alone, as an adjective, *redbrick* connotes a "self-made" image as opposed to the privileged, upper-class image of Oxford. See also **Oxbridge.**

redcap   **military policeman**

redemption fee   **prepayment penalty**
A term used in mortgage financing; the fee charged for paying off before maturity.

Red Indian   **Indian**
Meaning 'American Indian.' When a Briton says *Indian* he means a 'native of India.' If he has in mind an *American Indian,* he says *Red Indian.*

redirect, *v.t.*   **forward**
Directions to post office on envelope: *Redirect to...*

red rag   *Inf.* **red flag**
Inf. Usually in the phrase *a red rag to a bull.*

redundant, *adj.*   **(made or become) unemployed**
This is a harsh and dreadful word normally used in Britain to describe a person who
has lost his job because of automation, reorganization, or deterioration of economic
conditions generally, and not through any fault of his own. *Redundancy* is the equally
oppressive noun for the condition. To *make someone redundant* is, simply, to terminate
his employment, or, even more simply, to fire him, or, euphemistically, to let him go.
In the plural, *redundancies* means *unemployment generally*, in a sentence like: *There has
been a considerable increase in redundancies in that area*. *Redundant* is met with occasionally,
in British usage, in the sense of *superfluous*, as in *Home computers will make newspapers
redundant*, or *Improved widespread electronic communications systems will make daily trips to
the office redundant*. The word is not used that way in America. It is used, commonly in
Britain and exclusively in America, in its grammatical application, to indicate tautology
(as in *free gift*). One would wish that the British had avoided the unfortunate imagery
of superfluousness in the field of employment. *Redundancy pay* is the common term for
severance pay.

reel, *n.*   **spool**
Reel of cotton is *spool of thread*. See also **cotton**.

referee   **reference**
A *referee* is *one who gives you a reference* when you are applying for a job, admission to
a club, etc.

refer to drawer   **insufficient funds**
Although the British phrase (sometimes abbreviated R.D.) is much more elegant and
discreet, it imparts the same gloomy news as the American one. *No effects* was the old
term in Britain, but has been in disuse for many years, giving way to the euphemistic
legend *Refer to drawer*, discreetly written in red on the upper left-hand corner of the
face of the check (**cheque**). This is the customary procedure where the maker's bank
doesn't trust him, and as in America, returns the check to the payee's bank, which then
debits the payee's account. If the maker's bank trusts its depositor, the legend (still in
red ink) is lengthened to: *Refer to drawer; please re-present* (note hyphen). This invitation
to the payee's bank to try again reflects the bank's willingness to give its depositor a
chance to make good, when the payee, notified by his bank, gives the maker the bad
news. A third legend on a deposited check reads: *Effects not cleared*. This means that on
the face of it the maker had deposited enough money in check form to cover his own
check, but the deposit hasn't cleared yet. The American equivalent of *Effects not cleared*
is *Uncollected funds*. In this case, the impression is given that the maker's bank doesn't
quite trust him; but again, the payee's account is not debited unless the uncollected
funds remain uncollected. See also **overdraft**, which is quite another matter in Britain.
Refer to maker has now been adopted by American banks in certain cases. See also **Queer
Street**.

Reform Jew   **Conservative Jew**
See also **Liberal Jew**.

refuse tip   **garbage dump**
See also **tip**. *Refuse collector* has now been replaced by **sanitation officer**, the new
official name for **dustman** (garbage man).

(the) regions, *n. pl.*   SEE COMMENT
The country outside London and the **Home Counties**. This is a relatively new term
for what used to be called *the provinces*, born, it is believed, of the desire to get away
from the connotations of provinciality. It also has implications of **devolution** (home
rule) and local identity.

register, v.t.   **check**
The British *register* their *luggage*. The Americans *check* their *baggage*.

registered post. See **recorded delivery**.

Register Office   **marriage clerk's office**
Often incorrectly called *Registry Office* by the British. A *registry* is something quite different.

registrar, *n.*   **resident doctor**
Hospital term describing a doctor on call who is an assistant to a specialist.

registry, *n.*   **domestic employment agency**
Where you go if you still have the money and the courage to seek domestic servants.

relief, *n.*   **deduction; exemption**
Income-tax terminology. On your British income tax return you get *relief* for business expenses and *relief* for dependents. The analogous American terms would be *deductions* and *exemptions*. *Tax relief,* as a general term, would be called *tax benefit* in America.

relief, out- or **outdoor.** See **outdoor relief.**

remand home   **reformatory**
Reform school is used in both countries. See also **borstal.**

Remembrance Sunday   **Veterans' Day**
Formerly *Remembrance Day.* The Sunday nearest November 11, originally called *Armistice Day* in both countries, a day for honoring the memory of those who fell in World War I (the **Great War** in Britain). After World War II the concept was enlarged to embrace the additional victims and the names were correspondingly modified.

remembrancer, *n.*   SEE COMMENT
Still seen in the official titles *King's* (or *Queen's*) *Remembrancer,* an officer charged with the collection of debts due the monarch, and *City Remembrancer* (usually shortened to *Remembrancer*), who represents the City of London (see **City**) before committees of Parliament. With a lower-case *r* it has the same meaning in both countries: 'reminder,' 'memento.'

remission, *n.*   **time off**
For good behavior, presumably; a term in penology.

remould, *n., v.t.*   **retread**
The British *remould their tyres;* the Americans *retread their tires.*

removals, *n. pl.*   **moving**
Thus, on a business sign: J. SMITH & COMPANY, REMOVALS. On large moving vans it is common to see the phrase REMOVAL SPECIALISTS. See also **pantechnicon.**

remove, *n.*   **1. degree removed**
                                              2. partial school promotion
                                                      3. food course
1. This meaning is shared with America, where, however, it is seen much less frequently than in Britain. The British speak of something which is one *remove* from the **dustbin,** which means 'one step removed' from the garbage can, i.e., just about ready to be thrown out; or something may be based at *several removes* on something else, thus constituting a thinly disguised plagiarism in the arts, for instance.
2. A *partial promotion* at school, moving the student up a half-grade. It has nothing whatever to do with being removed from school. In some schools a *remove* does not mean the *promotion* but rather the *intermediate grade* itself to which the student is promoted if he is not poor enough to stay back but not good enough to go up a whole grade.
3. A distinct archaic meaning, used rather pretentiously in certain smart circles, is that of a 'dish' or 'course' at a meal, usually the one after the main dish.

renter, *n.*   **exhibitor**
In the special sense of 'film exhibitor,' one who owns or operates a motion picture house.

rent-protected, *adj.*   **rent controlled**
Referring to government protection of tenants.

repairing lease   **net lease**
Under which the tenant pays all the maintenance expenses, including real estate taxes (**rates**) and a net rental to the landlord. The complete technical label is *full repairing and insuring lease.*

reserve, *n.*   **1. surplus**
                                                                              2. reservation
1. Term used in corporate finance.
2. As in *game reserve; Indian reserve. Reservation* in this sense is strictly American.

reserve price   **upset price**
At auctions.

reset, *v.t., v.i.*   **receive (stolen goods)**
Used by itself intransitively, it means to 'act as a fence.'

resident, *n.*   **person registered at a hotel**
Nothing to do with domicile. See **non-resident.**

residual estate   **residuary estate**
A term relating to the administration of estates denoting what's left after expenses, debts, taxes, and specific and cash legacies.

responsions, *n. pl.*   SEE COMMENT
Oxford entrance examination, originally the first of three examinations for an Oxford B.A. and colloquially called **smalls**. The name was later applied to the entrance examination which was abolished in 1960. There are now two examinations: **moderations** (called *mods*) and *final schools* (called **Greats** when the subject is classics).

restaurant car   **dining car**
Another British name for this luxury, which is beginning to disappear in Britain, is *buffet car* (see **buffet**). The menu in a buffet car is, however, much more restricted. Many long distance trains have both.

resurrection gate. See **lich gate.**

resurrection pie, *Slang.*   **dish made of leftovers**

retrospective, *adj.*   **retroactive**
Describing the effect, e.g., of a statute applicable to past actions or events. But a retroactive pay raise would normally be described as *back-dated.*

return, *n.*   **round-trip ticket**
In Britain one might ask for a *return* to London on the train or bus, meaning a 'round-trip ticket.' A *day return* is valid only that day on certain trains; one can also purchase a *period return* where the return journey must be completed by a specific date. A one-way ticket is called a *single.*

return, *v.t.*   **elect**
The electorate *returns* a candidate. There is an echo of this usage in *election returns.*

return post   return mail

(the) Revenue, *n.*   **Treasury; I.R.S.**
The technical names of the central taxing authorities are *Inland Revenue Department* (Britain) and *Internal Revenue Service* (United States). The British often shorten their name to *the Revenue;* the common names in America are *the I.R.S* and *the Treasury. Revenue,* as the subject of a sentence, would be followed by a plural verb: *Revenue have expressed the opinion...*See **Appendix I.A.4.** Also **inland.**

reverse camber. See **camber.**

reverse-charge call. See **transferred charge call.**

reversionary interest   **remainder (interest)**
These are legal terms relating to trusts, a complicated field indeed, and if this kind of thing baffles you, read no further but show this to the family lawyer. In British law, a *reversionary interest* is an interest in property that vests after an intervening interest like a life estate or the right to income for a stated period. In American law, a *reversionary interest* or *reversion* is an interest retained by the creator of a trust, which takes effect after the termination of the trust. What the British call a *reversionary interest* would be called a *remainder interest,* or simply a *remainder* in America. If one considers the Latin origin, *reversio,* meaning literally a 'return before the journey is completed' as opposed to *reditus* meaning a 'return after the completion of a journey,' the American usage would appear to be correct and the British incorrect.

revise. See **revision.**

revision, *n.*   **review**
A school term for reviewing past work in preparation for examinations. Also, as a transitive verb, *revise* meaning *review.* Thus, *We are now revising our Latin verbs.* See also **prep.**

reynardism, *n.*   SEE COMMENT
A word coined by Siegfried Sassoon, who, according to his memoir, *The Weald of Youth* (Faber & Faber, London, 1942; see **Weald**), "was suffering from an overdose of *reynardism*" and needed "a spell of solitude and invigorative reading." He used it again (this time with an upper case *R*) in *Diaries 1923-1925* (Faber & Faber, London, 1985) when he "ceased to regret his exile from *Reynardism.*" The *reynard* in *reynardism* relates to the name given the fox in the medieval beast epic *Reynard the Fox.* For another Sassoon coinage, see **hurroosh.**

rhino, *n.*   *Slang.* **dough**
Slang. The wherewithal, possibly referring to the high value the Chinese place on rhinoceros horn, which they regard as an aphrodisiac. See also **ready; lolly; brass; corn.**

rhubarb, *n.*   **stage mob noise**
Inf. The actors murmur or shout 'rhubarb' to one another.

ribbon development   **linear suburban expansion**
Building development parallel to a highway, between villages or towns, containing residences, shops, necessary services, etc., instead of circular expansion, thus (theoretically) tending to preserve more of the green belt, but not looked upon with favor. Much talked about in the thirties.

rickle, *n., v.t.*   **haystack**
Mostly North of England, where it is also used more generally to mean a 'loose pile' of anything, like hay or brush. As a verb it means 'stack.'

ride, *n.* **forest riding-path**
There is an uncommon American use of *ride* as a noun denoting a road built especially for riding. As used in Britain, ther term implies that the road in question runs through the woods. Such roads anywhere help reduce the risk of forest fires. In Britain, there are some country lanes called 'Ride,' rather than 'Lane' or (Heaven forbid!) 'Street.' (See **close** for the British insistence on avoiding the lowly designation 'Street.') An illustration of the use of *ride* as a noun is found in the *Siegfried Sassoon Diaries, 1920– 1922* (Faber & Faber, London, 1981). Reminiscing about the "jolly old days of hunting in Sussex," Sassoon writes of the "early-morning chorus of...hounds in a large *well-rided* woodland." *Well-rided* sounds, at first blush, like baby-talk for *well-ridden,* but all it means is that those woods were crisscrossed with *rides,* though they were undoubtedly well-ridden as well.

ride bodkin. See **bodkin.**

riding, *n.* SEE COMMENT
Subdivision of a county. Not used except with respect to Yorkshire, which is understood in the names the *North Riding,* the *East Riding,* and the *West Riding.* The *South Riding,* like *East Dakota* and *West Carolina,* is nonexistent. There can be only three, because *riding* was originally *thriding,* meaning a 'one-third part.' *Thriding* lost its *th* because it was hard to pronounce after No*rth,* Eas*t,* and Wes*t.*

rigging screw **turnbuckle**
A nautical term, interchangeable with *bottle screw.*

right, *adj.* *Inf.* **real**
Inf. Used like *proper,* as in *He's a right hero,* or *She's a right friend.* Usually humorous; sometimes ironical, as in the case of a friend who turned out to be of the fair weather variety. See also **proper.**

righty-ho!, *interj.* *Inf.* **sure! O.K.!**
Inf. Also *rightio, righty-o, right ho, righto, right-oh.* These are all terms of assent to an order or proposal, not to a statement. *Right enough* means 'certainly,' as in *Look over there, that's George right enough.*

rig-out, *n.* *Inf.* **getup**
Inf. Usually applied to a person's unusual outfit or attire.

ring book **loose-leaf notebook**

ring doughnut. See **doughnut.**

ring-road; ringway, *n.* **beltway; by-pass**
A single route around a town; a *by-pass.* In a big city like London, it can consist of a succession of streets constituting a route arranged to avoid congested points. See also **orbital.**

rip, *n.* *Inf.* **hell raiser**
Inf. Literally, a *lecher,* a man of lax morals, but more commonly much less pejorative, with the emphasis on mischief and usually applied to youngsters.

ripping, *adj.* *Inf.* **great**
Slang. Ripping is also used as an adverb with *good*: one can have a *ripping* time or a *ripping good* time. Once in a while one hears the adverb *rippingly,* as in *Things went rippingly.* Used only by older folks and practically out of the language now. See also **rattling.**

rise, *n.*   **1. raise**
                                                                              2. gain
1. In salary.
2. On the stock market. And a *fall* is a *loss*. Some newspaper stock market reports list
the number of *rises* and *falls*, rather *gains* and *losses*.

rise, *v.i.*   **adjourn**
The House (of Commons) *rises* for the summer recess or at the end of a session.

rising, *adv.*   *Inf.* **going on**
Inf. Used only in expressions of age, as in *she is sixteen, rising seventeen*. Synonymous
with **coming.**

rising powder   **baking powder**
Both terms are used in Britain.

rising damp. See **damp course.**

risk, at. See **at risk.**

rithe, *n.*   **brook**
Rarely found.

riveting, *adj.*   **fascinating; absorbing**
A melodramatic participial adjective to describe something that attracts and holds
one's attention, to the exclusion of whatever else is happening; that glues one to his
chair or keeps one on the edge of it. *Too riveting* means 'terribly exciting.' *Positively
riveting* means 'utterly fascinating.'

roach, *n.*   **small carplike fish**
Caught for sport only in streams and an occasional moat. Eaten very rarely, if at all,
nowadays and then only experimentally.

road-metal. See **metalled road.**

road, *n.*   **way**
Inf. The British use *road* in a number of instances where Americans use *way*. *In
someone's road* means 'in someone's way,' and to *get out of someone's road* is to *get out of
his way*. In Gloucestershire, *anyroad* sometimes takes the place of *anyway*, in the sense
of 'nevertheless.' But rail*road* is the common term in America, rail*way* in Britain. The
accidents of language!

road-sweeper, *n.*   **street cleaner**

Road Up   **Road Under Repair**
Roadside warning sign.

roadway, *n.*   **pavement**
Pavement in Britain means 'sidewalk.'

ROAD WORKS   **MEN WORKING**
Roadside warning sign.

Robert. See **bobby.**

rocket, *n.*   *Slang.* **hell**
Slang. A *severe reprimand*. To *get a rocket* is to *catch hell*.

rod in pickle for. See **have a rod in pickle for.**

roger, *n., v.t.*   *Slang.* **screw**
Slang. Vulgar slang for the act of love.

rollie, also **rolley.** See **roll-up.**

roll-neck, *adj.*   SEE COMMENT
Applied to sweaters with a loose, rolled down collar. See also **polo-neck; turtleneck.**

roll-on, *n.*   **girdle**
A lady's undergarment.

roll-up   SEE COMMENT
A hand-rolled cigarette. Much more common in Britain, due to the price of cigarettes.
Also, *rollie; rolley.* See also **skin.**

roly-poly pudding   SEE COMMENT
Suet pudding wrapped in a cloth and steamed. Called **spotted dog** when improved
with currants or raisins.

roneo, *v.t.*   **duplicate**
Inf. On a roneo machine, a sort of mimeographing apparatus which may no longer
be extant.

roof, *n.*   **top**
In automobile context, a *roof* in Britain is a *hard top.* A soft one, i.e., a *convertible top,*
is called a *hood* in Britain. See **Appendix II.E.**

roofer, *n.*   *Inf.* **bread-and-butter letter**
Inf. Synonymous with **Collins.**

roof-rack, *n.*   **luggage rack**
See **Appendix II.E.**

roopy, *adj., Slang.*   **hoarse**

ropy, *adj.*   *Slang.* **cheesy**
Slang. Shabby, coming apart at the seams, like threadbare clothes or a nearly extinct
jalopy. It is occasionally used about oneself, as in *I'm feeling ropy as hell.* The usual
circumstance is a hangover. See also **grotty.**

rose, *n.*   *Inf.* **frog**
Inf. In the sense of a 'flower holder,' i.e., the article on the bottom of a shallow vase
into which you stick the stems. For another variety, see **maizie.**

rot, *v.t., v.i.*   **1. spoil**
                                                                          2. *Inf.* **kid**
1. *Slang.* To *rot* a plan is to *spoil* it.
2. *Slang.* Intransitively, to *rot* is to *kid around,* to *tease.*

rot, *n.*   **1. nonsense**
                                                                          2. SEE COMMENT
1. Common to both countries, but much oftener heard in Britain.
2. A term expressing a sudden series of failures in an endeavor (business, sport, etc.)
Thus, *A rot set in,* or (especially at cricket, when your **side** is collapsing) *Stop the rot!*

rota, *n.*   **roster**
List of persons acting in turn. *By rota* means 'in turn.' Saturday morning **surgery**
(definition 1) is taken *by rota,* by the three doctors in group practice in the author's
village.

rotten borough   SEE COMMENT
   In olden days, **Members** (of Parliament) represented *boroughs* (towns; *borough* comes from old English *burg*). A *rotten borough* was one which had degenerated in size, or even ceased to exist as a town, but continued to be represented in Parliament despite its lack of a constituency. They were abolished by the British Reform Act of 1832.

rough, *n.*   **1. heavy work**
                                                   2. *Slang.* **tough**
1. *Slang.* The *rough* is used to indicate the *heavy work* around the house. Thus, there might be a companion type of servant who did the cooking but somebody else in the household to do the *rough*.
2. *Slang.* Street rowdy; *tough guy.*

round, *n., prep., adv.*   **1. sandwich**
                                                   2. route
                                                   3. around
1. The British use the word *sandwich* the way the Americans do. After all, it was the Earl of Sandwich who is supposed to have invented the sandwich, because he ate meat between slices of bread during a twenty-four-hour gambling bout. But in a British pub you will more often hear the customers ask for a *round* of ham or a *round* of beef than for a *sandwich*. This is to distinguish a complete square from a diagonal half.
2. *Round* also means 'route,' in the sense of 'delivery route.' See also **country round; roundsman.**
3. In Britain, *round* is used in almost every case where *around* would be used in America. See also **about** for another British equivalent of the American *around.*

roundabout, *n.*   **1. traffic circle**
                                                   2. merry-go-round
2. See also **carousel.**

rounders, *n. pl.*   SEE COMMENT
   Children's game resembling baseball.

round on   **1.** *Inf.* **turn on**
                                                   2. *Slang.* **squeal on**
1. *Inf.* To make some kind of unexpected answer to someone, implying an angry retort; to *let him have it.*
2. *Inf.* To *peach* on him.

roundsman, *n.*   **delivery man**
   With a regular route; thus, the baker's *roundsman*, the milk *roundsman*. See **country round.**

round the bend   *Slang.* **crazy**
   Slang. Usually in the expression *drive round the bend*, meaning 'drive crazy.' Also, **round the twist.**

round the twist. See **round the bend.**

Rover ticket   *approx.* **unlimited travel ticket**
   A *Rover* or *Rover ticket*, purchased from a transportation company, provides unlimited travel for a given period within a given area. The term has been derived, of course, from the romantic verb to *rove*, but has clearly strayed from its origin in the term *Rover Pass*, meaning a sort of season ticket permitting one to park at a discount as often as one wishes in a particular garage for a specified period—which seems like an especially stationary way to rove. *Rover-ticket* has been extended to include *general admission* to certain sports events.

row-de-dow, *n.*   **uproar**
   Inf. Obsolescent.

rowlock *n.*　　　　　　　　　　　　　　　　　　　　　**oarlock**
(Pronounced ROLLOCK or RULLOCK).

Rowton House　　　　　　　　　　　　　　　　　　SEE COMMENT
A type of lodging for poor men, with better conditions than what the British call a *common lodging-house*, one usually fitted out with a dormitory with beds that can be rented for the night. *Rowton houses* were named after Lord Rowton, an English social reformer (1838–1903) who became interested in London housing conditions and devised a plan for a hotel for poor men. The first one opened in Vauxhall in 1892, and was so successful that a company was formed that built a chain of similar accommodations, which became known as *Rowton Houses*.

royal, *n.*　　　　　　　　　　　　　　　**member of the royal family**
Inf. Can also apply to foreign royalty, though there isn't much left.

Royal Commission　　　　　　　　　　　　　　　　SEE COMMENT
A body of persons appointed by the Crown to look into and file a report on some matter. Cf. **working party**. Sir Alan Herbert (A.P. Herbert) wrote some verses in the early thirties on the subject:
　　I am the Royal Commission on kissing,
　　　Appointed by Gladstone in '74.
　　The rest of my colleagues are buried
　　　or missing,
　　Our minutes were lost in the last
　　　Great War.
　　But still I'm a Royal Commission,
　　　My task I intend to see through,
　　Though I know as an old politician
　　　Not a thing will be done if I do.
It would appear that, unlike a working party, a Royal Commission is all too often a device created to give an indecent burial to a nagging question.

rozzer, *n.*　　　　　　　　　　　　　　　　　　*Slang.* **cop**
Slang. An outmoded term. The British share *fuzz* with the Americans. See **bobby** for synonyms.

RP. See **Received Pronunciation.**

R.S.M.　　　　　　　　　　　　　　　　　　　　SEE COMMENT
The initials stand for *regimental sergeant-major*, which in certain contexts has become a more or less generic bit of symbolism of the strict disiplinarian.

rub along　　　　　　　　　　　　　　　　　　　*Inf.* **get by**
Inf. As in *How do you manage without a maid? Oh, we rub along.*

rubber, *n.*　　　　　　　　　　　　　　　　　　　　　**eraser**
It does not mean 'contraceptive' in Britain.

rubbish!　　　　　　　　　　　　　　　　　　*Interj.* **nonsense!**
Interj. Or *tommyrot!* The British term is rarely used as an interjection in America.

rub up the wrong way　　　　　　　　　　　*Inf.* **rub the wrong way**
Inf. See **Appendix I.A.3.**

ruby, *n.*　　　　　　　　　　　　　　　　　　　　*approx.* **agate**
Type size of 5½ points.

ruck, *n.*   **1. common herd**
2. *Slang.* **also-rans**
3. rugby scrum
1. *Slang.* Usually seen in the phrase *common ruck,* or the phrase *ruck and truck.*
2. *Slang.* In a more limited sense, it refers to the main body of competition left out of
the running.
3. *Slang.* A specialized meaning. See **scrum.**

ruddy, *adj.*   *Slang.* **damned**
Slang. Ruddy came into use as a euphemism for **bloody.**

rude, *adj.*   **1. inconsiderate**
2. frank
3. *Inf.* **dirty (indecent)**
4. robust
Apart from its several common meanings shared with America, this adjective has
several uses in Britain not found in America:
1. *Inconsiderate,* as in: *It is rude of me not to let you know my plans sooner.*
2. *Frank, outspoken, indiscreet,* as in: *May I be rude and tell you that I don't like your new
hat?* Or, with a slightly different nuance, *May I be rude and ask you how much you paid for
that car?*
3. *Indecent, improper,* as applied, e.g., to a joke, or a picture or statue. A **nanny** of the
author's acquaintance refused to take her little charge into an Impressionist show at the
Tate Gallery in London because it was "full of *rude* paintings."
4. As used in the expression *rude health.*

rudery, *n., Inf.*   **piece of rudeness**

rug. See under **carpet.**

rugger. See **football.**

rum, *adj.*   *Inf.* **funny (peculiar)**
Slang. The usual meaning of *rum* is 'funny' in the sense of 'peculiar' or 'strange.' For
example: *What a rum way to dress!* But in combination with certain nouns, *rum* has other
meanings: a *rum customer* is a *dangerous customer,* a person not safe to meddle with; a
rum go is a *tough break*; a *rum start* is a *funny thing* of the sort that so often happens on
the way to the theater if one can believe comedians' patter; a *rum old do* is a *funny
situation,* a *bizarre happening*; a *mixed-up affair.* (*We started out, it began to rain, we ran inside,
the sun came out, we went out again, it began to pour with rain, we rushed back inside—it was
a rum old do!*) All three words in this idiom are Briticisms. See **do** in this connection.

rumble, *v.t.*   *Inf.* **see through**
Slang. To see the real character of a person; to get to the bottom of a situation.

rumble strip   **speed bump**
Also known, familiarly, as 'sleeping policeman'; one of those raised bumps placed
across a road to slow down motorists—a sensible precaution in both countries. See also
ramp, 1.

rumbustious, *adj.*   **rambunctious**
Inf. Obstreperous; unruly.

rum-butter, *n.*   **hard sauce**
More or less interchangeable with *brandy-butter,* containing, *inter alia,* soft brown
sugar, grated orange and lemon rind, butter, and rum. Served with rich fruit pudding,
baked apple, baked banana, mince pie.

rump steak, *n.*   **sirloin**
Butchers' terms are very confusing. The British use *sirloin,* but it refers to what the
Americans call *porterhouse.* See **Appendix II.H.,** and comment under **sirloin.**

rumpy, *n., Inf.*   Manx cat

run-away, *n.*   drain
Something to let the water through.

run in   *Inf.* **break in**
Inf. What one does to new automobiles. The British *break in* wild horses but *run in* new cars.

runner, *n.*   **stringer**
In the sense of part-time local newspaper correspondent.

runner beans   **string beans**
Often shortened to *runners.*

running account   **checking account**
Synonymous with **current account.**

running shed   **roundhouse**

run out   **put out**
A **cricket** term. One of the ways a player is put out in this game; too technical to go into here. The official cricket rule book runs to 47 pages.

run the rule over   **take a look at**
Inf. To *go over* something *cursorily*; examine it for correctness or adequacy. *This is my summary; would you be good enough to run the rule over it? (Rule* is probably short for *slide-rule).*

run-up, *n.*   SEE COMMENT
In British politics, the *run-up* to election is the period of the campaign approaching the vote. The term can be used to cover the period of approach to any event, e.g. the *run-up* to the Prime Minister's speech on a certain topic, referring to the period of feverish preparation. *Run-up* is borrowed from cricket, where the **bowler** acquires momentum by **running up** to the point at which he releases the ball.

rush, *v.t.*   *Slang.* **soak**
Slang. For instance: *How much did they rush you for that sherry?* To *rush* is to *charge,* with the distinct implication that the price was too high.

rush one's fences   *Slang.* **jump the gun**
Slang. To *go off half-cocked;* to act or react with undue haste.

rusticate, *v.t.*   **expel temporarily from university**
To be *permanently expelled* is, in Britain, to be **sent down.** *Rustication* occurs in the case of less serious offenses.

rux, *n., School slang.*   **tantrum.**

S

sack, *n., v.t.*   *1. n.* **dismissal**
                                                                       2. *v.t.* **fire**
                                                                       3. *v.t.* **expel**
1. *Inf.* As in, *get* or *give the sack.*
2. *Inf.* From a job. See synonyms under **give someone his cards.**
3. *Inf.* From a secondary school. From a university, the term for *expel* is *send down.*

safari bed. See **camp bed.**

safe storage   **safekeeping**

saffron bun   SEE COMMENT
   A delicacy of Cornish origin, bright yellow in color. If you should happen to look
into a 15th-century British cookbook (or *cokeryboke*, as they were called) you would find
that virtually all cakes and many breads were heavily "strewn forth" with saffron.

St. Lubbock's Days. See **bank holiday.**

St. Luke's summer   **Indian summer**
   Also called *Luke's little summer* and *St. Martin's summer.*

St. Martin's summer   **Indian summer**
   Also called *St. Luke's summer* and *Luke's little summer.*

saithe. See **Appendix II.H.**

...salad, *n.*   **...and salad**
   Chicken (ham, beef, etc.) *salad* on British menus means *chicken* (etc.) *and salad*: not the
chopped up variety familiar to Americans. In Britain you get a real piece of chicken or
other meat *and* a portion of salad.

saloon, *n.*   **1. sedan**
                                                                              2. parlor
1. A *saloon motorcar*, which can be shortened to *saloon* in proper context, is what Americans call a *sedan.*
2. *Saloon* is commercialese in Britain, except on a ship (and see *saloon bar* and **saloon-
car**). In the commercial idiom the British use the terms *hair-dressing, billiards,* etc., *saloon*
where the American term would be *parlor*; but in ordinary speech, a man would simply
refer to his barber, a woman to her hairdresser. *Saloon,* in America has a definitely
pejorative connotation linked with the image of brutish drunkards who let their wives
and children starve while they squander their wages on drink. Not so in the mother
country.

saloon bar. See **pub.**

saloon-car   **parlor car**
   Also *saloon-carriage.*

salt beef   **corned beef**
   Once a diet staple of the British army in the field, its army nickname is *bully beef.* See
also **corned beef.**

salting, *n.*   **1. salt marsh**
     2. tide-flat
1. Usually found in the plural.
2. Land periodically flooded by ocean or inlet tides.

sand, *n.*   **grit**
Inf. In the sense of *determination, courage,* steadfastness of purpose.

sandboy. See **happy as a sandboy.**

San Fairy Ann   **it doesn't matter**
Slang. British anglicization (World War I) of *ça ne fait rien.*
Obsolete, or almost so. See **mind, 2; I'm easy (about it).**

sanitation officer. See **refuse tip.**

sap, *n., v.i.*   **1.** *v.i., Slang.* **cram**
     2. *n., Slang.* **grind**
1. *Slang.* To *sap* is to *cram,* See also **mug; swot.**
2. *Slang.* A *sap* is a *grind,* in the two distinct senses of 'zealous student' and 'tough job.'
(The American slang meaning 'fool' is shared with Britain.)
One wonders whether this latter meaning reflects the anti-intellectual atmosphere that
gave rise to the objectionable term *egghead. Verbum sap.*

sapper, *n.*   **army engineer**
Engaged in the building of fortifications in the field, etc.

Sassenach, *n., adj.*   SEE COMMENT
From the Gaelic for *Saxon,* an opprobious term used by Scots, and sometimes by the
Irish as well, to designate and derogate the English.

sauce, *n.*   *Inf.* **cheek**
Inf. In the sense of 'impertinence.' Often heard in the phrase *bloody sauce.*

sauce-boat, *n.*   **gravy boat**

sausage, *n.*   *approx.* **weatherstripping**
Inf. Sausage-shaped form, velvet stuffed with sawdust, used to keep out under-the-
door drafts.

sausage roll   SEE COMMENT

1. Baked sausage meat in pastry. See also **pie; pasty; stargazey.**
2. *Inf.* Anything sausage-shaped, including people.

save one's bacon, *Slang.*   *Inf.* **save one's skin**

save the mark!   **God help us!**
Sometimes *God save the mark!* A sarcastic or scornful interjection. *He calls himself an
impressionist—God save the mark!*

savoury, *n.*   **tidbit**
A *canapé* or sometimes something larger served usually at the end of dinner, after
dessert; but the term also covers an *hors d'oeuvre* or *appetizer.* Examples might be a
sardine or anchovy on toast, a modest welsh rarebit, and so on. When served after
dessert, it is always hot.

say...   SEE COMMENT
Old-fashioned usage on solicitors' bills. Instead of itemizing his services, the lawyer
would simply put in a blanket sum, preceded by the word *say,* which amounted to *Shall
we say?* or, *Let's call it.*

say boo to a goose   *Inf.* **open one's mouth**
Inf. *Have the courage to start a conversation. Boo* is sometimes *bo; say* is sometimes *cry;*
goose is sometimes *battledore.* Usually in the negative: *He wouldn't say boo to a goose,*
meaning 'He was afraid to open his mouth (to say a word).' Describes a Milquetoast.

scarper, *v.i., Slang.*   *Slang.* **scram**

scatty, *adj.*   *Slang.* **whacky**
Slang. The closest Americans come to *scatty* is *scatterbrained.*

scene-shifter, *n.*   **stagehand**

scenic railway   **roller coaster**
See also **switchback.**

scent, *n.*   **perfume**
Not commonly used in America. A *scent spray* is an *atomizer.*

scheduled building   SEE COMMENT
(Pronounced SHEDULED.) Buildings earmarked by the British Government as Ancient
Monuments, or buildings of special architectural or historical interest. Some years ago,
the author received an official communication from the Office of the Home Secretary
announcing that his (the author's) modest cottage in Kent had become a *scheduled build-*
ing, as having special architectural or historical interest. (Indeed, the rumor is that
William Penn was reared there.) In any case, the letter listed all the things the owner
mustn't do, henceforth, in the way of alterations without the consent of the particular
department of the Home Office. It took a lot of campaigning to get a permit to thatch
the roof of the barn.

scheme, *n.*   **plan**
In Britain the noun does not always have the American connotation of 'slyness' or
'sharp practice' (in fact one may talk of government or private housing *schemes*), but
the noun *schemer* and the verb to *scheme* do have that connotation.

scheme of arrangement   **reorganization plan**
Of a corporation in financial difficulties.

schemozzle. See **shemozzle.**

scholar, *n.*   **scholarship student**
Learned persons are called *scholars* in both countries, but the word is not used in
America, as it commonly is in Britain, to denote a *student on a scholarship.* In the North
of England the term applies to any schoolboy, as it can in America, and once did all
over England. A literary correspondent who was brought up in the North writes: "On
the municipal buses was a charming notice: SCHOLARS PLEASE SIT THREE TO A SEAT.
This always invoked an incongruous image of Einstein, Wittgenstein, and A.J. Ayer
sitting with their elbows in each other's ribs."

school, *n.*   SEE COMMENT
An American may speak of Harvard as his *school;* no Briton would apply that term
to his university. The word is confined in Britain to the grades below college level (*college*
in the American sense; *university* in the British). For the distinction in Britain between
college and *university,* see **college.**

schoolboy cake   **cheap fruit cake**
Inf. Made with a minimum of fruit, and that consisting almost entirely of currants;
the type commonly served at boarding-schools and sold at railroad stations, cheap cafés,
etc. In earlier times, it was called *shouting cake,* and it is still so referred to jocularly by
older folk: the currants were so far apart they had to shout at one another—unlike
whispering cake, the ubiquitous fruit-laden British wedding cake, so richly laden that the
components were close enough to whisper to one another.

school-leaver, *n.* *approx.* **high-school graduate**
A student who has completed formal education at a secondary school level, is not going on to college, and is now ready to go to work for a living. The term usually comes up in a discussion of the labor market or youth problems. The shorter term **leaver** is occasionally used in **prep school** and **public school** circles to describe a student about to complete the curriculum there.

school treat, *n.* **school party**
Usually away from school, on private grounds thrown open for the occasion; but the practice is dying out.

schooner, *n.* **large sherry (port) glass**
An American *schooner* is a *tall beer glass*. In Britain, where beer is usually drunk in very large glasses as a matter of course (see **pint**), a *schooner* is a glass reserved for a more than usually generous portion of sherry, or sometimes port.

scoff, *n., v.t.* 1. *n., Slang.* **good eats**
2. *v.t., Slang.* **wolf**
1. *n., Slang.* A schoolboy term.
2. *v.t., Inf.* To *gobble* or *knock back* food, especially sandwiches.

sconce, *n., v.t.* *approx.* **fine**
Slang. A highly specialized Oxford i⸱ m, ⸱ plicable only to undergraduates dining in **hall** (i.e., while at dinner in the college di⸱⸱ng-room). To *sconce* a fellow student is to *fine* him a tankard of ale, or the like, for a breach of table etiquette. *Sconce,* as a noun, means the 'forfeit' so imposed. The table of offenses varies with the college. Characteristic misdemeanors are: gazing at or talking about a painting on the wall of the dining room (these are portraits of past worthies connected with the institution); looking at the "high table" (where the **dons** sit); talking shop, i.e., mentioning study subjects or homework; speaking in a foreign tongue; mentioning a girl's name (but aren't there girls in dining-hall nowadays, and do they come under the sconcing rules and regulations?). There is a sconcing order: upper classmen may sconce juniors, but not vice versa. Those of the same class may sconce one another, except that even here a pecking order prevails, in favor of those students who are **reading** (*majoring in*) subjects that have been taught the longest (e.g., theology vs. linguistics). The sconcer produces the full tankard of ale and challenges the offender to drink it down in one draught. If the offender succeeds (though he may become ill), the sconcer pays for the ale; if he stops for breath, he pays for it. Samuel Johnson, in his youth, wrote rather tartly to the Oxford don William Jorden, his tutor at Pembroke College: "Sir, you have *sconced* me twopence for non-attendance at a lecture not worth a penny." (That was in 1728, long before the *sconce* took the form of a tankard of ale.) Many years later, in his *Dictionary,* Sam Johnson wrote the following definition of the verb *to sconce*: "To mulct, to fine. A low word which ought not to be retained." But as you see, low or not, it was retained.

scone, *n.* *approx.* **baking powder biscuit**
(Should rhyme with JOHN though the long o is also heard in **non-U** circles. See **Appendix I.C.6.**) Usually served at room temperature, while the approximate American equivalent is served warm. The usual fare for *tea.*

scoop the pool *Slang.* **make a killing**
Slang. Originally a stock exchange term.

score off, *v.* **get the better of**
Inf. In an argument or in repartee.

Scotch egg SEE COMMENT
This is a pub delicacy consisting of a hard-boiled egg, coated with a blanket of pork sausage meat, which is then rolled in bread crumbs and deep-fried. Highly recommended.

Scotch foursome. See fourball.

Scotch woodcock   SEE COMMENT
Scrambled eggs (which the British sometimes call *buttered eggs*) on toast first spread
with anchovy paste. This is one of those fanciful food terms, comparable to *Welsh rabbit*,
now popularly spelled *rarebit* (a corruption), *Bombay duck* (a fish), and *Cape Cod turkey*,
which means 'codfish.' The recipe for Scotch woodcook in *Mrs. Beeton's Household Management* follows:

> *Scotch Woodcock (Anchois à l'Écossaise)*
> *Ingredients.*—The yolks of two eggs, one gill of cream (or cream and milk in equal
> parts), anchovy paste, toast, butter, cayenne, salt.
> *Method.*—Cut the toast into two-inch squares, butter well, and spread them with
> anchovy paste. Season the eggs with a little cayenne and salt; when slightly beaten
> add them to the hot cream, stir over the fire until they thicken sufficiently, then pour
> the preparation over the toast, and serve as hot as possible.
> *Time.*—Ten minutes. Sufficient for six to eight persons.

Scouse, *n.*   SEE COMMENT
Inf. (Rhymes with MOUSE.) Denotes both a native of Liverpool and the Liverpool
dialect.

scout. See **gyp.**

scraggy, *adj.*   **scrawny**

scray, *n.*   **tern**

scree, *n.*   **mountain slope**
But *scree* (or *screes*) can also be used to denote the pebbles or small stones and rocks
that dribble or slide down when people walk up a steep slope covered with loose gravel.

screw, *n.*   **1.** *approx. Slang.* **take**
                                                                    2. nag
                                                    3. *approx.* **twist; bit**
1. *Slang.* In the sense of 'salary.' It is hard to find an exact American slang equivalent.
Take may do, but it is broader than *screw* because it would cover the concept of *profit*
as well as that of *regular wages*. This term originated in the practice of handing over the
pay not in an envelope but in a *screwed up* piece of paper. See 3.
2. *Slang.* An old and shaky horse.
3. *Slang.* It is occasionally used to mean a 'rumpled-up ball of paper'—the sort thrown
into a wastebasket; at other times a 'bit of salt or tobacco,' or anything of that sort
contained in a piece of twisted paper.

screwed, *adj.*   *Slang.* **tight**
Slang. Loaded, picked, stinko, etc.

scribbling-block, *n.*   **scratch pad**
Also *scribbling-pad.*

scrimmage. See **scrum.**

scrimshank, *v.i.*   *Slang.* **goldbrick**
Military slang. To *shirk.* Originally a nautical slang expression alluding to the man
who idly swung the lead he was supposed to be taking soundings with. Medical humor:
a doctor fed up with signing excuses so that lazy employees could attend *soccer* matches
attested that a patient was suffering from *plumbum pendularum,* mock Latin for *lead
swinging.* (*Plumbum agitans* would have been closer.) See also: **skive; dodge the column;
swing the lead; swing it; skulk; slack; soldier; mike.**

scrip, *n.*   **temporary stock certificate**
In Britain a *scrip* is a *temporary certificate* issued to one entitled eventually to receive a formal stock certificate. In America *scrip* is applied to a formal certificate representing a fraction of a share. In the bad old days of U.S. company towns (mining towns were a prime example), one company would pay a *scrip* which could only be used in company-owned stores—now an illegal practice.

scrubber, *n.*   **loose woman**
Slang. At least, one who gives that impression. Not a nice thing to call a woman.

scruffy, *adj.*   **messy**

scrum, *n.*   **scrimmage; melee**
Inf. Short for *scrummage*, which is a variant of *scrimmage*. *Scrimmage* has the general meaning of 'confused struggle' or 'melee' in both countries. In British Rugby football, the *scrummage* is the mass of all the forwards surrounding the ball on the ground. As a sports term, the British usually use the shortened form *scrum*. Informally, *scrum* is used in Britain to denote the atmosphere of a group of people working in a state of confusion, whether it be a group of reporters competing for the attention of a celebrity, or a confused business conference with everybody working at cross-purposes. A British businessman pulled out of a smoke-filled conference room by a telephone call from his wife might say, "Sorry darling, but I've got to sign off now and get back in the scrum." A verbal use of *scrum* is found in the expression *scrum around (v.i.)* meaning 'fight your way through' as in a crowded tea tent at the Henley Regatta, trying to collect tea and goodies for the family.

scrummage. See **scrum.**

scrump, also **skrimp; skrump,** *v.t., v.i.*   **rob orchards**
Particularly apple orchards. *Scrumpy* is a rough, usually very strong cider. The name implies that it has been made from all the old apples lying around. Found in the West of England and, in fact, when you are used to it, very good. See also **cider.**

scrumpy. See under **scrump.**

scrutineer, *n.*   **ballot inspector**

scug, *n.*   *Slang.* **fink**
School slang. Extremely derogatory in the cruel way peculiar to children. It means a person with bad manners, unfriendly, a bad sport, and generally one to be shunned.

scullery, *n.*   **back kitchen**
Room for washing dishes.

scunner. See **take a scunner on.**

scupper, *v.t.*   *Slang.* **do (someone) in**
Slang. Scupper is a noun in both countries, meaning a 'drain in a ship' designed to carry water off a deck. As a British verb, *scupper* means 'ambush and wipe out.' In nautical circles, to *scupper* is to *sink a ship*, with the implication of finishing off the crew as well. In this sense, the slang British verb *scupper* would be about equivalent to *scuttle* and to the slang American verb *sink*, in the sense of 'do in,' as in, *We're sunk*.

scurf, *n.*   **dandruff**

scutter, *v.i.*   **scurry**

scuttle, *n.*   SEE COMMENT
A *scuttle* is a *coal pail*, usually called a *coal scuttle* in both countries. The word, however, has an exclusively British additional meaning: a 'wide shallow basket.'

S.E. See **Standard English.**

sea, *n.*   **beach**
Sea and *seaside* are used in Britain where Americans would usually say *beach*, or less commonly, *shore*, to mean a 'seaside resort,' like Brighton in Britain or Atlantic City in America. The classical Jack Sprat type of argument between spouses in America is based on the problem whether to take one's vacation in the mountains or at the *shore*. In Britain the *shore* would be the *seaside* (and the *vacation* would be a **holiday**). See **beach** for British use of the word. See also **front; bathe.**

sea fret   **sea fog**
A bit of dialectal nautical jargon.

sea front. See **front.**

season ticket   **commutation ticket**
In America one thinks of a *season ticket* as something entitling one to see all the games at a given ball park. In Britain it usually refers to train travel and can be valid for anything from a month to a year. In this sense, it is occasionally shortened to *season*, as in railroad station signs reading PLEASE SHOW YOUR SEASON. A *season ticket holder* is a *commuter*. *Season ticket* can also apply to a series of performances, in which sense it would be synonymous with *subscription*.

secateurs, *n. pl.*   **pruning shears**
(Accent on the first syllable, which rhymes with DECK.)

second, *n.*   **magna**
A university term. *Second* is short for *second-class honours* just as *magna* is short for *magna cum laude*. In some universities a second-class degree is further divided into an *upper* or (informally) *good second* and a *lower second* (also referred to as a *2.1* and *2.2*). See also **first; class.**

second, *v.t.*   **transfer temporarily; detail**
(Accented on the second syllable; SE-COND'.) Denotes a temporary transfer of an employee to another department of the company, or of a soldier to another unit. *Secondment* is the noun. *Detail* is military usage for assignment to a particular task.

secondary modern. See **eleven plus.**

secondary subject   **minor**
At college. In American colleges, students choose a *major* (in which they *major* or *specialize*) and usually a *minor*. In Britain, the student **reads** his main subject, and elects a *secondary subject*.

second class. See **first class.**

second eleven   **second rank**
Inf. Or *Grade B*—a term borrowed from **cricket**. See **eleven.**

secondment. See **second,** *v.t.*

see (someone) far enough   *Inf.* **see one in hell**
Inf. As in *I'll see him far enough before I invite him to dinner again.* Sometimes, to *see one further*.

see (someone) off, *Slang.*   *Slang.* **polish (someone) off**
Nothing to do with fond good-byes.

see (someone) out   **last for the rest of (someones's) life**
Inf. This coat will see me out, says the elderly woman who feels just a little guilty about an expenditure at a sale. *It'll outlive me,* she might have said.

see the back of   *Inf.* **see the last of**
Inf. Almost always after *I'll be glad to...*

self-selection, *n., adj.*   **self-service**
Applying to retail stores.

sell, *n.*   *Inf.* **letdown**
Inf. Commonly seen in the expression *What a sell!* It is used often as a reaction to the
gap between the promise and the performance.

sell (someone) a dummy   *Inf.* **put it over on (someone)**
Inf. A term borrowed from rugby.

sell (someone) a pup   *Slang.* **stick (someone)**
Inf. To *sell someone a pup* is to *stick him,* i.e., to cheat him, especially by getting a high
price for inferior merchandise.

Sellotape, *n.*   **Scotch tape**
Proprietary names.

sell the pass   **betray a cause** or **trust**
Inf. To cede the advantage to one's adversaries. Term borrowed from the language
of mountain warfare. After Parnell, the Irish patriot, had supported Gladstone's Irish
Home Rule Bill (1893), he was, in the words of James Morris (*Heaven's Command,* Faber
& Faber, London, 1973), "scorned by those who thought of mere Home Rule as supine
surrender." "Our general has betrayed us," wrote Archbishop Croke. "For his own
miserable gratification he has *sold the pass,* preferring an ignoble and licentious life in
London to the liberation and advancement of his too confiding countrymen." The charge
of licentiousness was the result of Parnell's affair with Katherine O'Shea, the wife of
one of Parnell's followers. He eventually married his Kitty, but that didn't matter to
the good Archbishop.

sell up   *Inf.* **sell out**
Inf. If a Briton were to sell his residence and also wanted to liquidate the furnishings
he would speak of *selling up* everything, i.e., *selling out* lock, stock, and barrel. It means
'sell out' also in the sense of 'sell out a debtor's property' in a forced sale.

semibreve, *n.*   **whole note**
Musical term. See **Appendix II.F.**

semi-detached, *adj.*   **two-family**
In America a *two-family house* may be divided horizontally or vertically. In Britain a
semi-detached residence is a one-family house joined to another by a common or party
wall. The two halves are often painted different colors. This euphemistic designation
genteelly stresses the detachment rather than the attachment, the British, in this case,
preferring to accentuate the negative in order to enhance the positive. When more than
two residences are joined together, the series is called a *terrace.*

semiquaver, *n.*   **sixteenth note**
Musical term. See **Appendix II.F.**

semolina, *n.*   **cream of wheat**

S.E.N.   **practical nurse**
Stands for *State Enrolled Nurse.* See also **sister.**

send down   **expel**
A term from university life. In referring to school, the British slang term is *sack.* See
also **rusticate.**

send (someone) spare   *Slang.* **drive (someone) nuts**
Slang. See also **go spare.**

send to Coventry   *Inf.* **turn one's back on**
Inf. To *ignore socially; give the cold shoulder to.* The primary factor of this punishment
is that nobody is to speak to the poor chap. There is a theory that this expression stems
from Coventry Gaol (Jail), to which the Royalists were confined by Cromwell's men.
Coventry is a city in Warwickshire 92 miles northwest of London.

send-up, *n.*   *Inf.* **take-off**
Inf. Or *put-on.* Hermione Baddeley introduced a number as *"a send-up of* an old music
hall song." Americans would have said "a take-off on..." Note the different preposition
(see **Appendix I.A.1.**). To *send* someone *up* is to *make fun of* him.

send up rotten   **pan**
Slang. To 'deprecate.' Lord Snowdon designed the large aviary in Regent's Park. In
an interview he said the people liked it now but when it was first opened to the public
many people *sent it up rotten.* Synonymous with **slate.**

senhouse hook   **pelican hook**
A nautical term denoting a hook on the end of a line or cable for insertion into an
eye, to make a firm connection which is nonetheless readily opened by hand. The British
call the hook by the name of the inventor; the Americans by the name of the bird whose
bill the hook resembles.

senior lecturer   **assistant professor**
Approximate equivalent in the teaching hierarchy. See **reader.**

Senior Service   **Royal Navy**
Americans should know that *Senior Service* means something more than a brand of
cigarettes.

Senior Wrangler. See **Wrangler.**

Senior Wrangler sauce. See **brandy-butter; wrangler.**

septillion. See **Appendix II.D.**

sergeant-major   **top sergeant**
See also **R.S.M.**

serve, *v.t., v.i.*   **wait on**
In a shop, to *serve* someone is to *wait on* a customer. *Are you being served?* (sometimes
shortened to *Are you served?*) would usually come out as, *Is someone helping you?* in an
American store. A British television comedy series entitled *Are You Being Served?* is about
life in a **draper's shop.**

servery, *n.*   *approx.* **service counter**
Generally a room from which, rather than in which, meals are served. Thus, at a pub
one might find a sign pointing to the GARDEN AND BAR SERVERY, indicating the room
to which one must go in order to obtain food and drink to be consumed in the garden
or the bar.

service engineer   **skilled mechanic**
A somewhat pompous epithet applied, e.g., to one experienced in refrigerators, dish-
washers, etc.

service flat, *n.*   **hotel apartment**
In the plural, *service flats* is seen in the expression *block of service flats,* which would
correspond to an American *apartment hotel* or *residential hotel.* See also **apartment; flat.**

service lift   **dumbwaiter**
This is rather tricky: **dumb-waiter** in Britain is what is known in America as a *lazy
Susan.*
service occupancy. See **vacant possession.**

serviette, *n.* napkin
Still used occasionally but (*dinner*) *napkin* is taking over. **Non-U**; see **Appendix I.C.6.**

servitor. See **sizar.**

set, *n.*
1. *approx.* **group**
2. **apartment; suite**
3. **paving block**
4. **badger's burrow**

1. A school term; thus the *A set*, the *B set*, etc., meaning 'group' (within a given grade or form) based on the ability of the students. In this sense, the word is giving way to a newer term, **stream.**
2. In this use, restricted to apartments in such exclusive and historic addresses as the residence known as *Albany* in London, with its sixty-nine *sets*, or to groups of rooms at the various **Inns of Court,** where *sets* is short for *sets of chambers.* See **chambers.**
3. Variant of *sett.*
4. Variant of *sett,* which can also mean badger's debris outside the burrow.

set about *Slang.* **lay into**
Slang. An expression that one *bovver boy* (member of a gang: see **bovver boots**) would be apt to use to encourage his undistinguished colleagues when about to take on a rival gang. *Let's set about that* **lot!**

set book, *n.* **required reading**
Specific reading assignment for an examination.

set down **let off**
A term used in transportation: passengers are *set down* in Britain and *let off* or *dropped off* in America. Signs seen in Britain: At a railroad station: PICK UP AND SET DOWN. NO PARKING. At bus stops: SETTING DOWN POINT ONLY (interchangeable with ALIGHTING POINT).

set fair **put up**
Stable term: to *set a horse fair* is to *put it up,* i.e., *get it all set* for the night.

set lunch **table d'hôte; prix fixe**
See also **set tea.**

set out one's stall, *Inf.*
display one's credentials

sett. See **set, 3.** and **4.**

set tea **afternoon tea**
Tea with little sandwiches and cakes, obtainable at hotels and restaurants; a complete tea at a fixed price. See also **tea.**

set the Thames on fire *Inf.* **set the world on fire**
Inf. Well, to lots of Britons the Thames *is* the world. A popular etymology is that *Thames,* in this expression, is a corruption of the old word (now dialect) *temse,* meaning 'sieve.' Thus, an indolent worker using a *temse* (for sifting meal, e.g.) would never set it on fire by vigorous action. Among the French, who have a similar saying about the Seine (mettre le feu à la Seine), there is an analogous popular theory that *Seine* in that expression comes from *seine* meaning 'fishing-net.' There is, however, nothing like *temse* or *seine* to explain the parallel German saw about the Rhine (*den Rhein anzünden*). Since the Romans used the same locution about the Tiber (*Tiberium accendere nequaquam potest*), it is more than likely that that is the source of all these expressions, each country referring to its own principal river.

sewer, *n.*   *Slang.* **louse**
Slang. Derived from the Hindustani word *sua* meaning 'pig,' and brought back to Britain by troops who had served in India. Perhaps an American slang equivalent would be *louse; bastard* might do, too. Some say, however, that the slang term is merely a figurative extension of the literal meaning, so that a closer equivalent might be *shit.* *Sewer* is Uncle Matthew's favorite expletive in Nancy Mitford's books.

sexillion, sextillion. See **Appendix II.D.**

shadow, *adj.*   SEE COMMENT
A term used in British political life in the following way: A *shadow cabinet* or *government* is a group of leaders of the party out of power who would be appointed to replace the current group if the outs became the ins. A headline in *The Times* (London) of March 12, 1974 reads: "Mr Carr appointed *shadow Chancellor...*" and the article, after speaking of *"shadow portfolios," "shadow minister without portfolio," "shadow Home Secretary,"* etc., makes a new departure and uses *shadow* as a verb: *"...*Mr Carr *shadows* Mr Healey at the Treasury...and Mr Rippon will *shadow* on Europe."

shake. See **in two shakes of a duck's tail.**

shake down   *Inf.* **put up (for the night)**
Slang. In Britain it is very hospitable of you to *shake* somebody *down.* In America, apart from its slang meaning of 'extortion,' a *shake-down* is an *improvised bed.* This use is reflected in the British use of *shake down.* None of this, of course, has anything to do with a *shakedown cruise,* which is a phrase used in both countries meaning a 'new ship's initial trip' made in order to break in both engine and crew.

Shakespearean university. See **Oxbridge.**

shambolic, *adj.*   **chaotic**
Inf. From *shambles.* Used to describe situations or places that are in a state of extreme disorder.

shammy. See **wash-leather.**

shandrydan, *n.*   **rickety vehicle**
Originally a chaise or shay, a light open two-wheeled horse-drawn carriage for two, sometimes with a hood; later applied to any ancient dilapidated vehicle. This term is hardly ever met with these days, and is of uncertain etymology.

shandy, *n.*   SEE COMMENT
A drink consisting of beer and lemonade or ginger beer in equal parts, which British children are (not legally) allowed to drink in their early teens in preparation for the eventual **pint.** Short for *shandygaff.*

shape, *n.*   SEE COMMENT
An old-fashioned word for any dessert like jello, blancmange, mousse, etc. shaped in a mold.

shared line   **party line**
The more fortunate have **exclusive lines.** Also called *shared service,* by the Post Office, which is in charge of telephones in Britain.

share-pushing   **stock touting**
Not necessarily fraudulent but with the implication of sharp practice.

share raid. See **raid.**

shares, *n. pl.*   **stocks**
Usual name for corporate equities. *Stock,* or *stocks,* in British financial circles, usually means 'government bonds,' but can mean 'corporate stock' as well, as in America; and

stockholder can refer to either type of security. *Tap stocks* are those which are always available. The term is applied also to government bonds which are sold by the government departments holding them when they reach a certain market price. They may be short-term or long-term. *Taplets* are small issues of this kind. In the summer of 1985 the Bank of England, according to *The Times* (London) announced "three more taplets totalling 600 million which will be available for sale Monday," and went on to describe the issues.

sharpen, *v.t.*   **sharp**
Musical term. See **Appendix I.A.3.**

shave hook   **paint scraper**

shaw, *n.*   **1. thicket**
                                                                                                          2. stalks and leaves
1. Mainly poetic.
2. Mainly Scottish, and referring particularly to turnip and potato crops.

sheaf, *n.*   *Inf.* **wad; bankroll**
Inf. Referring to paper money: *sheaf of* **notes** would be a *bankroll* or a *wad* in America.

shebeen, *n.*   *approx.* **speakeasy**
(Accent on the second syllable.) An unlicensed pub in Ireland. See **licensed.**

shelf company   SEE COMMENT
A corporation formed by a lawyer (**solicitor**) or an accountant, held available for the use of a client needing one.

sheltered trade   **domestic monopoly**
Describing a business that gets no competition from abroad, like a railroad.

shemozzle, *n.*   *Inf.* **mix-up; row**
Slang. A *mix-up*, a *mess*, a *confused situation* generally; in a narrower use, a *row*, in the sense of 'dispute,' a *rhubarb*, a *melee*. The British are Elizabethan in their spelling of this word; a sampling of variants: *schemozzle, shemozzl, shimozzel, chimozzle, shlemozzl, shlemozzle, schlemozzle, schlemazel*. Its origin is in London racetrack cant. The first *l*, and certainly the spelling *schlemazel*, crept in out of confusion with the totally unrelated Yiddish term *schlemaz(e) l*, meaning 'hard-luck guy.'

shepherd's pie   *approx.* **hash**
Not quite: a *shepherd's pie* is usually made of the remains of a roast (which in Britain is called a **joint**), ground up (**minced**), topped by a layer of mashed potatoes and baked in the oven.

sherbet. See **ice.**

shilling. See **Appendix II.A.**

shilling shocker   **dime novel**
Also known in Britain as a **penny dreadful** or a **penny blood.** All of these terms are old fashioned.

shingle, *n.*   **beach pebbles**
A beach so covered would be known as a *shingle beach* (as opposed to a *sandy beach*). In America it would be called a *pebble beach* or *pebbly beach.*

shipping order   **large order**
Inf. One of those interminable orders being given by the customer just ahead of you when you're in a mad hurry.

shipshape and Bristol fashion. See **Bristol fashion.**

shire, *n.*   SEE COMMENT
(Pronounced SHER, sometimes SHEER, when used as a suffix.) Old word for *county*, now rarely used except in the plural (the *Shires*) meaning the 'hunting country.' It is found mainly as a suffix in the names of most of the counties, as, for example, in *Hampshire, Yorkshire.*

shirty, *adj., Slang.*   **vexed**

shoal, *n.*   *Inf.* **raft**
Inf. A *multitude,* like a *shoal* (or *shoals*) *of correspondence* to attend to.

shock, *n.*   **sensation**
Inf. Common usage in journalism, especially on the garish daily posters at newsstands purporting to inform the public what today's big story is, but really only acting as a teaser. Thus: SHARES DROP SHOCK (Stock Market Collapse Sensation!); OLD BAILEY CONFESSION SHOCK (Murder Trial Confession—Wow!); BUDGET SHOCK (Terrible New Tax Bill!!), etc. A *shock result* in sports is an *upset.*

shocker, *n.*   **1.** *Inf.* **stinker**
                                                                        2. cheap novel
1. *Inf. Shocker* is used to describe a bad case of almost anything; a stretch of wretched weather, a new tax, an embarrassing utterance by a public figure, a dress in very bad taste, overcooked Brussels sprouts, an indescribably boring dinner party. Sometimes it is used in a rather exaggerated way, as in: *Isn't letter-writing a shocker!* See also **shocking.**
2. It can also mean a 'sensational novel' as opposed to a *thriller.*

shocking, *adj.*   *Inf.* **awful**
Inf. As in *Isn't it shocking?* (about the weather, etc.). *Shocking* is used in much the same way as **shocker, 1.**

shoeblack. See **boot.**

shoe mender   **shoemaker**
See also **mend.**

shoot, *v.t.*   **hunt**
A Briton *hunts* foxes and deer but *shoots* game birds and rabbits. Americans *hunt* quail, for instance. To *let the shooting* is to lease the right to hunt birds on your property.

shoot, *n.*   **1. shooting party**
                                                                    2. shooting expedition
                                                                    3. shooting practice
                                                                    4. shooting area

shoot a robin   *Inf.* **run into a streak of bad luck**
Slang. He must have shot a robin would be said of one suffering the lot of Job: one piece of bad luck after another. The Ancient Mariner was concerned with the albatross; a robin suffices in this quaint British expression. It's much worse than spilling salt, walking under a ladder, being crossed by a black cat; more like breaking a mirror.

shooting!, *interj.*   *Inf.* **good shot!**
Inf. A complimentary observation in certain sports like tennis, basketball, etc.

shooting-box, *n.*   **hunting-lodge**

shooting-brake, also **break** *n.* See **estate car.**

shoot the cat   *Slang.* **toss one's cookies**
Slang. To *throw up;* the common expression is **be sick.** See also **sick up; queer.**

shoot the crow   *Inf.* **decamp**
  Slang. To *take French leave,* which the French call *filer à l'anglaise,* naturally enough. Normally used to describe the sudden departure of someone else, rather than oneself. *Where's Jones these days? Shot the crow, it looks like.* See also **shoot the moon.**

shop the moon   *Slang.* **skip town by night**
  Slang. See also **moonlight flit; shoot the crow; hook it; leave (someone) to it.**

shop, *n.*   **store**
  A matter of usage. *Shop* is used in a few British informal expressions that one does not hear in America. *You have come to the wrong shop,* means 'I can't help you' (because you are applying to the wrong person). To *sink the shop* is to *keep mum* generally and more specifically to *keep your activities under wraps.* *All over the shop* means 'in wild disorder.' A *nation of shopkeepers* refers to Britain itself. *Shop-soiled* is *shop-worn* in America. To *have everything in the shop window* is to *four-flush,* to *play the big shot,* without having anything to back it up.

shop, *v.t.*   **1. jail**
                                            2. squeal on
  Slang. In the British underword to be *shopped* is to go to *jail,* and by extension to be *squealed on* by your accomplice so that you wind up in jail (spelled *gaol* in Britain, but pronounced like *jail*).

shop assistant. See **assistant; clerk.**

shopping-bag, *n.*   *Inf.* **pack; bunch; bagful**
  Slang. A *whole bunch* of something; a *miscellany.* The subject-matter itself may be omitted if the context is clear. 'She arrived with a shopping-bag,' says a doctor, meaning that the troublesome patient barged in with a plethora of ailments, a bagful of ills, all kinds of complaints. Also commonly used in America in reports describing the miscellany of munitions requested of the American government by visiting heads of state or their emissaries.

shop-walker, *n.*   **floorwalker**

short, *n.*   **straight drink**
  Inf. Of hard liquor, sherry, vermouth, etc., as opposed to a mixed drink (e.g., gin and tonic) or beer. This is pub terminology. Note that *straight,* in this context, is **neat** in Britain, and *hard liquor* is **spirits.** See also **double.**

short back and sides   **close haircut**
  Not a crew cut (which is called a **close crop** in Britain); rather, the normal British gentleman's style until World War II, and still, more or less, the Army private's, although that is changing in many parts of the world.

short commons   **short rations**
  Originally a university term denoting the daily fare supplied to students at a fixed charge. The phrase has become somewhat pejorative with the connotation of *subsistence living, meager pickings,* so that the person said to be *on short commons* might also be described as *on his uppers.*

shorthand typist   **stenographer**
  This term is now somewhat old-fashioned and is being supplanted by *secretary* even if the person involved is not properly speaking a *secretary* but only a *stenographer.* This is an example of the British tendency to pay honor to the dignity of labor—a trend very much in favor at the moment, which explains *shop* **assistant** for *salesperson, automotive engineer* for *garage mechanic,* etc. See also **P.A.**

shorthand writer   **court stenographer**

short list   **surviving applicants**
Those applying for a position who are still retained after initial screening and elimination. The fortunate ones are said to be *short-listed*.

shorts, *n. pl.*   **(outdoor) shorts**
Shorts, in Britain, are not underwear. In America the word can refer to either underwear or outdoor apparel, depending on the context. The British term for *underwear
shorts* is **pants,** sometimes *underpants*, though the *under* would seem to be superfluous
because the word *pants* alone implies that. *Pants*, in the American sense of 'outdoor
wear,' are *trousers* in Britain.

short-sighted. See under **long-sighted.**

short time   **part time**
As in, *Many workers are on short time...*, i.e., are still employed, but not on full time.
Does not apply to a regular part-time worker.

shot, *n.*   SEE COMMENT
Slang. Measure of upper cylinder lubricant. Thus, as you drive up to a gas pump
(petrol *station*) in Britain, you may ask for *two and two shots,* meaning 'two gallons of
gas and two shots of lubricant' which is mixed into the gas.

shot about   *Slang*. **beat**
Slang. In the sense of *exhausted; knocked out.*

shot of   **rid of**
Inf. Said to be a cockney version of *shut of*, but the variant appears to be in more
general use than the original. *Shut of* would seem to be used when referring to a person
who is a nuisance to be got rid of, while *shot of* can refer to persons or things one would
rather do without. *Shed of* would appear to be an Americanism derived from *shut of*.

shout, *n., v.i.*   **treat**
As a noun, one's *turn* to buy the drinks. *It's my shout this time* means 'This one's on
me.' As a verb, to *shout* is to *stand drinks*. Heard mainly down under.

shouting cake, See **schoolboy cake.**

shove-halfpenny   SEE COMMENT
Common pub game. Played by shoving well-polished old halfpennies (pronounced
HAY' PNEEZ) or token disks with the flat of the hand along a board separated into
horizontal sections having numerical values. Difficult to describe; much more fun to
play, although possibly the most frustrating game in the world.

show, *n.*   **1. chance**
                                                        2. affair
1. *Inf.* To say of someone that he had no *show* at all is to say that he had no *opportunity*
of proving or defending himself. One might plead, *At least give him a fair show!*
2. *Inf.* Speaking of his new, up-and-coming partner, the older man might say, *Jones is
doing well, but it's still my show*, i.e., *I'm still in charge around here*. See also **bad show;
good show.**

show a leg   *Inf.* **rise and shine**
Slang. Term used in the Royal Navy to rouse the sleeping sailor.

shower, *n.*   *Slang*. **washout**
Slang. When someone is referred to as a *shower*, or a *perfect shower*, he is a *total loss*,
a *washout*. See also **wet** and the opprobious **drip.**

show friendly to (someone)   act in a friendly manner
towards (someone)
Make a friendly gesture towards (someone). But see **friendly action**.

show-house, *n.*   model home
And *show-flat* is *model apartment.*

showing favour   SEE COMMENT
A term used in criminal law to describe the offense of giving aid and comfort to the criminal element, applied especially to police officers who accept bribes for helping them in their unlawful pursuits, e.g., by tipping them off about impending police raids.

show one's colours, *Inf.*   *Inf.* **stand up and be counted; reveal one's character or party**

shrewd, *adj.*   **1. sharp; biting**
2. severe; hard
1. Describing a wind, cold weather, pain, etc. A literary use; archaic in common speech.
2. Applying to a blow or a thrust. These meanings are in addition to the shared meaning of 'astute' or 'wise'.

shrimp. See under **prawn**.

shufty, *n.*   *Slang.* **gander; look-see**
Slang. (The *u* is pronounced like the OO in BOOK.) This word, of Arabic origin, with its variant *shufti,* is often used as a verb in the imperative: *Shufty!* meaning, 'Look!' Originally military stuff, but soldiers often take their special slang with them when they reenter civilian life, and it passes into general speech. See also **recce**.

shunting yard   switchyard

sick, *adv.*   sick to one's stomach
When a Briton says *sick* he means 'queasy,' not sick all over or sick generally. If that were the case he'd say **ill**. To *be sick* means to 'throw up.' See also **sick up; queer**. However, he uses *sick* in compounds with *bed, benefit, call, leave, list, pay, room,* etc. *Sick-making* (see **-making**) is slang for *sickening, disgusting.* See also **ill**.

sick as a cat   sick as a dog

sickener, *n.*   *Slang.* **bellyful**
Slang. After a long unpleasant experience: *I have had a sickener of that!*

sicker, *n.*   sick bay
Schoolboy slang. Infirmary. Very old, and not much heard any more.

sick up   throw up
Inf. A vulgar expression for *vomit.* The usual expression is *be sick; throw up* is hardly used. See also **sick; queer**.

side, *n.*   **1. team**
2. airs
3. English
1. To *let the side down* is to *be found wanting* at the crucial moment, in the clutch, so as to frustrate the good work of one's colleagues. The term originated, obviously, in sports, but can be applied to any situation.
2. *Inf.* To *put on side* is to *put on airs, put on the dog.*
3. A billiards term, synonymous with **spin**. In this usage, to *put on side* means to *put*

English on the ball. This appears to be the earlier meaning of *put on side* and there are those who believe that meaning **2.** evolved from meaning **3.** But why was the billiards technique called *English?* Anything to do with *angles?* After all, the first *Angles* were the Germanic folk who migrated to Britain in the fifth century and founded East Anglia. In the world of etymology, anything's possible.

sideboards, *n. pl.*   **sideburns**
    Inf. The British say *sideburns,* too.

sidesman, *n.*   **deputy churchwarden**
    Especially, one who passes the collection plate.

signal-box, *n.*   **switch tower**

sign off   **initial**
    In the sense of initialing a document as having read and disposed of it.

sign-posted, *adj.*   SEE COMMENT
    Applied to road directions, meaning that the route is clearly marked by road signs at all intersections where one must turn. "Not to worry, it's all sign-posted" is fairly reassuring, but better have the telephone number of the people you're aiming to get to.

sign the poisons book   SEE COMMENT
    When you buy certain medicines in Britain, the druggist (**chemist** or **dispenser**) has you *sign the poisons book* where appropriate. This is a handy arrangement, presumably, in connection with autopsies and other Agatha Christie-type situations. In America, an analogous record is maintained by the druggist himself.

silk, take. See **take silk.**

silverside, *n.*   **top round**
    Butcher's term.

Silver Streak, *Inf.*   **English Channel**

simnel cake   SEE COMMENT
    This is a fancy ornamental cake with a thick layer of marzipan and all kinds of decorations, served at Easter.

simple, *adj.*   *Inf.* **not all there**
    Inf. A term used more by village than city folk meaning something between 'silly' and downright 'feebleminded.' *Simpleton* and *simple-minded* are related; but *simple* used by itself means something a little stronger. One thus afflicted might be said to *have a screw loose, rocks in his head, bats in his belfry,* or to be *without the benefit of certain of his marbles.*

single, *n.*   **one-way ticket**
    See also **return** which is a *round-trip ticket.*

single cream. See under **double, 3.**

single cuff/double cuff   **barrel cuff/French cuff**

singlet, *n.*   **undershirt; T-shirt**
    Singlet is being replaced by *T-shirt,* and the common word for *undershirt* is *vest.*

single-track, *adj.*   **one-lane**
    Road term.

sink, *n.*   **kitchen sink**
A *sink*, in Britain, is a *kitchen sink*, not a bathroom one, which is called a **basin.**

sink differences, *Inf.*   *Inf.* **bury the hatchet**

sink the shop. See under **shop.**

sippet, *n.*   **crouton**

sirloin, *n.*   **porterhouse**
What Americans call a *sirloin* the British call a *rump steak.* There is a legend that King
Charles II, while stopping after hunting at Friday Hall in Chingford, near Epping Forest
(outside London), was so impressed by the roast loin of beef that he exclaimed, "By
St. George it shall have a title," and thereupon drew his sword and knighted it with
the words "Loin we dub thee knight, henceforth be *Sir Loin.*" Incidentally, two sirloins
in one roast are called a *baron of beef*, a *Baron* being much bigger stuff than a simple *Sir.*
It would be much more fun to believe in this etymological theory than in the prosaic
fact that *sirloin* (which was spelled *surloin* hundreds of years ago) came from the Old
French *sur longe, sur* meaning 'above' and *longe* meaning 'loin.' The wit of a king,
apocryphal or not, is so much more interesting than the anatomy of a steer.

sister, *n.*   **nurse**
The term *sister* is not applied to nurses in America except to nuns who nurse in
Catholic hospitals. Until a recent attempt at reorganizing the terminology, a *sister* was
the head nurse of a ward and there were *day sisters* and *night sisters. Theatre sisters* (the
theatre in question being an *operating-theatre*), were those who handed scalpels and
things to surgeons. The head nurse of a hospital was called *matron.* Except in the context
of medical practice, *nurse*, in Britain, would connote *children's nurse* (whence *nursery*)
rather than *hospital nurse.* See also **operating theatre; casualty ward; health visitor.**

sister company   SEE COMMENT
One of a number of subsidiaries of a parent company, in relation to the other subsidiaries. See **company.**

sit an examination   **take an examination**
Also **sit for an examination.**

sit bodkin. See **bodkin.**

sit down under   *Inf.* **stand for**
Inf. To *put up with.* What the British won't *sit down under*, the Americans won't *stand
for.* The British use *stand for* as well.

site, *v.t.*   **locate**
Large-scale industry is *sited* in the Midlands. Americans would have said *located* or
situated.

sitrep, n.   SEE COMMENT
Report on current situation; a military abbreviation.

sitter-in, *n.*   **baby-sitter**
For a child, not for a baby. Americans don't distinguish; they're all called *baby-sitters.*
Babysitter, in Britain, refers to one who takes care of a baby. See also **child-minder.**

sitting, *n.*   *approx.* **serving**
Some London restaurants have so many *sittings* a night; that is why it's so important
to **book** (reserve) in advance. Nobody rings up a restaurant and asks for this or that
sitting (which is simply a restaurateur's term) as one does, or used to, on large ships.

sitting, *adj.*   **incumbent**
In discussing American presidential elections, British television commentators and newspaper columnists invariably refer to the 'sitting president.' Americans call him the *incumbent*, using the adjective as a substantive to describe the one in office.

sitting-room, *n.*   **living-room**
Sitting-room sounds old-fashioned in America. *Living room* is coming into use as a synonym for **sitting-room**. See also **lounge; reception room; drawing-room.**

sitting tenant   **statutory tenant**
A tenant *in situ*, who is legally entitled to remain so despite the expiration of his lease.

situations vacant   **help wanted**
Advertisement page heading. As usual, the British phrase is somewhat grander. Synonymous with **vacancies.**

six, *n.*   SEE COMMENT
In cricket, a fly ball that lands beyond the **boundary** (the white line marking the outer limits of the playing field, or **ground**) scores six runs, as compared with a *boundary*, which scores only four. A *six* is the supreme achievement of a batsman, and rarely happens. It is far rarer than a home run in baseball. To *hit* (sometimes *knock*) a person *for six* is to *knock him for a loop, knock the daylights out of him*, in the sense of demolishing an opponent in an argument. One can *hit something* (as well as *someone*) *for six*: a weak argument from an adversary, for example. See also **batsman; cricket.**

sixpence, *n.*
See **Appendix II.A.**

sixth form   SEE COMMENT
The normal curriculum at a secondary school (ages 13–18, usually) consists of five **forms** (*grades*). A minority of pupils go into a higher form, called the *sixth form*, to prepare for university. This does not in all cases involve an extra year: gifted students may go directly from the fourth to the sixth. A pupil in this form is called a *sixth-former*. *See also* **A levels.**

sizar, *n.*   SEE COMMENT
Student at Cambridge, and at Trinity College, Dublin, on part or full scholarship. Originally, a *sizar* had to perform certain duties for other students that are now taken care of by paid employees of the College. *Servitor*, now obsolete, was the approximate equivalent at some Oxford colleges. See also **bursar; exhibition.**

skew-whiff, *adj., adv., Inf.*   **crooked(ly); askew**

skier. See **sky ball.**

skilly, *n.*   SEE COMMENT
Broth made of oatmeal and water, flavored with meat. A very thin type of gruel indeed. Also known as *skilligalee* and *skilligolee*, accented on the final syllable.

skimble-scamble, skimble-skamble, *adj.*   **confused, rambling, incoherent**
This lively adjective might describe a narration of a frightening experience, or an attempt to explain something somewhat beyond the speaker's power of comprehension. It is said to have developed as a reduplication of the dialectal word *scamble* (to scramble, shamble, sprawl, struggle or trample), or it may be simply a union of *scramble* and *shamble*. Shakespeare used it in *Henry IV, Part 1* (Act III, Scene 1), when Hotspur, angrily mocking the long-winded Glendower, says:

. . .sometimes he angers me
With telling me of the moldwarp [mole] and the ant,
Of the dreamer Merlin and his prophecies,

And of a dragon and a finless fish,
A clip-wing'd griffon and a moulten raven,
A crouching lion and a ramping [rearing] cat,
And such a deal of skimble-skamble stuff
As puts me from my faith...

(Hotspur ges on, and on, and on; it's well worth reading!) This uncommon word, in later days, was used by James Morris, in *Farewell the Trumpets* (Faber & Faber, London, 1978), in the expression 'treated with skimble-skamble deference,' to describe the way a throng might treat a great personage. In its sound, this adjective is reminiscent of **crinkle-crankle.**

skin, *n.*   **cigarette paper**
Slang. See also **roll-up.**

skinful, *n.*   *Slang.* **load on**
Slang. An awful lot to drink. To *have got a skinful* or *one's skinful* is to *be stinkin' drunk.*

skinhead, *n.*   *approx. Inf.* **young tough**
Slang. A special breed of hoodlum characterized by very closely cropped hair and **bovver** *boots.* See also **rough.**

skint, *adj., Slang.*   *Slang.* **broke**

skip, *n.*   **1. refuse container**
                                                        2. college servant
1. Large refuse container used by building contractors at the site. Cf. **skivvy-bin.**
2. See **gyp.**

skipper   **captain**
Inf. Of a cricket **side.**

skipping-rope, *n.*   **jump rope**
And to *skip* is to *jump rope*. See **Appendix I.A.3.**

skirt, *n.*   **flank**
Butcher's term; a *skirt* of beef.

skirting, skirting-board, *n.*   **baseboard**

skive, *v.i.*   *Slang.* **goldbrick**
Slang. Military slang, synonymous with **scrimshank** and **dodge the column;** to *goof off, shirk, get out of working.* A *skiver* is a practitioner of this type of evasion. See also **swing it; swing the lead.**

skivvy, *n., v.i.*   SEE COMMENT
Slang. A term of derogation of the order of *scullery maid;* the lowest on the scale (see also **slavey**). No American slang equivalent. Also used as a verb meaning to 'do any menial work'.

skivvy-bin, *n.*   **dumpster; public rubish receptacle**
Inf. About ten ton capacity; strategically placed by local authorities for dumping refuse that the regular **dustman** (*garbage man*—his title has recently been upgraded to *sanitation officer*) won't take away.

skulk, *n., v.i.*   **shirker; shirk**
As an intransitive verb *skulk* means to 'hide' or 'slink about' in both countries. A third meaning, to 'shirk,' is exclusively British. The noun *skulker* could apply to any of those meanings, but when it is shortened to *skulk* it means a 'shirker.' Synonymous with **slacker.**

sky ball   *approx.* **pop fly**
A cricket term, often informally *skier* (pronounced SKY' − ER).

slack, *v.i., Slang.*   *Slang.* **goof off**

slacker, *n.*   **shirker**
Slang. The usual connotation in America is evasion of military duty, so that *slacker* is
normally understood to mean *draft-dodger.* The word is the *-er* noun from the verb *slack,*
which is never heard (in the sense of *goof off*) in America. Synonymous with **skulk.**

slag, *v.t.*   **criticize**
Slang. Or *mock,* or *deride.* To *slag* someone *down* is to give him hell, let him have it.
Heard, but not commonly.

slang, *v.t.*   **abuse; revile**
Inf. A *slanging-match* is an *altercation,* a *helluva row,* in which everybody washes everybody else's dirty linen but nobody's gets clean.

slang, back. See **back slang.**

slant-tailed, *adj.*   **fast-back**
Automotive term. See also **Appendix II.E.**

slap, *adv.*   *Inf.* **right**
Inf. Examples: *slap through* is *right through; slap into* is *right into.* To walk *slap* into
someone is to *bump* into him.

slap-down, *adv.*   *Inf.* **one hundred percent**
Inf. As in: *I am slap-down on his side,* referring to a disagreement between two persons.
An American would be likely to say: *I am one hundred percent with him.*

slap-up, *adj.*   *Inf.* **bang-up**
Inf. First rate, great, terrific. The British once used both *slap-up* and *bang-up* commonly;
both would be considered old-fashioned now. A *slap-up do* meant a 'bang-up job,' a
first-rate piece of work, and especially a splendid party with no expense spared.

slash, *n., v.i., Vulgar.*   **piss**

slate, on the. See **on the slate.**

slate, *v.t.*   *Inf.* **pan**
Inf. To express a harsh criticism. Thus: *The reviewers slated the book unmercifully.* Syn-
onomous with **send up rotten.** But (especially in Lancashire) when a girl says *I am slated,*
she means something entirely different—that her petticoat is showing. Slate roofs are
common in that county; the slabs are affixed in layers, like shingles, and sometimes a
slab hangs over the edge when it is not supposed to. Somehow the unintentionally
exposed edge of a slip or petticoat reminded local wags of what must have been common
errors in roofing technique; hence this picturesque regional colloquialism. Another quaint
expression on the subject of slips showing is "Charley's dead!" which, when said to a
woman, means 'Your slip is showing.'

slate club, *n,*   **lodge**
In the sense of 'mutual aid society.' The members pay modest weekly dues, called
subscription in Britain.

slavey, *n.*   SEE COMMENT
Slang. A *maid of all work.* Usually connotes one employed in a rooming house (see
also **skivvy**). No American slang equivalent.

sledge, *n., v.t.*   **sled**
Children go *sledging* in Britain, *sledding*, or more commonly *coasting*, in America, where a *sledge* is a heavy vehicle used in pulling loads, usually over snow or ice.

sleep in   **sleep late**
Not used in the American sense of domestic servants who live with the family they work for.

sleeping partner   **silent partner**

sleeping policeman. See **ramp; rumble strip.**

sleep rough   **sleep in the open**
Inf. Out of doors, the way the youngsters do it for fun on the road, and the homeless do it because they're homeless.

sleepy, *adj.*   **overripe**
Of fruit, especially pears.

sleepy sickness   **sleeping sickness**
Encephalitis lethargica in both countries.

sleeve link, *n.*   **cuff link**

slice, *n.*   **bracket**
A term used in connection with British taxation. The rates go up as the *slices* go up. American rates follow a similar type of pattern, but the *slices* are known as *brackets*. Synonyms are **band** and **tranche** (the latter borrowed from the French).

slide, *n., v.i.*   **fall; drop**
Used of stock exchange prices when the news is bad.

sliding keel   **centerboard**
The British use *sliding keel* to refer to a hinged centerboard, and *centreboard* and *centreplate* for the kind that pull up vertically without pivots. Both countries used *daggerplate* for small *centerboards* that can be pulled up and out and stored when not in use.

slim, *v.i.*   **diet**
As in, *I mustn't have any butter on my toast; I'm slimming.* Am American would say: *I am dieting,* or more commonly, *I am on a diet.* See also **bant.**

slime, *v.i., Slang.*   *Inf.* **get away with it**

slinger, *n.*   **sausage**
Army slang. Can also mean *dumpling.* A more common slang term is **banger.**

slip, *n.*   **extreme side seat**
Theater term. There are *upper slips* and *lower slips* (depending on which gallery), too near the side walls to afford satisfactory vision.

slip-on shoes   **loafers**

slipover, *n.*   **sleeveless sweater**

slipper bath   SEE COMMENT
A bathtub in the shape of a slipper, with one covered end. Did they ever exist in America? Just about obsolete in Britain—but you never know.

slippy. See **look slippy!**

slip road   **access road**
The road by which one enters or leaves a parkway or turnpike.

slip seat   **jump seat**

Sloane Rangers   SEE COMMENT
Living in the vicinity of Sloane Square, they dress expensively and conservatively (silk scarves tied under their chins), work as well paid personal secretaries and spend weekends in the country hunting. They have, most of them, **double-barrelled** names. Not quite the old **Mayfair,** as the particular panache is lacking, but as close as one can get in these inflation ridden times.
Rosie Boycott tells us, in *Batty, Bloomers and Boycott* (Hutchinson, London, 1982), that the name was coined by Peter York of *Harper's and Queen* magazine. "The similarities in style, manners and dress of these jolly nice girls caught the attention of *Harper's and Queen,* which immortalized their existence in an article entitled 'The Sloane Rangers' published in October 1975. This describes *Sloane Rangers* as 'the nicest British girls. They wear Gucci not because they want to seem international girls, Eurogirls, but because there's something archaic, pageboyish about them, and Hermes scarves because they, too, are archaic and unmistakable...and navy blue because it Always Looks Good.'" For a witty and exhaustive (perhaps more than you really wanted to know) treatment of the subject, see *The Official Sloane Ranger Handbook,* by Ann Barr and the same Peter York (St. Martin's Press, New York, and Ebury Press, London, 1983), which includes a study of Sloane *men.*

slop, *n.*   **cop**
Slang. Slop developed as a shortened form of *ecilop,* which is *police* spelled backwards. This is an example of **back slang.** For synonyms see **bobby.**

slope off, *Slang.*   *Inf.* **sneak off**

slop out   SEE COMMENT
Slang. To *slop out* is to carry out one's chamber pot, or whatever vessel is provided in unsanitary, overcrowded prisons for the inmates. This is a hateful practice imposed on prisoners in antiquated quarters lacking proper toilet facilities, much protested by the inmates, according to newspaper reports of unrest and rioting in those institutions.

slops, *n. pl., Slang.*   **1. sailors' clothes and bedding**
                                                     2. sloppy clothes
1. Issued by the navy.
2. Ready-made, and uncared for.

slosh, *v.t.*   **smack**
Inf. In the sense of 'hit.'

sloshed, *adj.*   *Slang.* **smashed**
Slang. Tipsy, tight, squiffed, i.e., *intoxicated.* See also: **have one over the eight; skinful; squiffy; pissed.**

slot machine   **vending machine**
A distinction worth remembering, as the British phrase may well raise unfounded hopes in an American's (especially a Las Vegan's) breast. See also **fruit machine,** and expressions derived from *slot machine:* **penny in the slot; the penny dropped.**

slowcoach *n., Inf.*   *Inf.* **slowpoke**

slow off the mark,   *Inf.* **slow on the uptake**
Inf. See **off the mark.**

slow train   **local**
And **fast train** is the term for *express.* See also **stopping train.**

slut's wool   **dust balls**
Inf. The stuff that collects under the bed, behind the bureau, and other hard-to-reach places.

sly fox. See **Tom Tiddler's ground.**

smacker, *n.*   SEE COMMENT
Slang. Pound (currency). *Smacker* is also old-fashioned American slang for *dollar,* in this sense competing with *simoleon, bone,* and *buck.*

small ad   **classified ad**

small beer   *Inf.* **small time**
Inf. Insignificant.

smalls, *n. pl.*   **1.** *Inf.* **undies**
                                                             2. SEE COMMEENT
1. *Inf.* Even on fat ladies and gentlemen.
2. *Smalls* was the informal term for **responsions,** an Oxford examination procedure abolished in 1960.

smarmy, *adj.*   *Slang.* **oily**
Slang. In the sense of 'toadying.'

smartish, *adv.*   *Slang.* **on the double**
Slang. Tell the doctor to get here smartish! To walk *smartish* or *smartly* is to be going at a rapid pace. For a different and more common use of -ish, see **-ish.**

smash, *n.*   *Slang.* **smashup**
Slang. Traffic accident.

smashing, *adj.*   *Inf.* **terrific**
Inf. And a *smasher,* meaning 'something terrific,' usually refers to a girl, sometimes to a car. Adopted in America, to some extent.

smooth in   **get settled**
Inf. "I haven't smoothed in yet"—said by a man in a village antique shop when asked where the nearest **post-box** was. He'd been in the village only a week or so and hadn't settled in yet, found his way about, got to know the place, etc.

snag, *n.*   *Inf.* **trouble; catch**
Inf. When a Briton wants to explain what is holding something up, he very often starts the sentence with the phrase, *The snag is*...Americans tell you what the *catch is,* or the *hitch,* or the *problem,* or the *trouble.*

snap election. See **go to the country.**

snapper, *n.*   **snap**
Fastener used in dressmaking, also called **press stud.** An American *snapper,* the kind served at children's parties, is called a **cracker** in Britain. See also **popper.**

snap-tin, *n., Inf.*   **sandwich box**

snick, *n.*   SEE COMMENT
Inf. A cricket term for a ball not hit squarely but caught by the edge of the bat. See also **cricket; batsman.**

snicket, *n.*   **alley**
Synonymous with **twitten.**

snig, *n.*   **small eel**

snip, *n.*   **1. bargain**
                                                              2. *Inf.* **sure thing**
                                                                 3. *Inf.* **cinch**
                                                                 4. *Inf.* **steal**
1. *Inf.* An advantageous purchase.
2. *Inf.* In the sense of a 'cinch,' a 'certainty.' This usage originated in racing slang;
sometimes *dead snip.*
3. *Inf.* In the sense of 'anything easily done.'
4. *Inf.* In the sense of 'bargain.'

snob, *n.*   SEE COMMENT
   Slang. A *shoemaker,* for which there appears to be no slang American equivalent. This
usage is pretty well confined to oldtimers in the countryside. However, it is still sufficiently alive to have figured in *The Times* (London) crossword puzzle of May 11, 1976.
If you are not familiar with *The Times* crossword puzzle, it is too late to get started now:
they are masterpieces and nightmares of obfuscation and obscurantism. In that particular number, the definition of a four-letter word was "At last a worshipper of status."
The answer was *snob.* One who worships status is a *snob,* and *snobs* (*cobblers*) work *at
lasts!*

snog, *v.i., Slang.*   **neck**

snookered, *adj.*   *Slang.* **up the creek; in a tight spot.**
   Slang. (The OO is long, as in ROOF.) The British borrow their adjective describing this
unhappy condition from the game of *snooker,* a variety of pocket billiards.

snorter, *n.*   **1.** *Slang.* **humdinger**
                                                              2. punch in the nose
1. *Slang.* Anything outstanding.
2. *Slang.* But it can be used metaphorically, as in *I wrote him a snorter* (i.e., an angry
letter).

snorting, *adj.*   **fabulous**
   Slang. Rarely heard nowadays.

snotty, *n.*   **midshipman**
   Slang. Sometimes *snottie.* Midshipmen wear buttons on their sleeves. A naval joke is
that they are there to prevent the young sailors from wiping their noses on their sleeves....

snout, *n., Slang.*   **1.** *Slang.* **stoolie**
                                                                 2. *Slang.* **butt**
1. A police informer.
2. A *cigarette,* especially in prison argot.

snowboots, *n. pl.*   **galoshes**
   Slang. In Britain **galoshes** are what the Americans call *rubbers,* or *overshoes.* See also
gumboots; rubbers; Wellingtons; boots.

snowed up   **snowed in**
   See **Appendix I.A.1.**

snuff it   *Slang.* **croak**
   Slang. Synonymous with **drop off the hooks,** i.e., *kick the bucket.*

snug, *n.*   SEE COMMENT
   At some **pubs,** the bar-parlor, a room offering more privacy than the rest of the
establishment. Sometimes called the **snuggery.**

snuggery, *n.*   **den**
Slang. One's particular hideaway at home. Also applied to a bar-parlor in a **pub**. See **snug**.

sociable, *n.*   **S-shaped couch**
Designed for two occupants partly facing each other.

social contract   SEE COMMENT
Historically, this phrase has meant a presumed voluntary agreement among individuals pursuant to which an organized society is brought into existence, or an agreement between the community and the governing authority defining the rights and obligations of each party. Hobbes, Locke, and Rousseau all had a hand in this formulation. In Britain after 1874, it signified an unwritten arrangement between the Labour Government and the trade unions, whereunder, in consideration of **wage restraint** by the unions, the government carried out certain policies (such as price control, limitation of corporate dividends, maintenance of welfare benefits, etc.) in favor of the unions. See also **pay policy.**
Philip Howard (*Words Fail Me*, Hamish Hamilton, London, 1980) says:

> It was neither social nor a contract; and that passionate socialist and libertarian Rousseau, whose phrase was plagiarized (*Du Contrat Social* was published in 1762) would have denounced it as an antisocial and provisional bargain between unscrupulous individual power blocks against the general will.

sock drawer   SEE COMMENT
Inf. To put something into one's *sock drawer* is to secrete it in safekeeping, like a confidential document, not intended for another's eyes. The closest American expression might be the *cookie jar* where housewives secrete money snitched from the household budget.

sod, *n.*   *Slang.* **bastard**
Slang. This vulgar term of abuse should really not be used in mixed company (if at all). Technically, it cannot be applied to a woman (any more than **fanny** formerly could be applied to a man). The reason is that it is short for *sodomite.* However, British youth of both sexes, unaware of its origin, are now heard to use it of, or hurl it at, persons of either sex. According to a former employee of the Oxford University Press who later became the head of the American branch of another British university press, one of the titles considered for the *Shorter Oxford English Dictionary* was *Shorter Oxford Dictionary.* This was dropped in favor of the present title, solely to avoid the embarrassing initials S.O.D. Communication with the Oxford University Press revealed this tale to be apocryphal. *Sod all* is an intensification of *bugger all,* which is, in turn, an intensification of **damn all,** and means 'not a goddamned thing.' *Sod* means 'goddamn' in the expression *sod him (her, it, them).* *Sodding* is another way of saying *goddamned,* as in *sodding little bastard.*
There is a relatively new golf club at Chipping Sodbury, in the County of Avon (formerly part of Wiltshire). Members of older and grander clubs concocted a Spoonerism and gave the newer club the affectionately derisive title of *Sodding Chipbury.*

sodding. See under **sod.**

Sod's Law   **Murphy's Law**
Inf. If anything can possibly go wrong with a test or experiment, it will. Originally applied to the natural sciences, the use of this law has been extended to cover day to day living and reads simply, *If anything can possibly go wrong it will,* to which has been added, *and it will happen at the worst possible moment.* The French equivalent is *la loi d'emmerdement maximum.* Warning when in France: according to *Cassell's French-English Dicitionary,* emmerder is a "very coarse verb, not in decent use," and *emmerdement* isn't even listed. Various Britons have expressed themselves on the subject of this law which regulates human affairs, in letters to *The Times Literary Supplement.* Richard Boston's letter appeared there on December 14, 1973:

Sir,   I don't know when Sod's Law first appeared in print but it was certainly well before your review of *An Introduction to Confirmation Theory* (October 19). I myself wrote about Sod's Law in the *New Statesman* in October 1970, where I described it as the force in nature that makes it rain mostly at weekends, which makes you get flu when you go on holiday, and which makes the phone ring just as you've stepped into the bath. However, I am by no means claiming to have discovered the Law, which I first heard formulated in King's College, Cambridge, in about 1960. Needless to say, the principle involved was well understood long before that, as is shown by the proverb "The bread never falls but on its buttered side" which is quoted by the *Oxford Dictionary of English Proverbs* as a Lancashire proverb dating from 1871.

I imagine that the term Sod's Law may have developed from a phrase which I believe is used by demolition contractors. By its very nature demolition is a chancy business and when you're bringing down bridges or factory chimneys it's always possible that something may go wrong. Allowance has to be made for the unpredictable or, to use the technical term, the Buggeration Factor. I first heard mention of this in a television interview with (if I remember rightly) Alan Whicker on *24 Hours* (or was it called *Tonight* in those far-off days?) in the mid-1950's and that I should imagine was the first time this word was used on television.

S.O.E. See **fanny.** Comment 3.

soft furnishings   curtain material
In a British department store, if you wanted the drapery department, you would ask for *soft furnishings;* if you asked for the *drapery department* you would find yourself looking at dress materials. See also **drapers' shop.**

soft goods   textiles

soldier on   *Slang.* **stick with it**
Inf. To *soldier* (often *soldier on the job*) means to 'loaf on the job' in both countries, to 'shirk.' To *soldier on,* by itself, means to 'persevere doggedly,' to 'stay with it,' 'keep plugging' or whatever else one who resembles John Bull does in the face of hopeless odds.

soldiers, *n. pl.*   bread strips
Inf. Bread cut into strips, to be dipped into soft-boiled eggs; term used mostly by children. Grown-ups call them **fingers.**

solicitor, *n.*   lawyer
But it is not that simple; *lawyer* in the sense of 'general practitioner.' See also **barrister.** In America the use of *solicitor* in the British sense is restricted to the office of solicitor general of the United States and of certain individual states.

solitaire. See **patience.**

somerset, *n.*   padded saddle
Especially for a one-legged rider like Lord Somerset, who popularized this type of saddle. He died in 1855.

sonic bang   sonic boom

soon as say knife. See **as soon as say knife.**

SOP   Senior Officer Present
Inf. Not, as one might think from American usage, an abbreviation of *standard operating procedure.* This term originated as a response to the military *Who's in charge here?* It has come to be used by non-military personnel as well.

soppy, *adj., Slang.*   mushy

sorbet. See **ice.**

sorbo rubber   **sponge hard rubber**
Used in the manufacture of children's bouncing balls, dog's toy bones, as well as the interior of cricket balls.

sort of thing   *Inf.* **kind of; like**
Inf. Appended to a statement, it muddies or attenuates it somewhat, pulls its teeth a little, lessening its impact *ex post facto*, like *so to speak, more or less, practically,* and inelegantly, *kind of,* or (in the mouths of so many youths) *like,* both of which, however, more often come first. Thus: *He's a clever chap, but apt to get confused, sort of thing,* or, *The poor man is reduced to begging, sort of thing.* An ungrammatical and tiresome usage. To make matters worse, latterly, *sort of style* has raised its silly head.

sort out   **1. work out**
                                                                  2. take care of
1. Very frequently used by the British in the best tradition of muddling through. Things are always going to be *sorted out* later, or will *sort themselves out.* There is a lurking suggestion of *mañana* in this amiable expression.
2. Another meaning altogether is to 'straighten (someone) out,' to 'let him have it,' to 'give him a going over.' Junior has taken the car without permission and Senior suddenly needs it: *Just wait till he gets back, I'll sort him out!* An irate American daddy might say, *I'll straighten him out!* or, *I'll tell him a thing or two!*

souteneur. See **ponce.**

south of the Border. See **(the) Border.**

spadger, *n., Slang.*   **sparrow**

spaghetti junction   **cloverleaf**
Inf. Jocular, semi-pejorative for any cloverleaf, but particularly for a complex one. The epithet was first applied to an especially complicated one in Birmingham, which evoked the image of a mess of cooked spaghetti.

spanner, *n.*   **wrench**
A *spanner in the works* is a *monkey wrench in the machinery.* A *box spanner* is a *lug wrench.*

spare, bit of. See **bit of spare.**

spare, go. See **go spare.**

spare, going. See **going spare.**

spare, send (someone). See **send (someone) spare.**

spare ground   **vacant lot**

spare line   **allocated line**
But not yet connected. Telephone term.

spare room   **guest room**

sparking-plug   **spark plug**
See **Appendix II.E.**

spark out   *Slang.* **pass out cold**
Slang. Usually, to *pass spark out,* meaning to 'pass out,' whether from booze, fright, or exhaustion. In an extreme case, it can even mean to 'pass out for once and for all time; to die.' But see **pass out.**

spatchcock, *v.t.*   **interpolate**
Inf. A *spatchcock* is a fowl hurridly cooked after being killed. This curious word appears to be a shortening of *dispatchcock*—one quickly *dispatched* by being disposed of in a hurry. (Are there distant echoes of poaching in this?) Somehow *spatchcock* became a verb, meaning to 'insert' or 'interpolate,' with a hint that the insertion was the hurried result of an afterthought; and there is the implication that the interpolation changed the force and meaning of the original message. In *The Times* (London) of April 8, 1974, it was said that certain students of international affairs "thought it...irregular that Mr. Callaghan, the Foreign Secretary, should have *spatchcocked* in his formal statement to the Council of Ministers on the terms of membership of the EEC a long quotation from the Labour Party's election manifesto." *Spatchcock* is not under any circumstances to be confused with a *spitchcock,* an entirely different kettle of *eel* which has been *split and broiled.* One can also *spitchcock* (i.e., 'split and broil') a fish or a bird or a fowl, and thus we somehow get back to *spatchcock!*

spate, *n.*   **flood**
Used in America only metaphorically to mean an 'outpouring,' the word also refers to literal inundations in Britain.

speaking clock   SEE COMMENT
One dials a certain telephone number, and the 'speaking clock,' a usually very pleasant voice, answers with the correct time. In some parts of America, there is a 'time and weather number' one can dial, in other parts only a weather number, and sometimes the operator will slip one the correct time, though this is against the rules.

speak up!   **louder!**
An exhortation not to courage, not to candor, but simply to audibility.

spectators' terrace   **observation deck**
Airport term. See also **waving base.**

Speech Day   SEE COMMENT
Also *Prize Day.* An aspect of public, state, and prep school life. Prizes are given out, speeches are made, parents mill about, and tea is drunk.

spencer, *n.*   1. **thin shirt worn under dress**
                                            2. **short tight-fitting jacket**
                                                              3. **wig**
1. An old-fashioned garment, still sometimes worn by elderly ladies.
2. Either a short, sometimes fur-trimmed close-fitting jacket worn by women and children last century, or a short, tight jacket with collar and lapels sported by men in the late 18th and early 19th centuries, named after the second Earl Spencer (1758-1834), an English politician.
3. An English wig, named after Charles Spencer, third Earl of Sunderland (1674-1722), a British Prime Minister for a few years before his death.

spend, *n.*   **expenditure**
Verb now used as a noun in Britain in signify the amount a customer spends. Bemoaning the absence of American tourists in 1986 because of the fear of terrorism, the news reports, comparing the habits of American visitors and those from other countries such as Germany and Japan, showed that the average American *spend* was much greater. See **read** for another example of a verb used as a noun.

spend a penny   *Inf.* **go to the bathroom**
Inf. This is a term pertaining principally to ladies and derives from the fact that their arrangements, even in the simpler operations, in public places, are a little different from men's in that the little cabinets involved are locked and require the insertion of a coin

(it used to be a penny) in order to unlock them; just another bit of evidence to prove that it is still a man's world. A lady without a penny might well be a lady in distress. The cost has risen but the phrase goes on, and will. The term is less often used by men. Their euphemism is *have a* **wash.** The term is becoming old-fashioned and is used jocularly, nowadays, by the younger generation. The common euphemism is *use the* **loo** or *go to the loo.* In a restaurant or other public place, one would not inquire as to the whereabouts of the *loo*; the anxious patron would ask for the Gents' or the Ladies,' depending. See also **pee.**

spends, *n. pl.*   **expense account**
Inf. Headlinese: "Councillors to get extra *spends* for civic entertainment." Sounds like a bit of journalese that won't last.

spif(f)licate, *v.t.*   *Slang.* **crush**
Slang. To knock the hell out of.

spin, *n.*   **English**
Billiards term.

spinney, *n.*   **thicket**
A small bit of woods.

spirits, *n. pl.*   **hard liquor**

Spithead nightingale   **bosun**
Inf. In the Royal Navy. So called from *Spithead,* a naval anchorage near Portsmouth, the *nightingale* being a reference to a bosun's whistle.

spiv, *n.*   *Inf.* **sharp operator**
Inf. He lives by his wits, just managing to stay within the law. More specifically, a small-scale black market operator. Also applied to race track touts.

split-arse, *adv., Slang.*   *Slang.* **lickety-split**

split of a hurry, *Inf.*   *Inf.* **hell of a hurry**

split on   *Inf.* **squeal on**
Inf. See also **put (someone's) pot on; round on; grass; snout; shop, 2.**

spoil, *n.*   **rubble**
Rare in American, this British term is used to describe the dirt and rubble that comes out of a hole during excavation.

sponge bag   **toilet kit**
A small waterproof bag of toilet articles. The old ones were like miniature duffle bags with drawstrings. Nowadays they come with zippers.

sponge finger   **ladyfinger**

sport one's oak   SEE COMMENT
Inf. Originally (and still mainly) a university expression. An outside door would usually be of *oak*—or used to be, at any rate. *Sport,* in this curious usage, means 'show ostentatiously,' as in *sport a new shirt* (or a fancy waistcoat, or whatever—the implication being that the garment is rather showy). Thus, when you *sport the oak,* i.e., make a point of showing the outside of your front door to the public, you are *telling the world to stay out;* that you are busy and don't want to be disturbed, at any cost. Perhaps a closer definition would be *hang out the* DO NOT DISTURB *sign.*

Sports Day   SEE COMMENT
Sports Day is an annual function at most schools. On *Sports Day* the following things happen:
1. The parents are invited to watch the students engage in athletic competitions.

2. Tea is served in a huge **marquee** and the platters of goodies are distributed by well-scrubbed little boys.
3. It rains.

spot, *n.*   **1.** *Inf.* **bit**
                                                                        2. pimple
                                                          3. (decimal) point
1. *Inf.* E.g., a *spot* of lunch. A *spot of tea* means something more than just a cup of tea. It involves something solid as well, even if minuscule. A *spot to eat* is a *bite*. See **tea.**
2. *Inf.* Usually found in the plural. *Spotty* means 'pimply' in a phrase like *a spotty youth.*
3. Where an American would describe the number 123.45 as '123 point 45,' a Briton would say '123 *spot* 45.' This practice began in foreign exchange dealings but has begun to spread to domestic (**inland**) ones as well.

spot on, *adv.*   *Inf.* **on the nose**
   Inf. Meaning, 'in exactly the right place.' The British congratulated Messrs. Neil Armstrong & Co. for landing *spot-on target.* Also **bang on; dead on.**

spotted dog   SEE COMMENT
   Inf. Roly-poly *pudding* with raisins or currants. The image is that of a Dalmation. Sometimes called *spotted Dick.* See **roly-poly pudding.**

spring-clean, *n.*   **spring cleaning**
   For once, it's the Americans who add the *-ing;* usually it is the British. See **Appendix I.A.3.**

spring greens   **young cabbage**
   With their heads still unformed. Very tender and tasty and never come across by the author in America.

spring onion   **scallion**

spun, *adj.*   *Slang.* **fagged**
   Slang. Done in; *tuckered out.* Past participle of *spin,* in its sense of 'whirling someone around,' perhaps by delivering a blow that sends him spinning.

spunk, *n.*   *Slang.* **come**
   Slang. Seminal fluid. Although the meaning 'pluck' is the usual sense in both countries, there are situations where it would be advisable, in Britain, to seek a synonym.

squab, *n.*   **back of car seat**
   See **Appendix II.E.**

squailer, *n.*   **leaded stick**
   A not very common country term, denoting a stick with a metal knob which is used for throwing at small animals like squirrels; but nothing to do with the game of **squails.**

squails, *n. pl.*   SEE COMMENT
   A game played with small wooden disks called *squails,* on a round table called a *squail board;* but a **squailer** is not a squails player.

square, *n.*   **1. paper napkin**
                                                           2. mortar-board
1. *Inf.* See also **serviette.**
2. *Slang.* University jargon.

square, *adj.*   **even**
   Inf. As in *a square hundred (pounds,* e.g.), where an American would speak of *an even hundred.*

square-bashing, *n.* close order drill
But in a more general sense, loosely applied to any type of marching about on a military parade ground or barrack square, whence the name.

squareface, *n.* gin
Inf. From the squarish shape of the bottles in which gin was originally sold in South Africa, and often still is in Britain (*Bombay, Gordon's, Boodles,* etc.)

(the) Square Mile SEE COMMENT
The heart of the **City.**

squarson, *n.* SEE COMMENT
Combination of squire and parson, a **portmanteau** word.

squash, *n.* -ade
A soft drink. A *lemon squash* is a *lemonade,* an *orange squash* an *orangeade,* and so on. The drink is commonly made from a concentrate to which water (usually tepid) is added. See also **minerals.** *Squash* is also slang for a *crowded party* or *meeting.*

squashed fly biscuits. See **garibaldi.**

squib, damp. See **damp squib.**

squiffer, *n.* *Slang.* **squeeze-box**
Slang. Usually refers to a concertina rather than an accordion.

squiffy, *adj.* *Slang.* **tipsy**
Slang. Americans use *squiffed* which, however, indicates a somewhat more advanced stage of the curse of drink than *squiffy.*

squireen, *n.* SEE COMMENT
A *small landowner;* more commonly used in Ireland than England.

squitters, *n. pl., Slang.* *Slang.* **the runs**

S.R.N. SEE COMMENT
Common abbreviation for *State Registered Nurse.*

staff, *n.* personnel
The British use the word *staff* where the Americans would say *servants* or, in a business, *employees* or *personnel.* STAFF ONLY is a sign frequently seen on doors in business establishments visited by the public, particularly hotels, restaurants and the like. *Short-staffed* would be *short-handed* in America. *Staff finder* is occasionally seen as a heading in British newspapers where the American equivalent would be *help wanted.* *Staff vacancies* is another phrase meaning the same thing. *Staff bureau* and *staff agency* are somewhat more elegant terms for *employment agency.* In educational institutions, *staff* is used to denote the entire teaching body, as opposed to *faculty,* the equivalent American term. In Britain, **faculty** refers only to departments, like the *Faculty* of Medicine, of Law, of Engineering, etc.

staggerer, *n.* *Inf.* **blow**
Inf. In the sense of a 'riposte,' 'retort,' or a 'bit of repartee' that knocks the other fellow off balance. Sometimes used to describe an event that knocks the stuffing out of you.

staging post stopover
Inf. By extension, used to describe a major preparatory stage, e.g., *The talks may prove to be a staging post on the road to peace.*

stall, *n.*   **1. stand**
                                                                                2. orchestra seat
1. A *stall* generally is an *outdoor counter* or *stand* for the purveying of goods, particularly
food (see **coffee-stall**). See also **set out one's stall.**
2. A *seat in the orchestra.*

stalls, *n. pl.*   **orchestra**
The stalls are the equivalent of *the orchestra* as a description of that part of a theater,
concert hall, etc.

stall, set out one's. See **set out one's stall.**

stand, *v.i.*   **run**
A Briton *stands* for office; an American *runs* for it. One might wonder what the
sociological implications are in this disparity of usage. The following letter appeared in
The Times (London) on June 16, 1970.

> **Standing to sit**
> *From Mr. Richard Wood*
> Sir, Now you've spoiled it—by telling us that David Howell was "running" for
> election at Guildford. For years I have been telling American friends that, while they
> run, we stand.
> Yours faithfully,
> RICHARD WOOD, Standing for Bridlington.
> Flat Top House, Bishop Wilton, York.

standard, *n.*   **grade**
Still used to indicate the year (first, second, etc.) at school, but rather old-fashioned
now and more or less restricted to primary school. **Form** is generally used of secondary
and higher schools.

Standard English   SEE COMMENT
Commonly abbreviated to S.E. In the words of David Abercrombie (*Problems and
Principles,* Longmans, Green & Co. Ltd., London, 1955):

> Not only is it different from the dialects linguistically...it differs from them socially
> and politically also. Unlike the dialects, it is not tied to any particular region or country,
> but is a *universal* form in English; it is the kind used everywhere by educated people.
> This, moreover, is the *official* form of English, the only kind which is used for public
> information and administration. It thus has a quite different standing in the English-
> speaking world from the dialects...Although it is called "English" it no longer has any
> necessary connection with England...

standard lamp, *n.*   **floor lamp**
Other American equivalents are *standing lamp* and *bridge lamp.*

stand down   **1. retire; withdraw**
                                                                              2. postpone
1. To *retire* from a team, a job, the witness stand. Used both transitively and intransitively. In military circles, to *stand down* is to *go off duty:* in politics, to *withdraw one's
candidacy.*
2. To *postpone,* to *discontinue temporarily,* as in *Rescue operations had to be stood down because
of heavy seas.*

stand in (someone's) light, *Inf.*   **stand in (someone's) way**

stand off   **lay off**
To discharge temporarily employees who have become superfluous or, as they say
in Britain, **redundant.**

stand one's own   hold one's own

stand-up (piano)   upright (piano)

stang, *n.*   1. sting
                                                              2. beam
1. Or the resulting wound, in the North of England.
2. 'Wooden beam' or any wooden pole or stick.

stank, *n., v.t.*   dam
   Inf. This is a Gloucestershire term signifying a 'makeshift dam,' e.g., in a little brook
to make a drinking pool for cattle. It can be used as a transitive verb meaning to 'dam
up,' e.g., a brook, temporarily for any purpose. It is also used in the Midlands as a
technical canal term, as when a canal has to be *stanked* in order to lay an underground
pipe that has to travel under the bed of the canal.

starchy, *adj.*   *Inf.* stuffy
   Inf. As in the expression *nothing starchy about him!*

stargazey, *n.*   SEE COMMENT
   Inf. A kind of pie made in Cornwall with small fish (usually, with the heads looking
out through the pastry crust and, as it were, stargazing). Also *starrygazey.*

staring, *adj., adv.*   1. *Inf.* loud
                                                           2. *Inf.* raving
1. *Inf. Unpleasantly conspicuous, eye-shattering,* as a *staring* pink tie or a weird checked
vest.
2. *Inf.* Only in the common phrase *stark staring mad.*

starkers, *adj.*   stark naked
   Slang. Sometimes *starko.* See **Harry....**

stark ravers   *Slang.* **nuts**
   Slang. Raver by itself connotes homosexuality. As to the *-ers* in *ravers,* see **Harry...**
This is a rather old-fashioned term, giving way to **bonkers.**

start a hare   raise an issue
   Inf. Often a time-wasting one.

starters, *n. pl.*   appetizer
   Inf. As in, *What do you fancy for starters, love?* Slightly vulgar, more so than *afters.* Chi-
chi restaurants tend to use these terms self-consciously in the menus.

starting handle   crank
   Automobile term, now rather archaic. However, sometimes quite helpful. See **wind,**
v.t., and **Appendix II.E.**

star turn   *Inf.* **topnotcher**
   Inf. A **turn,** in vaudeville days, was an *act;* a *star turn* was a *headliner.* The term was
extended to include a *top performer* in any field: *the tops.* It is used to designate the chief
or central figure in any situation. When Sir Peter Ramsbotham, the British Ambassador
to the U.S., was relieved of that post in favor of the Prime Minister's son-in-law, and
posted to the governorship of Bermuda, there was an outcry and several of the newspapers and television commentators referred to him as a *star turn,* i.e., the glittering
gem in the diplomatic diadem. But *star turn* can at times—accented, perhaps, with a
shrug—be used pejoratively, to describe a person who is a *star* in a way that doesn't
do him any credit, like an outstanding bore, or lout. There are times when the emphasis
seems to be on an individual's propensity to get attention, someone with an idiosyn-
crasy who doesn't do anything to suppress it. Thus: *That Jones is a star turn; all he has
to do is walk into a room and things start happening.* In this use, the closest American
equivalent would be *humdinger.*

state school   **public school**
For the meaning of *public school* as used in Britain, see **public school.**

station calendar   **bulletin board**
On the wall at major railroad stations.

station-manager, *n.*   **station agent**
Formerly *station-master.*

statutory business   **official business**
Nothing to do with rape; a basis for avoiding parking tickets for government vehicles
in either country.

stay, *v.i.*   **live; reside**
Mainly Scottish: *I stay in Morningside, on the south side of Edinburgh,* or, *He comes from
Aberdeen. Really? Whereabouts does he stay?*

STD   SEE COMMENT
To be on *STD* means to be hooked into the automatic long-distance dialing system.
The letters stand for *Subscriber Trunk Dialling.* (See **trunk call.**)

steading, *n.*   **farmstead**
A *farm with buildings.*

step out   *Inf.* **step on it**
In England, to *step out* is to *hurry* or *hurry up.* Informally, it can also mean 'lead a
joyful social life.' In America, to *step out* is to go to a party or dance, or on a date;
sometimes, to go out on the town.

stew, *n.*   **fish tank**

stick, *n., v.t.*   **1.** *n.,* **pole**
                                                                   2. *n., Slang.* **guy**
                                                                   3. *v.t.,* **stake up**
                                                                   4. *v.t.,* **post**
                                                                   5. *v.t.,* **stand**
1. *n., Inf.* Ski terminology.
2. *n., Inf.* Particularly in an expression like, *He's not a bad old stick.*
3. *v.t., Inf.* Term used in gardening, with special reference to peas. A favorite expression
(and activity) of the wife of the poet laureate William Wordsworth.
4. *v.t., Inf.* Especially in the sign STICK NO BILLS. Sign alongside Hyde Park (London):
BILL STICKERS WILL BE PROSECUTED. See **hoarding.**
5. *v.t., Inf.* In the sense of 'bear' or 'tolerate,' as in, *I can't stick it a minute longer!*

stick, get the. See **get the stick.**

stick, give (someone) some. See **give (someone) some stick.**

stickjaw, *n.*   **chewy candy**
Slang. Life *taffy,* which is called **toffee** in Britain.

stick no bills! See **stick, 4.**

stick out, *v.i., Inf.*   *Slang.* **stick to one's guns**

stick up   **puzzle**
Slang. British robbers, as well as American, *stick up* their victims. But there is a second
British slang meaning which has its approximate American equivalent in the verb to
stick, meaning to 'stump,' or 'present someone with an unsolvable problem.' In this

connotation *stuck up,* in Britain, would mean 'completely at a loss,' the American equivalent being *stuck;* but it can also indicate unjustified superiority in Britain as well as in America. (The more usual term for this obnoxious attribute in Britain is **toffee-nosed.**)

stick, wrong end of. See **(have, get the) wrong end of the stick.**

sticky finish   **bad end**
Inf. The kind one should do his utmost not to come to.

sticky tape   **adhesive tape**
See also **Sellotape.**

sticky wicket   **tough situation**
Inf. A **wicket,** in **cricket,** is said to be *sticky* when it is drying out after rain. On such a wicket, the ball on its way to the **batsman,** after bouncing in front of him, behaves erratically, especially when bowled by a *spin-bowler,* one who is expert at imparting a twisting motion to the ball after it bounces. Obviously, a batsman batting on a *sticky wicket* is in a tough, tricky situation; and the term, like so many others from cricket, has been extended metaphorically to the general language. See **wicket.**

sting, *v.t.*   *Slang.* **soak**
Slang. To *sting* somebody such and such an amount for something is to 'soak' him, i.e., 'overcharge' him. Thus, in an antique shop, *What do you suppose he will sting us for that table?* Its use in America is normally confined to the passive participle (*stung*) in this context. In a sentence like, *I'd love champagne but I don't want to sting you,* the considerate young lady is telling her escort that she doesn't want the dinner check to get too big.

stock-breeder, *n.*   **cattleman**

stockbroker belt   **nouveau-riche suburb**
Stockbroker Tudor is *phony Tudor,* an architectural style in the manner of Anne Hathaway's Cottage. William Cobbett ("Peter Porcupine"), 1763–1835, the British political essayist and journalist in both countries, coined a different jocular pejorative for it: *tax-eater's showy.*

stockholder, *n.*   **livestock farmer**
In this usage, synonymous with **stock-breeder** and nothing to do with corporations; but it can have the usual American meaning as well.

stockinet, *n.*   **elastic knit fabric**
Used for undergarments.

stockist, *n.*   **retailer**
A shopkeeper who stocks the article in question.

stock-jobber, *n.*   **dealer in stocks**
In America, this word is most frequently used as a contemptuous reference to a stock salesman, particularly one who promotes worthless securities. In Britain it has no such shady connotation, describing merely an agent who acts as go-between or intermediary between brokers, never dealing directly with the public.

stocks. See **shares.**

stodge, *n., v.t., v.i.*   **1.** *n.,* **heavy food**
           2. *n.,* **glutton**
           3. *v.t., v.i., Inf.* **stuff**
1. *n., Slang.* Used especially of the puddings served at boarding-school that lie so heavily on the stomach.
2. *n., Slang.* Who overeats and feels *stodgy.*
3. *n., Slang.* In the sense of 'stuff oneself.' See also **pogged.**

stoker, *n.* **locomotive fireman**
The British and American usages are identical in shipboard terminology, but in Britain the term applies equally to train personnel.

stomach warmer **hot-water bottle**
Usage is regional and the American term is commonly used.

stone, *n.* See **Appendix II.C.1.f.**

stone cladding **stone facing**

stone the crows! *Inf.* **good heavens!**
Inf. A gentle expletive, now going out of fashion, except in Australia.

stonewall, *v.i.* *Inf.* **stall**
Inf. The unsportsmanlike practice of playing for time in cricket. The trick is for the **batsman** merely to defend his **wicket** rather than attempt to score runs, so that time will run out. Like *keeping possession* in American football and taking plenty of time to go into and out of the huddle with your eye on the clock, or *freezing the ball* in basketball. As with many cricket terms, it has been taken into the general language to describe *stalling for time,* which is close to, but not identical with the narrower American use of the term to mean 'obstruct discussion'.

stonk, *n.* *Inf.* **going over**
Slang. Literally, a *heavy shelling,* a word based upon a World War II military term for a highly specialized artillery technique (a 525-yard block of fire) christened *Standard Regimental Concentration,* a mouthful quickly shortened to *Stonk,* and then erroneously applied to just about any artillery action in the way professional jargon is so often misapplied by amateurs. The term passed into civilian use to describe anything that is devastating, like being thoroughly chewed out by the boss, for instance. Stronger than **rocket,** also originally military. Not a common usage by any means, but extant.

stony, *adj.* *Slang.* **broke**
Slang. Flat broke; stone broke, in fact.

stood out **postponed**
Procedural term, in law.

stooge about *Slang.* **kill time**
Slang. Somewhat more actively than, for example, playing solitaire; implies some activity, like a **pub-crawl,** or aimless driving around. See also **fossick; frig about.**

stook, *n.* **shock of grain**
Stack of sheaves of grain stood on end in a field so that they remain upright.

stop, *v.t., v.i.* **1. stay**
2. fill
1. Thus: *He stops in bed till noon,* or, *Why don't you stop at my house instead of the inn?* To *stop away* is to *stay away.* Also, *I'm happy and I want to stop like this* and *We'll knock this job off today if it stops fine,* but this usage is fading out. A good pal will *stop up* with you all night when you're in trouble. With a bad cold, you may want to *stop in* for a couple of days.
2. Dental terminology. Cavities are *stopped* or *filled* in Britain and a *stopping* is a *filling.*

stoppage, *n.* **deduction from wages**
E.g., withholding tax.

stopping train **local (train)**
An express is a **fast** train. Semi-antiquated usage; common term is **slow train.**

store, *n.*   **warehouse**
It is also used to mean a 'shop,' usually a large one. *Stores (n. pl.)* means 'supplies,' like food provisions at home, or *stock* in the sense of the 'inventory of a business.' A common sign on small shops in villages: POST OFFICE AND STORES, where *stores* means 'provisions and supplies.' *In store* means 'in storage,' but also has the same figurative meaning as the American usage: "What has the future in store for me?" *Cold store* is *cold storage.* See also **shop.**

storekeeper, *n.*   **employee in charge of supplies**
Supplies, parts, etc. There is a special use in American naval terminology, describing one handling naval stores and spare parts. The British equivalent of *storekeeper* in the usual American sense is *shopkeeper.* See **shop** and **store.**

stout, *n.*   **strong beer**
Dark brown; often asked for by the brand name "Guinness," among others less well known. See also **bitter.**

stove up, *v.t.*   **disinfect**
Slang. To disinfect generally, as to *stove up* clothing in a flop house; *delouse. Stove-up* is the noun describing the procedure.

straightened out   *Slang.* **fixed**
Slang. Describing an official 'on the take.'

straightforward, *adj.*   *Inf.* **cut-and-dried**
This word means 'frank' and 'honest' in both countries. A common additional British meaning is 'simple,' in the sense of 'presenting no complications.' Someone is presented with a contract to sign and after reading it through says that it seems perfectly *straightforward;* or a garage mechanic looks at some engine trouble and answers that the problem is perfectly *straightforward.*

straight on, *adv.*   **straight ahead**

streaky, *n.*   **bacon**
The kind commonly seen in America, less so in Britain.

stream, *n.*   **1. lane**
                                                                  2. SEE COMMENT
1. Traffic usually flows in *streams* in Britain rather than in *lanes* as in America. It is customary in Britain to speak of the left *stream,* the right *stream,* and the wrong *stream.* 2. *For school usage, see* **eleven plus.** *Stream* is also used as a verb in this connection meaning 'classify according to ability' and then divide into groups.

street, *n.*   **1.** *Inf.* **class**
                                                                  2. *Inf.* **alley**
1. *Inf. She's not in the same street as her sister* would be *She's not in the same class,* in America. And to be *streets ahead* of or *streets better* than someone is to *outclass him.* To *win by a street* is to *win by a mile.* This term originated in horse-racing and is used metaphorically in other pursuits. *Win by a distance* is also said in racing. 2. *Inf.* If something's *up your street,* it's *up your alley. Also down your street.* See also **line of country.**

street rough, *Slang.*   *Slang.* **toughie**

streets ahead of. See **street 1.**

strength. See **on the strength.**

'strewth!, *interj.*   *Inf.* **good God!**
Slang. Old-fashioned, but still heard. It is a contraction of *God's truth.* Also spelled *'struth.*

strike off   1. disbar
                                                               2. revoke license
1. Short for *strike off the rolls,* applying to lawyers.
2. Short for *strike off the register,* applying to doctors. But strangely, a doctor who is *struck off* in Britain may continue to practice, being deprived only of the right to prescribe dangerous drugs or to sign a death certificate.

striking price   SEE COMMENT
   When a new issue of stock is issued on a bid basis with a minimum price per share stated, and the issue is oversubscribed, the issuing company allocates the offered shares among the bidders on an equitable basis at a *striking price,* i.e., a figure at which the bargain is *struck,* near the highest bid. In the case of the British Government sale of 130 million shares of British Petroleum to the public in the summer of 1983, the minimum price per share was fixed at £4.05 (about $6.08 at that time). The *striking price* was fixed at £4.35 (about $6.53). There were 79,710 applications "at or above the *striking price,*" according to the Bank of England, which handled the affair for the Government.

Strine, *n., adj.*   SEE COMMENT
   Inf. Australian speech, its sounds and idioms. This word, coined by an Australian, represents the nasal and swallowed deformation of *Australian* in the accents of that country.

strip lighting   fluorescent lighting

strip-wash, *n.*
   Not often heard. The common term is **bed bath.**

stroke. See **oblique.**

strong, *adv.*
   The British sometimes speak of a *four-strong family,* i.e., 'a family consisting of four persons.' Americans would normally refer to a *family of four.* The phrase *one-strong family* is also seen, meaning a 'family of one' or 'a person living *solo.*' Americans use *strong* this way, too, but generally in the case of larger groups such as military forces, and the noun usually precedes the number followed by *strong as* in, *a detachment 200 strong; a working party 150 strong.*

strong flour
   Flour made from durum, or hard wheat. It is the kind used in the making of *pasta* products.

stroppy, *adj.*
   Slang. To *get someone stroppy* is to *rile* him, *get his goat, get his dander up.* A *stroppy* kid is one that needs licking into shape: aggressive and quarrelsome.

struck on, *Slang.*   *Slang.* **stuck on; nuts about**
   See synonyms under **mad on.**

strung up   *Inf.* **het up; strung out**
   Inf. On edge; nothing to do with lynching. *Strung* is seen in the American expression *highly-strung* (**high-strung** in Britain), but that describes a type of person, while *strung up* describes the condition of the moment. *Strung out* is the current vernacular in America, where it also means 'heavily addicted to drugs.'

stuck in. See **get stuck in.**

stuck up. See **stick up.**

stud. See **cat's-eyes.**

studentship, *n.*   **scholarship**
In the sense of an award of financial aid. *Scholarship* is the common term in both
countries, but *studentship* is used at some British colleges. See also **exhibition; bursar;
sizar; servitor.**

stuff, *v.t.*   *Slang.* **lay**
Slang. A particularly unattractive word for the sexual act. To *get stuffed,* in this sense,
would be the passive voice (if one can speak of the *passive* in connection with this
activity); but used as an expletive, *Get stuffed!* is simply an extremely vulgar way of
saying *Get lost!* See also **Stuff that for a game of soldiers!**

Stuff that for a game of soldiers!   **Screw that!**
This peculiar expletive sentence refers to any foolish or unprofitable enterprise the
speaker has finally decided to abandon. *How's that for a game of soldiers* means 'Whaddya
think of that mess?' in angrily describing a foul-up or sorry situation.

stumer, *n.*   *Slang.* **bum check**
Slang. By extension, a *counterfeit bill* or a *slug* (counterfeit coin); and by further extension, *anything phoney.*

stump, *n.*   **butt**
Cigar *stump* (also *stub*); cigarette **end.**

stumps. See **up stumps; wicket.**

stump up, *Slang.*   *Slang.* **pay up; come across**

sub, *n., v.i.*   **1.** *n.,* **advance**
                                                                          2. *v.i., Inf.* **make a touch**
1. *n., Inf.* An advance on future earnings or expectations, thus: *He had to take a £5 sub
on next week's pay.*
2. *v.i., Inf.* To *sub* is to *make a touch. Touch* somehow evokes the image of a reluctant
lender. This nuance is not inherent in the word *sub.* With *on, sub* becomes transitive,
taking as object the future earnings or the lender. Thus, one can *sub on* next month's
dividends, or *sub on* one's pal or daddy.
In all these uses, *sub* appears to come from *subsist money.*

subaltern, *n.*   SEE COMMENT
(Accented on the first syllable.) A military term, denoting á commissioned officer
below the rank of captain.

sub-editor, *n.*   **copy reader**
A newspaper term.

subfusc, *n., adj.*   **1. dull**
                                                                          2. SEE COMMENT
1. *adj.* Its common meaning is figurative: 'dull,' 'characterless.' *Subfusc* clothes are not
necessarily *drab;* in this sense the word may mean merely 'quiet' or 'modest.'
2. *n.* It also has the literal meaning of 'dusky' in both countries. It is rarely used in
America in either sense. It is a shortening of *subfuscous*—meaning 'somber; dusky.' At
some universities, including Oxford and Cambridge, *subfusc* is used as a noun meaning
the 'uniform worn for formal occasions,' such as commencement and the taking of
exams. For men it consists of dark suit, socks and shoes, white shirt and white bow
tie, gown, and mortarboard, the last being carried under the arm; for women, dark skirt
(long or short), black stockings and shoes, white shirt, black scarf or choker, gown, and
a beret in the shape of a soft mortar-board, with four points, so worn that one of the
points lies on or above the middle of the forehead.

subject, *n.*   **citizen**
A British *subject;* an American *citizen.* There is still enough loyalty to the British monarch to permit the use of a word which might be offensive to the American sense of
independence, at least since the Yorktown surrender. When a Briton speaks of himself

as a *citizen*, it is usually of a town or city. He would seldom be a *citizen* of Great Britain, except in formal language, though there is a category referred to as 'citizen of the United Kingdom and Colonies.' One correspondent suggests that *subject* is preferred to *citizen* because the latter is all too reminiscent of the French revolution. And while we're on the subject (no pun intended) of *citizen*, the dreadful euphemism *senior citizen* is now being heard in Britain, supplanting the time-honored **O.A.P.** and **pensioner.**

subscription, *n.*   **dues**
    A Briton pays his *subscription* to his club or other organization; never *dues*. *Subscription* is an American euphemism for *price of admission* to a dance, political dinner, charitable affair, etc., in which use the British settle for *ticket*.

subscription library   **lending library**

subway, *n.*   **pedestrian underpass**
    An American *subway* is called **underground** or **tube** in Britain. *Subways* in Britain are for getting to the other side of the street without peril to life and limb. They have them in Moscow and other civilized places, too.

sucking pig   **suckling pig**

sucks, *n. pl.*   *Slang.* **washout (fiasco)**
    Slang. Sucks! or *What a suck!* expresses derision at another's failure after a boast.

sucks to you!, *Slang.*   *Inf.* **so there!**

suffer an assessment for   **be taxed on**
    How descriptive!

sugar crystals. See **coffee sugar.**

sultana, *n.*   **white raisin**
    In Britain a *sultana* is a small seedless raisin, light yellow in color. *Sultanas* are used in puddings, cakes, buns, etc. (see **bath bun**). In America *sultanas* are a variety of grape, pale yellow in color, which when dried become what Americans call *white raisins*. They are also used as a source of white wine. With a capital *s*, *Sultana*, in America, is a trademark for a particular brand of seedless raisin, whether dark or white.

Summer Eights. See **Torpids.**

summer pudding   SEE COMMENT
    Line pudding bowl with crustless bread; fill with mush of any summer fruit and large chunks of bread without crust; cover top with bread; cool or freeze; turn out when mass is soaked and congealed.

summer time   **daylight saving time**
    Nothing to do with Porgy and Bess. The American term is also used in Britain but to British ears the familiar American phrase sounds rather old-fashioned. The British are on G.M.T. (Greenwich Mean Time), which is five hours later than Eastern Standard Time. See also **B.S.T.**

sump, *n.*   **crankcase**
    Automobile term. See also **Appendix II.E.**

sun-blind, *n.*   **(shop) awning**
    According to the February 19, 1976, issue of the *Calgary* (Alberta) *Herald*, "Ivan Bull, a six-foot, six-inch leather merchant, had been bumping his head on shop awnings— or *sunblinds*—for 15 years," in Newport, on the Isle of Wight, England. He complained to the police, and the sunblinds had to be raised to eight feet under an 1847 statute.

sunny intervals. See **bright periods.**

sun-trap, *n.*   **sunny, sheltered place**
   A phrase much used in travel advertising. The picturesque noun is an oblique reference to the elusiveness of the British sun which must be *trapped,* and sheltered from
the wind.

superannuation scheme   **pension plan**

super-elevated, *adj.*   **banked**
   Of roads and highways.

supergrass. See **grass.**

supplementary benefits. See **National Insurance.**

supply bill   **appropriation bill**
   A *supply bill* in Parliament is what Congress calls an *appropriation bill.*

supporter, *n.*   **best man**
   But only at a royal wedding. At that of Prince Andrew of England (now Duke of
York), his younger brother, Prince Edward, was uniformly referred to in the news
reports as Andrew's *supporter.*

supremo, *n.*   **governor; overseer**
   An official installed to take command over hierarchies previously established.

surely, *adv.*   SEE COMMENT
   In *The Strangers Are All Gone* (the fourth and final volume of Anthony Powell's te-
tralogical memoirs entitled *To Keep the Ball Rolling*—Heinemann, London, 1982), the
author starts a ruminative paragraph about the identity of 'The Friend' in Shakespeare's
sonnets with these words: *"Surely* (I use the adverb in the British interrogative sense
rather than the American usage of 'certainly')..." This would indicate that in British
English, *surely* beginning a sentence means something like 'Isn't it true (or likely) that...,'
the way *doubtless* sometimes implies, rather than eliminates doubt about what follows.
Powell's 'British interrogative sense' is clearly demonstrated in a sentence in Iris Murdoch's *The Philosopher's Pupil* (Chatto & Windus, London, 1983) that actually ends with
a question mark. Diane, the former prostitute, now mistress of George, the protagonist,
is reminiscing. George had been a client. "Then he fell in love with her, well, *surely* he
fell in love? George was rewriting history so fast, it was hard to remember what had
really happened." An earlier illustration of this British usage, complete with question
mark, appears in an adventure novel by Hammond Innes, *Gale Warning* (Harper & Row,
N.Y., 1947). Cpl. Vardy, being repatriated to England in March 1945, asks Jennifer, an
attractive passenger on the same wretched freighter *Trikkala* who had complained of
the chief engineer's drunken ogling, "What about [Warrant Officer] Rankin?...Does he
annoy you?" "Oh no," she replies with a little laugh. "He's not interested in women.
Surely you realized that?"

surgery, *n.*   **1. doctor's (dentist's) office**
                                    2. doctor's (dentist's) office hours
                                    3. day's schedule of doctor (dentist)
                     4. M.P.'s (lawyer's) session with constituents (clients)
                           5. M.P.'s (lawyer's) temporary outside quarters
1. A doctor's or dentist's office is always called his (her) *surgery* in Britain, never *office.*
2. *The period when he (she) is available at the office.*
3. *Doctor has a very large surgery today,* says the nurse through whom one is trying to
get an appointment. She means he has a very heavy schedule, i.e., lots of patients that
day.

4. *Inf.* When a Member of Parliament travels to his **constituency** (*district*) and holds a session at which he makes himself available to his constituents, he is colloquially said to *give a surgery*. The same usage applies to a lawyer who receives clients out of his office.
5. *Inf.* The place where this happens is also colloquially called a *surgery*.

surgical spirit   **rubbing alcohol**
This has nothing to do with zealous surgery.

surround, *n.*   **area surrounding**
A border around something, like a gravel walk around (or nearly all the way around) a rose garden, or a metal plate around an electric switch.

surveyor, *n.*   *approx.* **building inspector**
The general meaning is the same in both countries, but a *chartered surveyor* is a *licensed architect* and is usually engaged by a careful British prospective purchaser to look over the building before the contract is signed. If things go wrong later, the purchaser can sue the surveyor, who has received a fee for his written report. In this sense *surveyor* describes a privately engaged expert building inspector. A *building surveyor* is something different: a specialist in all aspects of real estate development, from negotiating for the purchase of the land through completion of the construction, including all aspects of financing, packaging and sale. There are large firms as well as individuals engaged in this activity, hired by the property developer usually at a fee equal to 10 percent of the total development cost.

sus law   SEE COMMENT
Inf. Sus, in this expression, is short for *suspect*. This troublesome law corresponded, to a certain degree, to the American vagrancy laws and was subtitled 'loitering with intent.' The law, about 150 years old, was repealed as of August 24, 1981. It permitted the police to question and even detain 'suspects' at random if they believed that there was reason to suspect that those involved might be planning a criminal act. Alleged overuse of this law was the cause of disturbances in various parts of England, notably Brixton in South London, known as the 'Harlem' of London.

suspenders, *n. pl.*   **garters**
Vertical ones, whether ladies' or men's; not the round kind like those worn by Knights of the Garter. *Suspenders,* the American term for the apparatus that holds up trousers, are called **braces** in Britain.

sus out   1. *Slang.* **case**
                                                                   2. *Inf.* **figure out**
1. *Slang.* As in *case the joint,* i.e., *reconnoiter* (British **recce**).
2. *Slang.* As in, *I'm trying to sus out what he means by it.*

swab, *n., Slang.*   **oaf;** *Inf.* **jerk**
See synonyms under **git.**

swacked, *adj.*   *Inf.* **tight**
Inf. From a Scottish verb *swack,* meaning 'drink heavily.'

swagger, *adj.*   *Inf.* **swell**
Inf. In the sense of 'smart,' but with the pejorative implication of ostentation. Old-fashioned.

swan, *n., v.i.*   *Slang.* **junket**
Slang. A trip of one sort or another whose ostensible purpose is official business, but whose primary motivation is pleasure. To *go swanning* is to take such a trip.

swan upping, *v.* SEE COMMENT
An annual function that goes back centuries: the taking up and marking of the swans that inhabit the Thames. There is an official swan-upping pennant which royal swan-uppers affix to their boats when they go out to take inventory of the sovereign's cygnets on the Thames from London to Windsor. A headline in *The Times* (London) of July 14, 1981, reads: 'Worst day of swan upping for centuries.' The report itself clearly establishes that there'll always be an England.

Worst Day of Swan Upping For Centuries
By Tony Samstag
Captain John Turk ies [sic] not a happy man this morning. Yesterday's swan upping, the opening of the annual procession of the Queen's randan and five Thames skiffs up the Thames from Sunbury to Pangbourne, was the worst in his dozen years as Royal Keeper of the Swans.

It was most probably the worst day of swan upping in the four-to-seven centuries this curious ritual is thought to have existed.

At Chertsey, the halfway point in yesterday's journey to Windsor, Captain Turk and his entourage, representing the Ancient Companies of Vintners and Dyers as well as the Crown, had seen not one cygnet and precious few adult birds. The second stage of the journey was a little better, but not much.

When one passer-by at Chertsey lock said she had seen three cygnets in a gravel pit near Shepperton, Captain Turk shook his head and said ruefully: "They must have known we were coming".

Swan upping, a corruption of "driving up", is nothing more or less than a census-taking, a legacy of the days when the bird was an important food source.

Each family of mute swans, pen, cob and cygnets, is caught and inspected for the nicked beak that indicates ownership by the Vintners and Dyers, or the unmarked beak that is the prerogative of the royal birds. Cygnets receive the same marks, or remain unmarked, as their parents.

Biologists, who are pleased to have the Crown carrying out this useful ecological survey for them, are unanimous in their opinion that lead poisoning is the cause of the swans' decline and that the most likely source of lead is anglers' weights. The anglers, not surprisingly, demur.

But until a satisfactory nontoxic substitute for the weights is devised, the decline of the swan and the controversy, will probably continue.

Coating the lead with various impermeable substances does not work. The fearsome digestive process of the swan grinds them away.

Happily, the mute swan as a species is not in danger of extinction, although the prospect of a Thames, or an Avon, for that matter, without them is depressing.

Not that the bird is universally popular; Lord Kingsale and Ringrone, writing to *The Times* in 1975, put the case against them forcefully and elegantly:

"In favour of swans it can only be said that they have a distinct ornamental value, and may, in some cases, keep water free of undesirable weed; against them the list of vices is formidable."

That list included damage to pastureland, destruction of fish spawn and young wildlife, and a generally malevolent disposition rare in the animal world.

Lord Kingsale's letter describes how "the mated cob . . . has been observed to pursue and destroy ten ducklings in as many minutes, and a pair of swans will in time clear the great majority of smaller water fowl from any stretch of water by incessant harrying and persecution.

"I have watched swans on several occasions tearing up the nests of grebes and drowning mallard ducklings, and have frequently intervened forcibly."

It may be some small consolation that the decline of the mute swan in the Thames was being deplored in *The Times* at least as long ago as 1928. It is indeed a grand tradition; and Captain Turk must be fervently hoping, as he continues to wend his doleful way up the Thames this week, that the swan upping of 1981 will not be the last.

The *randan* mentioned in the first paragraph is a rowboat (row*ing*-boat, in Britain; see **Appendix I.A.3**) for three men, the middle one using sculls, the other two regular oars.

swat. See swot.

swede, *n.*   yellow turnip

sweet, *n.*   dessert
Or *sweet course.* In America *dessert* is broad enough to include anything served as the
last course. In Britain *dessert* is generally a fruit course served at the end of dinner.
There is a good deal of Anglo-American confusion about this and a certain amount of
internal British confusion. It is impossible to resist setting forth in extenso the following
barrage of angry letters to *The Times* (London) (please note the headings), all of which
appeared between September 3 and September 9, 1971:

The dessert
From Mr John Russell
  Sir, When will Katie Stewart—and other writers of cookery recipes who appear to
be American—learn that there is no such course as *desserts* in an English meal? What
the Americans call *desserts* is what we English call *the sweet.* There is, however, the
dessert (singular) course in an English meal. It is the last course of all in a full course
dinner, and consists of fruit, nuts and trifling sweetmeats, and it is at this stage of the
meal that the port appears. It is a course which, for the ordinary household, has now
disappeared except for special occasions.
Yours, etc,
JOHN RUSSELL
Bures, Suffolk.
September 1.

The pudding
From Mr Robin McDouall
  Sir, "What the Americans call *desserts* is what we English call *the sweet"* writes Mr
John Russell of Bures (September 3). Let him speak for himself: others call it *pudding.*
I am, Sir, your obedient servant,
ROBIN McDOUALL,
2 Formosa Street, W9

The pudding
From Brigadier R.B. Rathbone
  Sir, Well done indeed, both Mr Russell (September 3) and Mr McDouall (September
6). "Pudding" certainly, but what is far more important is to kill (though alas I fear it
is too late) the gross misuse of the word "dessert." It appears in its American sense
not only in recipes but in restaurants and in ordinary conversation, sometimes by
those who should know better.
  Why, oh why, do we quietly absorb, instead of resisting, these unnecessary (and
in this case misleading) transatlantic importations which, far from enriching, nearly
always degrade our beautiful language?
I am, Sir, your obedient servant,
R.B. RATHBONE
Arreton, Blockley, Gloucestershire.
September 6.

From Mrs G.R.R. Treasure
  Sir, As an American, I should like to correct Mr John Russell (September 3) on the
subject of desserts. We call it dessert, period!—as in "Whadya gonna have for dessert?"
Yours faithfully,
MELISA TREASURE
3 The High Street, Harrow on the Hill,
Middlesex.
September 6.

From Major-General R.H. Allen
  Sir, Mr Russell may call it "The Sweet," Mr. McDouall may call it "Pudding," but

a considerable experience of driving for "meals on Wheels" has taught me that the recipients invariably called it "afters."
Yours faithfully,
R.H. ALLEN
The Pound House, 70 High Street,
Chinnor, Oxford.

sweet eff-all   *Slang.* **not a goddamned thing**
Slang. Seems to be a combination of **Sweet Fanny Adams** and **damn all,** but the *eff* is more likely the *f* in *fuck* than the *F* in **Fanny.** With those two idioms and this and **bugger all** and **sod all,** the British appear to have gone to a good deal of trouble to invent ways of saying *nothing at all.*

Sweet Fanny Adams   **nothing at all**
Slang. Fanny Adams was a real live girl who was killed two years after the end of the American Civil War. Her unpleasant murderer cut her into little pieces and threw them into a hop field (called **hop-garden** in Britain). The legend of that obscene crime led to the coining of the name *Fanny Adams* as military slang for 'tinned mutton.' This seems to have nothing whatever to do with *sweet Fanny Adams* meaning 'nothing at all.' Sometimes abbreviated to *Sweet F.A.,* and believed by some to be nothing more than the euphemism discussed in the preceding entry.

sweets, *n. pl.*   **candy**
Boiled sweets are *hard candy.*

sweet-shop, *n.*   **candy store**
Synonymous with **confectioner's.**

swept-out, *adj.*   **streamlined**

swimming-bath, *n.*   **swimming pool**
The American term is taking over.

swimming costume   **bathing suit**
Or **bathing costume.**

swing-door, *n.*   **swinging door**
A rare case of British preference for the shorter formation. See **Appendix I.A.3.**

swingeing, *adj., adv.*   *Inf.* **whopping**
Inf. Present participle of the archaic verb to *swinge,* meaning 'strike hard.'

swing it   *Slang* **goof off**
Slang. See **swing the lead.**

swing the lead, Slang.   *Slang.* **goof off**

swipes, *n. pl., Slang.*   *Slang.* **lousy beer**

Swiss roll   **jelly roll**

switchback, *n.*   **roller coaster**
Now more commonly called *scenic railway.* But *switchback railway* is a term describing zigzag railways for climbing hills. Synonymous with **big dipper.**

switched on   *Slang.* **turned on**
Slang. Interested, excited, by art, sex, nature, anything. The American expression is also used.

swizz, *n., Slang.*   **swindle**
The longer form, *swizzle,* can be used as a transitive verb meaning to 'swindle.'

swop, *v.t.*, *IN.f*   *Inf.* **swat**

swop, n., v.t., v.i.   **scythe**
   A country term. The scythe in question is a small one also known in the country as
a **bagging-hook**

swot, *n.*, *v.t.*, *v.i.*   *Slang.* **cram**
   Slang. Swot (also *swat*) means 'cram.' A *swot* is a *grind*, synonymous with **sap**. *To swot*
up is to *cram* or *bone up* and is synonymous with **mug up**.

T

ta   **thanks**
Slang. Heard increasingly. It may well have been given a new lease on life as a jocular expression, but used so much that the joke dissolved and the expression became respectable, as jocular-vulgar Cockney. One hears also "ta very much." Sounds like baby-talk, but used among Cockney adults. The Americans seem not to have developed any corresponding slang term. See also **ta-ta**.

table, *v.t.*   **submit for discussion**
This term means exactly the opposite of what it means in America, where to *table* an item is to *shelve* it or to postpone discussion of it, perhaps hoping it will never come up again.

table money   **cover charge**
Cover charge and (Fr.) *couvert* are used as well.

tack, *n.*   *Slang.* **chow; grub**
Slang. Good tack is *good eating.* Synonymous with **tuck**.

Taffy, *n.*   **Welshman**
One of those objectionable ethnic terms (e.g., *Paddy, Paki*). It comes from the old nursery rhyme:

Taffy was a Welshman, Taffy was a thief.
Taffy came to my house and stole a piece of beef.

Taffy is probably derived from the Welsh equivalent of *David: Dafydd.*

tail. See top and tail

tail-back, *n.*   *Inf.* **back-up**
Inf. Referring to traffic jams (**traffic blocks**). See also **nose to tail**.

tail-coat, *n.*   **cutaway**

take a brace. See duck, 1.

take a decision   **make a decision**

take against   **take a dislike to**

take (one) all (one's) time   **be all one can do**
Inf. It takes me all my time to pay for the food means *It's all I can do to pay for the food.* Thus, *He's so fat it takes him all his time to get up the stairs.*

take a rise out of, *Inf.*   *Inf.* **get a rise out of**

take a scunner at (against), *Slang.*   **take a dislike to**

to take away   **to go**
Referring to food which is prepared for consumption off the premises as in, *Sandwiches made up to take away.* Used attributively, without *to,* as in, *take-away coffee,* which would be *coffee to go* in America.

take down, *Inf., Slang.*   1. *Inf.* **take (a letter)**
                                                                              2. *Slang.* **take (cheat)**

take first knock   *Inf.* **go first**
Inf. A term taken from cricket; synonymous with **bat first.**

take in charge   **arrest**
See also **charge-sheet; detain, 1.**

take into care   SEE COMMENT
When a child is taken from its parents who are deemed unfit, in America the authorities are said to *take custody* of the child. In Britain, the child is *taken into care.*

take it in turns to   **take turns**
The British form is followed by the infinitive of the verb, the American form by a gerund. Thus in Britain two good friends of a sick man would *take it in turns to* sit by his beside, while in America they would *take turns* sitting there.

take no harm   **suffer no harm**

take on   *Inf.* **catch on**
Inf. Catch on is used in Britain as well.

take (someone's) point   **see (someone's) point**
I take your point rather than the American *I see your point* or *I get your point.*

take silk   SEE COMMENT
Become a Q.C. (or *K.C.*): *Q.C.* stands for *Queen's Counsel* and *K.C.* for *King's Counsel*, a specially recognized **barrister.** The title depends upon the sex of the sovereign. The word *silk*, by itself in this context, denotes such a counsel, thus: *John Jones, a silk, accepted the* **brief (i.e.,** *took the case*).

take the biscuit   *Slang.* **take the cake**
Slang. As in *That takes the biscuit!* To surpass all others, especially in stupidity, cheek, impudence, effrontery and the like. Also, but rarely, *the bun!*

take the mickey out of   *Inf.* **poke fun at**
Slang. Aggressively, to undermine self-confidence. Also, *take the mick out of; take the piss out of.* An illustration of the precise meaning of this phrase appears from the poignant story, reported in *The Daily Telegraph* (London) of September 20, 1980, of the mother of a young mass murderer on the run, who received in the mail from her son recent snapshots of himself and the other wanted man. She was quoted as follows: "Look at Jimmy in these pictures—not a care in the world...he is *taking the mickey out of* me like this. He is laughing at me and trying to upset me..."

take the piss out of. See **take the mickey out of.**

take the rise out of, *Inf.*   *Inf.* **get a rise out of**

take the shilling   **enlist**
Inf. From the days when the Recruiting Sergeant gave the new recruit a shilling, known as the *King's* (or *Queen's*) *shilling.*

take (make) up the running   **take the lead; set the pace**
A racing term, often used figuratively of, e.g., participants in a conversation. As used in the following TV film criticism by Nicholas Wapshott in *The Times* (London) of May 30, 1981, it would appear to mean something like 'take it from there':

> On Monday it is worth staying in to see Elizabeth Taylor in Butterfield 8 (BBC 19.25 pm), a part which she said she disliked but which won her her first Oscar. It is her last film with her husband Eddie Fisher as her next was Cleopatra and Richard Burton *took up the running.*

take (pull) your finger out   *Slang.* **get off the pot**
Slang. Delicacy forbids elucidation of the literal meaning of the expression, which
was used by no less a personage than the Duke of Edinburgh in a speech to British
industry.

taking, *n.*   *Inf.* **fit**
Inf. To be in a *taking* is to be *upset*, to be having a *fit* of anger or nerves. An old-
fashioned idiom.

talent spotter   **talent scout**

talk the hind leg off a donkey   *Inf.* **talk a blue streak**
Inf. Or *off an iron pot.*

talk through (out of) the
back of one's neck. *Inf.*   *Inf.* **talk through one's hat**

tally plan   **installment plan**
A *tally plan* or *tally system* was the method by which a *tally shop*, owned or serviced
by a *tallyman* or *tallywoman*, operated a retail business accommodating needy customers
who could not pay cash, the accounts being recorded in a pair of matching books, one
for each party, and usually paid weekly without billing. Except perhaps in quite depressed areas the practice has pretty well died out, giving way to regular installment
buying, called **hire-purchase**, or more popularly the **never-never**, in Britain.

tally plate   **nameplate**
Royal Navy usage.

tamasha, *n., Slang*   **show; fuss**
In the sense of an *exciting activity.* Adopted by the British army from Arabic/Persian.
Pronounced TA-MAH'-SHA.

tanner, *n.*   SEE COMMENT
Slang. The old sixpence, before decimalization. Not to be confused with a **tenner.** See
Appendix II.A.

Tannoy, *n.*   *Inf.* **P.A. system**
Inf. A proprietary name gone generic, like **hoover, hayter,** etc. The Tannoy is not the
only system in use in Great Britain, but every *Tannoy* speaker has a great TANNOY
conspicuously lettered around its edge, so that the name was the most likely candidate
for general adoption.

tap, *n.*   **faucet**
Tap (as a noun) is heard in America, *faucet* almost never in Britain; but Americans
speak of *tap*-water, never *faucet*-water.

taped, *adj.*   *Slang.* **nailed down**
Slang. One who *has it all taped* has thought of everything, and provided for all con-
tingencies; he's got it *all worked out*, and *buttoned down.*

taplets. See **shares.**

tap stocks, see shares

taradiddle, tarradiddle, *n., Inf.*   *Slang.* **fib**

tardy *adj.*   **sluggish**
Also has the American meaning of 'late,' but mostly in literary language.

tariff, *n.*   **schedule of charges**
In Britain, this word used alone can mean 'hotel' or 'restaurant charges.'

tarmac, *n.*   **1. tarroad**
                                                                           2. airfield
1. In America *tarmac* refers to the bituminous binder used in the making of tar roads.
Tarmac started out as a trademark for a binder for road surfaces, but now generally
refers to any bituminous road surface binder. It is a shortening of *tar macadam*, which
in America describes a pavement built by pressing a tar binder over crushed stone, and
in Britain a 'prepared tar concrete poured and shaped on a roadway to construct a hard
surface.' As a transitive verb, *tarmac* means to *tar* a road. See also **macadam.**
2. *Tarmac* has now acquired the specialized meaning of 'air-field,' especially the part
made of this material.

tart, *n.*   **1. pie**
                                                                        2. loose woman
1. What Americans think of when they recall Mom's apple pie or cherry pie would be
apple *tart* or cherry *tart* in Britain. For the meanings of British *pie* see **pie.**
2. Favorite epithet of jealous wives on the way home from a party. A stronger meaning
is 'prostitute.' But in the North of England it retains its original sense of 'sweetheart.'

tart up   *Slang.* **doll up**
   Slang. Often applied to interior decoration, and almost invariably pejorative, indicating that the décor was gaudy, and possibly tawdry as well. *He had his digs tarted up by
a Knightsbridge nance.* Also used in reference to writing style: *She writes a dreadfully tarted
up prose. Overdone* is the adjective that comes to mind, but perhaps it is stronger than
that. Can also be used hyperbolically to mean 'brighten up' or 'pep up,' as in *That soup
could do with some tarting up.*

ta-ta, *interj.*   *Inf.* **bye-bye**
   Inf. (First *a* as in HAT, second as in HAH, stress more or less equal). Grown-ups should
avoid such baby-talk, but it is heard among adult Cockneys, as is **ta.** To *go ta-ta's* is to
go for a walk.

tater, 'tatur, tatie, *n.*   *Slang.* **spud**
   Slang. The lowly *potato*, which by any other name would taste as good.

taters (taties) in the mould   **cold**
   Slang. Old-fashioned, but still in use; rhyming slang (see **Appendix II.G.3**). See also
tater.

tatt, *n., v.i.*   **1.** *n.* **frills**
                                                               2. *v.i.* **fritter away one's time**
1. *n., Slang.* The décor of the apartment was lovely and without tatt.
2. *v.i. Slang.* Doing more or less useless jobs just to pass the time.

tatty, *adj., Inf.*   **shabby**
   See **grotty.**

taws, *n.*   **lash**
   A thong, cut into narrow strips at the end, used for chastising children at school.
Also *tawse.* A Scottish word.

tax point, *n.*   **effective date**
   Example of this tax usage: **V.A.T.** on certain items went up from 8 percent to 25
percent May 1, 1975. An order for such an item is given April 25 for delivery May 2.
You pay 25 percent, says the tax office: the *tax point* is the delivery date, not the date
of the order.

tea, *n.*   SEE COMMENT
   In Britain, you can drink your tea or eat your tea. One drinks one's afternoon tea at
about 4:00 P.M., taken with **biscuits**, bread and jam, **scones**, and the like. But *tea* also
covers a **non-U** (see **Appendix I.C.6**) evening meal consisting of a light supper. In this
case you eat your tea. *Tea* is heard primarily among the working class and children,

and is really short for **high tea.** Not only children: a childless lady in the Essex countryside, excessively devoted to her half-Burmese male kitten named Tomson (no *h* or *p*; the name recognized the fact that the kitten was the offspring of an illicit, or at least unauthorized affair between the lady's pedigreed female and a local feline Casanova) explained the reason why she had to hurry home from an afternoon shopping excursion: "Tomson will be wanting his tea." In his column *moreover... in The Times* (London) of August 1, 1986, Miles Kingston, expressing shock at discovering something unexpected in a book he was reading, writes: "I put the book back on the shelf with a start. I looked distraught. I gave the cat its *tea* (much to its surprise—I had fed it 10 minutes previously) and I scratched my head." (Incidental note: This author is grateful to Mr. Kingston for another illustration of this British use of *tea*, but must express concern to the reference to one's cat as *it*. A cat is a noble being, and either a *he* or a *she*; never an *it*!)

teach someone's grandmother to suck eggs   **instruct an expert**
Slang. To attempt to instruct or advise someone more experienced than oneself, or to try to teach an expert on a matter within his field—like telling Albert Einstein how to approach the matter of relativity. Rebellious college students solemnly advising the faculty on "relevance" are a fair example.

tea lady   SEE COMMENT
The member of the staff at the office or shop who makes and brings around the tea at 11:00 A.M., and 4:00 P.M. There will be a **biscuit** (*cookie*) or two as part of the offering. It is considered good practice to suspend business discussion during the ceremony. Good for the nerves, too. Occasionally tea gives way to coffee, but the functionary in question will never be called the *coffee lady.*

team-ups, *n. pl.*   **separates**

tear a strip off (someone)   *Slang.* **bawl (someone) out**
Slang. The *strip* is a noncommissioned officer's stripe. The expression, in military circles, suggests demotion for a misdemeanor.

tearaway, *n.*   *Inf.* **hellraiser**
Inf. The term does not necessarily imply a bad character. A *tearaway* is a wild youngster who is probably going to straighten out in time.

tease, *n.*   *Inf.* **tricky job**
Inf. "It was quite a *tease*," said the Mr. Fixit, explaining why it took so long and cost so much for what had at first seemed the simple job of repairing the lawn mower. It had proved much more *exacting* once he got into it.

teat, *n.*   1. **nipple**
                                                               2. **bulb**
1. On a baby bottle.
2. The *rubber bulb* of a medicine dropper.

tea-towel, *n.*   **dish towel**
Also referred to as a **washing-up cloth.**

teetotalist, See **TT.**

telegraph pole   **telephone pole**
Both functions are served in both countries, which somehow assign different priorities to the respective wires.

telephone box. See **call-box; kiosk.**

telephonist, *n.*   **switchboard operator**
(Accent on the second syllable.)

telly, *n., Inf.*   *Inf.* **TV**
Also, **goggle box.** See also **have square eyes.**

temporary guest   transient
Hotel term.

ten. See twenty.

tenner, *n.*   sawbuck
Inf. A *ten-pound* note (*bill*). Not to be confused with tanner.

tension, *n.*   gauge
Usage restricted to the art of knitting, meaning the 'number of stitches to the inch.'

term, *n.*   trimester
On all education levels, the British divide the school year into three *terms*, separated
by long vacations. The American system generally prefers two, called *semesters*, separated by a very long summer vacation, but many American colleges have seen fit to
institute a trimestrial system, mainly to reduce the length of a college education below
four years, bringing it more in line with the three-year British university curriculum.
Term, in the British system, and *semester* and *trimester* in the American, are the respective
designations for fixed parts of the school year. To complicate matters still further, *terms*
often have quite different names in different British institutions. As only one example,
the three eight-week terms at Oxford are called Michaelmas, Hilary, and Trinity. At
Cambridge they are Michaelmas, Lent, and Easter. *Half-term* is a brief vacation occurring
about midway through the term in most British schools. *Term* can be short for *beginning
of term* as in, *The student returned from his travels in time for term.*

terminus, *n.*   terminal
A railroad or bus term. The British, however, use *terminal* to refer to the city center
where one picks up the bus to the airport.

terrace, *n.*   row of joined houses
A specialized British use of the word. Synonymous with link house. A *terrace house*
is known as a *row house* in America. See semi-detached.

terraces, *n., pl.*   standing room
Used only of a sports arena. Sometimes *terracing.*

Terylene, *n.*   Dacron
Trademark of Imperial Chemical Industries Ltd. (I.C.I.) as *Dacron* is of E.I. Du Pont
de Nemours & Co. (Du Pont). Both products are synthetic polyesters used as textile
fibers.

Test. See Test Match.

test bed, *n.*   proving-ground
Literally, an iron framework for resting machinery being tested.

Test Match   international match
This is principally a cricket term, now also applied to rugger. A *Test Match*, e.g.,
between England and Australia, has about the same importance in England as the *World
Series* in America. The English team is always referred to as the *England side*, never the
English side; but the Australians are always referred to as the *Australian side*, the West
Indians as the *West Indian side*, etc. *Test Match* is often shortened to *Test*: thus, *What
happened in the Melbourne Test?* See also cricket.

that cock won't fight   that excuse (plea, plan) won't work

that's it!   right!

that's the job!   *Slang.* that's the ticket!
Slang. Often *that's just the job!*

that's torn it! *Slang.* **that does it!**
Slang. Said in exasperation when things have gone wrong.

theatre, *n.* **operating room**
Short for *operating-theatre*; a *theatre sister* is an *operating-room nurse*; a *confinement theatre* is a *labor room*. See comments under **lint** and **sister**.

then? SEE COMMENT
A substandard idiomatic usage. *Then?* at the end of a sentence that is interrogative in form, but an observation or comment in substance, is little more than punctuation. "Been doing a bit of work, then?" says the gardener to the **guv'nor** as he notes a weeding job done in his absence. "Off on a holiday, then?" says your rustic neighbor, as he strolls by and catches sight of you lugging a valise to your car. *Then?* doesn't mean anything, except perhaps a bit of friendly jocularity.

theological college **divinity school; seminary**

there's a... **that's a...**
As in, *There's a good boy.*

there's no shifting it *Inf.* **it's unshakable**
Inf. About *idées fixes*, as in, *Once he's made up his mind, there's no shifting it.* Seems to be used only in the negative: *My mind's made up: don't confuse me with facts!*

thermic lance **blowtorch**

thick ear, *Slang.* **cauliflower ear**
See also **cloth-eared.**

thin on the ground **few in number**
Inf. Often used to mean 'short of help,' 'understaffed.'

third party insurance **liability insurance**

Third Programme SEE COMMENT
The BBC (British Broadcasting Company) broadcasts four different radio programs (note difference in spelling of *program*), Radio 1,2,3 and 4, in addition to two television programs, BBC 1 and BBC 2. In the early days, there were only three radio programs, known as the First, Second and Third Programmes. The last-named maintained a higher intellectual and artistic level than the other two, so that to *be Third Programme* was to be something of an intellectual, or to have leanings in that direction, and to be interested and more or less versed in the arts. Now it's *Radio 3* for the highbrows.

threap, *n., v.t.* **1.** *n.* **accusation.**
2. *v.t.* **scold**
Heard in Scotland and the North of England.

three star. See **four star.**

threshold agreement **union cost-of-living contract**

Throgmorton Street *approx. Inf.* **Wall Street; the market**
Inf. A street in the City of London whose name is used as a nickname for the London Stock Exchange, and the securities fraternity and their activities generally, just as nearby *Mincing Lane* is used for the wholesale tea business. The British often use the term **the City** to denote the financial community as a whole. See **city.**

throstle, *n.* **song-thrush**
Chiefly literary.

through, *adj.*   **1. connected**
                                               2. still in contention
1. This meaning is restricted to telephone operator usage. Thus, *You're through!* means 'Your party is on the line!' or 'You're connected!' When a British telephone operator says *You're through!* it sounds about as grim to an American as *Your time is up!* must sound to a Briton. In Britain the operator does not tell you when your time is up; instead there are three short beeps on a long distance call or a series of rapid pips on a local call from a pay station. No pips when you dial directly from a private telephone. 2. This meaning relates to elimination competitions in sports, called **knock-outs** in Britain. Thus (in cricket): *In the North, Yorkshire and Lancashire are through.* That means that they are 'still alive' in American sports parlance. *Through,* in American English, would more likely be taken to mean the exact opposite: 'finished,' 'eliminated.'

throw one's bonnet (cap) over the windmill   **throw caution to the winds**
     Evokes the Victorian atmosphere of a young lady involved in an impetuous elopement; but this expression is current usage.

throw out   **add on; build**
     Referring to adding an extension to a structure: to *throw out* a wing, thus enlarging a building or a room. The British also talk of *throwing out* a pier, i.e., building one out into the water.

throw-up, *n. Inf.*   **pin-boy**

thumping, *adj., adv.*   *Inf.* **enormously**
     Inf. Rarely used by itself to mean 'enormous,' as in *a thumping lie*; usually in combination with *great* or *big*; *a thumping great feast. Thumping good* means the same thing: a *thumping good* victory is an *overwhelming* one.

(The) Thunderer   SEE COMMENT
     Inf. Old-fashioned journalistic epithet for *The Times* (London), arising from its ponderous pronouncements on matters of national interest.

thundering, *adv.*   *Inf.* **mighty**
     Inf. In the sense of 'extremely'—a *thundering* good actor; a *thundering* good piece of mutton. An old-fashioned word.

thunder-mug, *n.*   **chamber pot**
     Slang. The commode which may contain it used to be referred to as a *thunder-box*. Like the commodities in question, the terms are not common; but they are heard now and then.

thundery trough   **line squall**
     A nautical term for a meterological phenomenon to worry about in any language.

tick, *v.t., v.i.*   **check**
     Please tick where appropriate, seen in instructions for filling out a form or on an advertisement coupon. A *tick list* is a *check list*. But see **on tick; tick off.**

ticket-of-leave, *n.*   **parole**
     A *ticket-of-leave man* is a *paroled convict.*

ticket pocket   **change pocket**
     Tailor's term.

ticket tout, *Slang.*   *Slang.* **scalper**

tickety-boo, *adj.*   *Slang.* **hunky-dory**
     Slang. Also spelled *tiggerty-boo.* Still heard but outdated.

tick, half a. See **half a tick.**

tickler, *n.*   *Inf.* **poser**
Inf. A delicate situation; a tricky problem.

tick off   1. **checkoff**
                                                                                       2. **tell off**
See **tick.**

tick, on. See **on tick.**

tick over   **turn over**
Referring to a car or other engine. Extended metaphorically, for example, to office or
business routine: *When he's away on holiday, things just tick over* (the activity slows down
to a trickle).

tic tac   SEE COMMENT
Inf. An arm-movement signaling system used by *tic tac men* at racetracks to flash the
changing odds to resident bookies.

tiddler, *n.*   **minnow**
Inf. This word is sometimes used informally an an epithet for little people, like kittens
and children, and can even be stretched to cover abstractions, like clues. "We haven't
found a tiddler yet," says the police investigator, meaning, "We haven't found the most
trifling clue."

tiddl(e)y, *adj., Inf.*   *Inf.* **tipsy**

tidy, *adj.*   **neat**
This is a matter of preference. *Tidy* is not heard much in America except, perhaps,
among genteel older ladies. It is common in Britain. KEEP KENT TIDY appeared on signs
all over that lovely county. A sign reading PLEASE PARK TIDILY adorns the parking lot
(**car park**) outside a pub in Gayley, Staffordshire. *Tidy-minded* means 'logical,' 'method-
ical.'

tied, *adj.*   SEE COMMENT
This word has different meanings in Britain depending upon the noun it modifies.
A *tied cottage* was one occupied by a farm worker at a nominal or no rent, as a perquisite
of his job; but he was not protected by the Rent Act covering most ordinary tenants
and making it virtually impossible for landlords to evict them. If he lost his job, he lost
his cottage. Many poignant situations arose as a result of the callous actions of farmer-
employers. This semi-feudal system has been abolished, and agricultural workers enjoy
the protection of the Rent Act like anybody else. In a television interview, Prince Philip
was asked about his living accommodations and he answered, "Buckingham Palace? A
tied cottage. It goes with the job." A sterling example of understatement. A *tied garage*
is one that serves one company exclusively. A *tied house* is a pub affiliated with a
particular brewery and serving only that brewery's brand of beer and ale. It is the
opposite of a **free house.**

tiepin, *n.*   **stickpin**
Synonymous with **breast-pin.**

tiffin, *n., v.i.*   **lunch**
Of Anglo-Indian origin, and hence obsolescent.

tig, *n.*   1. *Slang.* **tizzy**
                                                                                       2. *Slang.* **tag**
1. *Slang.* A *tizzy* in Britain was slang for *sixpence* (now no longer used; see **Appendix
II.A.**). The British use *tizzy* (in the sense of 'state of agitation') the way Americans do.
2. *Slang.* The children's game, so called from its primary meaning: a *light touch. Tag* is
used as well. See also **tig-tag.**

tiggerty-boo. See **ticketyboo.**

tights, *n. pl.* pantyhose
A term borrowed from the ballet world. A British salesgirl (shop **assistant**) would understand *pantyhose* but she and the customer would normally say *tights*.

tig-tag, *v.i.* 1. go to and fro
2. haggle
Slang. A combination of the two names of the children's game. See **tig, 2.**

tile-hung, *adj.* shingled with tiles
Describing country houses, particularly in the counties of Kent and Sussex, the roofs and sides of which are shingled with reddish-brown clay tiles, usually square or rectangular, occasionally rounded at the bottom or top.

till, *conj., prep.* through
In expressions of duration of time. *Till* (or *until*) a certain hour or date, in Britain, means 'through,' or, in the awkward American phrase, 'to and including.' At times, however, *till* doesn't literally mean 'through.' Thus, *He'll be away till Sunday* might mean 'He'll return some time in the course of Sunday.' Further questioning might clear up the ambiguity. See also **Appendix I.A.1.**

timber, *n.* lumber
In America *timber* means 'standing trees,' but the British use the term the way Americans use *lumber*. However, see **lumber** for British use of the word.

time!, *interj.* closing time!
Inf. The full phrase is: *Time, gentlemen,please!* See **during hours.** Pub terminology, of course.

time-limit, *n.* deadline

The Times SEE COMMENT
Never refer to this component of the **Establishment** as *The London Times* or *The Times of London*. This makes proper Britons huffy, and may evoke a reaction like: *The Times, sir! There is only one Times. There is also something called "The New York Times," I believe?*

.timetable, *n.* schedule
In British schools the list of periods and subjects is called a *timetable*. The Americans refer to it as the *schedule*.

time time and a half 2½ times pay
Overtime expression.

tin, *n.* can
A food container; and naturally the British say *tin-opener, tinned food*, etc. But *can* is fast replacing *tin*.

tinker, *n.* itinerant mender
Not much seen any more. The word is used informally as an approximate equivalent of *gypsy*.

tinker's cuss *Inf.* **tinker's dam(n)**
Inf. The *cuss* is slang for *curse*, of which *damn* is only one example. The British use *damn*, and sometimes even *curse*, in this connection. However, the *damn* is itself an error of folk etymology. The term is properly *dam*, the small clay guard that a tinker puts around a hole in a pot, for example, that is to be sealed with solder, to prevent the solder from running off the rounded surface of the pot until it has cooled. The hot solder dries out the clay, which is then thrown away. Thus there is hardly anything in the world worth less than a tinker's dam.

tinkle, *n.* *Inf.* **ring; 'phone call**
Inf. As in, *Give me a tinkle when you're next in town.*

tinpot, *adj.*   *Slang.* **crummy**
Slang. Heard in America in the expression 'tinpot politician.'

tin tack   **carpet tack**

tip, *n., v.t., v.i.*   **dump**
The British *tip* their *refuse* into a *refuse tip*. Americans *dump* their *garbage* into a *garbage dump*. A *tip-truck* is a *dump truck*. An American might well be mystified at the sight of a sign out in the open country reading NO TIPPING.

tipped, *adj.*   **favored**
As in *tipped to win the election* (or *the high jump*); or *tipped as the next Prime Minister.* Applied to cigarettes, *tipped* would mean only 'filter-tip.'

tip-top, *adj., Inf.*   **first rate**

tip-up seat   **folding seat**

tiresome, *adj.*   **annoying; irritating**
Not *boring*, the usual American meaning.

tit-bits, *n. pl.*   **tidbits**

titchy bit   **just a drop**
Inf. A *tiny bit* of anything.

tit in a trance   **restless soul**
Slang. Describes a person who jumps around from one chore to another, not knowing which to tackle first. Synonymous with **fart in a colander.**

tittup, *n., v.i.*   SEE COMMENT
A word rarely heard in America. A *tittup* is an extravagant prancing and bouncing sort of movement, characteristic of a spirited horse. To *tittup* is to move that way. *Tittup* is probably a combination of the dialectal word *tit* meaning 'jerk' and the *-op* of *gallop.*

tizzy, *n.*   SEE COMMENT
Slang. The old sixpence, now obsolete. *Tizzy* is a corruption of *teston* (also *testoon*), a term now obsolete and of interest only to numismatists, meaning certain European coins one side of which was decorated with a head. *Teston* was derived from *testone,* an augmentative of the Italian word *testa,* meaning 'head.' The term *teston* was specifically applied to a Henry VIII shilling which suffered from inflation and fell in value to sixpence. See also **Appendix, II.A.; tig, 1.**

toad-in-the-hole, *n.*   **sausage in batter**

tobacconist's shop   **cigar store**

Toc H. See **as dim as a Toc H lamp.**

tod. See **on one's tod.**

toff, *n.*   *Slang.* **swell**
Slang. More indicative of a way of life than wealth. It is a way of life that's gone, rendering the term old-fashioned.

toffee, *n.*   **taffy**
But *for toffee* means 'at all,' as in, *She can't play bridge for toffee.* i.e., *she plays very badly.* For *nuts* means the same thing.

toffee-nosed, *adj.*   *Slang.* **stuck-up**
Slang. Stuck-up is used in Britain as well, but see **stick up.**

to hand   **at hand; available**
   A shop will have certain merchandise *to hand*, or *ready to hand*, i.e., *available*. Your
letter *to hand*, however, used in old-fashioned correspondence, means 'Your letter received.' A notice on the quarterly telephone bill reads: "Any call charges not *to hand*
when this bill was prepared will be included in a later bill." See **Appendix I.A.1.**

toke, *n.*   *Slang.* **grub; chow**
   Slang. Food generally, but it has the special meaning of *dry bread*. Synonymous with
tack; tuck.

tol-lol (1), *adj.*   *Inf.* **so-so**
   Slang. Fair-to-middling. Apparently a corruption of *tolerable*, now obsolete.

tolly, *n., Slang.*   **candle**

Tommy, *n.*   SEE COMMENT
   Inf. A private in the British army. It is a shortening of *Tommy Atkins*. The original
Thomas Atkins was a private of the 23rd Royal Welch Fusiliers serving under Welling-
ton's command. (The spelling *Welch* for *Welsh* is peculiar to this regiment and one other,
The Welch Regiment). His name was chosen for a specimen question-and-answer form
in a soldiers' handbook around 1815. The term was not applied to colonial soldiers.
Hence it was believed by some that the name was derived from the initials *T.A.* (for
Territorial Army), but this appears to be error based on coincidence. The Territorial
Army, first known as the *Territorial Force*, was not founded until 1908, whereas *Tommy
Atkins* was in common use long before that. Apart from its use as a military designation—opposite number of a *GI* in the American army—*Tommy Atkins* has been used as
an epithet for a rank and file member of any type of organization. *Tommy*, by itself, is
also slang for *brown bread*, or *rations* generally, of the inferior sort that used to be handed
out to privates and laborers. An illustration of the use of *Thomas Atkins* is found in a
section of the British *Manual of Military Law* headed 'Illustration of Charges':

> Private Thomas Atkins is charged with...Disobeying a lawful command...in such
> manner as to show wilful defiance of authority, in that he...when personally ordered
> by Captain X upon parade to take up his rifle and fall in, did not do so, at the same
> time divesting himself of his equipment and saying, "I'll soldier no more, you may
> do what you please."

   Incidental intelligence: An Act of Parliament (the Army and Air Force Annual Act)
has to be passed every year to keep those bodies alive. This dates from the time of
Cromwell, when the army was extremely unpopular. The Royal Navy is, however, still
the Queen's and requires no such annual act to keep it going. (This information was
kindly supplied by the very same Brigadier R.B. Rathbone whose letter to *The Times*
(London) is quoted under **sweet.**)

Tom Tiddler's ground   **red light**
   A children's game: one stands in front, all the rest some distance behind him in a
line. The ones in back try to sneak forward. The one in front can turn around whenever
he chooses and if he sees anyone moving, he sends that one back to the starting line.
Also known as *sly fox* or *peep-behind-the-curtain* or *Grandmother's steps or footsteps*, depending on what part of Britain you're in.

ton, *n.* See **Appendix II.C.1.g.**

ton, *n.*   **100**
   Slang. The expression *the ton* means '100 m.p.h.' Thus the proud owner of a motorcycle says, *It can do the ton. Ton-up*, as an adjective (e.g., the *ton-up boys*) is a somewhat
derogatory term referring to the motorcycle set, the type that do 100 and scare you to
death. (When you get to know them, they can be charming.) In the British game of
darts, a *ton* is a score of 100 attained with the three darts that make up a single round.
This can be done by hitting the treble 20 with one dart and a single 20 with each of the

other two, or hitting the single 20 with one dart and the double 20 with each of the other two. It is an extremely rare achievement. In cricket, a *ton* is 100 runs by one **batsman**, also known as a **century**.

tone, *n.*   **whole tone**
Musical term. See **Appendix II.F.**

tongue sandwich, *Slang.*   *Slang.* **soul kiss**

tonk, *v.t., Slang.*   *Slang.* **clobber**

too good to miss   *Inf.* **too good to pass up**
Inf. See also **miss out.**

too right!   *Inf.* **definitely! and how!**
Inf. Mostly an Australasian usage.

toothcomb, *n.*   **finecomb**

toothful   *Inf.* **thimbleful**
Inf. A very small drink (of whiskey, etc.).

top, *n.*   **head (beginning)**
As, for instance, in the expression *top of the street.* See also **bottom.**

top and tail   SEE COMMENT
Inf. The process of pulling off the stem (*topping*) and nipping off the little brown tuft at the bottom (*tailing*) of gooseberries, to prepare them for cooking, especially, in the making of gooseberry **fool.** This can be done with the help of a knife, or, by the more adept, with the fingers. The term has been extended, perhaps somewhat jocularly, to the process of writing the salutation ('Dear Mr Wilson,') and the conclusion ('Yours sincerely' or 'Yours ever,') followed by the signature, in an otherwise entirely type-written letter, a practice believed by some to be helpful in personalizing a typewritten letter. (The absence of a period after *Mr* in the salutation is not a typographical error. See **Appendix I.D.6.**)

top gear   **high gear**
See also **Appendix II.E.**

top-hole, *adj.*   **great**
Slang. Anything the speaker regards as *first rate.* Now going out of fashion.

topliner, *n.*   **headliner**

top of one's bent   **heart's content**
See *Hamlet,* Act III, Scene 2.

top of the bill, *Inf.*   *Inf.* **headliner**

(at the) top of the tree   **(in the) highest rank**
Slang. At the higher reaches of one's profession.

topping, *adj.*   *Inf.* **great**
Inf. Simply terrific. Rather old-fashioned.

topside, *n.*   **top-round**
Butcher's term. Nothing to do with the bounding main when shopping for meat.

top up   **fill**
E.g., the gas tank, the crankcase, the battery, a drink. Heard at a cocktail party: "May I top you up?" Also used of salary. An unfortunate new use is found in the expression *top up the votes*, meaning 'stuff the ballot boxes.'

torch, *n.*   **flashlight**

(the) Torpids, *n. pl.*   SEE COMMENT
Oxford boat races. These are *bumping races* (see **May Week**). The Torpids are the Oxford equivalent of the Cambridge *Lent Races*. Oxford calls its equivalent of the Cambridge *May Races* the *(Summer) Eights*.

Tory, *n.*   SEE COMMENT
Inf. Member of the Conservative Party. A colloquialism favored in headlines; often used pejoratively.

tossed, *adj.*   *Slang.* **tight**
Slang. In the sense of *drunk.*

toss off, *Slang.*   *Slang.* **jerk off**

tosticated, *adj.*   **befuddled**
Slang. Perplexed, usually with the implication of drink. Sometimes *tossicated.* The noun *tostication* means *bewilderment* or *perplexity.* Obviously a corruption of *intoxicated,* possibly with a reference to **tossed** (slang for *drunk*) thrown in.

tot, *n.*   **dram**
Whiskey is often understood, but it can denote a small portion of any beverage.

tote betting   **pari-mutuel betting**

totem, *n.*   **hierarchy; order**
Inf. Used in expressions like 'I am a liberal-radical of the old totem,' i.e., *of the old order.* Apparently derived from the top-to-bottom order on totem poles.

to the wide   **utterly**
Inf. Done to the wide means 'done in' or 'dead drunk,' depending on the context, so be careful. To distinguish: Use *whacked to the wide* when you mean 'done in' (but still on one's feet) and *dead to the wide* or *sloshed to the wide* to describe the shameful condition of extreme intoxication, but *dead to the wide* can mean merely 'unconscious' (without the aid of liquor) if the context makes it clear.

totting-up procedure   **point system**
Whereby, on a cumulative basis, one's driving demerits reach a total sufficient to result in the suspension of one's license for a given period.

touch, *n.*   *Slang.* **thing**
Slang. In the sense of a particular 'sort of thing': *I don't go for the sports car touch.*

touch-lines, *n. pl.*   **sidelines**
Side boundaries in some sports.

tour of ops. See **ops room.**

tout, *v.i.*   **scout race horses**
American and British are both familiar with the racetrack *tout* who tells you how to bet. A special British meaning of the word as an intransitive verb is to 'spy' on racehorses in training to gain advance knowledge.

tower block. See **block.**

town, *n.*   SEE COMMENT
To someone in the **Home Counties,** *town* is *London,* even though London is not a town but a city. One has, e.g., spent the day *in town*; tomorrow one is going *to town* or *up to town* and the *town* in question is always London.

town and gown   SEE COMMENT
Non-university and university groups, respectively, at Oxford and Cambridge especially. *Town,* in this phrase, denotes those persons in the town who are not connected with the university as students, fellows, etc. *Gown* means the 'university people.' The phrase *town and gown,* with the same connotations, is not unknown in America and is used occasionally in some American college towns and cities. In Britain, *townee* is university slang for one of those persons who collectively constitute *town.* In American college towns, *townie* means the same thing, and like *townee,* is pejorative. The British use *gownsman* in contradistinction to *townee,* where one might have expected the apparently nonexistent form *gownee.* At Harvard College there are *townies* and *Harvies,* and the students at the affiliated women's college, Radcliffe, are *Cliffies;* at Yale there are *Yalies;* and this practice is undoubtedly widespread in America.

town boundary   city limits

track, *n.*   lane
A traffic term, referring to a particular lane of a highway.

trade, *n., v.i.*   (do) business
Trade is often used in Britain where Americans would say *business,* e.g., *He is in the necktie trade.* A *roaring trade* is a *rushing business. Trader* and *tradesman* mean 'shopkeeper' or 'craftsman,' as opposed to one engaged in a profession. A *trading estate* is a *business area,* sometimes more particularly a shopping center or a small factory zone. *Trading vehicles* are *commercial vehicles,* and *trade* plates are *dealer's plates.* To *be in trade* is to *keep a retail store. In trade* used to be a somewhat derogatory term used by the aristocracy. (Nowadays, even dukes open their estates to the public for gain.) See also **custom.** *Trade* is also used as a verb meaning 'do business' or 'conduct operations.' When Laker Airlines suddenly went into receivership (February 4, 1982), at the company's main ticket office in London, manager Mike Bridges read the following notice to stunned passengers: "We are now in the hands of the official receiver. Until we have had some instructions from the official receiver, we cannot *trade.*"

trade(s) directory book   yellow pages
The American term is now used in Britain as well.

trade(s) union   labor union
Shortened to *union* oftener in America than in Britain. The British name comes from the fact that membership is based on the worker's craft, rather than on the industry in which he is employed. See also **T.U.C.; social contract.**

trading estate, see **trade**

trafficator, *n.*   directional signal
See **winker.**

traffic block   traffic jam

traffic warden   traffic officer
Special officers particularly concerned with parking offenses who also assist the police in the regulation of traffic; recognized by their yellow hat-bands.

tram, *n.*   streetcar
Short for *tram-car,* which is never heard and never seen anymore, either, except in places like Blackpool and the Isle of Man.

tranche, *n.*
1. **bracket**
2. **block (of stock)**
(Pronounced TRAHNSH or sometimes TRONSH in imitation of the French pronunciation of the word.)
1. Fancy equivalent of **slice** and **band**, in tax terminology.
2. Part of a stock issue.

transfer, *n.*   **decal**
Decal is a shortening of *decalcomania.*

transferred charge call   **collect call**
This is the correct technical term for this operation in Britain. *Reverse-charge call* is a popular variant.

transport, *n.*   **transportation**
A Briton would ask, *Have you transport?* rather than *Have you (got) transportation?* A sign in an American hotel signifying an office making guests' travel arrangements would read TRANSPORTATION; in a British hotel, TRANSPORT. One possible reason why the British avoid *transportation* is that it may evoke unpleasant memories of *transportation* to a penal colony, e.g., Australia in the old days, the sense in which the word was then understood. In the old days, the transported convict was himself called a *transport.*

transport café   **truck drivers' all-night diner**
In Britain this might also be called a *lorry drivers' all-night pull-up.* See also **café.**

transport system   **transit system**

trapezium, *n.*   **trapezoid**
In America a *trapezium* is a quadrilateral having no sides parallel. In Britain it denotes a quadrilateral having two sides parallel, which in America is always called a *trapezoid.*

traps, *n., pl.*   *Inf.* **gear**
Inf. Traps means 'personal belongings,' especially 'luggage.' A Briton might ask a porter to get his *traps* into a taxi; Americans would say *my things* or *my stuff.*

traveller. See **commercial traveller.**

travelling rug. See **carriage rug.**

treacle, *n.*   **molasses**

(a) treat   *Inf.* **terrifically**
Inf. An old-fashioned Briton might say to the lady: *You dance a treat,* or he might say: *My wife is taking on a treat* (i.e., *making a terrific fuss*) about the lack of service. Sometimes lengthened to a *fair treat.* **Non-U** (see **Appendix I.C.6.**) or facetious.

treble. See under **double;** see also **quad,** adj.

trendy, *adj.*   *Inf.* **faddish, fashionable; with it**
Inf. Applies to clothes, furniture, ideas, anything. Sometimes used as a substantive to mean 'trendy person.' The connotations are usually mildly pejorative.

trews, *n. pl.*   **tartan trousers**
In the old days, short ones were worn by children under kilts. Now exclusively military wear.

trick cyclist   *Slang.* **head shrinker**
Slang. The British slang results from an attempt to approximate the difficult word *psychiatrist,* and is somewhat pejorative, reflecting mistrust.

trifle, *n.*   SEE COMMENT
A dessert. The base is sponge cake (or lady-fingers, called **sponge fingers** in Britain) soaked in liqueur, wine, sherry, or rum, to which custard and jam and fruit and rich milk or cream are added. Very sweet and very fattening.

trilby, *n.*   **felt hat**
Inf. From the novel *Trilby* by Gerald du Maurier.

trillion. See **Appendix II.D.**

Trinity. See under **term.**

Trinity House, London   SEE COMMENT
An institution begun under Henry VIII and still going strong. Responsible for pilotage and aids to navigation around the British coasts, such as lighthouses, pilot boats, beacons, licensing of pilots, etc. It corresponds more or less to the U.S. Coast Guard, without the latter's functions in the military or excise fields. Its members are known as *Trinity Brethren.* There used to be four more such institutions in other cities.

tripe and onions   *Inf.* **trash**
Inf. An intensive form of simple *tripe,* familiar to both countries in its abstract sense.

tripos, *n.*   SEE COMMENT
(Pronounced TRY'-POSS.) Honors examination at Cambridge University. The term is derived from the three-legged stool (*tripos*) on which the Bachelor of Arts sat to deliver his satirical speech in Latin on commencement day.

tripper, *n.*   *approx.* **excursionist**
A pejorative term for those who are having a day out at the shore, in the country, visiting stately homes, etc. The trip can last longer than a day, perhaps as long as a week or even two. See also **grockle.**

troilism, *n.*   SEE COMMENT
One ignorant of its pronunciation (TROY'LIZM) might have guessed that this word had something to do with Troilus, the Trojan hero and lover of Cressida. That he was exceptionally lovesick is attested by these lines from Shakespeare's *Troilus and Cressida*: "...I am mad/In Cressid's love/...Her eyes, her hair, her cheek, her gait, her voice;/...her hand/In whose comparison all whites are ink,/...to whose soft seizure/The cygnet's down is harsh/...I am giddy, expectation whirls me round,/The imaginary relish is so sweet/That it enchants my sense./Even such a passion doth embrace my bosom;/My heart beats thicker than a fev'rous pulse..." and an amateur etymologist might be forgiven for his guess that *troilism* denoted love-enslavement. But no: according to the *Oxford English Dictionary* it is nothing nearly so romantic, but rather "sexual activity in which three persons take part simultaneously"; and the *Collins English Dictionary* defines it as "sexual activity involving three people" (they omit the *simultaneously*) with a reference to *ménage à trois* and *dualism,* apparently with the suggestion that the *-l-,* far from that in *Troilus,* is nothing more than an echo from the one in *dualism.* (No mention is made of *pluralism, idealism, materialism,* or for that matter, *feudalism*; and there must be many more *-al* adjectives that grew into *-ism* nouns.) So we see that *troilism* is based simply on *trois,* and we wonder, did the French invent it—for there is no such word as *threelism, trelism, treslism* or *dreilism* that has come to this author's attention. Whatever the origin of the word, it is a far from common usage (we are not discussing the practice), and since in Victoria Glendenning's *Vita, The Life of Vita Sackville-West* (Weidenfeld & Nicolson, London, 1983), we find a quotation out of a communication from Virginia Woolf that includes the phrase "emotional troilism," one might conclude that *troilism* is (or was) nothing more than a bit of Bloomsbury cant. The *-l-* in *Troilus,* however seductive a clue to the amateur etymologist, turns out to be, alas, a red herring.

trolley, *n.*   **pushcart**
Trolley in Britain means also a 'hand-lever operated small truck' that carries railroad workers along the rails; but a *trolley-table* (sometimes shortened to *trolley*) is a *tea wagon.* *Trolley* is also the name given to the wheeled shopping carts used in supermarkets, as

well as the rolling luggage carriers supplied at airports, and in Britain, at some of the railroad terminals (railway **termini** or **terminuses,** in Britain). See also **barrow.** A *sweets trolley* is a *dessert cart.*

trooping the colour(s) SEE COMMENT
Annual ceremony on the Horse Guards Parade in Whitehall, London. The regimental flag (the *colour*) is borne aloft between lines of troops and handed to the sovereign. This ceremony occurs on the official birthday of the monarch, June 13. (She was born on April 21, a date on which the weather is uncertain. It has been known to rain on June 13.)

truck, *n.* **gondola car**
Truck is the term that would be used by the layman, whereas a more knowledgeable person would call it an **open goods waggon.** What Americans call a *truck* in railroad parlance is a **bogie** in Britain. The American *road truck* is a **lorry** in Britain.

truckle bed **trundle bed**

trug, *n.* SEE COMMENT
Originally known as *Sussex trug.* A convenient flattish garden basket coming in many sizes, made of thin woven slats.

trumpery, *adj.* **cheap**
In the sense of 'tawdry' or 'gaudy.' Sometimes also used as a noun denoting something that fits the description.

trumps, come up or **turn up.** See **come up trumps.**

truncheon, *n.* **billy**
Also known in America as a *nightstick* whether brandished by night or by day.

trunk call **long-distance call**
In the late Agatha Christie's *Murder on the Orient Express,* Hercule Poirot easily deduces that a suspect once lived in the United States because, as the great detective declaimed: "You said, 'I can always call my *lawyer long distance'* instead of 'I can always make a **trunk call** to my **solicitor'.**"

trunk enquiries **long-distance information**
England is a small country and when you want to ascertain an out-of-town telephone number, you dial 142 in London or 192 outside of London for a number anywhere in the United Kingdom and all of Ireland, whether long distance or local. See also **enquiries.**

trunk road. See **arterial road.**

try, *n.* *approx.* **touchdown**
In *rugger.* See **football.**

try it on *Inf.* **try it out**
Inf. With the strong implication that one is taking a shot at something in the hope of getting away with it. Hence the noun *try-on.*

TT, *n., adj.* **teetotaler; teetotal**
Inf. And the British occasionally say *teetotalist* instead of *teetotaller,* but it all points to the same degree of rectitude.

tube, *n.* **subway**
Synonymous with **underground. Goggle box** is the equivalent of the American slang use of *tube* for *TV.* See also **subway** for British use.

tub-thumper, *n., Inf.* *Inf.* **soapbox orator**

T.U.C.   SEE COMMENT
Stands for *Trades Union Congress*, much more closely linked to the Labour Party than the A.F.L.-C.I.O. is to any American party, and a much more powerful political force. See also **social contract; trade union.**

tuck, *n.*   *Slang.* **eats**
Slang. Indicating a big meal, particularly of the gourmet variety. Variants are *tuck-in* and, less commonly, *tuck-out*. *Tuck-in* is also a verb meaning to 'put on the feedbag,' i.e., 'eat hearty.' A *tuck-shop* is a *pastry shop* and a *tuck-box* is one for the safeguarding of goodies and is generally school jargon. To *tuck into* something in the food line is to *dig into* it. See also **tack; toke.**

tumble to   **catch on to**
Inf. To *tumble to* a concept, a hidden meaning, etc. is to *grasp* it, catch on to it, get the point of it. Synonymous with **twig.**

Tunbridge box   SEE COMMENT
Ornamental marquetry veneered box. Tunbridge Wells is a pretty, thriving town of about 40,000 souls in the county of Kent, 34¼ miles south by southeast of London. It is 5¼ miles south by southeast of another pretty, somewhat smaller Kentish town called Tonbridge. Both towns are on the main railroad line out of Charing Cross Station, London, to Hastings and other southeast coastal towns. Weekend guests unacquainted with the region coming down from London by rail, advised by their hosts to get off at Tunbridge Wells and look around for the green Daimler or the red Mini, quite often alight hastily and prematurely at Tonbridge, having spotted the station sign through the train window and assumed that the spelling difference was simply another case of British orthographical flexibility lingering from Elizabethan times. In fact, even despite explicit warnings simultaneously with the invitation, considerate hosts some-times dispatch emissaries to both stations. According to Richard Cobb, in *Still Life* (*Sketches from a Tunbridge Wells Childhood*—Chatto & Windus, London, 1983), in a passage emphasizing the 'singularity' of the town, "...Tunbridge Wells was not like other places, above all not like the wretched Tonbridge. (Tunbridge Wells prided itself on its 'u', and there could be no worse sin than to have spelt it wrong)." Tunbridge Wells is located in the borough of Royal Tunbridge Wells, which derives its name from the fact that it was once a favorite watering place of the English court, under the aegis of Beau Nash. Tunbridge Wells is famous for its ancient mineral wells, technically known as *chalybeate springs*, rediscovered in 1606 by Dudley, third baron North. They still produce an al-legedly health-giving drink which you used to be able to buy from an attendant for a pittance. The town is also famous for *Tunbridgeware*, a name given to small examples of the cabinetmaker's art, decorated with a kind of wood mosaic forming pictorial pat-terns; the most common category of this ware is the *Tunbridge box*. These boxes were first made in Tunbridge Wells around 1830 and were a thriving business until the middle of the 19th century. The boxes vary in size from two by three inches to two by three feet, and the veneer consists of extremely narrow rectangular pieces of multicolored wood, some of them as narrow as toothpicks. The art was imitated in many other English towns but wherever they were made the boxes were called *Tunbridge boxes*. Not all *Tunbridge boxes* are antiques: it is rumored that they are still being made today. *Tunbridge boxes* are used for a variety of purposes: the little ones usually for jewels; the big ones as hope chests; and the middle-sized ones for the secreting of illicit love letters by British lady characters in detective stories written by other British ladies.

tuppenny one   *Slang.* **sock on the jaw**
Slang. (*Twopence* and *twopenny* are pronounced TUPPENCE and TUPPENNY, and are sometimes slangily spelled that way.) One also hears of a *fourpenny one*, which appar-ently means the same thing as a *tuppenny one*, not necessarily twice as devastating.

tuppet, *v.i.*   *Slang.* **clickity-click**
Slang. A bit of onomatopoeia applied to ladies in spiked heels.

turf, *n., v.t.*   **sod**
Both terms, in both substantive and verbal uses, are synonymous in both countries, but turf is almost always used in Britain. One unit of the stuff (i.e., a standard size piece of ready made lawn) is called *a turf* in Britain, *a sod* in America. *Turves* are normally

1' × 3' in Britain; sods 1' × 1' in America. For wholly unrelated uses of both terms in Britain (and in particular, a good reason why not to use the American term there) see **sod**, *n.* and **turf**, *n.*

turf, *n.* *Inf.* **neck of the woods**
Inf. Preceded by a possessive pronoun, an expression that seems to transcend all class barriers, as in, *On me own turf, I sez wot's wot* or, *Let you give me lunch? Oh no, dear boy, we're on my turf now.*

turf accountant **bookmaker**
A preposterous euphemism for *bookie.* **Commission agent** is an equally euphemistic synonym.

turf out **throw out**
Slang. Usually applied to rubbish, whether a pile of old magazines or undesirable people; or even nice people after pub-closing time.

turn, *n.* **1. act (vaudeville)**
2. dizzy spell
1. This is a vaudeville term (remember vaudeville?). *Turn* in this sense is short for *variety turn* or *music hall turn* and by extension can denote the performer as well. See **star turn.** 2. Turn can mean 'shock' (*It gave me quite a turn*) in both countries. Less educated Britons also talk of having a *turn* to describe the experiencing of a *dizzy spell.*

turnabout, *adj.* **reversible**
Applied to overcoats.

turn and turn about **alternately**

turncock, *n.* **water main attendant**

turning, *n.* **turn**
The *first turning on the right* means the 'first right turn.' The British say, *Take the first turning on the right* and the Americans (when they are willing to bother), *Take your first right. Turning* has apparently come to mean *block,* i.e., the space between two *turnings* in the original sense of *turn.* It has been used in such phrases as *a medium length turning* (medium-sized block), *a short turning,* etc. See **Appendix I.A.3.**

turn out, *v.t.* **clean up**
In Britain one *turns out* a room or a closet by moving everything out of it, cleaning it up, and then moving everything back.

turn the Nelson eye on **turn a blind eye to**
Inf. To *wink at* (something); to overlook it, act as though nothing had happened. Admiral Nelson (1758–1805) lost the sight of one eye at Calvi in 1793 while in command of the *Agamemnon* during the French Revolutionary Wars. In 1801, while second in command under Sir Hyde Parker, he ignored Parker's order to cease action against the Danes at Copenhagen by putting his telescope to his blind eye and claiming that he hadn't seen Parker's signal. (He continued the battle and beat the Danes.) Hence, to *turn a Nelson eye* on something is to pay no attention to it, to ignore it, to pretend that nothing has happened.

turn-up, *n.* **1. trouser cuff**
2. upset
1. The term *cuff* in Britain is confined to sleeves. 2. In sports.

turn up one's toes, *Slang.* *Slang.* **kick the bucket**

turn up trumps. See **come up trumps.**

turtleneck, *adj.*   **round-neck**
Applied to sweaters with round collars skirting the base of the neck. For the American sense of *turtleneck,* see **polo neck.** See also **roll-neck.**

tushery. See **Wardour Street.**

twee, *adj.*   **arty**
Slang. Or *terrible refeened.* Usually seen in the phrase *fearfully twee.* Implies archness, affected daintiness, quaintness-for-quaintness' sake, and so on.

tweeny, *n.*   **assistant maid**
Inf. A maidservant, one who assists both cook and chambermaid, and whose position is thus *between* downstairs and upstairs. Also *tween-maid.* Just about obsolete.

twelfth man   **standby**
Inf. In **cricket,** the side consists of eleven players and a *twelfth man* who is present to take the place of an injured or otherwise unavailable player. The term has come into general use to signify a *standby* in any situation.

twenty   **a pack of**
Refers to cigarettes. In shops you ask for either *twenty* or *ten,* depending, e.g., on the state of your finances. Thus, *Tw ...ny P'ayers, please.* When you buy from a machine there may be any number of variations, seven, eight, twelve etc., depending on the machine. See also **packet.**

twenty shilling freeholder. See **freehold.**

twicer, *n., Slang.*   *Slang.* **double dealer**

twice running   **twice in a row**

twig, *v.t.*   *Inf.* **catch on to**
Slang. In the sense of 'understanding.' *Dig* is a common synonym (invented by jazz practitioners and enthusiasts) in America; sometimes heard in Britain as well. Synonymous with **tumble to.**

twin-bedded. See **double-bedded.**

twin with...   **linked with...; sister-citied with...**
Seen on roadside town signs to indicate a special formalized friendly relationship with a town abroad. A variant is the phrase *friendship town* followed by the name of a related community. Thus, driving along, you might see

CHICHESTER

TWIN WITH CHARTRES

or

ROYAL TUNBRIDGE WELLS

FRIENDSHIP TOWN
WIESBADEN

with the twin town usually chosen on the basis of similar industries or general interests and often quite similar in size.
Sometimes *twin* becomes *twinned,* as in

FOLKESTONE

TWINNED WITH BOULOGNE-SUR-MER

Chester and Roquefort have the cheese industry in common; Coventry and Volgograd (formerly Stalingrad) are linked by their common tragedy of woeful destruction in World War II; Liverpool and Odessa, like Bristol and Bordeaux, are seaport pairs; Cambridge is linked with both Leyden and Heidelberg, all university towns; Luton, in Bedfordshire, and Wolfsburg both manufacture automobiles. The practice is not confined to British communities, but often occurs among places in three or more countries. Puteaux, in

France, has links with ten towns in as many countries. Coventry may have set a record in twinning with not only Volgograd, but twenty-one others in seventeen countries, including Coventry in the United States and Parkes in New South Wales, Australia. Bishop's Stortford, in Hertfordshire, has linked with Villiers-sur-Marne, near Paris, and Friedberg, near Frankfurt—all three being commuting towns, called **dormitory** towns in Britain. In the United States, Seattle has twinned with Kobe; San Diego with Yokohama; Boston with Rome; and Montclair (N.J.) with Graz in Austria. This twinning or linking process is also called *jumelage* (from the French for 'twin': *jumeau*, fem. *jumelle*) and is a sort of municipal love affair for the furtherance of international contacts and goodwill. It was originally celebrated through the mutual visits of mayors, chambers of commerce, sports, church, and youth groups and such. Nowadays the activities have mushroomed with mutual visits of individual families who enjoy holidays abroad as guests of other families in the twin town, arranged through one's home town town-twinning organization: no hotel bills, only the fare and organization dues. This is an activity much to be encouraged. People of different nationalities get to know each other's countries and this can only help in a troubled world. It is pleasant to think about that *agent de police* being presented with a *bobby's* helmet on a dais in a square in Buxton, Derbyshire, at the official sealing of its twinning pact with Oignies, France. (The good people of Buxton might even one day learn how to pronounce Oignies.) Recently, the term *sister-cited* has come into American usage. In the October 8, 1974, issue of the London fortnightly *The Overseas American*, we read that as a result of recent détente, Baltimore, Md. was to be *sister cited* with Odessa, establishing the first relationship between U.S. and Russian cities.

A bit of cold water has been thrown on the twinning concept. The July, 1980 (Vol. 19, No. 7) issue of *Kent Life*, a monthly magazine devoted to the affairs of the County of Kent, in southeast England, carried this rather troubled editorial.

Is town twinning really worth it?

With our likely independence of other people's oil, our rows with France over agriculture, our disagreements with the Arab world, Great Britain looks set to become more insular than at any time since World War Two.

Nationalism is becoming fashionable. Not the climate, one would think, for the idea of twin towns.

Over the last 30 years or so, towns and even villages have set up these super penfriend arrangements with varying success.

Enthusiasm has blown hot and cold with the British probably blowing more coldly longer than the Continentals.

As an idea, twinning is good proving [sic] the links are forged firmly between ordinary people and not just junkets for the Town hall top brass. Visits between schools and sports clubs are splendid and the twinning idea in this sense is well worth developing.

But the odds are always stacked against it in this country. A classic case is that of Chatham, now part of the Rochester upon Medway set-up.

Early on in its life, the twinning arrangement with Valenciennes in Northern France resulted in much activity by the French.

They named one of their main public assembly halls in the civic centre and a mid-town pub after Chatham. Years later, after much prodding, Chatham reciprocated by calling a concourse at the Pentagon shopping centre after Valenciennes which is tantamount to a nothing as far as Chatham people are concerned.

Where will you find the name of Beauvais in Maidstone? A dozen years or so ago when it was decided to re-name the municipal theatre, the suggested name of Beauvais Theatre was given short shrift and a good opportunity was lost.

Apart from indifference, the financing of twinning militates against it. On the Continent, rich Chambers of Commerce are able to dip into their pockets to help in many ways. Not so here because Chambers of Commerce are organised differently and have little money muscle.

And with Town Halls looking at every penny and certainly not giving twinning much priority, the outlook looks grim.

So it appears we will soldier on with a few enthusiasts trying to make a go of a rickety notion.

Surely for towns which have links or are contemplating them, now is the time to consider seriously whether they can still go into the ventures wholeheartedly. If not the whole idea should be dropped completely.

However, the movement is far from dead. In fact, its geographical scope is increasing. The following letter appeared in *The Times* (London) of September 29, 1983:

Third World twins
From Mrs Jane Knight
Sir, To add to the information about twinning which David Walker contributed on September 19, you may be interested to know that there is more activity than he suggested in non-European twinning and linking.
There are forty communities in Britain either contemplating or in the process of linking with Third World communities. They range from Blewbury, in Oxfordshire linking with Azhagiamanavalam, in India; Marlborough with Gunjar, in the Gambia; and Leamington Spa with Bo, in Sierra Leone, just to name a few. These links range from town twinning to aid links to educational/cultural exchange and some have been going since 1980.
Third World twinnings are a very effective way of educating the public at both ends about our different ways of life and the many surprising similarities. This hopefully will break down the patronizing attitudes at this end and observing life in a developing country shows that we have a lot to learn from them about caring and sharing in the community.
There is to be a national conference for Third World linking communities in November.
Yours sincerely,
JANE KNIGHT
Community Link Adviser
Oxfam,
32A Bath Street,
Leamington Spa,
Warwickshire.
September 21.

In ignorance of the fact that Third World *twinning* was already a fait accompli, Major R.J. Wade (retired) wrote the following letter published in *The Times* (London) of September 19, 1986:

Twinning towns
From Major R. J. Wade, RE (retd)
Sir, Many British towns now advertise their twinning with continental cousins, usually in France or West Germany. How much more rewarding it might be if they could twin with places in the Third World, which could teach us so much of the forgotten philosophies of family togetherness, self-discipline, cheerfulness, courtesy, and optimism in exchange for the technical assistance and everyday necessities of which we have so much and they so little.
Yours sincerely,
JAMES WADE,
9 Catherine Close,
Shrivenham,
Swindon, Wiltshire.

A follow-up in *The Times* of September 29, 1986 responded to Major Wade's letter with evidence that Third World twinning was already in progress. In this case, a whole country in Africa—Lesotho, formerly Basutoland—was involved:

Third World twins
From Mr Paul Williams
Sir, Following the correspondence . . . about Third World town twinning, your readers may be interested to know that in March last year the then Lesotho High Commissioner came to Cardiff to launch the linking of Wales with Lesotho . . . The Lesotho High Commiossioner said that as far as he knew a linking on this scale was unique in the world.
To date 21 schools in Wales . . . have linked with corresponding schools in Lesotho. The Council of Churches for Wales is linked with the Lesotho Christian Council. Hospitals are beginning links. The Young Farmers, our leading women's organisa-

tions . . . some university departments . . . are involved. The Welsh TUC [Trade Union Congress] is making contact with the Lesotho Congress of Free Trade Unions.
    A primary headteacher from Morija, in Lesotho, wrote to a Bangor primary head:
    I was thrilled to hear that your school had become a twin to ours . . . Millions of pounds have been pumped to Africa, with disappointing results, and I feel sure that something like Dolen Cymru (Wales Link) will go a long way in establishing the real needs of the people here.
Yours sincerely.
PAUL WILLIAMS (Joint Secretary, Dolen (Cymru).
11 Min Menai.
Bangor, Gwynedd.

    And it has just (October 11, 1986) come to the attention of the author, courtesy of the World Service of the BBC on the eve of the Queen's visit to China, that the City of Edinburgh is already *twinned with* the City of Xian, ancient capital of China. Interplanetary *twinning* next?

twist, *v.t., Slang.*   swindle

twister, *n., Slang.*   *Slang.* **sharpie**

twit, *n.*   *Slang.* **jerk**
    Slang. The despicable variety.

twitten, *n.*   alley
    An enclosed type of narrow walk in a village or town, as opposed to open country, where it would be called a *footpath.* Mainly Sussex.

twizzle, *v.t., v.i.*   1. spin
                                                                          2. weave
1. *Slang.* No American slang equivalent. To *twizzle* somebody or something *around* is to *twist* or *spin* him (it) *around*, e.g., in order to examine from all angles.
2. *Slang.* Used intransitively, it means 'weave about,' 'meander.'

two (ten) a penny, *Inf.*   *Inf.* **a dime a dozen**

twopence coloured   gaudy
    Inf. Spectacular, with a slightly pejorative tinge. Said, for example, of Churchill's career by C.P. Snow. In common speech, the phrase usually comes out *twopenny* (pronounced TUP'-P'NY) *coloured;* its opposite is **penny plain.**

twopenny-halfpenny, adj.   *Inf.* **junky**
    Inf. (Pronounced TUP'-P'NY HAY'-P'NY.) It can mean 'worthless,' 'negligible,' 'nothing to worry about,' or even 'contemptible,' depending on the context. See also **grotty.**

two pisspots high, *Slang.*   *Slang.* **knee-high to a grasshopper**

two-seater, *n.*   roadster
    Does anybody under fifty still say *roadster?* Maybe *sports car* is closer in feeling, if not so accurate.

two-star. See **four-star.**

two-stroke, *n.*   oil and gasoline mixture
    Suitable for two-stroke engines. This term appears on many service station roadside signs. American friends who saw such a sign reading
TWO STROKE
TOILET
asked the author what a two-stroke toilet was.

two-up-two-down, *n., Inf.*   SEE COMMENT
    A small house with two floors, each having two rooms.

U

U   See Appendix I.C.6.

U.D.I.   **Unilateral Declaration of Independence**
As in the case of Rhodesia.

ulcer, *n.*   **canker sore**
Not used that way in America.

unbelt, *v.t., Slang.*   *Slang.* **shell out**

Uncle Tom Cobleigh and all   *Inf.* **the rest of the gang**
Inf. From an old ballad, "Widdicombe Fair," which begins:

> Tom Pearse, Tom Pearse, lend me your grey mare.
> All along, down along, out along lee.
> For I want for to go to Widdicombe Fair,
> Wi' Bill Brewer, Jan Stewer, Peter Gurney,
>   Peter Davey, Dan'l Whiddon, Harry Hawk,
> Old Uncle Tom Cobleigh and all.
> Old Uncle Tom Cobleigh and all.

Uncle Tom Cobleigh and all is used, usually at the end of a list of names, to indicate that the whole crew was there. Thus, a newspaper report of the **football** match in November, 1974, between West Ham United and Middlesborough (won 3-0 by West Ham United, in an upset) begins:

> Middlesborough returned to London yesterday with Spraggon and Foggon and Boam and Craggs, *old Uncle Jack Charlton and all,* but this time their raw north-eastern mixture, for all that chilling panoply of names, was not enough. West Ham, overwhelmed by Arsenal last week, were far too good for them.
> Jack Charlton is a veteran football player, one of the all-time greats, and the phrase *old Uncle Jack Charlton and all* is an echo of the refrain of the ballad.

undercut, *n.*   **1. tenderloin**
                                                                         2. uppercut
1. Butcher's term. The British use **fillet** (pronounced FILL'-IT) for the same cut. See **Appendix II.H.**
2. Boxing term.

underdone, *adj.*   **rare**
Referring to meat. The American term is now becoming current in Britain.

underground, *n.*   **subway**
Also called the *tube.* A *subway* in Britain is an *underground pedestrian passage.*

under observation   **patrolled**
Sign reading:

POLICE
THIS PROPERTY UNDER
OBSERVATION

means that the unoccupied house is being *patrolled* by the local police.

under offer   *approx.* **for sale**
For sale, but only if the owner chooses to reject a pending offer.

under the doctor   **under the doctor's care**
Don't be shocked, ladies. The British phrase is not to be taken literally. The same proprieties are observed *under the surgeon.*

under the harrow, *Inf.*   *Inf.* **in distress**

unfit, *adj.*   **unable to play**
Because injured or ill. Used in sports reporting and announcements at the game.

unharbour, *v.t.*   **dislodge**
A hunting term: to dislodge a deer from covert.

unit trust   **mutual fund**

university man   **college graduate**
The British make more of a fuss about one's having graduated from college. This is, of course, because college educations, which are beginning to be taken for granted in America, are still comparatively rare in Britain, although the trend is very much on the increase. The British are notoriously prone to putting lots of initials after people's names, particularly on business letterheads. These initials may refer to **Birthday Honours,** membership in a trade or professional association (anything from architects to veterinarian surgeons), or just college degrees. On an ordinary business letterhead it would not be uncommon to see listed *John Jones, B.A. (Oxon.), George Smith, B.Sc. (Cantab.),* etc. *(Oxon. and Cantab.* are abbreviations reflecting the Latin spellings of Oxford and Cambridge). See also **graduate,** the more common term for *college graduate.*

unmade road. See under **metalled road.**

unmetalled road. See under **metalled road.**

unofficial strike   **wildcat strike**

unseen, *n.*   **sight translation**
In an examination or classroom recitation: *He did well in his Latin unseens.*

unsocial hours   SEE COMMENT
Term used in industrial disputes to describe working hours that interfere with workers' social lives, like evenings, weekends, and holidays. Not overtime, which can occur in any job, but the regular hours in jobs like those of bus drivers, railroad personnel, night watchman, etc.

unstable verge. See **verge.**

up, *adv.*   **to London**
See also **down; down train.**

up, *adj.*   **out of bed**
Up, in America, is ambiguous, in that it can mean, simply, 'awake' or 'up and about.' In Britain it means the latter—'out of bed.' This can make for frustrating early morning telephone conversations between Americans and Britons.

up a gum tree   *Slang.* **up the creek**
Slang. In a pickle; in a fix. See also **in a cleft stick; on a piece of string; bunkered; under the harrow; snookered, up the spout.**

up for the Cup   **in town for the big occasion**
Slang. Originated in the North Country, where it is pronounced OOP FOR T'COOP (OO short as in HOOF, and the T' almost inaudible), and refers to coming up to London to support the team in the **football** (*soccer*) **Cup Final** at Wembley Stadium.

upper circle　　　　　　　　　　　　　　　　　　　**second balcony**
In a theater. See also **stall; pit; gods.**

upper ten　　　　　　　　　　　　　　　　　　　*Inf.* **upper crust**
Inf. The upper classes; short for the *upper ten thousand,* a phrase that originated in America.

uppish, *adj., Inf.*　　　　　　　　　　　　　　　　　　　*Inf.* **uppity**

upsides. See **get upsides with.**

up-stick, *v.i.*　　　　　　　　　　　　　　　　　　　*Inf.* **pack up and go**
Inf. This can describe moving one's entire ménage or simply clearing up after a picnic. From nautical slang (now obsolescent) meaning 'set a mast.' Cf. **pull up sticks.**

up stumps　　　　　　　　　　　　　　　　　　　*Inf.* **pull up stakes**
Inf. To *clear and leave.* One of the many terms derived from cricket. Not to be confused with **stump up.** *Draw stumps* means the same thing: *clear out.* **Stumps** are the three uprights in the ground supporting two small cross-pieces (**bails**), the whole structure constituting the *wicket* (See **wicket, 1.**). To *up* or *draw stumps* is to close the match, an operation which is extended figuratively to the *winding up* of a situation or phase.

up the junction　　　　　　　　　　　　　　　　　　　*Slang.* **up the creek**
Slang. In a tough spot; in a fix. How many people who use the American equivalent are aware of its taboo origin? The creek in question, in the original reference, flowed with excrement, and those caught upstream were bereft of a paddle. That version, in turn must have been a reference to Canto *XVIII* of *The Divine Comedy* of Dante Alighieri, according to which flatterers were confined to the Second Chasm of the Eighth Circle of Hell, which is filled with "excrement, that seemed as it had flowed from human privies." Wholly apart from these obscure origins, it appears that a distinguished, literate rock group known as "Squeeze" wrote and performs a song called "Up the Junction," involving a girl from Clapham Junction and an unhappy marriage. Clapham Junction is an important surburban railroad stop near London, and the phrase *up the junction,* describing the plight of the unhappy husband, must have arisen because of the familiarity of the songwriter with that station name. Apparently, the song came first, and from it the phrase, not too commonly heard, has come into the language.

up the pole　　　　　　　　　　　　　　　　　　　1. *Inf.* **dead drunk**
　　　　　　　　　　　　　　　　　　　2. *Slang.* **in a fix**
　　　　　　　　　　　　　　　　　　　3. **crazed**
1. *Slang.* In this meaning, the very opposite of the more or less rare American nautical usage in the sense of 'on the wagon.'
2. *Slang.* In a predicament.
3. *Slang.* By anything, not merely drink.

up the spout　　　　　　　　　　　　　　　　　　　*Slang.* **in a fix**
Slang. Used of any predicament, but, like *in trouble* in America, often understood to mean 'pregnant' when the context permits of the possibility of that interpretation.

up the wall. See **drive (someone) up the wall.**

up to the knocker, *Slang.*　　　　　　　　　　　　　　　　　　　*Inf.* **in great shape**

up train. See **down train.**

U.S., *adj.*　　　　　　　　　　　　　　　　　　　**unserviceable**
Slang. Not at all what one might think, seeing the word, always written as two capital letters: no dig at the U.S. at all. The term, always pronounced YOU ESS, originated in the Civil Service, in government laboratories. *Where's the Bunsen burner? Taken away; it's gone You Ess.* If you haven't guessed it, the *U* is the *un-,* and the *S* is for *-serviceable.* Also written *U/S.*

V

v. **very**
Common abbreviation in informal correspondence. See also **Appendix I.D.9.**

(the) V & A SEE COMMENT
The *Victoria & Albert Museum;* almost invariably so called.

vac, *n.* **college vacation**
(Pronounced VACK.) Less commonly, a school vacation. Simply a shortening. See also **come down; holiday.**

vacancies **help wanted**
Also, **situations vacant.**

vacant possession **immediate occupancy**
One sees in most real estate advertisements the expression *vacant possession on* **completion,** meaning 'immediate occupancy on closing title.' This is sometimes qualified by the addition of the phrase *subject to service occupancy* or less commonly, *service occupations,* meaning 'subject to the occupancy of part (rarely all) of the premises by persons living there and rendering services in payment of rent.' The purchaser can get them out by legal means, but it is an arduous process. It almost always applies to agricultural properties.

vacuum flask **thermos bottle**
See also **Dewar's flask.**

vains I! See **fains I!**

value. See **good value.**

value, *v.t.* **appraise**
Whence *valuer,* the usual term for *appraiser.*

Value Added Tax. See **V.A.T.**

valve, *n.* **tube**
Radio term. Transistors are making them obsolete, whatever they are called.

van, *n.* **1. closed truck**
2. baggage car
1. Large or small. In America usually restricted to big ones. See also **pantechnicon.**
2. Railroad term.

van, removal. See **pantechnicon; removals.**

variety, *n.* **vaudeville**
See also **music hall.**

variety turn. See **turn.**

varnish, *n.* **nail polish**

V.A.T. **sales** or **excise tax**
(Sometimes pronounced VEE-AY-TEE, sometimes VAT.) Sometimes *VAT,* abbreviation of *Value Added Tax,* effective April 1, 1973, replacing the old purchase tax and the selective employment tax, a sort of payroll tax in the service industries. *V.A.T.* resembles

the American Manufacturers' Excise Tax, and derives its *Value Added* label from the fact that at each successive stage of the production of an artifact, the person or entity involved is obliged to add a certain percentage (15% as of July 1, 1979) to his charge, which he collects on behalf of Inland Revenue (the national tax authority) and pays over to them at quarterly intervals. At the same time he can recover the V.A.T. amounts that other people have charged him on his acquisitions which go into what he is producing. Thus, a bicycle manufacturer passes on to the Inland Revenue the tax he has collected, but recovers the tax he has paid on, e.g., metal, tires, etc. V.A.T. applies not only to tangibles but to services as well. A writer passes on the percentage he has added to his fee, but gets back the percentage he has paid on writing-paper, telephone, and other things that he has had to pay for in order to perform his professional duties. Everyone in a profession or business doing anything above a (quite low) turnover has to go through this procedure, acting as a kind of unpaid tax collector. *Value Added Tax* is a Common Market system which Britain was prepared to introduce even if it hadn't joined the E.E.C.

V.C.   SEE COMMENT
Stands for *Victoria Cross*, the highest military distinction. Next in order are *C.M.G.* (Companion of the Order of St. Michael and St. George—Note: The C.M.G. joke discussed under the entry **K.** applies only to the civilian C.M.G.); *D.S.O.* (Distinguished Service Order); *M.C.* (Military Cross). *G.C.* stands for *George Cross*, awarded for extreme civilian bravery (dating from World War II).

(two) veg. See under **amenities.**

verge, *n.*   **grass shoulder**
Verges vary in width and are favorite spots for picnicking **trippers.** Making oneself at home on the *verge*, however narrow, is a British phenomenon. Americans are amazed to see the equipment employed in this happy activity: folding tables and chairs, ornate tablecloths, electric kettles, elaborate picnic baskets, deck chairs, too; everything but the kitchen sink. In Britain one sees parkway signs reading SOFT VERGES, but, when conditions are appropriate, HARD SHOULDER. Why *shoulder* in this case rather than *verge*, and why the singular, nobody knows. UNSTABLE VERGE, another common road sign, is another term for *soft shoulder.* See also **berm.**

vest, *n.*   **undershirt**
For what Americans mean by *vest*, the British say *waistcoat*. See also **singlet.**

vet, *v.t.*   **check**
Inf. With particular reference to candidates for a job, but now commonly used as well in security checking. By a logical extension, *vet* can mean 'authenticate,' referring to a work of art or a holograph, which is certified genuine after being checked up on. One can also *vet* a manuscript for accuracy. This term is derived from the practice of sending animals, especially race horses, to a veterinarian surgeon before purchase.

vice-chancellor, *n.*   **president**
A university term denoting the active head of the institution. The *vice-* is used because the **chancellor** is an honorary officer, always a prominent person, sometimes even royalty.

view, *v.t.*   **inspect**
In connection with selecting a residence. See **order to view.**

viewpoint, *n.*   **lookout point**
A special British meaning in addition to *point of view*, as in America. See **look-out.**

village, *n.*   *approx.* **town**
Village in Britain is more a description of a way of life than a label applied to a particular political subdivision. An article by Paul Jennings in the November 14, 1970, issue of *The Illustrated London News* bears the title "What is a Village?" and says, "Everyone knows what a village is...[but] there is no legal or official definition of a village in

Britain." The usual demographic distinction between *village* and *town* in Britain is based simply on population, and the break comes somewhere around 3,000. Hawkhurst, in Kent (pop. over 4,000) is said to be the largest village in Britain. For an American analogy, *small town* is about the best we can do. For excellent evocations of the image of a British village, see "A Day in the Life of Mediam," by Paul Jennings in the same issue of *The Illustrated London News*, and Ronald Blythe's *Akenfield* (Patheon Books, New York, 1969). While we're on the subject, a British *city* is a *town created by charter*. The popular legend is that the presence of a cathedral creates the distinction, but, as you might expect, there are cities without cathedrals and towns with cathedrals.

vinaigrette, *n.*   SEE COMMENT
   A small box, usually silver, with a fretwork inner lid; frequently Georgian, more often Victorian; now greatly prized by collectors. They originally contained vinegar or salts; ladies carried them to help them through the vapo(u)rs. They now make nice pill boxes.

visitors' book   **guest book; register**
   The American equivalent at a private home is *guest book*; at a hotel, *register*. The term applies not only to private homes, but also to very simple inns and boarding-houses. *Register* is the term commonly used in large British hotels.

viva, *n.*   **oral examination**
   Inf. (Pronounced VY'VA.) Short for *viva voce*, Latin for 'aloud.'

W

w.   **with**
Inf. A common abbreviation in informal correspondence. See also **Appendix I.D.9.**

Waac, *n.*   **Wac**
Inf. (Pronounced WACK.) A member of the Women's Auxiliary Army Corps (WAAC) in World War I. This became A.T.S. in World War II and is now WRAC, for Women's Royal Army Corps. The female branches of the air force and navy are, respectively, the WRAF (rhymes with GRAPH) and the WRNS (pronounced WRENS). See also **Wren.**

wadge. See **wedge.**

waff, *n.*   **puff**
A puff or blast of air or wind; heard mainly in Scotland and the North.

waffle, *n., v.i.*   **1.** *n., Slang.* **twaddle**
                                                           2. *v.i., Slang.* **pad**
                                                           3. *v.i., Slang.* **gabble**
                                                           4. *v.t., v.i., Inf.* **yelp**
1. *n., Slang.* As a noun *waffle* describes anything silly or useless.
2. *v.i., Slang.* To *waffle* in writing a paper at school is to fill up space, i.e., to *pad.*
3. *v.i., Slang.* To *waffle* conversationally is to engage in silly chatter; to *gabble, prate.*
4. *v.t., v.i., Slang.* To *waffle* a cry of pleasure is to *yelp* it. Rarely, *woffle.*
Reflecting uses 2. and 3., a British parliamentarian, writing on the art of *waffle*, describes it as the art of that which is superficially profound.

wage restraint   **wage control**
See also **pay policy; social contract.**

wage-snatch, *n., Inf.*   **payroll holdup**

wages sheet   **payroll**

wage stop, *n.*   SEE COMMENT
The policy of not allowing a person to receive more money from unemployment insurance than he would earn if he were working. Also used as a transitive verb, *wage-stop,* signifying the application of this policy.

waggon, *n.*   **car**
Railroad term, especially *goods-waggon,* meaning 'freight car.' A *waggon shed* is a *car barn.* The American spelling with one *g* is gaining precedence.

wag it   *Slang.* **play hookey**
Old-fashioned. Synonymous with **play truant.** Also, *play wag* or simply *wag.*

waistcoat, *n.*   **vest**
Waistcoat is rare in America, and when used is more often pronounced WESKIT than WASTECOTE. In Britain, it should be pronounced as spelled or with the first *t* silent, and the preferred American pronunciation is considered at least colloquial, or even vulgar, though it was considered "correct" not many decades ago. *Waistcoat* is used in Britain the way *hat* is used in America in expressions like to *wear several waistcoats* or *wear more than one waistcoat,* i.e., to act in a number of different capacities. In America, one is said to wear several *hats* to indicate activity in different capacities. For British meaning of *vest,* see **vest; singlet.**

waits, *n. pl.*   Christmas carolers

wait for it! *interj.*   1. *Slang.* **take it easy!; hold your horses!**
                                    2. *Slang.* **get this!; mind you!**
1. *Slang.* Extended from its use in the army by sergeants teaching new recruits the drill ("Present—wait for it—arms").
2. *Slang.* Further extended to mean 'wait till you hear this,' and used on the model of the army command as a pause word to underline the irony of the following statement.

wake-up operator   SEE COMMENT
If you have no alarm clock, or don't trust the one you have, you can dial the operator before retiring for the night and ask to be called at a fixed time next morning. The operator will ask you to hang up, after taking your number, and will ring you back, presumably to 'test your bell.' The operators are very pleasant indeed, and at a late hour, when business is slow, it is sometimes possible to have a nice little **natter** (*chat*).

walkabout, *n.*   campaign stroll
Inf. Taken by candidates for election; also by the Queen, on certain occasions.

walking stick. See **cane.**

walk out, *v.i.*   *Inf.* **go steady**
Inf. A courtship term, lower-class.

walk slap into. See **slap.**

walla(h), *n.*   *approx.* **-man**
A servant or employee charged with the performance of a particular service. Thus, the member of the household staff who worked the **punka(h)** was known as the *punka(h)-walla(h),* and so on. As you might suspect, this is an Anglo-Indian term and when the British left, the term became less common. Applying the term to American situations, *walla(h)* would appear to come out simply as *-man*: the individual who repairs your typewriter is the typewriter-*man*; cf. ice*man*, bar*man*, etc. A *bag-wallah*, in the old days, was a traveling salesman. Nowadays the term is either old fashioned or jocular, depending on the use.

wallpaper music   piped music
Inf. Muzak is the trademark in both countries.

wank, *v.i.*   *Slang.* **jerk off**
Slang. A metaphorical usage is explained in the following passage from *Jake's Thing,* by Kingsley Amis (Hutchinson & Co., London, 1978). It is part of a conversation between two Oxford dons:

> 'Damon, what's a wanker?'
> Lancewood hunched his shoulders with a jerk, showing that as well as being amused by the question he wasn't totally surprised by it....
> 'These days a waster, a shirker, someone who's fixed himself a soft job or an exalted position by means of an undeserved reputation on which he now coasts.'
> 'Oh. Nothing to do with tossing off then?'
> 'Well, connected with it, yes, but more metaphorical than literal.'
> 'That's a relief. Up to a point. Well, I got called it today.'
> 'Not really? By that pupil of yours?'
> 'No, by that picket of women's-lib women at the gate.'
> 'Oh yes of course. It's quite clever, all that, their campaign to make people feel old and senile and clapped out and impotent—that's where the literal part of wanker comes in.'

See **don; clapped out; toss off** (with which *wank* is synonymous).

want, *v.t.*   1. **take; require**
                                                     2. **need; lack**
1. Example: *It wants a bit of courage to sail the Atlantic alone.*
2. Example: *All the wheels want is a drop of oil; that picture wants to be hung higher; that child wants a good spanking.* In this connection a special use is found in archaic expression of time: *It wants ten minutes to twelve* meaning 'it is ten minutes to twelve.'
Richard II, in the great abdication speech (*Richard II,* Act III, Scene 3), says:

> Down, down, I come: like glistering Phaeton,
> *Wanting* the manage of unruly jades.

Phaeton (son of Helios, sun god of the Greeks) was permitted to drive the paternal chariot across the heavens for one day. He *wanted (lacked),* the *manage (management,* i.e., *control)* of the *unruly (uncontrollable) jades (vicious horses)* and was struck down by a Jovian thunderbolt lest he crash to earth and set it afire. The British tend to avoid *want* in the sense of 'desire' or 'wish,' for reasons of politeness. Where an American would say, *I want this changed,* or *Do you want a memo?* a Briton would usually say, *I would like this changed,* or, *Would you like to have a memo?* To Britons, *I want* may sound imperious, and *Do you want?* is less polite than *Would you like?* or *Do you wish?* A British usage rarely heard in America is *want* in the negative, for *shouldn't,* as in, *You don't want to oil this machine too often.* This usage means that 'it is not the best (or the right) way to treat it.'

want jam on it. See **have jam on it.**

warder, *n.*   **prison guard**

Wardour Street   *approx.* **movie business**
Inf. A street in London that is the center of the film industry and used figuratively to refer that business, the way Americans use *Hollywood.* The films themselves are shot elsewhere. Wardour Street used to be noted for its antique and imitation-antique shops, especially the latter, giving rise to the term *Wardour Street English,* meaning 'sham-antique diction,' the type common in inferior historical novels. This type of language is also called *gadzookery* or *tushery.*

wardship, *n.*   **custody**
Of minor children, in divorce matters.

ware wheat!   *Inf.* **look out for my corn!**
Inf. Ware...! (a shortening of *beware*) means 'look out for...!', and *wheat* is a jocular substitution for *corn.* All this is very old-fashioned stuff, probably a hunting term originally.

warned list   **ready calendar**
Procedural term in law.

warned off   **banned**
A euphemism, very much understating the case, applied to owners, trainers, jockeys, or bettors (**punters** in Britain) who break the rules of racing. The banning is effected by the Jockey Club, located at Newmarket, the headquarters of British racing, and deprives them of their right to enter any racetrack coming within the jurisdiction of the Jockey Club.

wash, *n.*   **use of the bathroom**
Inf. When your host asks whether you would *like a wash* he is offering you the use of *all* his bathroom facilities. See **have a wash.**

wash, *v.i.*   *Inf.* **stand up**
Inf. Always used in the negative: *It* (that story, that excuse) *won't wash.* See also **wear.**

(The) Wash. See **(The) Fens.**

wash-cloth, *n.*   **dishrag**
Also called **dish clout.**

washing-book *n.*   **account book**
Slang. An informal *account book*, for instance as between friends on a trip where one
pays all the expenses and there is a settlement at the end. It can also mean a 'running
score,' as during a social weekend of bridge. No American slang equivalent. One guess
is that this is derived from the concept of entries *washing* one another out, or it could
have come from the laundry or *washing book* with its contra entries of charges and
payments. This latter is a little notebook which is packed with the washing and travels
back and forth between home and laundry.

washing things   **toilet articles**

washing-up bowl   **dishpan**

washing-up cloth   **dish towel**
Sometimes called a *tea-towel.*

wash leather   **chamois**
Often shortened to *leather*; also known as *chamois-leather* and *shammy.*

wash up   **do the dishes**
Do the dishes would confuse a Briton no end because of the restricted meaning of **dish**
in his country: 'platter' or 'serving-dish.' Logically, he calls his *dishwasher* (if he has one;
they are far from ubiquitous) a *washing-up machine*. To him a *dish-washer* is a *water wagtail*,
a small bird (it comes in a variety of colors) equipped with a long tail that it keeps
wagging constantly, as though it were washing a platter. See **wash,** *n.*

waste bin   **wastebasket**

waste land   **vacant land**

wastepaper basket   **wastebasket**

watcher! *interj.*   *Inf.* **hi! howdy!**
Slang. Probably a corruption of *what cheer?*, an old greeting meaning *how's it going?*
There are those who say, however, that it is a running together of *what are you (doing
here, up to,* etc.). *Wotcher* is the preferred **Cockney** spelling.

watch-glass, *n.*   **crystal**
The American equivalent is used in Britain by jewelers but not by the general public.

watching brief, *n.*   SEE COMMENT
A law brief for a client indirectly involved in or concerned with a matter to which he
is not a party. Its technical use refers to the situation of a lawyer charged with the duty
of attending litigation in which the client is not directly involved, where, however, a
point of law affecting the client generally may be involved. To *have* (or *hold*) a *watching
brief*, broadly speaking, is to *keep aware* of a situation that may ultimately involve your
interests. Thus, a Briton asks, "Are you **in the picture**?" meaning 'Are you au courant?'
'Are you up to date?' 'Do you know what's going on?' And a Briton might answer, "I
have a *watching brief*," i.e., 'I'm keeping tabs' on the situation.

water, *n.*   **river; pond; lake**
One sees occasional river, brook, pond, or lake names in which *Water* (with a capital
W, as befits part of a proper noun) is used where *River, Brook, Pond*, or *Lake* would be
used in America. Thus, *Aften Water* and *Eden Water* (rivers), *Derwent Water* (a lake).

water-cart, *n.*   **sprinkling wagon**

watersplash, *n.*   **ford**
Shallow brook running across a road; only a couple of inches high, but there it is, and you drive through it slowly. Sometimes shortened to *splash.*

waving base   **observation desk**
At an airport. The British expression implies much livelier activity than just looking. At Scottish airports they call it by the rather stuffy term **spectators' terrace.**

Wavy Navy   **Royal Naval Volunteer Reserve**
Inf. Not to be confused with the Royal Naval Reserve. The name comes from the officers' cuff braid in the form of a wave, as opposed to the straight braid of the Navy or the approximately diamond pattern of the Naval Reserve.

wax, *n.*   **rage**
Slang. A *dreadful wax* is a *towering rage.* And *waxy* is *jumpy.* Old-fashioned.

way, *n.*   **dither; tizzy**
Inf. To be *in a way* or *in a great way* is to be *in a dither* or *in a tizzy.*

wayleave, *n.*   **easement**

Way Out   **Exit**
Ubiquitous sign in public places and nothing to do with the hippies. *Exit* signs seem to be confined to theaters and **car parks.**

way, permanent. See **permanent way.**

wayzgoose, *n.*   **printing company's annual picnic**

W.C.   **toilet**
Stands for *water closet.* One of many euphemisms. See **loo.**

w/e   **weekend**
Common abbreviation in informal correspondence for *weekend* (*week-end* in Britain). Not merely a designation of a part of the week, rather more the name of a social practice among the idle rich, as hinted at in the definition in the *Concise Oxford Dictionary:* "Sunday and parts of Saturday and Monday (occas. from Friday to Tuesday) as time for holiday or visit." But that definition was in editions prior to 1976. Times have changed—O tempora, O mores!—and the 1976 edition defines it a little differently: "Sunday and (part of) Saturday (occasionally longer period) as time for holiday or visit." See also **Appendix I.D.9.**

Weald, *n.*   SEE COMMENT
The *Weald* is a district in southern England including parts of the counties of Kent, Surrey, Hampshire, and Sussex, having a certain geological make-up. It is commonly heard in the phrase *the Weald of Kent. Wealden,* rarely seen, is the adjective.

wear, *v.t.*   *Inf.* **stand for**
Inf. As in, *Oh no, he won't wear that!* said, for instance, by a lawyer to a client who suggests an outrageous proposal to be made to the other side. Also in the sense of 'permit, tolerate': When something slightly irregular, though patently more efficient, is suggested to a bureaucrat, he won't *wear* it for a minute; or meaning 'accept' or 'see' as in: *I just can't wear him as capable of doing that sort of thing,* when people are discussing an unsolved murder and someone suggests a suspect. See also **wash,** *v.i.*

wear off   **wear out**
Of clothes.

weather-board, *n.*   **clapboard**
A *weather-boarded house* is a *clapboard house,* and *weather-boarding* is the *clapboard* itself, also known as *siding.*

web lettuce   **iceberg lettuce**
See also **cos lettuce.**

wedge, *n.*   *Slang.* **wad**
Slang. A *wedge* (of **notes**) is a *wad* (of *bills*). *Wedge* has thus come to mean 'money', as
in, "Got any *wedge*"? *Wodge* and *wadge* are variants. See also **lolly** for slang terms for
money.

weed, *n.*   *Slang.* **drip**
Slang. A pejorative, synonymous with **twit.**

...week   **a week from...**
The British say *today week* or *a week today* where the Americans say *a week from today;*
Tuesday week or *a week on Tuesday* where the Americans say *a week from Tuesday; last*
Sunday week where Americans say *a week ago last Sunday;* and the same difference in
usage applies to *fortnight.* See also **Appendix I.A.1.**

weekday. See **work-day.**

weepy; weepie, *n., slang.*   *Slang.* **tear jerker**

weighting, *n.*   **extra salary allowance**
A blanket upward adjustment to cover extra costs of living in certain areas. Under
London weighting, e.g., government employees living in inner London, i.e., within four
miles of Charing Cross, receive a certain increase, those in outer London a somewhat
smaller increment, etc.

weigh up   *Inf.* **weigh**
Inf. The British *weigh up* a situation. The Americans drop the *up.* So do the British
when they *weigh their words.* See **Appendix I.A.3.**

weir, *n.*   **dam**
A *dam* or any fixed obstruction across a river or canal. The water so backed up is
directed into a millstream or reservoir, with the excess going over the top of the *weir,*
or via a movable sluice gate, or both. On canals, the *weir* is off to one side and the
excess water runs down an incline into a reservoir.

well away, *Inf.*   **1.** *Inf.* **tipsy**
                                                          2. *Inf.* **off to a good start**
2. A term borrowed from horse-racing. At the outset of a long evening's drinking, one
would qualify, it seems, in both senses.

well bowled!   *Inf.* **nice going!**
Inf. The cricket (rough) equivalent of a pitcher in baseball is the **bowler,** and, like the
pitcher, he is a key figure. *Well bowled!* is a phrase borrowed from cricket which, especially in **public school** and university circles, is used to express approbation of ac-
complishments having nothing whatever to do with the game. Upper class and old-
fashioned; synonymous with the more common **well done** and **good show!** Cf. another
cricket term, applied in its literal sense to fieldsmen (*fielders*): *Well stopped, Sir!* said to
someone blocking an absurd proposal.

well breeched, *adj., Inf.*   **well heeled**

well cooked   **well done**
A description of how you would like your meat. The British use *well done* also. It may
be imagined that they would prefer *well cooked* in circumstances where it was important
to avoid giving the waiter the impression that he was being complimented (see **well
done!**).

well done!   *Inf.* **nice going!**
Inf. Attaboy! is not often heard in Britain.

Welliboots, *n. pl.* rubber boots
Slang. Variant of **Wellingtons.**

wellies. See **Wellingtons.**

Wellingtons, *n. pl.* rubber boots
See also **boots; rubbers; snowboots; galoshes; Welliboots; wellies.**

West Country SEE COMMENT
This term applies to the southwestern counties, Cornwall, Devon, Gloucestershire, etc. Englishmen never come from *the west* or have relatives or go on vacations *out west*, but rather the *West Country*, and have a *West Country*, rather than a *western* accent. Same goes for *North Country*, but not the South or the East. They also speak of the *North of England* and the *South of England* (and use *West-of-England* as an adjective), but never the East of England.

West End 1. SEE COMMENT
2. *approx.* **Broadway**
1. The shopping and theater center of London.
2. Used figuratively (like *Broadway*) to mean 'the theater,' as in *the West End season*.
But the term is also used in a more general way to denote the way of life characterized by theater-going, restaurant-dining, and parties. The term *Fringe Theatre* bears the same relationship to *West End* as *Off Broadway* does to *Broadway*, in the theater world.

wet, *adj.* *Slang.* **dumb**
Slang. Both countries use the scornful terms *drip* and *wet behind the ears*. What is the connection between stupidity and dampness? Is it a reference to a just slicked-up country bumpkin? or a new-born babe or animal? In Britain, *wet* is sometimes used as a noun, synonymous with *dumbbell.*

wet fish fresh fish
Sign in a fish-and-chips luncheon place which also functions as a fish store: OPEN FOR WET FISH 9.00 A.M. TO 3.00 P.M. ONLY. For the periods rather than colons in expressions of time, see **Appendix I.D.4.**

whack, *n.* 1. *Slang.* **gob**
2. *Slang.* **stretch**
3. **share**
1. *Slang.* A big *whack* of something is a *gob* of it, i.e., a *large hunk.*
2. *Slang.* Prison term.
3. *Slang.* To *pay your whack* is to *chip in*, as when the class buys the teacher a Christmas gift. For British use of *chip in*, see **chip in.**

whacked *Inf.* **done in; beat**
Inf. To be *whacked*, or *whacked to the wide*, is to be *beat, pooped*, etc. See **to the wide.**

whacko! *Interj.* *Inf.* **great!**
An expression of great satisfaction and joy; of Australian origin.

whale, *n.* *Slang.* **shark**
Slang. An American who is expert in a given field is said to be a *shark* at it. A Briton so skilled might be called a *whale on, at* or *for* it. There is an echo of the British usage in the expression *a whale of a...* Thus Jones is a *shark at math* in America, a *whale on, at* or *for maths* in Britain, and a *whale of a mathematician* anywhere. For prepositional usages, see **Appendix I.A.1.**

wharf, *n.* **dock**
See **dock** for British use of the word.

what?   **no?**

At the end of a sentence expecting the answer *yes*, like *nonne* in Latin, where Americans would say, *Isn't he?* or *Aren't they?* etc. Example: *"He's a clumsy chap, what?"* Now outdated. The sort of expression that might be used to caricature a relatively unintelligent member of the upper classes, as in *Jolly good show, what?*

what a sell! See **sell.**

what's the drill?   **what's the ticket?**

Inf. In the sense of 'what do we do?' *Drill*, apart from its ordinary meaning in the services, is a military term signifying *s.o.p.* (*standard operating procedure*), i.e., tactics worked out in advance so that everyone knows what to do in a given situation despite the stress of battle. From this background, *What's the drill?* developed the more general meaning 'What is the (proper) procedure?' For example: *What's the drill for getting tickets?* On leaving an oft-attended restaurant where one has a charge account and usually leaves a 15 percent tip, one might get a nod from the maître d' who regularly murmurs, *The usual drill, sir?* meaning, *Do I charge this to your account, adding the usual 15 percent tip? What's the form?* is not quite the same; it is more like *What's the situation?* or *What are the prospects?* or in current terms, *What's happening?*

what's the form? See under **what's the drill?**

wheeled chair   **wheelchair**

Usually called a **bath chair** or **invalid's chair** in Britain. See **Appendix I.A.3.**

wheeze, *n.*   **idea; scheme**

Slang. Idea in the sense of *expedient*, as in, *It would be a good wheeze to get an early start.*

When-I, *n.*   SEE COMMENT

Inf. Many, many Britons, now retired, have spent much of their lives in far-flung places, usually in what used to be the Empire and is now what is left of the Commonwealth. They like to reminisce, and these oral memoirs almost invariably start, *When I was in Singapore...*, *When I was in Bombay...*, *When I was in Hong Kong...*, etc. A number of these retired gentlemen live in tax-haven parts of the United Kingdom, like the Channel Islands, which include the Isle of Man where the term *When-I* is in current use to describe members of this group fortunate enough to find an audience. An American expression with similar connotations is *Way back when...* The author has read that in West Africa, a man who parades the fact that he has been to Britain is called a *been-to*, another lovely invention.

when it comes to the bone, *Inf.*   *Inf.* **when you come right down to it**

Where do we go for honey?   **Where do we go from here?**

Inf. What's the next step? (in, e.g., an investigation). A horribly coy expression, applied to the pursuit of a particular objective or advantage. Its meaning varies with the objective. In bridge, for example, it would mean *How shall I go about playing this hand?*

where the shoe pinches, *Inf.*   **where the difficulty** or **hardship lies**

Whig, *n.*   SEE COMMENT

Inf. Historically, a member of the political party that was the predecessor of the Liberal Party. It was composed of the aristocratic oligarchy. Today it is used informally as a label for one who has naive faith in progress. Cf. **Tory.**

whilst, *conj.*   **while**

Now used less frequently than *while* in Britain. See also **amongst.**

whin, *n.*   **thorny shrub**

Any prickly shrub, particularly **gorse** or furze.

whinge, See **winge.**

whinger, *n.*   **dirk**
(Rhymes with SINGER.)

whip, *v.t., Slang.*
                                                                  Slang. **swipe**

whip-round, *n.*   **1.** *Inf.* **passing the hat**
                                                              2. quick tour
1. *Inf.* A collection taken up, usually, for the purpose of purchasing a gift for someone.
Note sent around in a factory: 'Jennifer Whalen is getting married next Saturday. There
will be a *whip-round* next week to buy her a wedding present.' Also used of a collection
in a pub to pay for the next round of drinks.
2. *Inf.* A hurried bit of inspection of sightseeing of a place like a museum, a palace, a
city, a section of the country. *Let's have a whip-round of Parliament Square.* Or used verbally, as in *We whipped round Bloomsbury.*

whipsy, *n.*   **milk shake**
Slang. Not heard much any more. The American term has taken over.

whisky, *n.*   **Scotch**
Whisky (no *e* in Britain) is the term for *Scotch whiskey*. There is an *e* in Irish *whiskey*.
Whiskey, in America, must be qualified, to distinguish between Scotch and rye, which,
like bourbon, is little drunk in Britain. Bourbon, however, is increasingly found in
Britain's pubs and hotel bars. If you ask for 'whisky' *tout court*, you get Scotch.

whispering cake. See under **school boy cake.**

Whit, *adj.*   **Pentecostal**
Whit is short for *Whitsun*, which means 'Whit Sunday,' the seventh Sunday after
Easter. It used to be followed by a **bank holiday** known as *Whit Monday*, which has
been transferred to an early summer date independent of the religious calendar.

whitebait, *n.*   **SEE COMMENT**
Very small silvery fish, usually sprat, sometimes young herring, fried whole in batter
as caught, without being cleaned. Served in large quantities and extremely tasty.

white feather   **SEE COMMENT**
Slang. During the Boer War, "patriotic" ladies presented white feathers to young men
not in uniform. The taunt of cowardice was expected to shame them into enlisting. This
practice was revived during World War I. To *show the white feather* means to 'betray
cowardice.' The *Concise Oxford Dictionary* alleges that this term developed from the fact
that a white feather in the tail of a game bird betrays poor breeding. However, in an
enlightening and convincing article about common idioms in everyday speech stemming
from the sport of cock-fighting (*Verbatim* Feb. 1977), William Bancroft Mellor reports:

> *Show the white feather*, a phrase denoting cowardice...refers to the white fluff found
> at the base of the tail in many strains of game fowl, particularly those descended from
> the breeds which found their way here [America] 100 years ago from the North of
> England—the Whitehackles. When the tail of one of these birds is drooped during
> fight, and the cock thus acknowledges defeat, the white fluff, normally covered by
> the saddle and tail feathers, shows plainly.

white fish   **SEE COMMENT**
Generic term for all sea fish other than herring, salmon, and sea trout. In America it
refers to any one of several distinct freshwater species, written as one word.

Whitehall, *n.*   *approx. Inf.* **Washington (the government)**
Inf. The government, so-called because so many government offices are located on
Whitehall, a London street between Trafalgar Square and the Houses of Parliament. See
also **Number 10 Downing Street.**

White Paper. See **Paper.**

white spirit   **methyl alcohol**
Or denatured, for non-imbibing uses.

white stock   SEE COMMENT
A cooking term, describing chicken or fish stock, as opposed to **brown stock,** which
is beef stock.

white wax   **paraffin**
In Britain **paraffin** is what the Americans call *kerosene.*

wholemeal bread   **whole wheat bread**
See also **Hovis.**

W.I.   SEE COMMENT
Stands for *Women's Institute,* a national women's club with local branches doing excellent charitable work.

wick, get on someone's. See **get on someone's wick.**

wicket, *n.*   *approx.* **situation**
Inf. In cricket, *wicket* has two distinct technical meanings:
1. A set of three vertical stumps on which rest two horizontal bails which the **batsman**
defends against the **bowler.**
2. The space between the two sets of stumps and bails over which batsmen run to score
points.
    The physical condition of the *wicket,* in this sense, greatly affects the game and the
strategy of play. Since cricket is the British national sport, it is understandable that
many idiomatic expressions, having nothing to do with the game itself, have been taken
into the language, as in the case of baseball in America. Thus, derived from the second
meaning given above, to be on a *sticky wicket* is to be in a *bum situation* or *tough situation;*
to be on a *good wicket* with someone is to be *in favor* with him. In this use *wicket* means
'situation' generally; an article in *The Times* (London) spoke of "the American military
wicket in Vietnam." The British do not use the term *wicket* in croquet. Their equivalent
is **hoop.** See also **cricket; Test Match; sticky wicket.**

widdershins. See **withershins**

wide boy   *Slang.* **sharpie**
Slang. Shady character.

wide, to the. See **to the wide**

wife-battering   **wife-beating**
And **child-battering** is *child abuse.*

wifey, *n.*   SEE COMMENT
Sometimes *wifie,* occasionally *wify,* a term of endearment for one's sweet little wife
(regardless of size); but often, especially in Scotland, it appears in the expression *old
wifey,* used jocularly and the least bit pejoratively, to describe a somewhat addled woman
beyond her first flush of youth. On the train from Oban to Glasgow, the guard (brakeman), explaining a sudden stop: "Those two old wifeys back there had one or two over
the eight (see **have one over the eight**) and forgot to get off at their proper station.
We'll go back a few yards to let them off."

Wigan, *n.*   SEE COMMENT
Inf. A small manufacturing town in South Lancashire, population about 80,000; used figuratively in music hall patter as a prototype of small city architectural horror and cultural provinciality. To *come from Wigan* is to be *a small town hick*, like one's aunt in Dubuque, for whom the editors of *The New Yorker* declared at its inception that that sophisticated periodical was not intended. (By now things have undoubtedly changed in Dubuque, too.) America is so vast that every part of the country must have its *Wigan* and the names of a number of places occur to the writer, but fear of regionally restricted significance (to say nothing of retribution from local Chambers of Commerce) prevents their identification. However, network television being the unifying force it is, *beautiful downtown Burbank*, from the old *Laugh In* show, can now be boldly identified as the American national symbol closest in meaning to the figurative use of *Wigan*. The town has a pier although it is not on the seaside. Recommended reading is George Orwell's *The Road to Wigan Pier*, in which he writes, without sentimentality or snobbery, about the culture of the working classes.

wigging, *n.*   *Inf.* **dressing-down**
Inf. To give somebody a *wigging* is to give him *hell*. *Wig* is a transitive verb in both countries and means 'rebuke.' Its use as a verb is rare and it is usually found in the substantive form *wigging*.

wimpy, *n.*   **hamburger**
Slang. From *Wimpy*, the character in the *Popeye* comic strip, who could eat an infinite number of them. *Wimpy-Bar* is the name of a fast-food chain of hamburger joints, but the term *wimpy* has remained generic. It is, however, giving way to *hamburger* and *beefburger*.

win, *v.i.*   **succeed; gain**
Inf. In the sense of 'making progress,' 'getting there.' A gardener engaged in an unequal combat with weeds might say (if lucky), "We're winning." In a transitive British use, *win* can mean 'gain' in the sense of 'obtain': through advanced methods of mining, a company can *win* a larger amount of coal from the coal face.

wincey, *n.*   **type of cloth**
Consisting of a mixture of cotton and wool, or wool alone. *Winceyette* is a more finely woven version used for shirts, nightgowns, and so on.

wind, *v.t.*   **crank**
Once in a while a Briton still has to *wind* his car, though *crank* is the more usual term. See also **starting handle** and **Appendix II.E.**

wind. See **get the wind up; have the wind up; put the wind up; raise the wind.**

windcheater, *n.*   **windbreaker**

winding point   **turning-around place**
(The first *i* in *winding* is short, as in WINDLASS.) This is a canal term and denotes the place in a canal wide enough to permit the boat to turn around.

windle, *n.*   *approx.* **3 bushels**
An agricultural measure, used for grain. See also **Appendix II.C.1.h.**

window-gazing, *n.*   **window shopping**
The American term is now coming into general use in Britain.

windscreen, *n.*   **windshield**
See also **Appendix II.E.**

windy, *adj.*, *Slang.*   **1. flautulent**
                                                            2. *Inf.* **jumpy**

wine merchant's   **liquor store**

wing, *n.* **fender**
Automobile term but **fender** in England is *bumper* in America. A *wing mirror* is one attached to the fender. See **Appendix II.E.**

wing commander **lieutenant colonel**
In the British Air Force. There are *wings* in the U.S. Air Force, too, but the commander of a U.S. wing is called a *lieutenant colonel.*

winge, *v.i.* *Inf.* **gripe**
Slang. Also *whinge.* To *w(h)inge* is to *complain,* to *bewail one's fate.* In view of its uncertain spelling, the word must be a corruption of both *wince* and *whine.* Whatever its derivation, *w(h)inging* is hard on the listener. *The Times* (London) of July 6, 1981, contained an article on the extremely sensitive issue of the fallibility of cricket umpires' decisions, in which the following shameful intelligence is imparted: "England teams that lose in Australia are known as the 'whingeing Poms.'" (Note: For *England* [as opposed to *English*] in the quotation, see **Test Match.** *Pom* is Australian slang for *Englishman.*)

winker, *n.* **directional signal**
Slang. Also *winking lamp.* See **trafficator.**

winkie, *n.* **weenie**
Slang. Chlildren's slang for *penis.*

winkle, *n.* **periwinkle**
Or any edible sea snail.

winkle-pickers, *n. pl.* SEE COMMENT
Slang. Pointed shoes: the Americans seem not to have coined any slang to describe this sartorial lapse, which has now gone out of fashion.

winkle out, *v.t.* *Slang.* **squeeze out**
Slang. In both senses: for instance, to *winkle out* information by pumping a weak character previously sworn to secrecy; and to *winkle out* a rival by outmaneuvering him. To *winkle* one's way *out* of something is to *wriggle out* of it, and conversely to *winkle* one's way *in* is to *worm one's way in.*

win one's cap. See **blue,** *n.;* **cap.**

wipe off a score, *Inf.* *Inf.* **settle a score**

wipe (someone's) eye *Inf.* **steal a march on (someone)**
Slang. And *get the better of him.*

wireless, *n.* **radio**
Going out of fashion now in favor of the American term.

witch. See **Appendix II.H.**

with compliments. See under **compliments slip.**

withershins, widdershins, *adv.* **counterclockwise**
It is said to be bad luck to walk around a church *withershins,* a practice which sounds like one of those tiresome routines developed in black magic or witchcraft.

within cooee (coo-ee) of **within hailing distance of**
Slang. Within easy reach of (something). *Cooee, coo-ee* or *cooey,* with the *ee* sound long drawn out, is a very old Australian hailing cry, which spread to England, or at least London, over a century ago as both noun and verb (to *cooee,* to *hail*). To be *within cooee* of something, then, is to be not very far from it.

within kicking distance of, *Inf.*   **anywhere near**
For example, *I never got within kicking distance of that class of jockey.*

within the sound of Bow Bells. See **Bow Bells.**

with knobs on!   *Slang.* **in spades!**
Slang. The same to you with knobs on! is said, especially by youngsters, in retorting to
an insult.

with respect   **with all due respect**
In the sense of 'Excuse me, but...' Americans are careful to limit the degree of respect
in accordance with the qualifications of the individual addressed, while the British
diplomatically sidestep that issue by not modifying the noun, or go to the other extreme
by saying 'with all respect.' Philip Howard (*Words Fail Me*, Hamish Hamilton, London,
1980) calls *with (all) respect* a "Benedict Arnold phrase," and goes on:

> In academic circles, the man who begins his remarks *with respect* actually means 'I
> am about to demolish your argument and if possible you with a buzz-saw of disres-
> pect.' Alfred Friendly, the witty *Washington Post* journalist (not to be confused with
> Fred Friendly the American broadcaster and journalist), was disconcerted by the phrase
> when he took to spending half the year in London: 'When, in argument, an English-
> man says to me, "With all respect....", I know he means that he has no respect at all
> for what I have said. The expression is almost never heard in the United States, but I
> rather like it. In telegraphing the punch, it gives me a moment to prepare myself for
> the fact that he is about to knock the neck off a bottle and ream me a new arse-hole
> with what remains.'

With respect, the author begs to differ. *With respect* often has no more bite than *I
beg to differ.* After much of the last two decades in and about London, though often on
the receiving end of *with respect*, he remains blissfully unreamed.
A somewhat different interpretation is set forth in Henry Cecil's *Sober as a Judge*
(Michael Joseph, London, 1958), in connection with a colloquy between counsel and
the court:

> Every now and then [the judge] interrupted with a comment or a question. To which
> counsel would often reply:
> 'With respect, no, my Lord,' or 'With respect, my Lord, I would say,' etc., etc.
> Eventually [one of the judges] said:
> 'By "with respect", ... you mean, don't you, "Surely you're not serious when you
> say that"?'
> ' "With respect" is shorter, my Lord, ' said counsel.

Writing in the spring 1980 (Vol. VI, No. 4) issue of the language quarterly *Verbatim*,
Albert P. Blaustein, Professor of Law at Rutgers University, an authority and adviser
to new governments on constitutions, tells of some Anglo-American language problems
he had to contend with in negotiating and drafting the Zimbabwe constitution. The
negotiations were conducted "solely in the English language" which did not always
conform "to the principles of good American English." He mentions **table**, as one of
the troublemakers, and **at the end of the day** as an "overused trendy substitute," and
refers, as "jarring to the American ear," to the British practice of following a collective
noun, as subject, with a verb in the singular (see **Appendix I.A.4**). He singles out **whilst**
and **keen** as unfamiliar to American ears, and ends with the following paragraph on
with respect:

> But the words which came to be most dreaded are those which are innocent indeed
> to the American ear. When an African or Englishman begins his statement with the
> words *with respect*, you know very well that he disagrees with you entirely and is
> prepared to demolish your position.

witness-box, *n.*   **witness stand**
In America one *takes the stand* or is *on the witness stand*. In Britain one *enters the witness-
box* and is *in* it rather than *on* it because literally, one is in an enclosed *box* (save for the
top).

witter, *v.i.*   **ramble on**
See **rabbit on; blather.**

wizard, *adj.*   *Inf.* **terrific**
Slang. Synonymous with **super** and **smashing.** World War II slang in the R.A.F., usually applied to a successful mission.

wodge, *n.*   **chunk**
Inf. See also **wedge.**

wog, *n.*   SEE COMMENT
Slang. A *wog* originally meant an 'Arab.' Now it has been extended to include Mediterranean types and other dark-skinned foreigners. 'The *wogs* begin at Calais' has become an offensively racist slogan. Geoffrey Smith, a contemporary English writer and columnist, in *The English Companion* (Pavilion Books Ltd., London, 1984) suggests a possible derivation: an acronym built upon the fact that Egyptians working on the Suez Canal were issued shirts bearing the legend Working On Government Service. Disregard this and the false etymology: *westernized* (or *wily*) Oriental gentleman. It is short for *golliwog*, and unpleasantly racist. See also **coloured.**

wonky, *adj., Slang.*   *Inf.* **wobbly**

won't go   **won't work out**
Example: *Putting Jones in charge of that department won't go.*

wooden house   **frame house**

wooden spoon   *Inf.* **booby prize**
Inf. Derived from the quaint custom, originated at Cambridge, of awarding a *wooden spoon* to the student who came out last in the mathematics **tripos,** a custom which later spread to other universities and was applied in other fields.

wood wool   **excelsior**

The British name has nothing to do with sheep and the American name has nothing to do with banners bearing strange devices. Simply *wood shavings* by another name.

Woollies, *n.*   **F.W. Woolworth & Co.**
Inf. A joke name, like *Marks & Sparks.*

woolly, *n.*   **sweater**
Inf. Americans do not speak of a *woolly* but do use *woolies* to mean 'heavy underwear.' No equivalent American expression. See also **jumper; jersey.**

woolsack, *n.*   SEE COMMENT
Seat or divan in the House of Lords for the **Lord Chancellor.** It is stuffed with wool and covered with red baize.

word-spinning, *n.*   SEE COMMENT
Inf. There is no one precise sense in which this expression is used. *Spinning* connotes an endless production of words, and is usually used pejoratively to describe written or verbal verbosity. It can, however, mean 'word play' —using words in novel ways and combinations, in the manner of Joyce or Shakespeare. For another use of *spinning* see **money-spinning.**

workday, *n.*   **weekday**
Interchangeable in Britain with *weekday.* Where an American would use the expression *workday,* the British would say *working day.* It is worth noting that *weekdays* in rail and bus timetables includes *Saturday.* But see **w/e.**

workhouse, *n.*   **poorhouse**
Originally a charitable home for the poor, where the able-bodied were given work to do, and tramps could stay for the night in exchange for odd jobs about the place, this institution and the term itself are now obsolete, and the usual term is **almshouse** or *old people's home*, many of which have been converted into tasteful apartments for senior citizens who pay nominal rent. See **almshouse.** In America a *workhouse* is a *jail* for petty criminals. No such connotation ever attached to the word in Britain.

working party, *n.*   *approx.* **committee**
An informal group, typically of middle-rank officials, i.e., civil servants, to whom a government official or body refers a question for study and report. Usually, as the term suggests, it is less grand than a committee set up by a **minister** or Parliament. Cf. **Royal Commission.**

work in hand. See **in hand.**

works, *n. pl.*   1. **factory**
                                                                2. **machinery**
                                                                3. **operations**
A tractor *works* is a tractor *factory*. But the roadside sign ROAD WORKS means 'Men Working'; *sewage works* means a 'sewage system'; and a *spanner in the works* is a *monkey wrench in the machinery*. A *works convener* is a factory union official who *convenes* workers' meetings. Sometimes spelled *convenor*. *Ex-works* means 'from the factory'.

work to rule   **work by the book**
Describing what a union does when it takes advantage of the rule book technicalities to cause a slowdown. A form of protest, like a *job action*, short of a strike. See **industrial action.**

work to time, *Inf.*   *Inf.* **watch the clock**

worrying, *adj.*   **troubling**

worth a good deal of anybody's time   *Inf.* **a good sort**
Inf. A highly complimentary description of a person. See also **have time for.**

wotcher! See **watcher!**

wowser, *n.*   **fanatic puritan; spoilsport; teetotaler**
Slang. (Pronounced WOWZER.) A real Watch-and-Ward-Society type, intent on improving the "morals" of the community. Also called a *Mrs. Grundy*, from which is derived the word *Grundyism*, synonymous with prudery (from 'What will Mrs. Grundy [a neighbor] say?' in Thomas Morton's *Speed the Plough*, 1798). Originally Australian, its meaning has tended to narrow to 'teetotaler.'

WRAC   **Women's Royal Army Corps**
See **fanny.** Comment 3.

wrangler, *n.*   **mathematics honor graduate**
Formerly, at Cambridge University, the Senior Wrangler was the top man. From an obsolete sense of *wrangle*: to 'argue publicly on a thesis.'

wrap in cotton wool   **spoil; coddle**
Inf. **Cotton wool** is *absorbent cotton*. See also **live in cotton wool.**

wrap up!, *Slang.*   **shut up!**
For synonyms see **belt up!**

Wren, *n.*   **Wave**
Inf. A member of the Women's Royal Naval Service (WRNS). In praise of these patriotic ladies: *Up with the lark and to bed with a wren.* See also **Waac.**

write (someone) down as   **consider (someone) to be**
Inf. As in, *When she heard his reaction to the strike, she wrote him down as another armchair socialist.* An approximate informal American equivalent is to *put (someone) down as.*

writing down   **depreciation**
Tax terminology.

writ large   **1. (made) obvious**
                                                                          2. on a grand scale
1. As in, *He saw the end of his dreams writ large in the new policy.*
2. As in, *His suggestion was no more than the old policy writ large.*

WRNS. See **Wren.**

(get hold of the) wrong end of the stick   **miss the point**
Inf. With the implication that one hasn't got the facts of the case. Sometimes *have* instead of *get,* and sometimes *hold of* is omitted.

Wykehamist, *n.*   SEE COMMENT
    Graduate of (or student at) Winchester. William of Wykeham, Bishop of Winchester (1324–1404), founded Winchester, said by some to be the first British **public school** (though others claim that King's School, Canterbury, was founded much earlier—some time before 600), in 1382, and also New College at Oxford, which will continue to be called *New* forever. It was this William who said, "Manners Makyth Man." *Wykeham* is pronounced WIK'M.

YZ

(the) Yard   SEE COMMENT
Inf. Scotland Yard.

year dot   *Inf.* **year one**
Inf. Usually in the phrase, *Since the year dot,* meaning 'for ages.' See also **moons;**
donkey's years. *Year one* is astronomically incorrect, if we follow Philip Howard (*Words
Fail Me,* Chapter 19, Hamish Hamilton, London, 1980), who writes... "for those who
like to get things right: The Year Dot never existed except as a popular catch-phrase
meaning as long ago as anybody can remember. (It is true that astronomers invented
a zero for some calculations; but they identify it as the year of the consulship of Lentulus
and Piso, which historians call 1 BC.)"

years, donkey's. See **donkey's years.**

yield to redemption   **yield to maturity**
Financial parlance, describing a bond selling at a discount.

yell pen and ink   *Slang.* **yell blue murder**
Slang. Pen and ink is cockney rhyming slang (see **Appendix II.G.3.**) for *stink.* To *yell
pen and ink* is to *raise a stink, create an awful fuss, go into hysterics* and indulge in similar
types of unpleasant activities.

yeoman, *n.*   **1. small farmer**
                                                                       2. SEE COMMENT
                                                                       3. SEE COMMENT
1. Who cultivates his own land.
2. Member of the *yeomanry,* a volunteer cavalry force.
3. *Beefeater;* short for *yeoman of the guard* (see **beefeater**).
A *yeoman of signals* is a British petty naval officer having to do with visual signaling.
Yeoman's service or *yeoman service* is used figuratively in both countries meaning 'loyal
assistance,' 'help in need.' Hamlet used the expression in his conversation with Horatio.
(See line 36 of Act V, Scene 2.)

yobbo, *n.*   *Slang.* **lout; bum**
Slang. An extension of *yob,* **back slang** for *boy.*

Z car, *n.*   **police car**
(Pronounced, of course, ZED-CAR.) See also **jam sandwich; panda car.**

zebra, *n.*   **pedestrian crossing**
Inf. Sometimes *zebra crossing.* A passage across the road, marked with zebra-like stripes.
The *e* is either long or short. Once a pedestrian sets foot on a *zebra,* traffic must stop to
let him cross. See also **pelican crossing** and **belisha beacon.**

zed, *n.*   **(letter) z**
This explains the title!

zero norm. See **nil norm.**

zip, *n.*   **zipper**

zizz, *n., v.i., Slang.*   *Slang.* **snooze**

Appendices

[See Contents, page ix, for outline]

Appendix I — General Differences Between British and American English

A. Syntax

1. There are many differences between British and American usage in the use of prepositions. This is especially true of the prepositions *in* and *on*. Britons live *in* rather than *on* such and such a street (although they do live *on* a road); in Britain animals are *on* heat rather than *in* heat; the British say that predictable events are *on* the cards rather than *in* the cards; and athletes in Britain are *on* form rather than *in* form. Things that are on the way (in a stage of development) are described in Britain as *on* train as well as *in* train.

Different from is heard in Britain but *different to* is more commonly heard, and *other to*, although not frequently met with, is sometimes used where Americans would of course say *other than* (a usage, incidentally, in both countries that must have arisen from the mistaken belief that the ending *-er* in *other* indicated a comparative, and thus gave rise to the solecism *different than*).

Nervous *of* (doing something) for nervous *about*, the advantage *of* for the advantage *over*, an increase *on* rather than an increase *over*, frontage *to* instead of frontage *on*, *by* auction for *at* auction, membership *of* for membership *in* (but one is a member *of*, rather than a member *in* an organization in America as well as Britain), dry *off* for dry *out*, chat *to* for chat *with*, cater *for* rather than cater *to* (in the sense of 'kowtow' or 'pander to'), but sit *to* (in the sense of 'pose') rather than sit *for*, snowed *up* for snowed *in*, haven't seen him *in* rather than *for* six months, Monday *to* Friday (inclusive) for Monday *through* Friday (this sometimes confusing substitution occurs frequently in American English as well), a week *on* Tuesday (or Tuesday week) instead of a week *from* Tuesday, mad or crazy *on* rather than *about* (but the usual expression is *keen on* or *mad keen on*), *in* the circumstances rather than *under* them, visit *of* London for visit *to* London, infatuated *by*, not *with*, audience *of* the Pope rather than *with* him, the laugh *of* him for the laugh *on* him, liability *to*, not *for* (e.g.) income tax, special charges, etc., a study *of* rather than *in* (e.g.) courage (where *study* is used in the sense of *striking example*), something *on* rather than *along* those lines—these are all further examples. The verb *to notify* presents a special situation, involving something more than a difference in preposition usage. Americans notify someone *of* something. In Britain, one can notify something *to* someone. The subject matter, rather than the person notified, becomes the object of *notify*, thus: 'Please notify any change of address to your local post office.' Some authorities say this is substandard in Britain. It is unthinkable in American English. The verb *protest* (in the sense of 'object to,' as in to *protest a decision*) takes a direct object in American English, but is intransitive in Britain, requiring the preposition *at* or *against*.

2. Usage differs between the two countries in the matter of the definite article. Sometimes the British leave it out where Americans put it in. Thus, in Britain, you are *in hospital* or go *to hospital*; and if things are against you, you are *down at heel*. Americans *put on the dog*; Britons *put on dog* (or *put on side*). Sometimes they put it in where we leave it out. Americans, in formal documents, use the term *said* (without the article) as well as the *said* meaning 'aforementioned,' but in Britain the article is mandatory. Thus, a Briton will have *the gift of the gab*, or will visit a shop on *the High Street*, which is the equivalent of *Main Street*; and he will call an unidentified person *someone or the other*. **Ministers** (*cabinet members*) are referred to, for example, as *The Foreign Secretary, Lord,*

Sir or Mr So-and-so, or *The American Secretary of State, Mr So-and-So;* never (as in America) *Foreign Minister Lord, Sir or Mr So-and-So* or *Secretary of State So-and-So,* without benefit of the definite article. Sometimes the British use a definite article when we are content with the indefinite one. Thus, Britons go on *the* spree instead of on *a* spree, take *the* rise out of, not get *a* rise out of, someone, and something will cost forty pence *the* pound rather than forty pence *a* pound. They use both a *hell of a time* and *the hell of a time,* either of which can mean a 'terribly good time' or a 'terribly bad time,' depending on the context and the emphasis: *a hell of a time* usually means a 'rough time' and *the hell of a time* generally means a 'good time.' On occasion the *the* is not omitted but replaced by a possessive pronoun. Thus, *half his time he doesn't know what he is doing.* There is one instance, at least, where the British use the indefinite article in a way that seems peculiar to Americans. Both countries use the term *nonsense* in the same way, but the British also use the expression *a nonsense* in the sense of an 'absurdity,' i.e., a 'piece of absurd behavior,' a *fiasco,* a *muddle,* a *snafu.*

3. The British tend to lengthen (they feel that we tend to shorten!) the first word of many compound nouns, particularly by adding the ending *-ing.* Thus sail*ing*-boat, row*ing*-boat, dialli*ng*-code or tone, bank*ing* account, wash*ing* day, wash*ing*-basin, danc*ing*-hall, spark*ing*-plug, market*ing* research. This happens occasionally to single nouns as well: turn*ing* for *turn,* and part*ing* for a *part* in your hair as well as the sweet sorrow variety. Other examples are found in departmenta*l* store, cooker*y* book, and high*ly* strung. A similar practice is the adding of *-'s* in such Briticisms as barber*'s* shop, tailor*'s* shop, doll*'s* house (any little girl*'s,* not only the Ibsen variety), etc. *Innings* has an *-s* in the singular as well as the plural. There is a tendency often to pluralize, as in brain*s* trust, overhead*s,* removal*s* (the moving business), insurance*s* (as in 'Insurances Arranged' on insurance brokers' letterheads). An *-ed* is often added, as in the stocking*ed* feet, iced water, clos*ed* company for *close corporation* (in this case the British prefer the participial adjective to the noun phrase), wheel*ed* chair, twin-bedd*ed* room, wing*ed* collar, but *two-room flat* (note absence of *-ed* in *room*), the distinction here being that the *-ed* is used to indicate 'furnished with' but omitted where the concept is 'consisting of,' though Siegfried Sassoon, in *Diaries 1923–1925* (Faber & Faber, London, 1985), "proved" the rule by writing of a "four-room*ed* house." In the field of music, the British don't sharp and flat notes: they sharp*en* and flatt*en* them; and a music box is a music*al* box. Note, too, the British insistence on adding an object in certain expressions where the American usage is content with the verb alone: to *move house,* to *shower oneself,* although the object of the verb is occasionally omitted. Also note *pour with rain.* (What else would it pour with?) However, watch out: sometimes *they* do the shortening, as in *swing door* for *swinging-door, sunk garden* for *sunken garden, spring-clean* for spring *cleaning, long-play* for *long-playing* (record), *punch-bag* for *punching bag, drive* for *driveway.* On the subject of the length of words and the British preference for *short ones,* G. K. Chesterton expressed himself eloquently in his *Ballad of Abbreviations,* to the following effect:

> The American's a hustler, for he says so,
>   And surely the American must know.
> He will prove to you with figures why it pays so,
>   Beginning with his boyhood long ago.
> When the slow-maturing anecdote is ripest,
>   He'll dictate it like a Board of Trade Report,
> And because he has no time to call a typist,
>   He calls her a Stenographer for short.
> He is never known to loiter or malinger,
>   He rushes, for he knows he has "a date";
> He is always on the spot and full of ginger,
>   Which is why he is invariably late.
> When he guesses that it's getting even later,
>   His vocabulary's vehement and swift,
> And he yells for what he calls the Elevator,
>   A slang abbreviation for a lift.
> Then nothing can be nattier or nicer
>   For those who like a light and rapid style,
> Than to trifle with a work of Mr. Dreiser
>   As it comes along in waggons by the mile.
> He has taught us what a swift selective art meant

By description of his dinners and all that,
And his dwelling which he says is an Apartment,
Because he cannot stop to say a flat.
We may whisper of his wild precipitation
That its speed is rather longer than a span,
But there really is a definite occasion
When he does not use the longest word he can.
When he substitutes, I freely make admission,
One shorter and much easier to spell;
If you ask him what he thinks of Prohibition,
He may tell you quite succinctly it is Hell.*

4. A singular noun that describes an institution like a university or a political body is followed by a verb in the third person singular in America, third person plural in Britain. Thus, Harvard *plays* Yale, but Oxford *play* Cambridge; the American cabinet *meets*, the British cabinet *meet*; the American public *approves*, the British public *approve*. A headline in the *Daily Telegraph* (London) of August 15, 1981, about England's rout of the Australian side in the fifth **Test Match**, reads: *Australia Crash Again as England Seize Control*. In a sprightly article by Jack Smith in the *Los Angeles Times* entitled *Old-Timer Telling It Like It Is* ("Old-Timer" is an affectionate nickname for *The Times*), the subject of the proper number for verbs following collective nouns is treated as follows:

> By the way, in commenting the other day on a clipping from the Times about a group who picnicked on Chingford Plain to protest its proposed conversion to a golf course, I noted that the correspondent had written "the group has," [sic; *has* should be *was*] and I observed that the Times must have allowed this lapse of grammar as a courtesy to the correspondent, since it would have been the paper's style to treat *group* as a collective and use the plural verb *were*.
> I am challenged on that point by Helen Bacon of Northridge. She notes, correctly, that a collective or group noun may take either a singular or a plural verb, depending on whether the group is thought of as an entity, acting as a unit or as a collection of individuals, acting individually.
> "It seems clear that the group of protesters described in the Times acted as one as it 'strolled about and ate sandwiches in a militant fashion,'" Miss Bacon argues..."Also, I have no doubt that it (the group) chewed menacingly, tidied up the forest, and queued up at the Underground in unnaturally cheeful unison..."
> Miss Bacon and I do not disagree on the English grammar involved here; we disagree on the character of the English themselves. Despite the English reputation for discipline and solidarity in times of national peril, they remain a nation of free souls; and especially at a picnic, even one held in a common cause, I would expect them to disport themselves in their separate ways, some bowling, some skylarking, and some chewing sandwiches militantly, but never in unison.
> In its sports pages, by the way, the Times reported that "Crystal Palace have won succeeding games"; that "today Aston Villa defend their new status at Southampton," and that "Aberdeen have taken a brave practical approach to the problems of the age."
> In Pravda, a group is. In the Times of London, a group are.

On the subject of singular nouns followed by plural verbs, see the list in Marckwardt's *American English* (Oxford University Press, New York, 1958), Chapter 4, p. 77. He says that an American would be "downright startled, to see a sports headline reading 'JESUS ROW TO EASY VICTORY.'" (*Jesus* is the name of an Oxford college, and there is a *Jesus* at Cambridge as well). The British often use *look like* followed by a gerund rather than *look as if* or *look as though* followed by a subject and verb: *He never looked like being troubled* rather than . . . *as if he were in trouble*, or, *He looks like being successful in whatever he tries* instead of *He looks as if he would be successful* . . . *One another* incorrectly takes the place of *each other* in Britain when only two persons or things are involved:

*From *New Poems*, 1932. Pub. in *The Collected Peoms of G.K. Chesterton*, Methuen, London, 9th edn 1942.

Britain and America should treat one another as members of one family. James Morris (*Farewell the Trumpets,* Faber & Faber, London, 1978) writing of the first confrontation between General Allenby and Lawrence of Arabia: "They looked at one another with suspicion." For a peculiar use of *notify,* see **Appendix I.A.1.** There are other idiosyncratic solecisms, but a thorough study would be the subject of another book.

5. *Who* has become an acceptable British informal form of *whom.* On the other hand the objective case is used, informally but almost universally, for predicate nominative pronouns as in, *It's me; She's taller than him,* usages popular in America only in less educated circles. But getting back to *who,* the British often use it as a relative pronoun where Americans would use *which: the companies who pay well, the colleges who admit women.*

B. Pronunciation

1. The book is addressed to the written language. Pronunciation is another matter. The spoken language in London, let alone Devon or Shropshire, is often difficult for Americans. There is the matter of intonation generally, and there is a problem with vowels (the broad *a* and the short *o,* which is somewhere between the *o*'s in NOT and NOTE) and the diphthongs AE and OE, which are pronounced like a long E (as in EQUAL) in Britain and a short E (as in GET) in America. Thus, the diphthongs in *oecumenical* and *oedema,* which are permissible variants of *ecumenical* and *edema* in American English spelling, are pronounced EE in Britain and EH in America. The same is true with the second syllable of *anaesthetist* and names like *Aeschylus* and *Aesculapius,* in which the diphthong is not shortened in American spelling, as in the Greek-derived type of word mentioned above. See the letter in *The Times* (London) of July 21, 1986 quoted in **Appendix I.E.** The *time of day* becomes TOYM OF DIE in Kent and Sussex; *roundabout* (meaning a 'traffic circle' or 'merry-go-round') comes out RAYNDABAYT in those counties; and so it goes. In an amusing article ("Gaffes in Gilead," *The New York Times,* May 12, 1971), Gertrude M. Miller, a BBC pronunciation specialist, lists some horrendous examples, from which I select:

Place Names

Written:	Pronounced:
Prinknash	PRINNIJ
Culzean	K'LANE
Caius (a Cambridge college)	KEEZ
Magdalen (an Oxford college)	MAWDLIN
Magdalene (a Cambridge college)	MAWDLIN
Belvoir	BEEVER
Wemyss	WEEMZ
Kirkcudbright	KIR-KOO'-BRI
Dalziel	DEE-ELL'

Some notable omissions are:

Written:	Pronounced:
Wrotham	ROOT'M (OO as in BOOT)
Lympne	LIMM
Derby	DARBY
Hertford	HARFORD
Berkshire	BARKSHUH
Thames	TEMZ
Pall Mall	PELL MELL or PAL MAL
Marylebone	MARL'B'N
Beauchamp	BEECH'M
Warwick	WORRICK
Marlborough	MAWL'-BRUH

Family Names

Written:	Pronounced:
Ruthven	RIV'N
Leveson-Gower	LOOS-N-GOR
Menzies	MING-ISS or MINJIES
Cholmondeley	CHUMLEY
St. John	SIN-J'N

Featherstonehaugh	FANSHAW
Cokes	COOKS
Mainwaring	MANNERING
Home	HUME (HYUME)

Note: The Australian statesman and the London stationer's are pronounced *Menzies* as spelt; the *-ng-* in *Mingiss* is sounded as in *singer*.

Caution: To the surprise of some Americans, there are place names that are pronounced the way they are spelled, like Hampstead (pronounced HAMPSTED, not HEMPSTID); Berkhamstead (pronounced BURKHAM'-STED not BURK'-IMSTID); Cirencester (pronounced SIREN-SESTER, not half-swallowed like *Worcester, Gloucester*, etc.), but here one must again be careful, because SIS'-SETTER and SIS'-SESTER are still met with on occasion.

A special note on a few representative county abbreviations (there are many more, and county names are occasionally changed as counties are realigned, eliminated, merged, and renamed for allegedly greater administrative efficiency):

Bucks.	Buckinghamshire
Hants.	Hampshire
Lancs.	Lancashire
Wilts.	Wiltshire

These are Standard English if so written (and analogous to abbreviated American state names), and informal when so pronounced. Bucks., Hants., etc., in the spoken language are as confusing to Americans as Mass. is to a Briton.

For a full treatment of this subject, see the *BBC Pronouncing Dictionary of British Names* (Oxford University Press, Ely House, London, 1971), by G. M. Miller. Walter Henry Nelson, in Chapter V of his admirable *The Londoners* (Hutchinson & Co. Ltd., London, 1975) has some interesting things to say abut the mysteries of British pronunciation of their place names, and refers to Alistair Morrison's most amusing treatment of the pronunciation eccentricities of the denizens or habitués of London's chic West End, in *Fraffly Well Spoken* (Wolfe Publishing Ltd., London, 1968), where Berkeley Square (normally pronounced BARKLY, or more exactly, BARKLIH) becomes BOGGLEY and the British Empire comes out BRISHEMPAH. But these elisions and truncations are not confined to the West End, as any American making a telephone call through a British operator can testify after unraveling the arcana of *trangneckchew*, the solicitous operator's oft-repeated assurance that she is *trying-to-connect-you*.

2. It is not only place and family names that present difficulty. Many common nouns are normally accented or pronounced differently from the usual American way. Here are a few:

Accent only: *coroll'ary, labo'ratory, metall'-urgy, contro'versy* (the last two also as in America).

Written:	Pronounced:
ate	ETT
clerk	CLARK
figure	FIGGER
herb	sounding the H
lieutenant	LEFTENANT (army); LEH-TENANT or LEW-TENANT (navy)
missile	second i rhymes with EYE
privacy	i as in PRIVY
schedule	SHEDULE
solder	sounding the l
suggest	SUJJEST
vitamin	i as in BIT

Ate, privacy and *vitamin* are alternatively (though not often) pronounced the American way.

The British tend to accent the first syllable of certain words of French origin, where American speech normally refrains from doing such violence to the original: e.g., *ballet, brochure, café, consommé, garage, résumé, valet*, and the name *Maurice*. In words of three syllables, like consommé and résumé, they often offend American ears by accenting the *second* syllable: CON SOMM'EE, RAY ZOOM' EE! Differences in the pronunciation of Latin are another matter and of insufficient general interest to go into here. For enlightening discussion of the general area of pronunciation differences, see Marckwardt, *American English* (Oxford University Press, New York, 1958), Chapter 4, pp. 69–75, and

Strevens, *British and American English* (Collier-Macmillan Publishers, London, 1972), Chapter 6.

C. Spoken Usage and Figures of Speech

1. Certain usages in the spoken language are foreign to Americans. The telephone rings and the Briton may ask, *Who is that*? never, *Who's this*? Or he may ask, *Is that* (not *this*) *Bob Cox*? An example of this usage is seen in *An Improbable Fiction*, by Sara Woods (Holt, Rinehart & Winston, N.Y. 1971). The English amateur detective says: ". . .It seemed obvious that the [telephone] **caller** was an American . . . I never knew an Englishman to say, 'Is *this* Miss Edison speaking?'" An Englishman would have used *that*, not *this*. Another specially British habit is the use of a question to make a statement, either the kind that would be introduced in Latin by *num*, expecting a negative answer, or the type that would be introduced by *nonne*, expecting an affirmative reply. Thus, a man who happens to be illiterate, having ignored a printed notice, is called to account and asks (says, really), *Now, I can't read, can I*? Or Little Johnny, signaled by his impatient mother to hurry home, asks (says, really), *I'm coming home, aren't I*? Or a person who has slept through an incident which he might have observed if awake, asked about it by a police officer, replies, *Now, I was kipping [napping], wasn't I*? None of these "questions" implies that the listener knows the answer, nor does the speaker expect one. They are simply statements put in this form for emphasis. And the interrogative form is often used for purposes of delicacy, to underplay a statement: *You've come a long way, haven't you*? *It's not too difficult, is it*? And often in a shop the salesperson (*shop assistant*), with some knitting of brows, itemizes and tots up your bill, usually mumbling the words and figures with hardly more than a slight movement of lips, and then turns to you brightly and announces the result with eyes opened wide and a rising intonation, as though indicating surprise and apology for the unpleasant tidings. This happens frequently enough, all over Britain, to constitute a national mannerism. It doesn't save you any money but is rather touching; and it goes back to pre-inflationary days.
2. *Do* and *done* keep popping up in Britain in situations where they would be omitted in America. If you ask a British friend whether he thinks Charles has mailed your letters and he is not sure, he will answer, *He may have done*. An American would have said, *He may have*. If you said to a Briton: *Walking two miles before breakfast makes a fellow feel good*, he might reply, *Judging from your rosy cheeks, it must do*. An American would have left out the *do*.
3. I find that American usage tends to be more literal. We say *baby carriage* and the British say *pram* (an abbreviation of *perambulator*). The British would understand *baby carriage* but no recently arrived American (unless steeped in Christie, Sayers, and Allingham) would know what a pram was. The same would apply to *cleaning woman* and *char*, or *ball-point pen* and *biro*. There is no hard and fast rule. "One could retort," says E. S. Turner in a review of an earlier edition of this book in the *Times Literary Supplement* of March 20, 1981: "How is an untutored Englishman to know that a tuxedo is a dinner jacket?" But in general, it appears that American expressions are easier for Britons than the other way around. On the other hand, Walter Henry Nelson, in *The Londoners* (Hutchinson & Co. Ltd., London, 1975), discussing an upper-class characteristic which he calls "lack of equivocation," i.e., the freedom to call a spade a spade (his aristocratic host at one of the better clubs excused himself, within earshot of a lot of other people, saying that he had to pee: the nobility may "pee" while "their lessers go to wash their hands"), goes on to say that this directness has come into general usage in London. He gives examples: *Cripples' Crossing* (a street sign), where Americans might have preferred the gentler term *Disabled*; *Limb Fitting Centre* (rather than, perhaps, *Prosthetic Devices*?); *Royal Hospital and Home for Incurables* (would Americans resort to a euphemism like *Chronic*?) which Mr. Nelson characterizes as "a charming place to leave one's mother with reassurances about her future"; *Hospital for Sick Children*, "a nice no-nonsense name if there ever was one"—Americans would call it, simply, *Children's Hospital*, or, less simply, *Pediatric Hospital* (and one does wonder why the British bothered to include the word *Sick*, since well children don't need hospitals). Last of all, he refers to a London charity which sells Christmas cards painted by armless artists, and calls itself, in words sparse but graphic, *Mouth and Foot Painting Artists, Ltd.*
4. Inherent in many units of measure are figurative connotations which exist alongside their scientific functions. For years beyond the inevitable adoption of the metric system in the English-speaking countries, to their citizens things will inch, not centimeter, along; a miss will remain as good as a mile, not 1.609 kilometers; a ton of something

will create an image which its metric equivalent won't; 90°F will be a sizzler, while 32.2°C won't alarm anyone. A similar British-American image dichotomy exists in the case of some units. No matter how often an American tells himself a stone (applied to human beings) is 14 lbs., 15 stone does not evoke for him the image of a fat person; and even *a few hundred yards yonder* creates only a fuzzy notion compared with *about a quarter of a mile down the road*. (See also **Appendix II.C.**, p. 418.)

5. In money matters, before decimalization, percentages were often expressed in terms of so-and-so many *shillings in the pound*. Income-tax rates were always so expressed. Since there were 20 shillings to a pound, *40 percent* would be expressed as *8 shillings in the pound*. Since old shillings are still circulating, despite decimalization, this usage will undoubtedly linger for a time (See also **Appendix II.A.**, p. 417.)

6. For the subleties of variations in the vocabulary of spoken (and to a much smaller extent, written) British English based on class distinctions, the reader is referred to "U and Non-U, an Essay in Sociological Linguistics," by Prof. Alan S. C. Ross, of Birmingham University (England), which first appeared (1954) in a Finnish (of all things!) philological journal bearing the German name *Neuphilologische Mitteilungen* (which might be hard to find), later, in somewhat condensed form, in *Encounter*, and still later in *Noblesse Oblige*, a collection of articles edited by Nancy Mitford (Hamish Hamilton, London, 1956; Penguin Books Ltd., 1959). His article was commented on by Miss Mitford in *Encounter*, in a piece entitled "*The English Aristocracy*." (Living in France, she may have come across Ross in French translation, for she refers to the Finnish periodical as the *Bulletin de la Société Néo-Philologique de Helsinki*, or it may be that the article itself was in English, while the *Bulletin's* masthead or title was in several languages, including French. At any rate, *de Helsinki* should have been *d'Helsinki*.) She in turn was answered, still in *Encounter*, by Evelyn Waugh in "an Open Letter to the Honorable Mrs. Peter Rodd (Nancy Mitford) On a Very Serious Subject." The Mitford and Waugh articles, too, are included in *Noblesse Oblige*. All these comments gave currency to the concept of U and Non-U as linguistic categories constituting "class-indicators." They were followed by Ross's *What are U?* (André Deutsch, Ltd., London, 1969) and *U and Non-U Revisited*, a collection of essays by various authors, edited by Richard Buckle (Debrett's Peerage, Ltd., London, 1978). (The *U*, incidentally, doesn't stand for *You* as in *While-U-Wait*, but for *upper class*.) It is felt that these distinctions would be lost on most Americans, whose ears are not attuned to English class differences based on accent or vocabulary and who suffer from a feeling of inferiority equally in the spoken presence of London cabbies and Oxford dons. References to class differences in the text are therefore relatively few, but in one's eagerness to do as the Romans do, it would be well to take the trouble to avoid some of the more glaring shibboleths, like *lounge* (for *living room*), *serviette* (for *napkin*), *toilet* (for *lavatory*), *pardon!* (for *sorry!* or *what did you say?*) and *pardon me* (for *excuse me*).

D. Punctuation and Style

1. Punctuation differs in many respects. The British use the hyphen more frequently than the Americans. *No-one* is a conspicuous case in point, although the *Concise Oxford Dictionary* recommends *no one*. *Loop-hole* and *mast-head* are other examples of this practice. Fowler wrote in 1926, "In America they are less squeamish than we are, and do not shrink from such forms as *coattails* and *aftereffects*." The British still shrink, though *loophole* is now permissible.

2. Parentheses (which they call *brackets* or *round brackets*) are very much in evidence in company names to designate a particular region or field of activity, like *E.W. Ratcliffe (Timer Merchants) Ltd.; Samuel Thompson (Manchester) Ltd.* This is a useful practice in putting the public on notice and avoiding confusion.

3. The British often use single quotation marks (which they also call *inverted commas*) outside the quoted matter and double ones inside; thus: John said, 'Henry told me that he had heard Joseph say, "I won't go to school today"'. American usage puts the period (which the British call *full stop*), comma or other mark inside the final quotation mark: John said, "I told him not to worry," and then left. The comma would follow the final quotation mark in Britain: "... not to worry," and then left.

4. In telling time, the period, rather than the colon, is used between the hour numeral and the minutes: 6.30 rather than 6:30. When the minutes involved are less than ten, the zero before the digit is omitted: 9.5 rather than 9.05. And while we are speaking of expressions of time, it might be well to note the usage, on invitations, of expressions like *6.30 for 7.15*, which means "Dinner will be served

at about 7.15, but come as soon as you can after 6.30 for sherry or cocktails." It is good form to arrive any time between 6.30 and just before 7.15.
5. When dates are expressed in figures, the British follow the European method of day, month, year: thus, 10/27/69 becomes 27/10/69. *Next* often follows the name of the day in the expression of future time, as in, *See you Monday next*. In America it would be *next Monday*.
6. The period is usually omitted in *Mr, Mrs, Messrs, Dr*, but used in such abbreviations as *Prof., Rev., Hon.*, the rule appearing to be to use it where the abbreviation is simply a shortening of the word but to leave it out where the abbreviation consists of omitting letters from the middle of the word, as in *M(iste)r, D(octo)r*. However, it does appear in *St.*, the abbreviation of *Saint*.
7. *Mr* is the title of the common man in both countries. *Mr*, not *Dr*, is also the title of a surgeon or dentist, although Jones, your family physician, is *Dr* Jones. Correspondence that would be addressed to *Mr*. John Smith in America is usually addressed to John Smith, *Esq*. (with a period) in Britain, a quaint practice followed in America only in communications between lawyers. *Junior* (abbreviated to *Jr*.) and *II, III, IV*, etc. following the names of persons in the line of descent all bearing the same name are omitted in Britain. One would not address a letter to William A. Jones, Jr. or Samuel B. Smith II, as the case might be. In ordinary speech, if one were to mention a forthcoming visit to Fred Brown (there being a father and son of the same name), the listener might ask, "Senior or Junior?" But in correspondence, or in a formal listing such as a telephone directory, membership list and the like, the *Jr.* and Roman numerals are omitted.
8. In the names of rivers, the British put the word *River* first, the Americans last: *the River Thames*, the *Mississippi River*. The word *River* can of course be omitted in both countries.
9. Abbreviations are common in informal British correspondence. Some, but not all, have been included in the alphabetical listing. Some common ones are:

circs.	circumstances
hosp.	hospital
op.	operation
prb.	probably
s.a.e.	self-addressed envelope
s.a.p.	soon as possible
p.t.o.	please turn (the page) over
v.	very
w.	with
w/e	weekend

People's names are often abbreviated. A Briton in a hurry might write you that M. had been down for the w/e w. N. and would prb. return the favour soon, unless the circs. changed because N. had to go into hosp. for a v. minor op. s.a.p.
For the abbreviation of county names, see **Appendix I.B.1.**, p. 411.

E. Spelling
Where the only difference is one of spelling the item has generally been omitted, but it might be useful to point out that there are certain orthographical differences between the two countries. These fall into two main categories: word formation groups and individual words. Typical word ending peculiarities (sometimes only preferences) occur in the *-our* group (*colour, honour*); the *-re* group (*centre, theatre*); the *-ise* words (*criticise, agonise*; though *-ize* would now appear to be preferred); certain conjugated forms (*travelled, travelling*) or derived forms (*traveller, jeweller*) where the British double the final consonant; *-xion* words (*connexion*, [still used, though *connection* is now preferred], *inflexion*, but inconsistently, *confection, inspection*); *-ce* words (*defence, pretence; licence* and *practice* as nouns, but *license* and *practise* preferred as verbs); words of Greek derivation containing the diphthongs *ae* or *oe*, from which Americans usually drop the *a* or *o*, like *aetiology, anaesthesia, anaemia, oedema, oenology, oesophagus*. As to the treatment of diphthongs in words derived from the Greek, note the letter that appeared in *The Times* (London) of July 21, 1986:

Unkind cut

From Dr P. Furniss

Sir, What chance of survival has the diphthong when even you cannot spell "Caesarean" (leading article, July 11)? I note that you also prefer medi*e*val to medi*a*eval.

As an anaesthetist I must declare a partisan interest in the matter, but I am sure Aesculapius would add his support to my plea.

Sir, I beg you to protect the disappearing diphthong; it is an endangered English species!

Yours faithfully,

P. FURNISS.

10 Mile End Road, Norwich.

July 12.

Some common individual differences are found in *cheque* (see entry), *gaol* (jail), *kerb*, *pyjamas*, *storey* (meaning 'floor' of a building), *tyre*, *aluminium*, *grey*, *whisky* (but note Irish *whiskey*—see entry), *manoeuvre*, and again in the consonant-doubling department, *waggon*, *carburettor* (or *carburetter*), and others.

Appendix II —
Glossaries and Tables

A. Currency

Up to August 1, 1969, British coins in regular use were the halfpenny (pronounced HAY'PNY), penny, threepence (pronounced THRUH PNY, THRUPPENNY, THRUPPENCE, sometimes THREPPENCE; sometimes called THREPPENNY BIT), sixpence (nicknamed *tanner*, sometimes *bender*), shilling, florin (2 shillings), and half-crown (2½ shillings). Twenty shillings made a pound; 12 pence (plural of *penny*) made a shilling. Thus there were 240 pence in a pound. The farthing (¼ penny) was discontinued years ago; the halfpenny was demonetized on August 1, 1969; the half-crown on January 1, 1970. The *guinea* (see entry), existed only as a convenient way of denoting 21 shillings, i.e., one pound, one shilling. The symbol for pound is £, placed before the number, like the dollar sign; for shilling (or shillings) it was *s.*, for penny or pence *d.*; but there was also the oblique line and dash meaning *shilling(s)* written after the number; thus: 15/- meant 15 shillings. If there were pence as well, the dash was omitted; thus 15/9, orally *fifteen and nine*, meant 15 shillings and 9 pence. But on February 15, 1971, the British decimalized their currency, eliminating shillings as such, leaving only pounds and pence (now abbreviated to *p*), with 100 new pence to the pound. What used to be a shilling is now 5 new pence, a florin is now 10 new pence, and so on. (The *new* soon began to be dropped.) The old shillings and 2-shilling pieces (the same sizes as the new 5- and 10-pence pieces but different designs) are still in circulation but will gradually become collectors' items. What was one pound two shillings (£1-2-0) is now written £1.10. With the coming of the 100-pence pound, it became the fancy of some merchants, after adding up a column, to announce the total in terms of pence alone; thus: "111 pence" for £1.11 or "342, please," for £3.42. This custom is undoubtedly a hangover from the practice, in the old shilling days, of stating prices in shillings even when they exceeded a pound; thus: 102/6 or 200 s. Apparently, stating the price in smaller units is thought to make things sound cheaper. On decimalization day ("D-Day") the remaining old coins all became a thing of the past . . . or did they? Although the mint thereafter turned out only the new halfpennies (now discontinued), pennies and 2, 5, 10, and 50 pence pieces, lo! the old pennies, threepences, and sixpences were nevertheless at first allowed to circulate alongside the new coins for a year and a half (the old pennies and threepences were later excommunicated and the sixpences "restyled" 2½ p, as of September 1, 1971), either because they went into the old telephone and vending machine coin slots, or out of sentimental attachment to relics of the old regime, or because the British cannot resist the attraction for introducing into almost any situation a bit of amiably maddening confusion or something to grumble about. (Look out for nongriping Britons—they're getting ready to mutiny!) With sixpence temporarily worth less than threepence, there was bound to be a fair amount of consternation, indignation, error, high amusement, cries in Parliament of "Resign!," and general hilarity. Despite all this streamlining, however, it is to be doubted that the Polynesian idyll will be re-entitled *The Moon and Two and One-Half Pence*; and for a certainty, things will go on not being worth a farthing (see **farthing**) and ladies will go on spending a penny albeit a new one (see **spend a penny**). *Pee* is now the familiar pronunciation of *p (penny)* and 2 *pee*, rather than the old *tuppence* and 3 *pee* in place of the old *threepence*. (It may well be the case that this could not have happened when the other *pee* was more shocking than it is today. See **pee**.)

B. Financial Terms

For the benefit of those who follow the financial news, *stocks* are called *shares* in Britain, and *stocks* in Britain are *government bonds*. Stock prices are quoted in penny denominations, as are increases, decreases, averages, and the like. Thus, a stock quoted at 150 would be selling at 150 *pence*, or roughly around $2.25 per share (as of September, 1986). A *bonus issue* or *share* is a stock dividend. Preferred stock is called *preference shares*. *Scrip* means a *temporary stock certificate*, not a certificate for a fraction of a share, as in America.

C. Units of Measure
1. Dry Measure
a. Barrel
A *barrel* is a varying unit of weight (or other quantitative measure). It depends on what it is a *barrel* of. It works this way:

Commodity	Weight in lbs.
soft soap	256
butter	224
beef	200
flour	196
gunpowder	100

But careful: Applied to beer and tar, *barrel* is a unit of volume expressed in gallons and works this way:

Commodity	No. of gals.
beer	36
tar	26½

And remember, a *gallon* is an *Imperial gallon*, equal to approximately 120 per cent of an American gallon (1.20095 per cent is a little closer; see **gallon**). And to make things just a bit less certain, a *barrel* of fish is *500 fish!* For other examples of the British determination to keep things charmingly flexible, or doggedly inconsistent (as Mencken put it in *The American Language: Supplement I*, Alfred A. Knopf, Inc., New York, 1961, p. 495), see **score; stone.**
b. Hundredweight
112 pounds in Britain; 100 pounds in America. See also **stone.**
c. Keel
Weight of coal that can be carried on a *keel*, and still used as a wholesale coal measure. Since a British ton is 2240 lbs. and a British cwt. (hundredweight) is 112 lbs., a *keel* is, in American terms, 47,488 lbs., or a sliver under 23¾ tons, all of which is about to become totally immaterial under the fast-encroaching metric system.
d. Quart
1.20095 American quarts. See also **gallon.**
e. Score
i. 20 or 21 lbs, in weighing pigs or oxen. If you should happen to be in the British countryside and want to buy some pigs, don't think £2.99 a *score* is the bargain it seems: *score* doesn't mean 'twenty' in this usage. It is a unit of weight, regional, and applies especially to pig and cattle raising.
ii. 20 to 26 tubs in dispensing coal. *Tub*, incidentally, in various trades (butter, grain, tea, etc.) is a flexible unit of measure, depending on the commodity. This flexibility seems peculiarly British.
f. Stone
Generally, 14 lbs. British bathroom scales, as well as those in railroad stations and similar public places, are calibrated in *stones, half-stones*, and *pounds*, but Americans find it rather difficult to translate *stones* into *pounds* because 14 is a hard number to handle in mental arithmetic. To make things worse, a *stone* of meat or fish is 8 lbs., a stone of cheese is 16 lbs., etc. Eight 14-lb. stones make a *hundredweight*, which is 112 lbs. in Britain (more logically, 100 lbs. in America). Perhaps a table of terms used in the trade would help, showing the meaning of *stone* applied to various commodities.

Commodity	Weight in lbs.
hemp	32
cheese	16

potatoes	14
iron	14
wool	14*
meat	8
fish	8
glass	5

All of this will become a thing of the past with the complete adoption of the metric system.

g. Ton

2,240 lbs.; an American ton contains 2,000 lbs. Note that a British hundredweight contains 112 lbs. (not 100) so that 20 of them make up a British ton. It may be interesting to note that the Americans adopted British weights and measures in the early years, and then the British upped their "Imperial" standards in the early 1800s. See also **gallon**.

h. Windle

Approximately 3 bushels. An agricultural measure, used for grain.

2. Liquid Measure

a. Gallon

The standard British gallon is the *Imperial gallon*, equal to 277.420 cubic inches. The standard U.S. gallon is the old British *wine gallon*, equal to 231 cubic inches. Thus, the British gallon equals 1.20095, or almost exactly 1⅕ American gallons, a fact which makes the British price of gasoline (*petrol*) somewhat less grim for American visitors than the gas tank price signs indicate. This ratio follows through in liquid measure terms used in both countries for parts of a gallon, to wit: quarter (¼ gallon); pint (⅛ gallon); gill (1/32 gallon except that a gill is not uniform in all parts of Britain). And as to terms of dry measure, look out for the British quart, which equals 1.0320, rather than 1.20095, American dry quarts.

b. Gill

(The *g* is soft). When *gill* is used as a liquid measure in Britain, it usually means ¼ pint (i.e., ¼ of ⅛ of an *Imperial gallon*) and therefore 1.2 times as large as an American *gill*; but be careful, because in some parts of Britain it means ½ an *Imperial pint*, or exactly twice as much as in other parts of Britain. See also **gallon**.

c. Pint. See under **gallon**. See also **pint** under alphabetical listing.

d. Quart. See under **gallon**.

D. Numbers

billion

One followed by twelve zeros (which would be called *noughts* or *ciphers* in Britain). An American *billion* is only *one thousand million* (1,000,000,000), which is called a *thousand million* or a *milliard* in Britain. There are wholly different nomenclature systems in the two countries for numbers big enough to be stated in powers of a million. While this may not be material in computing your bank balance, it might prove important to mathematicians, astronomers, and astronauts, for whose benefit the following partial table is submitted:

English	American	Number	Formation
million	million	1,000,000	1 with 6 zeros
milliard	billion	1,000,000,000	1 " 9 "
billion	trillion	$1,000,000^2$	1 " 12 "
thousand billion	quadril- lion	$1,000 \times 1,000,000^2$	1 " 15 "
trillion	quintillion	$1,000,000^3$	1 " 18 "
thousand trillion	sextillion	$1,000 \times 1,000,000^3$	1 " 21 "
quadrillion	septillion	$1,000,000^4$	1 " 24 "
thousand quadrillion	octillion	$1,000 \times 1,000,000^4$	1 " 27 "
quintillion	nonillion	$1,000,000^5$	1 " 30 "

*Caution! 14 lbs. in sales to outsiders, but 15 lbs. in the case of sales to other growers or dealers.

thousand					
quintillion	decillion	$1,000 \times 1,000,000^5$	1	" 33	"
sextillion					
(sexillion)		$1,000,000^6$	1	" 36	"
septillion		$1,000,000^7$	1,	" 42	"
octillion		$1,000,000^8$	1	" 48	"
nonillion		$1,000,000^9$	1	" 54	"
decillion		$1,000,000^{10}$	1	" 60	"
centillion		$1,000,000^{100}$	1	"600	"

Warning note: see the following from *The Times* (London) of November 14, 1974:

How the Treasury Confuses Billions
The Treasury seems to be trying to make a significant change in the English language in a footnote to the Chancellor's Budget speech.

This defines the word "billion" as one thousand million—though since the philosopher John Locke first used the word in the late 17th century it has meant a million million here.

The United States, of course, uses the definition favoured by the Treasury. But the traditional English usage was confirmed in the Supplement to the Oxford English Dictionary published only two years ago.

Asked to explain, the Treasury confused things further. Informally within the Department, it seems, the word means a thousand million, "but the fact that officials use the term does not necessarily mean that it has been officially adopted."

And "it is probably safer to talk about a thousand million or a million million"— which of course is precisely what Locke and his contemporaries were trying to avoid when they coined the word in the first place.

Supplementary warning note: to confound the confusion and enhance the fun, see the following, from *The Times* (London) of October 29, 1975:

Complaint over 'billion' dismissed
Exercise in pedantry, the Press Council declares
To uphold a complaint about the misuse of the word "billion" would be no more than an exercise in pedantry, the Press Council said in an adjudication yesterday.

Mr. J. T. Anderson, of Rugby, complained that *The Times* misused the word "billion", having reported remarks by an MP and captain of industry showing "illiteracy and innumeracy".

Mr. A. D. Holmes replied that *The Times* agreed that billion in English meant a million million. However, the Business News section of the newspaper preferred to use the American style (a thousand millions) on the grounds that it was now general and that to translate it into British terms would be misleading. *The Times* was anxious to establish a uniform practice which would be acceptable to scientists, mathematicians, economists and financiers.

Mr. N. Keith, for *The Times*, wrote further to Mr. Anderson saying that it was incorrect to say that the business section preferred the American style. In fact it invariably preferred "X,000m", except when reporting a speech or when the term was used figuratively to mean large numbers. The *Financial Times* had formally adopted billion and informed its readers. *The Times* might be forced to do the same if inflation carried on at the present rate.

Mr. Anderson replied with a request that *The Times* should publish his letter but the newspaper replied that it regretted that it had not been possible to find a place for it.

The Press Council's adjudication was:

"The tongue which Shakespeare spoke (although in justice to him he did not employ the word "billion") has been, as some think, much mutilated in the centuries which have passed. The editor who chooses to use a word in a sense different from that accepted by others can hardly be accused of impropriety unless his use of it is calculated to mislead. No doubt the word "billion" as employed in England (but not in America or in the Continental languages) means, in a classical sense accepted here, a million million. In America it means a thousand million and the word is now increasingly used, like other American expressions, in this latter sense in economic and business matters.

"The Press Council notes that the editor of *The Times* seeks to establish a uniform practice, and considers that to uphold this complaint would be no more than an exercise in pedantry."

But wait: see the following, from *The Times* of November 19, 1975:

Billions and trillions
From Mr. R. H. Ramsford

Sir, Whether or not you were right in refusing to publish a letter criticizing the misuse of the word billion, the Press Council was certainly wrong to dismiss the criticism as an exercise in pedantry. Regrettably, this misuse is widespread and can—and does—lead to doubt and even outright misunderstanding.

What is particularly disquieting is that a body of the status of the Press Council is apparently so ill-informed that it has no hesitation in stating that billion is not used to signify a million millions in the continental languages. No extensive research would have been needed to reveal its mistake. The oldest edition of *Le Petit Larousse* I have at hand, the 1962 edition, already defines "billion" as "Un million de millions (10^{12}) ou 1 000 000 000 000/Autref., et encore aux Etats-Unis, syn. de MILLIARD". And its Spanish counterpart in 1972 simply defines "billón" as "Millón de millones".

The two main European countries that formerly used billion in the American sense were France and Portugal, but at a postwar International Conference on Weights and Measures, in 1948 if I remember rightly, they agreed to fall into line with Italy, Germany, England, and other countries that had always used it, even in common speech, to mean a million squared—and trillion to mean a million cubed, and so on.

There is no need to perpetuate the abuse, when we already have an unambiguous word for a thousand million: "milliard", which has long been widely used in Belgium, France and Italy at least. Alternatively, since the metric system is becoming more familiar, why not make use of its prefixes? "Megabuck" was in vogue some years ago, I have seen "kF" (for "kilo-francs") in official French writing, and I understand that "kilopounds" is beginning to be used in English. So why not adopt the prefixes giga (G) and tera (T) to signify the American and European billion respectively?

I hope *The Times* will decide to set the lead and popularize the use of one or other of the methods suggested above.

Yours sincerely,
R. H. RANSFORD,
11 Grovewood Close,
Chorley Wood,
Hertfordshire.
October 29.

And what's more (*Times*, same date):

From Dr. G. B. R. Feilden, FRS

Sir, In the current controversy over the misuse of the word billion it might help to note the dispassionate advice about the use of such words which is given in British Standard 350 *Conversion factors and tables*. Part 1 of the standard, published in 1974, states: "In view of the differences between European and USA practice, ambiguities can easily arise with the words 'billion', 'trillion' and 'quadrillion'; therefore their use should be avoided."

It is thus encouraging for us to know that *The Times* prefers the form X,000m and will continue to use it except when quoting less accurate sources.

Yours faithfully,
G. B. R. FEILDEN,
Director of General British Standards Institution,
2 Park Street, W1.
October 29.

The Economist weekly adopted the American usage years ago, to the annoyance of some readers. One wonders how long it will take for the British public to be won over to this adoption. As recently as December 7, 1979, the following letter appeared in *The Times*:

Billion dollar blunder
From Señor Francisco R. Parra
    Sir, Reference my letter "No 'ulterior motive' behind Venezuelan oil announcement" (November 29), we erroneously addressed you in American and said "billion" dollars. Understandably believing we were addressing you in English, you wrote out three more zeros (oops, "noughts"). Correct capital cost figures should be $3,500m to $4,000m for 125,000 barrels per day by 1988, and $20,000m by the year 2000.
Yours truly,
FRANCISCO R. PARRA,
Managing Director,
Petroleos de Venezeula
(UK) SA,
7 Old Park Lane,
London, W1.
November 29.

    Philip Howard, in Chapter 4, entitled 'Billion' of *Words Fail Me* (Hamish Hamilton, London, 1980), writes engagingly—as always—on this subject, and favors ending "the dangerous confusion by conforming to the American style of billion." And the BBC is having a hard time forcing *Centigrade* on its listeners and the die-hards are still (1985) counting money in shillings and old pence (see **Appendix II.A.**, p. 417.) So much for Progress!
    The British always put an *and* between 100 and a smaller number, as in *a/one hundred and twenty*, or *a/one hundred and ten thousand*. This *and* is normally omitted in America.

E. Automotive Terms

    The British equivalents of automotive terms in common use, such as *boot* ('trunk') and *bonnet* ('hood'), appear in the alphabetical listing below. For the benefit of car buffs or technicians and other specialists concerned with scientific automotive terminology, this list, kindly supplied by British Leyland Motors, Inc., and only minimally amplified by the author, may be of interest. The usual order followed in this book (English-American) is here reversed, on the theory that in this case the American reader knows the American equivalent and might thus more readily locate the relevant pairing.

AMERICAN	BRITISH
Body Parts	
bumper guard	*overrider*
cowl	*scuttle*
dashboard	*fascia panel*
door post	*door pillar*
door stop	*check strap*
door vent *or* vent	*quarter light*
fender	*wing*
firewall	*bulkhead*
hood	*bonnet*
license plate	*number plate*
rear seat back *or* backrest	*rear seat squab*
rocker panel	*valance*
skirt	*apron*
toe pan	*toe board*
trunk	*boot*
windshield	*windscreen*
wheelhouse *or* housing	*wheel arch*
Brake Parts	
parking brake	*hand brake*
Chassis Parts	
muffler	*exhaust silencer*
side rail	*side member*

Electrical Equipment

back up light	*reverse lamp*
dimmer switch	*dip switch*
dome light	*roof lamp*
gas pump *or* fuel pump	*petrol pump*
generator	*dynamo*
ignition wiring	*ignition harness*
parking light	*side lamp*
tail light	*tail lamp*
spark plug	*sparking plug*
turn indicator, blinker, directional	*trafficator*
voltage regulator	*control box*

Motor and Clutch Parts / Engine and Clutch Parts

carburetor	*carburetter*
clutch throwout bearing	*clutch release bearing*
engine block	*cylinder block*
hose clamp	*hose clip*
pan	*sump*
piston *or* wrist pin	*gudgeon pin*
rod (control) bearing	*big-end*

Rear Axle and Transmission Parts

axle shaft	*half shaft*
drive shaft	*propeller shaft*
grease fitting	*grease nipple*
ring gear and pinion	*crown wheel and pinion*

Steering Parts

control arm	*wishbone*
king pin	*swivel pin*
pitman arm	*drop arm*
steering idler	*steering relay*
steering knuckle	*stub axle*
tie bar *or* track bar	*track rod*

Tools and Accessories

antenna	*aerial*
crank handle	*starting handle*
lug wrench	*box spanner*
wheel wrench	*wheel brace*
wrench	*spanner*

Transmission Parts / Gearbox Parts

counter shaft	*layshaft*
emergency brake	*parking brake*
gear shift lever	*gear lever*
output shaft	*main shaft*
shift bar	*selector rod*
transmission case	*gearbox housing*

Tires

tire	*tyre*
tread	*track*

F. Musical Notation

In the past the British have shown a fine disregard for symmetry by turning their backs on the metric system. This trend is being reversed, a development which has not brought unalloyed joy to Anglophiles jealous of tradition. In musical notation the British have gone even further and rejected common fractions, as will be seen in the following table of equivalent terms in everyday use in the respective countries:

BRITISH	AMERICAN
breve	double whole note
semibreve	whole note
minim	half note
crotchet	quarter note
quaver	eighth note
semiquaver	sixteenth note
demisemiquaver	thirty-second note
hemidemisemiquaver	sixty-fourth note

The *semibreve* is the longest note in common use. How a half note, which is a pretty long note, got the name of *minim* is a great mystery to many people, especially since another (non-musical) British meaning of *minim* is 'creature of minimum size or significance,' and its non-musical American meanings have to do with aspects of minuteness. The answer is that at one time it was the shortest note in use. *Crotchet* is another funny one: it is derived from the Old French *crochet*, meaning 'little hook,' and everything would have been quite neat and tidy if the quarter note had a little hook, but it doesn't, and little hooks don't start until we get to eighth notes. *Quaver* is used in music in both countries to indicate a trill, and one can see a connection between trilling and eighth notes. A final mystery is the connection between *breve*—derived, of course, from *breve*, the neuter form of *brevis* (Latin for 'brief')—and a double whole note, a note no longer used in musical notation, which is the equivalent of two whole notes, and that makes it anything in the world but brief. The explanation is that in the Middle Ages there was a note even longer than the breve, something apparently called a *long*, compared with which a double whole note would, one supposes, seem brief.

G. Slang
1. Cant Terms
No attempt is made to include cant terms, a few of which are still current, peculiar to particular groups. The *taxi-drivers* of London have their own code: Charing Cross Underground ('subway') Station, recently renamed *Embankment* is the *Rats' Hole*; St. Pancras Station, the *Box of Bricks*; the Army and Navy Store in Victoria Street is the *Sugar Box*; the St. Thomas' Hospital *cab-rank* ('taxi stand') is the *Poultice Shop*; the one at London Bridge the *Sand Bin*; Harley Street (where doctor's offices cluster) is *Pill Island*; Bedford Row (where lawyers' offices proliferate) is *Shark's Parade*; and the Tower of London is *Sparrow Corner*. London busmen indulge in a lingo of their own: The last bus is the *Ghost Train*; to slow up (because of exceeding the schedule) is to *scratch about*; passengers on their way to the greyhound races are *dogs*; a busful is a *domino load*, and a *stone-cold* bus is an empty one; a plainclothes bus inspector is a *spot* and he can *book* ('report') a driver; passengers are *rabbits*; a *short one* is an unfinished trip; an accident is a *set*; to arrive late for duty is to *slip up*; a *cushy road* is an easy trip, and a busy one is known as *having a road on*. In the days when trolley cars competed, the British term *tramcar* became the rhyming equivalent *jam jar*. Sports talk is another matter. Any newspaper report or broadcast or telecast of a cricket or rugby match would be as unintelligible to an American as an American sportswriter's or announcer's commentary on a baseball game would be to a Britisher. To understand these categories of terminology, the reader must refer to technical works on the respective subjects.

2. London Slang
London slang is almost a language of its own, and to complicate matters, it keeps shifting all the time. George Orwell in *Down and Out in Paris and London* (1933) gives a list of cant words in this category including the following:

gagger	beggar; street performer
moocher	beggar
clodhopper	street dancer
glimmer	car watcher
split	detective
flattie	policeman
clod	policeman

toby	tramp
drop	money to a beggar
slang	street-peddler's license
the Smoke	London
judy	woman
spike	flophouse
lump	flophouse
deaner	shilling
hog	shilling
tosheroon	half-crown
sprowsie	sixpence
shackles	soup
chat	louse

3. Rhyming Slang

Rhyming slang is a type of cant which has developed from the peculiarly cockney game of replacing certain common words with phrases which end with a word that rhymes with the word replaced. Thus:

boat race	face
daisy roots	boots
German bands	hands
loaf of bread	head
mince pies	eyes
Mutt and Jeff	deaf
north and south	mouth
plates of meat	feet
tit for tat	hat
trouble and strife	wife
Uncle Ned	head
whistle and flute	suit

And many more. One doesn't run into these expressions very often, but when one does meet them, they can be pretty puzzling, especially when the cant phrase itself becomes truncated or otherwise corrupted through cockney usage. Thus *loaf of bread* is shortened to *loaf*, *mince pies* becomes *minces*, *tit for tat* turns into *titfer*, *whistle and flute* loses the *flute*, *German bands* winds up as *Germans*, and so on. The results: *loaf* for head, *minces* for eyes, *whistle* for suit, etc., come out as quite arbitrary substitutes miles removed from the words they stand for. One often heard outside the cockney world is *loaf*, particularly in the expressions, *Use your loaf!* (*Use your bean!*) and *Mind your loaf!* (*Low bridge!*). In certain cases there is a further hurdle in that the replaced word is itself a Briticism requiring explanation, like the case of *daisy roots* for *boots*, where *daisy roots* becomes *daisies*, *boots* would be shoes in America, and we wind up with *daisies* for shoes, an etymological riddle. For an exhaustive and very amusing treatment of this subject, see *A Load of Cockney Cobblers*, by Bob Alwin (Johnston & Bacon Publishers, London, 1973). *The Muvver Tongue*, by Robert Barltrop and Jim Wolveridge (The Journeyman Press, London, and West Nyack, N.Y., 1980) is an illuminating study of the social background of cockney rhyming slang as the vehicle of a working class culture. (For an explanation of *Muvver* as the pronunciation of *Mother*, see discussion under **bovver boots**.)

4. Poker Slang

all blue	flush
busted flush	four flush
broken melody	ruptured straight
Colonel Dennison	three tens
*Morgan's orchard**	two pair
pea green	flush
running flush	straight flush
*stuttering run***	broken straight

*Also means a count of four in cribbage. Apparently Morgan (whoever he was) had an orchard so poor that it bore only two pears.

**Missing one in the middle, like 7, 8, 9, jack, queen.

5. British Betting Terms

According to Bulletin No. 49 (April 1977) of the American Name Society, quoting *The Daily Telegraph* (London) of March 26, 1976, the British use the following terms in placing multiple race-track bets (which they call *punting*):

each-way: This is a quick way of writing two bets. It means a win bet on a selected horse and also a place bet on the same horse to an equal amount of stake money. Thus, *10p each-way* means a 10p win bet and 10p place bet. Total outlay: 20p.

double: Two horses are linked in one bet. If the first named horse wins, the stake money and the winnings are invested on the other horse.

treble: As a *double*, but with three horses linked together.

accumulator: As a *treble*, but with four or more horses. Advantage: stakes are kept low.

any-to-come (ATC) or **if cash:** Another type of wager where any cash (winning plus stakes) forthcoming from earlier bets finances further bets on selected horses. Examples of *ATC* or *if cash* bets follow:

round the clock: Three or more selections are each backed singly, with ATC bets on the others should there be enough cash available.

up and down: Two horses, each backed singly, with an ATC bet on the other.

rounder: Three horses backed singly. If cash, the other two horses are backed in a double.

roundabout: A rounder with double stakes on the double.

patent: Three horses backed in three single-win bets, three doubles, and a treble (seven bets).

round robin: Three horses linked in *up and down* bets on each pair, plus three *doubles* and a *treble* (10 bets).

Yankee: Four horses backed in six *doubles*, four *trebles*, and an *accumulator* (11 bets).

flag. Four horses. Each pair is backed *up and down* as well as all four horses in a *Yankee* (23 bets).

Canadian: Five horses backed in ten *doubles*, ten *trebles*, five four-horse *accumulators*, and one five-horse *accumulator* (26 bets).

Heinz (57 varieties): Name used in Britain (familiar through the grocery) for any kind of multiple mixture: a mongrel dog might be a *Heinz hound*, etc. Six horses backed in 15 *doubles*, 20 *trebles*, 15 four-horse and six five-horse *accumulators*, and one six-horse *accumulator* (57 bets).

H. Food Names

Food names are very puzzling and of butchers' terms only a few labels of specific cuts of meat are included. There are a good many that would baffle an American shopper: *rump steak* is sirloin; *sirloin* is porterhouse; a *baron* is a double sirloin; *silverside* is top round. It seems worse at the fish store (*fishmonger's*): here one can hear of *brill* (similar to a small turbot), *coalfish*, also called *coley fillet* and *saithe* (black cod), *witch* (resembling, but inferior to, lemon sole), *John Dory* (a flat fish with a big head), *huss*, also called *dogfish*, *rig*, and *robin huss* (similar to a small conger eel—and the *robin* is thought by fishmongers to be a corruption of *robbin'*, i.e., *robbing*, because the *huss* eats other fish and is thus robbin' the fisherman), and other strange species, to say nothing of unfamiliar seafoods like *winkles* and *prawns*. At the bakery one finds all kinds of goodies with alien names. Many are entries in the book; ignore the labels and purchase by sight and smell. See also the following entries: **capsicum, corn, courgette, cos lettuce, endive, squash, web lettuce.**

I. Botanical and Zoological Names

Botanical and zoological (especially avian) names present special difficulties, whether they are British names for shared species or simply names for those which do not include the United States in their habitats. There are exclusively British geological terms as well. British apple trees bear fruit called *Beauty of Bath, Cox, Granny Smith*, and *queening*. In the floral department, wild or cultivated, one finds the *cuckoobud, buttercress, kingcup, St. Anthony's turnip, blister-flower* (presumably because they have particularly acrid juices, which is why animals won't eat them), *horse gold, butter rose, butter daisy*, or *gold cup*; a fair collection of synonyms for the modest buttercup. Moreover, *cuckoobud* is not to be confused with the British *cuc-*

kooflower, a form of wild mustard with white or lilac flowers, and itself synonymous (in Britain) with *lady's smock* and *milkmaid* (actually the *cardamine pratensis*, if you must know), or with the *cuckoopint* (also known, collectively, as *lords and ladies*), which Americans call *jack-in-the-pulpit*, or (to stray for a moment from flora to fauna) with *cuckoospit*, the foamy mass in which various insects lay their eggs, often seen (to get back to flora) on Queen Anne's lace, which the British call *wild carrot*; and *cuckoospit* itself is usually known in America as *frogspit*. British *orange balsam* flowers, also known there as *swingboats* because the flowers are shaped rather like the carnival boats on some of the giant swings, are known as *jewelweed* or *touch-me-not* in America; *reed mace* is the United States broad-leaved *cattail*. Daffodils are *daffodils* in both countries, but are sometimes called *Lent lilies* by the British because of their time of blooming. *Butterbar, wild rhubarb*, and *bog rhubarb* are British synonyms for American *batterdock* (please don't confuse with *spatterdock*, a yellow water lily) or *umbrella leaves*. Still in the flora division, *wainscot* (the term for that type of paneling in both countries) is the British name for a superior type of oak imported from the Baltic region especially for wainscoting. To go entomological for a moment, the common British butterfly known there as the *Camberwell beauty* is our old friend the *mourning cloak* in America. With respect to avian terminology: a *butterbump* (not to be confused with *butterflies, butterbar, butter rose, butter daisy*, or, if this is getting too slippery, *butter fingers*) is a *bittern*; a *moorhen* is a *gallinule*; the *tree creeper* is the *brown creeper; windhovers* are *kestrels*. For devotees of the earth sciences we find *beck* and *burn* for *brook, rig* or *rigg* for *ridge, wold* for an open *tract* of uncultivated land, *moss* for *swamp, nick* for a small *valley* or water-cut *gorge, sea-fret* for thick *fog*, and *carr* for a dense *thicket*. Some of these terms are regional, some may be classified as dialect, some are assuredly standard, many will be strange even to British ears, but you never know when you're going to run into them.

J. *Britain, Briton, British, English,* etc.

Except in more or less official contexts, the inhabitants of the British Isles tend to think and speak of themselves as English, Scottish, Welsh or Irish first and British second. In *How To Be an Alien* (André Deutsch, London, 1946), George Mikes tells us that an alien may become British, but never English. By *British*, he means a naturalized subject of Great Britain; by *English*, he means English in culture, outlook, heart, and spirit. In a letter to *The Times* (London) on August 25, 1982, the distinction is made quite emphatically:

> **Race and crime**
> *From Mr D.K. Clarebrough*
> Sir, Dr Sandra Wallman (August 20) writes that "black people living in Brixton...are English by objective right as well as subjective preference." British they may be but English surely not. If I'm wrong, who then are the black or coloured people I see cheering West Indies, India or Pakistan, when they play the England cricket team on an English ground?
> We have a multiracial, multicultural and multinational society.
> Yours faithfully,
> DENIS CLAREBROUGH
> Southwood House,
> Hilltop Road,
> Dronfield,
> Sheffield.
> August 20.

The word *Briton* sounds historical or literary to them, and *Britisher* sounds like an Americanism. The *Concise Oxford Dictionary* says *Britisher* is the U.S. term for a British subject "as distinct from an American citizen" and goes on to say that it is "apparently of American origin but disclaimed by U.S. writers." *Britain* is used in Great Britain, of course, but English people are more likely to refer to it as *England*. To an older generation of the inhabitants of Britain, and still more, perhaps, to those of the white Commonwealth countries, the term *British* covers, as well, the former dominions, colonies, etc., at least those settled from the British Isles. *United Kingdom of Great Britain and Northern Ireland* is the official term for the country, and for alphabetical seating at the United Nations, it is listed as *U.K.*—in convenient proximity to the U.S. and U.S.S.R.

Historically, it is *Great Britain*, to distinguish it from Brittany in France. *Briticism* or *Britishism* is a term traced back to 1883 and is handy for distinguishing British idiom from the American, but in distinction to, e.g., French, the term would be *Anglicism*. A final oenological note: *English wine* is made from English grapes, grown on English vines. *British wine* (also called 'made wine') is fermented in Britain from foreign grape-concentrate. Never confuse the two: the English Vineyards Association (EVA) would never forgive you.

As to the inhabitants of Scotland: the variants are Scotch, Scots, and Scottish. According to Fowler (*A Dictionary of Modern English Usage*, 2nd edition revised by Sir Ernest Gowers, Oxford, 1965), *Scottish* is closest to the original form, *Scotch* was the English contraction, and *Scots* the one adopted in Scotland. The current favorite in Scotland is *Scottish*, next, *Scots*, with *Scotch* being more or less discarded. England has gone along with this, but in certain stock phrases, *Scotch* has been retained in both places and the rest of the English-speaking world, thus: *Scotch* whiskey (*whisky* in Britain), broth, tweed, egg, woodcock, mist, terrier, pine, beef; and Scotch House is a famous London shop dispensing Scottish textiles and apparel. The English call the dialect spoken in Scotland *Scotch*; the Scots usually call it *Scots*, and the dialect of the Lowlands *Lallans*, a corruption of *Lowlands*.

K. Cricket Terms

For the benefit of any Americans who may develop an interest in the English national sport, cricket, there follows a glossary which appeared in a cricket periodical published by *The Sun* (London, 1972). The definitions are themselves couched in cricketese and in turn need defining and translation in many cases, but here goes:

beamer: a delivery that goes through head high to the batsman without pitching after leaving the bowler's hand.

blob: one of various words used to denote an innings where the batsman has failed to score.

bosie: the Australian name for the googly, the ball that goes from off to leg instead of turning from the leg as with a normal leg break.

bouncer: has the same end product as a beamer in that the delivery goes through about head high to the batsman but is achieved by pitching short of a length.

boundary: four runs.

castle: the stumps.

century: 100 runs.

cherry: the ball, particularly when new and shiny.

Chinaman: this is bowled by a left-arm spin bowler who makes the ball turn into the right-handed batsman rather than the normal left arm spin delivery which turns away from the right hander.

Chinese Cut: this refers to the snick off the inside or bottom edge of the bat whereby the ball goes down the leg side close to the wicket instead of towards third man as the batsman intended.

cutter: a fast spinning delivery that moves quickly off the wicket when it pitches. Can be either off-cutter or leg-cutter.

drag: describes the action of the fast bowler when dragging his back foot along the ground in his delivery stride.

duck: no score.

finger spinner: a bowler who uses his fingers in order to impart spin on the ball, thereby making it change direction when it pitches. A right-handed finger spinner is an off spin bowler, making the ball move in from the off side.

flipper: a delivery from a leg break bowler which has top spin, making it hurry through quickly and straighten when it pitches.

gate: the gap between bat and pad when a batsman is playing a stroke.

googly: the more common term to describe a bosie, also known as "wrong'un."

hob: the stumps as in castle.

inswinger: the ball which swings through the air from the off side to leg.

king pair: falling first ball each innings of a two innings match.

length: the area in which the ball should pitch for a perfect delivery to prevent a batsman playing backwards or forwards with safety.

long hop: a short-of-2-length delivery that comes through at a nice height for a batsman to hit, generally on the leg side.

Nelson: all the ones as in 111. Considered unlucky for a batsman or a side to be on that figure. Double Nelson is 222.

nightwatchman: a lower order batsman who goes to the wicket just before close of play to save a recognised batsman from having to bat and possibly losing his wicket in the few remaining minutes.

outswinger: a ball that swings through the air towards the off side.

pair: signifies a batsman failing to score in both innings of a match.

sticky dog or **wicket:** a wicket on which the ball turns viciously as the wicket dries out under hot sun after being affected by the rain. It is not often that a true "sticky dog" is found in England but they have been known in Australia, notably Brisbane.

ton: a century.

wrist spinner: a bowler who uses his wrist to spin the ball making it come out of the back of his hand as with a leg break.

Yorker: an over pitched delivery which pitches near the batting crease and goes under the bat as the batsman starts to play his stroke generally moving forward.

L. Connotative Place-Names. The use of connotative place-names occurs in every language. The French author placing a character on the rue du Faubourg Saint Honoré, the German writing of the Kurfürstendamm, the Italian locating a scene on the Via Veneto or the Piazza San Marco are all using place-names to create a backdrop, an atmosphere. As for the English, the following might well perplex an American reader unfamiliar with Britain and British life:

Albany. A most exclusive apartment house (*block of flats*) in London, whose occupants always include many distinguished names. Originally Melbourne House (1770), it was converted in 1802.

Belgravia. A fashionable district of London. Its name is used metaphorically to mean the upper middle class.

Blackpool. A seaside resort in West Lancashire, in northwest England, known for its appeal to the masses.

Bloomsbury. A London district known as an intellectual center. The 'Bloomsbury Group' of artists, writers and intellectuals generally flourished there in the early 1920's and gave this place-name its cachet, implying quality, with a hint of preciosity.

Bow Bells. Literally, the bells of Bow Church in the *City* of London (a section of London housing, inter alia, the financial district). This place-name most frequently occurs in the expression *within the sound of Bow Bells*, which means 'in the City of London.' One born within the sound of Bow Bells is said to be a true Cockney.

Bow Street. Famed in British detective stories as the address of the principal London police court.

Brighton. A Victorian seaside resort, noted for massive hotels, endless rows of middle-class boardinghouses, the Prince Regent's 'Pavilion,' an antiques section known as 'the Lanes,' and other divertissements.

(The) British Museum. Often shortened to 'The B.M.,' to the discomfiture of many Americans. Britain's great library, museum and depository of priceless collections in the fields of history, art, archeology, etc.

Carnaby Street. A street in the Soho section of London, studded with apparel shops catering to the young with-it crowd in its heyday during the 1960s. *Carnaby* was used adjectivally to describe that type of attire.

Chelsea. A London district, center of the smart Bohemian set.

(The) City. Short for *the City of London.* See *Bow Bells* (above) and *(the) City* in the alphabetical text.

(The) Connaught. An elegant hotel full of ancient glory and still going strong.

Covent Garden. A London district which until recently housed London's vast, tumultuous vegetable and flower market, now removed to another part of the city, but still the location of the long-established theater bearing its name, famous for opera and ballet.

Dartington. A college devoted to the arts, very 'progressive,' avant garde and permissive.

Earl's Court. One of London's two great sports arenas. (See *White City*.) The Earl's Court section of London is known for its proliferation of 'bed-sitters,' tiny one-room housing units cut out of once great mansions.

(The) East End. A poor section of London, which includes the docks.

Eaton Square, Eaton Place. Very fashionable streets in London.

(The) Embankment. Road along the north bank of the Thames. Hotel rooms, offices, etc. which overlook it are the most desirable, but another connotation arises from the fact that it is the sleeping place of derelicts and tramps.

Eton, Harrow. Leading and venerable *public schools* (i.e., private schools) for ages thirteen to eighteen, whose playing-fields breed 'the future leaders of England,' according to Tory gospel.

Festival Hall. One of London's great concert halls.

Fortnum & Mason. Often shortened to 'Fortnum's.' A department store of great fame and elegance, with a famous tearoom catering to the upper classes.

Golders Green. A section of London much favored by middle-class Jews.

Hampstead. A borough of London frequented by practitioners of the arts.

Harley Street. A London street where the most expensive doctors, particularly specialists, have their offices, which do not participate in the National Health system. 'Harley Street doctor' has its analogue in 'Park Avenue physician.'

Harrods. A universal department store offering just about everything from antiques to comestibles, all of very high quality, at strictly non-competitive prices.

Harrow. See *Eton*.

Hyde Park. One of London's many beautiful parks. In one corner (the legendary Hyde Park Corner), speakers are permitted to address the public on just about any subject, with the emphasis generally against the *Establishment*.

Knightsbridge. London area characterized by elegant shopping.

Lord's. Short for *Lord's Cricket Ground*, the most famous of all cricket fields ('grounds'), home of the M.C.C. (Marylebone Cricket Club), the august body which controls and is the arbiter of all things relating to cricket.

Marks & Spencer. A chain store, just about ubiquitous, supplying chiefly wearing apparel but in many cases expanding into other fields, like food; noted for its very competitive prices, made possible because the organization manufactures many of the goods it sells. The name is often shortened to M & S, but its most popular form is *Marks & Sparks*, a sobriquet both jocular and affectionate.

Notting Hill Gate. A lower class area, unhappily too often the scene of racial unrest.

(The) Old Bailey. The chief criminal court of London.

(The) Old Vic. London's famous old repertory theater, known for its marvelous productions of Shakespeare. The scene has in large part shifted to the National Theatre, but the Old Vic still carries on. It has been refurbished and now enjoys a sparkling façade and elegant interior.

(The) Oval. London's other cricket ground. See *Lord's*.

Oxford Street. London's shopping street devoted to the needs of the common people, hard to navigate on foot because of the teeming multitudes.

(The) Palladium. London's leading vaudeville house (*music-hall*), scene of generations of memorable variety.

Park Lane. An elegant avenue bordering Hyde Park, location of many great hotels and superior shops.

Piccadilly. London's historic main thoroughfare, with elegant shops and hotels.

Portobello Road. Scene of the historic flea market, a center for relatively inexpensive antiques.

Regent Street. London's most elegant shopping street.

Roedean. Exclusive girls' *public school* (i.e., private school), attended by female scions of the best families.

Rotten Row. A fashionable equestrian track in Hyde Park, London. The name has been attributed to a number of derivations, the favorite of which is *route du roi*, the old route of the royal procession from the palace at Westminster to the royal hunting preserve. Others go back to the 18th century word, *rotan*, meaning 'wheeled vehicle' and derived from *rota*, Latin for *wheel*.

Sadler's Wells. A theater, the original location of the ballet company that bore its name and is now the Royal Ballet; still active as a dance center.

Savile Row. A London street, center of elegant *bespoke* (i.e., custom) tailoring for men.

(The) Savoy. One of London's oldest and most expensive hotels. Its best rooms overlook the Embankment. See *(The) Embankment.*
(The) Serpentine. A lake in Hyde Park, where people love to row.
(The) Tate Gallery. Almost invariably shortened to 'the Tate.' A fine permanent collection is housed in this gallery, which is also associated with avant garde shows of contemporary art.
(The) Victoria and Albert Museum. Usually shortened to 'The V. & A.' A museum noted, inter alia, for Victorian memorabilia.
Wembley Stadium. Always called 'Wembley;' a great *football* (i.e., soccer) field.
(The) West End. A part of London noted as the center of theater and chic restaurant life.
White City. Great indoor sports arena in London, home of the horse shows and other sports events and spectacles.
Wigan. A notoriously unattractive manufacturing town in South Lancashire, in the West of England.
Wilton's. A fish restaurant catering to the best people.
Winchester. A *public school* (i.e., private school), one of the oldest, with the highest academic standards.

M. Connotative Names of Periodicals. The names of certain leading periodicals can have connotative significance. One unfamiliar with the British scene, reading in a British novel, for instance, that So-and-so regularly takes a certain newspaper, or finds such-and-such a magazine in a house he is visiting, may not realize the connotative import of the author's choice of periodical. The following brief list of examples may help:
Country Life. An elegant magazine devoted to the interests of the upper classes, like history, stately homes, antiques, gardening, decrying 'progress' and saluting the good life according to Tory principles.
(The) Daily Telegraph. One of Britain's important national newspapers, of extremely conservative views, and beloved of the Tories.
News of the World. A daily of vast circulation, appealing to a wide segment of the public, the common man, rather like the New York papers of an earlier day, *The Mirror* and *The Graphic.*
Punch. The perennial weekly given mainly to humor and political satire.
(The) Tatler. A smart society magazine, with social notes from all over.
(The) Times. Britain's leading national daily, with a more or less "Labour" editorial slant in recent days. A component of Britain's **Establishment**, its letters-to-the-editors department and daily crossword puzzle have been, for many Britons over the years, an important part of daily life.

Index

A

a, 408
A,(B,C,), alpha (beta)
abandon, abandonment
abbreviations, 412, 415
a bed of roses, beer and skittles
able seaman, rating
a blue streak, nineteen to the dozen
about, -ish
above market value, over the odds
abscond, levant
absentee ballot, postal vote
absolutely, bang
absolutely sound, one hundred percent
  copper-bottomed
absorbent cotton, cotton wool
abuse, slang
Académie française, 2
accept the charge, pay for the call
access road, slip road
accident, 424
accident spot, black spot
acclimate, acclimatize
accommodations, accommodation
according to Hoyle, all Sir Garnet
account book, washing-book
accumulator, 426
accusation; scold, threap
AC-DC, double-gaited
a cinch, easy meat
ack-ack, archie
A Common Language, British and American
  English, 2
across the street, over the road
a crusher, one in the eye
act, come
act as chief prosecuting attorney, lead for
  the Crown
act in a friendly manner towards
  (someone), show friendly to (someone)
action for a declaratory judgment,
  friendly action
act (vaudeville), turn
ad, advert
add on, throw out
-ade, squash
adhesive tape, sticky tape
a dime a dozen, two (ten) a penny
adjourn, rise
adjourn Parliament, count out the House
adjustable table lamp, anglepoise lamp
adjusted to inflation, index-linked

adjuster, assessor
administration, government
admitted to practice, called to the bar
a dog's age, donkey's years
adoption of metric system, metrification
advance man, knocker-up
advantage, pull
advantage of/over, 408
adversary, adversarial
ae, 411
aerial, 423
Aeschylus,411
Aesculapius 411
affair; business, palaver
affair, show
aftereffects, 414
afternoon tea, set tea
afters, 3
agate, ruby
ages, moons
aggravation, aggro
aggressiveness, aggro
agonise, 415
a good sort, worth a good deal of
  anybody's time
agree,
agreement, articles
a horse of a different color, another pair
  of boots
airfield, aerodrome
airfield, tarmac
air mattress, li-lo
airplane, aeroplane
airs, side
aisle, corridor; gangway
aisles, 5
alcohol detector, breathalyser
ale and stout mixed, half-and-half
alert, on the spot
alfalfa, lucern (lucerne)
all aboard!, close the doors
all-around, all-round
all blue, 425
all decked out, (in) full fig
all dolled up, dressed to the nines; like a
  dog's dinner
all expenses paid, fully found
alley, luke; snicket; street; twitten
allocated line, spare line
all set, nailed on
all set?, fit?

433

almond taffy, hardbake
alongside, at the side of
alphabetical railroad guide, ABC
also-rans, ruck
alternately, turn and turn about
aluminium, 415
alumna, old boy; old girl
alumnus, old boy; old girl
A.M., ack emma
amateurish, prentice
ambulance chaser, accident tout
"American," 1
American English, 412
American Into English, 4
Americanism, 3
amicus curiae brief, watching brief
among, amongst
amorous weekend, dirty week-end
anaesthetist, 411
anchorman, link man
And how!, Rather!
...and salad, ...salad
Anglicism, 428
"Anglicization," xvii
Anglo-American Interpreter, xvii
annex, mediatize
anniversary, octingentenary
annoying, tiresome
Annual Meeting of Shareholders
   (Stockholders), Annual General
   Meeting
annuals, bedding
annulment, nullity
"An Open Letter to the Honorable Mrs.
   Peter Rodd On a Very Serious
   Subject," 414
another drink, (the) other half
another place, 5
answering machine, ansafone
(see articles), *articled clerk*
antenna, aerial
antenna, 423
any odd job?, bob-a-job?
anything, twp
anything goes, all in
any-to-come, 426
anywhere near, within kicking distance
   of
a pack of, twenty
apartment, flat; set
appetizer, starter
applaud, clap
apple trees, 426
appointment to look at, order to view
appraise, value
appropriation bill, supply bill
approximately, query
apron, pinny
apron 422
area surrounding, surround
aren't I, 413

argufy, argue the toss
arm of the law, limb of the law
armpit, oxter
Army and Navy Store, 424
army engineer, sapper
army stew, gippo
around, about
arouser, knocker-up
arrange for, lay on
arrest, detain; take in charge
arson, fire-raising
arty, twee
as a matter of fact, actually
as bright as a button, as bright as a new
   penny
as dead as a doornail, as dead as mutton
as easy as pie, as easy as kiss your hand
as follows, as under
as it turned out, in the event
as nice as pie, as nice as ninepence
as of, as from
ass, arse
ass-backwards, arsy-tarsy
assistant, bailiff
assistant maid, tweeny
assistant professor, senior lecturer
associate professor, reader
as soon as, directly
"A Tale of Two Cities," xv
at bat, on strike
ATC, 426
ate, 412
at full speed, flat out
at hand, to hand
at one's disposal, in hand; in one's gift
at the market, best offer
attic, loft
au courant, in the picture
auction, by/at, 408
audience of/with the Pope, 408
automatic airplane pilot, George
automobile, 5
Automobile Association, A.A.
automobile horn, hooter
Automotive Terms, 422
autopsy, post-mortem
available, to hand
a weak drink, maiden's (maid's) water
a week from..., ...week
a week on/from Tuesday, 408
awful, shocking
awful, 5
awfully, frightfully
A Word Geography of England, xxi
axle shaft, 423
aye, content

B

baby cardigan, matinee jacket
baby carriage, perambulator; pram; pushcart
baby carriage,   413
baby nipple, comforter
baby pacifier, dummy
baby-sitter, baby-watcher; sitter-in
backdrop, drop-scene
back kitchen, scullery
back of car seat, squab
backrest or *rear seat back,*   422
backside, fanny
backslang,   4
backstop, long stop
back to business, back to our muttons
back-up, tail-back
back-up light,   423
backwards, arsy-varsy
bacon, streaky
bad egg, bad hat
bad end, sticky finish
bad form, not on; off
badger's burrow, set
bad guess, bos
bad soldier or sailor, K.B.B.
bad tempered, liverish
baggage, luggage
baggage car, van
baggage room, left luggage office
baked, cooked
baked potato, jacket potato
Baker, Russell,   4
bakery, bakehouse
baking powder, rising powder
baking powder biscuit, scone
Ballad of Abbreviations,   409
ballet,   412
ballitraunt,   6
ballot inspector, scrutineer
ballpoint pen, biro
ballpoint pen,   413
balls, ballocks
balls, goolies
balmy, barmy
baloney, codswallop
baloney!, all my eye and Betty Martin!; rats!; rubbish!
Band-Aid, Elastoplast; plaster
bang (hit), bash
bangs, fringe
bang-up, slap-up
bank, camber
banked, super-elevated
banking account,   409
bank loan, overdraft
banknote,   6
bankroll, sheaf
banned, warned off
Bar Association, Law Society

barber shop, hairdresser's
barber's shop,   409
bargain, snip
barge, keel
barge operator, bargee
baron,   426
barrel,   418
barrel cuff/French cuff, single cuff/double cuff
bartender, barman
bartender's assistant, pot-boy
baseboard, skirting
basin, dock
basket-shaped boat, coracle
bastard, basket; by-blow; sod
Bath, Beauty of, 426
bathe, bath
bathing suit, bathing costume; swimming costume
bathrobe, dressing gown
bathtub, bath
batter, batsman
batterdock,   427
battery, accumulator
bawky-handed, xxi
bawl out, bollick
bawl (someone) out, tear a strip of
BBC Pronouncing Dictionary of British Names,   412
beach, sea
beach,   5
beach pebbles, shingle
beak,   6
beak (nose), boko; conk
be all one can do, take (one) all (one's) time
beam, stang
beamer,   428
bean (head), loaf
bean pole, pea stick
(be) a prostitute, (be) on the game (be) on the knock
beat, manor
beat, patch
beat, shot about; whacked
be a television addict, have square eyes
beat it!, cut away!
beat it, leg it
beat pole, quant
beat (tuckered out), knackered
beat up, banjo; clapper-claw
Beauchamp,   411
Beauty of Bath,   426
beauty parlor, hairdresser's
be a wise guy, come the acid
be baffled, go spare
be bumped off (get killed), get the chop
beck, 427
become, gone
bed, kip
bedbug, bug

bone up, gen up
bonnet,   422
bonus issue or *share,*   417
boo, barrack
booboo, bloomer
boob tube, goggle-box
bobby prize, wooden spoon
boodle, pot
book,   424
bookmaker, commission agent; turf
  accountant
bookstore, book seller
bookworm, mug
boom crutch, gallows
boor, bosthoon; bounder
boost, kiss of life
boot,   422
boots,   425
border, frontier
bore, bind
bosie,   428
boss, gaffer; governor
bosun, Spithead nightingale
Botanical and Zoological Names,   426
botch job, charley
bother, moider
bottom, inside (of a bus)
bouncer, chucker-out
bouncer,   428
bowel movement, motion
bowlegged, bandy-legged
bowl over, knock acock; pull up
bow to (someone), give (someone) best
box, cage
boxcar, covered goods-waggon
Box of Bricks,   424
box office, pay-box
boy, xviii
boycott, black
bracelets, darbies
bracket, band; slice; tranche
brackets,   414
brains trust,   409
brakeman, brakesman; guard
Brake Parts,   422
brass tacks, put-to
brawl, dust-up
brazier, fire-pan
bread-and-butter letter, Collins; roofer
bread and cheese, ploughman's lunch
bread box, bread bin
bread strips, fingers; soldiers
break in, chip in
break in, run in
break things off, part brass-rags
breve,   424
bribe, dab in the hand; dropsy
bricklayer, brickie
bridge foursome, bridge school
bridle trail, gallop
brill,   426

bring, fetch; make
bring charges against (someone), have
  (someone) up
bring (someone) up to date, put
  (someone) in the picture
brisk, rattling
Britain, Briton, British, English,
  etc.,   427
Briticism,   428
British,   1, 427,428
British and American English, xv,   413
British and American English Since 1900,   2
British Betting Terms,   426
Britisher,   427
Britishism,   428
Briton,   427
broad, judy
broad a,   411
broadcast over a network, network
broadcloth, poplin
broad forest path, ride
broads,   4
Broadway, West End
brochure,   412
broil, grill
broke, skint; stony
broken melody,   425
broken sizes, broken ranges; odd sizes
broken straight,   425
brokerage firm, broking firm
brook, beck; rithe
brook,   427
brown creeper,   427
brush aside, put by
brush (something) off, play (something)
  to leg
brush up on, brush up
buccaneer, filibuster
buck, jib
Buckinghamshire,   412
buckle under, lie down under
Bucks.,   412
buddy, butty; mate; mucker
bug, insect
bug (someone), get on (someone's) wick
build, throw out
building, house
building inspector, surveyor
building permit, planning permission
building supply firm, builder's merchant
built to order, purpose-built
bulb, teat
bulkhead,   422
bull, cock
bulletin board, notice board; station
  calendar
bulletproof, bandit-proof
bullhorn, loud-hailer
bum, yobbo
bumbershoot, brolly; gamp
bum check, dud cheque; stumer

bump, off-load
bump, ramp
bump; saddle, off-load
bumper, buffer
bumper, fender
bumper guard, 422
bumper to bumper, nose to tail
bumpkin, joskin
bums, 4
bum shot, bos
bun, bap; bread roll
bunch, lot
bureau, chest of drawers
bureaucrat, bumble
burglary, raid
burlap, hessian
burn, 301
burn one's bridges, burn one's boats
burst into flame, brew up
bury the hatchet, sink differences
bus conductress, clippie
bus fare zone limit, fare stage
bushel, 419
3 bushels, windle
business, custom; trade
business, xix 4
business suit, lounge suit
bust, damp squib
bust, frost
busted flush, 425
busy, engaged
but, bar
butcher shop, family butcher
butt, end; fag; gasper; snout; stump
butterbar, 427
butterbump, 427
buttercress, 426
butter daisy, 426
butterfly, 427
butter rose, 426
butt in, chip in
buzz saw, circular saw
by cloture, guillotine
bye-bye, ta-ta
by Jove, 6
by-pass, ring-road; ringway

C

cabinet member, minister
caboose, brake-van; guard's van
cadge, mump
Caesarean, Caesar
café, 412
Caius, 411
cajole, carny
calamity howler, dismal Jimmy
calendar, order paper
calendar clerk, list office
call box, 4

call off, cry off
calling party, caller
call (someone) out, give (someone) out
Camberwell beauty, 427
campaign stroll, walkabout
campus, college grounds; court; quad
can, tin
can, 4
Canadian, 426
Canadian bacon, back bacon
candidacy, candidature
candle, tolly
candy, sweets
candy store, confectioner; sweet-shop
canker sore, ulcer
canned pressed beef, corned beef
canned spiel, potted lecture
can (privy), jakes
Cant Terms, 424
cap and gown, academicals
captain, skipper
car, carriage; waggon
carburetor, 423
carburetter, 423
carburettor/carburetter, 416,423
care, mind
Carey, G.V., 4
cargo, freight
carnival slide, helter-skelter
carom, cannon
carpenter, chippie (chippy; chips); joiner
carpet tack, tin tack
carr, 427
carryall, holdall
car watcher, 424
car wrecker, car breaker
case, nutcase
case, sus out
cash, encash
casserole meal, fork supper
cassock, humpty
cast-iron, copper-bottomed
castle, 428
castles in the air, moonshine
castrate, doctor
catalogue, calendar
cat-boarding kennel, cattery
catch, snag
catch, 5
catch hell, get one's head in one's hand;
  get the stick
catch (in a mistake), catch out
catch on, take on
catch on to, tumble to
catch on to, twig
catch up with (someone), catch
  (someone) up
cater for/to, 408
cat food, cat's-meat
cathedral head, dean
catkins, lambs' tails

catnip, catmint
cattail, 427
cattle, beasts
cattle gate, kissing gate
cattleman, stock breeder
caught napping, caught on the wrong
    foot
caught short, caught on the hop
cauliflower ear, thick ear
-ce, 415
cent, bean
centennial, centenary
centerboard, sliding keel
centillion, 420
centre, 415
certified mail, recorded delivery
certified public accountant, chartered
    accountant
chaff, chip
chain store, multiple shops
chambermaid, housemaid
chamber pot, thunder-mug
chamber pot holder, commode
chamois, leather; wash leather
champagne, bubbly; champers
chance, earthly; show
change, chop
change pocket, ticket pocket
chaotic, shambolic
chap, 5
chapel, bethel
chapstick, lip-balm
char, 413
character, blighter, bod
charge, book
charge, put down
charge account, account
charter member, foundation member
Chassis Parts, 422
Chastenet, Jacques, 2
chat, 425
chatter; babble, chattermag; natter
chat to/with, 408
cheap, trumpery
cheap fruit cake, schoolboy cake
cheaply, on the cheap
cheap novel, shocker
cheap wine, plonk
check, bill; cheque
check, register; tick
check, vet
checkers, draughts
checking account, current account
check off, tick off
check strap, 422
cheek, sauce
cheers!, bung-ho!
cheesecake, maid of honour
cheesecloth, butter-muslin; muslin
cheese it!, nix!
cheesy, ropey

cheezit!, cave!
Chelsea, 4
cheque, 416
cherry, 428
Chesterton, G.K., 409
chewy candy, stickjaw
chick, bit of fluff
chick, bit of stuff
chicken, funky
chicory, endive
chief counsel, leader
Chief Justice, Lord Chancellor
child abuse, child-battering
Children's Hospital, 413
children's traffic guide, lollipop man
child's bib, feeder
child's nurse, nannie
chimney-corner, ingle-nook
Chinaman, 428
Chinese Cut, 428
Chin up!, Keep your pecker up!
chip in, pay one's shot
chock-full, bungfull; chockablock
chocolate sprinkles, chocolate vermicelli
Cholmondeley, 411
chop, cutlet
chopped meat, mince
chow, tack; toke
Christmas caroler, wait
chunk, wodge
church aisle, aisle
Churchill, Winston, 1
Church of England, C. of E.
church officer, clerk
cigarette butt, dog-end
cigarette paper, skin
cigar store, tobacconist's shop
cinch, doddle; pice of cake
cinema, 2
cipher, 419
Circle, Circus
circs., 415
circulation, general post
circumlocution, circumbendibus
circumstances, circs.
circumstances, 415
circumstances, in/under the, 408
Cirencester, 412
cited for bravery, mentioned in
    dispatches
citizen, subject
city editor, news editor
city hall, guildhall
city limits, city boundary; town
    boundary
civilian life, Civvy Street
clamp, cramp
clapboard, weather-board
Clark, John W., 2
Clark, William, 1
class, form

class, street
classical drama, legitimate drama
classified ad, small ad
clean, 5
cleaning woman, char; daily woman; Mrs
  Mop
cleaning woman, 413
clean up, turn out
clearance items, bunches
clear up, fine down
clerk, assistant
clerk, 412
clickity-click, tuppet
clicky-handed, 6
clipping, cutting
clobber, tonk
clod, 424
clod and stickin, 6
clodhopper, beetle-crusher
clodhopper, 424
close, level
close contract, exchange contracts
close corporation, 409
closed company, 409
closed season, close season
closed truck, van
close haircut, short back and sides
close order drill, square bashing
closet, cupboard
closing time!, time!
clothespin, clothes-peg
clothespole, clothes-prop
clotted cream, Devonshire cream
cloture, closure; guillotine
cloverleaf, spaghetti junction
clumsy, cack-handed
Clutch and Engine Parts, 423
Clutch Parts, Motor and, 423
clutch release bearing, 423
clutch throwout bearing, 423
clutter, lumber
coach, carriage
coalfish, 426
coal freighter, collier
coarse invective, billingsgate
coarse stone, rag
coattails, 414
coax, carny
cock, John Thomas
cock-eyed,skew-whiff
cockroach, blackbeetle
coddle, wrap in cotton wool
coed(ucational), mixed
coffee shop, café
Cokes, 412
cold, taters in the mould
coley fillet, 426
collar button, collar stud
collect call, transferred charge call
college department, faculty
college entrance examinations, A-levels

college graduate, graduate; university
  man
college monitor, proctor
college servant, gyp
college teacher, don
college vacation, vac
collision; crash
collision, 5
colon, 414
Colonel Dennison, 425
colour, 415
come, spunk
come across, stump up
comedy team, cross-talk comedians
come on!, Get out of it!; Give over!; play
  up!
come out on top, come top
come to a lot, come expensive
comforter, eiderdown
comfort station, public convenience
comicality, funniosity
coming along, in train
comma, 414
commencement, degree day
commercial bank, clearing bank
committee, working party
common, coarse
commoner, 3
common herd, ruck
Common Market, 2
common-room, combination-room
Commons, 5
common stock, ordinary shares
commotion, kerfuffle
community college, polytechnic
commutation ticket, season ticket
commuter, 3
commuting town, dormitory
company picnic, bean-feast
competition, (the) opposition
complaint, query
compound nouns, 409
concede, agree
concert master, leader
condemnation, compulsory purchase
conductor, guard
cone, cornet
confection, 415
confidence game, confidence trick
confined to quarters, confined to
  barracks
confine to quarters, gate
confused; rambling; incoherent, skimble-
  skamble
conger eel, 426
conglomerate, group of companies
conglomeration, mixed bag
congratulate, felicitate
conk out, pack up
con man, magsman
connected, through

connexion, 415
Connolly, Cyril, 1
conrod bearing, 423
conscientious objector, conchy
consent decree, agreed verdict
Conservative Jew, Reform Jew
conservatory (music school),
    conservatoire
consider (someone) to be, write
    (someone) down as
construction, construe
construction worker, navvy
consommé, 412
contact, make one's number with
contemptible, bloody
contract, private treaty
contractor, lumper
control arm, 423
control room, listening room
controversy, 412
conveniences, amenities; offices
conversant, au fait
convertible, drop-head
convertible sofa, put-U-up
convertible top, hood
coochy-gammy, 6
cook book, cookery book
(cooked) oatmeal, porridge
cookery book, 409
cookie, biscuit
cook up, bodge up
cool, fab; gear; kinky
cop, bobby; bogey (bogy); rozzer; slop
cops, busies
(the) cops, (the) filth; (the) Old Bill
copy reader, sub-editor
corn, maize
corned beef, salt beef
cornerstone, foundation-stone
corn meal, Indian meal
corn syrup, golden syrup
corollary, 412
corporate charter, memorandum and
    articles of association
corporation, company
corporation, limited company
correct(ly); exactly,
correspondence, 415
correspondence course, postal course
corridor, passage
corset cover, habit-shirt
cost estimate, bill of quantity
costs, costings
costume, livery
cot, camp bed
cotton candy, candyfloss
couch, divan
council flats, 4
councilman, councillor
counsel (legal), consultant

counterclockwise, anti-clockwise;
    withershins
counterfeit, forged
counterfeiter, coiner
counter shaft, 423
count on, let alone
countrywide election, general election
county fair, agricultural show
court sessions, assizes
court stenographer, shorthand writer
cover, mark
coverage, cover
coverall, boiler suit
cover charge, table money
covered approach to doorway, porch
cover with a large quantity, dollop
cover with soil, earth
covey of game birds, brown
cowherd, cattleman
cowl, 422
cow-pawed, 6
cowshed, byre
Cox, 426
Coxey's Army, Fred Karno's Army
cracked, crackers
cracker, bickie; biscuit
cracker barrel politician, ale-house
    politician.
crackers, 5
cram, sap; swot
crammer, grinder
cram school, crammer
crane fly, daddy-longlegs
crank, wind
crankcase, sump
crank handle, 423
crap (nonsense), balls
crash, 5
crash land (an aircraft), prang
crazy, mental; round the bend
crazy, 5
crazy about, mad on
crazy on/about, 408
cream of wheat, semolina
creek, fleet
creel, corf
crêpe-soled suede shoes, brothel-creepers
crest-fallen, chap-fallen
crew cut, close crop
crib, cot
cricket team, eleven
Cricket Terms, 428
crimes of violence, malicious wounding
criminal court judge, recorder
criminally assault, interfere with
crink, 6
Cripples' Crossing, 413
criticise, 415
criticize, slag
croak, snuff it
crone, faggot

crooked, bent
crooked(ly); askew, skew-whiff
crotch, crutch
crotchet, 424
crouton, sippet
crow, humble pie
crown wheel and pinion, 423
cruddy, grotty
cruise, crawl
cruise for a pickup, gutter-crawl
crummy, tinpot
crunch, put-to
crush, spif(f)licate
crystal, glass; watch-glass
cuckoobud, 426
cuckooflower, 426
cuckoopint, 427
cuckoospit, 427
cuff link, sleeve link
Culzean, 411
Cunliffe, Marcus, 1
cunning, dinky
crunny-handed, 6
cunt, fanny
cup of tea, cuppa
curate's egg, 5
curling iron, curling tongs
currant bun, Chelsea bun
currant cookie, garibaldi
Currency, 417
Current English Usage, xiv
curse, blind
curtain material, soft furnishings
curve, bend
cushy road, 424
custard sauce, custard
custodian, keeper
custody, wardship
custom made, bespoke
cut-and-dried, straightforward
cutaway, tail-coat
cut down to size, debag
cute, dinky
cutie, popsie
cutter, 428
cylinder block, 423
cylinder crankcase, 423

D

d., 417
dab, knob (of butter)
dab, lick
Dacron, Terylene
dad, governor
daffodil, 427
dago red, red Biddy
daisies, 425
daisy roots, 425
Dalziel, 411

dam barrage; stank; weir
damages, compensation
dame, bird
Dame, 5
damned, bally; bleeding; blind; blinking;
  bloody; blooming dashed; flaming;
  rattling; ruddy
damned!, jiggered
damned good, clinking
damn it!, blast!
damn! rats!, bother
dancing hall, 409
dandruff, scurf
darn, flipping
darning ball, darning mushroom
dashboard, fascia
dashboard, 422
dates, 415
davenport, 4
daylight saving time, summer time
day's route, country round
day's schedule of doctor (dentist),
  surgery
daytime babysitter, child-minder
D-Day, 417
dead, dead-alive
dead drunk in a fix; crazed, up the pole
dead duck, derby duck
dead-end residential area, close
dead-end street, blind road; cul-de-sac
deadline, time-limit
deaf, cloth-eared
deaf, 425
deal, do
dealer in stocks, stock-jobber
dean, doyen; head
deaner, 425
Dear..., My dear...
decal, transfer
decamp, shoot the crow
decarbonize, decoke
decillion, 420
decimalization day, 417
deck, pack
declare insolvent, hammer
deduction, relief
deduction from wages, stoppage
deep-dish pie, pie
defence, 415
definite article, 408
definitely! and how!, too right!
defroster, demister
DeGaulle, Charles, xvii
degree below 32°F, degree of frost
degree removed, remove
delay, hold-up
delayed acceptance penalty, contango
delayed delivery penalty, backwardation
delighted, chuffed
delightful, absolutely sweet

(delivery by) refrigerated truck, chilled distribution
delivery man, roundsman
dell, dingle
demisemiquaver,   424
demobilized, bowler-hatted
demonstration, demo
den, snuggery
denatured alcohol, methylated spirit
departmental store,   409
department store, departmental store
deposit slip, credit slip; paying-in slip
depreciation, writing down
deputy churchwarden, sidesman
Derby,   411
derby (hat), bowler
derrière, bum
desert, leave (someone) to it
desist, pack it in
dessert, afters; pudding; sweet
dessert,   3
destroy, perish
detail, second
detect, catch out
detective,   424
detour, diversion
deviltry, devilry
dialling code or *tone*,   408
diaper, nappy
diaphragm, cap
diarrhea, gippy tummy
Dibs on...! I dibsy! I claim!, bags I!
die laughing, fall about laughing
diet, bant; slim
Differences Between British and American English,   408
different from/to,   408
dig up, rake up
dime novel, penny dreadful; shilling shocker
dimmer switch,   423
diner, pull-up
dining car, restaurant car
diplomat, diplomatist
dip switch,   423
directional signal, trafficator; winker
director, producer
dirk, whinger
dirt floor, earth floor
dirty (indecent), rude
Disabled,   413
disagreeable, nasty
disappear, go missing
disbar, strike off
discard, cast
discharge, demob
discounter, bill broker
disgruntled, chuffed; choked
dish (desirable woman), crumpet
dish made of leftovers, resurrection pie
dish mop, dish-clout

dishonorable discharge, dismissal with disgrace
dishpan, washing-up bowl
dishrag, dish-clout; wash-cloth
dish towel, tea towel; washing-up cloth
dishwater, cat-lap
disinfect, stove up
dislike, down
dislodge, unharbour
dismissal, push; sack
dismissal with bonus, golden handshake
disorganized, rafferty
display one's credentials, set out one's stall
district, constituency
district attorney, public prosecutor
disturb, put (someone) off
dither, kerfuffle; way
dive, night-cellar
divided highway; dual carriageway
dividend, divi; divvy
divinity school; theological college
divvy up!, fair do's!
dizzy spell, giddy fit; turn
do, diddle
do,   3
dock wharf
doctor covering for another, locum
doctor's (dentist's) office, surgery
doctor's (dentist's) office hours, surgery
dodge, jink
dodo, bonce
do/done,   413
doesn't hold a candle to, (is) not a patch on
dogfish,   426
doggerel, rat rhyme
dogs,   424
dog tag, identity disc
doll's house,   409
doll up, tart up
dolmen, quoit
dome light,   423
domestic, inland; internal
domestic employment agency, registry
domestic monopoly, sheltered trade
domino load,   424
done dirt, hard done by
done for, snookered
done in, whacked
Do Not Enter, No Entry
don't exaggerate!, draw it mild!
Don't let it bother you!, Not to worry!
Don't mention it!, Pleasure!
doorman, commissionaire; porter
door pillar,   422
door post,   422
door stop,   422
door to door salesman, doorstep salesman; knocker
door vent or *vent*,   422

dope, griff
dope(fool), berk; gony; jobbernowl;
    juggins; mug; muffin; muggins; nit;
    poop
dopey, dozy; dozey
dormitory, hall of residence
do (someone) dirt, do (someone) down;
    do (someone) in the eye
do (someone) in, do (someone) up;
    scupper
do the dirty work, carry the can
do the dishes, wash up
double, large
double, 426
double boiler, double saucepan
double dealer, twicer
double portion, double
double sirloin, 426
double whole note, breve
double whole note, 424
dough (money), brass; corn; dibs; lolly;
    £. s.d.; oof; ready; rhino
do without (someone), give (someone
    something) a miss
down, mis; miz
down at heel, 408
down at the heels, down at heel
down shift, change down
draft, call-up
draft, 6
drafting room, drawing office
drag, fag; grind
drag, 428
drain, run-away
dram of whiskey, tot
Dr/Dr., 415
dreary, dree
dress, frock
dress, xix
dressed to kill, dressed to the nines
dresser, chest of drawers
dressing-down, wigging
dressing-room, changing-room
drip, weed
drive, hoy
drive, motor
drive/driveway, 409
driver's license, driving licence
driver's seat, driving seat
drive shaft, cardan shaft; propeller shaft
drive shaft, 423
drive (someone) crazy, drive (someone)
    up the wall
drive (someone) nuts, send (someone)
    spare
driveway, drive
drizzle, mizzle
drone on and on, jaw-jaw
drop, slide
drop, 425
drop arm, 423

drop dead, drop down dead
drop off course, bag
drudgery, donkey-work
drugstore, chemist's shop
drunken driving, drunk in charge
dry goods, Manchester
dry goods store, draper's shop
dry ice, hot ice
Dry Measure, 418
dry off/out, 408
dub, rabbit
duck, lough
duck, 428
dud, damp squib
duds, dunnage
due date, quarter-day
dues, subscription
dull, subfusc
dull, 5
dumb, wet; gormless
dumbwaiter; service lift
dummy bomb, proxy bomb
dump, tip
dune, dene
dunghill, midden
duplicate, roneo
durum flour, strong flour
dust balls, slut's wool
dustman, 2
dynamo 423

E

each other/one another, 410
each-way, 426
ear, lughole
early in the picture, early on
earn, knock up
earth sciences, 427
easement, wayleave
easy come easy go, light come light go
easy trip, 424
eat like a pig, pig it
eats, tuck
eat your cake and have it, have the
    penny and the bun
eccentric, 4
eccentric, cranky
-ed, 409
editorial, leader
editorialise, 3
editor in chief, chief editor
eel trap, buck
effective date, tax point
eggplant, aubergine
egg roll, pancake roll
eggs from uncooped hens, free-range
    eggs
eiderdown quilt, duvet
eighth note, quaver

eighth note, 424
Eisenhower, John, 1
elastic knit fabric, stockinet
elder, major
elect, return
election day, polling-day
Electrical Equipment (Automotive), 423
electrical socket, point
electric cord, flex
electric fan, punka(h)
electric heater, electric fire
electric power source, mains
electric tricycle, invalid carriage
elevator, lift
elimination contest, knock-out
Embankment 424
emcee, compère
emergency brake, 423
emergency room, casualty department
employ, engage
employee in charge of supplies,
 storekeeper
empty, peckish
Encounter, 414
endive, chicory
endless discussion, jaw-jaw
engaged, 5
Engine and Clutch Parts, 423
engineer, engine driver
engineer's and fireman's platform,
 footplate
England, 427
English, side; spin
English, 427
English Channel, Silver Streak
English horn, cor anglais
engrave, dye stamp
engraving, copperplate printing
enlist, take the shilling
enlisted men, other ranks
enormously, thumping
entail, attract
enter university, go up
enthusiastic, mustard-keen
enthusiastic about, keen on
entitled to the use of, free of
entrance, entry
eraser, rubber
error, misfield
escalator, moving stairway
escritoire, davenport
Esq., 415
estate or farm manager, bailiff
estate tax, death duties
European Economic Community, 2
eve, square, *adj.*
even, level
even money, evens
even Stephen, honours even; level
 pegging

everything but the kitchen sink,
 everything that opens and shuts
everything's hunky-dory, everthing in
 the garden's lovely
everything thrown in, all in
exaggerate, draw the long bow
excelsior, wood wool
except, bar
excise tax, purchase tax; V.A.T.
exclamation point, exclamation mark
excursion bus, charabanc
excursionist, tripper
executive, director
Executive Committee, (the) Executive
executive vice president, managing
 director
exemption, allowance
exemption, relief
exhaust, fag; knock up
exhaust fan, extractor fan
exhaust silencer, 422
exhibition game, friendly
exhibitor, renter
Exit, Way Out
expel, sack; send down
expel temporarily from university,
 rusticate
expense account, spends
expenses, outgoings
expensive, pricey
expensive suburb, gin and Jaguar belt
explode, create
express, fast
express company, carrier
express post, 4
extension, flex
extension courses, extra-mural studies
extension school, college of further
 education
extortion, demanding money with
 menaces
extortionate rent, rackrent
extra, gash
extra measure, long pull; pull
extra salary allowance, weighting
extremely slow, dead slow
extreme side seat, slip
exult riotously, maffick
eyes, 425

F

4F, C Three
fabulous, snorting
face, 425
face annihilation, on a hiding to nothing
face card, court card
face cloth, flannel
fact-finding board, court of inquiry
factor, bill broker

factory, works
factory whistle, hooter
faddish,. trendy
fagged, flaked out; spun
faintest, foggiest
fair, fête
fair-haired boy, blue-eyed boy
fair with occasional showers, bright
  periods
fake, duff
fall, slide
fall on one's face, come a purler;
  put up a black
fanatic puritan, wowser
fancy, 5
farm equipment and machinery,
  dead stock
farmhand, agricultural labourer
farmstead, steading
farsighted, long-sighted
farthing, 417
fascia panel, 422
fascinating; absorbing, riveting
fashionable, trendy
fashion show, dress show
fast-back, slant-tailed
fasten, pop
fast one (swindle), do
fat and squat, fubsy
father, Pater
fatty, podge
faucet, tap
favored, tipped
favorite (horse racing), pot
faze, fuss
Featherstonehaugh, 412
fed up, chocker
feeding, feed
feel like, feel
fee(s), dues
feet, 425
fellow, bean; chap; cove
felt hat, trilby
fender, wing
fender, 422
few in number, thin on the ground
fey, airy-fairy
fiasco, lash-up; (a) nonsense
fib, taradiddle
fiberglass, glass fibre
field, ground
fielder, fieldsman
field hockey, hockey
fifth wheel, gooseberry
figure, 412
figure out, sus out
fill, make up; stop; top up
fillers, balaam
fill in, gen up
fill out, fill in
financial district, (the) City

financial editor, City editor
Financial Terms, 417
fine, champion
fine, sconce
finecomb, toothcomb
fine grave, grit
finely granulated sugar,
  castor-sugar
fingerprints, dabs
finger spinner, 428
finicky, dainty
finish, put paid to
finished, gone for a burton
fink, scug
fire, sack
firecracker, banger
fire department, fire brigade
fire insurance company office, fire
  office
fireplace implements, fire-ions
fire-screen, fire-guard
firewall, 422
fireworks display, Brock's benefit
firm beach, hard
first balcony, dress circle
first-class mail, letter post
first name, Christian name
first rate, tip-top
fiscal year, financial year
fish and seafood, fish
*fishmonger's,*426
fish sticks, fish fingers
fish store, fishmonger's
fish tank, stew
fit, taking
fit (of anger), bait
fitted with storm windows,
  double-glazed
fit-up, pick up
five, fiver
five hundred pounds, monkey
fix, nobble
fix (spay), brick up
fixed, straightened out
fixtures, fitments; fittings
flag, 426
flair, panache
flank, skirt
flashlight, torch
flashy, flash
flat, puncture
flat broke, (in) Carey Street
flat cakes, dampers
flatten (notes), 409
flatter, flannel
flattery, flannel
flattie, 424
flatulent, windy
flicks, 5
flight by night, moonlight flit
flipper, 428

flirt, carry on
flood, spate
floor, pair
floor lamp, standard lamp
floor space, carpet area
floorwalker, shop-walker
flop house, casual ward; doss-house
flophouse, 425
florin, 417
flout, drive a coach and horses
   through
flower frog, maizie
flowers. See **Botanical and
   Zoological Names,** 426
fluff (dust ball), fug
flunk, plough
fluorescent lighting, strip lighting
flush, 425
fly, flies
fog, 427
fogy, buffer
fold, put the shutters up
folding seat, tip-up seat
fondle, nurse
food course, remove
food cupboard, meat-safe
Food Names, 426
fool, flat; goat; juggins; mug;
   muggins
fool, 6
fool around, rag
foot (far end), bottom
ford, watersplash
foreman, charge-hand
forest-riding path, ride
for free (gratis), buckshee
for sale, under offer
for that matter, for the matter of
   that
fortuitous, chance-come
fortune, bomb
for (used for), in aid of
forward, redirect
foul line, crease
foul up, bugger
founding, foundation
Four Corners, Four Wents
four flush, 425
foursome, fourball
Fowles, John, 1
Fraffly Well Spoken, 412
frame house, wooden house
frank, rude
Frayn, Michael, 3
free, gash
free-for-all, donnybrook
freight, carriage; goods
freight elevator, hoist
freighter, cargo boat
freight train, 2
French fried potatoes, chips

French tab, draw tab
fresh fish, wet fish
freshman, fresher
fried bread, French toast
fright, guy
frills, tatt
fringe benefits, perks
fritter away one's time, tatt
frock, 5
frog, rose
frogspit 427
from the word go, from the off
frontage to/on, 408
front desk, reception
front yard, forecourt
frozen food, frosted food
fruit and vegetable pushcart vendor,
   costermonger; pearly
fruit basket, chip
fruit course at end of meal, dessert
fruit seller, fruiterer
fry, fry-up
fuck, poopnoddy
fuel or *gas pump*, 423
full approval, full marks
full of pep, cracking
full regalia, (in) full fig
full stop, 414
full time, full out
funny, 5
funny (peculiar), rum
furnish, issue
furze, gorse
fuss, carry on; kerfuffle; tamasha
F.W. Woolworth & Co., Woollies

G

gabble, waffle
gag, rag
gagger, 424
gain, rise; win
galley (on the deck of a ship),
   caboose
gallinule, 427
gallon, 419
gallon, Imperial, 418
galoshes, snowboots
gamble, flutter; game
game, gammy
game, match
gander, shufty; dekko; recce
gang foreman, ganger
gaol, 416
gappermouth, 6
garage, 412
garbage, gash
garbage can, dustbin
garbage dump, refuse tip
garbage man, dustman

garbage truck, dustcart
garters, suspenders
gasoline, petrol
gas or *fuel pump*, 423
gate, barrier
gate, 428
gaudy, twopence coloured
gauge, bore; tension
gear, clobber; traps
gearbox housing, 423
Gearbox Parts, 423
gear lever, 423
gearshift, gear-lever
gear shift lever, 423
gee!, cool!; cor!; oo-er!
geezer, josser
gelatin-type dessert, jelly
general delivery, poste restante
generator, dynamo
generator, 423
genuine, pukka
German bands, 425
Germans, 425
German shepherd, Alsatian
get along with, get on with
get a move on, look smart!
get anywhere with, get much
    change out of
get a rise out of, take a
    rise out of; take the rise
    out of
get away with it, slime
get a word in edgewise, put
    one's hoof in
get back on, get one's own back on
get by, rub along
get down to brass tacks, come to the
    horses
get even with, get upsides with
get going, get one's skates
    on; get on with it; get
    stuck in; get weaving;
    pull one's socks up
get in (someone's) hair, get up
    (someone's) nose
get lost!, cheese off!; On your bike!
get moving, push along
get off, alight
get off the pot, take your finger out
get out of an automobile, debus
get settled, smooth in
get (someone) out, dismiss
get (someone) riled up, get across
    (someone)
get (someone's) back up, put
    (someone's) back up
get some shut-eye, have a doss; put
    one's head down
get something going, put up the
    hare
get (something) under way, have

(something) put in hand
get somewhat tight, have one over
    the eight
get sore (angry), go spare
get the best of, get the better of
get the better of, score off
get the gate (be fired), get the chop
get things started, open the bowling
get this!, wait for it!
get tired of, go off
get-up, clobber
Ghost Train, 424
GI, tommy
giant, lambert
gibble-fisted, 6
gift of the gab, the 408
gill, 419
gimpy, dot and carry one
gin, mother's ruin; squareface
gingersnap, ginger biscuit
gin mill, gin-stop
girdle, belt; roll-on
Girl Scout, Girl Guide
give a hoot, care a pin
give a yell at, chi-ack
give (someone) hell, give (someone)
    some stick
give (someone) his pink slip, give
    (someone) his cards
give (someone) the gate, give
    (someone) the bird
giving services for board and lodging,
    au pair
glimmer, 424
gloomy Gus, dismal Jimmy;
    Jeremiah
Gloucester, 411
glove compartment, cubby; globe
    locker
glutton, stodge
go AWOL, go spare
gob, whack
go (become), come over
go berserk, go spare
go-between, link man
goddamned, bleeding; bloody
goddamned fool, b.f.
God help us!, save the mark!
God's country, blighty
God willing, D.V.
gofer, dog's body
go first, bat first; take first knock
going on, coming; rising
going over, stonk
going places, on the up and up
going too far, (a) bit thick
    over the top
go into bankruptcy., put up the
    shutters
Goldberg, Sylvia, xviii
goldbrick, scrimshank; skive

gold cup, 426
gondola car, open goods-waggon; truck
good and bad, good in parts
good at, hot on
good eats, scoff
good God!, 'strewth!
Good heavens!, Crikey!; stone the crows!
good shot!, shooting!
good show, xxi
good spell, good innings
good trains, xiv
good stuff, good value
good thing, good job
goof, boob
goof off, dodge the column; mike; slack; swing it; swing the lead
goofy, bonkers
googly, 428
gooseberry, goosegog
goose egg, duck
gooseneck lamp, flexible (table) lamp
goose pimples, chicken-flesh
gorge, live like a fighting cock
gorge, 427
go steady, walk out
go the limit, make all the running
go to and fro, tig-tag
go to bed early, have an early night
Go to hell!, Go to bath!
go to the bathroom, spend a penny
go to the dogs, go to the bad
go to the races, go racing
goulies, goulash
government bonds, 417
government bonds, gilts
government employee, civil servant
(Government Insurance System), National Insurance
government lottery bond, premium bond
government official, politician
Government Printing Office, Her Majesty's Stationary Office
government publication, Paper
governor, supremo
grab bag, lucky-dip
grade, class; form; standard
grade crossing, level crossing
grade (hill), gradient
grade school, elementary school
graduate, come down; pass out
graduate, post-graduate
graduate from, leave
graduating student, leaver
graft, backhander
grain, corn
Granny Smith, 426
grass shoulder, verge

gravel, beach
gravy boat, sauce-boat
grease fitting, 423
grease nipple, 423
great, rare; ripping; top-hole; topping
Great Britain, 428
great! fine!, lovely!; whacko!
great fun, all the fun of the fair
"Greek", double Dutch
Greek, xiv
green arrow, filter sign
greenhouse, glasshouse
green-looking, cabbage-looking
green pepper, capsicum
green thumb, green fingers
Greenwich Mean Time, G.M.T.
green woolen cloth, Kendal green
grey, 416
Grey, Anthony, xxi
greyhound racing, greycing
griddle, girdle
grind, cad; kibble; mug; sap; aesthete
gripe, bind; winge
grit, sand
ground, earth
ground fog, 6
group, lot; set
grub (food), bait; tack; toke
grudge match, needle match
gruel, skilly
gruesome, curly
guard, keeper
guck, jollop
grudgeon pin, 423
guest book, visitors' book
guest room, spare room
gum, chewing gum
gurgle, guggle
guy, bean; beggar; bloke; chap; cove; johnny; stick
gym suit, gym slip (gym tunic)

H

haberdashery, draper's shop
haggle, tig-tag
Haire, Suzanne (Lady Haire of Whiteabbey), 3
hairpin, hair grip
hair spray, lacquer
half a minute (right away), half a tick
half-cocked, at half-cock
half-crown, 417,425
half note, minim
half note, 424
halfpast, half
halfpenny, 417

half shaft, 423
ham, gammon
hamburger, wimpy
hamburger roll, bap
Hampshire, 412
Hampstead, 412
handball, fives
handbill; large-sized newspaper,
    broadsheet
hand brake, 422
handle, do
handle by hand, manhandle
handling and mailing, postage
    (posting) and packing
hands, 425
hand (someone) a line, chat up
handwriting, hand
hang around, mouch
hand up, put down the 'phone
hanky-panky, jiggery-pokery
Hants., 412
happy as a clam, happy as a
    sand-boy
hard-boiled, hard-baked
hard boiled, hard-cooked
hard candy, boiled sweets
hard cider, cider
hard labor, hard
hard liquor, spirits
hard-luck guy, lame duck
hard sauce, brandy-butter;
    rum-butter
hard up, in low water; (in) Queer
    Street
hardware, fixings; gongs
hardware store, ironmonger's
Harley Street, 424
Harris, Jed, 3
Harry, Dixon, 1
harum scarum, rackety
hash, shepherd's pie
hat, 425
hatchet man, butcher
(have a) ball, (have a) rave-up
have a general election, go to the
    country
have an affair, have it off
have a screw loose, have
    a slate loose
have high hopes, fancy one's
    chances
have it easy, have jam on it
have no use for, have no time for
have plenty to do, have enough on
    one's plate
have (someone) at one's mercy,
    have (someone) on toast
have (someone) under one's thumb,
    put the comether on (someone)
have (something) going, have
    (something) on

have (something) lined up, have
    (something) in one's eye
have the inside dope, know the form
having a liquor license, licensed
have a road on, 424
having a telephone, on the
    telephone
hawker, cheapjack
hawthorn, may
hayseed, chaw-bacon
haystack, rickle
head, 425
head (beginning), top
headboard, bed-board
head cheese, brawn
headfirst, neck and crop
headlight, headlamp
headliner, topliner; top of the bill
head nurse, charge-nurse
head over heels, arse over tip
head shrinker, trick cyclist
health inspector, health visitor
heaping, heaped
hearing aid, deaf aid
heart's content, top of one's bent
heated argument; noisy party, ding-dong
heater, fire
heaven, land of the leal
heavy, double
heavy cream, double cream
heavy favorite, long odds on
heavy food, stodge
heavy linen or muslin, dowlas
heavy work, rough
Hebrew, 2
hedge clippings, brash
Heinz (57 varieties), 426
held for questioning, assisting the police
hell, bean; rocket
hell of a hurry, split of a hurry
hell of a time, a/the, 409
hell raiser, rip; tearaway
help wanted, situations vacant; vacancies
hem and haw, hum and ha
hemidemisemiquaver, 424
herb, 412
here's how!, cheers!
Herter, Christian, 1
Hertford, 411
het up, in a flap; strung up
he was shot down, he bought the farm
hey! look here!, hi!
hey! (what's going on?), hullo!
hide-and-seek, hy-spy
hideaway, bolt-hole; hidey-hole
hiding place, hide
hierarchy; order, totem
highbrow, Bloomsbury
highest rank, (at the) top of the tree
high fur hat, busby
high gear, top gear

high-hat, come a heavy over
highly strung, 409
high rise, multi-storey
high-school graduate, school-leaver
High Street, the, 408
high-strung, highly-strung
high tension tower, pylon
highway robbery, daylight robbery
high-wheeler, penny-farthing
hi! howdy!, watcher!
hillside valley, coomb
hillside woods, hanger
hire, engage
his/the, 409
hit, job
hitch, 5
hitch, hiccup
hit (success), knock
hoarding, 4
hoarse, roopy
hoax, legpull
hob, 428
hobo, layabout
hock (pawn), pop
hog, 425
hold one's own, stand one's own
hold the bag, hold the baby
hold your horses!, wait for it!
hole in one's sock, potato
holy mackerel!, blimey!
Home, 412
home away from home, home from
 home
home economics, domestic science
homely, plain
home rule, devolution
homestretch, home run
homework, prep
homey, homely
homosexual, bent; ginger
Hon., 415
honey, duck; love
honky-tonk, gaff
honorary university head, chancellor
honors, four honours
honour, 415
hood, bonnet
hood, 422
hoodlum, hooligan
hope, earthly
hope chest, bottom drawer
hopeless, clueless
hop field, hop-garden
hop sack, bin
hops kiln, oast
hop to it, jump to it
horny, randy
horse around, cod
horse chestnut, conker
horse chestnut game, conkers
horsefly, cleg

horse gold, 426
horselaugh, laugh like a drain
horse sense, gump
horse show, gymkhana
horse stall, loose-box
horse trader, coper
horsie, gee
Horwill, H.W., 3
hose clamp, 423
hose clip, 423
hosp., 415
hospital, 415
hospital, in/to 408
hospitalise, 3
hot, fallen off the back of a lorry
hot and bothered, mithered
hotel apartment, service flat
hotel bootblack, boots
hotel maid, chambermaid
hot-water bottle, stomach warmer
hot water heater, immersion tank
hour, 414
house call charge, call-out charge
house call, domiciliary
house (dormitory), college
household refuse, dust
house-sitter, homeminder; houseminder
house trailer, caravan
housing or wheelhouse, 422
how'd it go?, good party?
How have you been?, How are you
 keeping?
humbug, gammon
humdinger; punch in the nose, snorter
humorous comic, comic
hundredweight, 418
hunky-dory, ticketyboo
hunt, shoot
hunter, gun
hunting-lodge, shooting-fox
hurts me like hell, gives me gyp (gip; jip)
huss, 426
hut; small cottage, bothy
hyphenated, double-barrelled

I

I beg to say that . . ., I have to say
 that . . .
I bet, I'll be bound
iceberg lettuce, web lettuce
ice cream, ice
ice cube, block of ice
iced water, 409
idea, wheeze
idiot box, box; goggle-box
if cash, 426
ignition harness, 423
ignition set, 423
I (he, etc.) got the message, (the)

penny dropped
immediate occupancy, vacant possession
impassive, po-faced
Imperial pint, 419
impose tax on (something), charge
(something) to tax
impracticable, not on
improve, buck up
improvement assessment,
betterment levy
improvisation, lash-up
imputed income, notional income
in, 408
in a fix, up the spout
in a foster home, in care
in a mess, all over the shop
in a pickle, in a cleft stick
in a spot, in baulk
in a tight spot, on a piece of string
in a tizzy, in a fuzz
in between, between whiles
In Britain, 6
incidental, by the way
incinerator, destructor
inconsiderate, rude
increase on/over, 408
incumbent, sitting
Incurables, Royal Hospital and Home for,
413
in danger, at risk
independent contracting, (the) lump
in desperate straits, past praying for
index card, record card
Indian, Red Indian
Indian summer, Luke's Little Summer;
St. luke's Summer; St. Martin's
Summer
in dutch with (someone), in (someone's)
bad books
inflexion, 415
info, griff
in for it, for it; for the high jump
in form, on form
information, enquiries
-ing, 409
in good order, Bristol fashion
in good shape, landed
in great shape, up to the knocker
ingrown, ingrowing
in heat, on heat
in high spirits, in a merry pin
in hot water, in low water; under the
harrow
initial, sign off
initiation fee, entrance fee
inlet, creek; loch
inn, hostelry
innards, gubbins
inner-spring, interior-sprung
inning, innings
innings, 409

inn keeper, landlord
in raptures, over the moon
insane, certified
insect, creepy-crawly
inside dope, gen
inside of loaf, crumb
in spades!, with knobs on!
inspect, view
inspection, 415
installment plan, hire-purchase; never-
never; tally plan
instant replay, action replay
instruct an expert, teach (someone's)
grandmother to suck eggs
instructions, book of words
instructions to trial lawyer, brief
instructor, lecturer
insufficient funds, no effects; R.D.; refer
to drawer
insulating layer, damp course
insurance, assurance
insurances, 409
inswinger, 428
intensive search, comb-out
inter-city bus, coach; motor coach
interfere with (someone), mess
(someone) about
intermission, interval
intern, houseman
internal, inland
international match, Test Match
interpolate, spatchcock
intersection, crossroads
intersection area, box
in the cards, on the cards
in the clutch, at the crunch
in the driver's seat, in the driving seat
in the running, in the hunt
in the same situation, in the same case
in the soup, in the cart
in the works, on the stocks
intonation, 411
in town for the big occasion, up for
the Cup
in two shakes of a lamb's tail, in two
shakes of a duck's tail
inverted commas, 414
investigation, enquiry
investment bank, merchant bank
invisible onlooker, fly on the wall
involve, attract
in wild disorder, all over the shop
Irish, 427
irritating, tiresome
I.R.S., (the) Revenue
-ise 415
islet, ait
Is someone helping you?, Have you been
served?
Is that/this—?, 413
it doesn't matter, San Fairy Ann

itinerant mender, tinker
It's all the same to me, I'm easy (about
    it)
It's incredible!, It isn't true!
it's unshakable, there's no shifting it
It's up to you, (the) ball's in your court
-*ize*,   415

just about, as near as dammit; as near as
    makes no odds; just
just a drop, titchy bit
Just a minute!, Hold on!
just what the doctor ordered, meat and
    drink
justice of the peace, magistrate

J

jabber away, rabbit on
jack, knave
jack-in-the-pulpit, cuckoo-pint; lords and
    ladies
jack-in-the-pulpit,   427
jack up, gazump
jail, boob; bridewell; shop
jailbird, lag
jalopy, banger; granny waggon
jam jar,   424
Jane Austen fan, Janeite
janitor, caretaker
jelly doughnut, doughnut
jelly roll, Swiss roll
jerk, charlie; clot; git; hoick; jobbernowl;
    nit; poon; swab; twit
jerk off, toss off; wank
Jesus College,   410
jeweller,   415
jewelweed,   427
jimmy, jemmy
jitters, (the) needle
job, job of work; lark; ploy; type of
    activity
jock, hearty
Joe Doakes, Joe Bloggs
John Doe, A.N. Other
John Dory,   426
Johnson, Keith R.,   4
john (toilet), bog; loo; petty
join up, club together
joke, cod
jolly,   5
joufin-head,   6
judgment roll, docket
judy,   425
juggle, cook; fluff
jumping the gun, early days
jump rope, skipping rope
jump seat, slip seat
jump the gun, rush one's fences
jumpy, nervy; windy
June bug, cockchafer
junior varsity player, colt
junk, clutter; lumber
junket, swan
junkman, rag-and-bone man
junky, twopenny-halfpenny
jurisdictional dispute, demarcation
    dispute

K

kay-neived,   6
keel,   418
keep, detain
keep after, chevy
keep an eye on, keep obbo on
keep going, carry on
keep still!, be quiet!
keep still, be said
keep your eyes peeled, keep your
    eyes skinned
kerb,   416
kerosene, paraffin
kestrel,   427
kick hard; take a decisive step, put the
    boot in
kickoff, K.O.
kick the bucket, drop off the hooks; peg
    out; turn up one's toes
kid, chip; rally; rot
kid (someone), have (someone) on
kid (tot), kipper; nipper
killed, gone for a burton
kill time, stooge about
kindling, firewood
kind of, sort of thing
kind of thing, game
kingcup,   426
king pair,   428
king pin,   423
kiosk,   4
Kirkcudbright,   411
kitchen sink, sink
kitchen stove, aga
kittaghy,   6
kitty, mog; moggy; moggie
knee-high to a grasshopper, two
    pisspots high
knight, baronet
knitted wrist cuff, muffetee
Knittel, Robert,   1
knock, pink
knocked up, in pod; preggers
knocked up, preggers
knock holes in, drive a coarch and
    horses through
knock-kneed, baker-legged
knock oneself out, graft; knock
    oneself up
knock oneself out at, put one's back into
knockout, raver

Knowler, John,   6
K.O. blow, oner

L

laboratory,   412
laboratory assistant, demonstrator
labor union, trade union
lab test, practical
lack, want
ladybug, golden-knop; ladybird
ladyfinger, sponge finger
lady in waiting, maid of honour
lady's flat compact, flapjack
lady's smock,   427
lady's suit, costume
lady's woolen undershirt, spencer
Laetare, Mothering Sunday
lake, loch; mere; water
Lallans,   428
lame, gammy
Lancashire,   412
Lancashiremen,   6
Lancs.,   412
landscaped ground, policy
landslide, landslip
lane, stream; track
lap robe, carriage rug
larder, buttery
large building, block
large fern, bracken
large order, shipping order
large public room, hall
large sherry (port) glass, schooner
large tent, marquee
large truck, juggernaut
lash, taws
last for the rest of (someone's) life,
   see (someone) out
late autumn, back-end
Latin,   2, 412
laundry boiler, copper
lavatory,   414
law apprentice, devil
lawyer, solicitor
lawyer's assistant, clerk
lawyer's office, chambers
lay, grind; prang; stuff
lay into, set about
lay it on thick, come it rather strong; pile
   on the agony
lay off, stand-off
layshaft,   423
lazy Susan, dumb-waiter
lead balloon, damp squib
leaded stick, squailer
lean bacon, griskin
lean over backwards, fall over backwards
lease, contract hire
leather dressing, dubbin

leatherneck, jolly
leave (a message), pass
leave (as an estate), cut up for
leave well enough alone, leave well
   alone
left-handed, leftarm
left-handed,   6
leftist, lefty
legal fiction, legal figment
legal holiday, bank holiday
legislative report, blue book
lemon sole,   426
lending library, subscription library
length,   428
Lent lily,   427
Less Than Kin,   1
let alone, leave alone
letdown, sell
let off, set down
let (someone) have it, have (someone's)
   guts for garters; put it across
   (someone)
letterhead, headed paper
letter (in athletics), blue; cap
letter man, blue
letter opener, paper knife
leverage, gearing
Leveson-Gower,   411
liability insurance, third party insurance
license/licence,   415
licensed architect, chartered surveyor
license plate, number plate
license plate,   422
license to sell bottled alcoholic beverages,
   off licence
lickety-split, split-arse
lick (vanquish), flog
lie, fluff
lie low, go to ground; lie doggo
lieutenant,   412
lieutenant colonel, wing commander
life jacket, life vest
life preserver, life-belt
lifesaving service, humane society
lift, elevator
light out, bunk
light supper, high tea; knife-and-fork tea
light waterproof jacket, anorak
like, sort of thing
like,   5,410
like a house afire, like old boots
like it or not, choose how
like taking candy from a baby, money for
   jam
lima bean, broad bean
Limb Fitting Centre,   413
limits, boundary
line, free line
line, line of country
line, queue

linear suburban expansion, ribbon
   development
line of schoolchildren, crocodile
line squall, thundery trough
line up, queue
Linguistic Atlas of England, 6
link arms with, link
linked with..., twin with...
linoleum, lino
lint, fleck; fluff
liquidation sale, closing-down sale
Liquid Measure, 419
liquor store, wine merchant
literal usage, 413
literary hack, devil
little devil, limb
little hill, mole
little old lady from Dubuque, Aunt
   Edna
live, stay
live a sheltered life, live in cotton wool
live like a pig, pig it
liverwurst, liver sausage
livestock farmer, stockholder
live to a ripe old age, make old bones
living room, drawing-room; lounge;
   sitting-room
living room, 414
Lloyd, Selwyn, 1
load on, skinful
loaf, 425
loafer, layabout
loafers, slip-on-shoes
loaf of bread, 425
loan share; loan stock, bond
loathe, bar
local, branch
local tax, rate
local (train), slow train; stopping train
locate, site
location of the john, geography of the
   house
locker-room, changing-room
lock-up, glasshouse
locomotive fireman, stoker
lodge, slate club
lodging, digs
lollypot, 6
London, 424
London Bridge cab-rank, 424
Londoners, The, 411
(the) London Police, (the) Mets
London Slang, 424
long-distance call, trunk call
Long-distance Information, Trunk
   Enquiries
long hop, 428
Longitude 30 West, 2
long life, good innings
Long play, 409
longshoreman, docker

long term, long-stay
long-winded story, circumbendibus
look, look-round
look as if..., look like...
look like + gerund, 410
look out for my corn!, ware wheat!
lookout point, viewpoint
look-see, shufty
look up, look-up
loony, dotty; loopy
loophole, let-out
loop-hole/loophole, 414
loose gravel, loose chippings
loose-leaf binder, file
loose-leaf notebook, ring book
loose woman, scrubber; tart
'loose woman,' 3
loot, pewter
Lord, lud
"Lord Disgusted," 3
lords and ladies, 427
Lordy!, Lawk(s)!
lose one's balance, overbalance
lose out, kick the beam
lost, landed
lost and found, baggage service; lost
   property office
lotsa luck!, (the) best of British luck!
lottery computer, Ernie
loud, staring
louder!, speak up!
lounge, 414
louse, nasty piece (bit) of work; sewer
louse, 425
lousy!, bad show!
lousy, bloody; filthy
lousy beer, swipes
lout, yobbo
lout, 4
love child, chance-child; come-by-chance
lower class, down-market
low gear, bottom gear
Lowlands, 428
lug, hump
luggage rack, roof-rack
lumber, deals; timber
lump, 425
lunch, tiffin
lunch coupon, luncheon voucher
Lympne, 411

M

machine operator, machinist
machinery, works
Macmillan, Harold, 1
(made or become) unemployed,
   redundant
made to order, bespoke

made vicar, appointed to the cure of souls
made work, hospital job
magazine rack, canterbury
Magdalene, 411
maggot, gentle
magician, conjuror
magistrate, beak
magna, second
magnifying glass, reading glass
maid of all work, general servant
maid of honor, chief bridesmaid
mail, post
mailbox, letter-box; pillar-box; post-box
mail car, postal van
mailing and handling, dispatch
mailman, postman
mail order buying, postal shopping
mail order house, catalogue company
main road, arterial road
main shaft, 423
Main Street, High Street
Main Street, 408
maintenance man, clerk of the works
Mainwarings, 412
major in, read
majority, clear majority
major league, first class
make a booboo, drop a brick
make a case for, make out a case for
make a decision, take a decision
make a fourth, make a (the) four up
make a fuss, create
make a fuss (row), cut up rough
make a gaffe, drop a clanger
make a hash of, make hay of
make a killing, scoop the pool
make (a long story short), cut (a long story short)
make an error, misfield
make a play for, make a dead-set at
make a touch, bring off a touch; sub
make fun of, make game of
make it, have it off
make (suduce), pull
make tea, brew up
make the rounds (of pubs), pub-crawl
mall, hyper-market
mallet, club-hammer
mama, mummy
-man, walla(h)
manoeuvre, 416
Mansbridge, Ronald, xv
mantelpiece, chimney-piece; mantelshelf
Manx cat, rumpy
map reference system, grid
Marckwardt, Albert H., xv, 412
Marlborough, 411
marriage certificate, marriage lines
marriage clerk's office, Register Office
Marylebone, 411

mashed potatoes, creamed potatoes; mash
mass-media public, admass
master-at-arms, jaunty
master of ceremonies, compère
mast-head/masthead, 414
mat, mount
match in a tinderbox, cat among the pigeons
materials appraiser, quantity surveyor
math, maths
mathematics honor graduate, wrangler
Maurice, 412
maybe, 3
Mayes, Herbert R., 3
Measure, Dry, 418
Measure, Liquid, 419
measure, units of, 413, 418
meat department, butchery
meat-pie, pie
mechanic, fitter
mechanical pencil, propelling pencil
median divider, centre strip
me/I, 411
meet, meets, 410
melee, scrum
member of college governing body, Fellow
member of the royal family, royal
membership of/in, 408
memo, chit
Memoirs, 4
Memoirs of the Second World War, 1
Mencken, H.L., 1
menstruate, come on
MEN WORKING, ROAD WORKS
Menzies, 412
merry-go-round, giddy-go-round; roundabout
mess, balls; charley; cock-up; mess-up; muck; mull
mess around, fossick; frig about
messes up, bunkered
Messrs/Messrs., 415
mess up, make a balls of; mull
messy, scruffy
metallurgy, 412
met-by-chance, chance-met
methyl alcohol, white spirit
"mid-Atlinguish," 1
Mid-Lent Sunday, Mothering Sunday
midshipman, snotty
mid-years, collections
mighty (very), jolly; thundering
military officer's servant, batman
military policeman, redcap
milkmaid, 427
milk shake, whipsy
milk truck, milk float
milliard, 419
million, 419

mimic, hit off
mince pie, mincemeat tart
mince pies, 425
minces, 425
mind you, mind
mind you!, wait for it!
mine bucket, kibble
minim, 424
Mini Minor, mini
minnow, tiddler
minor, secondary subject
mint candy, humbug
minutes, 414
misprint, literal
miss, miss out
missile, 412
miss the point, catch hold of the wrong
  end of the stick
mister, governor
Mitford, Nancy, 2, 414
mixture, omnium gatherum
mix-up, box-up; shemozzle
model home, show-house
moderator, link man
molasses, treacle
molest by stealing or damaging tools,
  ratten
moll, bint
molotov cocktail, petrol bomb
mommy, mummy
Monday to/through Friday, 408
moneymaking, money-spinning
money market, Lombard Street
money pouch, purse
money raising, money-spinning
money (to a beggar), 425
money transfer order, banker's order
mongrel, Heinz hound; pyedog
monitor, prefect
moocher, 424
moorhen, 427
more dead than alive, dead-alive
more power to him, more power to his
  elbow
Morgan's orchard, 425
morning coffee break, elevenses
Morris, William, 1
Morrison, Alistair, 412
moss, 427
most valuable player, man of the match
mother, Mater
mother's helper, mum's help
"Mother Tongues," 6
Motor and Clutch Parts, 423
motor-car, 5
motorcycle, motor-bike
motorman, driver
mountainside hollow, corrie
mountain slope, scree
Mountbatten, Admiral Lord Louis,
mourning cloak, 427

mouth, 425
Mouth and Foot Painting Artists, Ltd., 413
mouth to mouth resuscitation, kiss of life
move, flit; move house
move house, 409
movie, film
movie business, Wardour Street
movie camera, cinecamera
movie house, cinema
movies, flicks; pictures
movies, 2
movie trailer, dreadful warning
moving, removals
moving van, pantechnicon
M.P.'s (lawyer's) session with
  constituents (clients), surgery
M.P.'s (lawyer's) temporary outside
  quarters, surgery
Mr., Esq.
Mr/Mr., 415
Mrs/Mrs., 415
mucilage, gum
muddle, cock-up; (a) nonsense
muddy bottom, putty
muffin stand, curate's assistant
muffler, 422
multicolored sprinkles, hundreds and
  thousands
multiple plus, adapter
municipality, corporation
municipal or public housing unit, council
  house
Murphy's Law, Sod's Law
mushy, soppy
musical box, 409
Musical Notation, 423
muslin, calico
mustard, wild, 427
musty, frowsty
Mutt and Jeff, 425
mutual fund, unit trust
mutual insurance group, friendly society
My!, I say!

N

nab, nobble
nag, screw
nailed down, nailed on; taped
nail polish, nail varnish
name for, call after
nameplate, talley plate
names, 415
Names, Botanical and Zoological, 426
napkin, serviette
napkin, 414
narrow ditch, grip
national passenger train timetable,
  Bradshaw
native, local

naughts, 419
navy yard, dockyard
nay-voter, non-content
near, nr.
neat, tidy
neat, 5
neck, snog
neck of the woods, turf
need, want
neighborhood bar, local
Nelson, 429
Nelson, Walter Henry, 412
nerve, neck
nervous of/about 408
net lease, repairing lease
Newman, Edwin, 1
newscaster, newsreader; presenter
newsdealer, newsagent
newsstand, bookstall; kiosk
next, 415
N.G., N.B.G.
nice going!, well bowled!; well done!
nice to hear your voice, nice to hear you
nice work!, good show!
nick, 427
nickname, middle name
nigger, nig-nog
night on the town, night on the tiles
nightstick, baton
nightwatchman, 429
nine of diamonds, curse of Scotland
nip, drain
nipple, teat
no?, what?
no alternative, nothing (else) for it
no answer, no reply
Noblesse Oblige, 414
no-building zone, green belt
no fuss or feathers, nothing starchy
no great catch, not much cop
no luck, no joy
nominate, adopt
non-Anglican, chapel; nonconformist
non-Church of England, dissenter
nonillion, 419,420
nonne (Latin), 413
nonsense, rot
Nonsense!, Rubbish!
nonsense,a, 409
non-white, coloured; immigrant
noodle, bonce; conk; napper; noddle
no-one/no one, 414
no-parking thoroughfare, clearway
Norfolk, 6
north, norland
north and south, 425
nose out, pip; pip-at-the-post
no soap, in the basket
not a damned thing, damn all; not a
    sausage

not a goddamned thing, bugger all;
    sweet eff-all
not all there, (a) bit missing; simple
not applicable, N/A
notary public, Commissioner for Oaths
not at all, not half
not by a long shot, not by a long chalk
not care a rap about, have no mind to
note, 6
notebook, exercise book; jotter
not feeling up to par, feeling not quite
    the thing
not funny, past a joke
nothing, nil
nothing to write home about, nothing to
    make a song about
no through trucks, except for access
notion, clue
notions, fancy goods
notions store, haberdashery
not nearly, not half
not so bad, not so dusty
not think much of, have no time for
not too happy, not best pleased
noughts, 419
nouveau-riche suburb, stockbroker belt
no way!, not on your nelly
nudist, naturist
number, bit of goods
numbering, strong
number plate, 422
Numbers, 419
num (Latin), 413
nurse, sister
nursery, crèche
nustletripe, 6
nut, nutcase; nutter
nut (head), chump; crumpet
nuts, bonkers; crackers; doolally; stark
    ravers
nuts about, struck on
nutty, potty
nutty, 5

O

oaf, muff; swab
oarlock, rowlock
oatmeal (uncooked), oats
observation deck, spectators' terrace;
    waving base
obstreporous, stroppy
obstruct, mess (someone) about
(obtaining money) under false
    pretenses,
(obtaining money) by deception
obvious, writ large
occasional, odd
occupant, occupier
ocean, 5

octillion,   419,420
odd, kinky
oddball, queer card
odd-job man, jack
odds and ends, oddments
oe,   411
oecumenical,   411
oedema,   411
off color, near the knuckle
office, reception
officer holder, placeman
office of school principal or college dean,
  headship
office or store worker, clerk
officer, official
Officer Commanding, O.C.
officer risen from the ranks, ranker
official business, statutory business
off limits, out of bounds
off one's rocker, off one's chump;
off one's dot; off one's onion
off the rack, off-the-peg
off the record, on a lobby basis
off to a good start, well away
off to a start, off the mark
oil and gasoline mixture, two-stroke
oilcloth, American cloth
oily, smarmy
O.K., landed
old bean,   6
old duffer, dug-out; gaffer
old hand, old soldier
old man, old cock
old people's home, almshouse
old soldier, old sweat
old-timer, old party
old tomato.   3
oleo, marge
on,   408
on a grand scale, writ large
(on) parole, (on) license
on approval, on appro
on a silver platter, on a plate
once in a while, once in a way
one another/each other,   410
one-horse town, one-eyed village
one hundred percent, slap-down
one hundred runs, century
one hundred thousand pounds, plum
one-lane, single-track
one of a kind, one-off
one-pound bill, bradbury
one room apartment, bed-sitter
one-story house, bungalow
one-way ticket, single
on one's own, off one's own bat; on
  one's pat; on one's tod
on sale, on offer
on second thought, on second thoughts
on tenterhooks, on thorns
on the cuff, on the slate; on tick

on the double, smartish
on the loose, going spare
on the nose, bang on; dead on; spot-on
on the payroll, on the strength
on the reverse side, overleaf
on the right track, on the right lines
on the wagon, on the hob; on the teapot
on top of the world, cock-a-hoop
oomph, comeback
op.,   415
open account, running account
open house, omnium gatherum
open one's mouth, say boo to a goose
open-toed shoes, peep-toes
open watercourse, leat
operating room, operating-theatre;
  theatre
operation,   415
operations, works
operations planning room, ops room
oral examination, viva
orange balsam,   427
orchestra, stalls
orchestra seat, stall
orderly,   5
ordinance, by-law
Orient, East
or nearest offer, o.n.o.
Orton, Harold,   6
other to/than,   408
-our,   415
out, get-out
outdo oneself, push the boat out
outdoor bowling game, bowls
outdoor painting, external painting
(outdoor) shorts, shorts
outfit, kit
outlook, look-out
out of bed, up
out of luck, landed
output shaft,   423
outside, outwith
outstanding person or thing, oner
outswinger,   429
over, on
over, P.T.O.
overall, coverall
overcase, dull
overheads,   409
overlaps,   6
overpass, fly-over
overrider,   422
overripe, sleepy
overseas shipping, export carriage
overseer, supremo
overstock, backlog
Oxbridge,   4
oyster wrapped in bacon, angel on
  horseback

P

p.   417
pacifier, comforter
pack, look-out
package, packet
package,   3
package store, off licence
pack; bunch; bagful, shopping bag
packed full of, packed out with
pack up and go, up-stick
pad, drum
pad, waffle
padded saddle, somerset
paid hospital bed, pay bed
pain, blighter
pain in the ass, Gawdelpus
paint, decorate
painting of the Last Judgment, doom
paint scraper, shave hook
paint with a size base, distemper
pair,   429
Pakistani, Paki
pal, cully
Pall Mall,   411
pan, send up rotten; slate
pan, send up rotten; slate
pan,   423
pansy, poof
panties, knickers
pantry, larder
pantyhose, tights
paper back, xv
paper napkin, mortar-board; square;
   stand down
par, level par
paraffin, white wax
parcel,   3
pardon!,   414
parentheses,   414
parenthesis, bracket
pari-mutuel betting, tote betting
parking brake,   422, 423
parking light,   423
parking lot, car park
parking space, parking bay
parlor, saloon
parlor car, saloon-car
parlor pink, armchair socialist
parochial school, demonimational school
parody, cod
parole, ticket-of-leave
part, parting
partial school promotion, remove
parting/part,   409
part time, short time
party line, shared line
party not in power, (Her Majesty's)
   Loyal Opposition
pass, overtake
passage, passing

passengers,   424
passing grade, pass
passing lane, off-side lane
passing the hat, whip-round
pass out cold, spark out
pass (something) up, give (someone *or*
   something) a miss
past the crisis, off the boil
P.A. system, Tannoy
patent,   426
patrol cars, mobile police
patrolled, under observation
patrolman, constable
patsy, Aunt Sally
paved road, metalled road
pavement, roadway
paving block, set
pay a fortune, pay the earth
pay as you go, P.A.Y.E.
payroll, wages sheet
payroll holdup, wage-snatch
pay (someone) peanuts, pay
   (someone) in washers
pay spot cash, pay on the nail
pay up, stump up
pea green,   425
peanut, ground-nut; monkey nut
(peanut) heaven, gods
pear cider, perry
pebble-coated stucco, pebbledash
pebbling, garneting
peculiar, odd
peddler, chapman
peddler of faked merchandise,
   duffer
pedestrian crossing, pelican
   crossing; zebra
pedestrian underpass, subway
Pediatric Hospital,   413
pee,   413, 417
Pei, Mario,   2
pelican hook, senhouse hook
pence,   417
penny,   417
penny-pinching, cheese-paring
pension benefits, pension cover
pension plan, superannuation
   scheme
Pentecostal, Whit
pep, bean
pepper shaker, pepper castor;
   pepper pot
pep talk, ginger-up
perambulator,   413
percentages (expressed),   414
perfectly okay, by all means
perfectly safe, as safe as a bank; as
   safe as houses
performance record, league table
perfume, scent
perhaps,   3

"Perils of the Spoken Word," xviii
period, full stop
period, 415
periodical room, news-room
periwinkle, winkle
personal, private
personal exemption, personal
  allowance
personal luggage, dunnage
personnel, staff
person registered at a hotel, resident
person-to-person call, personal call
pest, blighter
pester, play (someone) up
peteman, peterman
petrol pump, 423
petty cash fund, float
pharmacist, dispenser
pharmacy, chemist's shop
pheasant, Norfolk sparrow
pheasant brood, nide
'phone call, tinkle
phonograph, gramophone
phys. ed., P.T.
picayune, fiddling
pick on, pitch upon
pick up, beat up
picky, dainty; faddy
picture card, court card
picture window, look-out
  window; look-through
  window
pie in the sky, jam tomorrow
pie, tart
pig food, pannage
pigheaded, bloody-minded
pig's cheek, bath chap
piles of..., bags of...
pill, 5
Pill Island, 424
pimp, ponce
pimple, spot
pin-boy, throw-up
pinch, lag; nick
ping, pink
piston or *wrist pin*, 423
pint, 419
pint of milk, pinta
piped music, wallpaper music
pipe down!, cheese it!
piss, slash
pitcher, jug
pitman arm, 423
place (rooms), digs
places, please!, beginners!
plaguing, poxing
plain as the nose on your face, plain
  as a pikestaff
plan, scheme
plank, item
plant (a rumor), put about

planted grove, plantation
plates of meat, 425
platform, programme
platter, dish
played down, hole-in-the-corner
play fair, keep a straight bat; play a
  straight bat
play hookey, play truant; wag it
play/plays, 410
play safe, play for safety
playtime, breaktime 426
(see Appendix II.H), 426 brill
play up on (someone) (go wrong),
  play (someone) up
pleasant, bright
Please..., I shall be glad if you will...
please turn (the page) over, 415
plexiglass, perspex
plod, flog it
pluck, bottom
plug along, peg away
plumber, fitter
plumbing, drains
plump, pudsy
plum pudding, plum duff
plurality, majority
plural verb, 410
P.M., pip emma
pocket notebook, pocketbook
Pocket Oxford Dictionary, xv
point system, totting-up procedure
poison, hemlock
poke fun at, quiz; take the mickey
  out of
poker session, poker school
Poker Slang, 425
poky, choky; quod
pole, stick
police blotter, charge-sheet
police car, jam sandwich;
  panda car; Z car
Police Constable, P.C.
police dog, Alsatian
police lineup, identification parade
policeman, constable
policeman, 424
police wagon, prison van
polish (someone) off, see (someone)
  off
political journalist, lobbyist
political party committee, caucus
political platform, party manifesto
political scientist, politician
Pollyannna, Mark Tapley
pond, water
pony, crib
pool, club together
pool, lasher; pond
poolroom, billiards-saloon
pooped, jiggered
poorhouse, workhouse

pope's nose, parson's nose
pop fly, lofty catch; sky ball
pop over, nip round
pork and beans, beans and bacon
portable bassinet, carrycot
porterhouse, sirloin
porterhouse, 426
poser, facer; tickler
position, 5
post, stick
postcard, P.C.
postpaid, post-free
postponed, stood out
potato chips, crisps
pot-holder, kettle-holder; oven
  glove
pottie, jerry; po
Poultice Shop, 424
poultry dealer, poulterer
pound, nicker
pound, 417
pounds (measure), 418
pound note(s), ...of the best
pour, pour with rain
pour (the tea), be mum
pour with rain, 409
POW camp, bag
powdered sugar, icing sugar
practical nurse, S.E.N.
practise/practice, 415
pram, 413
prawns, 426
prb., 415
preferred stock, preference shares
pregnancy, pudding club
premium, five-star
prepayment penalty, redemption
  fee
prepositions, 408
pre-preparatory school, prep school
presented by..., introduced by...
present (gift), prezzy
president, vice-chancellor
president (of a corporation),
  chairman (of a company)
pressed for, pushed for
press publication restriction,
  D-Notice
pretence, 415
prick, hampton
Priestly, J.B., 1
prime rate, base rate
prime time, peak viewing time
Prince Albert, frock-coat
principal, head
Prinknash, 411
printing, impression
printing company's annual picnic,
  wayzgoose
prison guard, warder
privacy, 412

private hospital, nursing home
private line, exclusive line
private school, public school
Privy Councillor, P.C.
prix fixe, set lunch
PR man, P.R.O.
probably, 415
problem, 5
proctor at school examinations,
  invigilator
proctor's assistant, buller
prod, job
producer, manager; producer
Prof., 415
professional pallbearers, mutes
promenade, parade
promptly, like one o'clock
pronto, bang off
Pronunciation, 411
proofreader, corrector
propane gas, Calor gas
propeller shaft, 423
Prosthetic Devices, 413
provide, lay on
proving-ground, test-bed
prune wrapped in bacon, devil on
  horseback
pruning shears, secateurs
pry, prize
p.t.o., 415
pub, pot-house
pub keeper, landlord
public issue, offer
  for subscription
public open-air swimming pool,
  lido
public rubbish receptacle,
  skivvy-bin
public school, council school; state
  school
pudding, 3
puff, waff
pull (bring) it off, have it off
pullover, jersey; jumper
pull rank on, pip
pull (someone's) leg, rally
pull up stakes, pull up sticks; up
  stumps
pumps, court shoes
punching bag, punch-bag
Punctuation and Style, 414
punishment task, impot
punting, 426
push, flog
pushcart, barrow; trolley
push-up, press-up
put in place, offer-up
put it over on (someone), sell
  (someone) a dummy
put (oneself) out to, lay (oneself)
  out to

put one's head down, get one's
  head down.
put on the dog, put on side
put out, run out
put out (be a nuisance), put about
put (someone) out, dismiss
put to sleep, put down
put up, field
put up, set fair
put up (for the night), shake down
puzzle, stick up
pyjamas,   416

Q

quadrillion,   419
quadruple (stamps), quad
quality, county
quart,   418, 419
quarter light,   422
quarter note, crotchet
quarter note,   424
quarter of a pound, quarter
quaver,   424
queasy, queer
Queen Anne's lace,   427
queening,   426
queer,   5
quick and lively, like one o'clock
quick as a wink, quick as thoughts
quick tour, whip-round
quiet down, go off the boil; quieten
quilt, eiderdown
quintillion,   419
quippy,   6
Quirk, Randolph,   2
quit, pack up
quite a..., fair old...
quite a dish, nice bit of work
quiz, mug
quotation marks, inverted commas
quotation marks,   414

R

rabbit, rebate
rabbits,   424
racetrack, race course
racist, racialist
racket, dodge; ramp
radio, wireless
radio,   2, 7
radio-phonograph, radiogram
raft, shoal
rage, wax
railroad switch, point
rails, metals
rain cats and dogs, bucket down;
  rain stair-rods

raincoat, mac
rain (of) blows, fib
raise, keep
raise, put up
raise an issue, start a hare
ramble on, witter
rambunctious, rumbustious
rancor, gall
rare, underdone
rat cheese, mouse-trap
Rathbone, Brigadier R.B.,   3
rather, -ish
rat on, nobble
rats!, blast!
Rats' Hole,   424
rattled, in a flat spin
raving, gill
raving, staring
razat,   6
-re,   415
read up on (someone; something),
  read (someone; something) up
ready calendar, warned list
ready-made, reach-me-down
ready to go, ready for off
ready-to-wear, off-the-peg
real, proper; right
real estate, property
real estate broker, estate agent; land
  agent
real-estate developer, developer
real estate development, estate
Rear Axle and Transmission Parts,   **423**
rear light,   423
rear of orchestra, pit
rear seat back or *backrest*,   422
rear seat squab,   422
reasonably sure, morally certain
rebuke, call to order
receive (stolen goods), reset
recess, break; playtime
recording, recordal
record on license, endorse
red as a beet, red as a turkey-cock
redbrick,   4
red flag, red rag
red herring, Norfolk capon
red-legged crow, chough
Red Light, Tom Tiddler's Ground
reduced (in price), cheap
reed mace,   427
refer, pass
reference, referee
reforest, reafforest
reformatory, borstal; remand home
Reform Jew, Liberal Jew
reform school, approved school
refrigerator, fridge
refuel, bunker
refuse container; college
  servant, skip

register, visitors' book
registered identification mark, monomark
registered nurse, hospital nurse
regular, ordinary; proper
reinforcement, long stop
relax, put one's feet up
religious organization, fraternity
remainder (interest), reversionary interest
remnant, off cut
remote sewage disposal pipe, long sea outfall
removable bridge, denture
removals, 409
rent-a-car, hire-and-drive
rent (horse and carriage), job
reorganization plan, scheme of arrangement
repair, mend
represent, act for
require, want
required reading, set book
requisition, indent
research scientist, boffin
reservation, reserve
reserve, book
reside, stay
residence farm, home-farm
resident doctor, registrar
residential development, housing estate
resident student, boarder
residuary estate, residual estate
responsions, 7
rest area, lay-by
restaurateur, caterer
restless soul, fart in a colander; tit in a trance
rest room, convenience
résumé, 412
retailer, stockist
retain, instruct
retarded, m.d.
retire; withdraw; postpone, pack it in, stand down
retirement present, leaving gift
retread, remould
retroactive, back-dated; retrospective
return mail, return post
Rev., 415
reveal one's character or party, show one's colours
reverse lamp, 423
reversible, turnabout
review, crit; notice
review, revision
revile, slang
revoke license, strike off
Rhyming Slang, 425

ridge, 427
ridicule, guy
rid of, shot of
rig (fish), 426
rig, rigg, 427
right, just; slap
right!, that's it!
right and day, chalk and cheese
right away, straight away
right here, just here
right with you!, just a tick!
rigid, clench
ring, bell; tinkle
ring gear and pinion, 423
rise, change
rise and shine, show a leg
river, water
river, 415
river bend, gut
river or port commission, conservancy
river-widening, broad
river-widening, 4
roadbed, permanent way
road hog, crown stroller
road maintenance man, lengthman (lengthsman)
roadster, two-seater
Road Under Repair, Road Up
road without speed limit, de-restricted road
roast, joint
roasted, frazzled
robin huss, 426
rob orchards, scrump
robust, rude
rock, 3
rocker panel, 422
road (conrog) bearing, 423
roke, 6
roller coaster, scenic railway; switchback
roll of toilet paper, lavatory roll
romaine, cos lettuce
roof lamp, 423
rookie, colt; erk
rookies, intake
room in a rooming-house, kip
rooming-house, kip
Ross, Alan S.C., 414
roster, rota
rotary mower, hayter
rotating conveyor belt, carousel
rotten, mankie
rough time, bad patch
roundabout, 411, 426
roundabout route or method, circumbendibus
round brackets, 414
rounder, 426

roundhouse, running shed
round-neck, turtleneck
round robin,   426
round the clock,   426
round-trip ticket, return
round up, organize
route, round
row, hoo-ha; schemozzle; bother
row hard, bucket
rowing boat,   409
row of joined houses, link houses;
    terrace
Royal Academy of Dramatic Art,
    R.A.D.A.
Royal Air Force, R.A.F.
Royal Naval Volunteer Reserve,
    Wavy Navy
Royal Navy, Senior Service
rubber, conker; conqueror
rubber boots, gumboots;
    Welliboots; Wellingtons
rubberneck, nosey-parker;
    prodnose
rubbers, galoshes
rubbing alcohol, surgical spirit
rubbish, bumf (bumph)
rubbish heap, laystall
rubble, spoil
Rube Goldberg, Heath Robinson
rub the wrong way, rub up the
    wrong way
ruching, frilling
ruckus, do
ruddle (reddle), keel
rudeness, rudery
rugby scrum, ruck
rumble seat, dickey
rummage sale, jumble sale
rump steak,   426
run, ladder
run, stand
run along, cut along
run for office, put up
run into a streak of bad luck, shoot
    a robin
runner (sled), hob
running flush,   425
run rings around (someone),
    hit (someone) all over
    the hop
run through (money), make off with
run to earth, earth
runt-of-the-litter pig,   6
run up; put together
    roughly, cobble, *v.t.*
Runyon, Damon,   3
ruptured straight,   425
Ruthven,   411

S

s.,   417
-'s,   409
sacred cow,   2
saddled with, lumbered with
saddle (someone) with, land
    (someone) with
s.a.e.,   415
safe and sound, home and dry
safekeeping, safe storage
sailing boat,   409
sailors' clothes and bedding, slops
saithe,   426
saleslady, assistant
salesman, assistant
salesman,   5
sales person, counter-jumper
sales tax, V.A.T.
saleswoman,   5
sally forth, eddy forth
saloon keeper, publican
salt marsh, salting
same old story, mixture as before
sanctimonious piety,
    God-bothering
Sand Bin,   424
sandbox, play-pit
sandpaper, glasspaper
sandwich, round
sandwich box, snap-tin
sandy stretch by the sea, dene
Santa Claus, Father Christmas
s.a.p.,   415
Saturday Review,   3
sausage, banger; slinger
sausage in batter, toad-in-the-hole
save by a hair, drag from the
    burning
save one's skin, save one's bacon
savings account, deposit
    account
savings and loan association,
    building society
savvy, nous
sawbuck, tenner
Say!, I say!
scab, blackleg
scab (strikebreaker), knob
scads, lashings
scallion, spring onion
scalper, ticket tout
scavenger, mudlark
schedule, timetable
schedule,   412
scheduled sporting event, fixture
schedule of charges, tariff
scheme, wheeze
schlepp, hump
schnozzle, hooter
scholarship, studentship

scholarship student, bursar; scholar
Scholastic Aptitude Tests (S.A.T.),
  A-levels
school, college
schoolmaster, beak
school party, school treat
(school) recess, inty
School Zone, Patrol
score, record
score, 418
scorecard, matchcard
Scotch, whisky
Scotch, 428
Scotch tape, Sellotape
Scots, 428
Scottish, 428
scout race horses, tout
scram, buzz off
scram!, push off!
scram, scarper
scrambled eggs, buttered eggs
scrap coal, dross
scratch about, 424
scratch pad, scribbling-block
scrawny, scraggy
screw, poke; roger
Screw that!, Stuff that
  for a game of soldiers!
scrimmage, scrum
scrip, 418
scroochy, 6
scrounge, nobble
scurry, scutter
scuttle, 422
scythe, swop
sea, 5
sea-fret, 427
sea level, ordnance datum
sea mist, haar
seaside promenade, front
secondary issue, offer
  for sale
second balcony, upper circle
second-class mail, newspaper post
second floor, first floor
second rank, second eleven
second-story man, cat burglar
secretary, bureau
secretary, P.A.
Secretary of Labor, Employment
  Secretary
Secretary of the Treasury,
Chancellor of the Exchequer
secured bond, debenture
sedan, saloon
See?, Follow?
Seeing Eye dog, guide dog
see one in hell, see one far enough
see (someone's) point,
  take (someone's) point
see the last of, see the back of

see through, rumble
select, look-out
selector rod, 423
self-addressed envelope, 415
self-service, self-selection
sell illegally, flog
sell out, sell up
semiannual, half-yearly
semiannually, half-yearly
semibreve, 424
seminary, theological college
semiquaver, 424
send up, lag
send up a trial balloon, fly a kite
senior citizen, O.A.P.
Senior Officer Present, SOP
sensation, shock
sense of direction, bump of
  direction
sentenced to an indeterminate term,
  detained during the Queen's
  (King's) pleasure
separates, team-ups
septillion, 420
serve in large quantities, dollop
serve time, do bird; do porridge
service, approach
service, (the) forces
service counter, servery
serviette, 414
serving, sitting
serving dish, dish
set, case
set; impose, lay
set, 424
set eyes on, clap eyes on
set of deadbeats, long firm
set the ball rolling, open the
  bowling
set the world on fire, set the Thames
  on fire
settle a score, wipe off a score
settle down, hang up one's hat
sewerage system, drains
sewing gear kit, housewife
sexillion, 420
sextillion, 420
sexually unconventional, kinky
sexy, dishy; fruity
shabby, tatty
shackles, 425
shake, judder
shaky (queasy), dicky
shallow, fleet
shape, nick
shape up, pull one's socks up
share, whack
shares, 417
shark, whale
Shark's Parade, 424
sharp, downy; fly

sharp, sharpen
sharpen (notes),   409
sharpie, twister; wide boy
sharp operator, spiv
shell, cartridge
shell out, unbelt
shelve,   1
shift bar,   423
shiftless, come-day-go-day
shilling,   425
shine, black; clean
shingle, brass plate
shingled with tiles, tile-hung
Shinkman, Bernard F.,   1
ship, forward
shirk, skulk
shirker, skulk; slacker
shirt (worn under the
   dress); (short) jacket;
   wig, spencer
shock of grain, stook
shoe, boot
shoemaker, shoe mender
shooting area, shoot
shooting expedition, shoot
shooting-match, boiling
shooting party, shoot
shooting practice, shoot
shop,   5
shop assistant,   5
(shop) awning, sunblind
shopping bags, carrier bag
short coat, coatee
short hairs, curlies
short jacket, bum-freezer
short o,   411
short one,   424
short rations, short commons
shoulder, berm
show, house
show, tamasha
shower oneself,   409
shrewd, cute
shut up, belt up; put
   a bung in it
Shut up!, Go to bed!; wrap up!
sick as a dog, sick as a cat
sick bay, sicker
Sick Children, Hospital for,   413
sick joke,   2
sick note, aeger
sick to one's stomach, sick
sideburns, sideboards
sidecheck, bearing-rein
side lamp,   423
sidelines, touch-lines
side member,   422
side rail   422
sidewalk, footway; pavement
side with (someone), play for
   (someone's) side

sight, guy
sight translation, unseen
sign, board
silencer, exhaust,   422
silent partner, sleeping partner
silver set, canteen of cutlery
silverside,   426
simple, penny plain
simpleton, looby
single room, apartment
sing out, give (someone) a shout
singular noun,   410
sink, basin
sirloin, rump steak
sirloin,   426
Sir Michael & Sir George,   1
sister-citied with..., twin with...
sit down, put one's arse to anchor
sit in, (be a) fly on the wall
sit to/for,   408
situation, position; wicket
situation room, incident
   room
situation,   5
sixpence,   417, 425
sixteenth note, semiquaver
sixteenth note,   424
sixty-fourth note,
   hemidemisemiquaver
sixty-fourth note,   424
skiffy,   6
skilled mechanic, service engineer
skip, hunt; miss out
skip town by night, shoot the moon
skirt,   422
slacks, bags
slang,   6, 7
Slang,   424
slash, oblique
slattern,   6
sled, sledge
sleep, kip
sleeping sickness, sleepy sickness
sleep in the open, sleep rough
sleep late, lie in; sleep in
sleeveless sweater, slipover
slicker, loose waterproof
slingshot, catapult
slipcovers, loose covers
slippery, greasy
slip up, put a foot wrong
slip up,   424
slip (vanishing act), guy
sloping stone jetty, hard
sloppy clothes, slops
slot machine, fruit machine
slow lane, near-side lane
slow on the uptake, slow off the
   mark
slowpoke, slowcoach
sluggish, tardy

sly, carny; pawky
smack, slosh
small box, casket
small bundle of kindling, pimp
small carplike fish, roach
small eel, grig; snig
small farmer, yeoman
small fruit basket, punnet
small hill, how
small landholding, croft
small parakeet, budgie
small pork sausage, chipolata
small rented garden area, allotment
small scythe, bagging-hook
small shrimp, prawn
small spongy cake, muffin
small time, small beer
smart cookie, long-head
smashed, sloshed
smash hit, bomb
smashup, smash
"Smithson, Charles", 1
smock, coverall
Smoke, the 425
snack bar, buffet
snag, 5
snap, popper; press stud; snapper
snapper, cracker
snappy, nippy; parky
sneakers, gym shoes; plimsolls
sneak off, slope off
snooze, zizz
snowed in, snowed up
snowed up/in, 408
soak, rush; sting
soapbox orator, tub-thumper
soccer, football; footer
soccer team, eleven
socialized medicine, National
   Health Service
social worker, almoner
sock on the jaw, fourpenny one;
   tuppenny one
sod, turf
sofa, chesterfield; divan
soft drink, mineral
soft-soap, flannel
solder, 412
soldier in the ranks, ranker
Sold Out, House Full
solicit, importune
solitaire, patience
so long!, bung-ho!
someone or the other, 408
something special, bobby-dazzler
somewhat, -ish
sonar, Asdic
song-thrush, throstle
sonic boom, sonic bang
son of a gun, beggar
soon as possible, 415

sophisticatedly off-beat, kinky
sop up, mop up
sore, narked
sore 6
sorry!, 414
sort of, -ish
so-so, tollol
so there!, sucks to you!
soul kiss, tongue sandwich
sound, copper-bottomed
soup, 425
south end of a northbound horse,
   east end of a westbound cow
spanner, 423
sparking plug, 423
spark plug, sparking-plug
spark plug, 423
sparrow, spadger
Sparrow Corner, 424
spatterdock, 427
spatula, fish slice;
   palette-knife
speakeasy, shebeen
speak to, have a word with
special delivery, express
special delivery, 7
special election, by-election
specialist, jobber
specialist (medical), consultant
specs, gig-lamps
speed bump, rumble strip
Spelling, 415
spending spree, mucker
spiced meatball, faggot
spicey, fruity
spike, 425
spill, mucker
spin, birl, twizzle
spit, gob
split, 424
split-off, hive off
spoil; kid, rot
spoil, wrap in cotton wool
spoiled, off
spoilsport, wowser
spoil the record, blot one's
   copybook
**Spoken Usage and Figures of
   Speech,** 413
sponge bath, bed bath; blanket
   bath; strip-wash
sponge hard rubber, sorbo rubber
spoof, cod
spool, reel
sports, athletics
spot, 424
spread the gory details, pile on the
   agony
spree, razzle
spree, the/a, 409
spring-clean, 409

spring cleaning, spring-clean
sprinkling wagon, water-cart
sprowsie, 425
spud, tater
spuds, praties
squabble, argy-bargy; barney
squabblers, Kilkenny cats
squander, make off with
squash, marrow
squeal (inform), grass
squal on, round on; shop; split on
squeal on (someone), put
  (someone's) pot on
squeeze-box, squiffer
squeeze out, winkle out
squelch, quench
squirrel, bun
S-shaped couch, sociable
stagehand, scene-shifter
stage left, prompt
stage mob noise, rhubarb
stage right, opposite prompt
stake up, stick
stalks, haulm
stalks and leaves, shaw
stall, stonewall
stand, stall; stick
standby, twelfth man
stand for, sit down under; wear
standing room, terraces
stand in one's way, stand in one's
  light
stand up, wash
stand up and be counted, show
  one's colours
Stanhope, Henry, 4
St. Anthony's turnip, 426
star, principal boy
stark naked, starkers
start, off
starting handle, 423
starve, clem
state, agricultural show
State Department, Foreign Office
state employment office, labour
  exchange
station agent, station-manager
station house, nick
station-to-station call, ordinary call
station wagon, estate car
statutory tenant, sitting tenant
stay, stop
stay out of it, hold the ring
steaks and chops, grills
steal a march on (someone), wipe
  (someone's) eye
steeplechase rider, jump
  jockey
steering idler, 423
steering knuckle, 423
Steering Parts, 423

steering relay, 423
stem-winder, keyless watch
stenographer, shorthand typist
steno pad, jotter
step on, cram on
sticker, label
stick it out, carry one's bat
stickpin, breast-pin; tiepin
stick (someone), sell (someone) a
  pup
stick to one's guns, stick out
stick with it, soldier on
sticky dog or *wicket*, 429
still in contention, through
sting, stang
stingray, fire-flair
stingy, mean
stink, pong
stinker, shocker
St. John, 411
stockade, glasshouse; jankers
stock dividend, bonus issue (bonus
  share); free issue of new shares
stock exchange defaulter, lame duck
stocking cap, jelly-bag cap
stockinged feet, 409
stocking feet, stockinged feet
stock market transaction, bargain
stocks, shares
stocks, 417
stock touting, share-pushing
stoit, 6
stone, 3, 418
stone-cold 424
stone facing, stone cladding
stone wall, brick wall; hedge
stoolie, snout
stool pigeon, nark
Stop, Halt
stop at, call at
stop bugging me!, get knotted!
stop off at..., break a journey at...
stopover, staging-post
stopper, guard
storage room, box-room;
  lumber-room
store, shop
store, 5
store sign, fascia
storey, 416
stove, cooker
stow it!, put a sock in it!
St. Pancras Station, 424
straight, neat
straight ahead, straight on
straight drink, short
straight flush, 425
straight man, feed
straight razor, cut-throat
straw hat, boater
straw mattress, palliasse

take, screw
take, want
take a dislike to, take against; take a
  scunner on
take (a letter), take down
take a look at, run the rule over
take an examination, sit an
  examination
(take a) pee, pumpship
take a powder, cut one's lucky;
  hook it
take as a deduction,
  claim against tax
take a shot at, have a bash at
take a tumble, come a cropper
take care of, sort out
take (cheat), take down
take drugs, drug
take it easy!, wait for it!
take it on the lam, bunk
take off, beetle off
take-off, cod; send-up
take (someone) in, do (someone)
  brown
take the bull by the horns, grasp the
  nettle
take the lead; set the pace,
  take (make) the running
take to one's bed, lie up
take to the pottie, pot
take turns, take it in turns to
talent scout, talent spotter
talk a blue streak, talk the hind leg
  off a donkey
talking to, jaw
talk nonsense, blether (blather);
  haver
talk one's way out, flannel
talk show, chat show
talk through one's hat, talk through
  (out of) the back of one's neck
tamp, pun
tamper with, nobble
tanner,   417
tantrum, paddy; rux
tape needle, bodkin
taps, last post
tar, macadam
tar road, tarmac
tartan trousers, trews
tastes like more, (it's) mor(e)ish
taxi stand, cab-rank
taxi stand,   424
tea, char
teacher, master
team, side
tea maker, kettle-boy
tea party, bun-fight
tear down, pull down
tear jerker, weepy; weepie
tease, cod; rag

teed off, brassed off; cheesed off
teen-age,   2
teetotal, TT
teetotaler, TT
teetotaler, wowser
telephone, blower
telephone booth, call-box; kiosk
telephone pole, telegraph pole
telephone repair department, faults
  and service difficulties
Teleprompter, Autocue
teller, cashier
tell off, tick off
telly,   2
temporary mailing address,
  accommodations address
temporary pasture, ley
temporary school leave, exeat
temporary stock certificate, scrip
temporary stock certificate,   418
tenderloin, fillet; undercut
that excuse won't work,
  that cock won't fight
ten-foot pole, barge pole
ten or more, double figures
ten to one, (a) guinea to a
  gooseberry
terminal, terminus
tern, scray
terrible,   5
terribly exciting, too rivetting
terribly (very), beastly
terrific, imperial; smashing, wizard
terrifically, not half; (a) treat
textile dealer, mercer
textiles, soft goods
Thames,   411
thanks, ta
that does it!, that's torn it!
that's a..., there's a...
That's incredible! It isn't true!
that's the ticket!, that's the job!
the,   408
the ace of spades, old mossyface
the Ashes,   5
theatre,   415
the blues, hip
the City,   5
the diamond industry, Hatton
  Garden
(the) dumps, (the) hump
The English Aristocracy,   414
The French Lieutenant's Woman,   1
The Gulag Archipelago,   4
the/his,   409
The Literature of the United States,   1
The Loved One,   1
the market, Throgmorton Street
the press, Fleet Street
The Random House Dictionary,   4
the rest of the gang, Uncle Tom

Cobleigh and all
there you are! that's it! voilà!, Bob's
 your uncle!
thermos bottle, Dewar's flask;
 vacuum flask
the runs, squitters
the works, lot
thick, dim
thick, double
thicket, shaw; spinney
thicket, 427
thick-headed, as dim as a Toc H
 lamp; dim
thimbleful, toothful
thin copy paper, flimsy
thin down, fine down
thing, touch
thingamajigs, gubbins
third-class mail, printed paper rates
third degree squad, heavy gang
thirty-second note, demisemiquaver
thirty-second note, 424
Thomas, Dylan 1
thorny shrub, whin
thread, cotton
threepence, 417
three tens 425
through, till
throw caution to the winds,
 throw one's bonnet (cap)
 over the windmill
throw money around, lash out
throw out, turf out
throw together, knock up
throw up, be sick; honk; sick up
thumb one's nose, cock a snook
thumbtack, drawing-pin; push pin
 thwart, queer the pitch
tick-tack-toe, noughts and crosses
tidal bore flood, eagre
tidal stream, lough
tidbit, savoury
tidbits, tit-bits
tide-flat, salting
tidy, 5
tie bar or *track bar*, 423
tied up, 5
tight, elephant's tight, screwed; tossed
tight (stingy), mingy
time, 414
time and charges, A.D.C.
time of day, 411
time off, remission
tin, 4
tinker's dam(n), tinker's cuss
tip, drop
tip (on the races), nap
tipsy, cut; squiffy;
tiddle(e)y; well away
tire, 423
Tires, 423

titfer, 425
tit for tat, 425
title, freehold
title closing, completion
titles (honorary), 415
tits, Bristols; charlies (charleys)
tizzy, fret; tig; way
toady, clawback
to a T, like one o'clock
to be fresh to, cheek
toboggan, luge
toby, 425
toe board, 422
toe pan, 422
to go, to take away
(to) have had it, (to) have had one's
 chips
toil, fag
toilet, W.C.
toilet, 414
toilet articles, washing things
toilet bowl, closet; pedestal
toilet kit, sponge bath
toilet paper, bumf (bumph)
tollfree number, free fone
to London, up
(to) make matters worse,
 (to) cap it all
ton, 419, 429
tone, note
tongue-tied, mumchance
tons 4 cwt., keel
tons of, masses of
too, as well
too good to pass up, too good to
 miss
took the bait, penny in the slot
Tools and Accessories, 423
too soon, early days
toot, razzle
toot, 6
top, roof
top boy, head boy; head girl
top girl, head boy; head girl
topnotcher, star turn
top of the bottle, head
top round, silverside
top-round, topside
top round, 426
top secret, most secret
top sergeant, sergeant-major
torrent, gill
tosheroon, 425
toss one's cookies, shoot the cat
tot, kipper
to take the best (men) out of
total loss, poor tool
tote bag, dorothy bag
to tell the truth, actually
touch and go, dicey; dodgy
touchdown, try

touch-me-not, 427
touch, corner-boy; keelie; rough
tough break, bit of a knock
tough going, against the collar
toughie, street rough
tough luck!, bad show!; Hard
  cheese!
tough on, hot on
tough situation, sticky wicket
tout, chant
tow car, recovery van
Tower of London, 424
town, council; parish; village
town hall, guildhall
town officer, clerk
tow truck, ambulance; breakdown
  van
toy, ploy
track, line
track, 423
track bar or *tie bar*, 423
tracklayer, platelayer
track rod, 423
track socket, chair
track (someone) down, lay
  (someone) by the heels
tract, 427
trade, 5
trade in, give in part exchange
trafficator 423
traffic circle, roundabout
traffic jam, hold-up; traffic block
traffic officer, traffic warden
traffic policeman, pointsman
traffic post, bollard
trailer truck, articulated lorry;
  bender
tramcar, 424
tramp, 425
transfer temporarily, second
transient, non-resident; temporary
  guest
transient or occasional worker,
  casual labourer
transit system, transport system
transmission, gearbox
Transmission and Rear Axle Parts, 423
transmission case, 423
Transmission Parts, 423
transom, fair-light
transportation, transport
trap, cakehole; gob
trapezoid, trapezium
trash, tripe and onions
trash basket, litter bin
traveling salesman, bagman;
  commercial traveller
traveling show, mobile production
travelled, traveller, travelling, 415
tread, 423
Treasury, (the) Revenue

Treasury Department, Exchequer
treat, jam
treat, push the boat out
treat, shout
treat (someone) right, do (someone)
  well
treble, 426
tree creeper, 427
trellis, pergola
trial balloon, Aunt Sally
trial calendar, cause-list
trial lawyer, barrister
trifle, ha'p'orth
trillion, 419
trimester, term
triple achievement, hat trick
trot, crib
trouble, bother; snag
trouble, 5
trouble and strife, 425
troublesome; annoying,
  awkward
trouble spot, black spot
troubling, worrying
trouser cuff, turn-up
truck, lorry
truck drivers' all-night diner,
  transport café
truck farm, market garden
trucking company, haulage
  contractor
truckman, haulier
truck (non-driving locomotive
  wheels), bogie
trudge, foot-slog
tvundle bed, truckle-bed
trunk, 422
trunk (of an automobile), bot
Trust an Englishman, 6
try, go
tri it out, try it on
try one's luck, chance one's arm
T-shirt, gym vest; singlet
T-shirt, 2
tub, 418
tube, valve
tube, 3
tuckered out, clapped out; cooked;
  creased
tummy, little Mary
tuppence, 417
turbot, 426
turn, go
turn, turning
turn a blind eye to,
  teach the Nelson eye on
  (see Appendix I.C.6) 414, U
turnbuckle, bottle screw; rigging
  screw
turned, gone
turned on, switched on

turn in, give in part exchange
turn in, kip
turn indicator,   423
turning-around place, winding
   point
turning/turn,   409
turnkey deal, package deal
turn on, round on
turn one's back on, send to
   Coventry
turn out well, come up trumps
turn over, tick over
turnpike, motorway
turn (someone) in, give (someone)
   in charge
turn up, knock on
turtleneck, polo neck
tuxedo, dinner-jacket
TV, telly
TV,   2
twaddle, waffle
twenty-five pounds, pony
twice in a row, twice running
twin-bedded room,   409
twist, screw
twisted, kinky
two-and-a-half times pay, time time
   and a half
two-family, semi-detached
two pair,   425
two-room flat,   409
two shakes of a duck's tail,
   (in a) brace of shakes
two-toned shoes, co-respondent
   shoes
two weeks, fortnight
type of cloth, wincey
typesetter, compositor
type (sort), mark
tyre,   416, 423

U

*U and Non-U, an Essay in
   Sociological Linguistics*,   414
U.K.,   427
umbrella leaves,   427
unable to play, unfit
Uncle Ned,   425
uncollected funds, effects not
   cleared
unconventional, bolshy
uncouple, hook off
under control, in hand
underground,   424
underhand, hole-and-corner
underpants, liners; pants
undershirt, singlet; vest
undertaker, funeral furnisher
under the doctor's care, under the

doctor
under the weather, pulled
   down
undies, frillies; smalls
unemployment benefits, (the) dole
unfit, C Three
unholy mess, dog's breakfast
Unilateral Declaration of
   Independence, U.D.I.
unilateral deed, deed-poll
union cost-of-living contract,
   threshold agreement
union protest activity, industrial
   action
union suit, combinations
*United Kingdom of Great Britain and
   Northern Ireland*,   427
Units of Measure,   418
unlimited travel ticket, Rover ticket
unlisted, ex-directory
unpleasant, beastly
unprepared, caught on the hop
unserviceable, U.S.
unskilled hunter, postman's knock
   man
up and down,   426
uplands, downs
upper crust, upper ten
uppercut, undercut
uppity, uppish
upright (piano), stand-up
   (piano)
upright telephone, candlestick
   telephone
uproar, row-de-dow
upset, cut up
upset, turn-up
upset price, reserve price
upstairs hall, landing
up the creek, jiggered; up
a gum tree; up the junction
up to snuff, quite
urinate, pee
urination, pee
use of the bathroom, wash
Use your loaf!,   425
USO, ENSA
utterly, to the wide

V

v.,   425
vacant land, waste land; spare
   ground
vacation, holiday
vacation time, hols
vacuum (clean), hoover
vacuum cleaner, hoover
valance, pelmet
valance,   422

wheelchair, bath-chair; invalid's
chair; wheeled chair
wheeled chair, 409
wheelhouse or *housing*, 422
wheel wrench, 423
when all is said and done, at close of
play; at the end of the day
when the time comes, on the day
when you come right down to it,
when it comes to the bone
Where do we go from here?, Where
do we go for honey?
where the difficulty or hardship lies,
where the shoe pinches
whew!, lumme!
which/who, 411
while, whilst
while-U-wait shoe repair shop, heel
bar
whimper, grizzle
whimsical structure, folly
whip, cane
whipping, cat
whirlwind tourist, Pagett
whisky/whiskey, 428
whistle, 425
whistle and flute, 425
Whitacker's Almanack, 1
white collar, black coat
white cottom cloth, calico
white-faced cow, hawkie
whitener, blanco
white raisin, sultana
whiz, dab
Who is that/this? 413
whole note, semibreve
whole note, 424
wholesaler, merchant
whole tone, tone
whole wheat bread, brown bread;
whole meal bread
whopping, swingeing
whorehouse, knocking-house
ho wants this? Quis?
who/which, 411
who/whom, 411
wicked, naughty
wicket, hoop
wide necktie, kipper tie
wife, dutch
wife, 425
wife-beating, wife-battering
wig, jasey
wild, on the loose
wild carrot, 427
wildcat strike, unofficial strike
Wilde Oscar, 1
wild open land, heath
wild rhubarb, 427
willies, jim-jams
Wilts., 412

Wiltshire, 412
win a bet, have it off
windbreaker, windcheater
windfall, bunce
windhover, 427
winding, crinkle-crankle
windle, 419
window shade, blind
window shopping, window-gazing
windscreen, 422
windshield, windscreen
windshield, 422
wine gallon, 419
wing, 422
wing (wound), pip
winkles, 426
wireless, 2, 7
wise guy, clever Dick
wishbone, 423
witch, 426
with, w.
with, 415
with a double bed, double-bedded
with all due respect, with respect
within hailing distance of,
within cooee of
with it, trendy
witness stand, witness-box
wobbly, wonky
wold, 427
wolf, scoff
woman, 425
Women's Royal Army Corps, WRAC
won't work out, won't go
Wood, Frederick, 3
wooded vale, dene
wood silver, chip
wood (wooded area), copse
woolen helmet, Balaclava
woolen scarf, comforter
woozy, muzzy
Worcester, 412
"Word Sanctuary," 3
Words in Sheep's Clothing 2
work, answer
work by the book, work to rule
work in vain, plough the sand(s)
work like mad, do one's nut
work out, sort out
World War I, Great War
World War II, Hitler's War
worn-out rope, junk
worthless paper, bumf(bumph)
wow (impress), knock
wrapper, dressing gown
wreck, crash
wreck, crock
wrecking crew, breakdown gang
wrench, spanner
wrench, 423
wretched, 5